COOPER'S
OUTLINES OF
INDUSTRIAL LAW

SIXTH EDITION

BY

JOHN C. WOOD, C.B.E., LL.M.

OF GRAY'S INN, BARRISTER; PROFESSOR OF LAW IN
THE UNIVERSITY OF SHEFFIELD

LONDON
BUTTERWORTHS
1972

FIRST EDITION	. . .	October, 1947
REPRINTED .	. . .	May, 1948
SECOND EDITION .	.	November, 1954
THIRD EDITION	. . .	October, 1958
FOURTH EDITION .	. .	August, 1962
REPRINTED .	. .	December, 1963
FIFTH EDITION	. . .	June, 1966
REPRINTED .	. . .	October, 1967
REPRINTED .	. .	November, 1968
SIXTH EDITION	. .	September, 1972

©

BUTTERWORTH & CO. (PUBLISHERS) LTD.
1972

ISBN—Casebound : o 406 56651 8
Limp : o 406 56652 6

Printed in Great Britain by
Hazell Watson & Viney Ltd., Aylesbury, Bucks

OUTLINES OF
INDUSTRIAL LAW

ENGLAND·   BUTTERWORTH & CO. (PUBLISHERS) LTD.
           LONDON : 88 Kingsway, WC2B 6AB

AUSTRALIA· BUTTERWORTHS PTY. LTD
           SYDNEY : 586 Pacific Highway, Chatswood, NSW 2067
           MELBOURNE : 343 Little Collins Street, 3000
           BRISBANE : 240 Queen Street, 4000

CANADA :   BUTTERWORTH & CO. (CANADA) LTD.
           TORONTO : 14 Curity Avenue, 374

NEW ZEALAND : BUTTERWORTHS OF NEW ZEALAND LTD.
           WELLINGTON : 26-28 Waring Taylor Street, 1

SOUTH AFRICA : BUTTERWORTH & CO. (SOUTH AFRICA) (PTY.) LTD.
           DURBAN : 152-154 Gale Street

PREFACE TO SIXTH EDITION

Rarely can a new edition of a legal text book have required less justification. The changes in the subject, the controversy surrounding many of these changes and above all the fundamental challenge to the strength of the law made by the changes all involve a need for revision. Industrial law is a grouping of somewhat diverse areas of law—contract, tort, health and safety, social security, trade unions, industrial relations and so on. Differing periods bring attention to one or other of these areas, often regrettably to the neglect of the others. The bias and strengths of text books obviously vary considerably. Some plainly select areas at the expense of others. At the present moment the great activity and attention is directed to the area of trade unions and industrial relations. The Industrial Relations Act, 1971 looms disproportionately large. It has made great changes but its full effect will not be known for many years. Unfortunately these years are not likely to be less stormy. The whole area is very fluid indeed, a fluidity potentially increased by the party political controversy surrounding the new law. The fundamental legal rules and legal method will be much affected by what happens: and their importance becomes that much greater.

Attention must not, however, be diverted away from those areas where change and debate are less vigorous. The balance will undoubtedly not remain as it is at present. Before this book reaches the reader the Robens Committee Report on Health and Safety at Work will have been published. This will inevitably bring a debate on the place and effectiveness of the law in this area: it will most likely lead to fundamental legislative reform.

When this book was first published it was possible, outside the major parent subjects of contract and tort, to include in a book of this size most of the relevant law in some detail. Such is the change that now every chapter and indeed many topics alloted to a section within a chapter are now covered by a text book, or books in their own right. Inevitably the result is that this edition has had to turn more to principle, to exclude much detail and to aim at selection rather than comprehensiveness. It is nevertheless remarkable that the scheme adopted by Sir W. Mansfield Cooper in 1947 in writing this book has survived the test of time. His was a notable pioneering effort with outstanding judgment and balance. Many have benefited and built on his work. Inevitably fairly radical changes have been made and will increasingly be made as the conspectus changes. It is to be hoped that the reader will not lose sight of the important basis of this book.

At the time of writing the process of development of the Law, if anything, accelerates. By the time the book is in the reader's hands the National Industrial Relations Court and the appeal courts will have had a great deal to say on the Industrial Relations Act.

On a more mundane plane the contracts of employment provisions in the Contracts of Employment Act, 1963, the Redundancy Payments Act, 1965 and the Industrial Relations Act, 1971 will have been consolidated in a new Contracts of Employment Act, 1972. Students will find its table of derivations useful.

Preparation of this edition has taken place in a period of frenetic legal change and debate. It could not have been completed without the assistant editorship of Dr. M. R. Kay of Manchester University. He has undertaken special responsibility for the trade union and industrial injuries sections as well as giving unstinting general help throughout. His contribution is indeed a substantial one. It should be obvious too that particular thanks are due to the publishers. Their judicious use of help, exhortation and encouragement was both essential and appreciated.

MAY, 1972.   JOHN C. WOOD.

PREFACE TO FIRST EDITION

The author of a students' text book on Industrial Law is relieved of one, at least, of the anxieties which fall upon a person responsible for the publication of yet another book. He need not make too abject an apology or offer too elaborate a justification for the book's appearance. The great development of the subject during the last decade, the clear indication of the increasing scope of the influence of government in industry, and the absence of any students' text book on the subject designed to assist the law student and the student who is not otherwise studying law, lead to the hope that the present work may be of use to teachers of Industrial Law.

In any students' text book the problems of election is paramount. Some years' experience in teaching students who have no background of legal knowledge has increased my conviction that there is no substitute for the approach by means of the study of the common law. It is possible for teachers of genius so to interpret statute law that its study is capable of instructing and maintaining the interest of the student. For the rest of us, the study of the common law provides an invaluable introduction and affords a body of principle to which, in the main, later statutory developments can be related with interest and profit.

The book has been written in what have proved to be the odd moments of an unduly active existence and under conditions which the writer had not visualised when he agreed to attempt the work. Whatever merits it is found to possess may, with complete justice, be ascribed to many friends who have interested themselves in its preparation. My debt to Professor R. A. Eastwood, LL.D., Dean of the Faculty of Law in the University of Manchester, has assumed dimensions to which it has become almost an impertinence to refer. His interest in this book, his readiness at all times to discuss and criticise, are but special instances of the encouragement he has given continuously to the writer for twenty years. My friend, Mr. M. H. Fairclough, LL.B., of the Northern Circuit, has read the book in manuscript and saved me from many errors. I have received valuable suggestions from Professor B. A. Wortley, O.B.E., LL.D., Professor of Jurisprudence and International Law in the University of Manchester, and from Mr. Henry Hartley, B.Sc. (Econ.), lately Lecturer in Administration in the University of Manchester. My colleague, Mr. Vincent Knowles, M.A., has given me much assistance with the proofs. The active interest of the publishers has been such as to fall little short of collaboration, and I should wish to express, in particular, my gratitude to Mr. J. W. Whitlock and Mr. N. P. Shannon. My wife has helped at every stage of the book's progress and, usually, it must be confessed, in the most laborious and least interesting aspects of its making.   It remains to add that I alone am responsible for what follows, but it is not unnatural that my sense of responsibility is the more acute in the many instances in which I have not found it possible to accept the suggestions of my friends.

MARCH, 1947.   W. MANSFIELD COOPER.

CONTENTS

ix

TABLE OF STATUTES

References in this Table to *Statutes* are to Halsbury's Statutes
of England (Third Edition) showing the volume and page at
which the annotated text of the Act will be found.

Table of Statutes

TABLE OF CASES

This Table includes Selected Decisions of the Umpire, under the Reinstatement in Civil Employment Act, 1944, which are published by H.M. Stationery Office, R.E. Code 1.

A

PAGE

PAGE

PAGE

PAGE

PAGE

PAGE

PAGE

PAGE

PAGE

PAGE

I.L.—2*

H

PAGE

PAGE

PAGE

PAGE

PAGE

M

PAGE

PAGE

PAGE

Table of Cases

lix

PAGE

PAGE

PAGE

PAGE

I.L.—3*

PAGE

PAGE

CHAPTER 1

INTRODUCTORY

1. General Considerations

The law of England is, in both its content and its sources, a unity. An instrument, fashioned by the needs of a people, compounded of centuries of organic growth, it cannot be divided into those neat and comprehensive compartments favoured by the theorist. Any exposition, therefore, of the law relating to the citizen in his role as servant, any effort to treat of him as producer in factory, mine, quarry, shop or office will take us far afield. We shall be concerned, in some detail, with the law of contract and of tort; we shall glance, more generally, at the law of crime and of property. We shall gain some knowledge of the law of procedure and remedies; we shall see the courts wrestling with the problem of the meaning to be given to words and so become acquainted with some of the principles of interpretation. And if the attempt to discover what is the present state of the law involves so discursive an effort, so too does an investigation of its sources. The student might imagine that since industrialism is so modern, the law concerning it would be found in statute. Such a hope would be realised in part only. For though industrialism is a modern phenomenon, service and employment are as old as mankind, and we shall be compelled to seek the sources of our study in the common law and in equity as well as in legislation.

By the common law is meant that mass of customary and case law which is the peculiar and, indeed, the unique possession of the English legal system. Legal custom arose from the ordinary, peaceable habits of the English folk. Once the King's Judges went on assize, they gradually united the divergent customs, achieving, in the course of time, a law common to the whole realm. They would follow their own earlier decisions in subsequent cases and these decisions would be recorded by beginners in the study of the law; student scribblings very often helped to lay the foundations of our notable collection of law reports.

We shall constantly refer, in this book, to the views of the common law on particular topics and shall document these views by reference to cases, some ancient and some modern, but rarely arising, whatever their period, out of formal legislation. Occasionally we shall contrast with the common law view that of equity. We shall consider, for example, the equitable view of fraud in the formation of a contract and the scope of the equitable remedy of injunction.

But though we shall contrast common law and equity, they are not to be regarded as antithetical forces.   They are, in fact, supplementary.   As Maitland has assured us, equity represents a collection of appendices to the common law.[1]   Had these appendices been abolished we might have got on tolerably well.   Had the common law gone the result would have been anarchy.

We shall also seek our law in statute.   Every duly passed Act of Parliament is binding law, and against its authority neither custom nor precedent can prevail.   Legislation, indeed, is the instrument which, in the modern state, most easily keeps the law in some degree of conformity with changing economic and social needs.   The bulk of the law covering the health and safety of the worker is the result of statute, and the torrent of legislative activity which was a characteristic of the last century is the most telling monument to the growing importance of the topics we shall discuss in this book. Indeed, that torrent has engulfed Westminster and we shall frequently find our law, not directly in statute, but in rules and orders which some Act of Parliament empowers a minister to make. Legislation, however, cannot stand by itself.   However carefully drafted an Act may be, its operation in all the diverse circumstances to which it will be applied will necessarily raise difficulties.   The legislature cannot hope to do more than deal with a general problem; the interpretation of the resulting Act will be a matter for the courts, and we shall sometimes find an entire body of case law arising out of statutory words and phrases which, of themselves, seem clear and unambiguous enough.   Thus Parliament and the courts are complementary instruments and the final unity of our law is demonstrated when it is shown that the courts, in interpreting statutes, have recourse to principles of interpretation whose origins lie deep in the springs of the common law.[2]   Indeed an important principle is that, as far as possible, the courts will interpret statutes so as to give effect to the general principles of the common law.

Although, strictly construed, the function of the lawyer stops at an understanding of the appropriate statute and case law, this can no longer be regarded as enough.   The law of employment concerns a vital part of the national economy.   The Government's concern that the economy should be sensibly planned and managed leads it along interventionist paths.   Often, and with increasing frequency, as we shall see, this takes the form of statute law which is absorbed within the traditional framework of the law.   But it may fall short of legislation: government plans often take the form of white papers published with the hope of influencing the areas they cover but falling

---

[1] *Equity: A Course of Lectures*, Cambridge University Press, 1910, 1st Ed., p. 19.
[2] The whole question of the relationship between statute law and common law has been brought into sharp focus by the Industrial Relations Act, 1971.   The judgments of the N.I.R.C. and its impact as a whole will be a most interesting jurisprudential study.

short of formal legal regulation. Their existence must be acknowledged and their effect upon the legal framework assessed.

2. Scope of the Subject

Most legal subjects are a collection of topics gathered together for reasons of convenience within a general concept of relevance. This underlying similarity, their practical connections, historical development may all serve to determine the topic chosen. The decisions as to what is to be included, what excluded, are often arbitrary and parts of the subject are bound to have close links with its neighbours so that these decisions can be challenged. Indeed such interrelationship spreads over the boundaries of discipline. Thus the exact boundary between industrial relations and industrial law has always been difficult to determine. Recent development, in particular the Industrial Relations Act, 1971 and especially the Code of Practice made under it, have made the distinction even more tenuous.

Each decade tends to bring emphasis to a new part of the subject so helping to determine its form and shape. But the basis of industrial law is firmly rooted in the law of contract and the law of tort. These topics must form the backbone of this book. Statutory developments have caused important sections to be added. Safety legislation must be dealt with, as must those statutes of social welfare having a direct effect on the worker. In the same way the subject must embrace trade union law and those parts of industrial relations with a clear legal content. Each of these additional topics deserves, and indeed has received, separate treatment in its own right. Here they are treated together so that the reader and student may get a conspectus of the law which regulates the workman in relation to his employment. It is for this reason that the starting point of the subject must be the law of master and servant—an old-fashioned sounding description of the underlying legal bond between employer and employed.

3. Relationship of Master and Servant

(1) Nature.—The relationship of employer and employed,[1] of master and servant, is, according to the common law, a voluntary relationship into which the parties may enter on terms laid down by themselves within limitations imposed only by the general law of contract. A man agrees expressly or by implication to be a servant or an apprentice and there is no other way in which the relationship can arise. The faintest doubt cast upon the voluntary character of the relationship would be sufficient to secure the active aid of the courts. "My Lords," said Lord ATKIN, addressing the House of Lords in a case in which it had been argued that an Act of Parliament

---

[1] Terminology is difficult. Master and servant is old-fashioned. Employer and employed begs the self-employed difficulty. Indeed, the Industrial Relations Act, 1971, makes a vital distinction between "employee" and the wider "worker". See s. 167.

gave power to transfer the employees of one company to the service of another,

> "I confess it appears to me astonishing that apart from overriding questions of public welfare, power should be given to a court or to anyone else to transfer a man without his knowledge and possibly against his will, from the service of one person to the service of another. I had fancied that ingrained in the personal status of a citizen under our laws was the right to choose for himself whom he would serve and that this right of choice constituted the main difference between a servant and a serf."[1]

Although the relation is firmly based in contract, suggestions have been made that it might be possible and even desirable to introduce elements of the concept of status into the legal nature of the employer–employee relationship.[2]   One of the chief effects would be to enable the law to continue the worker's right to work even in the face of opposition from the employer.   This type of approach can be seen in the very special statutory dock labour scheme[3] but it is, as yet, completely alien to the present legal concept of employment.

(2) **Test.**—Let us suppose that the owner of a factory proposes to build extensions.   Two courses are clearly open to him.   He may engage bricklayers, plasterers, tilers and the like, and be himself responsible for carrying out the work, or he may, and more usually will, place the work in the hands of a builder.   If he chooses the first course he will contract to engage a number of servants and he will control the manner in which their work will be done.   If he chooses the second course he will contract for a desired result with one who, in law, is known as an independent contractor.

In the first place there will be a contract of service, in the second a contract of services.   The distinction is of basic legal importance and we shall see it arising at many points—employers' liability, social security.   It is difficult to make.[4]   "It is often," remarked one Judge,

> "easy to recognise a contract of service when you see it, but difficult to say wherein the difference lies."

---

[1] *Nokes* v. *Doncaster Amalgamated Collieries, Ltd.*, [1940] A.C. 1014 at p. 1026; [1940] 3 All E.R. 549 at p. 556.   The Redundancy Payment Act, 1965 raises the question of transfer of employment.

[2] For example, Wedderburn, *The Worker and the Law*, 2nd. Ed. 1971, p. 81. The concept of a worker having a "property right " in his job is one that academic writers have seized upon.   See *A Proprietary Right in Employment*, E. G. H. Clayton, (1967) Jo. Bus. Law 139.   *The Contract of Employment*, R. W. Rideout (1966), 19 Current Legal Problems 111 is a good critique of the present approach.   An attempt to see a marked shift from contract to status in current developments has as yet little real foundation but is a point to keep in mind.

[3] Considered judicially in *Vine* v. *National Dock Labour Board*, [1957] A.C. 488; [1956] 3 All E.R. 939.   A case with similar distinctive features is that dealing with University office holders—*Vidyodaya University* v. *Silva*, [1964] 3 All E.R. 865, [1965] 1 W.L.R. 77.

[4] The best treatment is to be found in Atiyah, *Vicarious Liability in the Law of Torts*. Chs. 3–8. *Stevenson, Jordan and Harrison, Ltd.* v. *MacDonald and Evans*, [1952] T.L.R. 101, *per* DENNING, L. J., at p. 111.

It is necessary, in consequence, to point out guiding factors used and acknowledged by the Judges in arriving at their decisions whilst emphasising the overriding lack of precision. One of the most frequently quoted judgments is that of McCARDIE, J., in *Performing Right Society, Ltd.* v. *Mitchell and Booker* in which this passage occurs:

> " The nature of the task undertaken, the freedom of action given, the magnitude of the contract amount, the manner in which it is to be paid, the powers of dismissal and the circumstances under which payment of the reward may be withheld, all these questions bear on the solution of the question. . . . It seems, however, reasonably clear that the final test, if there be a final test, and certainly the test to be generally applied lies in the nature and degree of detailed control over the person alleged to be a servant."[1]

There has been, in a large number of cases that have been reported, a search for a sound delineation of the tests to be applied. That the question is one of remaining uncertainty can be copiously illustrated. It may be that the only satisfactory conclusion is the one indicated in the passage just cited; there must be a large number of tests all of which are applicable where the circumstances permit. In that case the paramountcy of the control test was advocated, other tests have however, been suggested.[2]

Control.—Many of the earlier cases are susceptible to solution by use of the control test.

In *Jones* v. *Scullard*[3] the defendant owned horses, harness and a brougham which he kept at certain livery stables. Whenever the defendant wished to use the carriage the owner of the stables supplied one of his men to drive. The same man had in fact been supplied for six weeks and had been provided (by the defendant) with a livery. On the occasion in question he drove negligently so as to injure the plaintiff. In *Quarman* v. *Burnett*[4] the defendants owned a carriage for which, when they wished to drive, they hired both horses and a driver from a job master. For three years the same driver had been supplied (he was, indeed, the only one available) and the hirers had supplied him with a livery which he kept at their residence. He was, in fact, returning the hat to the house when the horses started and caused injury to the plaintiff and his carriage. The facts in the two cases are sufficiently alike to cause difficulty and the difficulty is perhaps increased when it is known that in

---

[1] [1924] 1 K.B. 762 at p. 767.

[2] There is an interesting essay on this problem by Dr. R. W. Rideout, printed as Appendix III to the Report of the Committee of Inquiry under Professor E. H. Phelps Brown into Certain Matters concerning Labour in Building and Civil Engineering, (1968), Cmnd. 3714. This report deals in part with the labour only contract—a phenomenon to which attention will be given ; see *infra*, p. 13.   [3] [1898] 2 Q.B. 565.

[4] (1840), 6 M. & W. 499. For a recent case where there was no control, see *Norton* v. *Canadian Pacific Steamships, Ltd.*, [1961] 2 All E.R. 785 ; [1961] 1 W.L.R. 1057, which concerned licensed luggage porters on a Liverpool landing stage.

Jones v. *Scullard* the driver was held to be a servant of the defendants, whilst in *Quarman* v. *Burnett* it was held that he was not. In *R.* v. *MacDonald*[1] the accused was employed as a cashier at a salary of £150 per annum. He was, in addition, to receive a commission on profits though he was under no liability to contribute towards losses. He was held to be a servant. The prisoner in *R.* v. *Negus*[2] was employed to solicit orders. Apart from a covenant that he would give his exclusive services to his employers he had a complete discretion as to how and when he would seek business. He was to receive a commission on all orders which resulted from his activities. But though Negus was held not to be a servant (despite his covenant as to exclusive services), one who performed the single transaction of clearing out a drain was, in *Sadler* v. *Henlock*,[3] found to be so.

Such decisions show the question of service, in the case of contracts not evidenced by writing, to be one of fact and, consequently, a matter for the jury in all cases in which a jury is sitting:

> "The greater the amount of direct control exercised over the person rendering the services by the person contracting for them, the stronger the grounds for holding it to be a contract of service and, similarly, the greater the degree of independence of such control the greater the probability that the services rendered are of the nature of professional services and that the contract is not one of personal service."[4]

In *Quarman's* case and in *R.* v. *Negus* the necessary control was not present, while in *Jones* v. *Scullard, R.* v. *MacDonald* and *Sadler* v. *Henlock* it was.

Whenever, therefore, it is necessary to discover whether or not one man is the servant of another one, inquiry must be directed towards finding who has the power to control. Other factors may help. It may be material to know how and by whom a person is paid; by whom and in what circumstances he may be dismissed. But these things, though helpful, are not conclusive. For a man may be the servant of another though he receives no payment, as often happens in family enterprises,[5] and someone other than his legal master may have power to dismiss him,[6] whilst the number of

---

[1] (1861), Le. & Ca. 85.

[2] (1873), L.R. 2 C.C.R. 34. *Cf. R.* v. *Bailey* (1871), 12 Cox 56, with almost identical facts Bailey was held to be a servant. The distinction lay in that Negus, although exclusively working for the complainant, could choose when he worked whereas Bailey had to give all his working time. There have been numerous cases in criminal law arising from the crime of embezzlement which was a crime committed by a "clerk or servant," Larceny Act, 1916, s. 17, involving this same problem of definition. It has now receded into the mists of history with the repeal of larceny and its replacement by theft which does not heed this distinction. See Theft Act, 1968.

[3] (1855), 4 E. & B. 570.

[4] *Simmons* v. *Heath Laundry Co.*, [1910] 1 K.B. 543, *per* FLETCHER MOULTON, L.J., at p. 550.

[5] *R.* v. *Foulkes* (1875), L.R. 2 C.C.R. 150.

[6] *Reedie* v. *L. & N.W. Ry. Co.*, (1849), 4 Exch. 244.

places in which a man may work will, in many cases, furnish little aid in tracing his master.

Between complete control and complete independence the richest variety of circumstances may exist, and the law recognises that many types of service will involve wide fields of initiative and discretion being left to the servant. The question, therefore, is not whether the control is exercised; it is "where is the right to control?" The distinction between the physical ability to control and the right to control may be important. Under modern industrial conditions the actual control is, more often than not, in the hands of a foreman or manager who is himself a servant. Control by the master—who may be a large corporation—is often physically impossible. Contemporary economic organisation rests upon an organised hierarchy of delegation and there thus arises the rule that a superior servant is not, for the purposes of liability, the master of his subordinates no matter how exalted may be the character of the services. The captain of a merchant vessel may well be able to assert *de facto* control over the crew, but he is not legally its master (though a merchant captain is so called); they are fellow servants.[1] In all such circumstances the superior servant is merely the agent of the person who has the right of control and that person alone will be the master. On the other hand, the mere fact that a master from time to time engages in activities usually performed by a servant will not change the relationship in any way; it will still be that of master and servant.

Often whether a servant or an independent contractor is employed will depend on the employer's knowledge and experience. It is generally no use my employing a servant over whom, because of my ignorance and inexperience, I cannot exercise control other than the ultimate power of dismissal for blatant lack of skill. For that reason a patient's contract with his doctor will rarely be a contract of service, for an effective control cannot be asserted. And this difficulty of controlling professional service is responsible for the problems which have been before the courts in relation to doctors employed by or working in hospitals,[2] though there is no doubt a teacher is the servant of the local authority by whom he is employed. Within the boundaries of these two examples every degree and variety of control may be found. A further factor which is of great importance to the employer who wishes to choose between employment of a servant or an independent contractor is the amount of work he has to offer. Where full-time service is required it is usual to have a contract of employment and the relationship of master and servant despite the drawbacks mentioned above. So doctors, lawyers, chemists and advanced technicians of all types are

---

[1] *Hedley* v. *Pinkney & Sons Steamship Co.*, [1892] 1 Q.B. 58, see Lord ESHER, M.R., at p. 62; affirmed, [1894] A.C. 222.
[2] See pp. 13 *et seq.*

to be found in employment even though the nominal control resting
in the master is made almost illusory by his lack of the particular
skill involved.[1] For this reason control cannot be advanced as the
sole determining test.   This has been emphasised in recent case law.
In *Morren* v. *Swinton and Pendlebury Borough Council*, for example,
a resident site engineer was selected by consulting engineers who
supervised him.   He was paid by the local authority for whom the
works were being constructed and there was a contract of service.
Despite the local authority not having control it was held that the
site engineer was their servant.[2]

Industrial injuries insurance is based upon a similar concept in that
insurable employment is defined as employment under a contract of
service or apprenticeship.[3]   In *Whittaker* v. *Minister of Pensions
and National Insurance*, where the claimant was a trapeze-artiste,
MOCATTA, J., said,

> " It seems clear from the more recent cases that persons possessed
> of a high degree of professional skill and expertise, such as surgeons
> and civil engineers, may nevertheless be employed as servants under
> contracts of service, notwithstanding that their employers can,
> in the nature of things, exercise extremely little, if any, control over
> the way in which such skill is used.   The test of control is, therefore,
> not as determinative as used to be thought to be the case, though no
> doubt it is still of value in that the greater the degree of control
> exercisable by the employer, the more likely it is that the contract
> is one of service."[4]

Control over a trapeze artiste is plainly illusory, but the lady in
question also did other things including acting as an usherette.   She
was held to be, taking her position as a whole, acting under a contract
of service.

Ready Mixed Concrete (South East), Ltd. v. *Ministry of Pensions
and National Insurance*[5] is perhaps the most interesting of this line
of cases.   In 1963 Latimer agreed to collect, carry and deliver ready
mixed concrete as an owner-driver.   He bought an appropriate
vehicle on hire-purchase from a finance company associated with the
ready-mixed concrete firm.   The terms of his contract declared him
to be an independent contractor.   In his judgment MACKENNA, J.,
analysed a contract of service in some detail.   He found that there
were three necessary conditions—(i) an agreement by a servant to

---

[1] The courts have recently considered the position of an architect who was
directing building operations, and held that he was not a servant on the facts
of the case.   He was an agent for certain purposes such as ordering materials
but control was lacking.   See *Clayton* v. *Woodman & Son (Builders), Ltd.*,
[1961] 3 All E.R. 249; [1961] 3 W.L.R. 987 at pp. 992–3.   The decision that
he was liable in tort was reversed on appeal, [1962] 1 W.L.R. 585.
[2] [1965] 2 All E.R. 349; [1965] 1 W.L.R. 576.
[3] National Insurance (Industrial Injuries) Act, 1965, Schedule 1, Part 1,
para. 1.   See *infra*, Ch. IX.
[4] [1967] 1 Q.B. 156, at p. 167.
[5] [1968] 2 Q.B. 497, [1968] 1 All E.R. 433.

provide his work and skill in the performance of some service for his master in consideration of a wage or other remuneration; (ii) an agreement, either expressly or impliedly, to accept the master's control; and (iii) other provisions not inconsistent with the relationship being that of master and servant. This last condition was considered by the Judge at some length. He gave five illustrations. In the first, there is an agreement to build providing at the expense of the builder the plant and materials. Even though the builder uses only his own labour and accepts a high degree of control, this is not a contract of service but a building contract. The labour only type of building-contract will be considered later.[1] In the second, there is an agreement to carry goods with the carrier providing everything needed for the performance. This is a contract of carriage. In the third, there is an agreement by a labourer to work for a builder and to provide his own simple tools. Despite this provision of tools, where the labourer accepts the builder's control this is a contract of service. In the fourth, there is an agreement to work for another, to accept his control but to provide one's own transport. This provision of transport is not a sufficiently important matter to affect the contract of service. In the fifth example, the same agreement provides that a person shall work for another under his control and also that he shall sell him land. The first part of this is a contract of service and the radically different obligation under the second part does not affect it.[2]

Having put these examples, MACKENNA, J., summarised his view, saying,

" An obligation to do work subject to the other party's control is a necessary, though not always a sufficient, condition of a contract of service. If the provisions of the contract as a whole are inconsistent with its being a contract of service, it will be some other kind of contract, and the person doing the work will not be a servant. The judge's task is to classify the contract . . . He may, in performing it, take into account other matters besides control."[3]

He found that Latimer had sufficient freedom in the performance of his obligation to make him an independent contractor and not a servant.

There can be no doubt about the rejection of the control test as the sole or even as the supreme or crucial test. In *Argent* v. *Minister of Social Security*,[4] ROSKILL, J., emphasised that no single test was decisive. He was considering the case of a part-time drama teacher whom he held not to be a servant on the particular facts. A part-time interviewer was considered in *Market Investigations, Ltd.* v. *Minister of Social Security*[5] and again the control test was held not

---

[1] See *infra*, p. 13.
[2] See *Amalgamated Engineering Union* v. *Minister of Pensions and National Insurance*, [1963] 1 All E.R. 864; [1963] 1 W.L.R. 441.
[3] [1968] 2 Q.B. 497, at p. 516.
[4] [1968] 3 All E.R. 208; [1968] 1 W.L.R. 1749.
[5] [1969] 2 Q.B. 173; [1968] 3 All E.R. 732.

to be decisive. It was emphasised that the opportunity to use individual skill and personability is often present under a contract of service and the lady in question was held to be a servant even though she had considerable control over her own pattern of working.

Integration.—An alternative way of looking at the problem might be described as the integration test. In *Stevenson, Jordan and Harrison, Ltd.* v. *MacDonald and Evans*, in his judgment, DENNING, L. J., found that employment as part of a business was a feature which ran through contracts of service whilst under a contract of services the work

> "although done for the business, is not integrated into it, but is only an accessory to it."[1]

It would seem to indicate that where a man works as part of a business he will almost invariably be a servant. On the other hand it is also clear that a contract of service may arise in respect of a single isolated transaction which cannot be said to be integrated into the business, provided always that the necessary element of control is present. Again in *Westall Richardson, Ltd.* v. *Roulson*[2] the court considered the situation in the Sheffield cutlery trade of the " outworker." The system is that the outworker occupies a workshop in a factory. He is supplied from the factory with cutlery to polish. The outworker provides his own tools and employs and pays any labour he considers necessary. The court was of the opinion that the outworker was not a servant of the cutlery manufacturer although, in one sense at least, he is an integral part of the business carried on in that factory.

The test was discussed in the *Ready Mixed Concrete* case. An earlier *dictum* of DENNING, L. J., was cited. In *Bank Voor Handel en Scheepvaart N.V.* v. *Slatford*,[3] he said,

> " In this connection I would observe that the test of being a servant does not rest nowadays on submission to orders. It depends on whether the person is part and parcel of the organisation."

MACKENNA, J., raised the query about the exact meaning of " part and parcel of the organisation." He plainly did not regard it as a useful or clear test.

On the other hand COOKE, J., appeared to find this approach useful in the *Market Investigations* case. He said that he found it to be of assistance, as was the test to be found in a Canadian case, *Montreal* v. *Montreal Locomotive Works, Ltd.*,[4] where Lord WRIGHT in the Privy Council said,

---

[1] *Stevenson, Jordon and Harrison, Ltd.* v. *MacDonald and Evans*, [1952] T.L.R. 101, *per* DENNING, L.J., at p. 111.
[2] [1954] 2 All E.R. 448; [1954] 1 W.L.R. 905.
[3] [1953] 1 Q.B. 248, at p. 295.
[4] [1947] 1 D.L.R. 161.

" It has been suggested that a fourfold test would in some cases be more appropriate, a complex involving (1) control; (2) ownership of tools; (3) chance of profit; (4) risk of loss",

and in an American case, *United States* v. *Silk*[1], where it was suggested that the question was one of economic reality. Despite this approach the general conclusions support a multiplicity of tests,

" The most that can be said is that control will no doubt always have to be considered, although it can no longer be regarded as the sole determining factor, and that factors which may be of importance are such matters as whether the man performing the services provides his own equipment, whether he hires his own helpers, what degree of financial risk he takes, what degree of responsibility for investment and management he has, and whether and how far he has an opportunity of profiting from sound management in the performance of his task."[2]

The problem continues to come before the courts. In *Construction Industry Training Board* v. *Labour Force, Ltd.*,[3] COOKE, J., returned to the question of the appropriate test. His view is summarised in two sentences in his judgment,

" First, that no list of tests which has been formulated is exhaustive, and that the weight to be attached to particular criteria varies from case to case. Secondly, although the extent of the control which the alleged employer is entitled to exercise over the work is by no means a decisive criterion of universal application, it is likely in many cases to be a factor of importance."

In *Global Plant, Ltd.* v. *Secretary of State for Health and Social Security*[4] the workers under review drove earth-moving machines and the situation was a typical one of ambiguity between a contract of service and one of services. Again the same tests were discussed. Lord WIDGERY, C. J., accepted the views expressed in the judgments of COOKE, J. He did amplify the test that the opportunity to deploy management skills and make money by doing so indicates a contract of services. He did not regard this as a weighty factor, but accepted that where a man agrees to do work for a fixed sum, and will gain if it is completed quickly and lose if it is late, he is *prima facie* independent.

(3) Transfer of Servant—Who is the Master? A servant may be hired to another so as to make that other his master even whilst the general contract of service with the one who has lent the servant persists. In *Donovan* v. *Laing, Wharton and Down Construction Syndicate*,[5] the defendants contracted to lend a crane and its driver to a firm which was loading a ship at their wharf. The crane driver received directions as to how he should work from the firm and *not* from the defendants. It was held that though the driver remained in

---

[1] (1946), 331 U.S. 704.
[2] [1968] 3 All E.R. 732 at p. 738.
[3] [1970] 3 All E.R. 220.
[4] [1972] 1 Q.B. 139; [1971] 3 All E.R. 385.
[5] [1893] 1 Q.B. 629.

the general service of the defendants they had, for the purposes of this particular transaction, parted with the power to control him and to that extent he became the servant of the firm.[1]

Donovan v. *Laing* was considered and distinguished in *Mersey Docks and Harbour Board* v. *Coggins and Griffith (Liverpool), Ltd.*,[2] in which case the Harbour Board let a crane to stevedores for the purpose of loading a ship and also provided a man to work the crane. The conditions of hiring provided that a craneman in such circumstances should be the servant of the hirers though the Board continued to employ and pay the man and retained the right to dismiss him. The craneman was negligent and injured a third person. The House of Lords held that the Harbour Board as the permanent employer was liable and that, for the purposes of liability for negligence, the craneman remained their servant. One important aspect of the case is that it established that the question of liability for negligence is not to be determined by any agreement between the permanent employer and the person to whom the servant is lent, but will depend on all the circumstances of the case. The general principles governing the loan or transference of servants from one master to another were discussed fully in *Chowdhary* v. *Gillot*.[3] The plaintiff had left his car with the second defendants (the Daimler Co., Ltd.) for repairs and asked a servant of the Company to drive him to the station. Gillot, another servant of the Company, was told to drive the plaintiff and his wife and whilst he was doing so the car collided with a lorry driven by Jones, the third defendant. It was held that Gillot throughout remained the servant of the Company, and did not, on driving the car, come under the control of the plaintiff. STREATFEILD, J., in his judgment laid down five propositions. The presumption, he affirmed, in cases where the transfer of a servant is in issue, is against there being such a transfer, and the burden of proof, which is heavy, is on the general employer to prove that control has passed to the transferee. The general employer must prove that there is such a transference as passes the right to control the servant in the manner of the execution of the act in question. Whether there has been such a transference will be a question of fact[4] and finally, there cannot be such a transference

---

[1] See also *Gibb* v. *United Steel Company, Ltd.*, [1957] 2 All E.R. 110; [1957] 1 W.L.R. 668, where it was emphasised that the mere fact that the general employer continued to pay the servant's wages does not dispose of the question.

[2] [1947] A.C.1; [1946] 2 All E.R. 345.

[3] [1947] 2 All E.R. 541.

[4] See *Garrard* v. *A. E. Southey & Co. & Standard Telephones and Cables, Ltd.*, [1952] 2 Q.B. 174; [1952] 1 All E.R. 597; *O'Reilly* v. *I.C.I.*, [1955] 1 W.L.R. 839, [this case has been rendered of little effect by the Occupiers Liability Act, 1957 under which O'Reilly would have an action whether a servant or not] and *Denham* v. *Midland Employer's Mutual Assurance, Ltd.*, [1955] 2 Q.B. 437, where the transference with authority to control did not take place. *Herdman* v. *Walker (Tooting), Ltd. & City Plant Hirers, Ltd.*, [1956] 1 All E.R. 429; [1956] 1 W.L.R. 209, where control was specifically transferred and *Gibb* v. *United Steel Company, Ltd.*, [1957] 2 All E.R. 110; [1957] 1 W.L.R. 668, where the court held that control had passed.

without the servant's consent.   It has been suggested that such a transference " rarely if ever " takes place when a man is lent with a machine or when a skilled man is lent, but "does sometimes take place " where the man is unskilled.[1]   In *Baxter* v. *Central Electricity Generating Board*[2] there was an interesting attempt to extend the duties of a master to the servant of another who voluntarily helped the master's workmen.   It was held that this could not be done and the servant failed to bring his case within the rules of the master's duty. For a clear example of a transfer see *McArdle* v. *Andmac Roofing Co.*[3]

(4) Special Situations—*Labour Only Contracts.*—The building and civil engineering industries have always had a pattern of employment with distinctive features.   One of these was the labour only contract under which the main contractor supplies the materials and a sub-contractor either individually or as the leader of a gang carries out the work.   This type of arrangement is used in other types of work, in agriculture for example, but it was in the building and civil engineering fields that it came into great prominence. During the 1950's there was a great increase in its use.   There were several reasons for this: the employment pattern, the attitude of the Unions concerned, the taxation structure.[4]   The matter became one of concern for the regulation of employment was most often based on the assumption that there would be the more normal relationship of employer and employee.   The growth of the number of independent contractors meant that many aspects, such as safety and hours of work, were escaping the intended regulation.   The position in the building and civil engineering industries was considered by a Committee of Inquiry under Professor Phelps Brown.[5]

It fell to the courts in several cases to consider the labour only sub-contract.   Union hostility to the system was made clear in *Emerald Construction Co., Ltd.* v. *Lowthian*.[6]   The defendants were officers of the Amalgamated Union of Building Trade Workers.   The plaintiff company had secured a labour only sub-contract in connection with the construction of a large power station.   The Union told the main contractors that unless all bricklayers were directly employed they would advise their members to strike.   No action was taken in response to this threat which was put into operation by means of various forms of industrial action.   An interim injunction was sought against the Union.   This raised the question whether the protection of the Trade Disputes Act, 1906 which speaks of

---

[1] *Denham* v. *Midland Employer's Mutual Assurance, Ltd.*, [1955] 2 Q.B. 437; [1955] 2 All E.R. 561, *per* DENNING, L.J., at p. 444.   *Savory* v. *Holland, Hannen and Cubitts (Southern), Ltd.*, [1964] 3 All E.R. 18; [1964] 1 W.L.R. 1158 is an example of the non-transfer of a specialised workman—a shot-firer.
[2] [1964] 2 All E.R. 815; [1965] 1 W.L.R. 200.
[3] [1967] 1 All E.R. 583.
[4] See recent provisions of Finance Act, 1971, ss. 29–30.
[5] July 1968, Cmnd. 3714.   Especially Chapter VI.
[6] [1966] 1 All E.R. 1013; [1966] 1 W.L.R. 691.

inducement to break a contract of employment applied to such
threats against labour only contracts. This meant that the Court
of Appeal had to consider the juridical nature of the labour only
contract. It was made clear that the contract was perfectly lawful.
It was held that a labour only contract, between main contractor and
sub-contractor, was not a contract of employment even though it was
a contract for the supply of labour.

The same problem came to be considered in a rather unusual way.
A company of building contractors which employed labour only
gangs went into voluntary liquidation.   There was an overdraft with
the bank guaranteed by the directors which related in part to
payments that had been made to such gangs.   The priority of such
a debt under the Companies Act, 1948 depended upon whether it
was on account of wages or salary.   The liquidator did not think it
was.   The guaranteeing directors took out a summons to test this
view.   PLOWMAN, J., applied the *Emerald Construction* case and held
that the labour only contract could not be a contract of employment for the purposes of the Companies Act.[1]

Hospital Service.—The growth of employment by the State and
particularly the employment by the State of professional men, as in
the hospital service, has led to a reconsideration by the Judges, not
of the principles governing the distinction between services and
service, but of the impact of these principles on the changing conditions of professional employment.   *Hillyer's* case[2] had laid down
that the surgeons, physicians and anaesthetists who gave their
services to a hospital were not its servants, and that, in consequence,
the hospital would not be liable for their negligence; they were

" professional men employed by the defendants to exercise their
profession to the best of their abilities according to their own discretion; but in exercising it they are in no way under the orders or
bound to obey the directions of the defendants."[3]

The case went further and laid down that though nurses and theatre
attendants were in general the servants of the employing hospitals,
they were not so when they were working under the control and
subject to the orders of the surgeons. " No surgeon," it was said,

"would undertake the responsibility of operations if his orders
and directions were subject to the control of or interference by the
governing body."[4]

The decision was not without its difficulties and has been the
subject of considerable judicial comment.   Indeed it is now authority
only for the proposition that a hospital will not be responsible for
a doctor whom it does not employ even though he uses services

---

[1] *Re C. W. & A. L. Hughes, Ltd.*, [1966] 2 All E.R. 702; [1966] 1 W.L.R.
1369.   For a more recent illustration of the borderline between employed
and self-employed, see *Inglefield* v. *Macey*, (1967), 2 K.I.R. 146.
[2] *Hillyer* v. *The Governors of St. Bartholomew's Hospital*, [1909] 2 K.B. 820.
[3] *Ibid.* FARWELL, L.J., at p. 825.   [4] *Ibid.* FARWELL, L.J., at p. 826.

provided by the hospital. In *Collins* v. *Hertfordshire County Council*[1] a resident house surgeon was held to be a servant of the employing hospital. A medical officer, owing to a mishearing on the telephone had sent to a surgeon a lethal drug (cocaine instead of procaine) which the surgeon had used on the patient with fatal results. The court held that the County Council, as the authority responsible for the conduct of the hospital was guilty of permitting a dangerous system to operate and that the surgeon and resident house surgeon were negligent. The County Council, however, was held not to be liable for the actions of the surgeon, whose work it could not control, even though he was a part-time employee, but it was able to control the work of the resident house surgeon for whose negligence it was liable. The case had certain weaknesses as an authority, for the resident surgical officer might be said not to be a person of professional standing. She was a student in her final year of training—and the legal status of a fully professional person was still in some doubt. Happily the courts resisted the temptation to draw a distinction between full-time and part-time employees. Nothing but ambiguity and difficulty could arise from any such distinction. HILBERY, J., preferred another line of argument:

> " . . . a consulting surgeon who is on the staff of one of the teaching hospitals or, indeed on the staff of an ordinary hospital . . . goes . . . to perform operations, voluntarily giving services to the hospital. He can refuse to perform an operation and he can come as often as he likes or as seldom as he likes, although, of course, for the convenience of running a hospital he has his days for operating to which he adheres. But he does not do any of that contractually; he does it as a matter of arrangement to which he honourably adheres. It may be that the situation of such a surgeon can be distinguished from the situation of qualified persons employed to fulfil the obligation undertaken by the hospital to give the necessary treatment to a patient."[2]

Whether or not this was an adequate statement of the position before the introduction of a national health service is open to doubt. It is quite inadequate to-day when " ordinary hospitals " are managed by regional boards and teaching hospitals by boards of management on which laymen and medical practitioners are jointly represented. The medical staff of the hospitals, whether resident or consultant, whether full-time or part-time, are appointed by and subject to the general control of the members of the boards acting as agents for the Ministry of Health. But the medical members of the boards would not wish, nor the laymen be competent, to control the method of treating a patient.

The case of *Cassidy* v. *Ministry of Health*[3] enabled the Court of Appeal to look at the effect of the changes in the organisation of

---

[1] [1947] K.B. 598; [1947] 1 All E.R. 633.
[2] [1947] K.B. 598 at p. 618; [1947] 1 All E.R. 633 at p. 640.
[3] [1951] 2 K.B. 343; [1951] 1 All E.R. 574.

hospitals with the result that it was held that a hospital authority is liable for the negligence of doctors and surgeons employed under a contract of service. SOMERVELL, L.J., and SINGLETON, L.J., found that a contract of service existed between the hospital and the whole-time assistant medical officer and Dr. Ronaldson, the house surgeon whose negligence had caused the action to be brought. DENNING, L.J., in a judgment of much interest, went further. He would not accept the view that the question of liability depended on whether there was a contract of service or of services. Liability, he thought, depended on

> " Who employs the doctor or surgeon—is it the patient or the hospital authorities? If the patient himself selects and employs the doctor or surgeon, as in *Hillyer's* case, the hospital authorities are, of course, not liable for his negligence, because he is not employed by them. But where the doctor or surgeon, be he consultant or not, is employed and paid, not by the patient but by the hospital authorities, I am of the opinion that the hospital authorities, are liable for his negligence in treating the patient."[1]

Thus, there is no doubt that where a hospital employs a physician or surgeon under a contract of service the hospital will be liable for his negligence in the course of the employment and the employee, on his side, can enforce his rights against the hospital as his master.[2] Strictly speaking, the legal position of the consultant has not yet been before the courts and the Judges in *Cassidy's* case took care to differentiate the facts with which they were dealing from the position which might arise if the negligence of a consultant were in question. It is true that DENNING, L.J., said in the passage cited above that the hospital would be liable wherever it paid and employed the doctor whether he were consultant or not, but he had also said earlier in his judgment referring to *Gold's* case (*vide infra*) that once hospital authorities were held responsible for nurses and radiographers, he could see no possible reason why they should not also be responsible for the house surgeons and resident medical officers on their permanent staff.

Thus the position of the part-time consultant is not yet certain and the test of by whom he is selected and paid, if it prevails, would seem likely to fasten upon the hospital authorities, a widening field of liability. More patients will, with the aid of their general practitioners select their consultant, into whose hands they will pass when they enter the hospital, but they will not pay the consultant and the consultant will, in the great majority of cases be in the hospital by the authority of and under contract with the hospital authority. Thus, once the test of a hospital authority's inability to control the method in which a professionally trained person does his work is

---

[1] [1951] 2 K.B. at p. 362; [1951] 1 All E.R. at p. 586.
[2] *Edwards* v. *West Herts Group Management Committee*, [1957] 1 All E.R. 541; [1957] 1 W.L.R. 415 where a house physician was held to be a servant but his particular claim failed on the facts. See *infra*, p. 87.

abandoned, and it is clearly no longer valid, there seems no reason, either in logic or expediency, to draw a distinction between consultant part-time and resident full-time services and the emphasis of DENNING, L.J.'s judgment becomes significant. In fact, the judgment is not inconsistent with a statement made by Viscount HAILSHAM, L.C., in *Lindsey County Council* v. *Marshall*,[1] when he said,

"I can see no difference in principle between the employment of a doctor to advise on medical questions and the employment of any other skilled person to advise upon any other questions."

What then, of the hospital nursing and ancillary services of a professional or semi-professional character? At one time it was held that, so far as a nurse was concerned, a distinction was to be drawn between those services which she rendered in her professional capacity and as to which she was held not to be subject to the control of her employers, and her general and routine services, in which she was held to be so subject. This development of the law was almost completely fruitless[2]. So it was held that a nurse who misread a prescription, giving the patient a drug in what proved to be fatal quantities was not capable of such control by her employers as to make them liable for her negligence,[3] but a nurse who injured herself whilst preparing a poultice for administration to a patient was held to be a servant, at least for the purposes of the Workmen's Compensation Acts.[4] Such decisions opened the prospects of unending litigation in the effort to define what were and what were not professional services. However, *Gold* v. *Essex County Council*[5] cut the knot and laid down firmly that a radiographer employed at a hospital owned by the respondents was their servant and that they were responsible for his negligence, even when acting in a professional capacity. Thus it would seem that since patients do not choose their nurses and since nurses are employed under contract of service or of education and training, the hospital will normally be liable for their negligence, and it is unlikely that judicial *dicta* to the contrary now represent true statements of the law.

Other Examples. These general principles may be varied by statute. A pilot, for example, is an independent contractor and is not subject to control when in charge of a vessel.[6] Yet though this is so, the owner or master will, in all those cases where a pilot is compulsory, be liable for his acts as though he were a servant. By

---

[1] [1937] A.C. 97 at p. 107; [1936] 2 All E.R. 1076 at p. 1081.
[2] See "Hospitals and Trained Nurses," by A. L. Goodhart, 54 *L.Q.R.* p. 553; "Hospital Authorities and Locatio Operarum," by J. J. Gow, *Juridical Review*, Vol. LXII, No. 2, Aug. 1950, p. 169, and " The Liability of Hospitals for Negligence," by C. J. Hamson in " The Law in Action," p. 19; and see *Roe* v. *Minister of Health*, [1954] 2 All E.R. 131; [1954] 1 W.L.R. 128.
[3] *Strangways-Lesmere* v. *Clayton*, [1936] 2 K.B. 11; [1936] 1 All E.R. 484.
[4] *Wardell* v. *Kent County Council*, [1938] 2 K.B. 768; [1938] 3 All E.R. 473.
[5] [1942] 2 K.B. 293; [1942] 2 All E.R. 237.
[6] *The Bonvilston* (1914), 30 T.L.R. 311, *per* BARGRAVE DEANE, J., at pp. 311–12.

the operation of the Pilotage Act, 1913, the old defence of compulsory pilotage has gone.[1]   Again, in London, as a result of the London Hackney Carriages Act, 1843, as far as the public are concerned the relationship between the driver-hirer of a cab and the proprietor of the cab is that of master and servant, and it is of no moment that but for the operation of the Act the actual relationship of the parties would be that of bailor and bailee.[2]   The Town Police Clauses Act, 1847, produces the same effect in the provinces in all those circumstances to which the Act applies.   The effect of these three statutes is to create for certain purposes a relationship of master and servant where, applying the normal criteria, none exists, but exceptions from the general principle may run in the other direction.   So it has been held that a police constable, though appointed and in some measure controlled by the local Watch Committee, is not a servant of that body at any rate when he is engaged in the performance of duties laid upon him by statute or common law.[3]

More generally, the position of the company director and the service agreement has attracted dispute and discussion.[4]

4. COMPARISON WITH SIMILAR RELATIONSHIPS

(1) Independent Contractors.—There are certain relationships which, sharing characteristics in common with that of master and servant, are yet to be distinguished from it because of the differing legal consequences.   In the previous section we have discussed the boundary between the servant and the independent contractor. An independent contractor is a person doing that which a principal wishes to delegate, but doing it unfettered by any control except as to the end to be achieved.

Where such a contractor sub-contracts, as in the case of the builder who, instead of hiring tilers, plumbers and the like, contracts with a master tiler or a master plumber, there is no relationship of master and servant between the contractor (the builder of our example) and the sub-contractors, though of course the relationship will be established between any of the latter and the men they employ to work to their orders.

(2) Agents.—The relationship of principal and agent is one which often overlaps that of master and servant.   Agency springs from the fundamental rule that a man is generally able to exercise his rights through another and that other's act will be regarded as his own—*qui facit per alium facit per se.*   The definition of agent as " a person who is authorised to act for a principal and has agreed so to act, and who has power to affect the legal relationship of his principal with a third

---

[1] S. 15.
[2] *King* v. *London Improved Cab. Co.* (1889), 23 Q.B.D. 281. at p. 284.
[3] *Fisher* v. *Oldham Corporation*, [1930] 2 K.B. 364.
[4] See for example, *Lee* v. *Lee's Air Farming Ltd.*, [1961] A.C. 12.

party "[1] emphasises that the kernel of agency is the adjustment by the agent in some way, by contracting or giving a receipt, for example, of the relationship of the principal and another person called the third party. The principal may choose to appoint as his agent either a servant or an independent contractor, depending very much on considerations similar to those discussed above.[2] Care must be taken to avoid confusion in the field of tort where the master's responsibility for the acts of his servants is often based on the same fundamental idea as that of agency. In a sense the workman who is told by his master to dig a hole is the master's agent for so doing, and will often be so described. It will be seen when vicarious liability is discussed that the relationships of servant, independent contractor and person authorised to act although not in contractual relationship are of paramount importance. To analyse these relationships in terms of agency easily leads to confusion, and there would be much less if the idea of agency were restricted to the field of contract. The difficulty of distinguishing servant and agent usually arises where there is an informal relationship. In the field of criminal law, the appropriation of property by an agent will be either theft by a bailee or fraudulent conversion, whereas taking by a servant will be a different head of theft. There are, therefore, in this field cases which illustrate this relationship.

So where workmen arranged that one of their number should collect the wages due to them in gross from their employer, from whom also the chosen worker would learn how the sum was to be distributed amongst them, it was held that he received the money as agent for the workers and not in his capacity as a servant.[3] An art dealer engaged to sell a carpet and furniture on commission was held to be an agent and not a servant,[4] as was a person employed to sell coal and collect accounts and to attend an office for the purpose of accounting for receipts, but who had the most complete liberty to go where he pleased for the orders.[5] The method of remuneration is not conclusive, for a servant may be paid a varying commission and an agent may receive a fixed salary.

(3) Service Tenancies.—We have next to discuss the position where a person lives in a house owned by his employer. For certain purposes it is necessary to know whether the occupier holds as servant or as tenant.[6] If he occupies in the latter capacity the rights and duties of a tenant accrue to or fall upon him. If he occupies only as servant then, from the standpoint of the law, he has no independent

---

[1] *The Law of Agency*, by R. Powell, 2nd Ed. (1961). For a full discussion of the relationship, servant, agent and independent contractor, see pp. 7 *et seq.*
[2] See p. 7, *ante.*
[3] *R. v. Barnes* (1866), L.R. 1 C.C.R. 45.
[4] *Lowther* v. *Harris*, [1927] 1 K.B. 393.
[5] *R. v. Marshall* (1870), 21 L.T. 796.
[6] *Ramsbottom* v. *Snelson*, [1948] 1 K.B. 473; [1948] 1 All E.R. 201.

occupation of the tenement at all; his apparent occupation is, in law, occupation by his master.[1] His possession is of a mere physical character, lacking that " exclusive " character which is essential to a true tenancy.   The distinction between occupation as a tenant and occupation as a servant may be extremely fine,[2] but it is generally true that where a person is permitted

> " to occupy premises by way of reward for services or part payment his occupation is that of a tenant, but that where he is required to occupy them for the better performance of his duties, though his residence there is not necessary for that purpose, or if his residence there be necessary for the performance of his duties though not specifically required, his occupation is not that of tenant."[3]

(4) Partnerships.—Questions of some nicety arise also between service and partnership.   The Partnership Act, 1890, makes specific reference to the topic by enacting[4] that a contract for the remuneration of a servant or agent of a person engaged in a business by a share of the profits of the business does not of itself make the servant or agent a partner in the business.   Sharing in profits is a valuable test as to whether the agreement constitutes partnership rather than service, and an agreement to share losses is perhaps more so.[5]   The sure guide is the intention of the parties and here, the terms which the parties use are not conclusive.   So where a son lived with his father and helped in the father's business which traded under the name of Rushworth and Son, it was held that he was not a partner though he and his father had entered into a deed in which they described themselves as co-partners.[6]   The court decided that whatever the position between the parties and the world at large they were not partners *inter se*, for though the son kept the firm's books of account there were no entries as to division of profits and no proof of the son's contributing capital or taking a share of the profits.   In *Stocker* v. *Brockelbank*[7] a firm exploited a process which their manager had discovered.   The manager's contract of service provided that his employment should be irrevocable during the period for which the process was licensed, that he should be remunerated by the payment of a percentage of the profits and that he should be able to buy the business on agreed terms.   It was held that the manager was a mere servant.   For none of the incidents of partnership were present;

---

[1] This has important consequences under the Rent Acts, see Service Occupiers, *The Rent Acts*, by R. E. Megarry, 10th Ed.

[2] *Cf. Bent* v. *Roberts* (1877), 3 Ex. D. 66 with *Martin* v. *West Derby Assessment Committee* (1883), 11 Q.B.D. 145.

[3] *Fox* v. *Dalby* (1874), L.R. 10 C.P. 285.

[4] S. 2 (3) (b).

[5] *R.* v. *MacDonald* (1861), Le. & Ca. 85.   *Walker* v. *Hirsch* (1884), 27 Ch.D. 460.

[6] *Radcliffe* v. *Rushworth* (1864), 33 Beav. 484.

[7] (1851), 3 Mac. & G. 250.

" he is to contribute no capital, sustain no loss, his credit is not to be pledged, he is to manage the trade according to the direction of the defendants, and he has no uncontrollable discretion. . . ."[1]

We have already noted that where the owner of a vehicle hires it to one who drives it for profit the relationship is technically one of bailment though statute may, as far as the general public is concerned, give the association the legal effects of a master and servant relationship.[2] In *Keen* v. *Henry*[3] the plaintiff's mare had been killed by a driver who bailed a cab daily for the purpose of plying for hire. KAY, L.J., had no doubt about the position.

"The plaintiff whose mare has been killed has nothing to do with the relation between the proprietor and the driver, but whatever that relationship may be he is entitled to look to the proprietor for an indemnity."[4]

The principle affects third parties only and, as between themselves, the proprietor and driver are not master and servant, so where the driver of a vehicle which he had bailed was injured the House of Lords held that he was not a workman within the Workmen's Compensation Acts and could not recover from the proprietor.[5]

---

[1] (1851), 3 Mac. & G. 250, *per* LORD TRURO, L.C., at p. 263.
[2] As to bailor-bailee relationship, see *ante*, p. 180.
[3] [1894] 1 Q.B. 292.
[4] *Ibid.*, at p. 295.
[5] *Smith* v. *General Motor Cab. Co., Ltd.*, [1911] A.C. 188.

CHAPTER II

FORMATION OF THE CONTRACT OF SERVICE

We have already seen that the relationship of master and servant arises out of a contract. We have now to consider the character of that contract, its formation, its duration and its termination.

A contract is an agreement by which two or more persons agree to regulate their legal relationships, recognised and, generally speaking, enforced by the law. Before the law will recognise an agreement as a contract, certain essential conditions must be fulfilled. They are as follows:—

(i) One party must agree expressly or impliedly to perform an undertaking and the other party agree to accept such performance. There must, that is to say, be offer and acceptance.

(ii) Both parties must intend that the agreement shall give rise to a legally recognised obligation.

(iii) Both parties must be persons whom the law acknowledges as competent to enter into contracts. They must have capacity.

(iv) The agreement must be supported by consideration or entered into according to certain prescribed forms.

(v) The objects of the contract must be legal.

These conditions are essentials of the law respecting every type of contract. They will be discussed in this book only in their relevance to the contracts of service and apprenticeship. For a discussion of their wider aspects the reader is advised to refer to the standard works on the law of contract where he will find them more comprehensively treated.

1. Offer and Acceptance

(1) General Principles.—No contract can arise until the minds of the parties are brought together in agreement. Such agreement is evidenced by the making of an offer by one party (the offeror) and the acceptance of that offer by the other party (the offeree).[1] Until that process is complete there can be no binding obligation between the parties. The offer must be sufficiently precise in its terms as to be capable of acceptance, so that when A agreed that, should a certain play go to London after a provincial tour, he would engage B to play a part "at a West End salary to be mutually arranged between us" no action could be successfully brought.

---

[1] *Hudspeth* v. *Yarnold* (1850), 9 C.B. 625.

The parties were taken to intend there to be no binding contract until a defined or clearly ascertainable salary had been offered and accepted.[1]

Offers are either particular or general. Particular offers are addressed to a specified person and may be accepted by that person only. If A offers employment particularly to B, there can be no binding agreement if C purports to accept it, except where he does so on B's behalf within cases covered by the law of agency. A would be free to regard C's purported acceptance not as an acceptance but as an offer, and the right of acceptance or rejection of such offer would lie with A. General offers may be made either to individuals within a specified group or to the world at large. Numerous examples of offers made to the members of a specified class have occurred during the two recent European wars. Corporations and companies of various kinds announced their readiness to pay to such of their employees as should serve in His Majesty's Forces the difference between the remuneration paid by the corporation to the employee in question and that received by him whilst in the service of the Crown. Such offers were clearly addressed to the employees as a class and could be accepted only by them. Enlistment in such cases would amount to an acceptance of the offer by conduct.[2] An offer made to all the world will bind the offeror as soon as it is accepted in the mode which he indicates. The evidence in *Williams* v. *Carwardine*[3] showed that an advertisement had been published which offered a reward to anyone giving such information as would enable the murderer of A to be discovered. B supplied the information and was held to be entitled to the reward even though she was prompted to give the information, not by the reward offered but as the result of other motives. It seems clear that B knew of the offer of the reward.[4]

The acceptance must conform unconditionally with the terms of the offer. Consequently where A, who intended to enter the service of B, received from B a letter stating "yours of yesterday embodies the substance of our conversation and terms. If we can define the terms a little more clearly it may prevent mistakes, but I think we are quite agreed on all. We shall therefore expect you on Monday," it was held that there was not a binding contract, since B's acceptance was qualified and in fact amounted to a counter offer.[5] An

---

[1] *Loftus* v. *Roberts* (1902), 18 T.L.R. 532. *Cf. Powell* v. *Braun*, [1954] 1 All E.R. 484; [1954] 1 W.L.R. 401, where the court were willing to quantify an agreed bonus. See *infra*, p. 28, and see *N.C.B.* v. *Galley*, [1958] 1 All E.R. 91; [1958] 1 W.L.R. 16.

[2] See *Davies* v. *Rhondda District Urban Council* (1917), 87 L. J. K.B. 166. *Shipton* v. *Cardiff Corporation* (1917), 87 L. J. K.B. 51.

[3] (1833), 5 C. & P. 566, subsequent proceedings (1833), 4 B. & Ad. 621; see also *Edgar* v. *Blick* (1816), 1 Stark. 464.

[4] *Williams* v. *Carwardine* (1833), seems to be inadequately reported in 4 B. & Ad. 621.

[5] *Appleby* v. *Johnson* (1874), L.R. 9 C.P. 158. *Cf. Homeward Bound Extended Gold-Mining Co., Ltd.* v. *Anderson* (1884), 3 N.Z.L.R. 266.

intention to accept is not sufficient, but the acceptance need not be a formal acceptance.   It may, indeed, be evidenced by conduct,[1] provided that whether it be formal or by conduct it is notified to the offeror by those competent to do so.   In *Powell* v. *Lee*[2] the court was concerned with what amounted to the unauthorised notification of an acceptance.   Powell and others had applied for the post of headmaster, and the school managers, by resolution, appointed Powell to the vacancy provided he married a lady having the qualifications to become a schoolmistress.   The decision was not communicated to Powell.   A meeting was called later, the matter was re-opened and a competing candidate selected.   Powell then learned of the position, and one of the managers assured Powell that "he would stand by him."   The court decided that there was no contract, and emphasised the principle that only an authorised acceptance of Powell's offer could make the transaction into a binding contract.   The person making the offer cannot make silence an acceptance by saying, "If I do not hear from you I shall take this as acceptance."[3]   Acceptance must be notified but where post is an accepted method of reply to an offer, acceptance will date from the time of posting.[4]

Acceptance or rejection closes the offer and there can be no renewal of negotiations thereafter except by agreement.   Should the offer not be accepted it may be revoked by the offeror at any time and it will lapse by the death of either party, by the making of a counter offer and by the effluxion of time where a time has been named, or where no provision has been made as to time, at the end of a reasonable period of time.   What is reasonable in such cases will vary with the type of service involved.

The law regards the contract of employment as a personal matter between the two parties.   It follows that agreements arising from collective bargaining between employers and trade unions do not *ipso facto* become part of individual contracts of employment.   The terms agreed, however, will be acted upon by the two sides and will then by implication be incorporated as terms in each appropriate contract of employment.   Only in an indirect sense does the system of collective negotiation have legal effect on the individual's contract of service.   The legal status of the collective bargain is now affected by the Industrial Relations Act, 1971.[5]

(2) Mistake.—The consent of the parties to a contract must be a genuine consent, and anything which renders the consent illusory or unreal will affect either the formation or the performance of the contract.   The elements usually affecting consent arise from mistake, misrepresentation (either innocent or fraudulent), duress

---

[1] *Paynter* v. *Williams* (1833), 1 C. & M. 810.
[2] (1908), 99 L.T. 284.
[3] *Felthouse* v. *Bindley* (1862), 11 C.B. N.S. 869.
[4] *Byrne* v. *Van Tienhoven* (1880), 5 C.P.D. 344.
[5] Ss. 34 *et seq.*

and undue influence. These have, however, varying effects, and though, in relation to the contract of service there is a scarcity of authority on them, they require consideration in some detail.

The legal effect of mistake on a contract will be found expounded with great clarity in *Bell* v. *Lever Bros., Ltd.*[1] and *Solle* v. *Butcher*.[2] Not every kind of mistake will affect a contract; where it does so it will, at law, operate either to negative or in some cases to nullify consent. Mistake may arise either as to the identity of the parties or as to the existence or quality of the subject matter. Mistake concerning the identity of the parties will not affect a contract at law except where the identity of one of the parties is a paramount consideration.

Clearly in most contracts of service the personal element will be paramount and a mistake as to identity will make any purported agreement void *ab initio*. Mistake as to the existence of the subject matter is not likely to arise in contracts of service, but the courts have in recent years discussed quite acute problems arising from what is, in effect, mistake as to the quality of the subject matter. The cases, it is true, do not involve a continuance of the contract. They are concerned only with its discharge, but they are none the less instructive. A mistake as to the quality of the subject matter

" will not affect assent unless it is the mistake of both parties and affects the existence of some quality which makes the thing without the quality essentially different from the thing as it was believed to be."[3]

In *Bell* v. *Lever Bros., Ltd.*,[4] two points arose for decision. The appellant and another had been paid the sum of £50,000 by the company in consideration of an agreement to determine their contracts of service, of which part of the term was still to run. After this the company sought rescission of the second contract on the grounds of mistake and non-disclosure. It appeared that both appellants had acted in breach of their service agreements, and, had the company known, the contracts might have been terminated without compensation. Clearly there was a mistake as to subject matter; the question before the court was whether it was mistake of such a kind as to make the thing contracted for different from the thing secured. In Lord ATKIN's words, "Is an agreement to terminate a broken contract different in kind from an agreement to terminate an unbroken contract?"[5] His Lordship thought not.

"The contract released is the identical contract in both cases, and the party paying for the release gets exactly what he bargains for. It seems immaterial that he could have got the same result in another way, or that if he had known the true facts he would not have entered into the bargain."[6]

---

[1] [1932] A.C. 161, at pp. 217 *et seq.*
[2] [1950] 1 K.B. 671; [1949] 2 All E.R. 1107.
[3] *Bell* v. *Lever Bros., Ltd.*, [1932] A.C. 161, *per* Lord ATKIN at p. 218.
[4] *Ibid.*   [5] *Ibid.*, p. 223.   [6] *Ibid.*, pp. 223-4.

The second point requiring decision is suggested by the last sentence, namely : was there no duty of disclosure on the part of the appellants? The answer is that no such general duty exists. Unless the law lays a specific duty of disclosure on a party he may keep silent even as to matters which he knows would influence the other. In three sets of circumstances only does the duty to disclose arise.[1] In the first the duty of disclosure may arise out of the relationship of the parties as is the case, for example, with principal and agent, trustee and beneficiary. Such relations are said to be fiduciary. *Bell's* case shows clearly that no such duty arises in the case of master and servant.[2] In the second place there are certain contracts—said to be *uberrimae fidei*—in which one of the parties has peculiar means of knowledge and upon whom the law lays an obligation to make the most complete disclosure. But again the contract of service is not such a contract. The third class of cases may involve contracts of any kind. If a party to negotiations innocently makes a statement which he later discovers to be false he is under a duty to correct it, and where a true statement is made which later becomes, to the knowledge of its maker, false, there is also a duty to correct it.[3]

Mistake which negatives or nullifies consent makes the contract void *ab initio*. There is a considerable body of case law and periodical literature upon the topic of mistake and in particular upon that aspect concerning mistaken identity.[4] Most mistake cases arise because the plaintiff, if successful, will recover goods which had apparently passed to an innocent purchaser, for no property can pass under a void contract or, with certain well defined exceptions, thereafter. Recovery of the goods in this way is obviously preferable to an action in fraudulent misrepresentation against the rogue. Such action is often collaterally available but will generally prove to be worthless. It follows from the particular significance played by the question of the passing of property that the cases have little relevance to a contract of master and servant. In such cases the right to determine the contract is what is sought and this follows from the fraud without need for an enquiry into the application of the rules of mistake. One case which does show the possible application of the rules is *Boulton* v. *Jones.*[5] Here an order for leather hose was

---

[1] This analysis of the law is based upon the judgment of FRY, J., in *Davies* v. *London and Provincial Marine Insurance Co.* (1878), 8 Ch.D. 469, at pp. 474–5 particularly.

[2] See also *Healey* v. *Société Anonyme Française Rubastic*, [1917] 1 K.B. 946 and *Swain* v. *West (Butchers), Ltd.*, [1936] 3 All E.R. 261; but see *Cork* v. *Kirby MacLean, Ltd.*, [1952] 2 All E.R. 402, in the field of tort..

[3] *Davies* v. *London and Provincial Marine Insurance Co., supra.*

[4] Articles of note include C. J. Slade, " The Myth of Mistake in the English Law of Contract," 64 *L.Q.R.* 230; J. F. Wilson, " Identity in Contract and the Pothier Fallacy," 17 *M.L.R.* 515 and the reply by J. Unger, 18 *M.L.R.* 259; K. O. Shatwell, " The Supposed Doctrine of Mistake in Contract, a Comedy of Errors," 33 Canadian Bar Review, 164.

[5] (1857), 2 H. & N. 564.

sent to Brocklehurst but was accepted by the plaintiff, who had taken over the business from Brocklehurst. Jones refused to pay saying that he had intended only to deal with Brocklehurst. The reason for this seems to have been that Jones had a set-off against Brocklehurst. Jones was held not to be liable for the price and it can be assumed that in a similar case where the purchaser addresses his offer to another because of his particular skill, as a painter or carver for example, a similar decision would be reached where that person's successor purported to accept.

(3) **Misrepresentation.**—The representations of parties to a contract may either induce a person to enter into the contract or introduce terms into the contract. A representation which is false may, as we have seen, lead to mistake of such a character as will prevent a contract coming into existence. Misrepresentations which do not prevent the formation of a contract are either innocent or fraudulent. A misrepresentation must, of course, mislead, and will be innocent if the untrue statement of fact is made in an honest belief that it is true. It will be fraudulent where it is made knowingly, or without a belief in its truth or recklessly, careless whether it be true or false.[1] Rescission has always been a remedy for both innocent and for fraudulent misrepresentation. An action for damages would also lie where the misrepresentation was fraudulent. Since the Misrepresentation Act, 1967 a court can now award damages in a case of innocent misrepresentation where there is negligence. Should the misrepresentation become a term of the contract —which is a matter of construction for the courts[2]—it will be a warranty or a condition. A warranty is a term collateral to the main agreement, a violation of which gives rise to an action for damages but not to a right to repudiate. So in *Bettini* v. *Gye*[3] a term in a contract of service that a singer would reach this country so as to have six days for rehearsal was held to be a mere warranty. When the singer arrived having only two such days, it was held that there was no right of repudiation. A condition is a term vital to the contract, breach of which entitles the injured party to damages and gives him also " another and higher remedy; namely, that of treating the contract as repudiated."[4] The right to rescind will be lost where the injured party has, by unambiguous words or acts, after knowledge of the misrepresentation, affirmed the contract, or if, before the contract has been avoided, innocent third parties have secured rights under

---

[1] *Derry* v. *Peek* (1889), 14 App. Cas. 337, *per* Lord HERSCHELL at p. 374. The failure of a servant to disclose his own misdoing will not amount to fraud; *Bell* v. *Lever Bros., Ltd.*, [1932] A.C. 161; *Healey* v. *Société Anonyme Française Rubastic, supra.*

[2] *Behn* v. *Burness* (1863), 3 B. & S. 751, *per* WILLIAMS, J., at p. 754.

[3] (1876), 1 Q.B.D. 183; see also *Richards* v. *Hayward* (1841), 2 Man. & G. 574.

[4] *Wallis, Son and Wells* v. *Pratt and Haynes*, [1910] 2 K.B. 1003, *per* FLETCHER MOULTON, L.J., at p. 1013.

it,[1] or if the misrepresenting party cannot be restored to his original position.

(4) Duress and Undue Influence.—Any contract of service induced by duress or undue influence is voidable at the option of the party suffering the compulsion. Duress involves the use of violence or the threat of violence or imprisonment. It must be directed by one party or his agent to the other party, his spouse or his children. Undue influence arises where one party exerts such influence over another that the will of that other is unconscionably influenced. The remedy is available, not to those who are the victims of their own folly, but to those who are victimised by others.[2] Duress differs from fraud in that in duress the victim is aware of the true state of facts and his knowledge precludes a right of action in deceit. Both fraud and duress differ from undue influence in that a person alleging either is put to the strictest proof, whilst, where one party is known to have had much influence over another, the onus of disproving its unfair use will fall on him who is said to have possessed it. Indeed, in those relations which we have already described as fiduciary the law presumes such influence. Master and servant does not, as we know, constitute such a relationship, though master and apprentice may.[3] Undue influence, however, does not arise only in the case of fiduciary relationships.

" Wherever the courts find one of two persons exercising undue influence over the other it will not allow a transaction to . . . stand."[4]

So in *Collins* v. *Hare*,[5] where a clerk had coerced his master into paying a substantial portion of the premium on an insurance policy for the benefit of the clerk, it was held that an assignment to the clerk of that part of the policy covered by the master's premiums was void.

Money paid under the compulsion of the law, even though mistakenly, will not, of course, support a claim for duress or undue influence.[6]

2. INTENTION OF THE PARTIES

"To create a contract there must be a common intention of the parties to enter into legal obligations. . . ."[7] Where the subject matter of the agreement is social, the law will presume that no legal obligation is intended, but where the parties agree as to their business relations the contrary presumption will prevail.[8] In

---

[1] This would appear to be impossible in the case of the contract of service.
[2] *Allcard* v. *Skinner* (1887), 36 Ch.D. 145, *per* LINDLEY, L.J., at p. 182.
[3] *Peacock* v. *Kernot* (1848), 10 L.T. (O.S.) 517.
[4] *Fowler* v. *Wyatt* (1857), 24 Beav. 232, *per* ROMILLY, M.R., at p. 237.
[5] (1828), 1 Dow & Cl. 139. *Cf. Barnes* v. *Richards* (1902), 7 L.J. K.B. 341.
[6] *William Whiteley, Ltd.* v. *R.* (1909), 101 L.T. 741.
[7] *Rose and Frank Co.* v. *J.R. Crompton and Bros., Ltd.*, [1923] 2 K.B. 261, *per* ATKIN, L.J., at p. 293.
[8] *Ibid.* at pp. 282, 288, 293.   *Edwards* v. *Skyways, Ltd.*, [1964] 1 W.L.R. 349 is an interesting illustration of this point.

Taylor v. *Brewer* the point at issue was whether the members of the committee of a club had legally bound themselves by a resolution

> " that any service to be rendered by W shall, after the third lottery, be taken into consideration and such remuneration be made as shall be deemed right."[1]

The court was of opinion that this was a mere engagement of honour not amounting to a contract.   Similarly, the relationship existing between the Salvation Army and its officers is, apparently, not a contractual relationship, so that where such an officer was injured whilst working on premises occupied by the Salvation Army, that organisation was held not liable under the Workmen's Compensation Acts.[2]   The parties did not intend, the court believed, to confer upon one another rights and obligations which are capable of enforcement in a court of law.   On the other hand, where an employer offered, in return for added responsibility and past faithful service, a bonus on the net trading profit but did not state the basis on which the bonus was to be calculated, the Court of Appeal distinguished *Taylor* v. *Brewer* and held there was a binding agreement and awarded the plaintiff £25.[3]

3. CAPACITY

Principles of law are, in general, designed to operate in normal circumstances on persons who are not subject to legal disabilities. Yet, though this is generally so, every legal system must make provision for those who, because of their status or condition, require exceptional treatment.   The categories which require special treatment from the point of view of capacity or immunity are : (i) the Crown and its servants; (ii) foreign sovereigns and their diplomatic agents; (iii) aliens; (iv) corporations; (v) infants; (vi) mentally disordered persons and drunkards; (vii) partners.

(1) The Crown and Its Servants.   Historically the Crown occupied a position of high preference in the law of contract in that it could not be sued in its own courts, and though this position has now been amended, the special situation of the Crown as party to a contract requires comment.   In addition a contract of service with or under the Crown has characteristics peculiar to itself.

For many centuries there existed no right of action against the Sovereign and even when the harshness of the rule was so clear as to prompt the granting of a petition of right, such a grant was of grace, "of extreme grace", but not of right.   In 1947, the Crown Proceedings Act was passed and this provides, amongst other things, that where a person has a claim of right against the Crown and, if the Act had not been passed, the claim might have been enforced,

---

[1] *Taylor* v. *Brewer* (1813), 1 M. & S. 290, at p. 291.
[2] *Rogers* v. *Booth*, [1937] 2 All E.R. 751.
[3] *Powell* v. *Braun*, [1954] 1 All E.R. 484; [1954] 1 W.L.R. 401.

subject to the consent of the Crown, by petition of right, or might have been enforced by a proceeding provided by any statutory provision repealed by the Act, then, subject to the provisions of the Act, the claim may be enforced *as of right* by proceedings taken against the Crown for that purpose in accordance with the provisions of the Act.[1]

Thus many former procedural difficulties are ended but only in relation to those claims which, before the passing of the Act were enforceable, by petition of right or under the terms of some statute. The right to sue the Crown for breach of contract is, therefore, still a right subject to limitations. And it is at this point that the peculiar characteristics of a contract of service with or under the Crown must be considered.

A contract of service with the Crown is terminable without notice at the Crown's pleasure except in those cases where statute otherwise provides. The petitioner in *Dunn* v. *R.*[2] was engaged by the Commissioner for Nigeria as a consular agent for a period of three years certain. He was dismissed within that period and on action brought it was held that he could not recover for breach of contract. Under the same principle it has been held that a term in a contract which purports to nullify the rule that a Crown servant is dismissible at pleasure, will be invalid. In *Denning* v. *Secretary of State for India in Council*,[3] a clause stipulating for notice of dismissal except in the case of misconduct was unavailing. But of course the power of the Crown may be restricted by statute,[4] and the Privy Council in *Reilly* v. *R.*[5] expressed the view, that quite apart from statute

> "if the terms of the appointment definitely prescribe a term and expressly provide for a power to determine 'for cause' it appears, necessarily, to follow that any implication of a power to dismiss at pleasure is excluded."

Such a view is not binding on English courts and should be treated with caution, for the general trend of decisions does not give it support. Thus in the recent case of *Riordan* v. *War Office*[6] the plaintiff was employed on terms laid down in Army Council Regulations which provided for a period of notice of dismissal. This term was held to be void and the Crown's right to dismiss without notice was confirmed.

In the case of *Lucas* v. *Lucas and High Commissioner for India*[7] the wife of an Indian civil servant sought to attach her husband's

---

[1] Crown Proceedings Act, 1947, s. 1.
[2] [1896] 1 Q.B. 116.
[3] (1920), 37 T.L.R. 138.
[4] *Gould* v. *Stuart*, [1896] A.C. 575.
[5] [1934] A.C. 176, at p. 179.
[6] [1959] 3 All E.R. 552; [1959] 1 W.L.R. 1046, affirmed by the Court of Appeal, [1960] 3 All E.R. 774; [1961] 1 W.L.R. 210.
[7] [1943] P. 68; [1943] 2 All E.R. 110.

"overseas pay" paid to him through the High Commissioner for India against arrears of alimony, but it was held that she might not do so. To succeed she would have to show that there was a debt owing or accruing to her husband from the Crown. The court said this was not so, for Mr. Lucas could not maintain an action for unpaid salary against the Crown.[1] A different conclusion was reached by the Privy Council in a Ceylon case, Kodeeswaran v. A.—G. of Ceylon, where a civil servant's right of action against the Crown was accepted.[2]

It has moreover been suggested that the reason that contracts of service with the Crown should be terminable at will is to be found in the still wider principle that a necessary characteristic of the doctrine of the sovereignty of Parliament is that future executive action cannot be fettered. Such indeed was the argument in *Rederiaktiebolaget Amphitrite* v. *R.*[3] but the case has not found wide acceptance and was distinguished in *Robertson* v. *Minister of Pensions*[4] wherein it was held that an army officer was entitled to rely on an assurance from the War Office that his disability was to be attributed to military service and that such an assurance bound the Crown. DENNING, J., pointed out that the doctrine of executive necessity was in fact unnecessary for the decision in the *Amphitrite* case:

> "because the statement there was not a promise which was to be binding, but only an expression of intention. . . . In my opinion the defence of executive necessity is of limited scope. It only avails the Crown where there is an implied term to that effect or that is the true meaning of the contract."[5]

Despite these rules the Industrial Relations Act, 1971 applies the rules of unfair dismissal, which are not dependent on the question of notice to Crown servants with the exception of the armed forces[6] and certain employees who may be covered by a certificate issued by a Minister of the Crown on the grounds of national security.[7]

A contract with the Crown may not be enforced against Crown servants so as to make them liable in their official capacities. Where the Deputy Commissioner of Natal had taken over certain wagons and oxen an effort to make him personally liable failed.[8] When servants of the Crown act publicly there is a presumption that they

---

[1] "A Civil Servant and His Pay," by D. W. Logan, July 1945, 61 *L.Q.R.* 240; Crown Proceedings Act, 1947, by H. Street, 2 *M.L.R.*, 1948, No. 2, at pp.130–131.

[2] [1970] A.C. 1111.

[3] [1921] 3 K.B. 500.

[4] [1949] 1 K.B. 227; [1948] 2 All E.R. 767, but see *Commissioners of Crown Lands* v. *Page*, [1960] 2 Q.B. 274; [1960] 2 All E.R. 726, especially DEVLIN, L. J., at pp. 291, 735 respectively.

[5] *Ibid.*, p. 231, and p. 770 respectively.

[6] S. 162(2), (3d).

[7] S. 162(7).

[8] *Palmer* v. *Hutchinson* (1881), 6 App. Cas. 619. See also *Macbeath* v. *Haldimand* (1786), 1 Term Rep. 172.

act as agents and the normal rules of agency apply and it will require the most unambiguous language to make them personally liable. "No doubt," said Viscount HALDANE in *Commercial Cable Co.* v. *Government of Newfoundland*:

> "if he chose in unambiguous language to bind himself by contract personally, the Governor could do so and take the consequences, but he could not, by doing so, bind the Parliament and the people."[1]

But though in the main the principles of the law of agency apply where Crown servants act in their representative capacity, one further difference should be noted. The agent of a private principal is liable on a contract made as the result of his assertion of an authority he does not, in fact, possess; an agent of the Crown will not, it has been suggested, be so liable,[2] but the rule is not without its critics.[3]

The extension of public enterprise makes the delineation of Crown service a matter of great importance. The traditional field of Crown service is those tasks of government which originally lay within the royal prerogative and covers the Ministers of State and their subordinates.[4] The creation of commercial corporations has given rise to a further list. The corporation will only be a Crown servant if Parliament in the Act creating it has indicated that it is to act on behalf of the Crown.

> " In the absence of any such express provision, the proper inference, in the case, at any rate, of a commercial corporation, is that it acts on its own behalf, even though it is controlled by a government department."[5]

In this sphere, commercial undertakings directly under the Crown and those expressly protected[6] gain Crown immunity. They are in contrast to the National Coal Board, the airways corporations and so on.

(2) Foreign Sovereigns and their Diplomatic Agents.— Foreign sovereigns, the diplomatic representatives of foreign powers and their servants have a full capacity to contract but have also a complete immunity from the jurisdiction of our courts unless, with the permission of their superior, they waive their privilege.

---

[1] [1916] 2 A.C. 610 at p. 616.
[2] *Dunn* v. *MacDonald*, [1897] 1 Q.B. 555.
[3] See *Governmental Liability* by H. Street, C.U.P., 1953, at p. 93.
[4] *Bank voor Handel en Scheepvaart N.V.* v. *Administrator of Hungarian Property*, [1954] A.C. 584; [1954] 1 All E.R. 969.
[5] *Tamlin* v. *Hannaford*, [1950] 1 K.B. 18, *per* DENNING, L.J., at p. 25; [1949] 2 All E.R. 327 at p. 330.
[6] *E.g.* Regional Hospital Boards, Board of Governors of a Teaching Hospital and Hospital Management Committees:— National Health Service Act, 1946 (9 & 10 Geo. 6, c.81) ss. 12, 13(2). Central Land Board :— Town and Country Planning Act, 1947 (10 & 11 Geo. 6, c. 51) s. 3(2).

This represents the position both at common law[1] and by statute.[2] The immunity extends even to commercial transactions;[3] it covers a British subject accredited to Great Britain by a foreign power,[4] and will extend for such time after the appointment of a successor as is reasonably necessary to enable the privileged person to wind up his affairs.[5] To constitute a waiver of privilege there must be actual submission in face of the court, for example, by appearance in answer to a writ.[6] Applying these principles to the contract of service, it will be seen that though foreign sovereigns, their diplomatic staffs and servants have capacity to enter into such contracts, an injured party will not be able to obtain redress should the contract be broken unless (i) there is waiver of privilege, or (ii) the contract makes provision for a surety who is within the jurisdiction and who may consequently be made liable.

There is now a tendency, with the growth of international organisations and the like, to extend the principles of diplomatic immunity. The International Organisations (Immunities and Privileges) Act, 1950,[7] and the Diplomatic Immunities (Commonwealth Countries and Republic of Ireland) Act, 1952,[8] have respectively given powers to grant immunities to international organisations, Judges, counsel, suitors, etc. of the international court and representatives of powers at international conferences, and to representatives of the Commonwealth countries and the Republic of Ireland. On the other hand the Diplomatic Immunities Restriction Act, 1955,[9] provides for some restriction. Where countries do not grant similar rights immunity may be withdrawn from their representatives and the Act excludes from such immunity citizens of the United Kingdom and Colonies except for these enjoying it at the passing of the Act.

(3) **Aliens.**—An alien, that is a person who is not a British subject, has, in peacetime, the same contractual rights as a British subject.[10] On the outbreak of hostilities the position changes and a class of "enemy aliens" comes into being. The class is artificial in the sense that it is a creation of the law and will not necessarily include all those of hostile nationality. It consists of persons who voluntarily reside in or carry on business in an enemy country.[11] Thus a British subject, or the subject of a neutral state who does

---

1 *Taylor* v. *Best* (1854), 14 C.B. 487.
2 Diplomatic Privileges Act, 1708.
3 *Magdalena Steam Navigation Co.* v. *Martin* (1859), 2 E. & E. 94.
4 *Macartney* v. *Garbutt* (1890), 24 Q.B.D. 368.
5 *Musurus Bey* v. *Gadban*, [1894] 2 Q.B. 352.
6 *Mighell* v. *Sultan of Johore*, [1894] 1 Q.B. 149; *Dickinson* v. *Del Solar*, [1930] 1 K.B. 376.
7 14 Geo. 6, c. 14.
8 15 & 16 Geo. 6 and 1 Eliz. 2, c. 18.
9 4 Eliz. 2, c. 21.
10 He may not however own a British ship or part thereof: Merchant Shipping Act, 1894, s.1; Status of Aliens Act, 1914, s.17.
11 *Porter* v. *Freudenberg*, *Kreglinger* v. *S. Samuel and Rosenfeld*, *Re Merten's Patents*, [1915] 1 K.B. 857.

either of these things, unprotected by the licence of the Crown, is as much an enemy alien as one of hostile nationality who also fulfils the conditions, and, conversely, an enemy national who does not trade in or with the hostile country nor reside there, will not, for the purposes of the law, be an enemy alien.

At common law an enemy alien is the object of many disabilities, and under modern conditions may well find his disabilities increased as the result of legislation.   On the outbreak of war all commercial and similar intercourse with enemy aliens becomes illegal except where permitted by the Sovereign.   Permission, granted with some freedom in earlier times, is now severely restricted and will be accorded only where the paramount needs of the State demand it.

" There may be occasions on which such intercourse may be highly expedient.   But it is not for individuals to determine on the expediency of such occasions . . . it is for the State alone."[1]

Thus a purported contract of service entered into with an enemy alien not under protection of the Crown will be void and no action may, at any time, be brought upon it in the courts.

Where a contract is entered into before the outbreak of war and requires further performance involving intercourse with an enemy alien (as would, for example, a contract of service), it will be dissolved on the outbreak of war.   Public policy demands such dissolution, and a clause by which the parties attempt to suspend performance until the conclusion of hostilities will be invalid.[2]   The courts will not apply the doctrine of severance and so enforce parts of a contract of this sort which do not offend the basic reason for dissolution, benefit to and intercourse with the enemy.[3]   A contract already executed is not dissolved, but no action may be brought upon it on the initiative of an enemy alien during the war; where such an alien is the plaintiff in proceedings interrupted by the outbreak of war his right to appeal is suspended, except, apparently, that a British defendant has the right to ask for and receive dismissal of an action against him which is obviously ill-founded.[4]   Thus, an enemy alien may be sued in the Queen's courts during the continuance of the war, but he may not sue. If he is sued he will be accorded the fullest opportunities of defence and, should he desire to appeal, he may do so. The rule preventing an enemy alien from suing is directed at the alien; it is not directed against British subjects and friendly neutrals and it will not apply where its enforcement would result in any injustice to these.[5]

(4) Corporations.—A corporation is an artificial person created by law and must conform, generally speaking, in its contractual as in its other activities, to the instrument which governs it.   A

---

[1] *The Hoop* (1799), 1 Ch. Rob. 196, *per* Sir WILLIAM SCOTT, at pp. 199, 200.
[2] *Ertel Bieber & Co.* v. *Rio Tinto Co.*, [1918] A.C. 260.
[3] *Kuenigl* v. *Donnersmarck*, [1955] 1 Q.B. 515; [1955] 1 All E.R. 46.
[4] *Eichengruen* v. *Mond*, [1940] Ch. 785; [1940] 3 All E.R. 148.
[5] *Rodriguez* v. *Speyer Bros.*, [1919] A.C. 59 at p. 69.

statutory corporation must keep within the terms of its statute, a company incorporated under the Companies Acts within the terms of its Memorandum of Association. Should such corporations act beyond their powers any resulting contract will be void.[1] With a chartered corporation the matter is rather different, and though such a corporation enters into a contract in excess of its powers the contract will be binding. The corporation risks, however, forfeiture of its charter.[2]

Because of its artificial character a corporation can act only through its agents. Formerly most contracts had to be under seal. This requirement has now been removed.

The contractual powers of trading companies incorporated under the Companies Act, 1948,[3] are as follows :—

> 32(1) . . . (a) A contract which, if made between private persons would be by law required to be in writing, and if made according to English law to be under seal, may be made on behalf of the company in writing under the common seal of the company :
> (b) A contract which, if made between private persons, would be by law required to be in writing, signed by the parties to be charged therewith, may be made on behalf of the company in writing signed by any person acting under its authority, express or implied :
> (c) A contract which if made between private persons would by law be valid although made by parol only, and not reduced into writing, may be made by parol on behalf of the company by any person acting under its authority, express or implied.

Other corporate bodies are now basically in the same position as individual persons. The Corporate Bodies' Contracts Act, 1960,[4] provides that where private persons can contract in writing signed by the parties or orally, then a corporate body can do so.[5]

(5) Minors.[6]—The contractual capacity of an infant rests upon a common law basis as modified, and in some directions restricted, by the Infants' Relief Act, 1874. The first section of the Act provides that three types of contracts made with an infant are absolutely void : namely, contracts for the repayment of money lent, or to be lent, for goods (other than necessaries) supplied or to be supplied, and contracts on accounts stated. The section affirms the common law position that contracts in respect of necessary goods sold and delivered to an infant shall be binding upon him, as also are contracts into which he could validly enter at the date of the Act and which were not voidable by him. This latter category represented contracts which were for his benefit and included chiefly the contracts with which we are concerned: namely the contracts of

---

[1] *Ashbury Railway Carriage and Iron Co.* v. *Riche* (1875), L.R. 7 H.L. 653.
[2] *Jenkin* v. *Pharmaceutical Society of Great Britain*, [1921] 1 Ch. 392 at p. 877.
[3] S. 32.   [4] 8 & 9 Eliz. 2, c. 46.
[5] *Ibid.*, s. 1.
[6] See Family Law Reform Act, 1969. ss. 1, 9, which reduced the age from 21 to 18.

service and apprenticeship. These are *prima facie* binding,[1] and if they are, on the whole, for the infant's benefit at the time they are entered into, they will bind him. "The question is this," said FRY, L. J.,

> "Is the contract for the benefit of the infant? Not, Is any one particular stipulation for the benefit of the infant . . . the court must look at the whole contract having regard to the circumstances of the case. . . ."[2]

The principle involved is not difficult to state or to apprehend, none the less its application has not been without difficulty. Two modern cases show the general attitude of the courts. The plaintiff in *Olsen's* case,[3] aged seventeen years, entered into a deed of apprenticeship with the defendants by which, in consideration of a premium of £100, they covenanted to teach him the profession of aeronautical ground engineer. The contract contained a clause exempting the defendants from all liability in respect of injuries, howsoever arising. The plaintiff was injured, and the question of the validity of the contract was raised. If the contract as a whole were for his benefit he might well be bound. But if this were not so the whole contract, including the offending clause, would be void. The court had no difficulty in holding this to be so:

> "Taking into consideration every suggested advantage that may still accrue to the plaintiff . . . the deed is so wide in the extent to which it purports to relieve the defendants that it is not for the benefit of the plaintiff and is therefore void."[4]

In *Doyle* v. *White City Stadium, Ltd.*[5] the infant plaintiff was a boxer of considerable repute who applied for a licence from the British Boxing Board of Control. It was a condition of the grant of the licence that he should strictly adhere to the rules of the Board, one of which provided that a boxer's remuneration might be withheld only where he was disqualified for a deliberate foul, did not try, or retired without sufficient cause, or where the referee gave a "no contest" decision. Unknown to the plaintiff this rule was altered to one which gave to a disqualified boxer mere travelling expenses until the Board made its decision known, when it might deal with the prize moneys at its discretion. The plaintiff, subsequently to the grant of the licence, entered into a contract to box for the defendants for the sum of £3,000 win, lose or draw. At the contest he was disqualified for hitting below the belt. As a result the Board withheld the prize money from the plaintiff, who brought action to recover it. There were, of course, two contracts, and it was under the first—that connected with the issue of the

---

[1] *Wood* v. *Fenwick* (1842), 10 M. & W. 195; *De Francesco* v. *Barnum* (1890), 45 Ch.D.430.

[2] *De Francesco* v. *Barnum*, (1890), 45 Ch.D. 430, at p. 439.

[3] *Olsen* v. *Corry and Gravesend Aviation, Ltd.*, [1936] 3 All E.R. 241.

[4] *Per* GREAVES, L.J., at p. 249.

[5] [1935] I K.B. 110; *Chaplin* v. *Leslie Frewin (Publishers), Ltd.*, [1966] Ch. 71.

licence—that the penalty attached. This, it was argued, was not a contract of service or education, nor was it one involving necessaries, and therefore it could not bind the infant. The Court of Appeal rejected this point; the first contract was held to be so closely connected with the contract of service that, provided it was, on the whole, for his benefit, he must be bound:

> "It is as much in the interests of the plaintiff himself as of any other contestant that there should be rules for clean fighting, and that he should be protected against his adversary's misconduct in hitting below the belt or doing anything of that sort."[1]

There, then, we find the court applying to a modern situation a principle which had been laid down with great clarity by Lord ESHER, M.R., almost fifty years earlier:

> "It is impossible to frame a deed as between a master and apprentice[2] in which some of the stipulations are not in favour of one and some in favour of the other. But if we find a stipulation in the deed which is of such a kind that it makes the whole contract an unfair one, then that makes the whole contract void."[3]

Wherever a stipulation, though repugnant, does not make the whole contract unfair, and is severable from the rest, it will, in fact, be severed and the remainder of the contract, being for the infant's benefit, will bind him.[4] An infant agreed that he would not, during the three years following the termination of his contract of service, engage in certain occupations, including that of restaurant keeper, within a certain distance of East Clacton. His employer was not a restaurateur though he hoped to extend his business activities in that direction. The court held that this covenant did not invalidate the entire contract. The infant was only employed for the business then carried on, and the agreement:

> "in so far as it seeks to restrain the defendant from engaging in the business of restaurant keeper, goes beyond what was necessary for the protection of the business. . . ."[5]

In both *Bromley* v. *Smith*[6] and *Doyle* v. *White City Stadium, Ltd.*[7] the court made use of a principle which has often been used, to discover whether the contract was for the infant's benefit. "What would be the position," the courts have frequently enquired, "if the offending clause were not in the contract at all?" Would the infant be able to enter into a contract of equal or greater benefit? Or, to put much the same test in a different manner, "Is the clause

---

[1] [1935] 1 K.B. 110, *per* Lord HANWORTH, M.R., at p. 126.
[2] The word may be read as "infant," as was pointed out by A. L. SMITH, L.J., in *Clements* v. *London and North Western Ry. Co.*, [1894] 2 Q.B. 482 at p. 495.
[3] *Corn* v. *Matthews*, [1893] 1 Q.B. 310, per Lord ESHER, M.R., at p. 314.
[4] *Bromley* v. *Smith*, [1909] 2 K.B. 235.
[5] [1909] 2 K.B. 235, *per* CHANNELL, J., at p. 241.
[6] *Supra.*
[7] [1935] 1 K.B. 110.

usual in infants' contracts of this particular type?" In *Doyle'*
case it was felt that:

> "the result would be that no infant could ever obtain a licence
> from this society (*i.e.* the British Boxing Board) because it would
> be very unlikely that they would give him one unless he, in his
> turn, was bound to some obligation of proper fighting, and he
> would be debarred for ever from taking part in any boxing contests
> at all."[1]

And with reference to the stipulation in *Bromley* v. *Smith*, CHAN-
NELL, J., said:

> " The defendant could not get employment on any better terms . . .
> and I think it was for his benefit to get employment on those
> terms . . . and it is quite right that when leaving that service he
> should forgo the right of soliciting customers whom he would
> never have known but for that service."[2]

So, a clause which is usual in a particular trade or industry will not
generally be against the infant's benefit.

As to contracts of education, the law takes a liberal view, and
training, from singing at one extreme to billiard playing at the other
has been regarded as activities beneficial to an infant and by
which he may contractually be bound. In *Mackinlay* v. *Bathurst*[3]
the infant defendant contracted with the plaintiff that he should,
at a fixed premium and during a period of three years, teach her
to sing. During these years and for seven years afterwards the
plaintiff was to be the defendant's business manager and be
remunerated by a commission on his pupil's earnings. When of
full age the defendant did not repudiate the agreement, but the
following year she refused to pay any further commission. She was
held to be bound by the agreement. Similarly, in *Roberts* v. *Gray*[4]
the defendant, an infant who hoped to make the playing of billiards
his profession, agreed to travel with Roberts on a world tour.
Again, on his failure to do so he was held liable in an action for
breach of contract. Such cases demonstrate clearly the wide view
of education—and, ultimately, of service—which the law takes.

(6) Mentally Disordered Persons and Drunkards.—A mentally disordered person or a drunkard will be bound by a contract of
service unless he can prove that he was so disabled or so drunk as to
be incapable of understanding what he was doing, and that the other
party had knowledge of the disability or drunkenness.[5] Where,
however, necessaries are sold and delivered to a person who by reason

---

[1] [1935] 1 K.B. 110, *per* SLESSER, L.J., at p. 133.
[2] [1909] 2 K.B. 235, *per* CHANNELL, J., at p. 242; for use of same test see
also *Leslie* v. *Fitzpatrick* (1877), 3 Q.B.D. 229, and *De Francesco* v. *Barnum*
(1890), 45 Ch. 430.
[3] (1919), 36 T.L.R. 31.
[4] [1913] 1 K.B. 520.
[5] *Matthews* v. *Baxter* (1873), L. R. 8 Exch. 132; *Imperial Loan Co.* v. *Stone*,
[1892] 1 Q.B. 599.

of mental incapacity or drunkenness is incompetent to contract, he must pay a reasonable price therefor.[1]

(7) Partners.—A partner has authority in the absence of express prohibition to enter into contracts of service relating to the partnership which will bind the firm.[2] So a servant may be, for certain purposes, the servant of each partner.[3] The dissolution of a partnership may amount to a breach of a contract of service or apprenticeship.[4]

4. FORM OR CONSIDERATION

(1) Form.—According to a doctrine peculiar to English law a contract must be under seal or be based upon consideration. A promise gratuitously to perform services will not be actionable unless it be by deed. Subject to this, however, at common law a contract of service may be entered into orally. Statute has modified the position, and certain defined contracts must be written. The contract of service does not fall into this category, but there are certain contracts which do and which are so closely connected with service that they should be mentioned now, even though a fuller discussion of them is left to later chapters. So under the Truck Act, 1831,[5] master and servant are permitted, provided the contract be in writing and signed by the worker, to enter into arrangements whereby the cost of certain goods and services owing to the master are deducted from the worker's wages, and under the Truck Act, 1896,[6] similar agreements are rendered possible in respect of fines for damaged materials and the like. The London Hackney Carriages Act, 1843, section 23, provides that an agreement made between the driver or conductor and the proprietor of such a vehicle as to the payment of a sum of money on account of the earnings of the carriage will be unenforceable unless it is in writing.

The contracts of merchant seamen have long been regulated by statute. The principal Act for over 70 years was the Merchant Shipping Act, 1894. The whole question of employment in the shipping industry was the subject of a very important committee of inquiry[7] under the Industrial Courts Act, 1919 with Lord Pearson as Chairman. Its Report provides a thorough going study of employment in an industry with special employment problems and long traditions.

The Merchant Shipping Act, 1970[8] applies to ships registered in

---

[1] Sale of Goods Act, 1893, s. 2.
[2] Partnership Act 1890, s. 5; also see s. 9. *Drake* v. *Beckham* (1843), 11 M. & W. 315.
[3] *R.* v. *Leech* (1821), 3 Stark. 70.
[4] *Titmus and Titmus* v. *Rose and Watts*, [1940] 1 All E.R. 599.
[5] Section 23; see further Chapter IV, pp. 152 *et seq.*
[6] Ss. 1–3; see further Chapter IV, pp. 157 *et seq.*
[7] Final Report of the Court of Inquiry, 1967, Cmnd. 3211.
[8] After a lengthy sojourn on the statute book likely to be put into force early in 1973.

the United Kingdom.   It replaces the existing statutory provisions on matters such as engagement, discharge, discipline—special offences are laid down[1]—trade disputes and disqualification.   The justification for the special provisions arises from the nature of the merchant service and a full discussion of the individual points is to be found in the Pearson report.   Special attention is paid to the form of crew agreements.   Each person employed as a seaman in a ship registered in the United Kingdom has to have a written agreement.   The agreement has also to be signed by both the seaman and by a person on behalf of his employers.[2]

All the agreements with individual seamen must be collected together into one document, known as the crew agreement.   The crew agreement must be in terms approved by the Department of Trade and Industry.   This is not meant to be a standard form contract, because different provisions and forms may be approved in different circumstances.[3]   There is power vested in the Department of Trade and Industry to grant exemptions for specified types of ship or descriptions of seamen.   This can be done by regulation or in respect of individual employees or seamen where the Department is satisfied that there is adequate protection without a crew agreement.   These provisions replace the old rules under the 1894 Act but in recognition of the growth of trade unions and collective agreements provide for greater flexibility.   The details of permissible crew agreements are governed by regulations[4] for the Act is basically an enabling Act leaving detailed regulation for subordinate legislation.   There is, however, an intention of relaxing provisions of the old law.   It was for example necessary for an official known as a superintendent to be present both at a signing on and a discharge.   The Pearson Report indicated that this was an unnecessary safeguard in modern conditions.

The Act itself, by its provisions, determines a basic content of the contract of service and in that sense is unusual.   A group of sections[5] deal with wages.   Earnings up to £50 must be paid in full on discharge and sums over £50 must be paid within seven days[6].   Failure to pay entitles the seaman to a day's wage whilst he is unpaid up to 56 days and any sums unpaid thereafter carry the punitive interest of 20 per cent.

(2) **Notice of Terms of Employment.**—Although English law is basically informal about the form of a contract of service the recent Contracts of Employment Act, 1963, has provided that an employee to whom the Act applies must be given written particulars

---

[1] Ss. 27–32.
[2] Section 1(1).
[3] Section 1(3).
[4] Section 2.
[5] Ss. 7–18.
[6] Section 7(2).

of the salient terms of his employment.[1]   This statement must be
kept up to date.   It is not the contract of service but is important in
defining and perhaps incorporating terms.   This is shortly but
importantly discussed in *Camden Exhibition and Display, Ltd.* v.
Lynott.[2]

An employee is defined for the purposes of this Act as an individual
who has entered into or works under a contract with an employer,
whether the contract is for manual labour, clerical work or otherwise
and whether the contract is express or implied, oral or in writing
and including contracts of apprenticeship.[1]   This is a fairly comprehensive definition and is much wider than the definition of workman found in some other Acts.   Certain categories of workman are
excluded.   The Act does not apply to the Crown, so all Crown servants are excluded as are dock workers under the Dock Workers
(Regulation of Employment) Act, 1946, unless they are engaged on
work other than dock work; a master or seamen in ships of eighty
tons or more or workers employed to do work about such a ship
in port of a kind normally done by a seaman; and skippers or
seamen on fishing boats.[4]   The Act also does not apply to any
period when an employee is working mainly or wholly outside
Great Britain unless he ordinarily works in Great Britain and is
working for the same employer.[5]

Wherever the Act applies the employer is given the fairly generous
period of thirteen weeks in which to deliver to his employee the
necessary written statement.[6]   The Act provided for this to be done
to all existing employees and thereafter for a statement to be issued
at the commencement of any period of employment.   Where there
is subsequent to the giving of notice of particulars a change in them
the employer has one month in which to issue a statement of the
change.[7]   The original statement must be given to the employee but
a notice of changes need not be given for retention as long as the
employee is afforded reasonable access to it and the opportunity to
read it.

The rules do not apply, there being special exemption, where the
employee is a close relative of the employer, that is to say father,
mother, husband, wife, son or daughter.[8]   They also do not apply
where there is a written contract of service covering the statutory
requirements in existence but this exemption is limited to cases
where the employee has a copy of the written contract or at least a

---

[1] For the other provisions of this Act relating to notice, see below, Chapter III,
p. 73.

[2] [1966] 1 Q.B. 555; [1965] 3 All E.R. 28.

[3] Section 8(1).

[4] Contracts of Employment Act, 1963, s. 6(2).   The Minister is given power
in s. 6(6) to vary these by regulation.

[5] *Ibid.*, s. 9(1).

[6] Contracts of Employment Act, 1963, s. 4(1).

[7] *Ibid.*, s. 4(4).

[8] *Ibid.*, s. 6(3).

reasonable opportunity of reading a copy.   If the terms change then a statutory notice must be given in the usual way within one month.[1]

The initial notice must contain the following particulars: the name of the parties; the date on which employment began; the scale or rate of remuneration or the method of calculating remuneration; the intervals at which remuneration is paid—*e.g.* weekly; any terms and conditions relating to working hours or to normal working hours; any terms or conditions relating to holidays including public holidays, and holiday pay, and with sufficient information to enable the entitlement to be precisely calculated, incapacity for work due to sickness or injury and pensions and pension schemes; the length of notice which the employee must give and is entitled to receive to determine the contract of employment.[2]   Since 1971 the notice has also to contain an indication of the worker's rights in relation to trade union membership and activity and non-membership under s. 5 of the Industrial Relations Act, including the effect of any approved closed shop or agency shop agreement.   In addition, the worker's individual grievance procedure must be outlined and the person to whom he has to apply to seek redress specified.[3]   The provision as to pension rights does not apply where there is a statutory scheme which itself provides for information to be given to the employees.[4]   Where the contract has no terms about holidays, incapacity or pensions, this fact must be stated.[5]   If the contract is for a fixed term its date of expiry must be stated.[6]

There are various provisions which relieve the employer of the full duty to place into every employee's hands full details.   These may detract from the aim of the statute but they relieve the employer of a very onerous burden.   Thus the written statement given to the employee may refer to another document to which the employee is given reasonable access and a reasonable opportunity of reading during the course of his employment.[7]   It may also indicate that future changes in matters contained in the document to which the employee has been referred will be made in that document within the permissible period of one month without the employee being notified.[8]   This introduces the somewhat unsatisfactory notion of constructive notice.

No corps of enforcement officers has been established.   The Redundancy Payments Act, 1965,[9] has however indicated a tribunal to which an employee may have recourse if he is not given a statement in due time.   It is then for the tribunal to determine what

---

[1] Contracts of Employment Act, 1963, s. 6(4).
[2] *Ibid.*, s. 4(1) as amended by Industrial Relations Act, s. 20(1).
[3] Industrial Relations Act, 1971, s. 20(2).
[4] *Ibid.*, s. 4(1).
[5] *Ibid.*, s. 4(2).
[6] *Ibid.*, s. 4(3)
[7] *Ibid.*, s. 4(5)
[8] *Ibid.*, s. 4(6).
[9] S. 38.

particulars ought to have been given or referred to in the statement. Where a statement is given and the employer or an employee feels that a question arises as to the particulars which ought to have been given, these too may be referred to the tribunal. The regulation of the tribunal is set out in the Industrial Relations Act,[1] the tribunal itself is set up by the Industrial Training Act, 1964.[2]

(3) Consideration.—We have already seen that, except in the case of a deed, an agreement will not become a contract unless it is supported by valuable consideration. Deeds will themselves usually contain a provision as to consideration, but if A promises gratuitously to perform services for B, B can enforce the promise only where the agreement is under seal. In all other cases, some consideration is necessary. An interesting contribution has been made to the law by the decision of DENNING, J., in *Central London Property Trust, Ltd.* v. *High Trees House, Ltd.*[3] The plaintiffs by a lease under seal had let a block of flats to the defendant for a term of ninety-nine years at a ground rent of £2,500 per annum. In January, 1940, as a consequence of war conditions making it impossible to let many of the flats, the plaintiffs gave a written agreement to reduce rent to £1,250 and the defendants continued to pay at this rate until 1945, when the receiver for the debenture holders of the plaintiff company claimed that the original rent of £2,500 was due and a friendly action was brought to test the position. The plaintiff alleged that if there was a new agreement in 1940, it was void for want of consideration. DENNING, J., agreed that there was no consideration, but he went further and pointing to the developments in the law he said—

> " They are cases in which a promise was made which was intended to create legal relations and which, to the knowledge of the person making the promise, was going to be acted upon by the person to whom it was made, and which was in fact, so acted upon. In such cases the courts have said that the promise must be honoured. . . . The courts have not gone so far as to give a cause of action in damages for the breach of such a promise, but they have refused to allow the party making it to act inconsistently with it."

The principle in the *High Trees* case cannot, however, be said to do otherwise than modify the rules of consideration over a narrow field. The limitations were clearly shown in *Combe* v. *Combe*[4] where a wife tried to enforce such a unilateral promise against her husband. The principle in the *High Trees* case was regarded as a shield and not as a sword[5] and the right to sue on a promise of this type was rejected.

---

[1] See *infra*, p. 430. [2] Section 12.
[3] [1947] K.B. 130; see also *Robertson* v. *Minister of Pensions*, [1949] 1 K.B. 227; [1948] 2 All E.R. 767.
[4] [1951] 2 K.B. 215; [1951] 1 All E.R. 767.
[5] See the judgment of BIRKETT, L.J., at pp. 224, 772 respectively.

What then is consideration? It has been defined variously as consisting

> " either in some right interest, profit or benefit accruing to one party or some forbearance, detriment, loss or responsibility given, suffered or undertaken by the other,"[1]

or as requiring

> "that something of material value shall be given or some other detriment shall be sustained by the recipient of a promise in order to make that promise enforceable."[2]

The consideration may consist of mutual promises; A, that is to say, may agree to work for B in consideration of B's promise of suitable remuneration, in which circumstances the consideration is said to be executory on both sides; or it may consist in a promise by A in return for some act on the part of B, the most frequently cited example of which is the offer of a reward. Supposing that A offers a reward in return for information, there is a general offer which is made into a contract when B supplies the information. And here something of a difficulty arises, for a consideration which is past will not support a contract, and it is necessary sharply to distinguish an executed consideration from a past consideration. In the example of a reward just given, the consideration is not past, since the act of providing the information itself constitutes an acceptance of the offer, and the acts of the parties are simultaneous. If, however, A promised B £x in consideration of a service already rendered, there could be no contract except where it could be shown that the service was performed at the request, express or implied, of the person whom it is sought to make liable when a reasonable sum would be recoverable.[3] If there were no such request the consideration would be nugatory and no contract could exist.

Consideration in the contract of service will usually take the form of the performance of service on the one side and the payment of wages on the other, but it may take other forms. The grant of food and lodging may amount to consideration,[4] as may enlistment in the Forces where an employer has promised reinstatement after, and payment of half wages during a war, to such of his employees as enlisted.[5]

Consideration, then, must exist. It must also have value in the eyes of the law, and nice questions have arisen as to what constitutes such value. A promise to do that which a party is already under a duty to do will not amount to valuable consideration. In

---

[1] *Currie* v. *Misa* (1875), L.R. 10 Exch. 153, *per* Lush, J., at p. 162.

[2] Law Revision Committee, 6th Interim Report, p. 14; see also *Dunlop Pneumatic Tyre Co., Ltd.* v. *Selfridge and Co., Ltd.*, [1915] A.C. 847 at p. 855.

[3] *Lampleigh* v. *Brathwait* (1615), 1 Sm. L.C., 13th Ed., 148; Hob. 105. *Jewry* v. *Busk* (1814), 5 Taunt. 302. *Bryant* v. *Flight* (1839), 5 M. & W. 114.

[4] *R.* v. *Foulkes* (1875), L.R. 2 C.C.R. 150. *R.* v. *Worfield* (*Inhabitants*) (1794), 5 Term Rep. 506.

[5] *Budgett* v. *Stratford Co-operative and Industrial Society, Ltd.* (1916), 32 T.L.R. 378.

Stilk v. *Myrick*,[1] seamen contracted to do all that was necessary to bring the ship to port. Because of certain desertions the number of the crew was reduced and the master promised to divide the absentees' wages amongst those who had remained loyal. The plaintiffs brought action to enforce this promise, but the court held that they had done no more than they were enjoined to do by the terms of the original contract, so that there was no consideration to support the new promise. Again, where a servant has, under the orders of a superior servant, done unlawful things and is induced to provide information as to the acts of that other on promise that he will not be discharged, he will have no remedy if he is discharged, for the servant may already be under the duty of reporting acts hostile to his employers, and there would, in such circumstances, be no consideration for the promise of immunity from dismissal.[2] But though the consideration must have value, the court, following the principle that it will not make bargains for the parties, is not concerned about its adequacy,[3] provided that the inadequacy is not such as to import the element of servility into the contract. So, granted that consideration for a covenant in restraint of trade exists, the court will not be concerned that it is not equal or proportionate to the restraint.

> " It is . . . enough that there actually is a consideration for the bargain; and that such consideration is a legal consideration of some value. . . ."[4]

Moreover, the flow of the consideration determines the parties to the contract so far as rights of action are concerned, in that no stranger to the consideration can sue. A may contract with B that B will serve C, but C will not be able to sue B for breach except where A contracts merely as C's agent. In all other cases the person entitled to sue must be a party to the consideration. Finally, the consideration must be legal. An illegal consideration will avoid the contract.[5]

5. LEGALITY OF OBJECT

All contracts having objects contrary to statute or common law, or which entail the passing of an illegal consideration, are void. So an agreement by which an employee purports to permit his employer to make deductions from his remuneration will be void unless there is compliance with the provisions of the Truck Acts.[6] So, too, will a purported agreement to waive a breach of duty

---

[1] (1809), 2 Camp. 317; *cf. Hartley* v. *Ponsonby* (1857), 7 E. & B. 872.
[2] *Swain* v. *West (Butchers), Ltd.*, [1936] 3 All E.R. 261; but see *High Trees* case, *supra*.
[3] *Pilkington* v. *Scott* (1846), 15 M. & W. 657; see also *Gaumont-British Picture Corporation, Ltd.* v. *Alexander*, [1936] 2 All E.R. 1686.
[4] *Hitchcock* v. *Coker* (1837), 6 Ad. & El. 438, *per* TINDALL, C.J., at p. 457.
[5] This topic is discussed in the following section.
[6] *Kearney* v. *Whitehaven Colliery Co.*, [1893] 1 Q.B. 700; see also Chapter V.

imposed by statute on an employer.[1]   A contract of hiring entered
into on a Sunday does not, apparently, offend the Sunday
Observance Act, 1677.[2]

But it is the group of contracts void as being against public policy
which is of immediate interest to us, and we shall notice the most
important of these in the remainder of this section.

Any agreement by which a man promises not to serve in Her
Majesty's Forces will be void, for the security of the State must
always be a paramount concern of public policy.[3]   For the same
reason agreements having for their object unjustifiable interference
with the ordinary course of judicial proceedings will be illegal.
Consequently an undertaking by which a servant who has committed an offence against his master promises to pay a sum of money
in consideration of his employer's promise not to prosecute, will
be contrary to the law,[4] and the same is true though the person
who promises not to prosecute is not the victim of the felony.[5]
The compromise of criminal proceedings is illegal, and it is immaterial
that a Judge has consented.[6] But where the offence, though public
in character, involves damages in respect of which a party might
maintain an action, that party may compromise or settle his private
damages in whatever way he pleases. It follows that the receipt of
securities by an employer from his servant, in respect of the latter's
defalcations, is not of itself illegal, provided it is not accompanied
by an agreement to abstain from prosecuting.[7] Agreements between
master and servant by which part of the salary is to be treated, for
taxation purposes, as expenses are also void as against public policy.[8]

It is a well-established principle of the common law that a
contract of service must not contain servile incidents.   "The law
of England allows a man to contract for his labour or allows him to
place himself in the service of a master, but it does not allow him
to attach to his contract of service any servile incidents."[9]   This,
indeed, is one of the reasons why there cannot be an assignment
of a contract of service, though moneys due under such a contract
are assignable.[10]

Servile incidents arise most usually in relation to covenants in

---

[1] *Baddeley* v. *Earl of Granville* (1887), 19 Q.B.D. 423; for a fairly strong case
see *Wheeler* v. *New Merton Board Mills, Ltd.*, [1933] 2 K.B. 669; [1933]
All E.R. Rep. 28.

[2] *R.* v. *Whitnash* (*Inhabitants*) (1827), 7 B. & C. 596.

[3] *Re Beard, Reversionary and General Securities Co., Ltd.* v. *Hall, Re Beard,
Beard* v. *Hall*, [1908] 1 Ch. 383.

[4] *Lound* v. *Grimwade* (1888), 39 Ch.D. 605. *Jones* v. *Merionethshire Permanent Benefit Building Society*, [1891] 2 Ch. 587.

[5] *R.* v. *Burgess* (1885), 16 Q.B.D. 141.

[6] *Windhill Local Board of Health* v. *Vint* (1890), 45 Ch.D. 351; see also *Keir*
v. *Leeman* (1846), 9 Q.B. 371.

[7] *Flower* v. *Sadler* (1882), 10 Q.B.D. 572.

[8] *Napier* v. *National Business Agency, Ltd.*, [1951] 2 All E.R. 264.

[9] *Per* Bowen, L.J., in *Davies* v. *Davies* (1887), 36 Ch.D. 359 at p. 393.

[10] *Russell & Co., Ltd.* v. *Austin Fryers* (1909), 25 T.L.R. 414.

restraint of trade but they may also arise in other connections. So though an assignment of salary may be valid,[1] it will not be so when its effect may be to deprive the assignor of his means of support[2] and an agreement, in consideration of money borrowed, that the borrower will not, *inter alia*, determine his engagement with his employers without the consent of the lender, is also void,[3] though an agreement to serve for the remainder of the covenantor's life may be good.[4]

Servility is to be construed in relation to the contract as a whole and will vary according to the type of service involved. In the theatrical and cinematograph industries it is not unusual for a contract of service to include personal covenants of a quite intimate character. An actress has been held to be bound by a contract containing obligations to keep her weight at or below a certain figure, and to maintain herself in such a state of health that her employers might effect a normal insurance, and which gave to her employers the right to suspend or to terminate the contract should she so conduct herself in her private life as to become disgraced or held in contempt.[5] Stipulations of this character are usually binding because they are of value to both parties. The essence of servility is a want of mutuality; a want which could clearly be seen in *Hepworth Manufacturing Co.* v. *Ryott*.[6] The defendant, an actor, had contracted with the plaintiff to perform as a cinema actor. He was to use an assumed name which name was to be the sole property of the plaintiff. The actor covenanted not to use the assumed name for any purpose, nor to act for new employers except on their agreeing not to announce or advertise his appearance under the pseudonym. Under this assumed name ("Stewart Rome") he achieved a considerable reputation—such, indeed, that his estimated market value without it was reduced by one-half. He became employed by other film producers, used the name despite his covenant and was faced with an action for an injunction against him. The court had no difficulty in deciding that the contract was unreasonable whether it was in restraint of trade or not. Clearly the stipulation as to the name lacked all mutuality. On the same grounds the pseudonym under which a journalist writes has been held to be his own property though the presumption of ownership may here be displaced by agreement to the effect that it belongs to his employers.[7]

Restraint of Trade.—The modern law as to restraint of trade is

---

[1] *Re Mirams*, [1891] 1 Q.B. 594.
[2] *King* v. *Michael Faraday and Partners, Ltd.*, [1939] 2 K.B. 753; [1939] 2 All E.R. 478.
[3] *Horwood* v. *Millar's Timber and Trading Co., Ltd.*, [1917] 1 K.B. 305.
[4] *Wallis* v. *Day* (1837), 2 M. & W. 273.
[5] *Gaumont-British Picture Corporation, Ltd.* v. *Alexander*, [1936] 2 All E.R. 1686.
[6] [1920] 1 Ch. 1.
[7] *Forbes* v. *Kemsley Newspapers, Ltd.*, [1951] 2 T.L.R. 656.

set out in *Nordenfelt* v. *Maxim Nordenfelt Guns and Ammunition Co.,*[1] wherein it was held that all covenants in restraint of trade are, in the absence of specially justifying circumstances, void as being contrary to public policy.   The only special circumstance which will justify the restraint is that it is reasonable in reference alike to the parties and to the public.   Thus, whenever an effort is made to restrain the trading or labouring activities of another, the overriding test is that of reasonableness, and, since the presumption is against the validity of the restraint, the onus of proving it to be reasonable is on the person alleging it to be so.   It has been found, however, that the criterion of reasonableness varies as between contracts for the sale of the goodwill of a business and contracts of service and employment. The purchaser of a business might seek to protect himself from the competition of the vendor over such area and within such time as would secure to him the fruits of the purchase he had made, for he will have paid to ensure that the vendor does not compete against him under the head of goodwill.   But though an employer, as we shall see, might protect himself in other directions, he could not enforce a covenant which was aimed at the competition of his servant.

> " I cannot find any case in which a covenant against competition by a servant or apprentice has, as such, ever been upheld by the court."[2]

The reason for the distinction was laid down by Lord SHAW, who, after showing that where a business is sold the law will usually enforce the seller's covenant not to compete, since generally " the public interest cannot be invoked to render such a bargain nugatory," went on:

> "In the case of restraints upon the opportunity of a workman to earn his livelihood a different set of considerations comes into play. No actual thing is sold or handed over. . . .   The contract is an embargo upon the energies and activities and labour of a citizen, and the public interest coincides with his own in preventing him, on the one hand, from being deprived of the opportunity of earning his living, and in preventing the public, on the other, from being deprived of the work and service of a useful member of society. In this latter case there is not a something already realised made over to and for the use of another, but there is something to be created, developed and rendered to the individual advantage of the worker and to the use of the community at large."[3]

If, then, the master cannot by covenant protect himself from the competition of his servant, to what protection is he entitled?   In the first place the employer is fully entitled to protect his trade secrets and processes.   Indeed,

---

[1] [1894] A.C. 535.

[2] *Herbert Morris, Ltd.* v. *Saxelby,* [1916] I A.C. 688, *per* Lord PARKER at p. 709.

[3] *Ibid., per* LORD SHAW at p. 714.   The wider aspects of the doctrine were discussed in a leading case not dealing with employment, *Esso Petroleum, Ltd.* v. *Harper's Garage* (Stourport), Ltd., [1968] A.C. 269.

" no employee is entitled to filch his employer's property in whatever form that property may be, whether it is in the form of a
secret process or whether it is in some other form."[1]

In *Haynes* v. *Doman*,[2] an employee was held to be bound by his
covenants not to divulge the trade secrets of his master or the
manner in which he conducted his business and also not to serve
any other person or firm engaged in a similar business within a
radius of twenty-five miles unless the consent of the employer
was obtained. So that, in the second place, whilst an employer
is not entitled to secure himself from the normal competition
of one who was at one time his servant, he may, by covenant,
ensure that his old customers are not enticed from him. The
prohibition against disclosing trade secrets may well be worthless
without the restriction against entering the service of rivals.[3]
None the less, in practice, it is less difficult to show the reasonable
character of a clause restraining the violation of a secret process
than it is to show the reasonable character of a clause protecting
a trade connection. All that can be said is that the facts of each
particular case, together with the location of the business[4] and the
area within which it operates, must be carefully considered. A
connection which is world-wide may justify a restraint which is
world-wide in its incidence,[5] but a firm with a local connection cannot
prohibit its servants' competition outside the area of that connection. When a butcher in Cambridge sought to prevent his employee
from being concerned in similar business in his own or other persons'
interests within five miles of the shop, the restraint was held to be
unenforceable because, though an area agreement was quite proper
in such a case, five miles was too wide.[6] A promise not at any time
either during or after the period of service to solicit or entice away
any person in the habit of dealing with the employer, and not, after
the termination of the engagement, to advertise the fact that she
had served with her late employer ("Late with ——") has been
held to be unenforceable because its construction would not permit
of its being narrowed merely to include those who were customers
during the period of the employee's service.[7]

Another consideration in testing the validity of the restraint is

---

[1] *Triplex Safety Glass Co.* v. *Scorah*, [1938] Ch. 211; [1937] 4 All E.R. 693,
per FARWELL, J., at pp. 215 and 697. And see *Commercial Plastics, Ltd.*, v.
Vincent, [1965] 1 Q.B. 623; [1964] 3 All E.R. 546 where the judge thought it
reasonable to protect against the servant later dredging up secret processes
from the recesses of his memory. The covenant in question was too wide.

[2] [1899] 2 Ch. 13.

[3] [1899] 2 Ch. 13, *per* LINDLEY, M. R., at p. 23. *Home Counties Dairies Ltd.*
v. *Skilton*, [1970] 1 All E.R. 1227.

[4] See in particular *Mason* v. *Provident Clothing and Supply Co., Ltd.*, [1913]
A.C. 724; the speech of Lord SHAW, at pp. 736–7.

[5] *Nordenfelt* v. *Maxim Nordenfelt Guns and Ammunition Co., Ltd.*, [1894]
A.C. 535.

[6] *Empire Meat Co., Ltd.* v. *Patrick*, [1939] 2 All E.R. 85.

[7] *Konski* v. *Peet*, [1915] 1 Ch. 530.

the character of the business concerned. In *Mason* v. *Provident Clothing and Supply Co., Ltd.*,[1] the defendants carried on the business of "check and credit" tailors and drapers. They operated chiefly by means of canvassers of whom the plaintiff was one. He had covenanted that he would not within three years of the termination of his agreement become employed by, or engaged in any manner with, any similar business within a twenty-five mile radius of London. This was held to be too wide, though quite clearly a canvasser of this kind has unique opportunities of enticing customers away. Indeed, it has been suggested that where an employer carries on his business by means of a constant succession of new customers, the courts will watch the restraint with greater jealousy than where an employer seeks to protect a connection which is relatively fixed.[2] Moreover, *Mason's* case justifies the postulation of a third principle, namely, that a servant's personal aptitudes and skill are his own possession, and the law will not permit the operation of a covenant which is unreasonably restrictive of their use. Here, at any rate,

> "the public interest coincides with his own in preventing him on the one hand from being deprived of the opportunity of earning his living, and in preventing the public, on the other, from being deprived of his work and service . . . a man's aptitudes, his skill, his dexterity and his manual or mental ability may not, nor ought to be, relinquished by an employee. They are not his master's property, they are his own, they are himself."[3]

The position of the servant is also a matter for consideration. The closer his contacts with customers or prospective customers the easier it will be to justify a restraint.[4] Similarly the higher the servant is in the hierarchy of servants the easier it will be. So in *M. and S. Drapers* v. *Reynolds*[5] where the restraint was imposed on a collector salesman, the court rejected the analogy with a managing director based on *Gilford Motor Co.* v. *Horne*,[6] and held that in the light of its particular circumstances the restraint was unreasonable. It is nothing more than a question of fact for again, in *G. W. Plowman & Son, Ltd.* v. *Ash*,[7] a restraint on a sales representative was accepted

---

[1] [1913] A.C. 724; Viscount HALDANE, L.C., was of opinion that the clause in question was badly drafted and that the defendants could have protected themselves had more care been exercised.

[2] See, *e.g. Fitch* v. *Dewes*, [1921] 2 A.C. 158; *Bowler* v. *Lovegrove*, [1921] 1 Ch. 642; but see *Routh* v. *Jones*, [1947] 1 All E.R. 758 and *Gledhow Autoparts, Ltd.* v. *Delaney*, [1965] 3 All E.R. 288; [1965] 1 W.L.R. 1366, where the objectionable width was not as to geographical area but as to the total inclusion of all within that area, whether they were the employer's customers or not.

[3] *Hepworth Manufacturing Co.* v. *Ryott*, [1920] 1 Ch. 1, *per* ASTBURY, J., at p. 12. The judgment in this case provides a most cogent analysis of the law.

[4] It was felt in *S. W. Strange, Ltd.*, v. *Mann*, [1965] 1 All E.R. 1069; [1965] 1 W.L.R. 629 that a bookmaker's clerk built up no real contact with clients as business was largely conducted on the telephone.

[5] [1956] 3 All E.R. 814; [1957] 1 W.L.R. 9.

[6] [1933] Ch. 935; [1933] All E.R. Rep. 109.

[7] [1964] 2 All E.R. 10; [1964] 1 W.L.R. 568.

as valid. On the other hand the restraint may extend to future activity in any capacity within the permitted area. So where the part owner of a magazine sold his share and subsequently took part in the production of a competing magazine as an employee it was held that the covenant " not for five years . . . directly or indirectly carry on or be engaged or interested in any business similar to or competing with the business of the partnership " was enforceable.[1]

The fourth rule is that the question whether a restraint is reasonable is a question of law for the judge; neither the jury nor witnesses will be heard to give their opinion on the question.[2]

Fifthly, if the contract is reasonable at the time it is entered into it will be enforced. It is not the business of the court "to look out for improbable and extravagant contingencies to make it void."[3] On the other hand, an employer cannot hope to enforce a contract restraining his employee from entering into a business differing from that on which he is employed, on the ground that the employer may himself, at a later date, want to set up in that business.[4]

An interesting type of agreement in restraint of trade was considered in *Kores Manufacturing Co., Ltd.* v. *Kolok Manufacturing Co., Ltd.*[5] Usually the covenant is part of the contract of employment made between master and servant either at the commencement of employment or at some later stage. In this case the agreement was between two manufacturers in the following terms:

> " In consideration of your agreeing not without written consent to, at any time, employ any person who, during the past five years, shall have been a servant of ours, we undertake not, without your written consent to, at any time, employ any person who, during the past five years, shall have been a servant of yours."

The defendants broke this agreement by employing a chief research chemist of the plaintiffs. The Court of Appeal refused to enforce the agreement on the ground that it was too wide and so unreasonable.[6] A similar rule of a trade protection society, the Mineral Water Bottle Exchange and Trade Protection Society, Ltd., which required written consent before the employee of a fellow member could be employed until a two year period had elapsed, was described by CHITTY, J., as "a harshly conceived absolute agreement" which did not protect the employer's business and so was unreasonable and void.[7] The

---

[1] *Ronbar Enterprises* v. *Green*, [1954] 2 All E.R. 266; [1954] 1 W.L.R. 815.
[2] *Dowden and Pook, Ltd.* v. *Pook*, [1904] 1 K.B. 45; *Mason* v. *Provident Clothing and Supply Co., Ltd.*, [1913] A.C. 724.
[3] *Rannie* v. *Irvine* (1844), 7 Man. & G. 969, *per* TINDAL, C.J., at p. 976.
[4] *Bromley* v. *Smith*, [1909] 2 K.B. 235.
[5] [1959] Ch. 108; [1958] 2 All E.R. 65.
[6] The much more interesting point of its consistency with the public interest was left open. In the lower court LLOYD-JACOB, J., had stressed this aspect in refusing to enforce the agreement. See [1957] 3 All E.R. 158 at p. 162.
[7] *Mineral Water Bottle Exchange & Trade Protection Society* v. *Booth* (1887), 36 Ch.D. 465, at p. 469.

court did distinguish the case where a similar agreement had the purpose of protecting knowledge confidentially obtained.[1]

A whole system of employment came under review in *Eastham* v. *Newcastle United Football Club, Ltd.*,[2] when the Football League's " retain and transfer " system was challenged by the plaintiff as being in restraint of trade.   The court was firmly of opinion that the retain system, by which a club kept a footballer on its books without paying him because he had been put on the transfer list at the end of the season, was illegal.   The transfer system might have been justifiable but the Football League failed to convince the court that it protected a legitimate interest.   Taken with the retain system it was clearly in restraint of trade and illegal.   A further point of interest in the case is that the court recognised that a servant could take action when affected by an agreement between *employers* as in the *Kores* case discussed above.

Finally, where a contract in restraint of trade contains stipulations which are void and others which are valid, the void stipulations may be severed and the valid stipulations enforced.[3]   But this will only obtain where each stipulation is distinct in itself; where, in fact, the act of severance is an act of the parties, not of the court.[4]   The principle that the courts will not make a bargain for the parties prevents the extraction from a void promise of a part which would be enforceable.

> " It would in my opinion be *pessimi exempli*, if when an employer had exacted a covenant deliberately framed in unreasonably wide terms, the courts were to come to his assistance and, by applying their ingenuity and knowledge of the law, carve out of this void covenant the maximum of what he might validly have required."[5]

An illegal contract is void and a party cannot invoke the assistance of the law in respect of the illegality.   Such a principle is inevitable though it may produce cases of considerable hardship.   It follows that any moneys paid or securities transferred in respect of an illegal contract cannot be recovered, but to this rule there are exceptions.   In the first place where no part of the illegality has been carried out, either party may recover money paid or securities already transferred.   Secondly, where the parties are not *in pari delicto* the innocent party may recover what he has paid.   The parties will not be *in pari delicto* where one has entered into the contract because of the fraud or duress or improper influence of the other, or where the contract is made illegal by a statute the

---

[1] See *supra*, pp. 47-48.

[2] [1964] Ch. 413; [1963] 3 All E.R. 139.

[3] *Bromley* v. *Smith*, [1909] 2 K.B. 235; *Macfarlane* v. *Kent*, [1965] 2 All E.R. 376; [1965] 1 W.L.R. 1019.

[4] *Putsman* v. *Taylor*, [1927] 1 K.B. 637.

[5] *Mason* v. *Provident Clothing and Supply Co., Ltd.*, [1913] A.C. 724, *per* Lord MOULTON, at p. 745; *Hepworth Manufacturing Co.* v. *Ryott*, [1920] 1 Ch. 1, see ASTBURY, J., at pp. 11-12.

object of which is the protection of one class of persons from the transactions of another class, and the plaintiff falls within the protected class. It will be for the court to pronounce on the innocence or guilt of the party seeking relief. In *Stokes* v. *Twitchen*[1] the plaintiff had executed a deed of apprenticeship which, contrary to statute, did not contain a note of the consideration and was not stamped, though a printed notice defining these requirements had been attached to the deed. The court held that the plaintiff was not, in these circumstances, an innocent party and could not recover the premium though the consideration had failed.

Finally, it should be noted that where an agreement is not wholly illegal and it is possible, by applying the principles of severance already outlined, to sever the good from the bad parts of the contract, those parts which do not offend will be enforced by the courts. The plaintiff in *Kearney* v. *Whitehaven Colliery Co.*,[2] a servant of the defendants, had agreed to permit his employer to make certain illegal deductions from his wages, and had also agreed to give fourteen days' notice of his intention to leave the service. The court held that the illegality as to wages did not vitiate the entire contract, and that the obligation to give fourteen days' notice still bound the plaintiff. The apparent difficulty of deciding whether a contract is made wholly illegal or whether severance can be allowed has been greatly simplified by two recent cases, outside the law of master and servant.[3] Where the illegality is a fundamental wrong, such as a crime, there can be no severance.[4] Where, however, the illegality is more in the nature of a breach of rules severance will be allowed provided that the illegal promise is not substantially the only consideration given. Covenants in restraint of trade do not of course form a substantial part of a contract of employment and nothing in the recent formulation of the rules detracts from the court's usual practice of severing such agreements.

6. CONTRACT OF SERVICE AND RACIAL DISCRIMINATION[5]

The common law, with its concept of contractual freedom, placed no fetters on employment policies which might be developed to exclude coloured workers, or indeed to select on other grounds such as religion. Such case law as there is points to a completely unsatisfactory position. Thus it might be possible, where several people are involved, for example, an employer and a trade union to

---

[1] (1818), 8 Taunt. 492.

[2] [1893] 1 Q.B. 700.

[3] *Bennett* v. *Bennett*, [1952] 1 K.B. 249; [1952] 1 All E.R. 413; *Goodinson* v. *Goodinson*, [1954] 2 Q.B. 118; [1954] 2 All E.R. 255.

[4] *E.g.*, to defraud the revenue, *Napier* v. *National Business Agency, Ltd.*, [1951] 2 All E.R. 264.

[5] For a full study of this problem see *Race, Jobs and the Law in Britain*, 2nd Ed. (1970), by Bob Hepple; and *Race and Law*, by A. Lester and G. Bindman.

sue for conspiracy.[1]   It might also be possible to seek a declaration, but the remedy is of little avail.[2]

The Race Relations Act, 1968 has attempted to deal with the situation.   Section 3 relates to employment and provides that it is unlawful for an employer, or anyone concerned with the employment (a phrase which makes the employer clearly vicariously liable for actions of his servants), to discriminate against another person. Discrimination means treating a person less favourably on the grounds of colour, race or national origin.[3]   Separate but equal is defined as less favourable.[4]   The actions referred to in section 3 are refusing or deliberately omitting to employ a person seeking work for which he is qualified; failing to offer like terms or conditions of work; failing to afford like opportunities for training and promotion.   Also covered is dismissing the person in circumstances where others would not be dismissed.

These provisions extend gradually to smaller units of employment. For the first five years, employers with twenty-five or less employees are excluded, and for the following two years, those with ten or less. There is also a provision that discrimination may be justified if it is done in good faith to secure or preserve a reasonable balance.[5]   The Act also excludes employment in a private household.[6]

It only remains to explain the effect of making these actions unlawful.   It brings them within the machinery of the Act which involves reference to a conciliation committee and ultimately to a civil action in the county court.   It seems to be envisaged by the Industrial Relations Act, 1971 that where there is discrimination which may be an unfair industrial practice under that Act, for example a dismissal chiefly on racial grounds, then the matter should be dealt with in this way.[7]   If a breach of the Race Relations Act is disclosed, the Secretary of State or the Race Relations Board may seek a written assurance against repetition, and if this is broken, may take action under the Race Relations Act.

7. Industrial Relations Act—Effect on Formation of Contract of Service

The Industrial Relations Act, 1971 breaks new ground by laying down rights as to trade union membership of an employee.   In a key section, s. 5, it provides that every worker has the right to be a mem-

---

[1] *Scala Ballroom (Wolverhampton)* v. *Ratcliffe*, [1958] 3 All E.R. 220; [1958] 1 W.L.R. 1057.

[2] *Eastham* v. *Newcastle United Football Club*, [1964] Ch. 413, [1963] 3 All E.R. 139.

[3] S.I.   Note that it does not include religion: a possible problem, for example is Northern Ireland.

[4] S.1(2).

[5] S.8.

[6] For the full range of exclusions, see s.8(7) (8).

[7] Industrial Relations Act, 1971, s.149.

ber of such trade union as he may choose. The wording must be carefully noted. In the Act, the term trade union indicates a registered trade union.[1] The aim of the provision is to outlaw action by an employer to prevent his worker joining such a trade union. To the industrial relations specialist, the term " as he may choose " appears odd in that it allows a free choice of trade union. In most situations there will be one, or a group of appropriate trade unions, and although the notion of appropriateness might be hard to define it is practically sensible to expect the choice to be so restricted. Once he is a member, the Act also protects the worker's right to take part in its activities, including seeking election as an official and acting as one if elected.[2] Such right is merely limited by the phrase " at any appropriate time." The Act defines this as outside working hours or at times agreed with his employer.[3] The Code[4] has a section dealing with employee-representation at the workplace which stresses the need for clarity and agreement upon the facilities, including time off, to be allowed.[5]

The Act introduces a balancing right[6] that a worker has a right to belong to no trade union or organisation of workers[7] or to refuse to belong to any particular trade union or organisation of workers. This right may be modified by the establishment of an agency shop agreement which will be discussed below.

To protect these rights the Act creates unfair industrial practices which lay the employer open to an action for compensation before an Industrial Tribunal.[8] It should be noted here that the definition of worker is such as to include applicants for work.[9] This has the effect of protecting the worker who applied for a job which he can establish he failed to get for one of these reasons. The employer's action which became unfair industrial practices covers action preventing or deterring the worker from exercising the basic rights set out in s. 5(1), or dismissing him, penalising him or discriminating against him for exercising these rights or refusing to engage him on the ground of his membership or non-membership of a trade union. It is specifically provided that a benefit offered selectively on the grounds of membership or non-membership is discrimination.[10] On the other hand it is important to note that encouraging a worker to join a trade

---

[1] For a discussion of " registered ", see below at p. 459.
[2] S.5. 1(a).
[3] S.5(5).
[4] Industrial Relations Code of Practice, made under s.2 of the Act.
[5] *E.g.* Para. 116.
[6] It is strongly argued by some that it is not a true balance because the encouragement of union membership and the development of collective bargaining is an ideal. This right militates against that aim.
[7] The Act's jargon for unregistered trade union: see footnote 1.
[8] S.5(2) and s. 106.
[9] S.167.
[10] S.5(4).

union with negotiating rights is not to be construed as unfair.[1]   It should be noted that section 5 lays down rights between an employer and his workers.   It is these that are protected.   It would not appear to be unfair for an employer to suggest to another with whom he contracts that only union, or non-union labour (it will usually be the former) be sent to his premises under the contract.

Pressure on an employer to commit these unfair industrial practices is dealt with by section 33.   The employer is not able to hide behind this pressure as a complete defence.   Indeed the matter is to be determined as if no such pressure had been exercised.   It is, however, an unfair industrial practice on the part of the person, including a trade union or organisation of workers or their officials, to exert such pressure provided that it can be shown that the principal purpose was knowingly to induce the employer to commit one of the unfair practices, under section 5, under the rules relating to unfair dismissal[2] or under the provision making the pre-entry closed shop agreement void.[3]

The action covered is calling, organising, procuring or financing a strike, or threatening to do so, or similarly organising, procuring or financing any irregular industrial action short of a strike.[4]   Irregular industrial action is further defined as any concerted course of conduct carried on by a group of workers with the intention of preventing, reducing or interfering with the production of goods or the provision of services in a situation where such action is a breach of contracts of employement or terms and conditions of service.[5]   These provisions which are fundamental to the Act and recur throughout will no doubt attract their share of interpretative case law.   For example the line between financing a strike and say helping a striker's family must be narrow.   The provisions will also lead to action to rearrange contractual positions.   It might, for example, be thought advantageous by a trade union to have the liability to do overtime made voluntary and therefore any refusal to work overtime as an industrial weapon would not be caught under the definition of irregular industrial action.   It will plainly cover a sit-in, a go slow, certain types of non-co-operation, but probably not a work to rule.

(1) Closed Shop.—The result of section 5 is to make the maintenance of a closed shop impossible because under its provision compulsory membership of a trade union cannot be enforced.   This

---

[1] S.5(3).   In accordance with the general policy of the Act, this clause is narrowly drawn—it does not specifically cover non-registered organisations or trade unions without rights.   A good employer might well want to do this, certainly in the case where a union is building up its strength prior to recognition.

[2] See below, p. 105.

[3] Discussed below.

[4] S.33(2).

[5] S.33(4).

indeed is the intention of the legislation and this is strengthened by a special provision relating to pre-entry closed shop agreements. These are agreements made between employers and unions under which the employer promises not to engage workers who are not already union members or who are not already members of a specific trade union. This is casually called a pre-entry closed shop agreement. It may also take the form of the employer agreeing not to engage workers who have not been recommended or approved by the trade union. These types of agreement are made void by the Industrial Relations Act.[1] A worker who feels that he has been refused engagement by an employer because of the operation of such an agreement may apply to the Industrial Court[2] to have such an agreement declared void.

It was recognised when the Bill was passing through Parliament that there were several special situations where the ending of the closed shop would present severe problems and would damage collective bargaining already established. The most obvious example was the acting profession[3] where the number of aspirants to a job is so great that industrial relations would suffer if there were not some regulation. This situation has been met by the provisions allowing approved closed shop agreements.[4] Such an agreement is made between employers and trade unions—again note this means registered trade unions. Under such agreement it is to be provided that a worker, if not already a member of the trade union must join unless specially exempted.[5] The effects of such an agreement are to supersede the section 5 rights discussed above. The worker is under a duty to join[6] and if he fails to do so the employer does not commit an unfair industrial practice if he dismisses him or commits any of the other acts forbidden in section 5. An approved closed shop agreement has to be sanctioned by the Industrial Court.[7] The rules are set out in Schedule 1 to the Act. Briefly they envisage a joint application by employer and trade union where it is proposed to enter into such an agreement. The draft agreement has to be examined by the Commission on Industrial Relations with a view to satisfying themselves that such an agreement is necessary to enable the workers to be organised or to continue to be organised; to maintain reasonable terms and conditions of employment; to promote or maintain stable arrangements for collective bargaining, and to prevent bargains being frustrated.[8] If it is satisfied on these

---

[1] S.7(1).
[2] For a discussion of the institutions set up by the Industrial Relations Act, see below, p. 428.
[3] The merchant sea service is another.
[4] Ss. 17–18.
[5] *E.g.* under a conscience clause.
[6] Note the form allowed is *post*-entry not *pre*-entry.
[7] S.17(1) (c).
[8] Schedule 1, para. 5.

points, and also that the alternative agency shop agreement is not appropriate, the Commission must report favourably to the court. If it does not think so, the application fails.   Where the report is favourable, the court lays down a period[1] during which a ballot may be requested.   If no ballot is requested, the order approving the closed shop agreement is made.   Part II of the Schedule sets out the procedure to be followed where a ballot is requested.   Such ballot requires a majority of those eligible to vote or at least two-thirds of those actually voting for subsequent approval of the agreement by the court.[2]   Part III allows an established agreement to be challenged.   Such a challenge cannot be made successfully within two years of a previous ballot and it must be requested by at least one-fifth of the workers covered by the agreement.   It requires the same majorities to ensure the continuance of the approved closed shop—that is to say a majority of those entitled to vote or two-thirds of those actually voting.[3]

(2) **Agency Shop.**—The provisions on the closed shop have been regarded with disfavour by trade unionists and some employers. Abolition has not, however, been total and the concept of an agency shop agreement is introduced by the Act and provides a device somewhat similar to a post-entry closed shop.   This is the agency shop agreement.   The big difference is that it provides for a category of workers in the shop who are not union members but who must pay dues to the union.

An agency shop agreement is made on the one side by an employers' association, employers or a single employer, and on the other by a trade union or several trade unions.   Again it must be noted that the trade unions must be registered under the Act.   The agreement specifies that workers of a particular description or descriptions must, as part of the terms and conditions of their service, either be a member of the trade union or trade unions, or agree to pay contributions to them or be acceptable as on conscience grounds paying similar contributions to a charity.[4]

The first point to note is that the Act envisages the agreement covering groups of workers.   It will be an industrial relations judgment as to the appropriate area to be designated as the agency shop.   The Act envisages that the agreement will be made voluntarily.   The result of such an agreement is that section 5 rights are modified.   The worker is required to fall into one of the three categories and he loses the protection of section 5 if he refuses.[5]   He may, for example, be dismissed by the employer without this being an unfair industrial practice.   The three categories do not present

---

[1] 1–3 months.
[2] Schedule 1, para. 14.
[3] Schedule 1, para. 20.
[4] S.11.
[5] S.6.

real difficulty. The worker may choose trade union membership. Where there are joint agreements, nothing apparently affects his right to choose which of the unions he will join. He may instead choose not to become a member. He must then pay contributions to the agent trade union. The exact nature of these appropriate payments are laid down in the Act.[1] They may include an initial payment and periodical payments.[2] Finally the worker may try to be accepted as permitted to pay to a charity. He has to show that he objects on the grounds of conscience both to being a trade union member and to paying contributions in lieu of membership.[3] He must make his submission to the trade union which can then agree to accept his plea and approve the amount he has to pay and the charity selected as recipient.[4] Disputes relating to the contribution payable under section 8 by the non-member or as to the acceptability of the claim to pay as a conscientious objector, as to the amount or the charity, are to be determined by the Industrial Tribunal.[5]

In this way the Act recognises as a major exception to section 5 the agency shop agreement. It goes further and provides a procedure by which application may be made to the Industrial Court for the imposition of such an agreement. In the past, trade unions have often found closed shops hard to obtain. The agency shop agreement procedure promises to be easier. Application to the court may be made by a registered trade union, or registered trade unions, or a joint negotiating panel of trade unions or by an employer.[6] It must specify the workers to be covered and the proposed parties to the agreement. The Industrial Court then has to satisfy itself that the applicants have been already granted negotiating rights and that the applicant is not barred by the rules designated to prevent continual applications[7] and if it does so, the Commission on Industrial Relations is asked to organise a ballot. If the Commission feels that the application hides a recognition dispute, that is to say a battle between unions as to who should be recognised as able to negotiate for particular groups of workers, this must be reported to the court and the recognition procedure invoked.[8] Once satisfied that this is not so, the Commission then has to consider the appropriate group of workers to be balloted. It may report to the court that the application should apply to a narrower or to an extended group.[9] Once this point is settled a ballot is taken. The majority required is a simple majority of those eligible to vote or two-thirds of those actually voting.[10] If this is achieved, the employer has a duty to

[1] S.8.
[2] S.8 goes into some detail.
[3] S.9(1) (b).
[4] S.9(2).
[5] S.10.
[6] S.11(2).
[7] S.13(4) and s.15(3).
[8] This is discussed in Ch. X, below, p. 427.
[9] S.12(2).
[10] S.13.

make the appropriate agency shop agreement, and a duty of carrying it out.   This duty to carry it out is protected by the Act making it an unfair industrial practice to induce or attempt to induce[1] an employer not to carry it out.[2]   If the ballot fails to show the requisite majority in favour, the Industrial Court must make an order making any purported agency shop agreement covering the parties void for two years after the results of the ballot were reported.[3]

The Act also provides for a challenge to be made in respect of an existing agency shop.   Any worker within the shop may apply, but the application must have the written support of one-fifth of the workers if it is a voluntary agreement and two-fifths if it has been imposed by the Industrial Court[4].   Again the Commission on Industrial Relations has to hold the ballot.   The same majorities are required to ensure continuance—a simple majority of those eligible or two-thirds of those actually voting.   If these are not achieved, the Industrial Court must order that the agreement be rescinded.   The parties to the agreement cannot then enter into an agency shop agreement for two years thereafter and any such purported agreement is void.[5]

Balloting is protected from an unfair industrial practice.   An employer by lock-out must not attempt to prevent an application for an agency shop agreement or for a ballot to test an existing one. A trade union or official or any person also commits an unfair industrial practice if by strike or irregular action[6] an attempt is made to force the employer to enter into an agreement once an application has been made under section 11, or to stop the employer himself applying.[7]

8.   CONTRACT OF APPRENTICESHIP

It is necessary to look specially at the contract of apprenticeship, which combines elements of training and education as well as of service.   In the words of WIDGERY, L. J., in a recent case

" A contract of apprenticeship is significantly different from an ordinary contract of service. . . . A contract of apprenticeship secures three things for the apprentice: it secures him, first, a money payment during the period of apprenticeship; secondly, that he shall be instructed and trained and thus acquire skills which will be of value for him for the rest of his life; and thirdly, it gives him status. . ."[8]

---

[1] By the methods discussed under s.33: see *supra*, p. 56.
[2] S.13(2).
[3] S. 13(4).   No further application can be made in this two-year period.
[4] S. 14(1), (2), (3).
[5] S. 15(3).   No fresh application is allowed during this two-year period for the same or substantially the same group of workers.
[6] Again the terms are those of s. 33.   [7] S. 16.
[8] *Dunk* v. *George Walker & Son, Ltd.*, [1970] 2 Q.B. 163 [1970] 2 All E.R. 630.

It will be readily imagined that a great deal of the case law relating to apprenticeship is of considerable age. There is some difficulty in assessing accurately the modern law.[1] In this section the principal distinctive features of a contract of apprenticeship fall to be considered.

The relationship between a contract of service and a contract of apprenticeship has been summarised in these terms:

> " It may be that an apprentice does to some extent do the class of work which would be done by a servant, but he does not do it as a servant. His relation to his employer is one of apprenticeship and not of service and carries with it certain special incidents and, in particular, that of being entitled to instruction as well as to the food or wages to which a servant would be entitled."[2]

As in every other contract the five essential elements must be present. There must be offer and acceptance clearly showing the agreement of the parties. The parties must intend to establish a legally binding relationship. They must have capacity; there must be form or consideration and, of course, the agreement must be free from all taint of illegality.

(1) Parent and Infant.—The parties to a contract of apprenticeship are usually the master (who may himself be an infant[3]) the apprentice and the latter's parent or guardian. The apprentice must be party to the apprenticeship or it will be invalid.[4] The apprentice must consent to be bound as an apprentice; a parent cannot bind him without his consent.[5] This consent must be real and anything in the nature of undue influence will operate to avoid the contract, for the relationship of master and apprentice may be fiduciary.[6] There are special provisions to protect seamen who are under 18.[7] The participation of the parent or guardian in the indenture is not necessary and his liability is usually restricted to guaranteeing the apprentice's performance of his undertakings.

The common law was apparently silent as to the minimum age of apprenticeship. The question is now dealt with by statute which regulates both the minimum age of work and of apprenticeship. The Children and Young Persons Act, 1933[8] provides that no children two years under the school leaving age may be employed. This provision may be regulated by local authority byelaw. These provisions, and the school leaving age,[9] obviously place a lower limit on the age of apprenticeship.

---

[1] Thus in *Dunk's* case, two nineteenth-century cases were over-ruled.
[2] *Horan* v. *Hay Loe*, [1904] 1 K.B. 288, per KENNEDY, J., at p. 291.
[3] *R.* v. *St. Petrox (Inhabitants)* (1791), 4 Term Rep. 196.
[4] *R.* v. *Ripon (Inhabitants)* (1808), 9 East 295.
[5] *R.* v. *Arnesby (Inhabitants)* (1820), 3 B. & Ald. 584.
[6] *Peacock* v. *Kernat* (1848), 10 L.T. O.S. 517.
[7] See Merchant Shipping Act, 1970, s. 51.
[8] S. 18 as amended.
[9] 15, to be raised to 16 in 1972.

(2) Form.—A contract of apprenticeship must be in writing.[1]
A deed is no longer required but is often executed although the law
is satisfied as long as the contract is in writing and signed by the
apprentice.[2]   The Merchant Shipping Act, 1970 has special provision
as to sea service.[3]   The contract is one in which consideration is
present as a matter of course but if it is exclusively composed of a
duty on the part of the master to teach and no corresponding
promise to serve, the agreement is not binding unless under seal.[4]

(3) Discharge.—The contract of apprenticeship is based on
personal performance.   So the death of the master ends the contract.[5]   Unless there are special provisions, the apprentice will not
be bound to others in this event.[6]   The master's illness, if it prevents performance, will also terminate the contract.   The master
will be excused performance by permanent illness of the apprentice.[7]
Where the master is adjudged bankrupt then if either the master or
apprentice gives written notice to the trustee, the apprenticeship
will be discharged.   The trustee in such circumstances may repay
an appropriate part of the premium.[8]   The trustee has also power
to arrange the transfer of the apprenticeship.[9]

The position arising where a partnership is dissolved depends upon
the exact circumstances.

(4) Termination.—If the master desires the right to dismiss
his apprentice for misconduct, he must specifically reserve power to
do so in the indenture for no such power exists at common law,[10]
though apparently there is in London a customary right to do so.[11]
There is some evidence to suggest that when the misbehaviour of
the apprentice is such as to amount to positive danger—as where a
student assistant to a chemist was too intoxicated to compound the
drugs so that a shop boy had to do it[12]—the apprentice may be
dismissed.   It cannot be doubted that the decision was correct,
though it is true that in the case quoted, the wrong doer was not
merely an apprentice but an assistant as well.   It is submitted that
should similar circumstances arise in the case of one who was simply

---

[1] The Contracts of Employment Act, 1963 applies to apprenticeship contracts.
[2] *R.* v. *Ripon* (*Inhabitants*) (1808), 9 East 295; *Kirkby* v. *Taylor*, [1910]
1 K.B. 529.
[3] S. 1.
[4] *Lees* v. *Whitcomb* (1828), 5 Bing. 34.
[5] *R.* v. *Peck* (1698), 1 Salk. 66.
[6] *Cooper* v. *Simmons* (1862), 7 H & N. 707; *Baxter* v. *Burfield* (1747), 2 Stra.
1266.
[7] *Boast* v. *Firth* (1868), L.R. 4 C.P. 1.
[8] Bankruptcy Act, 1914, s. 34(1).   For an example, see *Re Richardson,
Ex parte Gould* (1887), 35 W.R. 381.
[9] S. 35(2).
[10] *Winstone* v. *Linn* (1823), 1 B. & C. 460.
[11] *Woodroffe* v. *Farnham* (1693), 2 Vern. 291.
[12] *Wise* v. *Wilson* (1845), 1 Car. & Kir. 662.

an apprentice the decision of the courts would be the same.[1] A master may dismiss an apprentice who is an habitual thief,[2] but insubordination, although an embarrassment to the master and fellow-workmen alike, will not entitle the master to dismiss him.[3]

Where the master relies on a covenant to dismiss he should remember that he is dealing with a young man, for the courts are likely to view the youth's peccadilloes more generously than they would those of one of more mature years. In *Newell* v. *Gillingham Corporation*[4] the plaintiff, an infant, brought action for wrongful dismissal. He was a conscientious objector whose behaviour, it was found, might irritate his colleagues and lead to loss of working time, but the behaviour was held not to be such as, in a young man, would justify dismissal. Should the conduct of the apprentice be such that it is impossible for the master to instruct him, the master will have a complete defence to any claim the dismissed apprentice may make, "inasmuch as the capability of the apprentice to be instructed, maintained and provided for by the master is naturally a condition precedent to the master's teaching him."[5]

As to termination by the voluntary act of the parties, there is no doubt that though an infant apprentice cannot dissolve the contract unless the dissolution is for his benefit,[6] nevertheless, if it is for the infant's benefit and all parties consent, the agreement may be terminated.[7] The act of the infant alone is inoperative unless he benefits thereby, for if it is beneficial that he be bound apprentice it will rarely be for his benefit to dissolve the connection.[8] He may, however, avoid the contract on reaching his majority or within a reasonable time thereafter. What is a reasonable time in such circumstances is a question of fact.[9] Lord KENYON has pointed out that if the right of election to be discharged on reaching his majority were not given to the infant, an infant who unwisely bound himself to the age of fifty or upwards would be compelled to serve until that time.[10] An infant who elects to avoid the apprenticeship must give his master reasonable notice and the mere fact that the apprentice has absented himself will not amount to such notice.[11] A third party

---

[1] It is urged that this reasoning would apply where the apprentice was negligent. *Therman* v. *Abell* (1688), 2 Vern. 64, is against such a view in that the court compelled a tradesman who had dismissed his apprentice for negligence to refund part of the premium. But the case was heard in the seventeenth century, and since then the adoption of machinery has given the negligence of workers (including apprentices) a more sinister significance.

[2] *Cox* v. *Mathews* (1861), 2 F. & F. 397; *Learoyd* v. *Brook*, [1891] 1 Q.B. 431.

[3] *McDonald* v. *John Twiname, Ltd.*, [1953] 2 Q.B. 304; [1953] 2 All E.R. 589.

[4] [1941] 1 All E.R. 552.

[5] *Raymond* v. *Minton* (1866), L.R. 1 Exch. 244; 4 H. & C. 371, *per* MARTIN, B., at p. 373, citing *Addison on Contracts*, 4th Ed., p. 440.

[6] *Waterman* v. *Fryer*, [1922] 1 K.B. 499; *Smedley* v. *Gooden* (1814), 3 M. & S. 189.

[7] *R.* v. *Weddington* (*Inhabitants*) (1774), Burr. S.C. 766.

[8] *R.* v. *Great Wigston, Leicester* (*Inhabitants*) (1824), 3 B. & C. 484.

[9] *Wray* v. *West* (1866), 15 L.T. 180.

[10] *Ex parte Davis* (1794), 5 Term Rep. 715 at p. 716.

[11] *Coghlan* v. *Callaghan* (1857), 7 I.C.L.R. 291.

who has joined in the contract as guarantor of the infant's behaviour cannot successfully plead, in an action on his covenant, that the infant has elected to avoid the contract. So, a father who was a party to the indenture of his son's apprenticeship was held liable for breach when his son failed to serve an agreed seven years because of his election, when reaching the age of twenty-one, no longer to be bound.[1]

(5) Remedies.—A master could moderately chastise an apprentice who misbehaves,[2] but the change in social circumstances makes the case law very unreliable.

Where an apprentice by his conduct commits a breach of contract, the master may have rights against the apprentice and, in addition, against any person who has become surety for the infant's performance of his undertaking. No action for damages will lie against an infant apprentice though, as we shall see, he may be brought before the court under the provisions of the Employers and Workmen Act, 1875. An apprentice of full age is fully liable on the contract and may be sued for part of the premium though he entered into the contract when he was an infant.[3]

Generally, the master will prefer to move against the surety, and he will be entitled to damages up to the time of action brought[4] but not thereafter. "The apprentice may come back to-morrow; and the master cannot therefore recover . . . damages beyond the time of the action."[5] Where the breach is by the master to the prejudice of the apprentice, the master will be liable in damages from the date of breach to the time of bringing the action.[6] For a recent case on measure of damages see *Dunk* v. *George Waller & Son, Ltd.*[7]

An action for specific performance will not lie at the suit of either party to the instrument of apprenticeship[8] but, though an injunction will not be granted during the apprenticeship, the courts have power to restrain breaches of restrictive covenants after the period of apprenticeship is concluded.[9]

Money paid as premium by or on behalf of the apprentice will be recoverable by means of an action for money had and received only where there is a complete failure of consideration. So if A pays £50 as premium and receives neither instruction nor any other relevant benefit under the contract, an action will lie. But if he receives any benefit at all, no part of the premium will be recoverable

---

[1] *Cuming* v. *Hill* (1819), 3 B. & Ald. 59.
[2] *Gylbert* v. *Fletcher* (1629), Cro. Car. 179;   *Penn* v. *Ward* (1835), 2 Cr. M. & R. 338.
[3] *Walter* v. *Everard*, [1891] 2 Q.B. 369.
[4] *Lewis* v. *Peachey* (1862), 1 H. & C. 518.
[5] *Russell* v. *Shinn* (1861), 2 F. & F. 395, *per* BYLES, J., at p. 396.
[6] *Addams* v. *Carter* (1862), 6 L.T. 130.   [7] [1970] 2 Q.B. 163.
[8] *De Francesco* v. *Barnum* (1890), 45 Ch.D. 430
[9] *Evans* v. *Ware*, [1892] 3 Ch. 502.

at common law.[1] Where, under the provisions of the Employers and Workmen Act, 1875, the court rescinds an instrument of apprenticeship, it may order the repayment of the whole or any part of the premium paid when the apprentice was bound.[2]

A court of summary jurisdiction has, under the terms of the Employers and Workmen Act, 1875, power to hear and determine any dispute between an apprentice to whom the Act applies and his master.

---

[1] *Whincup* v. *Hughes* (1871), L.R. 6 C.P. 78; *Olsen* v. *Corry and Gravesend Aviation, Ltd.*, [1936] 3 All E.R. 241.
[2] S. 6.

CHAPTER III

DISCHARGE OF THE CONTRACT OF SERVICE

Having considered the way in which a contract of service is formed, we must now discuss how the obligations so created may be discharged. Discharge will normally be by performance, and we shall thus be concerned with the quality of performance which will be required to satisfy the law. The parties, instead of performing, may decide to rescind or vary the terms of the contract, setting up a substitute manner of performance. Such rescission or variation is only possible where all parties agree. Failing such mutual agreement the refusal by either party to perform may amount to repudiation giving rise to rights of action. These rights, in turn, may be discharged only in certain clearly defined ways. The varying ways in which the rights of the parties, created by or out of the contract, can be extinguished, must now be discussed.

1. PERSONAL PERFORMANCE

Performance must be by the person, at the time and in the place and manner agreed upon by the parties or enjoined by the law.

The rule that performance must be by the person indicated in the contract has led to two propositions of outstanding importance. The first is that a contract of service, unless there be specific agreement to the contrary, is performable only by the parties thereto, so that neither party can assign the contract. In *Nokes* v. *Doncaster Amalgamated Collieries, Ltd.*,[1] the appellant was a miner employed by a company on which an order had been made under the Companies Act, 1929,[2] transferring it, its liabilities and assets to the respondent company. The appellant, unaware of the order, worked for some time, then absented himself and was charged and found guilty by the lower courts of an offence under section 4 of the Employers and Workmen Act, 1875,[3] namely, breach of his contract of employment. The House of Lords, however, rejected this finding, and in no uncertain terms affirmed the right of a workman to choose his own employer.

> "It will be readily conceded that the result contended for by the respondents in this case would be at complete variance with a fundamental principle of our common law—namely, that a free citizen, in the exercise of his freedom, is entitled to choose the employer

---

[1] [1940] A.C. 1014; [1940] 3 All E.R. 549.
[2] Now repealed and replaced by Companies Act, 1948.
[3] Also repealed.

whom he promises to serve so that the right to his services cannot be transferred from one employer to another without his assent."[1]

Thus the sale of a company by a receiver operates to terminate contracts of employment. This was so even when sale was to a subsidiary company.[2]

The second principle is that because the contract is one of personal service it will be discharged by the death of either master or servant. The dissolution of a partnership may operate in the same way. Conversely the master's bankruptcy will not discharge the contract, but this is entirely due to technical difficulties which would render it inequitable to the servant were the master so easily to escape liability.

(1) Death.—Death will bring a contract of service to an end, whether it be the death of the servant[3] or of the master, as in *Farrow* v. *Wilson*,[4] where the personal representatives were held not to be liable to continue the engagement of the servant. The servant is discharged from further performance on the death of the master, not in breach of the contract, but as the result of an implied condition that the continued existence of the parties is an essential of the contract. But though death dissolves the contract, it does not divest the deceased's representatives of any rights of action which had already accrued before the date of death.[5]

(2) Dissolution of Partnership.—Where a partner dies and there is a consequent dissolution of the partnership, the contract of service will be discharged wherever it is one related to the personal conduct of the deceased person. In *Harvey* v. *Tivoli, Manchester, Ltd.*,[6] the death of a member of a troupe of three music-hall artists was held to discharge the contract though he had been replaced, and the troupe was ready to appear. In *Phillips* v. *Alhambra Palace Co.*,[7] one of the defendant partners had died after a contract had been entered into with the plaintiffs, who also were music-hall artists. In this case it was held that the obligation continued despite the death of the partner, for the obligation was not of a personal character, and the partners, when they booked the artists to appear, were not individually known. In the first case the contract was with three specific persons—in the second case it was with a company and the personal element was not paramount. A dissolution of a partnership on account of the retirement of a partner

---

[1] *Nokes* v. *Doncaster Amalgamated Collieries, Ltd.*, [1940] A.C. 1014, *per* Viscount SIMON, L.C., at p. 1020.

[2] *Re Foster Clark Ltd.'s Indenture Trusts*, [1966] 1 All E.R. 43; [1966] 1 W.L.R. 125, but the appointment of a receiver does not have this effect. *Re Mack Trucks (Britain), Ltd.*, [1967] 1 All E.R. 977; [1967] 1 W.L.R. 780.

[3] *Stubbs* v. *Holywell Ry. Co.* (1867), L.R. 2 Exch. 311; *Graves* v. *Cohen* (1929), 46 T.L.R. 121.

[4] (1869), L.R. 4 C.P. 744.

[5] *Stubbs* v. *Holywell Ry. Co.*, *supra*, *per* KELLY, C.B., at p. 313.

[6] (1907), 23 T.L.R. 592.

[7] [1901] 1 K.B. 59.

will operate as a wrongful dismissal,[1] but a continuance of service under a firm containing some of the old partners will amount to a waiver of rights of action.[2]   A dissolution of a partnership may amount to a breach of a contract of apprenticeship.[3]

(3) **Bankruptcy.**—The bankruptcy of the master or of the servant does not dissolve a contract of service,[4] but since the contract of service may be personal in character, it does not follow that the rights of the master under such a contract will pass to his trustee in bankruptcy.   So where publishers, who had agreed to publish a book written by their reader and adviser, were adjudicated bankrupt, it was held that the trustee in bankruptcy had no right to reprint and publish the book.[5]   An order by the court to wind up a company operates as notice to the servants.[6]   Where a manager and receiver was appointed by the court, it was held that

> "the result of such an appointment is to discharge the servants from their service to their original employer, and . . . there is a wrongful dismissal."[7]

In *Measures Bros., Ltd.* v. *Measures*,[8] a service agreement with a director contained an undertaking that he should hold office for seven years, and that for seven years thereafter he would not engage directly or indirectly in any similar business.   Within the seven years' service a receiver and manager were appointed as a result of a debenture holder's action.   The receiver gave the director notice and the latter then engaged in a similar undertaking.   It was held that he was entitled to do so.   The plaintiff company, not being themselves willing to perform, could not enforce the performance by the servant.   If the winding-up of a company, not merely acted as notice but dissolved the contract of service, the result would be, as has been pointed out, to enable any company by the simple device of voluntary liquidation to put an end to its contracts.[9]

(4) **Illness.**—Illness may or may not terminate the contract. Regard must be had, in every case, to the terms of the agreement, to the custom of the service,[10] and to the surrounding circumstances. If the effect of such considerations is to frustrate the object of the engagement the contract will be ended.[11]   In *Robinson* v. *Davison*[12]

---

[1] *Brace* v. *Calder*, [1895] 2 Q.B. 253.

[2] *Hobson* v. *Cowley* (1858), 27 L. J. (Ex.) 205.

[3] *Titmus and Titmus* v. *Rose and Watts*, [1940] 1 All E.R. 599.

[4] *Thomas* v. *Williams* (1834), 1 Ad. & El. 685.

[5] *Lucas* v. *Moncrieff* (1905), 21 T.L.R. 683.

[6] *Re General Rolling Stock Co., Chapman's Case* (1866), L. R. 1 Eq. 346.

[7] *Reid* v. *Explosives Co.* (1887), 19 Q.B.D. 264, *per* Lord ESHER, M.R., at p. 267.

[8] [1910] 2 Ch. 248.

[9] *Re Patent Floor Cloth Co., Dean and Gilbert's Claim* (1872), 41 L. J. (Ch. 476, *per* BACON, V.C., at p. 477.

[10] *O'Grady* v. *M. Saper, Ltd.*, [1940] 2 K.B. 469; [1940] 3 All E.R. 527.

[11] *Storey* v. *Fulham Steel Works Co.* (1907), 24 T.L.R. 89; *Condor* v. *Barron Knights, Ltd.*, [1966] 1 W.L.R. 87.

[12] (1871), L.R. 6 Exch. 269.   *Cf. Bettini* v. *Gye* (1876), 1 Q.B.D. 183.

a wife contracted as agent for her husband, that she should sing at a certain concert. Owing to sickness she could not do so, and the plaintiff brought an action for breach of contract. It was held that her illness excused performance and that no action would lie.

" This was a contract for the performance of a service which could alone be undertaken by the defendant's wife. She could not depute it to anyone else, as it depended on her own personal skill,"

said KELLY, C.B.,[1] and he went on to state that the true rule had been laid down by POLLOCK, C. B., in *Hall* v. *Wright*[2]:

". . . a contract by an author to write a book or by a painter to paint a picture within a reasonable time would, in my judgment, be deemed subject to the condition that if the author became insane or the painter paralytic and so incapable of performing the contract . . . he would not be liable personally in damages any more than his executors would be if he had been prevented by death."

In such cases the illness clearly frustrates the contract with the result that it is discharged.

What degree of illness will frustrate the agreement is a question of fact. Where the sickness is such that it compels the master to engage a substitute or otherwise involves a radical change in the master's plans, the undertaking is obviously brought to an end. This happened in *Poussard* v. *Spiers and Pond*.[3] The plaintiff's wife, an opera singer, was under contract to sing for the defendants; she became ill during rehearsals, and the defendants entered into a contract with another singer who completed the rehearsals and sang at the opening and at three subsequent performances. The plaintiff then recovered but the defendants refused to re-employ her, and she brought action for breach. The court held that her sickness went to the root of the contract and entitled the defendants to rescind

". . . if no substitute capable of performing the part adequately could be obtained except on the terms that she would be permanently engaged at higher pay than the plaintiff's wife . . . it follows as a matter of law that the failure on the plaintiff's part went to the root of the matter and discharged the defendants."[4]

Bettini v. *Gye*[5] might usefully be compared with *Poussard's* case, for here, too, the plaintiff was a singer and he had agreed to be in London for the purpose of rehearsals six days before the opening performance. Owing to illness he did not arrive until two days before, and the defendant refused to receive him into his service. It was held that the condition as to rehearsals did not go to the root of the contract, and the defendant could only seek redress through a cross claim for damages.

---

[1] *Robinson* v. *Davison* (1871), L.R. 6 Exch. 269 at p. 274.
[2] (1859), E. B. & E. 765 at p. 793.
[3] (1876), 1 Q.B.D. 410.
[4] *Poussard* v. *Spiers and Pond* (1876), 1 Q.B.D. 410, *per* BLACKBURN, J., at p. 415.
[5] (1876), 1 Q.B.D. 183.

It may be that frustration applies only to contracts envisaging a short period of highly paid employment, for it seems that where a contract of service is in progress of performance and the servant is absent through illness, that illness will not of itself terminate the contract.   The master can, of course, in the absence of any agreement to the contrary, end the contract by giving due notice.   Until he does so he remains liable on the contract, that is to say he has to pay the agreed wages.   Such illness has been considered in an illuminating judgment of PILCHER, J., in *Orman* v. *Saville Sportswear, Ltd.*[1]   The terms of the contract may provide for illness and they will be enforced.   Failing express terms the parties may by their conduct have established an understanding which will also be enforced by the courts.   Thus where a Commissionaire had never been paid during previous absences through illness the Court of Appeal held that he was not entitled to be paid, for he was working on the understanding that this would be the position.[2]   The court may also be willing to imply a term covering illness.   This, it seems, will only be done where the court is satisfied that had the parties considered the matter they would have reached an agreement in the terms implied.[3]   Where none of these consideration apply, as in *Orman* v. *Saville Sportswear, Ltd.*,[4] the employer remains liable to continue paying wages until determination of the contract by due notice.   These rules will apparently be applied even where the illness is the result of the servant's personal wrongdoing[5] or the result of an accident.[6]

2. DURATION OF PERFORMANCE

As to the time of performance, the first point to be discussed is the question of the duration of the contract.   The general rule is that the contract will endure for such time as the parties have agreed upon, so that where a time has been stipulated no difficulty is likely to arise.   Most contracts of service, however, have no fixed duration. They continue until the appropriate notice is given by one party or the other.   The old notion of general hiring—that an indefinite hiring was for a year, has slipped into history.[7]

A contract of service with or under the Crown persists, as we have already seen, only during the pleasure of the Crown[8] and the same is generally true of contracts between local authorities and their

---

[1] [1960] 3 All E.R. 105; [1960] 1 W.L.R. 1055.
[2] *O'Grady* v. *M. Saper, Ltd.*, [1940] 2 K.B. 469; [1940] 3 All E.R. 527.
[3] *Reigate* v. *Union Manufacturing (Ramsbottom) Co. Ltd.*, [1918] 1 K.B. 592. This was not so in *Orman's* case.
[4] See also *Marrison* v. *Bell*, [1939] 2 K.B. 187; [1939] 1 All E.R. 745.   The headnote of this case has attracted criticism.
[5] *K—.* v. *Raschen* (1878), 38 L.T. 38.
[6] *Warburton* v. *Co-operative Wholesale Society, Ltd.*, [1917] 1 K.B. 663.
[7] *Richardson* v. *Koefod*, [1969] 3 All E.R. 1264; [1969] 1 W.L.R. 1812.
[8] See *ante*, pp. 29 *et seq.*

servants,[1] though in certain cases power to dismiss is dependent upon the concurrence of the Home Office.[2] Where, however, the contract of service with the local authority requires an agreed period of notice by either party, the provision must be observed.[3]

(1) Impossibility.—A contract of service will be terminated wherever, owing to a change in the law or in the relevant circumstances, performance becomes impossible. In either of these events the parties will be excused further performance. A member of the crew of a British ship caught in an enemy port on the outbreak of war has been held to lose all right to wages.[4] For this no fault lay upon him, but neither did any lie upon his employer, and the court deemed it inequitable to make the master liable for wages when the servant could not perform his promise to assist in the working of the ship. So, too, where a servant is to be paid a commission on work resulting from his activities, the right to commission will generally cease when he is embodied under compulsory enlistment Acts.[5] In *Unger* v. *Preston Corporation*[6] an alien, employed as an assistant school medical officer, was interned in June, 1940, and not released until March, 1941. The executive action of internment was held to have frustrated the contract so as to release the master from his obligations, but in *Nordman* v. *Rayner and Sturges*[7] the internment of an Alsatian of French sympathies for one month was held not to end the contract.

The defendant in *Morgan* v. *Manser*[8] was a music hall artist who had entered into an agreement appointing the plaintiff his manager for a period of ten years. The plaintiff was to secure engagements for the defendant who was not to offer his services to anyone else. During the ten-year period the defendant served with the Forces, and after discharge had entered into agreements with agents other than the plaintiff. The defendant successfully pleaded that the period of military service had frustrated the original contract.

The test in all these cases will be whether the change of law or of circumstances is such as to bring about a substantial frustration, the operation of which test was described by STREATFEILD, J., in *Morgan* v. *Manser* in the following terms :

"If there is an event or change of circumstances which is so fundamental as to be regarded by the law as striking at the root of the contract as a whole, and as going beyond what was contemplated by the parties and such that to hold the parties to the contract would be to bind them to terms which they would not have made

---

[1] Local Government Act, 1933, s. 105 (2).
[2] *Ibid.*, ss. 100(1), 103(3).
[3] *Ibid.*, s. 121.
[4] *Horlock* v. *Beal*, [1916] 1 A.C. 486.
[5] *Marshall* v. *Glanvill*, [1917] 2 K.B. 87.
[6] [1942] 1 All E.R. 200.
[7] (1916), 33 T.L.R. 87.
[8] *Morgan* v. *Manser*, [1948] 1 K.B 184; [1947] 2 All E.R. 666.

had they contemplated that event or those circumstances, then the
contract is frustrated by that event immediately and irrespective
of the volition or the intention of the parties, or their knowledge as
to that particular event, and this even although they have continued for a time to treat the contract as still subsisting. In those
circumstances the court would grant relief and pronounce that the
contract has been frustrated either by implying a term to that
effect or otherwise. Their own belief and their own knowledge and
their own intention is evidence, and evidence only, upon which the
court can form its own view whether the changed circumstances
were so fundamental as to strike at the root of the contract and not
to have been contemplated by the parties."[1]

Where that impossibility arises from the deliberate act of one party,
for example, the employer, that will be dismissal, not impossibility.[2]

(2) Termination by Notice.—The next question which arises
is, "within what time may a contract, indefinite as to duration, be
brought to an end?" A contract may, of course, be indefinite as to
the time during which it is to endure, and yet stipulate the length
of notice to be served. Such stipulation must be observed, except
where statute demands a longer period, and a deviation from its
terms will constitute a breach. Where there is no stipulation as to
notice the law draws an interesting distinction. Servants are either
menial or not so. All contracts are, in the absence of agreement or
custom, terminable by reasonable notice.[3] In one case twelve
months' notice was held to be reasonable on the discharge of an editor,[4]
in another an editor was held entitled to six months only.[5] Twelve
months was held to be reasonable notice for the chief engineer of an
ocean liner,[6] whilst the foreign correspondent of a newspaper,[7] a journalist,[8] and a controller of cinemas have been held entitled to six
months' notice.[9] Three months was deemed reasonable for a
" salesman-specialist,"[10] a company director,[11] a commercial traveller,[12] and a private tutor,[13] whilst one month sufficed to end the
services of an advertising and canvassing agent,[14] a woman journ-

---

[1] [1948] 1 K.B. 184; [1947] 2 All E.R. 666, at pp. 191, 670 respectively.
[2] *Denmark Productions, Ltd.* v. *Boscobel Productions, Ltd.*, [1969] 1 Q.B.
699; [1968] 3 All E.R. 513.
[3] *Creen* v. *Wright* (1876), 1 C.P.D. 591; *Re African Association, Ltd. and Allen*,
[1910] 1 K.B. 396.
[4] *Grundy* v. *Sun Printing and Publishing Association* (1916), 33 T.L.R. 77.
[5] *Fox-Bourne* v. *Vernon & Co., Ltd.* (1894), 10 T.L.R. 647.
[6] *Savage* v. *British India Steam Navigation Co., Ltd.* (1930), 46 T.L.R. 294.
[7] *Lowe* v. *Walter* (1892), 8 T.L.R. 358.
[8] *Chamberlain* v. *Bennett* (1892), 8 T.L.R. 234; *Bauman* v. *Hulton Press, Ltd.*,
[1952] 2 All E.R. 1121.
[9] *Adams* v. *Union Cinemas, Ltd.*, [1939] 3 All E.R. 136
[10] *Fisher* v. *Dick & Co., Ltd.*, [1938] 4 All E.R. 467.
[11] *James* v. *Thos. H. Kent & Co., Ltd.*, [1951] 1 K.B. 551; [1950] 2 All E.R.
1099.
[12] *Grundon* v. *Master & Co.* (1885), 1 T.L.R. 205; see also *Moor* v. *Brown
and Co., Ltd.* (1911), 131 L.T.Jo. 467.
[13] *Wilson* v. *Ucelli* (1929), 45 T.L.R. 395.
[14] *Hiscox* v. *Batchellor* (1867), 15 L.T. 543.

alist,[1] the editor of a film news reel,[2] and a stationery clerk in a telegraph office.[3] Chorus girls and musicians have been held to be entitled to a fortnight's notice[4] and a hairdresser's assistant to one week.[5] In rather special circumstances an engineer has been held entitled to at least six months.[6]

3. CONTRACTS OF EMPLOYMENT ACT

These common law rules proved to be inadequate in that they made no distinction for the long-serving employee. Thus a man on a weekly contract was only entitled to a week's notice whether he had worked for his employer for one week or for forty years. Large scale redundancies, particularly in the motor industry, emphasised this defect. The Government at first encouraged individual firms to establish redundancy schemes with advanced notice of redundancy and payments to mitigate its severity based upon length of service. Some valuable agreements were negotiated[7] but the pace was too slow and the problem had to be tackled by legislation. Two statutes now govern the position: the Contracts of Employment Act, 1963,[8] lays down minimum periods of notice and protects employees during the periods of notice, whilst the Redundancy Payments Act, 1965, provides for redundancy payments.[9] This last Act also contains some amendments of the Contracts of Employment Act.

Although the surrounding rules are complicated the scheme of the Contracts of Employment Act is simple. It provides that an employer has to give the following periods of notice:—to an employee with continuous employment, of thirteen weeks but less than two years, one week; of two years but less than five years, two weeks; of five years but less than ten years, four weeks; of ten years but less than fifteen years, six weeks; of fifteen years or more, eight weeks.[10] There is no reciprocal period against employees. Although the bill proposed the same periods for both sides, this would have had grave disadvantages, particularly the prolonging of strike notices, and so the Act merely provides that an employee who has been continuously employed for twenty-six weeks or more has to give one week's notice.[11] There are no longer periods laid down.

The Act applies to any individual who has entered into or works under a contract with an employer, whether the contract is for manual labour, clerical work or otherwise and whether the contract is

---

[1] *Re Illustrated Newspaper Corporation* (1900), 16 T.L.R. 157.

[2] *McCabe* v. *Pathé Frères Cinema* (1919), 35 T.L.R. 313.

[3] *Vibert* v. *Eastern Telegraph Co.* (1883), Cab. & El. 17.

[4] *Thomas* v. *Gatti* (1906), *The Times*, June 22nd; *Gubertini* v. *Waller*, [1947] I All E.R. 746.   [5] *Manubens* v. *Leon*, [1919] I K.B. 208.

[6] *Hill* v. *C. A. Parsons & Co. Ltd.*, [1972] Ch. 305.

[7] See *Security and Change*, H.M.S.O., 1961.

[8] Amended by the Industrial Relations Act, 1971, s. 19.

[9] A detailed consideration of this Act will be found in Chapter V.

[10] Contracts of Employment Act, 1963, s. I(I). Industrial Relations Act, 1971, s. 19.   [11] *Ibid.*, s. I(2).

express or implied, oral or in writing and whether it is a contract of service or one of apprenticeship.[1] The new right of the employee is based on the notion of continuous period of employment and detailed rules as to the calculation of this period are set out in Schedule 1 to the Act. The basic period for calculation is the week and a week is defined as a week ending on a Saturday.[2] It is necessary to establish weeks that count towards continuous employment. Those which do not will generally break the period and the employee must start his period of qualification all over again.[3]

(1) **Weeks which Count.**—1. The basic week, called a normal working week. This is any week in which the employee is employed for twenty-one hours or more.[4]

The week is defined so narrowly that an employee can be concurrently aggregating the minimum period for two, or exceptionally even three, employers.

2. A week governed by a contract of service requiring the employee normally to work for twenty-one hours or more.[5]

Here the test is not the hours actually worked but the existence of a contract requiring at least twenty-one hours' work from the employee. It will be of regular and frequent occurrence in many trades. Periods of sickness where the contract is not terminated by notice are covered.[6] So are temporary lay-offs.[7] The use of the word " normally " in the rule also means that holiday periods are included under this head. Although twenty-one hours' work are not required during holiday weeks they are nonetheless normally required under the existing contract. It has been said that " loan " to another employer did not break the contract of service.[8]

3. A week where twenty-one hours of work are not performed and there is in existence no contract of employment if the employee is:

(a) Incapable of work through sickness or illness.[9] Incapable has been held to refer to the job in question and a temporary lighter job need not break the continuity.[10] Absence from work does not normally, in default of express provision in the contract, terminate the contract.[11] If the contract has not been determined then the weeks of absence count under the previous head. This head is an extension stretching into the period after the contract has been determined. It is limited to twenty-six weeks after a week counting under the previous heads. It must be followed by a week counting under the previous heads. Theoretically an employee can have a

---

[1] *Ibid.*, s. 8(1).   [2] Para. 11.

[3] Section 1 requires continuous **employment.**   [4] Para. 3.

[5] Para. 4., e.g. *Middle* v. *Edward Saunders & Son, Ltd.*, [1966] 1. T.R. 361.

[6] *Tarbuck* v. *L. E.Wilson & Co., Ltd.*, [1967] I.T.R. 157—service with absence.

[7] *Harris* v. *H. G. Wickington, Ltd.*, [1966] I.T.R. 62.

[8] *Proctor* v. *J. & R. Anderson*, [1967] I.T.R. 334.

[9] Para. 5(1) (a).

[10] *Collins* v. *Nats (Southend), Ltd.*, [1967] I.T.R. 423.

[11] See *Orman* v. *Saville Sportswear, Ltd.*, [1960] 3 All E.R. 105; [1960] 1 W.L.R. 1055.

solitary week of employment followed by twenty-six weeks of illness and a further week of employment which both maintains the continuity and permits a further twenty-six weeks of absence through illness to count. The rules appear to fail to provide for the employee who returns at the end of his twenty-sixth week of absence to find a lock-out in progress. The point is perhaps an academic one but it illustrates the difficulties of detailed regulation of the type undertaken here.

(*b*) Absent from work on account of a temporary cessation of work.[1] The phrase "temporary cessation of work" is not without difficulty. No time limit is laid down. The phrase was considered in the House of Lords in *Fitzgerald* v. *Hall Russell, Ltd.*[2] It relates to a cessation of the *employee's* work. There is no need for his employer to stop activity. The employee has to be "stood off" in the sense that he is later recalled. The fact that a job is taken in this period of cessation does not destroy the position.[3] It is expressly said not to include absence through strikes.[4] It plainly is not meant to cover the situation where an employee moves to a new employer, fails to settle, and quickly moves back to his old job. It covers situations such as extra holiday periods taken with the employer's agreement at the employee's expense. It covers periods when the work-place is closed or no work is available. This may arise through many causes such as a natural calamity like a fire, or the disruption of supplies of materials. A lock-out is covered and so are non-strikers laid off because a strike has disrupted production so that work is not available.

(*c*) Absent from work in circumstances such that, by arrangement or custom, he is regarded as continuing in the employment of his employer for all or any purposes.[5] Under this head any unique local practices are taken care of. Without it there may have been unfortunate breaks in continuity where an employee left and went to Canada but returned after a few months and was allowed continuity of benefits schemes, holidays and pension rights, it was held that this rule did not apply and that the work was not continuous.[6] There apparently has to be an understanding at the time that employment is continuing.[7]

4. A week where before July 6th, 1964,[8] the employee was absent for the whole or part of a week because of a strike or lock-out.[9]

---

[1] Para. 5(1) (*b*).
[2] [1970] I.T.R. 1. For an example of the opposite situation see, e.g., *Lane* v. *Wolverhampton Die Casting Co., Ltd.,* [1967] I.T.R. 120.
[3] *Thompson* v. *Bristol Channel Ship Repairers and Engineers, Ltd.,* [1969] I.T.R. 262.
[4] Para. 5(3); for a special situation where that does not apply, see *McCartney* v. *Sir Robert McAlpine & Sons, Ltd.,* [1967] I.T.R. 399.
[5] Para. 5(1) (*c*).
[6] *Murray* v. *Kelvin Electronics Co.,* [1967] I.T.R. 622.
[7] But see *Cann* v. *Co-operative Retail Services, Ltd.,* [1967] I.T.R. 649.
[8] The date upon which the provision came into force by Ministerial Order.
[9] Para. 6.

It has already been noted that the Act was used as a vehicle to discourage unlawful strikes.   No attempt was made to be retrospective in this and this rule makes this plain.   The position of industrial disputes is important enough to merit separate discussion.

Industrial Disputes.—The Schedule defines lock-outs and strikes, using markedly similar language.[1] A lock-out involves the closing of a place of employment, the suspension of work or the refusal by the employer to continue to employ any number of his employees. A strike involves cessation of work by a body of employees acting in combination, a concerted refusal to continue work.   In the case of both strikes and lock-outs these actions must be in consequence of a dispute and in each case the aim of the action must be to coerce the employees or employers, as the case may be, to accept or not to accept terms or conditions of or affecting employment.   Both definitions also expressly include similar action taken to aid other employers or employees in dispute.

The distinction between a lock-out and a strike is now, in consequence of the Act, of great importance.   If newspaper reporting of industrial disputes is any guide, this may well lead to considerable argument on the facts of particular disputes.

A period of lock-out, whether the lock-out is lawful or not, that is to say whether due notice is given or not, counts towards the period of continuous employment.   The period before July 1964 is covered by rule 4 above[2] and the period after by rule 3(*b*).[3]   It is interesting to note that since this Act the period of notice to constitute a lawful lock-out will in all probability be four weeks to satisfy the statutory provisions as to notice to longer-serving employees.

A period of strike before the commencement of the Act also counts towards the continuous employment.[4]   Strikes after the Act came into force fell into two categories.   Where the strike was lawful, that is to say called after due notice, which will generally be of one week, the period of strike does not count towards the period of continuous employment but it does not break the continuity. Where the strike was unlawful the week did not count and the period was broken.   It followed that employees who had served for more than twenty-six weeks would, by taking part in wild-cat or lightning strikes, lose their accrued right to longer periods of notice.   This provision was plainly an attempt to help check this type of industrial activity.   It was thought that the longer-serving worker would act as a restraining influence when he realised that precipitate industrial action would put him in the position of the newly employed as far as his right to notice was concerned.   Whether the right was important enough to serve as a serious consideration is open to doubt and it has been pointed out elsewhere that one of the terms of the

---

[1] Para. 11(1).
[2] Para. 6.
[3] Para. 5(1) (*b*).
[4] Para. 6.

settlement of the unlawful strike might well properly be a promise by the employer voluntarily to give rights similar to the statutory rights lost.[1] The Redundancy Payments Act, 1965, has ended this attack on unlawful strikes and has changed this rule so that it no longer has any effect and the worker who may have suffered by having his period of service restarted is reinstated to the position he would be in under the new rule.[2]

National Service.—There is an important rule, of somewhat limited application,[3] which provides that where the law of reinstatement applies to a National Serviceman and he rejoins his former employer within six months after the end of his service he may join his previous period of employment to the subsequent period.[4]

Change of employment.—The continuous period of employment presupposes employment with the same employer. There are, however, changes in the actual parties to a contract of employment which in common sense cannot be regarded as true changes. The Act makes special exceptions to protect the employee.[5] Four categories of formal change of this type do not break the continuity of employment. These are:

(*a*) where the trade or business or undertaking is itself transferred;

(*b*) where an Act of Parliament causes one corporate body to replace another as employer;

(*c*) where the employer dies and the personal representative carries on the business;

(*d*) where the employer is a partnership, personal representatives or trustees and they change.

This area has been the subject of considerable difficulty both under this Act and under the Redundancy Payments Act, 1965 which has to make similar provisions.[6] Difficulty has arisen over the concept of a transfer of a business. The term business itself gave trouble, for the concept of business is a multi-factor one, covering buildings, fixtures, stock, goodwill and so on.[7] Thus a variety of situations have had to be considered by the tribunals. They will be discussed at great length when redundancy payments are considered.[8]

(2) **Rights in Period of Notice.**—The rights of the employee who is under notice, as laid down by the Act, whether given by himself or by his employer are set out in the Second Schedule.[9] These rules do not apply if the contractual notice is at least one week greater than the statutory period.[10] The rights cannot, on the other hand,

---

[1] See Grunfeld (1964), 27 *M.L.R.* 70.

[2] S. 37. See also Industrial Relations (Continuity of Employment) Regulations, 1972, S.I., 1972 No. 55.

[3] But application considered in *Binks and Kersley* v. *Weymann's, Ltd.,* [1966] I.T.R. 265.

[4] Para. 9.   [5] Para. 10.

[6] Redundancy Payments Act, 1965, s. 13(1).

[7] *Tucker* v. *Cox*, [1967] I.T.R. 395.

[8] See *infra* p. 126.   [9] S. 2.   [10] S. 2 (3).

be excluded or limited by contractual agreement, and any attempt to do so is void.[1]

The purpose of the rules is to establish and guarantee to the worker whilst under notice a minimum rate of payment. The rules are not set out with any real clarity and this part of the Act exhibits some of the worst features of Parliamentary draftsmanship. There are two major defects.

1. The aim of the rules is to ensure that an employee does not suffer by being given inadequate wages during a period of notice. It is basic, but never made clear, that he must be paid for all work done and problems only arise where he is unable to work at least a minimum period.

2. Where he is not working normally then some rules for the calculation of a minimum wage are required. The Schedule provides these but in doing so hides a clear statement of liability in the rules of calculation. It would have improved the clarity beyond measure if the basic rights had been expressed in the section and the Schedule had been reserved for rules of calculation.

These rules of calculation turn upon the existence or otherwise of a normal working week. This concept of normal working hours per week is not defined by the Act. In the majority of cases it will presumably be clear and the contract of employment will be for say forty, forty-two or forty-four hours per week. The Schedule does deal with the situation where overtime pay commences after a stated number of hours have been worked. Then that stated number of hours shall be the normal working hours.[2] This is not so, however, where that number is smaller than the minimum number of hours of the working week stated in the contract of employment. Then the number of minimum hours will be taken.[3] Thus fixed overtime is included whilst voluntary overtime is not.[4] The concept of fixed overtime has given difficulty and a distinction made between a situation where it is obligatory[5] and one where it is only obligatory if available and offered: there being no duty on the employer to provide it.[6] Both parties have to be bound, one to provide, the other to work overtime.[7]

Employment with normal working hours.—Where there are, relating to an employee, normal working hours and during the statutory period of notice the employee is, during any part of those normal hours,

---

[1] S. 2 (4).

[2] Para. 1(1).

[3] Para. 1(2).

[4] *Turriff Construction, Ltd.,* v. *Bryant,* [1967] I.T.R. 292. *Armstrong Whitworth Rolls* v. *Mustard,* [1971] 1 All E.R. 598.

[5] The best discussions are in cases which did not succeed, e.g. *Pearson and Workmen* v. *William Jones, Ltd.,* [1967] I.T.R. 471; but see *Pioli* v. *B.T.R. Industries, Ltd.,* [1966] I.T.R. 255.

[6] *Ministry of Labour* v. *Country Bake, Ltd.,* [1968] I.T.R. 379.

[7] *B.T.R. Industries* v. *Spicknell,* [1967] I.T.R. 298.

(*a*) ready and willing to work but no work is provided by his employer;

(*b*) incapable of work because of sickness or injury;

(*c*) absent in accordance with the terms of his employment on holiday,[1] then the employer is liable to pay the employee for the normal working hours which would otherwise have been worked.[2] In simple language, which hereabouts is at a premium, the worker is entitled to the usual wage for normal hours provided that he either works them, or is denied work through the action of his employer, or cannot work because of sickness, injury or due holidays.[3] This rule naturally can only be applied where the wage is a flat rate, independent of the nature of the work done. Where the wage rate varies, as in piece rates, then a second formula is required. This is that the rate of remuneration shall be at the average hourly rate paid in the four weeks fully completed before notice.[4] The hourly rate is arrived at by taking only the hours when the employee was working and only the remuneration payable for, or apportionable to, those hours.[5] If these hours involved greater remuneration than normal because they were not normal working hours, and weekend working would be an example, then the basic rate is to be substituted.[6] That is to say, the employer has to count back from the Saturday before notice four full weeks and take the hourly average rate of pay for that period and apply it to the normal working hours calculated in the same way as when there is a flat rate of pay. If the previous weeks were for one reason or another not full weeks the employer must take into account enough earlier days to make the period up to four full weeks.

The employer is, of course, entitled to subtract from the sum calculated any money he has paid under sickness pay schemes or by way of holiday pay.[7] The right to these moneys where the employee gives his week's notice does not arise until the notice has expired and he has left.[8]

Employment with No Normal Working Hours.—Here the system of averaging previous earnings is used and the employee is entitled to a sum not less than his average weekly rate over the period of twelve weeks counting back from the last full week before notice.[9] Earnings have been held to include regular bonuses and allowances

---

[1] Para. 2(1) (*a*), (*b*) and (*c*).

[2] Para. 2(2).

[3] The artificial nature of the amount has been emphasised in a redundancy payment case, *British Transport Hotels, Ltd.* v. *Minister of Labour*, [1967] I.T.R. 165.

[4] Para. 2(3).

[5] Para. 2(4).

[6] Para. 2(44) added by s. 39 Redundancy Payments Act, 1965.

[7] Para. 2(5).

[8] Para. 2(6).

[9] Para. 3(2); the definition of earnings has been considered in several redundancy payment cases.

not dependent upon amount of work done.[1]   But this rule does not include receipts such as tips[2] though a tronc or service charge payment is different.[3] Travelling expenses[4] and payment in kind[5] are not included.   Weeks in which less than twenty-one hours were worked have to be ignored.[6]   If this reduces the number of weeks that count in the last twelve to less than eight, earlier weeks must be added until the number averaged is eight.[7]   The obligation to pay is subject to the condition that the employee is ready and willing to do work of a reasonable nature during the period of notice.[8] This does not apply where the employee is sick or injured and unable to work, nor where he is absent from work on holiday in accordance with the terms of his employment.[9]   Any payment by the employer in such circumstances can be taken into account in determining the minimum pay for the period of notice.[10]   Sickness and industrial injury benefits taken into account in determining such pay are to be included.[11]   There is a similar provision too that the right does not accrue until after the notice expires and the employee leaves where it is the employee who has given notice.[12]

There are various situations in which the right to this guaranteed minimum wage does not arise or is lost.   The employer is not liable to pay if the employee is on leave of absence at his own request.   It is lost if, after notice is given and before it expires, the employee takes part in a strike of employees of the employer.[13]   The rights do not deprive the employer of the right to dismiss forthwith for cause during the period of notice.   Then, only the period before the transgression shall be subject to the guarantee of a minimum remuneration.[14]   If, on the other side, the employer breaks the contract during notice, payments made under these rules will serve to mitigate the employee's loss and this must be taken into account.[15]

4. PLACE OF PERFORMANCE

The authorities as to the place in which the contract of service should be performed are, in English law, very meagre.   The determining factor is the intention of the parties, to be gathered from the character of the service and the circumstances of the case.

---

[1] *Skillen* v. *Eastwoods Bros, Ltd.*, [1967] I.T.R. 112. *Collin* v. *Flexiform*, [1966] I.T.R. 253.

[2] *Hall* v. *Honeybay Caterers, Ltd.*, [1967] I.T.R. 538.

[3] *Tsoukka* v. *Potonec Restaurants, Ltd.*, [1968] I.T.R. 259.

[4] *Barclay* v. *Richard Crittall (Electrical), Ltd.*, [1968] I.T.R. 173; but contrast *S. and U. Stores, Ltd.* v. *Lee*, [1969] I.T.R. 227.

[5] *Lyford* v. *Turguard*, [1966] I.T.R. 554; but see *Pierce* v. *Bathes, Ltd.*, [1966] I.T.R. 263.

[6] Para. 3(3).

[7] Para. 3(3).

[8] Para. 3(4).

[9] Para. 2(5) (a) and (b).

[10] Para. 2(5).

[11] Para. 34.   See Industrial Relations Act, 1971, Schedule 2.

[12] Para. 2(6).

[13] Para. 5.

[14] Para. 6(1).

[15] Para. 6(2).

Clearly a personal servant such as a valet or a secretary must be
prepared to attend the person of his master in whatever place he
may be, but where the service is territorial rather than personal the
master cannot unreasonably demand that his servant move from
place to place.   Yet if a request to move is not unreasonable it must
be obeyed.   So, where a platelayer was, after a day's work, ordered
to attend at another station at 11 p.m. and to travel there by trains
which entailed travelling in his own time it was held that his suspension on refusal to obey was justified.   There was no evidence,
it was said, to show that the order was not reasonable and proper.[1]

The distinction between territorial and personal service is apparently recognised by the law of Scotland and would doubtless
influence the courts in this country.[2]   The whole topic has been
but little discussed in our courts.   In *Royce* v. *Charlton*[3] an apprenticeship deed contained the usual covenant by the master to teach
the apprentice.   It was silent as to the place where the instruction
was to be given.   At the time of the execution of the agreement the
master was in business at Mansfield, but, for business reasons, he
transferred the business to Leicester, forty miles away.   The court
would not imply a stipulation that performance was to be at the
place where the master had his business when the deed was executed
—even though, as was the case, the mother of the apprentice had
agreed to provide food and lodging.   This case, however, was
overruled in *Eaton* v. *Western*.[4]   A firm situated in London agreed to
instruct an apprentice and did so for some time.   The partnership
was then dissolved, two partners remaining in London and two setting up a new business in Derby.   The court held that a stipulation
could be implied that the contract was to be performed in the place
where the business was carried on and the parties resided at the time
of the making of the indentures.   " I do not say," said LINDLEY,
L. J., " that the removal of the business to a small distance would
be material, but when the removal necessitates a change in the place
of residence of the apprentice, I think it is contrary to the intention
of the parties."[5]

The problem is one which has been discussed in cases under the
Redundancy Payments Act, 1965, which must be taken into consideration.[6]

5. MANNER OF PERFORMANCE

Wherever the contract itself makes provision, as it usually will,
for the manner in which it is to be performed, its stipulations must
be scrupulously followed by the parties.   In addition the law lays
upon the parties duties which arise out of the peculiar character of
the relationship of master and servant.

---

[1] *Beale* v. *Great Western Ry. Co.* (1901), 17 T.L.R. 450.
[2] See MacDonell, *Law of Master and Servant*, 2nd Ed., pp. 190–1, citing
Fraser's *Law of Personal and Domestic Relations*.
[3] (1881), 8 Q.B.D.1   [4] (1882), 9 Q.B.D. 636.   [5] *Ibid.* at p. 642.
[6] See *infra*, pp. 126 *et seq.*

(1) Duties of the Master.—These duties have their origin in three separate ways.   The legislative tendency for the last century has been to place on employers of labour increasingly heavy obligations as to the safety and health of their employees and much of the remainder of the book will be spent discussing them.   The development in the courts of the tort of negligence has also imposed duties of care both on masters and servants and has provided a remedy for either if injury occurs as a result of the other's negligence.   This branch of the law will be discussed in Chapter VII.   Finally the parties to the contract of employment are bound by the contractual promises which they have expressed or which the law deems to be implied in the contract.   It will be appreciated that the same duty may arise in all three fields and the injured servant will have a choice of the way in which he frames his action, although in practice he will plead all possible heads in the alternative.   An interesting practical point arising from this choice is illustrated by *Matthews* v. *Kuwait Bechtel Corporation*,[1] where leave to serve a writ outside the jurisdiction under R.S.C., Order 11, r. 1(e),[2] depended upon whether the plaintiff's action could be said to sound in contract.   The action was for injuries caused by an alleged unsafe system.   But the plaintiff sought to base his action upon an implied term of the contract as an alternative to the tort of negligence.   The Court of Appeal were satisfied that an action in contract was available.   It is the contractual aspect which is relevant here, and the rules expounded are those which the law will apply in default of express provision to the contrary in the contract.

The implied duties can be usefully grouped into two sections: those which cover the performance of the contract by the master, and those which are aimed at protecting the servant.   The first group comprises methods such as medical treatment, board and lodging and the provision of work.   The second group covers the protection of the servant's person and property whilst he is engaged in the work itself.

Although at one time there was some authority for the proposition that a master was "obliged to provide for his servant in sickness and in health," with a consequent liability to pay for medicines supplied to his servant,[3] this is no longer so.[4]   Nor is a master liable, in default of obligations arising under contract or by statute, to pay for the services of a doctor attending a servant who has met with an accident in his service,[5] though it is otherwise where the master adopts the surgeon's services or brings in his own surgeon.   And in cases of need, though the master has no liability to meet the costs,

---

[1] [1959] 2 Q.B. 57; [1959] 2 All E.R. 345.
[2] See now R.S.C., Ord. 11, r. 1(f).
[3] *Scarman* v. *Castell* (1795), 1 Esp. 270.
[4] *Sellen* v. *Norman* (1829), 4 C. & P. 80; *R.* v. *Smith* (1837), 8 C. & P. 153.
[5] *Wennall* v. *Adney* (1802), 3 Bos. & P. 247; *Cooper* v. *Phillips* (1831), 4 C. & P. 581.

he must call in medical assistance to his sick or injured servant. So it was held to be negligent of a master not to call a doctor to a servant who had suffered a severe injury,[1] and in another case, where the servant died from what proved to be double pneumonia, the duty of the master was described in these terms:

> "It was the duty of the defender, I do not say to provide medical attendance for the girl, but to obtain for her the medical assistance to which she was entitled by calling in her panel doctor, and was thus in breach of his duty at common law to take such steps to relieve the girl as were reasonable and practicable in the circumstances."[2]

In default of contract a master is under no duty to provide board and lodging for his servant; in domestic service a term will be implied[3] making the master so liable and would have to be deliberately excluded if this were desired. Conversely where a youth goes to a master on approbation, with a view to apprenticeship, but remains merely to serve and is not apprenticed, the master will have no claim for the expenses of lodging and feeding him.[4] To succeed in such a claim the master would have to prove an agreement to that effect.[5]

It is an implied term of the contract of service that the master will reimburse his servant for all expenses which the latter properly incurs within the scope of his employment and will indemnify him against liabilities and losses.[6] This will be so wherever the master appears to have the right to authorise the acts of the servant,[7] though the purported authorisation results in the commission of illegal acts by the servant. The defendants in *Burrows* v. *Rhodes*[8] were the authors of the Jameson raid and by means of a fraudulent statement they had induced the plaintiff to re-enlist in the armed forces of the British South Africa Company. The plaintiff believed that the venture in which he was to engage was a lawful one, and it was held that he had a right of action for damages in respect of injuries he had received. If the servant is aware of the illegal character of his acts he cannot hope to be indemnified.[9]

There is no general duty on the part of the master to provide work. The majority of contracts of service are such that the master fulfils his obligation by continuing to pay wages irrespective of whether he provides work or not. In such contracts no breach will arise upon the master's failure to do so. In *Konski* v. *Peet* the

---

[1] *Jeffrey* v. *Donald* (1901), 9 S.L.T. 199.
[2] *M'Keating* v. *Frame*, 1921 S.C. 382.
[3] *Liffen* v. *Watson*, [1940] 1 K.B. 556; [1940] 2 All E.R. 213.
[4] *Harrison* v. *James* (1862), 7 H. & N. 804.
[5] *Attwaters* v. *Courtney* (1841), Car. & M. 51.
[6] *Re Famatina Development Corporation, Ltd.*, [1914] 2 Ch. 271.
[7] *Adamson* v. *Jarvis* (1827), 4 Bing. 66.
[8] [1899] 1 Q.B. 816.
[9] *Shackell* v. *Rosier* (1836), 2 Bing. N.C. 634.

master gave his servant a week's salary in lieu of notice and the court held that the master was free to do so.[1]   Such also was the decision where the employers of a representative salesman were prepared to pay him his wages but would not find work for him.[2]   The law, however, has always recognised that, in a minority of contracts, the opportunity to work is of the essence of the contract and the failure of the master to provide work goes to the root of the contract and may constitute a repudiation.[3]   It is, for example, of the utmost importance that a singer should keep her name before the public, that a surgeon should be given the opportunity of practising his craft, that a person employed on a commission or piece rate basis should be provided with the means of earning the agreed rates. In modern contracts of this character it is usual to stipulate that work or publicity should be provided, but the duty may arise in the absence of a specific stipulation.   Consequently where the proprietors of a newspaper sold it, during the currency of its editor's service agreement, to a company which did not use the editor's services though continuing to pay him, there was a breach of contract on the ground that

" the defendants engaged the plaintiff not to perform at large the sort of work commonly performed by any chief sub-editor. . . . They engaged him to fill the office of chief sub-editor of a specific Sunday newspaper.   By selling that newspaper they destroyed the office to which they had appointed him."[4]

In these anomalous cases the master's duty may not only be to provide work but to provide work of a specific kind.   In *Herbert Clayton and Jack Waller, Ltd.*, v. *Oliver*[5] the appellants, who were theatrical producers, had engaged Oliver to play the lead in one of their productions—Oliver undertaking not to appear elsewhere except with their consent.   A part was offered which Oliver insisted was not a leading one and he therefore refused to appear and sued on a breach of contract.   The House of Lords was firmly of opinion that since the appellants had not offered a part answering the description on the contract the respondent must succeed.

A master need not provide a servant with a testimonial, nor need he answer questions from interested parties as to the servant's character.[6]   If he does give a testimonial the document may be either a general testimonial which the servant retains and which becomes his property or it may be addressed to some interested party who will then no doubt become the owner of it.[7]   If the testi-

---

[1] [1915] 1 Ch. 530.
[2] *Turner* v. *Sawdon & Co.*, [1901] 2 K.B. 653.
[3] *Devonald* v. *Rosser & Sons*, [1906] 2 K.B. 728.
[4] *Collier* v. *Sunday Referee Publishing Co., Ltd.*, [1940] 2 K.B. 647, *per* ASQUITH, J., at p. 651 ; [1940] 4 All E.R. 234.
[5] [1930]A. C. 209; see also *McLaren* v. *Chalet Club, Ltd.* (1951), 101 L. Jo. 598.
[6] *Carrol* v. *Bird* (1800), 3 Esp. 201.
[7] *Wennhak* v. *Morgan* (1888), 20 Q.B.D. 635.

monial remains the property of the servant it must not be maliciously defaced or an action will lie.[1]

If a master gives his servant a testimonial or supplies information to a prospective employer he may incur obligations (a) to the State (under, for example, the Servants' Characters Act, 1792, or similar enactments) or (b) to third parties or (c) to the servant himself. The duty owed to the State will be discussed when we consider the contract of service in relation to the criminal law.[2] As to third parties an action in deceit will lie wherever a master recommends his servant in terms which he knows to be false and, though he acts without malice or hope of reward, the subsequent misconduct of the servant recommended will render him liable in damages.[3] He may also in circumstances where he knows his testimonial is going to be relied upon be liable in negligence. The liability for negligent mis-statements is of recent origin.[4] As to his liability to the servant, a master will incur no liability in making a statement, oral or written, as to his servant's character wherever the statement is true. To succeed in an action against the master arising out of a testimonial the servant must prove not only falsehood but malice,[5] for a communication between one master and another is qualifiedly privileged and the privilege will be destroyed only by proof of malice. We have, then, to discover the limits of the privilege accorded to the master and what evidence of malice will be accounted an abuse of that privilege so as to render him liable in an action for defamation.

A communication will be privileged wherever it can "be fairly said that those who made it had an interest in making such a communication and those to whom it was made had a corresponding interest in having it made to them."[6] Such an interest may clearly be a legal interest, but as the case of *Stuart* v. *Bell* shows, it may also be a mere social or moral interest.[7] Stuart was a valet and he was accompanying his master, who was staying in Newcastle as the guest of the defendant, who was a city magistrate. The Chief Constable of Newcastle showed to the defendant a letter he had received from the Edinburgh police to the effect that suspicion rested on the plaintiff in respect of certain articles stolen from an hotel at which he had lately stayed. The defendant then told Stuart's master of the theft and of the suspicion and a little later Stuart was dismissed. It was held that the occasion was privileged. "A privileged communication," said LINDLEY, L.J.:

"is one made on a privileged occasion and fairly warranted by it and not proved to have been made maliciously. A privileged

---

[1] *Ibid.*   [2] See Chapter VI, p. 213, *post.*

[3] *Foster* v. *Charles* (1830), 6 Bing. 396.

[4] *Hedley Byrne & Co., Ltd.* v. *Heller & Partners, Ltd.*, [1964] A.C. 465; [1963] 2 All E.R. 575. *Mutual Life and Citizens' Assurance Co., Ltd.* v. *Evatt*, [1971] A.C. 793.

[5] *Weatherston* v. *Hawkins* (1786), 1 Term Rep. 110.

[6] *Hunt* v. *Great Northern Ry. Co.*, [1891] 2 Q.B. 189.

[7] [1891] 2 Q.B. 341.

occasion is one which is held in point of law to rebut the legal implication of malice which would otherwise be made from the utterance of untrue defamatory language."[1]

Such a definition would protect the master who, dismissing his servant for dishonesty, did so in the presence of a third party as a witness of what transpired—a precaution which CAMPBELL, C.J., thoroughly applauded.[2] It would include the statements of the directors of a limited company to the shareholders[3] and of the chairman of a co-operative society to the members assembled in meeting.[4] It would cover communications which, as it were, looked backward to a former employer or to the Registry from which the servant had been originally engaged,[5] and one written by a former master referring to the behaviour of the servant after his period of service.[6] Finally the privilege persists:

> "as long as anything is discovered before unknown to the master; as, for instance, if I give a good character to a servant and next day discover that the servant is dishonest . . . it becomes my duty to communicate my discovery to the person to whom I have given the character."[7]

"Malice," it has been said,[8] "is not confined to personal spite and ill will, but includes every unjustifiable intention to inflict injury on the person defamed," or, in the words of BRETT. L.J., "every wrong feeling in a man's mind."[9] So where the master communicates statements which are, to his knowledge, untrue, or, in the truth of which he does not believe, he will defeat his privilege,[10] as he will where his actions are not straightforward,[11] or his language is excessive or violent.[12]

The scope of the second group of duties is illustrated by the claim in *Lister* v. *Romford Ice and Cold Storage Co., Ltd.*[13] This action, brought by the insurers of the appellant company, was to recover damages paid to a servant of the company as a result of injury caused by the negligent driving of Lister, the respondent, who was employed by the company to drive their lorry. It was argued on

---

[1] *Ibid.*, at p. 345. A ship's master who makes an entry in the ship's log defamatory of a seaman does so on a privileged occasion: *Moore* v. *Canadian Pacific Steamship Co.*, [1945] 1 All E.R. 128.

[2] *Taylor* v. *Hawkins* (1851), 16 Q.B. 308, at p. 321.

[3] *Lawless* v. *Anglo-Egyptian Cotton Co.* (1869), L.R. 4 Q.B. 262.

[4] *Stott* v. *Evans* (1887), 3 T.L.R. 693.

[5] *Dixon* v. *Parsons* (1858), 1 F. & F. 24; *Farquhar* v. *Neish* (1890), 17 R. (Ct. of Sess.) 716.

[6] *Child* v. *Affleck* (1829), 9 B. & C. 403.

[7] *Gardner* v. *Slade* (1849), 13 Q.B. 796, *per* Lord DENMAN, C.J., at p. 799.

[8] *Stuart* v. *Bell*, [1891] 2 Q.B. 341 at p. 351.

[9] *Clark* v. *Molyneux* (1877), 3 Q.B.D. 237.

[10] *Murdoch* v. *Funduklian* (1886), 2 T.L.R. 614.

[11] *Kelly* v. *Partington* (1833), 4 B. & Ad. 700.

[12] *Fryer* v. *Kinnersley* (1863), 15 C.B. N.S. 422.

[13] [1957] A.C. 555; [1957] 1 All E.R. 125.

behalf of Lister that it was an implied term of the contract of service
that the master impliedly agreed to indemnify the employee, where
the master was insured, or where as a reasonably prudent employer
he ought to have been insured. This argument was supported by
reference to *Semtex, Ltd.* v. *Gladstone*,[1] in which FINNEMORE, J.,
although holding that the plaintiffs, who were floor contractors, had
not impliedly agreed in the contract of employment with the defendant by insurance to indemnify the driver of the plaintiff's shooting
brake, had said:

> " I think there is implied in a contract a term that the law will be
> observed and that the driver will not be called upon to do an
> unlawful act—in other words that the employer will have taken
> steps which he is bound to take under the Road Traffic Act, 1930."

Section 35 of that Act, however, only makes it a criminal offence
to drive a vehicle on the road without having in force a valid policy
of insurance which covers injuries to third parties injured by the
vehicle. The House of Lords, as the Court of Appeal,[2] was divided
as to whether this term indemnifying the driver was implied, but
the majority decision was that there was no such term.[3] The
problem to be decided is clearly posed by Viscount SIMONDS in the
following way:

> " . . . the question must be asked and answered whether in the
> world in which we live to-day it is a necessary condition of the
> relation of master and man that the master should, to use a broad
> colloquialism, look after the whole matter of insurance."[4]

The reasons advanced for the rejection of this view are not unim-
peachable. For instance one of these reasons, *i.e.* that to remove
the sanction from the employee of liability for negligence might lead
to irresponsibility, is almost entirely nullified in practice by the
fact, which Viscount SIMONDS himself recounts, that this sanction,
although it has been in existence for centuries, has been rarely used.[5]

In *Edwards* v. *West Herts Group Hospital Management Committee*[6]
a resident house physician sued his employers because some of his
belongings were stolen from his room. It had already been decided
in *Deyong* v. *Shenburn*[7] that a master in somewhat similar circum-

---

[1] [1954] 2 All E.R. 206; [1954] 1 W.L.R. 945.
[2] DENNING, L.J., dissenting.
[3] Viscount SIMONDS, Lord MORTON of HENRYTON and Lord TUCKER,
Lord RADCLIFFE and Lord SOMERVELL of HARROW dissenting.
[4] [1957] A.C. 555 at p. 576; [1957] 1 All E.R. 125 at p. 132.
[5] *Ibid.*, at pp. 579 and 134 respectively. For a full analysis of this case
see "Vicarious Liability and the Master's Indemnity," Glanville Williams, 1957,
20 *M.L.R.* 230, where the need for legislation or for trade union action on
standard terms of contract is foreseen as a result of the use of this action. And
see Ministry of Labour, Interdepartmental Committee Report on *Lister* v.
Romford Ice & Cold Storage Co., Ltd., and, on this Report, Gerald Gardiner,
1959, 22 *M.L.R.* 652.
[6] [1957] 1 All E.R. 541; [1957] 1 W.L.R. 415.
[7] [1946] K.B. 227; [1946] 1 All E.R. 226, see *supra*, p. 16.

stances was not liable in tort for negligence and so the plaintiff sought
to rely on an implied term in the contract of service that the master
would take care of the servant's goods.   The Court of Appeal refused
to find that in the circumstances such a term could be implied.[1]

(2) **Duties of the Servant.**—Paramount amongst the duties
which the servant owes to his employer is the duty of faithful service.   Clearly, the content of such a duty will defy definition; it will
vary with every type of service though certain acts constituting its
breach will be common to all:

> "Suppose the plaintiff had conducted himself on all occasions in a
> negligent and lazy spirit, there may be insuperable difficulty in
> a legal definition of the plaintiff's conduct and yet the defendant
> would be justified in discharging him. . . ."[2]

Those breaches of the duty which are common to all industry will
constitute the obvious but not legally interesting examples—such
things as persistent laziness, bad timekeeping and the innumerable
offences the mere recital of which would be of little value.   The
reports provide, unfortunately perhaps for the employer, but fortunately for the student, more luminous and compelling examples.

Any act which is inconsistent with the terms of the contract,
express or implied, and which is injurious to the master and his
interests will amount to a breach of the duty of faithful service.   A
manager whose acts were injurious to the interests of the theatre he
was employed to manage was held to have been rightly dismissed.[3]
Conversely the court saved from attachment a servant who refused to produce material documents in his possession which he
held merely in his character of servant.   The court would not infer
that he could produce the documents without violating the duty he
owed to his employer.[4]   Nor must a servant place himself in a
position in which his own interests conflict with his duty to his
employer.   A confidential clerk, advising on securities, found to be
dealing in Stock Exchange differences was held to be rightly dismissed. Because of his speculations he could not give his employers
disinterested advice.[5]   The clash of interest and duty can be seen
most clearly in *Boston Deep Sea Fishing and Ice Co.* v. *Ansell.*[6]
The defendant had been employed as managing director of the
plaintiff company, and he had contracted with a firm of shipbuild-
ers for the supply of certain vessels and had taken from them a
commission in respect of the transaction, of which his employers

---

[1] An action might lie, independent of contract, under s. 59 of the Factories
Act, 1961, which provides for " adequate and suitable accommodation " for
clothing not worn during working hours: *McCarthy* v. *Daily Mirror Newspapers,
Ltd.,* [1949] 1 All E.R. 801.
[2] *Lomax* v. *Arding* (1855), 10 Exch. 734.
[3] *Lacy* v. *Osbaldiston* (1837), 8 C. & P. 80.
[4] *Eccles & Co.* v. *Louisville and Nashville Railroad Co.,* [1912] 1 K.B. 135.
[5] *Pearce* v. *Foster* (1886), 17 Q.B.D. 536.
[6] (1888), 39 Ch.D. 339.

knew nothing. He also possessed shares in an ice-making and fish-carrying company which paid bonuses to those of its shareholders who, being owners of fishing vessels, used the company's ice or its services as a carrier. He was held to the strictest accountability, but, apart from that, there was clearly a breach of his duty faithfully to serve, since the temptation to use the company's ice or its services as a carrier conflicted or might conflict with his duty to consider his employers' interests in preference to his own.

It is a breach of the duty of faithful service for a servant to use, in a manner hostile to his employer or former employer, any materials collected or knowledge of persons acquired during the period of service. So a servant who solicits for himself or a prospective employer the custom of his master's clients, will commit a breach of contract even though it is not suggested that any transfer should take place until after the determination of the existing contract of service.[1] To use materials obtained in the service of one employer in promotion of the interests of another was held in *Lamb* v. *Evans* to be contrary to good faith, the materials in question being certain printing blocks;[2] and where a servant, two days before leaving his employer's service, compiled a table of measurements of engines manufactured by them, this was held to be a breach of confidence.[3] His new employers produced an engine of similar dimensions. It is true that, had the latter cared to purchase engines made by the former employers they could themselves have collected the relevant information. But the information did not exist in the compendious form in which it was abstracted by the servant. A servant, similarly, must not reveal or use information which he collects when working upon secret processes, and it is immaterial whether he has stored the information in his memory or by other means.[4] The position is the same whether the information be collected directly by the individual himself or be transmitted to him by another. A partner who was under covenant not to communicate a certain secret process used by the partnership communicated information to his son. The son was held to be a mere volunteer deriving benefit under what was, in fact, a breach of faith. He could gain no title by it, though the court conceived that the result might have differed had he been, as he claimed, a purchaser for value without notice of any obligations affecting the information.[5] The rule does not apply, however, where there is a public interest to have the information disclosed.[6]

In most contracts of service where a man is likely to be brought into contact with confidential information a clause will be included

---

[1] *Wessex Dairies, Ltd.* v. *Smith,* [1935] 2 K.B. 80; [1935] All E.R. Rep. 75.
[2] [1893] 1 Ch. 218.
[3] *Merryweather* v. *Moore,* [1892] 2 Ch. 518.
[4] *Amber Size and Chemical Co., Ltd.* v. *Menzel,* [1913] 2 Ch. 239.
[5] *Morison* v. *Moat* (1851), 9 Hare 241.
[6] *Initial Services, Ltd.* v. *Putterill,* [1968] 1 Q.B. 396; [1967] 3 All E.R. 145.

defining his duty in unambiguous terms.   This, though advisable, is not absolutely necessary, for such duties will be implied in all contracts which place the servant in a confidential position.[1]   They will apply to that " part of the employee's stock of knowledge which a man of ordinary honesty and intelligence would recognise to be the property of his old employer ".[2]   But no kind of legally recognised relationship, however confidential, can destroy the right of a man to use the experience and the skill which he has acquired as the result of his service.   The courts have attempted to draw distinctions between disclosing and using information which a man could not help acquiring[3] and knowledge dishonestly and surreptitiously obtained, but the distinction cannot be said to have emerged very clearly.   All that can be said is that it will be for the jury to determine whether the servant's behaviour does or does not amount to a breach of faith.[4]   So that where an accountant sold the copyright of a book on business management, based in part on information gained generally as a servant, and in part as a consequence of a special and particular assignment to which he had been directed under his contract of service, it was held that his employers could restrain publication only of those parts of the manuscript which related to the latter event.[5]

Whether a breach of faith has or has not arisen, will always be difficult whenever the question concerns a man's use of his own knowledge and skill.   For in such cases the courts are reluctant to interfere, even though the knowledge and skill have been acquired in the service of his employers.   Such interference would, in most cases, savour of restraint of trade.

They will, however, interfere where the use of the knowledge and skill harms the employer.   This was the situation in *Hivac, Ltd.* v. *Park Royal Scientific Instruments, Ltd.*[6]   Certain employees of the plaintiff company worked in their spare time on similar kind of work for the defendant company, the two firms being in direct competition.   There was no evidence that any of the workmen (who were not parties to the action) had divulged any confidential information.   It was found that the employees had agreed to do and had

---

[1] *Robb* v. *Green* (1895), 2 Q.B. 315, *per* Lord Esher, M.R., at p. 317; *Alperton Rubber Co.* v. *Manning* (1917), 86 L.J.Ch. 377; *Bents Brewery Co., Ltd.* v. *Hogan*, [1945] 2 All E.R. 570.

[2] *Printers and Finishers, Ltd.* v. *Holloway*, [1964] 3 All E.R. 54; [1965] 1 W.L.R. 1 *per* Cross, J., at p. 5.

[3] *E.g. United Indigo Chemical Co., Lt.* v. *Robinson* (1931), 49 R.P.C. 178, *per* Bennett, J., at p. 187.

[4] See *Worsley & Co., Ltd.* v. *Cooper*, [1939] 1 All E.R. 290, for a case where no breach of faith occurred.

[5] *Stevenson, Jordan and Harrison, Ltd.* v. *MacDonald and Evans*, [1952] 1 T.L.R. 101, C.A.

[6] [1946] Ch. 169; [1946] 1 All E.R. 350, C.A.   This case is discussed by Professor Kahn-Freund in 9 *M.L.R.*, 1946, at p. 145 and by Professor W. A. Lewis, *ibid.* at p. 280.   For a recent example see *Cranleigh Precision Engineering, Ltd.* v. *Bryant*, [1964] 3 All E.R. 289, [1965] 1 W.L.R. 1293.

done, work which they knew must harm their employers and had done so without informing their employers, that this was a breach of their duty of fidelity and that the defendant company would be restrained from employing them. The court made something of the fact that because of the abnormality of the times and the operation of an essential work order, the workmen could not easily be dismissed. But it is doubtful how far this is relevant. Any highly skilled workman who moves, or is compelled to move elsewhere, is a loss to the firm first employing him. But this must be regarded as one of the risks of trade. It is only where the workman harms his employer that the law will interfere.

> "The law would, I think, be jealous of attempting to impose upon a manual worker restrictions, the real effect of which would be to prevent him utilising his spare time. He is paid for five and a half days in the week. The rest of the week is his own, and to impose upon a man, in relation to the rest of the week, some kind of obligation which really would unreasonably tie his hands and prevent him adding to his weekly money during the time, would, I think, be very undesirable."[1]

And again . . .

> "it would be most unfortunate if anything we said should place an undue restriction on the right of the workman, particularly a manual workman, to make use of his leisure for his profit. On the other hand, it would be deplorable if it were laid down that a workman could, consistently with his duty to his employer, knowingly deliberately and secretly set himself to do in his spare time, something which would inflict great harm on his master's business."[2]

The servant cannot defend his action by saying that an approach or offer was made to him and he was not the initiator of, say, leaving employment and accepting work from an existing client of his master.[3]

The same considerations apply to patent rights acquired by a servant as a consequence of his service. Most contracts with workers likely to discover new processes will contain explicit references to the ownership of any discoveries likely to be made. But the principle is the same whether there is an express contract or not. So where a contract which contained no express covenant as to patents was terminated by the dismissal of the servant, an injunction was granted to his former employers restraining the servant's infringement of certain patents taken out in his own name during the course of the service agreement.[4] To have allowed the patentee, in the circumstances of the case, the benefits of his patent, would

---

[1] *Hivac, Ltd.* v. *Park Royal Scientific Instruments, Ltd., per* Lord GREENE, M.R., [1946] Ch. 169 at p. 174; and [1946] 1 All E.R. 350 at p. 354.
[2] *Hivac, Ltd.* v. *Park Royal Scientific Instruments, Ltd.,* [1946] Ch. 169; [1946] 1 All E.R. 350, at pp. 178 and 356 respectively.
[3] *Sanders* v. *Parry*, [1967] 2 All E.R. 803; [1967] 1 W.L.R. 753.
[4] *Worthington Pumping Engine Co.* v. *Moore* (1902), 19 T.L.R. 84.

have amounted to the regularisation by the courts of an act of bad faith. Originally the position was that an application for a patent might be made only by the "true and first inventor of an invention"[1] but this has now been modified in that the application for a patent may now be made not only by the first inventor but also by any person being his assignee or by that person either alone or jointly with any other person.[2] Hitherto it has been usual for a servant likely to make discoveries to agree to do all those things necessary to secure the granting of patents and to assign such grants to his employer. In future the assignee himself will be able to take out the patents and some of the difficulties which have arisen hitherto will be avoided.

But whether there is agreement or not, the benefits of a discovery will, at common law, accrue to the employer wherever it would be contrary to good faith for the discoverer to take these benefits; a proposition which has been stated in the following terms :

> "It is a term of all employment, apart altogether from any express covenant, that any invention or discovery made in the course of the employment of the employee in doing that which he is engaged and instructed to do during working hours and using the materials of his employer, is the property of the employer and not that of the employee, and that having made such a discovery or invention the employee becomes a trustee . . . of that invention . . . and is bound to give the benefit of such discovery or invention to his employer. . . ."[3]

Not all the inventions of a servant will belong to the master though they be discovered in what was, nominally, the master's time, nor will all his inventions belong to himself because they were made outside his formal working hours. The test is in every case this test of faithful service.

> "Whether . . . the benefit of the patent . . . belongs to him or his employers (depends on whether it is) inconsistent with the good faith that ought properly to be inferred or implied as an obligation arising from the contract of service that the servant should hold the patent otherwise than as trustee for his employer."[4]

The application of these principles where there is a written contract of service can be seen very clearly in *British Celanese, Ltd.* v. *Moncrieff*.[5] The defendant was employed as a research chemist by the plaintiff, under the terms of a contract which provided, *inter alia*, that he would, so long as he was bound by the agreement, communicate all his discoveries to the company. These would then, without further payment, become the sole and exclusive property of the plaintiffs if they desired them. Later the parties entered into

---

[1] Patents Act, 1907 (7 Edw. 7, c. 29), s.1.   [2] Patents Act, 1949, s.1(1).
[3] *Triplex Safety Glass Co.* v. *Scorah*, [1938] Ch. 211, *per* FARWELL, J., at p. 217; [1937] 4 All E.R. 693, at p. 698.
[4] *British Reinforced Concrete Engineering Co.* v. *Lind* (1917), 86 L.J. Ch. 486.
[5] [1948] Ch. 564; [1948] 2 All E.R. 44.

a leaving agreement, the purpose of which was to free the defendant from his duties under the contract of service, but imposed certain obligations as to matters to be treated as confidential for a further term of five years. During his period of service with the plaintiff company he had, jointly with another employee, made certain discoveries and before the termination of his employment with the plaintiffs, the defendant had done all that was necessary to secure patent protection in respect of these discoveries in Great Britain, the United States and Canada. When he had left them, the company desired him to join in making application for patents for the inventions in certain foreign countries not included in the original applications. The defendant did not claim any beneficial interest in the discoveries but refused to make application for the new protection. It was held that he was under a duty to do so. For though the basis of the agreements between the parties was contractual, in fact, something in the nature of a trust had arisen because of the undertaking by the defendant that the discoveries should become the exclusive possession of the plaintiff company.

An even wider application is illustrated in *British Syphon Co., Ltd.* v. *Homewood*,[1] where a chief technician, whilst in the plaintiffs' employment, and not at their express request, invented a low pressure syphon system. After leaving their employment he started to take out a patent and the plaintiffs sought an injunction and an assignment of the invention. ROXBURGH, J., held that as the invention was made whilst he was chief technician it became the property of his employers, for although they had not asked him to work on that problem it would be a breach of faith for him, having solved it, to keep it to himself or, *a fortiori*, to sell it to a rival. In *Sterling Engineering Co., Ltd.* v. *Patchett*[2] an attempt to show a variation of the term under which the employer has the sole benefit of an invention made by a servant relating to and during his employment failed because the understanding relied upon was held to be less than a binding agreement.

A servant must act reasonably and carefully when in charge of his master's property and must show reasonable skill in the performance of his employment. Where a servant accepts a particular employment his acceptance constitutes an implied warranty that he possesses the necessary skill.[3] If the undertaking involves special expertise he must display that expertise or he will be liable to dismissal.[4] Moreover though a single lapse from the necessary standard of care may involve a servant in dismissal it will have to be a lapse involving negligence.[5]

---

[1] [1956] 2 All E.R. 897; [1956] 1 W.L.R. 1190.
[2] [1955] A.C. 534; [1955] 1 All E.R. 369.
[3] *Harmer* v. *Cornelius* (1858), 5 C.B.N.S. 236.
[4] *Heaven* v. *Pender* (1883), 11 Q.B.D. 503.
[5] *Savage* v. *British India Steam Navigation Co., Ltd.* (1930), 46 T.L.R. 294, but see the new action for unfair dismissal *infra*, pp. 100 *et seq.*

It is the duty of an agent—and the term will include a servant—
to render proper, clear, and full accounts to his master.[1] The wilful
and fraudulent failure to do so will render the servant liable to dismissal or to such other appropriate remedy as the master may
pursue.[2] In particular a servant must disclose and account for any
secret benefits he may take, for it is inconsistent with good service
that he should make any personal benefits from the service except
such as are known to and approved by the employer.[3] This rule
appears to apply to unauthorised borrowing where this destroys the
necessary confidence.[4]

Reading v. *A.-G.*[5] deals with the problem of secret gains in ways
which, to say the least, must be regarded as memorable, and though
the petitioner, Sergeant Reading was, at the operative time, a member of His Majesty's forces stationed in Egypt and was not, in
consequence, properly to be regarded as a servant, the principles
upon which his litigation was decided are applicable, in their entirety,
to the relationship of master and servant. For, as Lord NORMAND
said,

> "though the relation of a member of His Majesty's forces is not
> accurately described as that of a servant under a contract of
> service or as that of an agent under a contract of agency . . . he
> owes to the Crown a duty as fully fiduciary as the duty of a servant
> to his master or of an agent to his principal and, in consequence . . .
> all profits and advantages gained by the use or abuse of his military
> status are to be for the benefit of the Crown . . ."[6]

Reading then, whilst stationed in Cairo, agreed on a number of
occasions to accompany lorries to certain destinations, his uniform
guaranteeing that such lorries would avoid inspection by the police.
These lorries contained illicit spirits and as a result of his services
Reading secured almost £20,000. Ultimately, the military authorities
arrested him, impounded many thousands of pounds and secured
his conviction for conduct prejudicial to good order and military
discipline. The enterprise which had first led Sergeant Reading into
these adventures did not desert him, for on his release from prison
he secured the grant of a petition of right by which he claimed the
return of the moneys seized. It was urged amongst other things, on
his behalf, that to allow the Crown to retain the money would be
to make the Crown a participant of Reading's crime, but it was
countered that it was not for Reading who had gained the advantage
by his service in the forces, to set up his own wrong against the

---

[1] *Thompson* v. *British Berna Motor Lorries, Ltd.* (1917), 33 T.L.R. 187, *per*
McCARDIE, J., at p. 188.
[2] *Willets* v. *Green* (1850), 3 Car. & Kir. 59.
[3] *Boston Deep Sea Fishing and Ice Co.* v. *Ansell* (1888), 39 Ch.D. 339; *Swale*
v. *Ipswich Tannery, Ltd.* (1906), 11 Com. Cas. 88.
[4] *Sinclair* v. *Neighbour*, [1967] 2 Q.B. 279; [1966] 3 All E.R. 988.
[5] [1951] A.C. 507; [1951] 1 All E.R. 617.
[6] *Ibid.*, at pp. 517 and 621 respectively.

claim of the Crown. The money therefore quite properly remained with the Crown.

Where it is usual for the servant to receive benefits from third parties, as, for example, where a servant is permitted to receive tips and the master is generally aware of this, the servant will not be under a duty to account.[1]

The duty to disclose personal benefits of a financial character raises the question whether a servant has a general duty to disclose facts which might prove inimical to the master. The question is not without its difficulties. We have already discussed the duty of disclosure as affecting the formation of a contract.[2] We have seen that provided the parties obtain substantially that which they bargained to obtain, mistake arising from non-disclosure will not affect validity. This was the case in *Bell* v. *Lever Bros., Ltd.*[3] In *Fletcher* v. *Krell*[4] a governess who had described herself as a spinster whereas she was in fact a divorcee was held not to be under any duty to disclose, and the same result was reached in the case of a commercial traveller whose employment compelled him to use his car for the carriage of samples.[5] When his licence was suspended for three months by the court, his employers instantly dismissed him. They maintained that he ought to have informed them of a previous conviction of drunkenness whilst in charge of a motor car. But the court held that he was under no such duty.

> " In some cases it might be the essence of the contract that the man himself had to drive the motor car, but there was nothing in this case to show that the plaintiff had put it out of his power to perform his duties."[6]

He might indeed arrange with another to drive the car on his behalf.

The foregoing cases are perhaps not more than specialised applications of the principle *caveat emptor*; of the rule that he who sets out to buy labour is not different from the person who buys any other commodity, must look after himself and cannot generally complain that the seller did not reveal defects in the article he was selling. Rather different considerations may arise now (*a*) where a workman tries to make his employer liable for the result of defects in the workman which he has not revealed and (*b*) where an employee is aware of conduct amongst fellow servants inimical to the master.

In *Cork* v. *Kirby MacLean, Ltd.*[7] the plaintiff, a workman employed by the defendants, was injured by a fall partly caused by a breach of statutory duty on the part of his employers and partly because

---

[1] *Holden* v. *Webber* (1860), 29 Beav. 117; *Baring* v. *Stanton* (1876), 3 Ch.D. 502.
[2] See *ante*, pp. 29 *et seq.*
[3] [1932] A.C. 161.
[4] (1872), 42 L.J.Q.B. 55.
[5] *Hands* v. *Simpson, Fawcett & Co., Ltd.* (1928), 44 T.L.R. 295.
[6] *Ibid., per* FINLAY, J., at p. 297.
[7] [1952] 2 All E.R. 402.

an illness from which he suffered caused him to have the fall. He sued his employers, who discovered that he suffered from epilepsy and had been ordered by his doctor not to work above ground level but had not informed his employers of this. It was held that he had been in fault in not informing his employers and that the damages awarded to him would be reduced by one half.

The case, so far as one is aware, is the first case which implies that the *caveat emptor* rule must be modified where contracts of service are concerned and, of course, if a general duty of disclosure were laid on those applying for work, a quite new vista of English law would be opened up. In fact, these aspects of the case were not canvassed. SINGLETON, L.J., considered the point only in these terms :

> "A man who knew himself to be in the condition in which Mr. Cork knew that he was ought to have told his employers. However anxious he was to get work he owed a duty to himself and his fellow workmen, and failure to inform the employers, followed by instructions from them to work at some height above ground, involved risk to the other workmen as well as to himself."

The Judge was thus confident that his act was a "fault" within the meaning of section 4 of the Law Reform (Contributory Negligence) Act, 1945.

The case, however, does not lay down any general duty of disclosure and is authority only for the proposition that a workman who withholds information from his employers cannot make them fully liable for any harmful consequences arising therefrom.

Moreover there is no general duty to disclose to the employer any improper conduct on the part of fellow-servants. In *Swain* v. *West (Butchers), Ltd.*[1] a servant had expressly promised to do all in his power to promote the interests of the employing company. Under the direction of the managing director he had done certain unlawful acts and, when this was discovered, the chairman of the board had promised that, should he provide evidence of the manager's illegalities, he (the servant) would not be dismissed. The court held that because of the express promise he was under the duty of disclosing acts inimical to the company and there was no consideration to support the promise not to dismiss. The interest of the case, from this particular angle, is that the Court of Appeal took some care not to enunciate the principle that a general duty existed in such cases.

> " I do not decide that in every case where the relation of master and servant exists it is the duty of the servant to disclose, or to disclose upon inquiry, any discrepancy of which he knows of his fellow servants."[2]

We have already observed that a master is under the duty of indemnifying his servant in respect of all expenses which the latter

---

[1] [1936] 3 All E.R. 261.
[2] *Swain* v. *West (Butchers), Ltd.*, [1936] 3 All E.R. 261, *per* GREER, L. J., at p. 264.

properly incurs in the scope of his employment. The subject of the servant's indemnity to the master has recently been discussed in circumstances where the master was jointly responsible as a tort-feasor for causing the damages and in circumstances where the fault was that of the servant alone. The plaintiff in *Jones* v. *Manchester Corporation*[1] was the widow of one William Jones, an employee of the Corporation, who sustained burns during the course of his employment and died as the result of the administration of an anaesthetic by a young doctor (the second defendant) who was employed by the Regional Hospital Board (the third defendant). Minimal damages were awarded against the employers but damages amounting to almost £1,500 were awarded against the doctor and the Regional Hospital Board, the latter being ordered to indemnify the doctor. It was against the order that they should indemnify their servant that the Hospital Board appealed and, indeed, claimed an indemnity or contribution from the second defendant. For, on their behalf, it was argued that arising out of their contractual relationship with the doctor an undertaking on her part to indemnify the Board against her negligent conduct must be implied, and though, on the record, there was a denial that the doctor was a servant of the Board the point was not, in fact, raised either at first instance or on appeal. In such circumstances SINGLETON, L.J., found it difficult to deal with the claim under this head, but found that the Board was responsible in negligence because it had failed to provide adequate supervision for an inexperienced physician. He thought that there might be circumstances in which a servant who caused damage to his employer might be held liable to that employer—but if the damage arose because, either directly or by implication, the master asked the servant to do work not really within her capacity then the employer would not be entitled to an indemnity. Thus SINGLETON, L.J. thought that though there might be a right of indemnity in a master against the liability he has incurred because of the tortious act of his servant, this right would be defeated if the master himself had in any way contributed to the damage or bore some part of the responsibility therefor. In consequence he had no difficulty in rejecting the Board's claim for an indemnity.

DENNING, L.J., as might be expected, was more forthright. He contested the view that a master has a right of indemnity against the consequences of his servant's negligence. Though there were writings in support of such a proposition, in the absence of agreement he could see no contractual basis for such an indemnity.

"A servant promises, no doubt, to do his duty to his master to the best of his ability, but he does not promise to indemnify him against liability to third persons and I see no reason why any such promise should be implied. The master's claim against the servant,

---

[1] [1952] 2 Q.B. 852; [1952] 2 All E.R. 125.

if it exists at all, must, I think, be based not on a promise of indemnity, but in damages for breach of contract."[1]

The third Judge, HODSON, L.J., disagreed with his brethren. He did not find evidence of negligence on the part of the Board, the doctor alone was negligent and he found that the Board was entitled to the relief for which they asked, though, of course, his opinion did not prevail.

The position where the master is in no way at fault has now been considered by the House of Lords in *Lister* v. *Romford Ice and Cold Storage Co., Ltd.*[2] It is clear from this case that there is an implied term in a contract of employment that the workman will " perform his duties with proper care."[3] The dicta in this case show that this duty applies to every servant, and is not merely restricted to those who bring some particular skill, such as the lorry driver. All the judges in the House of Lords accepted that there was this implied term and the dissenting opinions were based on the implication of a further term that the employer would protect his servant by insurance.[4]

The case has been distinguished, in *Harvey* v. *R. G. O'Dell, Ltd.*,[5] where a storekeeper was chosen to take a fellow workman to an outside job because the storekeeper had available a motor-cycle combination. Although the storekeeper had used his motor-cycle on his employer's business from time to time, he had been given an expense allowance based on the cost of public transport. McNAIR, J., held that the proposition in the *Romford Ice* case did not apply to a person driving a vehicle in the course of his employment, when such action was not work he was employed to do but was merely a special occasion on which the servant had assisted his employer by undertaking an unusual task.

In the *Romford Ice* case DENNING, L. J.,[6] went further than he had done in *Jones* v. *Manchester Corporation* and held that a man does not even warrant that he will use reasonable care when he is working. Here DENNING, L. J., was delivering a dissenting judgment in the Court of Appeal, and the House of Lords have firmly rejected his view. Where the master is not at fault, the implied term in the contract of employment plainly makes the servant liable to indemnify his master. Where the master is also at fault, through giving his servant a job beyond his known skill for example, then the decision

---

1 *Jones* v. *Manchester Corporation*, [1952] 2 Q.B. 852, at p. 868; [1952] 2 All E.R. 125, at p. 131.

2 [1957] A.C. 555; [1957] 1 All E.R. 125.   See p. 86, *supra.*

3 *Per* Viscount SIMONDS at pp. 572 and 130 respectively.

4 Lord RADCLIFFE and Lord SOMERVILLE of HARROW, and see p. 86, *supra.*

5 [1958] 2 Q.B. 78; [1958] 1 All E.R. 657.   For a discussion of the decision in this case see *infra*, p. 174.

6 *Romford Ice & Cold Storage Co., Ltd.* v. *Lister*, [1956] 2 Q.B. 180, at p. 187; [1955] 3 All E.R. 460, at p. 464.

in *Jones* v. *Manchester Corporation* will bind the courts, subject to the question being considered at some future time in the House of Lords.

Finally a servant must obey all the reasonable and lawful commands of his master,[1] and it is an implied term of a contract of service that the servant shall not be required to perform an illegal act.[2] The orders which command obedience must be reasonable not only in relation to the particular type of service to be rendered but also in the general sense, and last century a defence to a claim for wages that the servant had obstinately refused to work was rejected by the courts. It did not show a disobedience to reasonable orders:

> " if the plaintiff's wife had been requested to work during church time and had obstinately refused that would have been to her credit."[3]

What is reasonable will be a question of fact.[4] The Redundancy Payment Act cases give many useful factual examples.

A servant is not bound to serve at the peril of his life;[5] so that the order to go home to a domestic servant so ill as to be unable to move from her bed was demonstrably unreasonable,[6] as was an order to remain in a house where a contagious disease was raging.[7] The onus of proving that the order was unreasonable will lie on the servant. The respondent in *Ottoman Bank* v. *Chakarian*[8] was an Armenian employed in the Smyrna branch of the bank and was sent, during troubled times, to Constantinople. Whilst there he informed his employers that, owing to Turkish hostility to Armenians, his life was in danger and he suggested a transfer to some branch outside Turkey. This was refused, whereupon he left Constantinople, was dismissed and brought an action for wrongful dismissal. The court held that he had discharged the onus of proving that his life was in danger and was thus entitled to succeed. It was otherwise where, the general situation being the same, the respondent failed to discharge the onus of showing that his life was in danger.[9]

A servant may, indeed must, disobey an order of his master where it conflicts with his legal duties, but a moral duty will not justify a servant's act of disobedience. In *Turner* v. *Mason*[10] a servant whose mother had suffered a seizure and was believed likely to die, was refused permission by her employer to visit her. Notwithstanding this the servant absented herself and, dealing with

---

[1] *Spain* v. *Arnott* (1817), 2 Stark. 256.
[2] *Gregory* v. *Ford & Others*, [1951] 1 All E.R. 121.
[3] *Jacquot* v. *Bourra* (1839), 7 Dowl. 348.
[4] *Price* v. *Mouat* (1862), 11 C.B.N.S. 508.
[5] *Limland* v. *Stephens* (1801), 3 Esp. 269, *per* Lord KENYON, at p. 270.
[6] *M'Keating* v. *Frame*, 1921 S.C. 382.
[7] *Turner* v. *Mason* (1845), 14 M. & W. 112, *per* ALDERSON, B., at p. 118.
[8] [1930] A.C. 277.
[9] *Bouzourou* v. *Ottoman Bank*, [1930] A.C. 271.
[10] (1845), 14 M. & W. 112.

A
344.42

the visit to the mother, the court said,

> " It is very questionable whether any service to be rendered to
> any other person than the master would suffice as an excuse; she
> might go, but it would be at the peril of being told that she could
> not return."[1]

6. RESCISSION, VARIATION AND REPUDIATION

It is open to the parties to show that they have mutually agreed
upon rescission or variation of the contract at any time before breach
of the contract.   Where a new contract follows, there is some
difficulty in deciding whether there has been rescission or mere
variation.

Rescission demands a variation so fundamental as to clearly
extinguish the original contract.[2]   In the case of the total rescission
of the contract the agreement may be oral.[3]   This is so even though
the original agreement was in writing or even by deed, for though at
law a document under seal could be rescinded only by seal the courts
of equity did not, in this matter, follow the law and, as a result of
the Judicature Act, 1873, the rules of equity must prevail over the
rules of law wherever they conflict.[4]

Where a party unjustifiably refuses to perform or makes it
impossible for himself or for the other party to do so he will be said
to have repudiated the contract.   That other party will then have
a right of action for damages and, in appropriate circumstances, the
right to regard himself as excused from further performance.   The
servant's rights where the employer dismisses him unfairly have been
extended by the right to sue for unfair dismissal.[5]   The law discussed below still governs the contractual relationship but is likely
to be superseded in many respects by the new remedies.   The most
obvious examples in the contract of service arise where a master
wrongfully dismisses his servant or the servant wrongfully leaves his
employment.

(1) Wrongful Dismissal.—Wrongful dismissal has been described
as a mere illustration of the general legal rule that an action will lie
for an unjustifiable repudiation of a contract,[6] but it is not every
wrongful act which will enable the injured party to regard himself as
excused from further performance.   The House of Lords considered
the topic in relation to the contract of service in *General Billposting
Co., Ltd.* v. *Atkinson,*[7] where the respondent was dismissed without
notice.   The House accepted and applied the test laid down by
Lord COLERIDGE, C. J., in *Freeth* v. *Burr,*[8] viz.

---

[1] *Ibid., per* POLLOCK, C. B., at p. 116.
[2] *Marriott* v. *Oxford and District Co-operative Society, Ltd.* [1970] 1 Q.B. 186;
[1969] 3 All E.R., 1126; [1969] 3 W.L.R. 984.
[3] *Price* v. *Dyer* (1810), 17 Ves. 356.   [4] *Berry* v. *Berry,* [1929] 2 K.B. 316.
[5] Industrial Relations Act, 1971. See below, p. 105.
[6] *Re Rubel Bronze and Metal Co. and Vos,* [1918] 1 K.B. 315, at p. 321.
[7] [1909] A.C. 118.   [8] (1874), L.R. 9 C.P. 208, at p. 213.

"the true question is whether the acts and conduct of the party evince an intention no longer to be bound by the contract." Again, "in every case the question of repudiation must depend on the character of the contract, the number and weight of the wrongful acts or assertions, the intentions indicated by such acts and words, the deliberation or otherwise with which they are committed or uttered and on the general circumstances of the case."[1]

Clearly, then, we should know in what circumstances a master is justified in dismissing his servant or a servant is justified in leaving his employment. For unless the act be justified a right of action for damages will accrue, together with the right to treat the contract as discharged. The discharge of the contract will excuse further performance—a point of some importance, for example, where the servant has, before the master's repudiation, still to perform covenants, perhaps in restraint of trade.[2] On the other hand there are circumstances where dismissal is wrongful and because of the position of monopoly of the employer the servant seeks reinstatement. He may in such circumstances seek a declaration that the dismissal was wrongful. Such a declaration will only be granted in exceptional circumstances, of which the facts in *Vine* v. *National Dock Labour Board*[3] provide a good example. Vine was a dock labourer and his dismissal was held to be invalid because the Board had delegated power of dismissal to a disciplinary committee when there was no power to do so. The House of Lords took the view that the dock labour scheme made a declaration appropriate. In the same way an order of certiorari is not available.[4] In *Hill* v. *C. A. Parsons and Co., Ltd.*[5], the Courts of Appeal granted an injunction to restrain employers from terminating a contract of employment. They had been under pressure from a trade union to dismiss their workers who did not belong to that union. They issued notices which were challenged. The impending Industrial Relations Act made the case special.

To justify the dismissal of a servant there must be either misconduct, pecuniary or otherwise, wilful disobedience or wilful neglect.[6] The degree of misconduct, disobedience or negligence justifying dismissal cannot be legally defined; it is a matter for the jury, as

---

[1] *Re Rubel Bronze and Metal Co. and Vos*, [1918] 1 K.B. 315, *per* McCardie J. at p. 322.

[2] *S. W. Strange, Ltd.* v. *Mann*, [1965] 1 All E.R. 1069; [1965] 1 W.L.R. 629.

[3] [1957] A.C. 488; [1956] 3 All E.R. 939. *Ridge* v. *Baldwin*, [1964] A.C. 40; [1963] 2 All E.R. 66 is a similar example of a different relationship: the case concerned a Chief Constable. But *cf. Barber* v. *Manchester Regional Hospital Board*, [1958] 1 All E.R. 322; [1958] 1 W.L.R. 181, where despite the contract of a consultant having " a strong statutory flavour " it was held to be an ordinary contract of master and servant where such a declaration was not appropriate.

[4] *Vidyodaya University of Ceylon* v. *Silva*, [1964] 3 All E.R. 865; [1965] 1 W.L.R. 77.

[5] [1971] 3 All E.R. 1345; [1971] 3 W.L.R. 995.

[6] *Callo* v. *Brouncker* (1831), 4 C. & P. 518.

will also be the question whether the dismissal was *bona fide* on those grounds.[1] Yet where the employer is genuinely dissatisfied with his servant and dismisses him the dismissal may be justified though there were, in fact, no grounds for that dissatisfaction.[2] The employer must, however, prove dissatisfaction, which may be difficult. In such circumstances the employer would clearly be likely to have committed the unfair industrial practice of unfair dismissal.

Misconduct, then, may or may not justify dismissal. Insubordination, even on a single occasion, for example, may justify the extreme step being taken, as in *Churchward* v. *Chambers*,[3] where a messman was held properly discharged on his refusal to send up dinner though it was admitted that the incident occurred in a period of exasperation and was followed by an apology. A single act of insubordination would, it is submitted, justify dismissal only where it was such that the parties could not continue on the old terms.[4]

> "Their Lordships," said the Judicial Committee of the Privy Council, "would be very loath to assent to the view that a single outbreak of bad temper, accompanied, it may be, with regrettable language, is sufficient ground for dismissal. Sir JOHN BEAUMONT, C.J.,[5] was stating a proposition of mere good sense when he observed that in such cases we must apply the standards of men and not of angels and remember that men are apt to show temper when reprimanded."[6]

The court went on to make two observations which students—and employers—might bear in mind. The first was that summary dismissal is a strong measure to be justified only in exceptional circumstances; the second, that the test to be applied in determining whether the dismissal was justified "must vary with the nature of the business and the position held by the employee and that decisions in other cases are of little value. . . ."[7] The modern test is whether the misconduct goes to the root of the contract so as to indicate an unwillingness to continue to be bound upon the original terms. Thus in *Laws* v. *London Chronicle (Indicator Newspapers), Ltd.*,[8] a journalist who left a meeting at the request of her immediate superior but against the orders of the chairman was held not to have repudiated the contract by her act and her dismissal on account of it was wrongful. Many of the nineteenth century cases should be read with caution for they rest upon a very different social background and

---

[1] *Clouston & Co., Ltd.* v *Corry*, [1906] A.C. 122; *Smith* v *Allen* (1862), 3 F. & F. 157.
[2] *Diggle* v. *Ogston Motor Co.* (1915), 84 L. J.K.B. 2165.
[3] (1860), 2 F. & F. 229.
[4] *Edwards* v. *Levy* (1860), 2 F. & F. 94.   [5] In the lower court.
[6] *Jupiter General Insurance Co., Ltd.* v. *Ardeshir Bomanji Shroff*, [1937] 3 All E.R. 67, *per curiam*, at p. 74.   [7] *Ibid.*
[8] [1959] 2 All E.R. 285; [1959] 1 W.L.R. 698.

would probably be decided differently to-day.[1] For a rather picturesque and clear indication of unwillingness to be bound, see *Pepper* v. *Webb*.[2]

Immorality, again, will justify dismissal, but it must be the immorality of a servant whose service is intimate to the master or his household or whose continued presence in the employment of the master constitutes a danger to the household or to other employees. So, an unmarried maid may be discharged on being found to be with child,[3] as may a man-servant who is the father of the bastard child of another servant.[4] A clerk who assaulted with intent to ravish his master's maid-servant was held to have properly been summarily dismissed,[5] but where a servant married a woman already with child this was held not to justify dismissal.[6] A master has no right to insist upon the medical examination of a servant whom he suspects to be pregnant.[7]

As to inebriety in a servant, the law has been stated by the Judicial Committee of the Privy Council in these words:

". . . when the alleged misconduct consists of drunkenness there must be considerable difficulty in determining the extent or conditions of drunkenness which will establish a justification for dismissal. The intoxication may be habitual or gross and directly interfere with the business of the employer or with the ability of the servant to render due service. But it may be an isolated act committed under circumstances of festivity and in no way connected with or affecting the employer's business. In such a case the question whether the misconduct proved establishes the right to dismiss the servant must depend upon fact and is a question of fact."[8]

No more need, nor could, be added.

Incompetence is always a valid reason for dismissal and the failure of a servant to provide the skill which, by accepting the employment, he has held himself out as possessing, is a breach of duty entitling the master summarily to discharge him.[9] Indeed the right to discharge might well become a duty and would be so in those cases where the incompetence of a servant created danger to his fellow servants. To that situation the words of PARK, J., in a case involving dismissal for theft, might well be adapted,

". . . if he is negligent in his business and injures his master, I am not prepared to say that the master may not dismiss him, as if he

---

[1] See for example, *Spain* v. *Arnott* (1817), 2 Stark. 256.
[2] [1969] 2 All E.R. 216; [1969] 1 W.L.R. 514.
[3] *R.* v. *Brampton (Inhabitants)* (1777), Cald. Mag. Cas. 11; *Connors* v. *Justice* (1862), 13 I.C.L.R. 451.
[4] *R.* v. *Welford (Inhabitants)* (1778), Cald. Mag. Cas. 57.
[5] *Atkin* v. *Acton* (1830), 4 C. & P. 208.
[6] *R.* v. *Hanbury (Inhabitants)* (1753), Burr. S.C. 322.
[7] *Latter* v. *Braddell* (1881), 50 L.J.Q.B. 448.
[8] *Clouston & Co., Ltd.* v. *Corry*, [1906] A.C. 122, at p. 129.
[9] *Harmer* v. *Cornelius* (1858), 5 C.B.N.S. 236; *Searle* v. *Ridley* (1873), 28 L.T. 411.

were kept it might be very injurious, as he might do the business very carelessly when he knew he was not to be kept longer."[1]

Neglect in certain circumstances justifies dismissal but raises the question of the degree of negligence which must be shown. Manifestly it would be unfair to hold the threat of instant dismissal over the head of every servant guilty of acts of negligence, however trifling. In *Gould* v. *Webb*,[2] the plaintiff, who was the European correspondent of a newspaper, had neglected to send a letter containing news material which he had collected and, being dismissed, had brought action for wrongful dismissal. He was successful, the court being of opinion that the breach of the agreement did not go to the root of the contract. The master's remedy was a counter-claim for damages. The servant's act did not entitle him to regard the entire contract as discharged. Negligence is often a matter of forgetfulness and the courts have frequently had to inquire how far one failure to remember will justify dismissal. Wisely they have refused to enunciate any general principle. A signal-man who forgot to pull the lever at the proper moment would probably be guilty of negligence so grievous as to amount to incompetence. For a servant who damaged an expensive machine it was urged that mere forgetfulness could not amount to neglect, but it was answered: "I think that to forget to do a thing which it is of great importance you should remember may well show such a careless regard to your master's interests as amounts to neglect."[3]   But the Judge was quick to add :

" I do not say it would be a good ground for dismissal in every case. Some trivial acts of forgetfulness might not even justify a complaint or remark."[4]

The courts have rightly seen the injustice of, and have consequently rejected, the notion that the seriousness of an act of negligence is always to be measured by its consequences. The test is often not the consequences but the nature of the act.[5]

When the master instantly dismisses his servant, the cases indicate that he is under no duty to give reasons. Indeed if a cause for dismissal exists it is of no moment that the master when dismissing was unaware of it.[6]   The right to sue for unfair dismissal means that these cases can no longer be safely followed. If, however, the master intends to discharge his servant, he should do so on the occasion

---

[1] *Cunningham* v. *Fonblanque* (1833), 6 C. & P. 44, at p. 49.

[2] (1855), 4 E. & B. 933.

[3] *Baxter* v. *London and County Printing Works*, [1899] 1 Q.B. 901, *per* DARLING, J., at p. 903.

[4] *Ibid.* See also *Blenkarn* v. *Hodges' Distillery Co., Ltd.* (1867), 16 L.T. 608, *per* BYLES, J., at p. 608.

[5] *Savage* v. *British India Steam Navigation Co., Ltd.* (1930), 46 T.L.R. 294, *per* WRIGHT, L.J., at p. 295.

[6] *Ridgway* v. *Hungerford Market Co.* (1835), 3 Ad. & El. 171, at p. 177; and sec *Cyril Leonard & Co.* v. *Simo Securities Ltd.* [1971] 3 All E.R. 1313; [1972] 1 W.L.R. 80.

of the wrongdoing.[1] If, with knowledge or suspicion, he continues to employ the servant, he will not be able to dismiss him
subsequently, for he will be deemed to have elected to waive his
right.[2] It would be otherwise if he did not know or believe that the
servant had done wrong, for it is impossible to condone a wrong
which a man does not believe to have occurred. The practical thing
to do in any case of doubt is to pay the servant any sums due to him
together with wages in lieu of notice. This will not amount to
wrongful dismissal.[3]

Finally, repudiation may arise where the servant himself refuses
to conform to the terms of the contract. Yet, just as, in the case
of the master, there are circumstances which justify a master in
preventing a servant from completing performance, so there may be
circumstances which justify a servant in leaving the service of the
master without giving the required or customary notice. If the
master breaks the contract the servant may be excused further
performance, as where the master of a ship failed to supply the
seaman with the provisions agreed upon;[4] or where the fulfilment of
the contract entails unexpected dangers to life,[5] or where the
servant is subjected to unnecessary or unreasonable punishment.[6]
And the same is true if the risks anticipated by the parties are
increased owing to changed circumstances. In one case,[7] the
Japanese government, having purchased a warship in this country,
engaged a ship master who in turn engaged the plaintiff to assist, as
a member of the crew, in its navigation to Japan. During the voyage
Japan declared war on China and the plaintiff left the ship. It was
held that he was justified in so doing since the change of circumstances had imported new perils which the seaman had not covenanted to undergo.[8]

(2) Unfair Dismissal.—Quite separate from these basic contractual rights, and in addition to them, the Industrial Relations
Act, 1971 has created for every employee the right not to be unfairly
dismissed by his employer.[9] To dismiss unfairly is an unfair industrial practice by the employer and a complaint can be made within
four weeks to an Industrial Tribunal.

Dismissal.—It is irrelevant whether the dismissal is with or without due notice. As long as the contract of employment is terminated
by the employer this is dismissal. So too is failure to renew a fixed
term contract.[10] It is not a dismissal if the employee leaves of his

---

[1] *Horton* v. *McMurtry* (1860), 5 H. & N. 667, *per* BRAMWELL, B., at p. 675.
[2] *Phillips* v. *Foxall* (1872), L.R. 7 Q.B. 666, *per* BLACKBURN, J., at p. 680.
[3] *W. Dennis & Sons, Ltd.* v. *Tunnard Bros. and Moore* (1911), 56 Sol. Jo. 162.
[4] *The Castilia* (1822), 1 Hag. Adm. 59.
[5] *Ottoman Bank* v. *Chakarian*, [1930] A.C. 277, but *cf. Bouzourou* v. *Ottoman Bank*, [1930] A.C. 271.
[6] *Edward* v. *Trevellick* (1854), 4 E. & B. 59, *cf. Renno* v. *Bennett* (1842), 3 Q.B. 768.
[7] *O'Neil* v. *Armstrong, Mitchell & Co.*, [1895] 2 Q.B. 418.   [8] *Ibid.*
[9] Industrial Relations Act, 1971, s. 22.   [10] S. 23.

own accord, even if the employer's action has contributed to this.[1] Only during a period of obligatory notice is the employee able to leave without losing his dismissal rights, and then the employee must give a written notice to his employer terminating the employment at an earlier date.[2] Although non-renewal of a fixed term contract is a dismissal, the rights may be excluded, where the period is for two years or more provided that before the term expires the employee waives his rights in writing.[3]

Unfair.—The Industrial Relations Act, 1971 sets out, in fairly general terms what is fair. The employer has the duty to show that the principal reason for the dismissal comes under the definition of fair or was another substantial reason of a kind enabling him to justify his dismissal.[4] It follows that the onus is on the employer in the first place. No reason for dismissal is made plainly unfair.

Fair is said to be a dismissal by reason of capabilities, or qualifications for performing the kind of work the employee was employed to do or by reason of conduct, or for redundancy[5] or for loss of the right to perform the work under a statutory rule, for instance through loss of a licence.[6] Capability is expanded as meaning assessed by reference to skill, aptitude, health or any other physical or mental quality and qualifications are said to include degrees, diplomas and other such qualifications. It will be appreciated that these definitions are far from specific. They will allow room for wide variations depending upon the particular circumstances surrounding the dismissal. Some of the points raised in redundancy payments cases will obviously be relevant. For example, in *North Riding Garages* v. *Butterwick*[7] the duty of a workman to keep up with technical progress in his job was considered. Many of the current reasons for dismissal, particularly of managers, under formulae such as " lack of initiative " or " fails to fit into the company pattern " will have to be argued under the general provision of some other substantial reason.

The approach to the determination of fairness is to be that of common sense. Thus it is provided that the overriding consideration of reasonableness shall be used and cases determined in accordance with equity and general merits.[8] It follows, for example, that a case apparently falling within the definition of fair might easily be deemed unfair because of surrounding circumstances. Where for example a worker lacks capability, it is doubtful if it would be fair to dismiss him where it could be shown that he had been denied a reasonable amount of necessary training.

---

[1] *Cf.* the rules in redundancy, Redundancy Payments Act, 1965, s. 3(1) (*c*).
[2] Industrial Relations Act, 1971, s. 23(2).
[3] S. 30.   The Act does not apply to fixed term contracts other than apprenticeships made before it came into force.   [4] S. 24(1).
[5] This keeps the two codes—redundancy payments and unfair dismissal separate.   There is one minor overlap, see s. 24(5).   [6] S. 24.
[7] [1967] 2 Q.B. 56; [1967] 1 All E.R. 644.   [8] S. 24(7).

The designation of redundancy as fair has the effect of keeping the claim for a redundancy payment[1] separate from the claim for compensation for unfair dismissal. Obviously a complete overlap would have been chaotic, and as it is the rules of procedure will have to cope with the borderline case which might arguably be either. There are two cases, however, where unfair dismissal is relevant in a redundancy situation. These arise where it is necessary because of a redundancy situation to select those to be made redundant from a group of workers in a similar position. If the selection can be shown to have been made on the grounds of the exercise, or the expressed intention to exercise, rights protected by section 5(1) of the Act[2] or if there is a customary or an agreed selection procedure and this has been contravened without good cause, then the dismissed worker can claim that he has been unfairly dismissed.[3]

Dismissal and Industrial Disputes.—The effect of strike action without due notice is usually to constitute a breach of the contract of service. It follows that the employer is able to regard the contract as terminated. He can, incidentally, sue the striking worker for the breach, an action rarely contemplated let alone taken. It follows that dismissal during strike action is legally permissible. Even where strike notice is given—that is to say the worker gives the length of notice required to terminate his contract—the logic of the situation is that the contract of service comes to an end. There is no need for a dismissal. The possibility that there might be a distinction between notice to terminate and strike notice was discussed at length in *Morgan* v. *Fry*.[4] It was held in that case by Lord DENNING that the effect of strike notice was merely to suspend the contract of service and not to terminate it. This approach has now been incorporated into the Industrial Relations Act.[5] But it is clear that the employer is entitled to terminate the contract. No question of unfair dismissal arises.

The employer's action will be unfair dismissal, however, if the ground for dismissal is taking part in a strike or other irregular industrial action and other employees in the same position were not similarly dismissed or other strikers were offered re-engagement whereas the complainant was not. This selection for dismissal or non-re-engagement must be shown to have been on the grounds of the claimant's exercising or threatening to exercise his rights protected by section 5(1). In simple language the employer will be responsible for unfair dismissal if he " victimises " particular employees because of their conduct in relation to lawful trade union activity.[6]

---

[1] For this, see *infra*, p. 126.
[2] To belong or not to belong to a trade union: to take part in trade union activities, see *supra*, p. 54.
[3] S. 24(5).
[4] [1968] 2 Q.B. 710; [1968] 3 All E.R. 452.
[5] S. 147. See *infra*, p. 111.
[6] S. 26.

A lock-out presents the similar picture in reverse, with the breach of contract being committed by the employers. Again such action involving dismissal by way of lock-out is not *ipso facto* unfair. It is only where at the resumption of work re-engagement is not offered that the quesiton of unfair dismissal arises. Provided that re-engagement is offered by the original employer or his successor or an associated employer in his same position or a different but reasonably suitable one then there is no unfair dismissal. If, however, there is no re-engagement then the provisions in the Act as to what is fair and what is not are applied. The non-re-engagement is treated in exactly the same way as a dismissal.[1]

Application.—The rules as to unfair dismissal apply to employees. An employee is defined as an individual who has entered into or works under a contract of employment.[2] Certain classes are excluded.[3] These are those employed in an undertaking with less than four employees including the claimant, those employed by a husband or wife or close relative,[4] registered dock workers, share-fishermen, certain Scottish teachers. More generally, part-time workers who are employed for less than twenty-one hours weekly are also excluded, as are those who under their contract of employment ordinarily work outside Great Britain. This last exclusion does not apply to those working on board a ship registered in the United Kingdom unless the employment is wholly outside Great Britain or the employee in question is not ordinarily resident in Great Britain. The dismissal provisions apply to the termination of Crown employment[5] which is defined as employment under or for the purposes of a Government department but does not include those serving in the armed forces.[6]

There are important qualifications. The claimant must be able to show that he was continuously employed for at least one hundred and four weeks up to the effective date of the termination.[7] This date is, where notice is given, when it expires; where no notice is given, the actual date of termination; and where there is a fixed term contract, the expiry date.[8] There is also an upper age limit. The rights do not apply once the employee has passed the normal retiring age which may be either one special to the employment or the usual national one of sixty-five for a man and sixty for a woman.[9]

Of these exclusions, that relating to small undertakings below four and those relating to qualifying period and retirement age do not operate where the dismissal is for the reason that the employee used the rights protected by section 5(1).[10]

---

[1] S. 25.
[2] S. 167.
[3] S. 27.
[4] The list is in s. 27(4).
[5] S. 162(3) (*b*).
[6] S. 162(2).
[7] S. 28(*a*).   [8] S. 23(5).   [9] S. 28(*b*).   [10] S. 29.

Procedures and Remedies.—The person dismissed to whom the rules apply must complain to an Industrial Tribunal.[1] The complaint has to be made within the four weeks following the effective date of termination, unless the Tribunal is satisfied that it was not practicable to do so.[2] A copy of the complaint is then sent to a conciliation officer and the complainant and employer are notified of the availability of a conciliation officer. The proceedings must be postponed to give an opportunity for settlement by conciliation.[3] A settlement between employer and dismissed employee is void if it tried to preclude a complaint being made to the Industrial Tribunal.[4] This does not apply, however, where the conciliation officer has been concerned and has reached a settlement as directed by the Act.[5] If conciliation fails the Tribunal is able, if it finds the case proved, to recommend that the complainant be re-engaged on terms it considers reasonable.[6] Such recommendation has to be considered both equitable and practicable.

It would obviously be wrong to make such a recommendation where all available posts were filled, however strong the grounds. The Tribunal may also make an award of compensation either as an alternative to re-engagement or, where re-engagement is not thought appropriate, by itself.[7] The compensation is to be paid by the employer who has dismissed unfairly, to his ex-employee.

There is a section of the Act setting out general principles as to the assessment of compensation.[8] The aim is to cover the loss sustained by the complainant in so far as that loss is attributable to the employer. This loss is to include expenses that have been reasonably incurred and loss of benefit that might have been expected. The Tribunal must reduce the assessment to the extent that it feels the complainant has caused or contributed to the loss. There is also the duty to mitigate the loss, as is usual under the common law. So the dismissed worker must actively seek another job and take one if offered provided it is suitable.[9] This will lead to considerable argument with the employer in a difficult position as far as getting evidence.[10] In this respect special mention is made of an unreasonable refusal of an offer of re-engagement made under the Tribunal's recommendation. On the other hand failure to make such an offer in unreasonable circumstances may be taken as an aggravation of

---

[1] S. 106.
[2] Schedule 6, para. 5.
[3] Schedule 6, para. 6.
[4] S. 161(1) (*b*).
[5] S. 161(2) (*d*). The conciliation officers duties are set out in s. 146(3).
[6] S. 106(4).
[7] S. 106(5).
[8] S. 116.
[9] See *Brace* v. *Calder*, [1895] 2 Q.B. 253.
[10] There is a similar problem of alternative employment in redundancy but as this is offered by the employer he has full details.

the damage.   The employer is not allowed to shelter behind an excuse that trade union pressure has been put on him.[1]   Where there is such pressure a contribution may be ordered.[2]

The amount of compensation is subject to an overall limit.   It cannot exceed one hundred and four weeks' pay with an absolute maximum of £4,160, that is to say a weekly limit of £40.[3]   The exact method of calculating a week's pay for this purpose is laid down in regulations.

The difference between these rules of compensation and those under the redundancy payments scheme are remarkable.   This latter scheme bases its computation of redundancy pay not upon actual loss but on length of service.   There will obviously be factual situations where the facts might arguably fall within either head.   It will be a problem for the Tribunal to decide: the parties will clearly be influenced by the differing amounts of compensation accruing under each head.   This difference is hard to justify logically.

Exclusion.—An agreement to preclude the application of the rules of unfair dismissal is void under the Act.[4]   It does however provide that a joint application may be made by parties to a procedure agreement designating that agreement as a substitute for the statutory scheme of unfair dismissal.[5]   Application is to be made to the Industrial Court (note not the Tribunal which deals with dismissal cases).   The court has to be satisfied that the remedies under the agreement submitted in substitution are on the whole as beneficial though they need not be identical.   The procedure must provide for arbitration or an independent reference where the balance of interests may mean a deadlock.   Once an exclusion order is in force, the parties or the Secretary of State may apply to the Industrial Court for its revocation.   This will be done if all the parties wish it, or if the court is satisfied that the conditions for exclusion no longer exist.[6]

This procedure apart, an employer cannot contract out of his liability.[7]   Generally there are special rules for fixed term contracts.[8]

Relationship with Wrongful Dismissal.—It must be emphasised that these rules of unfair dismissal have not superseded the rules set out in the previous section on wrongful dismissal.   These will still decide the entitlement to notice and the occasions when the employer can dismiss instantly.   They will offer an alternative cause of action which, because of the financial limit of £4,160 (£40

---

[1] This would be an unfair industrial practice, s. 33(1).
[2] S. 119.
[3] S. 118.   An official of a trade union is not to be made to contribute; his trade union may be.
[4] S. 161(1).
[5] S. 31.
[6] S. 32.
[7] S. 161.   [8] S. 30.

per week) may still be attractive to the highly paid worker. This cause of action will not, for a time at least, be brought in an Industrial Tribunal although there is provision for their jurisdiction to include, coincidentally with the other courts, actions for breach of the contract of employment.[1]

(3) Strike Notice.—The effect of a strike, and of strike notice has been dealt with by the Industrial Relations Act, 1971. It provides that where notice is given by or on behalf of an employee of his intention to strike it will not, unless it expressly provides otherwise, be regarded as notice of termination of the contract of employment nor as a repudiation of the contract.[2] This will be especially so if the contract clearly contains a " no strike " clause which in its usual form will require certain procedures to be gone through before strike action is taken. Such a clause is not uncommon in a collective agreement between an employer and a trade union. It may be expressly or impliedly incorporated in the individual's contract of service. This becomes of great importance because the Act provides that a strike following due notice is not to be regarded as a breach of contract for the purposes of actions for breach, proceedings in tort, section 5 of the Conspiracy and Protection of Property Act,[3] and section 96 of the Industrial Relations Act which governs unfair industrial practices by way of inducing a breach of contract.[4] This does not apply, however, if the employee is acting contrary to a term of his contract of employment which excludes or restricts his right to take part in a strike.[5]

Due notice is defined as a period not less than that required on his part to terminate his contract of employment. This period may be set out in his contract of service[6] and failing that is governed by the Contracts of Employment Act, 1963 which, whilst setting out increasing periods in relation to the employer's notice, provides for a week's notice only for the worker.[7]

7. Remedies

(1) General Considerations.—A breach of contract may arise either on or after the due date of performance or before that date arrives. In the first case the breach is said to be actual, in the second

---

[1] S. 113. It will not relate to damages for death or personal injury.
[2] S. 147 (1). The law had reached this point in *Morgan* v. *Fry*, [1968] 2 Q.B. 710; [1968] 3 All E.R. 452.
[3] See *infra*, p. 502.
[4] See *infra*, p. 505.
[5] S. 147 (3).
[6] A professor has usually to give three months' notice of termination which rather inhibits lawful strike action.
[7] Contracts of Employment Act, 1963, s. 1(2).

case, anticipatory. From the moment the contract is broken without adequate excuse a right of action arises and the injured party may seek his remedy though the date of performance has not been reached. This rule can be seen in *Hochster* v. *De la Tour*[1] and *Batty* v. *Melillo*.[2] De la Tour had agreed to employ Hochster as a courier, the service to commence at a future date. Before that date arrived Hochster was told that his services would not be required. In *Batty* v. *Melillo* the defendant and his wife had agreed on July 7th to serve the plaintiff as equestrian performers at a weekly salary for a period of three months at "Astley's Amphitheatre or elsewhere." The plaintiff set up his entertainment at Peebles but the defendant did not appear, so that a writ was issued on August 23rd, *i.e.*, before the end of the period of service, within which, of course, the defendant might have presented himself for duty. It was held none the less that the facts disclosed a good cause of action. The reason for the rule was stated by Lord CAMPBELL to be

> " that where there is a contract to do an act on a future day, there is a relation constituted between the parties in the meantime by the contract, and that they impliedly promise that in the meantime neither will do anything to the prejudice of the other inconsistent with that relation."[3]

Though, in the case of an anticipatory breach, action may be brought before the date of performance has arrived, there is no compulsion on the injured party to do so.[4] If he does not seek his remedy the contract persists for the benefit and at the peril of both parties. So that had the courier in *Hochster* v. *De la Tour* elected not to sue until the date of entering into his master's service had arrived and between the master's announcement that he would not require the courier's services and the date of performance the master had died, the courier would have been deprived of the remedy.[5] The innocent party may ignore the repudiation and perform his side of the bargain. He will then be in a position to claim the full contract price.[6] This very unusual decision has possibly wide implications. Although the innocent party cannot force his performance upon the repudiator, where the repudiator's acceptance or co-operation in some way is needed, the principle is wide enough to embrace an expert who insists upon carrying out a survey in distant lands or even, by analogy, a servant who merely remains available, if allowed to work.

---

[1] (1853), 2 E. & B. 678.   [2] (1850), 10 C.B. 282.

[3] *Hochster* v. *De la Tour* (1853), 2 E. & B. 678, at p. 689.

[4] *Shindler* v. *Northern Raincoat Co., Ltd.*, [1960] 2 All E.R. 239; [1960] 1 W.L.R. 1038.

[5] *Frost* v. *Knight* (1872), L.R. 7 Exch. 111.

[6] *White & Carter (Councils), Ltd.* v. *McGregor*, [1961] 3 All E.R. 1178; [1962] 2 W.L.R. 17; attention should be paid to the dissenting opinions of Lord MORTON and Lord KEITH; see also "Measure of Damages when a Contract is Repudiated" by A. L. Goodhart, (1962), 78 *L.Q.R.* 263.

Special statutory provision is made by the Employers and Workmen Act, 1875, as to proceedings between an employer and workmen. The Act gives jurisdiction to the courts of summary jurisdiction and to the County Courts in disputes arising out of or incidental to the relationship of master and servant. The courts of summary jurisdiction may, in respect of any dispute brought under the Act, hear and determine the cause and order the payment of any sum whether as wages due or damages and exercise the powers conferred by the Act on the County Court. But the amount claimed must not exceed £10 in respect of each cause and the court must not order payment of a greater sum than this exclusive of costs.[1]

The powers of the County Court are set out in section 3. The court may adjust and set off claims on the part of either the employer or workman whether the claims are for wages, damages, or otherwise and whether they be liquidated or unliquidated.[2] It may rescind any contract between employer and employed on such terms as to the apportionment of wages or other sums due thereunder, and as to the payment of wages or damages, or other sums due as it thinks fit.[3] The court has the power to order damages for breach of contract but its power to take security for the performance of the unperformed part of the obligation, with the consent of the plaintiff, has been ended by the Industrial Relations Act.[4] That Act specifically states that no court may order specific performance of a contract of service nor use an injunction so as to compel an employee to work or to attend at his place of work to do so.[5]

The remedies available to a party who is injured by breach of contract (and the breach itself, apart from any resulting damage, amounts to nominal injury) are damages, or an injunction, or both. In addition, the servant may be able to sue on a *quantum meruit*. Only where there is a specific agreement in the contract to this end may a master retain wages due but not paid to his servant. The appropriate remedy where a servant breaks his contract and wrongfully leaves the service of his master is an action by the master for damages.[6]

The courts have laid down the sphere of the two remedies of damages and injunction and the circumstances in which they will be awarded.[7] The court will ask, whether the injury can be sufficiently recompensed by the payment of damages and whether the damages can be awarded once for all in reasonable and exhaustive satisfaction of the breach. If the answer is in the affirmative damages

---

[1] S. 4; *Parker* v. *Doncaster Collieries, Ltd.* (1946), 174 L.T. 391.
[2] S. 3(1).
[3] S. 3(3).
[4] S. 128(2).
[5] S. 128(1).
[6] *M'Kenzie* v. *Sheffield Cutlery Service*, [1950] S.L.T. (Sh. Ct.) 81.
[7] *Doherty* v. *Allman* (1878), 3 App. Cas. 709, *per* Lord CAIRNS, L.C., at pp. 720–721.

will be awarded, but if the injury is likely to continue, and the award of damages will not genuinely compensate the plaintiff, the court may, by injunction, restrain the defendant from doing those things which he has promised not to do. And where a breach involves both sets of conditions both damages and injunction may be sought.

(2) **Damages.**—Where a master commits a breach of contract, the servant may either treat his act as determining the contract and sue for damages or sue on a *quantum meruit* for services rendered. He may choose the latter (for he cannot pursue both remedies) even though he has not completely performed his promise. This was the situation in *Planché* v. *Colburn*[1] where the plaintiff was employed to write a book, but before he had finished doing so he was informed by the defendants that they no longer intended to publish the work. Despite his own lack of completion it was held that he might recover for the work he had actually done. The amount recoverable will depend entirely on whether the contract is one in which the right to remuneration vests at intermediate periods or only on completion of the full work.   If the plaintiff is to be paid an agreed sum on completion and the failure to complete is due to the defendant, the plaintiff will be entitled to recover the whole sum.[2]   More generally the remuneration will vest at intermediate periods and though the plaintiff will be entitled to a sum covering his services to the date of dismissal, he will not be entitled on a *quantum meruit* to recover anything in respect of the remainder of the period during which he might have earned remuneration had there been no breach.   For in such circumstances his right depends on his performance, which he will be unable to prove.[3]   Nor can he hope to achieve the same purpose by deferring his action until the end of the period for which he was engaged.   Finally the action on a *quantum meruit* will lie only where the original contract is closed, for, as was said in *Planché* v. *Colburn*,[4] " When a special contract is in existence and open, the plaintiff cannot sue on a *quantum meruit.*"   The obligation is quasi-contractual.   The original contract is gone and the right to recovery is based on the justice of compelling the defendant to pay for such performance as he has accepted.[5]

Because of such considerations the servant will usually found his action on damages for breach of contract.   The master must necessarily do so.   The compensation recoverable by way of damages will be for those injuries which either arise naturally from the breach or, where they cannot be said to arise naturally,

---

[1] (1831), 8 Bing. 14.

[2] *O'Neil* v. *Armstrong, Mitchell & Co.*, [1895] 2 Q.B. 418, *per* Lord ESHER, M.R., at p. 421.

[3] See review of the authorities in the notes to *Cutter* v. *Powell* (1795), 2 Smith L.C. 1.   Clearly, wherever possible in these circumstances he will sue on the contract itself.

[4] (1831), 8 Bing. 14, *per* TINDAL. C.J., at p. 16.

[5] Winfield : *Province of the Law of Tort* (1931), p. 158.

are such as might reasonably be supposed to have been in the contemplation of the parties as the probable result of its breach when they made the contract.[1] The first principle will cover the majority of contracts; the second will cover those in which damage of unusual incidence flows from the breach. Consequently it was held in *Addis* v. *Gramophone Co., Ltd.*[2] that a wrongfully dismissed servant is entitled to damages covering the wages he would have earned during the period within which the master might have terminated the contract by notice and the estimated amount of commission he might have earned. But none would be awarded either in compensation of injured feelings or for any difficulty which might be experienced in obtaining new employment elsewhere. In other words, the damages will be an estimate of his actual pecuniary loss[3] whether the loss be in wages, or in gratuities,[4] or in publicity and reputation.[5] Since this is so, the damages recoverable will be lessened by any amount which the plaintiff has earned between the date of the breach and the date on which the contract would have terminated but for the breach or on which the damages were assessed.[6] So, where the breach arose out of the dissolution of a partnership, it was proper, in assessing the damages, to consider the fact that the continuing partners were ready at all times to maintain the plaintiff in employment, for there is a duty on the servant to mitigate the loss.[7]

The parties may include in their contract a figure to be payable as damages in the event of breach. This was done in *Kemble* v. *Farren* where the court said :

> "we see nothing illegal or unreasonable in the parties by their mutual agreement, settling the amount of damages, uncertain in their nature, at any sum on which they may agree. In many cases, such an agreement fixes that which is almost impossible to be accurately ascertained; and in all cases it saves the expense and difficulty of bringing witnesses to that point."[8]

---

[1] *Hadley* v. *Baxendale* (1854), 9 Exch. 341, *per* ALDERSON, B., at p. 354.

[2] [1909] A.C. 488.

[3] *Lindsay* v. *Queen's Hotel Co.*, [1919] 1 K.B. 212.

[4] *Manubens* v. *Leon*, [1919] 1 K.B. 208.

[5] *Marbe* v. *George Edwardes (Daly's Theatre), Ltd.*, [1928] 1 K.B. 269; *Herbert Clayton and Jack Waller, Ltd.* v. *Oliver*, [1930] A.C. 209; *cf. Withers* v. *General Theatre Corporation*, [1933] 2 K.B. 536; [1933] All E.R. Rep. 385.

[6] *Jackson* v. *Hayes Candy & Co., Ltd.*, [1938] 4 All E.R. 587.

[7] *Brace* v. *Calder*, [1895] 2 Q.B. 253. And see *British Transport Commission* v. *Gourley*, [1956] A.C. 185.

[8] (1829), 6 Bing. 141, *per* TINDAL, C.J., at p. 148. In this case the defendant, an actor, was paid £3 6s. 8d. for each night on which a theatre was opened and was to pay £1,000 if he broke his contract. The latter figure was held to be a penalty because of the disproportion between the two sums. Such a view would no longer be taken by the courts: see *Imperial Tobacco Co. (of Great Britain and Ireland), Ltd.* v. *Parslay*, [1936] 2 All E.R. 515. A figure will be a penalty only where it is unconscionable and there is a grave disproportion between the figure stipulated and any damages likely to flow.

The legal effect of any figure stipulated by the parties to be paid as damages will vary according to whether the court regards it as liquidated damages (*i.e.*, a genuine pre-estimate of loss) or as a penalty.   If it be construed as the former it alone will be recoverable whatever the actual loss ensuing.   If it be a penalty the parties may recover such sum as they can prove to have suffered as a loss consequent upon the breach, and estimated according to the principles outlined above ; the penalty is ignored.

(3) Injunction.—Though there are early authorities to the contrary, the remedy of specific performance is not available to the parties to a contract of service.   This is so partly because the character of the contract prevents the courts exercising any effective supervision but chiefly because the courts will not permit themselves to become an instrument whereby the voluntary character of the agreement might be invaded.

"I should be very unwilling," said FRY, L.J., in *De Francesco* v. *Barnum*,

> "to extend decisions the effect of which is to compel persons who are not desirous of maintaining continuous personal relations with one another to continue those personal relations.   I think the courts are bound to be jealous lest they should turn contracts of service into contracts of slavery; and . . . I should lean against the extension of the doctrine of specific performance and injunction in such a manner."[1]

The courts will, however, grant an injunction in appropriate cases, the first principle being that *prima facie* an injunction will not be issued to restrain wrongs in cases in which damages would be the proper remedy.[2]   An injunction is an order of the court issued to the defendant with the object of restraining him from committing or continuing some act which is wrongful (when the injunction is said to be prohibitory) or with the object of restraining his continuance of some wrongful omission (when it is said to be mandatory).   So where a contract of service contains a promise by either party not to do a given act, the courts will hold the party to his promise.   The scope of the remedy was outlined by Lord ST. LEONARDS in *Lumley* v. *Wagner* :—

> "Wherever this court has not proper jurisdiction to enforce specific performance, it operates to bind men's consciences, as far as they can be bound, to a true and literal performance of their agreements, and it will not suffer them to depart from their contracts at their pleasure, leaving the party with whom they have contracted to the mere chance of any damages which the jury may give."[3]

---

[1] *De Francesco* v. *Barnum* (1890), 45 Ch.D. 430, at p. 438, but note that the courts under the Employers and Workmen Act, 1875, s. 3 (3) have a restricted power of ordering performance of a contract.
[2] *London and Blackwall Ry. Co.* v. *Cross* (1886), 31 Ch.D. 354.
[3] (1852), 1 De G.M. & G. 604, at p. 619.

The defendant had agreed to sing for the plaintiff and not to sing for any one else without his permission. Her counsel advanced the argument that an injunction would prevent her appearance at any other theatre without having power to compel her to sing for the plaintiff. The argument was not acceptable to the court.

" . . . but she has no cause of complaint if I compel her to abstain from the commission of an act which she has bound herself not to do and thus, possibly, to cause her to fulfil her engagement."[1]

The distinction between a negative covenant which may be the object of an injunction and a positive one which may not, can be seen in *Rely-a-Bell Burglar and Fire Alarm Co., Ltd.* v. *Eisler.*[2] The defendant Eisler covenanted that he would not, during his employment by the plaintiffs, enter into any other employment at all or be interested in the business of any other company dealing with burglar or fire alarms. The restriction was held to be a valid one but the court would not restrain Eisler from continuing to be employed by a rival company nor restrain that company from employing him. It did, however, grant an injunction restraining him from being interested in the rival or any similar company dealing with burglar and fire alarms. Clearly the law would not permit an injunction restraining Eisler from continuing to be employed, and to have granted one against the rival company or any subsequent company employing him would, in fact, amount to enforcing the specific performance of the original contract. The courts are always reluctant to grant an injunction where the effect is to compel the servant to perform his contract or starve. None the less in *Eisler's* case an injunction restraining his interest in the company would be quite proper for it related, not to his employment, but to his holding as a shareholder.

A covenant negative in form but positive in essence will not be enforced. In *Davis* v. *Foreman*[3] the employer undertook not to dismiss his servant except for misconduct or other breach of contract. The servant was given notice and brought an action. The court held that the covenant though negative in form was positive in substance and an injunction could not be granted. Conversely, where the form is positive but the essence negative, an injunction will be granted. An actor joined a theatrical company on terms *inter alia*, that

" no member of the company is allowed to act, sing, or appear publicly at any other theatre without special permission of the management."

An injunction restraining the actor from appearing elsewhere was granted on the ground that the contract contained a negative stipulation.[4]

---

[1] *Ibid.*
[2] [1926] Ch. 609.
[3] [1894] 3 Ch. 654.
[4] *Grimston* v. *Cuningham*, [1894] 1 Q.B. 125.

The remedy is a discretionary one and the court will limit the terms of the injunction to what it considers reasonable in the circumstances of the case.   In *Warner Bros. Pictures Inc.* v. *Nelson*[1] a film actress covenanted exclusively to serve certain producers for 52 weeks (the contract to be renewable for a similar period) and not, during the tenure of the engagement, to give her services to any other person.   The court granted an injunction to the producers, but limited it, as to place, to the area of the jurisdiction of the court, and as to time, to the period of three years or the continuance of the contract, whichever was the shorter.

An injunction, as we have seen, will be awarded only where damages are not an adequate remedy.   This was clearly so in *Hill* v. *C. A. Parsons and Co., Ltd.*[2] where the breach by the employer was in giving too short a notice.   Longer notice would have completely changed the worker's position since it would not have been effective until the Industrial Relations Act, 1971 came into force.   Thus an injunction was thought to be appropriate.   The remedies are not in the alternative and the court has power to grant both damages and an injunction.[3]

(4) Discharge of Rights of Action.—Once a right of action has accrued to a party it may be discharged only by judgment of the court, by release, by accord and satisfaction or by the lapse of time.

The judgment of an English court of record arising out of breach of contract will completely discharge rights of action issuing from the same breach between the same parties.   Otherwise the release of a right of action is required to be by deed, whether the contract out of which it arises is a simple contract (oral or written) or a formal contract under seal.

Accord and satisfaction implies a new contract by which the person in whom the right of action lies agrees to accept some new consideration in discharge of his right, whether that right arises out of a simple or a specialty contract.   This agreement represents an "accord" but will not, of itself, discharge the right of action. More is required and there can be no "satisfaction" until the consideration is actually transferred.

The working of the principle can be seen in *R.* v. *Harberton* (*Inhabitants*)[4] where the master of an apprentice with some time still to run under his indentures received £4 in satisfaction of his release of the apprentice.   There was complete agreement and a receipt was given.   In addition the master offered to deliver up

---

[1] [1937] 1 K.B. 209; [1936] 3 All E.R. 160; see also *Marco Productions, Ltd.* v. *Pagola*, [1945] K.B. 111; [1945] 1 All E.R. 155.
[2] [1971] 3 All E.R. 1345; [1971] 3 W.L.R. 995.
[3] *Leeds Industrial Co-operative Society, Ltd.* v. *Slack*, [1924] A.C. 851, *per* Viscount FINLAY, at p. 863.
[4] (1786), 1 Term Rep. 139.

the indentures, but this did not take place until a considerably later date. This, said the court, amounted to an accord and satisfaction and the indentures must be considered as ceasing to exist from the time when the consideration changed hands.

The consideration, however, may consist in the mere giving of a promise, for though the general principle is that an accord without satisfaction has no legal effect, and that the original cause of action is not discharged as long as the satisfaction agreed upon remains executory, yet where

> " it can be shown that what a creditor accepts in satisfaction is merely his debtor's promise and not the performance of that promise, the original cause of action is discharged from the date when the promise is made."[1]

A creditor's promise to accept a smaller sum than the amount owing is of no legal value.[2] If A wrongfully discharges B who is entitled to a sum of £20 wages, B's agreement to accept £10 in full settlement will not amount to an accord and satisfaction and, should he feel so disposed, B may sue on the original cause of action for the remaining £10. For there is no consideration for the renunciation of the £10.[3] This will obtain, however, only where the amount of the debt is known; where there is a dispute as to liability, or the amount of the liability, the acceptance of the smaller sum will discharge the right of action, as will the acceptance of a negotiable instrument in place of legal tender, or the acceptance of any other consideration.[4] Similarly, the right of action is discharged where the creditor accepts a lesser sum from the hands of a third party on the debtor's behalf,[5] or when he accepts a smaller sum from the debtor himself before the due date of payment.[6]

Finally a right of action arising by way of contract may be discharged by lapse of time. Under the terms of the Limitation Act, 1939, an action founded on a simple contract shall not be brought after the expiration of six years from the date on which the cause of action accrued,[7] whilst an action founded on a specialty[8] or on a judgment[9] debt may not be brought after the expiration of twelve years from the date on which the cause of action accrued or the judgment became enforceable. By the Law Reform (Limitation of Actions, etc.) Act, 1954, the period is three years if damages are claimed for personal injuries caused by the breach of a contractual duty.[10]

---

[1] *Morris* v. *Baron & Co.*, [1918] A.C.1, *per* Lord ATKINSON, at p. 35.

[2] As accord and satisfaction. Such a promise may well give rise to an estoppel. See the discussion of the *High Trees Case, supra*, pp. 43, *et seq.*

[3] *Foakes* v. *Beer* (1884), 9 App. Cas. 605.

[4] *Goddard* v. *O'Brien* (1882), 9 Q.B.D. 37.

[5] *Bidder* v. *Bridges* (1887), 37 Ch.D. 406.

[6] *Pinnel's Case* (1602), 5 Co. Rep. 117a.

[7] S. 2 (1) (a).

[8] S. 2 (3).

[9] S. 2 (4).

[10] S. 2 (1).

CHAPTER IV

WAGES

Although it will be obvious from the foregoing chapters that the contract between master and servant is largely a matter for the common law and is hardly touched by legislation, this is not so true for the important aspect of wages and their payment. There has been a considerable body of legislation dealing with wage fixing, the protection of wages and the allied subject of unemployment insurance. These topics will be considered in the second half of this chapter following a summary of the attitude of the common law to the question of wages.

1. COMMON LAW

(1) **Fixing of Wages.**—Perhaps the most important part of a contract of service, particularly from the workman's point of view, is the fixed wage. Although the wage clause, like any other, is in law a matter for bargaining between the individual employer and workman, in practice a large number of wage rates are fixed by agreement between employers' associations and trade unions or groups of trade unions. This process is known as collective bargaining and it has become a familiar feature of industrial organisation. It is, in fact, government policy to encourage the use of collective bargaining. " Since the 1870s the Government has recognised collective bargaining," as the normal means of settling wages and working conditions and more recently has actively encouraged the establishment of joint agreed machinery of negotiation and consultation in industry."[1] These agreements predominantly deal with wage rates and the allied subject of hours of work but there is a markedly growing tendency for them to embrace wider aspects of conditions of employment.[2] The law has not as yet recognised collective bargains as fully effective. The common law, with its doctrine of privity of contract, has always excluded strangers to a contract from participation either in its formation or in the enforcement of its terms. It follows that agreements between employers and workmen cannot be directly affected by agreements by associations and unions. The problem of the relation between

---

[1] Ministry of Labour, Industrial Relations Handbook, 1961, p. 3. And see the particularly valuable chapters dealing with joint negotiating machinery in private industry and in the nationalised industries.

[2] The Industrial Relations Code of Practice delineates topics which should or may be dealt with in collective bargains: paras. 90–95. The tendency is for them to deal with a wider case.

the collective bargain and the individual contract between employer and workman is a considerable one to which we must now
turn.[1]

In *Young* v. *Canadian Northern Rly. Co.*[2] the judicial committee
of the Privy Council had to consider this point for the appellant's
claim that he had been wrongfully dismissed depended upon the
incorporation of an agreement between employers and Union in his
own contract of service. It is noteworthy that the employers were
accepted as having acted, up to the point in issue, in compliance
with the terms of this agreement. It was held however that the
agreement was not incorporated and that compliance with the
terms did not establish contractual liability. This is clearly a
restrictive and strict interpretation of the rules of incorporation.
It is a matter which must depend very much upon the individual
facts of each case. Thus, in *Tomlinson* v. *L.M. and S. Ry.*,[3] it was
held that a similar type of agreement providing for conciliation
machinery had been incorporated. Apart from these cases the matter is devoid of real authority from which principles may be drawn
and the opinions of writers vary.[4] The problem is one that is met
afresh when each individual situation is considered for the basic rule,
that the terms of a collective bargain do not affect the individual
contract between employer and workman unless expressly or by
implication incorporated in that individual contract, demands
interpretation with each different situation. It may well be that
the restrictive dictum in *Young's* case that acceptance of terms in
practice does not necessarily establish contractual liability may
itself be restrictively applied and that the ever increasing use of
collective bargains as the basis for hiring and continuing the hiring
of workmen may lead to judicial acceptance of a readier assumption
of incorporation. So in *National Coal Board* v. *Galley*[5] it was held
by the Court of Appeal that it was unnecessary to decide whether
there was incorporation by continued acceptance of the terms by
both employer and workman since the contract of service in question
expressly provided for incorporation. An interesting objection to
incorporation was, however, argued by the defendant. It was
claimed on his behalf that an agreement of a national kind, being
by its very nature wide and general, could not be held to be intended
to be enforceable. This argument was rejected and the Court were
of the opinion that it was the intention that the agreement should be
enforceable. Until there is more certainty on the point of incorp-

---

[1] For an excellent treatment of this topic see especially " Legal Framework"
by O. Kahn-Freund which is Chapter II of " The System of Industrial Relations
in Great Britain," edited by Flanders and Clegg, 1960.
    [2] [1931] A.C. 83.   [3] [1944] 1 All E.R. 537.
    [4] Compare the attitude of Gayler, " Industrial Law," 1955, particularly pp.
170–186, with that of Professor Kahn-Freund. See recent treatment in
Joel v. *Cammel Laird*, (1969) I.T.R. 206.
    [5] [1958] 1 W.L.R. 16.

oration it can only be regretted that the common law doctrine of privity seems to create some unreality about this section of the law.[1]

(2) Equal Pay Act 1970.—Although the preamble of this Act says that its purpose is to prevent discrimination, as regards terms and conditions of employment, between men and women its real aim is to improve the position of women who in many sectors of work perform comparable jobs for a lesser rate of pay. The Act is unusual in that it is meant to do most of its work before it comes into force, at least as far as changes in practices are concerned. It received the Royal Assent in May 1970 but does not come into force until December 29th, 1975.[2]

The Act applies to both men and women. Employers must give equal treatment as regards terms and conditions of employment. The terms and conditions of one sex must not be more favourable than those of another where they perform like work or where the work is rated as equivalent.[3] The Act frames the provisions to secure this in terms of women being equivalent to men but it points out that the reverse applies. The practical difficulties of the application of the Act will arise from the two areas: like work and work rated as equivalent.

Like work is said to cover a situation where a woman's work is of the same, or a broadly similar nature to that of a man. If there are differences these must not be of practical importance in relation to the terms and conditions of employment. To determine this, not only the nature of the differences but also their frequency must be considered.[4] The application of these new rules calls for a categorisation of jobs. Only once this is done can the relative position of men and women be assessed. Clearly there will be areas in which it is extremely difficult to draw up an acceptable series of categories.

Work rated as equivalent arises where a woman's job and a man's have been the subject of a job evaluation, where the terms and conditions of employment are based on that evaluation and where the jobs have been given equal value. A job evaluation is a study undertaken to assess in terms of demand made on the worker under various headings the jobs to be done by all or some of the employees. If the job evaluation has had, as part of its scheme, a different rating for men and women, that is to say if the evaluation scheme itself has discrimination built into it, this must be ignored and the results adjusted.[5]

The area of comparison is of importance. This is defined as with

---

[1] For examples, see *Maclea* v. *Essex Line, Ltd.* (1933). 45 Lloyds L.R. 254; *London Passenger Board* v. *Miscrop*, [1942] 1 All E.R. 97.
[2] S. 9. This is power vesting in the Secretary of State to put ss. 1 and 2 into force on December 31st, 1973, if he feels it is expedient to do so to secure orderly progress towards the final aims.
[3] S. 1(1).
[4] S. 1(4).
[5] S. 1(5).

men in the same employment which is expanded to cover men employed by her employer or by an associated employer at establishments in Great Britain. Where more than one establishment is included in the comparison the terms and conditions of employment have to be common.[1] Employed means employed under a contract of service or apprenticeship and covers a person who works outside the establishment but is based on it, a salesman for example.[2] Associated employers include a company controlled by another, or two companies both under the same control.[3] The Act applies in respect of these rules set out in section 1 to Crown servants other than the armed forces. Special provision is made for the protection of the armed forces[4] and also for the police.[5]

Once the Act comes into force[6] a dispute as to the right to equal treatment may be referred to an Industrial Tribunal. Either the complainant or the employer against whom the claim is made may take the matter for settlement to the Tribunal.[7] Where it is not reasonable to expect a woman herself to take the matter to a Tribunal, the Secretary of State for Employment may refer the matter.[8] A claim may be lodged up to six months after the employment in question has been terminated[9] and may relate to a period of not more than two years up to the date the proceedings were started.[10]

Once the right to equal pay is established the employer has the duty of justifying any variations between an individual man and woman. Greater remuneration or material advantages may be justified on personal grounds. Thus a long service or good conduct bonus enjoyed would not offend these rules. It is, however, for the employer to satisfy the Tribunal that the difference does not arise from a class differentiation between men and women.

The Act also provides for the amendment and variation of existing agreements and pay structures. A collective agreement, made either before or after the Act comes into force, may be referred by either of the parties to it or by the Secretary of State for Employment to the Industrial Arbitration Tribunal[11] if it contains a provision applying specifically to men only or women only[12] The Industrial Arbitration Tribunal is given power to make amendments. It may

---

[1] S. 1(2).
[2] S. 1(6) (a) (b).
[3] S. 1(6) (c).
[4] S. 7.
[5] S. 8.
[6] December 29th, 1975.
[7] S. 2(1).
[8] S. 2(2). So may another court which finds itself faced with an equal pay question s. 2(3).
[9] S. 2(4).
[10] S. 2(5).
[11] Before the Industrial Relations Act 1971 this body was known as the Industrial Court.
[12] S. 3(1).

make such amendments as are needed to extend provisions applying to only one sex to include the other and to remove any resulting duplication without in any way establishing less favourable terms than those agreed.[1]   The Industrial Arbitration Tribunal has no power to widen the application of an agreement beyond the express category to which it applies.   Within that category it may extend a provision to the other sex; it cannot extend the provision outside the category.   Nor where there is a rate expressed to apply to one worker only in a category and there is no provision for the other sex can the agreement be extended to cover them.   The rate must however be raised at least to the level of the lowest men's rate in the agreement.[2]   It must be emphasised that these amendments relate not only to rates of pay: they also cover other terms and conditions of employment.   The powers relate not only to collective agreements but also to an employer's pay structure.   This is any arrangement which fixes common terms and conditions of employment for employees or a class of employee which is known or open to be known to the employees affected.[3]   Reference of such a structure may only be made by the employer himself or by the Secretary of State for Employment.   Provision is also made in the Act for reference to the Industrial Arbitration Tribunal of wages regulation orders[4] or agricultural wages orders.[5]

The Act applies to all workers of whatever age.[6]   It is not to be taken as altering the law relating to the employment of women[7] nor does it apply to any special treatment in respect of childbearing.[8] It does not apply to terms and conditions relating to retirement,[9] marriage or death.[10]

(3) **Right to Wages.**—It need not be emphasised that the courts will always adhere to the express agreement between the employer and workman.   The rules to be discussed are those that arise when the express agreement is not clear upon a particular point.   There is no basic right to be paid for work which will be automatically incorporated into any contract.[11]   An agreement which gives the employer the right to fix remuneration has been interpreted as giving no right to *any sum* if the employer decides to pay nothing.[12] It seems, however, that these cases were based on a rule that such

---

[1] S. 3(4).
[2] S. 3(4).
[3] S. 7(6).
[4] S. 4, made under the Wages Councils Act, 1959.
[5] S. 5, made under the Agricultural Wages Acts.
[6] S. 11(2).
[7] S. 6(1) (*a*), *e.g.* under the Factories Acts.
[8] S. 6(1)(*b*).
[9] Whether voluntary or not on the grounds of age, length of service or incapacity.
[10] S.6(1)(*b*).
[11] *Reeve* v. *Reeve* (1858), 1 F. & F. 280.
[12] *Taylor* v. *Brewer* (1813), 1 M. & S. 290; *Roberts* v. *Smith* (1859), 4 H. & N. 315.

discretions meant there was no contract at all,[1] and more significance must now be attached to the line of cases in which reference to remuneration[2] or the understanding that there would be remuneration[3] would at least support an action for *quantum meruit*.

The question of commission and bonuses is one which has been the subject of some litigation. In *Powell* v. *Braun*[4] where the employer had offered a bonus instead of a pay rise and this had been accepted by the employee who had received such a bonus until 1952 the Court of Appeal allowed an action for *quantum meruit*. The argument of the defendant, based on the type of case mentioned above, was rejected and the appellant was awarded a reasonable sum. The determination of the proper amount of commission payable depends upon the terms of the agreement but it appears that if the commission is stated to be based upon each year's profits then losses in a particular year mean that there can be no commission in that year, but the losses cannot be carried forward to the following year to defeat a claim to commission based upon that year's profits.[5] Where an advance of commission has been paid to the employee his liability to return such of the advance as proves not to have been earned at the termination of his contract of service depends upon the particular provisions of the contract of service. The general rule is that there must be repayment[6] but it is recognised that an individual contract may be so drafted as to prove an exception to this rule and to allow the employee to retain an advance which had not been earned.[7]

It follows from what has already been said about the effect of illness upon a contract of service that since the contract is not terminated the right to wages and commission and bonuses will continue until express termination. The case in which the question of illness has recently been discussed, *Orman* v. *Saville Sportswear, Ltd.*,[8] was, in fact, a claim for both wages and bonus and the amount claimed was recovered.

Perhaps the problem upon which there has relatively been most attention devoted in the courts is that of apportionment of wages over an incompleted part of a contract of service. The leading case is *Cutter* v. *Powell*[9] which clearly illustrates the injustice of the

---

[1] See the explanation of these cases by Vaughan Williams, L. J. in *Loftus* v. *Roberts* (1902), 18 T.L.R. 532.

[2] *Bryant* v. *Flight* (1839), 5 M. & W. 114.

[3] *Higgins* v. *Hopkins* (1848), 3 Exch. 163.

[4] [1954] 1 All E.R. 484; [1954] 1 W.L.R. 401.

[5] *Phillips* v. *Curling* (1847), 10 L.T. O.S. 245.

[6] *Rivoli Hats, Ltd.*, v. *Gooch*, [1953] 2 All E.R. 823; [1953] 1 W.L.R. 1190; *Bronester, Ltd.* v. *Priddle*, [1961] 3 All E.R. 471; [1961] 1 W.L.R. 1294.

[7] *Clayton Newberry, Ltd.* v. *Findlay*, [1953] 2 All E.R. 826; [1953] 1 W.L.R. 1194n.

[8] See *supra*, p. 114.

[9] (1795), 6 Term Rep. 320. Followed in *Sinclair* v. *Bowles* (1829), 9 B. & C. 92 and *Vigers* v. *Cook*, [1919] 2 K.B. 475. For an excellent treatment of this topic see Smith's Leading Cases, 7th Ed., Vol. 2, pp. 1–53.

rule arising. In that case the plaintiff's husband, a sailor, was promised thirty guineas if he acted as second mate on a voyage from Jamaica to Liverpool. Cutter died in the course of the voyage and his widow sued for a portion of the money in proportion to Cutter's service before death. She failed and the Court held that partial performance of an entire obligation did not give rise to any right to remuneration and so Cutter was not due any portion of the agreed sum. It is then of importance to the workman to establish that an agreement is divisible and not entire. Failing this it may be possible to argue that the defendant has received substantial performance of the contract[1] for if this is so he cannot refuse to pay merely because the work does not exactly fulfil that promised in the contract.[2] Similarly if it is the defendant who himself has prevented complete performance then the plaintiff will be able to recover for that proportion of the work that he has done on a *quantum meruit*.[3]

(4) **Payment on Redundancy.**[4]—The scheme for redundancy payments is laid down in great detail by the Redundancy Payments Act, 1965.[5] The aim is to secure for an employee a redundancy payment where he finds his present work, at which he has been employed for some time, is failing to provide continuous full employment, or his job is disappearing altogether. The scheme is closely allied to the Contracts of Employment Act provisions for adequate notice which were aimed at giving him a fair period of time to obtain other work.[6] It aims to provide a cushion of monetary compensation linked with the length of service he has had with his employer, to tide him over the social upset of losing his job. The method of doing this which has been chosen is by Act of Parliament covering all the possible variations in circumstance which the width and complexity of employment may throw up. The result is that the provisions of the Act, which implement the simple notion, are detailed and complicated. They may form part of a workers' charter in one sense but they cannot be regarded as a clear, simple understandable enactment of rights. The principal features must be considered.

Redundancy.—Redundancy is defined as being dismissed by an employer where that employer has ceased or intends to cease carrying on business for the purpose of which the employee was employed, or where the needs of that business for employees to carry out work of a particular kind, or in a particular place, have ceased or diminished or are expected to cease or diminish.[7] The application of this

---

[1] *Hoenig* v. *Isaacs*, [1952] 2 All E.R. 176.
[2] *H. Dakin & Co., Ltd.* v. *Lee*, [1916] 1 K.B. 566.
[3] *Planché* v. *Colburn* (1831), 5 C.P. 58.
[4] For a detailed study of the law and the wealth of reported Tribunal decisions, see Grunfeld, *The Law of Redundancy* (1971).
[5] 1965 *c.* 62. The appointed day on which the Act came into force was December 6th, 1965.
[6] See *supra*, pp. 72 *et seq.*
[7] Redundancy Payments Act, 1965, s. 1(1) and (2).

definition to differing facts has led to a large number of Tribunal decisions and appeals on points of law. Thus the significance of the definition of cessation as applying to temporary as well as permanent cessation has been considered.[1] A period of thirteen weeks' closure has been held to be temporary cessation.[2] The definition has also been held to apply to dismissal during the " running down " period.[3] Another area which has presented a difficult factual distinction is the application of the concept of place of work imposed by the provision that redundancy relates to work " in the place where the employee was so employed ". This requires an often difficult contractual and factual interpretation. Thus an electrician working in and around Liverpool was within the company's administrative north-west area. Work declined in Liverpool but was available in Barrow. It was held that Barrow did not fall within his place of work.[4] In a contrasting case the right to transfer between South Wales and Chard in Somerset was accepted as the proper interpretation of the contract in question which thus created a wide " place of work."[5]

Cessation is a fairly clear type of redundancy. Far greater difficulties arise where the basis is a surplus of workers. The recent concentration upon increased productivity, review of job structure by consultants, capital investment in advanced labour saving machines, have all added to the more traditional cause, decline in trade. The reports have considered numerous variations and have thrown up a number of basic problems.[6] An example is the introduction of a new system of doing the same work which is beyond the capabilities of the employee concerned. Such dismissal will usually be a redundancy[7] subject to the general consideration that the employee must keep up with normal developments in the skills of his job.[8] Reorganisation may lead to the dismissal of a man in an area not affected by diminution of work because one of the surplus men is moved and displaces another.[9] This sensibly has been brought within the definition.[10] Just as some of the cases seem to amplify the definition, so there are others which delineate the boundary beyond which a redundancy cannot be claimed. Again only examples can be given. The most obvious type of case is that

---

[1] S. 25(3).

[2] *Gemmell* v. *Darngavil Brickworks, Ltd.*, [1967] I.T.R. 20.

[3] As a result of the phrase " intends to cease "—*R. J. Hewitt (Wholesale Fruiterers), Ltd.* v. *Russell*, [1969] I.T.R. 260.

[4] *O'Brien, Pritchard and Browning* v. *Associated Fire Alarms*, [1968] I.T.R. 182.

[5] *Parry* v. *Holst*, [1968] I.T.R. 317.

[6] E.g. *Brown* v. *Dunlop Textiles, Ltd.*, [1967] I.T.R. 531; *Dutton* v. *C. H. Bailey, Ltd.*, [1968] I.T.R. 355.

[7] *Whiles* v. *H. Wesley, Ltd.*, [1966] I.T.R. 342; *Louden* v. *Crimpy Crisps, Ltd.*, [1966] I.T.R. 307.

[8] *North Riding Garages, Ltd.* v. *Butterwick*, [1967] 2 Q.B. 56.

[9] *W. Gimber & Sons, Ltd.* v. *Spurrett*, [1967] I.T.R. 308.

[10] E.g. *Essen* v. *Vanden-Plas (England), 1923, Ltd.*, [1966] I.T.R. 186.

concerning personal misconduct[1] or incompetence.[2] It might be thought that one of the conclusive tests of redundancy was the evidence whether the dismissed employee has been replaced. Although it is indeed strong evidence, it is not necessarily conclusive. Replacement will normally rebut redundancy,[3] but not necessarily so if other factors, such as the state of trade, indicate that at the time of dismissal there was a need for less staff that has since changed.[4]

Dismissal.—The Act also defines dismissal. It covers a situation where the contract of employment is terminated by the employer, with or without notice; where the contract is for a fixed term and that term expires and is not renewed under the same contract and where the employee terminates his contract without notice where he is entitled to do so, consequent upon his employer's conduct.[5] It is immaterial whether the dismissal is with or without notice as long as the dismissal is accepted.[6] Although dismissal is defined in section 3(1), attention must also be paid to section 22(1) which defines constructive dismissal. It covers the death, dissolution, liquidation or receivership of the employer. Dismissal does not occur where the employee has the provisions of his contract renewed or he is re-engaged under a new contract and where the terms as to capacity and place in which he is employed and as to other matters do not differ from the previous position. The renewal or new contract must take effect immediately on the ending of employment under the previous contract. Otherwise, if the renewal or re-engagement is in pursuance of an offer in writing made before the previous contract has expired there is no dismissal if the new employment takes effect immediately or after an interval of not more than four weeks. For the purposes of the computations, to allow for four- or five-day weeks, employment ending on Friday, Saturday or Sunday may be counted as ending on the Sunday night so that re-employment on the Monday is continuous and likewise the four-week period extends to the Monday. These rules on dismissal have also attracted their fair share of reported case law. One of the most important points that has arisen concerns prior warning of redundancy. In the leading case the firm put the worker who was to be redundant in touch with another employer. He started there at the end of his notice. The actions of the firm were said to be advance notice of redundancy, not of dismissal. To qualify as the latter, a date of dismissal must be

---

[1] *Ibid.*

[2] *Hindle* v. *Percival Boats, Ltd.,* [1969] 1 W.L.R. 174; [1969] I.T.R. 86.

[3] *White* v. *Chapman,* [1967] I.T.R. 320; *Kirkby* v. *Fred Peck, Ltd.,* [1970] I.T.R. 229.

[4] *Ford* v. *Westfield Autocar, Ltd.,* [1967] I.T.R. 404.

[5] *Ibid.,* s. 3. This section does not include termination by the employee without notice where he is entitled to do so because of a lock-out by his employer.

[6] *Marriott* v. *Oxford and District Cooperative Society, Ltd.,* [1968] I.T.R. 121.

given or ascertainable.[1] An example of where it was has been considered.[2]

One situation which is likely to occur was anticipated by the Act. This is the problem facing the employee who is under notice of dismissal and finds he could start a new job before he has served out his notice. He is able to leave for the new job without destroying the dismissal provided that he gives his employer a written notice to terminate his contract at an earlier date.[3] This earlier date then becomes the relevant date for the purpose of redundancy payment.[4] The employer can himself serve a written counter-notice before that date.[5] This will bar a claim for redundancy payment but the right to a payment may still be granted by a Tribunal which has weighed the merits of the employee's desire to leave early and the employer's view that he must stay.[6] The Legislature's insistence that the notice of the employee should be in writing is a hardship, for it is the type of formality which a worker might easily overlook. But the need for writing has been strictly applied[7] although there is no need for a special form as long as the contract is clear.[8] Another difficulty is that the notice must be given during the obligatory (*i.e.* contractual or Contracts of Employment) period of notice. If longer notice is given, the obligatory period is counted from the date of termination so that a notice might be given *too early*. This is a paradox as well as a difficulty for the employee.[9]

An important feature of the law is the definition of dismissal as including a situation where the employer's action justified the employee leaving.[10] A clear case arises where the employer fails to fulfil his contractual obligations, by failing to pay wages for example.[11] No less clear but perhaps harder to establish, is a situation where the employer insists that the employee does things that he is not bound under his contract of employment to do. Transfer to a junior post is a good example of this.[12] Changes in major features of the employee's work would similarly justify self-

---

[1] *Morton Sundour Fabrics, Ltd.* v. *Shaw*, [1967] I.T.R. 84.

[2] *Hicks* v. *Humphrey*, [1967] I.T.R. 214.

[3] S. 4(1).

[4] S. 4(2).

[5] S. 4(3).

[6] S. 4(4).

[7] *Brown* v. *Singer Manufacturing, Ltd.*, [1967] I.T.R. 213.

[8] See *e.g. Hudson* v. *Fuller Shapcott*, [1970] I.T.R. 266.

[9] *Lobb* v. *Bright Son & Co. (Clerkenwell), Ltd.*, [1966] I.T.R. 566.

[10] S. 3(1) (c). It is interesting to note that this head of the definition of dismissal is not repeated in the unfair dismissal provisions of the Industrial Relations Act, 1971. See s. 23.

[11] *Broadhurst* v. *H. Buchan & Son*, [1969] I.T.R. 247.

[12] *Skillen* v. *Eastwoods Froy, Ltd.*, [1967] I.T.R. 112. For decisions on the other side of the line, see *e.g. Jones* v. *W. C. Youngman, Ltd.*, [1966] I.T.R. 463; *Atherton* v. *John Crankshaw Co., Ltd.*, [1970] I.T.R. 201.

dismissal. It would be not only as to status but would also apply to changes in hours[1] or place of work.[2]

Offer of New Employment.—The entitlement to redundancy pay for a dismissal is destroyed if before the relevant date the employee has refused an offer of re-engagement or renewal to take effect before that date. The terms, including capacity and place of employment, must not differ.[3] A similar provision applies where an offer is made in writing before the relevant date of re-engagement and renewal on terms which differ but which nonetheless constitute suitable employment in relation to the employee.[4] Again the offer must take effect before the relevant date. It will be obvious that a provision of this type is bound to cover a lot of situations in which opinions as to suitability differ and indeed there have been very many reported cases. Those on section 2(3) which relate to the offer of the same terms have given rise to no difficulties of principle.[5] The same cannot be said of section 2(4) and different terms of employment. It has been decided that the terms and conditions must be certain so that the employee can make a proper judgment.[6] He has no obligation to ferret out information.[7] The matter is to be looked at in the light of information to hand when the terms were offered. If the Tribunal is then satisfied as to suitability it must then determine whether the refusal was reasonable. Then the personal position of the employee becomes relevant.[8] In practice it is impossible to keep the two considerations separate. The obvious point of consideration is pay and there have been very many cases reported.[9] There are difficulties. The opportunity to work overtime makes a comparison of basic rates unreal. But overtime may not be certain.[10] The same problem applies to future prospects which might soon recoup and perhaps surpass an initial drop in earnings.[11] Similarly travelling expenses are a factor in the monetary comparison.[12] Apart from monetary considera-

---

[1] *Spelman* v. *George Garnham*, [1968] I.T.R. 370.

[2] *Strachen* v. *William Jones Clifton, Ltd.*, [1966] I.T.R. 552; *Mumford* v. *Boulton Paul (Steel Construction), Ltd.*, [1970] I.T.R. 222. But *contra* see *Stevens* v. *Stricker & Sons, Ltd.*, [1966] I.T.R. 456; *Stevenson* v. *Teesside Bridge & Engineering*, [1971] 1 All E.R. 296.

[3] S. 2(3).

[4] S. 2(4); Not necessarily personally—a notice on an appropriate board has been held to suffice. *McCreadie* v. *Thomson & MacIntyre (Patternmakers)*, [1971] 2 All E.R. 1135; [1971] 1 W.L.R. 1193.

[5] *E.g. Reilly* v. *South Mills (Rayon), Ltd.*, [1967] I.T.R. 161.

[6] *J. & J. Maybank, Ltd.* v. *Edwards*, [1970] I.T.R. 189.

[7] *Roberts* v. *Essoldo Circuit (Control), Ltd.*, [1967] I.T.R. 351.

[8] *Carron Co.* v. *Robertson*, [1967] I.T.R. 484.

[9] *E.g.* two early cases, *McNeil* v. *Vickers, Ltd.*, [1966] I.T.R. 180; and on the opposite side of the line, *Souter* v. *Henry Balfour & Co., Ltd.*, [1966] I.T.R. 383.

[10] *Ryan* v. *Liverpool Warehousing Co., Ltd.*, [1966] I.T.R. 69.

[11] *Farnell* v. *Howard & Bullough, Ltd.*, [1967] I.T.R. 11.

[12] *McIntosh* v. *British Rail*, [1968] I.T.R. 26.

tions, attention has been given to status[1] and health[2] and prospects.[3] A factor relating more to the reasonableness of the matter is that the use of Tribunals is intended to allow commonsense judgment to be applied to each individual set of contested facts. The price to be paid is some inconsistency.

Lay-off and Short-time.—Where an employee is laid off or kept on short-time for four or more consecutive weeks or for six or more weeks within a period of thirteen weeks, he is also entitled to lay a claim for a redundancy payment.[4] Lay-off occurs under the Act where an employee works under a contract on terms that his remuneration depends on his being provided with work of the type he is employed to do and because his employer has not found work for him he is entitled to no remuneration in any week.[5] The Tribunals have had to distinguish between lay-off which amounts to dismissal and gives rise to an immediate claim, and one which qualifies only under these rules.[6] Short-time occurs where diminution of work provided by the employer of the appropriate type means that the employee is entitled in a particular week to less than half a week's pay.[7] The method of calculating the week's pay is set out in the Second Schedule and is done by reference to the method set out in the Second Schedule to the Contracts of Employment Act, 1963,[8] which lays down the method of calculating minimum weekly remuneration. The right to a redundancy payment through lay-off or short-time only arises where the employee has given his employer written notice of his intention to claim such payment, called a notice of intention to claim, and before giving that notice has either (*a*) been laid off or on short-time for four or more consecutive weeks of which the last ended not more than four weeks prior to the service of the notice, or (*b*) been laid off or kept on short-time for a series of six or more weeks, of which not more than three were consecutive (otherwise head (*a*) would apply) within a period of thirteen weeks where the last week of the series ended not more than four weeks prior to the service of the notice.[9] In each example the last day of

---

[1] *Taylor* v. *Kent County Council,* [1969] 2 Q.B. 560; [1969] 2 All E.R. 1080.
[2] *Tyler* v. *Cleveland Bridge & Engineering Co., Ltd.,* [1966] I.T.R. 89.
[3] *James and Jones* v. *National Coal Board,* [1969] I.T.R. 70. *Freer* v. *Kayser Bondor, Ltd.,* [1967] I.T.R. 4; and contrast *Brown* v. *James Keiller & Co., Ltd.* [1966] I.T.R. 546.
[4] Redundancy Payments Act, 1965, s. 6(1).
[5] *Sneddon* v. *Ivorycrete (Builders), Ltd.,* [1966] I.T.R. 538; *Jones* v. *Harry Sherman, Ltd.,* [1969] I.T.R. 63.
[6] *Ibid.,* s. 5(1). Week here means a week ending on Saturday except where renumeration is calculated as ending on another day when the week runs to that day instead.
[7] *Ibid.,* s. 5(2).
[8] See above at p. 77.
[9] Redundancy Payments Act, 1965, s. 6(1). The weeks in either series may be mixed lay-off and short-time: s. 7(2). Weeks of strike or lock-out are ignored: s. 7(3).

the period of weeks counted is known as the relevant date.[1] Where the employee gives his notice of intention to claim he must also, to qualify for a redundancy payment, give one week's notice[2] terminating his contract of employment within the time limit laid down.[3] He will not qualify under these rules even if he is dismissed by his employer—the rules governing dismissal will then apply.[4] So that the procedure outlined above is not applied at the end of a period of short-time or lay-off, it is provided that if on the date of service of intention the reasonable expectation is that within four weeks at the most the employee will enter on a period of thirteen consecutive weeks without lay-off or short-time then the right to a redundancy payment fails.[5] This will be raised by the employer giving within seven days of receiving the notice a written counter-notice.[6]

Where there is notice followed by counter-notice and during the next four weeks following the notice there is a lay-off or short-time then the counter-notice fails. Where the counter-notice does not fail in this way or is not withdrawn the entitlement to a redundancy payment will depend on a decision of the tribunal.[7]

Requisite Period.—The Act requires an employee to have been continuously employed for 104 weeks before the dismissal or notice of intention to claim. Weeks before the employee is eighteen do not count.[8] The method of computation of this period is that laid down in Schedule 1 to the Contracts of Employment Act, 1963. The onus of disproving continuity is on the employer.[9] Continuity covers a succession of different contracts with the same employer.[10] The only additional rule is that where there is renewal of employment or re-engagement with up to four weeks interregnum this period will count. Where a change occurs in the ownership of a business or part of a business by which a person is employed and the old owner immediately before terminates the employment, with or without notice, but the new owner renews the engagement or re-engages the employee then the employment is continuous. A business is defined as including a trade or profession and any activity carried on by a body of persons whether corporate or incorporate.[11] Transfer involves many factors, because of the numerous component parts of the concept of business, buildings, name, stock, and so forth; but evidence of the transfer of good will is strong but not conclusive evidence of such a transfer.[12] Special situations have been considered,

---

[1] *Ibid.*, s. 6(2).   [2] Or more if his contract demands it.

[3] The time limit is three weeks after the notice unless there is a counter notice (see below) when it is three weeks after it is withdrawn, where there is withdrawal, or three weeks after the tribunal decision where there is no withdrawal, s. 7(5).   [4] *Ibid.*, s. 6(3).   [5] *Ibid.*, s. 6(4).   [6] *Ibid.*, s. 6(5).

[7] *Ibid.*, s. 7.   For the tribunal, see below p. 428.   [8] *Ibid.*, s. 8(1).

[9] S. 9(2).   For discussion of Schedule 1 to the Contracts of Employment Act, 1963, see below at p. 73.

[10] *Re Mack Trucks (Britain)*, [1967] 1 W.L.R. 780; [1967] 1 All E.R. 977.

[11] S. 25(1).

[12] *Kenmir* v. *Frizzell*, [1968] 1 W.L.R. 329; [1968] 1 All E.R. 414; [1968] I.T.R. 159.

e.g. farming. Here special customs apply, there usually being a separate transfer of the land and the stock. There is no real good will. Nevertheless after some hesitation the law now recognises the normal farm sale, that is to say land and buildings, as a transfer.[1] Cases which have fallen outside the scope of transfer of business have included a franchise operation,[2] physical assets only,[3] share capital.[4] Where the employee refuses the offer of renewal or re-engagement his right to a redundancy payment will lapse under the rule in section 2 as if the offer had been made by the previous owner.[5]

Weeks where an employee is outside Great Britain and where no contribution is paid do not count unless under the National Insurance rules a contribution should have been paid.[6]

Exceptions.—The Act does not apply to persons who at the time of redundancy are over 65 for men and 60 for women.[7]

The Act does not apply to registered dock workers under the Dock Workers (Regulations of Employment) Act, 1946, unless it is employment which is wholly or mainly not dock work as defined in the Scheme. It does not apply to the master or members of the crew of a fishing vessel if remuneration is solely by a share of the profits. It does not apply to an employee who is the spouse of the employer. Nor does it apply to various public offices,[8] employment in the civil service or in a list of health service employees set out in the Third Schedule. The Act does not apply to those employed by a foreign government. There is ministerial power to add to or alter these exceptions.[9]

A redundancy payment is not an entitlement under the Act where the employee is abroad on the date such entitlement should arise, known as the relevant date, unless he ordinarily worked in Great Britain.[10] On the other hand an entitlement will arise where an employee normally employed outside Britain happens to be in Great Britain in accordance with his employer's instructions on the relevant date.[11]

The Act does apply to domestic servants but the list of excepted relatives is longer than that for a general employment as it also includes father, mother, grandfather, grandmother, stepfather, son, daughter, grandson, granddaughter, stepson, stepdaughter, brother,

---

[1] *Lloyd* v. *Brassey*, [1969] 2 Q.B. 98.

[2] *E.g.* petrol filling station: *Bumstead* v. *John L. Cerns, Ltd.*, [1967] I.T.R. 137.

[3] *Dallow Industrial Properties, Ltd.*, v. *Else*, [1967] 2 Q.B. 449; [1967] 2 All E.R. 30.

[4] *Cameron* v. *Hector Finlayson & Co., Ltd.* [1967] I.T.R. 110.

[5] Redundancy Payments Act, 1965, s. 13. These provisions apply to retrospective situations. [6] *Ibid.*, s. 17.

[7] *Ibid.*, s. 2(1). The section says "immediately" before. That word cannot be given logical meaning.

[8] As defined in s. 7 of Superannuation (Amendment) Act, 1965.

[9] *Ibid.*, s. 16.

[10] *Ibid.*, s. 17(1). This rule does not apply to mariners, that is to say a master, seaman or apprentice on a British ship who is ordinarily resident in Great Britain, s. 20. [11] For 'relevant date' see p. 134 n. 2 *infra.*

sister, half-brother or half-sister. This applies only to domestic service in a private household.

Computation of Redundancy Payment.—The amount of the redundancy payment is to be calculated according to the provision of the First Schedule.[1] The basis of calculation is the period of continuous employment which stretches back from the relevant date. The term " relevant date " is one of art and is established by reference to the appropriate of three possible subsections.[2] For dismissal it is: (a) where dismissal is by notice—the date on which the notice expires; (b) where termination is without notice and by either side—the date termination takes effect; (c) where the contract is for a fixed term— the date of expiry of that term.[3] For anticipating notice by the employee under the Act it is the date at the end of the employee's notice.[4] Finally where there is an appropriate period of lay-off or short-time, under the first head of four or more consecutive weeks —at the end of that period[5], and under the second head of six or more weeks within a period of thirteen—the end of the sixth or last week.[6]

The period of continuous employment is to be calculated according to the complex rules laid down in Schedule 1 of the Contracts of Employment Act, 1963.[7] In addition to these rules no weeks before an employee was 18 years old will count and a short period between renewal of employment or re-engagement will count.[8]

The first and fundamental qualification is that the employee must have been continuously employed for a "requisite period" of 104 weeks prior to the relevant date. Weeks before the employee is 18 years old, it has just been observed, do not count.[9] So the employee must have, counting back from the relevant date, at least two years continuous employment since he became eighteen. Having established this basic right to a redundancy payment it is necessary to calculate how much. Again reckoning backwards from the relevant date the following additions are to be made:

(a) For each year of continuous employment in which the employee was for every week over 41 years old—one and a half week's pay.

(b) For each year not covered by this in which the employee was in every week over 22 years old—one week's pay.

(c) For any other year—a half week's pay.[10]

---

[1] Redundancy Payments Act, 1965, s. 1(1).

[2] *Ibid.*, s. 3(4), s. 4(2) or s. 6(2). For the head under which a particular redundancy falls see the discussion above.

[3] *Ibid.*, s. 3(4).

[4] *Ibid.*, s. 4(2). Anticipating expiring notice is where the employee during notice by the employer gives written notice to the employer to terminate on an earlier date.

[5] *Ibid.*, s. 6(2)(a).   [6] *Ibid.*, s. 6(2)(b).

[7] As amended by this Act. For details of the Contracts of Employment Act, 1963, see pp. 73 *et seq.*

[8] *Ibid.*, s. 8(3) and s. 1(1); s. 1(2)(b) allow up to 4 weeks to count.

[9] *Ibid.*, s. 1(1) and s. 8(1).   [10] *Ibid.*, para. 2.

The maximum number of years which may be counted is twenty.[1] So the maximum sum for an elderly employee who falls redundant with twenty or more years continuous employment after he was forty-one is 30 weeks' wages.

It will be recalled that a man who has attained 65 or a woman 60 before the relevant date is not entitled to a redundancy payment.[2] Where the relevant date falls in the last year of normal working life, i.e. after the man is 64, the woman 59, the payment will be calculated according to the normal rules but will then be reduced by the fraction $\frac{x}{12}$ where x is the number of months from the 64th or 59th birthday to the relevant date.[3] But otherwise he will retain a fraction of his redundancy payment equivalent to the fraction of the year between his 64th and 65th birthdays (59th and 60th for a woman, of course) which followed his becoming redundant—the relevant date. So if he is made redundant at the end of the third month he is entitled to $\frac{9}{12}$ of the payment, at the end of the ninth month, $\frac{3}{12}$ and so on.

To complete the computation it is necessary to determine the financial sum to be used as the weekly basis. It is the minimum remuneration to which he would be entitled in the week immediately preceding the relevant date.[4] Naturally as the employee may have been on short-time, or laid off in this week, for example, the sum in question is a purely nominal one bearing no relation to wages actually paid. It is to be calculated according to the rules laid down in Schedule 2 to the Contracts of Employment Act, 1963. These rules are not fully appropriate so, as we shall see in a moment, certain suppositions are to be made. Schedule 2 has been discussed fully elsewhere.[5] It is merely necessary to say by way of summary that there are basically three types of employment. Those involving a normal working week with normal hours which determine the wage paid. Normal hours here mean those for which no overtime pay is available. In the vast majority of cases it will be the advertised 40, 42, or 44 hour week. Secondly there are those who work a normal week but whose wages are not calculated according to hours—the piece-rate worker. Here the average hourly rate is calculated from the four weeks ending with the last complete week before notice. Finally if there is no normal working week the weekly rate is to be calculated by reference to the period of twelve weeks ending with the last complete week before notice was given. There are various points where the rules are not applicable and the Redundancy Payments Act gets round these by saying that, whether it is so or not, the following, where appropriate, will be presumed: the contract is terminable by notice and has been so terminated; the employee was ready and willing to work during the week in question but no

---

[1] *Ibid.*, para. 3.
[2] *Ibid.*, s. 2(1). The section says " immediately " before. This word cannot be given a logical meaning.
[3] *Ibid.*, para. 4.
[4] *Ibid.*, Schedule 2, para. 5(1).   [5] See above, pp. 77 *et seq.*

work was provided; the employee was willing to do work of a reasonable nature and amount to earn the average piece-rate figure; the employee was not absent from work without leave of his employer. Finally the rules apply even if the employee would be excepted under the Contracts of Employment Act.[1]

There is a general rule that a redundancy payment cannot be computed on a weekly basic wage of more than £40.[2]

Special Provisions.—It will already have been appreciated that the legislation is an attempt to cover every type of employment and every combination of circumstances. This leads inevitably to complexity and wealth of detail and some of the special rules are better discussed separately from the main scheme.

Provision is made for the situation where an employee who is under notice by his employer or who has himself given notice under the rules relating to lay-off and short-time[3] takes part in a strike. It may well be that the action gives the employer the right to terminate the contract of employment immediately. If the employer exercises that right then the employee falls into one of the categories of those excluded from the right to a redundancy payment.[4] The Act provides that he will not in these circumstances be excluded.[5] Where under similar circumstances, the employee is dismissed forthwith by his employer[6] whilst under notice he may ask the tribunal[7] to look at his case and the tribunal may allow him the whole or part of his redundancy payment as it thinks fit.

The Minister has power to exempt from the redundancy scheme employees who are covered by an agreement with their employers either individually or through bargains by associations and unions, which provides for payments on the termination of their employment.[8] Their provision prevents unnecessary duplication where there is in existence a satisfactory agreed redundancy scheme. The Minister must not exempt unless the parties are willing to allow disputes as to right of payment and amount of payment arising out of the scheme to be submitted to the tribunal. There is a similar Ministerial power to exclude the right to a redundancy payment where the employee has a right or claim to a periodical payment or lump sum by way of pension, gratuity or superannuation allowance from his employer.[9] This applies to situations where such payments are determined by reference to his employment and begins to be paid when he leaves employment.[10] Where there is a statutory

---

[1] Redundancy Payments Act, 1965, Schedule 1, para. 5(2).

[2] *Ibid.*, para. 3, the sum may be varied upwards by Ministerial Order. Since the maximum number of years that can count is 20, the most that can be awarded is £1,200 (20 × 1½ × £40) as compared with £4,160 under the unfair dismissal rule.

[3] *Ibid.*, s. 6.

[4] *Ibid.*, s. 2(2).   [5] *Ibid.*, s. 10(1).

[6] The grounds are set out in s. 2(2).

[7] *Ibid.*, s. 10(3).   [8] *Ibid.*, s. 11.   [9] *Ibid.*, s. 14(1).

[10] Regulations may lay down a permitted lapse of time before payment begins.

entitlement to a lump sum on termination of employment this need not exclude the employee from right to a redundancy payment. Here the position may be regulated by Ministerial regulations under which there may be exclusion, or the redundancy payment may be set off against the statutory right.[1]

Strikes during Notice.—It may happen that a strike takes place whilst an employee is under notice given by his employer. This position is dealt with in s. 40. If, after the notice, which is referred to as notice of termination, the employee begins to take part in a strike the employer can serve on him a notice of extension. This notice asks the employee to extend his contract of employment beyond the expiry date by a number of days equal to the number of working days lost by the strike. The notice must make it clear that if he complies with the request or satisfies the employer that he cannot comply because of sickness or injury or because it would not be reasonable for him to do so his claim for a redundancy payment will not be contested by the employer.[2] The notice of extension will be satisfied, not only by the employee working on the extra days but also by his attending at his place of employment, ready and willing to work and he need not have given written assent to the extension. If he does not comply with the notice he loses his right to a redundancy payment unless the employer chooses to pay nonetheless.

Tribunal.—Any questions arising out of the rules that have been discussed— those set out in Part I of the Act[3]—as to the right of an employee to a redundancy payment or as to the amount must be referred to a tribunal.[4] The tribunal is that set up under s. 12 of the Industrial Training Act, 1964.[5] The constitution of the tribunal is governed by regulations made under that Act. Its procedure is also governed by regulation and the Act sets out various topics upon which regulations may in particular be made.[6] There are three substantive points affecting the tribunal laid down in the Act. The first two shift the burden of proof and provide that where there is a reference a person's employment is presumed to be continuous unless the contrary is proved and a dismissal is presumed to be by reason of redundancy unless the contrary is proved.[7] Finally where the reference covers lay-off or short-time[8] the matters referable to the tribunal may include any question whether an employee is entitled to a redundancy payment where he is not dismissed but terminated his contract himself under the terms of the Act.[9]

---

[1] Redundancy Payments Act, 1965, s. 14(2) and s. 47(1).

[2] The wording is vague and wide. A good example of the type of case which might fall under that head would be where the employee has made all the arrangements to emigrate. The matter is one for the tribunal which may award full or partial payment.

[3] *Ibid.*, ss. 1 to 25.   [4] *Ibid.*, s. 9.
[5] *Ibid.*, s. 56(1).   [6] *Ibid.*, s. 46(2).
[7] *Ibid.*, s. 9(2).   [8] *Ibid.*, s. 9(3).
[9] That is under s. 6(3).

Redundancy Fund.—The liability to pay a redundancy payment is placed by the Act upon the employer.[1] There are rules of limitation which provide that entitlement will lapse unless the payment has been made or agreed, or a claim has been made to the employer in writing or the matter has been referred to the tribunal within the six months following the relevant date.[2] In addition the Act establishes a Redundancy Fund under the control of the Secretary of State.[3] The Fund is to be built up by the levying upon employers of a Redundancy Fund contribution whenever they are liable to pay an employer's national insurance contribution for any person over 18.[4] The weekly sum levied is regulated by the Secretary of State.[5] Rebates are paid from the fund to an employer in three circumstances:[6] where he has made a redundancy payment to an employee under the terms of the Act;[7] where he has made a payment under one of the private schemes which has been accepted by the Secretary of State as giving exemption from the statutory scheme[8] and where he has made a terminal payment to an employee by virtue of an award of the Industrial Court.[9] In the last two instances there will be no rebate unless the right to the payment made was based upon employment of the requisite period—that is to say 104 weeks. The amount of the rebates is calculated according to Schedule 5 which was amended to reduce the amount from about 70% to 50% by the Redundancy Rebates Act, 1969. The rules again are detailed but the basis of the calculation is that the employer is entitled to three-quarters of a week's pay for each year of employment which counted towards the redundancy payment where the employee was 41 or over, one-half of a week's pay for each year where he was 22 or over and one-quarter of a week's pay for other years.[10] It will be appreciated that these sums are less than the redundancy payment figures which are $1\frac{1}{2}$, 1 and $\frac{1}{2}$ respectively. Where the full redundancy payment is not made under the rules the rebate will be similarly scaled down.[11]

As well as the rebate the Secretary of State is also empowered to pay out of the Redundancy Fund a redundancy payment direct to an employee who has taken all reasonable steps, other than legal action, to recover payment from his employer and has failed to have his rights established fully, or has found that his employer is insolvent.[12] Thus the Fund becomes an insurance that employees will be paid even where they fail to get satisfaction from their employer.

---

[1] Redundancy Payments Act, 1965, s. 1(1).   [2] *Ibid.*, s. 21.
[3] *Ibid.*, s. 26.   [4] *Ibid.*, s. 27(1).
[5] *Ibid.*, s. 27(2).   It started at fivepence for a man and twopence for a woman.
[6] *Ibid.*, s. 30.
[7] This is a normal situation under s. 1(1).
[8] See s. 11.   There is a similar provision relating to payments to other excluded employees, see s. 31(1) and (2).
[9] See s. 12(2).   [10] Para. 2.
[11] *E.g.* by a tribunal or where the employee is in his 64th year, paras. 3 and 4.
[12] *Ibid.*, s. 32.

Disputes arising from questions relating to payments out of the Redundancy Fund might be referred to the tribunal.[1]

2. STATUTORY REGULATION OF WAGES[2]

Legislation concerned with the fixing of remuneration is not new in our law. But in modern, as opposed to medieval, times any effort by the State to determine a " just " wage in a comprehensive sense has been resisted as much as has any attempt to impose a " just " price for commodities. The characteristic of our own times so far as the wage structure of the country is concerned is the growth of collective bargaining between capital and labour and the growth of legislation to implement such bargaining where, for example, trades unionism is weak and there is a consequential disparity of power between the parties. Such wage regulating legislation is of two kinds. It is either general or particular according to whether it is aimed at the protection of classes of workers irrespective of the industry in which they are engaged, or whether it is aimed at protecting wage earners in a particular industry. Thus in this section, we shall discuss legislation operating generally upon prescribed classes of workers and also that which is restricted in scope to workers following particular vocations. The Wages Councils Act, 1959, is an excellent example of the former, whilst the provisions of the Acts relating to the payment of wages to workers in mining is an example of State intervention in a particular industry.[3]

(1) Wages Councils.—The Trade Boards Act, 1909, was the first of a series of Acts designed to deal with so-called sweated industries by creating machinery for the regulation of wages. The original Act applied to four industries[4] but the list has been constantly increased during the intervening years.[5] Consolidation of the earlier legislation took place with the Wages Councils Act, 1945. Trade Boards were converted into wages councils and the new scheme was conceived in wider principles than the earlier Acts. Councils could now fix guaranteed weekly wages and periods of holidays with pay.[6] This Act was later amended by the Wages Councils Act, 1948, which brought into the scheme a substantial part of those employed in road haulage, and the Terms and Condi-

---

[1] Redundancy Payments Act, 1965, s. 34.

[2] For the law as to particulars of piece work and wages in factories, etc., see Chapter VII, *infra*, p. 309.

[3] Prior to 1959 catering wages were similarly dealt with by the Catering Wages Act, 1943, but they are now assimilated into the general structure of Wages Councils.

[4] Certain aspects of tailoring, box-making, lace-making and chain-making.

[5] It is estimated that in 1961 three and a half million workers were covered by Councils: Industrial Relations Handbook, p. 155. There are at present just over 50 Wages Councils.

[6] S. 10.

tions of Employment Act, 1959, which integrated those employed in the catering industry.   Further consolidation took place with the Wages Councils Act, 1959, and it is in this statute that the current law is to be found. It has been slightly amended by the Industrial Relations Act, 1971.[1]

Power to establish wages councils is vested by the Act[2] in the Secretary of State for Employment.   The power to make an order may be exercised after initiative that may arise in three ways.   The Secretary of State himself may act on his own initiative because no adequate machinery exists for the effective regulation of wages amongst the workers described.[3]   He may act following the application of a joint industrial council or other similar body representing workers and employers, or of any organisation of workers and employers which claims that it habitually takes part in the settlement of remuneration and conditions of employment.[4]   He may, on receiving such application, if satisfied that there are sufficient grounds submit the application to a commission of inquiry.   If the commission of inquiry recommends the setting up of a wages council then the Secretary of State, if he thinks fit, may make an order accordingly.   The third initiative arises where the Secretary of State refers a case to the Commission of Industrial Relations himself on the ground that he feels that no adequate machinery exists or that existing machinery is likely to break down or cease to be adequate in the future so that a reasonable standard of remuneration will not be maintained.[5]   It will be noted that reference under this head is wider in that it applies also to a state of affairs that may exist in the future.

The Commission of Industrial Relations under the Act is not restricted in its deliberations to the immediate reference submitted by the Secretary of State.   It may consider any other question relevant to that reference, and it may, in particular, consider whether there are any other workers allied with those forming the subject of its immediate reference, whose position ought to be considered.   The Commission may either make what is known as a " wages council recommendation " for the establishment of such a council or report that existing machinery is adequate or inadequate.   In the latter case it may make suggestions for the improvement of the existing machinery.[6]

The Secretary of State may not make a wages council order without publishing a notice of his intention so to do, specifying a place where draft copies of the order may be obtained and the time, being not less than forty days, within which objections may be made.   Objections must be in writing and must state not only the grounds of objection but also the variations in the order which are asked for.   If there are no objections, or if, after considering objec-

---

[1] Schedule 3, para. 40, Scheds. 8 (amendments) and 9 (repeals).
[2] Wages Councils Act, 1959, s. 1(1).   [3] *Ibid.*, s. 1(2)(*a*).
[4] *Ibid.*, 1959, s. 1(2)(*b*) and s. 2.   [5] *Ibid.*, 1959, s. 1(2)(*c*).   [6] *Ibid.*, s. 3.

tions, the Secretary of State is of opinion that they have already been considered by the Commission itself and dealt with expressly in the report of the Commission or will be met by modifications he proposes to make, or are frivolous, he may make the order. Failing this he may substantially amend the order giving to the amended order the notice and period for the receipt of objections required in the case of the original order or he may refer the draft order to a commission of inquiry. When the commission has reported he may promulgate the draft order or make an order with such modifications as he thinks fit.[1] Where a commission of inquiry embodies two or more wages councils recommendations in the same report it may recommend the establishment of a central co-ordinating committee in relation to all or to any of the councils to which the recommendations relate.[2] A wages council order will come into effect on the date it is first published or on such later date as may be specified by the order.[3]

The Secretary of State may, subject to certain provisions, abolish or vary the field of operation of a wages council, again after due notice and the consideration of objections,[4] but an order which abolishes or varies the field of operation of one or more wages councils may include provision for the establishment of one or more wages councils operating in relation to all or any of the workers in relation to whom the first mentioned council or councils would have operated, but for the order, and such other workers if any as may be specified by the order.[5] If there is a central co-ordinating committee established the Secretary of State will not make an order for abolition or variation without consulting that body and where the order abolishes a wages council and directs that another wages council already in existence shall operate, but does not otherwise affect the field of operation of any wages council the provision of section five of the Act does not apply, but the Secretary of State must consult the wages councils concerned.[6]

Applications for the abolition of a wages council may be made to the Secretary of State either by a joint industrial council, conciliation board or other similar body which represent substantial proportions of the workers or employers concerned, or jointly by organisations of workers and organisations of employers which represent substantial proportions of the workers and employers concerned on the ground that the bodies making the applications jointly provide machinery adequate for the effective regulation of wages.[7] Where such an application is made the Secretary of State must refer the matter to

---

[1] Wages Councils Act, 1959, Sched. I.
[2] *Ibid.*, s. 7.
[3] *Ibid.*, Sched. I.
[4] *Ibid.*, s. 4.
[5] *Ibid.*, s. 4.
[6] *Ibid.*, Sched. I.
[7] *Ibid.*, s. 5. Unilateral application was added by the Industrial Relations Act, 1971.

the Commission on Industrial Relations[1] and he may do so where he is considering abolition under his powers contained in s.4. The Commission may report recommending abolition or a narrowing of the field of operations or, where the inquiry is as to variation it may make recommendations concerning this.[2]

The wages councils envisaged by the Act are constituted under the Act as having not more than three independent persons from whom will be appointed the chairman and deputy chairman. The representatives of employers and workers must be equal in number and will be chosen after such consultation as is considered necessary with representative organisations of employers and employed who are not concerned with the matters to be investigated by the Commission.[3]

The wages council, when appointed, will consider such matters as are referred to it by the Secretary of State or any government department with reference to the industrial conditions prevailing amongst the workers and employers in relation to whom the council operates. It reports to the Secretary of State or department, or it may, on its own motion, make recommendations to either the Secretary of State or a department, which recommendations must forthwith be taken into consideration.[4]

A central co-ordinating committee may be established in relation to two or more wages councils and a power exists in the Secretary of State to abolish or vary the field of operation of a central co-ordinating committee. This device is novel. In the case of the original trade boards, a board itself might set up district trade committees[5] for the purpose of dealing with local conditions. The district board might exercise the powers and functions of the trade board excepting those which related to the fixing of general minimum time and piece rates, guaranteed time rates, piece work basic time rates, and overtime rates. Under the Wages Councils Act, 1959, however, the machinery of co-ordination works, as it were, from the base upwards, and in the creation of a co-ordinating committee the effort is made to secure a general equality of condition between wages councils concerned with workers amongst whom some identity of need is to be found. A wages council may also request the Secretary of State to set up an advisory committee so that the council may refer matters to it to obtain reports and recommendations.[6]

A wages council has power to submit to the Secretary of State proposals known as wages regulation proposals, for fixing wages to be paid to the workers either generally or for any particular work, and

---

[1] Substituted for an *ad hoc* Commission by the Industrial Relations Act, 1971, Sched. 3, para. 20.
[2] Wages Councils Act, 1959, s. 6.
[3] *Ibid.*, Sched. II.
[4] *Ibid.*, s. 10.
[5] Trade Boards Act, 1909, s. 12 (1).
[6] Wages Councils Act, 1959, s. 2 and Sched. III.

for requiring any such workers to be allowed holidays by their employers. Proposals for allowing holidays to a worker must not be made unless both the working and holiday rates of remuneration have been fixed, and any proposal must provide for the length of the holidays to be related to the period during which such worker has been employed or engaged to be employed by the employer who is to grant the holidays. The proposals may make provision for the times at, or periods within, which the holidays are to be taken and those relating to holiday remuneration may contain provisions as to the times at which and the conditions subject to which the remuneration shall accrue and become payable and for securing that any remuneration which may have accrued to the worker will, in the event of his ceasing to be employed before the date of the holiday, nevertheless become payable by the employer.[1] There are the usual rules concerning the publication of proposals, the making of representations and similar matters.[2]

The term " worker " is defined[3] as one who has entered into or works under a contract with an employer, whether the work be manual or clerical, whether the contract be express or implied, oral or in writing. The contract may be a contract of service, or of apprenticeship or a contract personally to execute any work or labour, but the definition does not include one who is employed casually and otherwise than for the employer's business.

The definition was discussed in *Westall Richardson, Ltd.* v. *Roulson*[4] where the defendant was engaged in the cutlery industry upon terms that he paid a rent for the room he occupied in another's factory, employed his own assistants and determined his own and their conditions of employment. The factory owner paid for his work on terms mutually agreed. He claimed holidays and holiday pay from the owners of the factory by virtue of s. 10 of the 1945 Act. The court held he could not succeed on the grounds that the relationship between the company and the defendant was outside the provisions of the Act.

> " In the case of the defendant in my judgment while there may be (and indeed I think there is) some element of service or servitude in his position, there is a far greater element of independence and freedom. In the case of other out-workers, the balance may incline the other way."[5]

On the receipt, by the Secretary of State, of any wage regulation proposals, he will, unless he refers them back for consideration, make an order, known as a wages regulation order, giving effect to the proposals. Where they are referred back, the council will re-

---

[1] *Ibid.*, s.11 (1), (2).
[2] *Ibid.*, s. 11 (3).
[3] *Ibid.*, s. 24.
[4] [1954] 2 All E.R. 448.
[5] *Ibid.*, at p. 452 *per* VAISEY, J. The use of the word "servitude" is open to some criticism ; see *ante*, p. 38.

consider the proposals and re-submit them to the Secretary of State
with or without amendment. Where the order has been made the
Secretary of State must notify the wages council, but no order can
have effect so as to prejudice any rights to remuneration or holidays
conferred by any other Act of Parliament. Any remuneration,
including holiday remuneration, fixed as the result of an order becomes the statutory minimum remuneration. The legal result is that
if any worker has contracted for a remuneration less than the statutory minimum his contract will have effect as though the statutory
minimum remuneration were imported into the contract in place of
the lesser remuneration agreed upon by the parties. Failure to pay
the statutory minimum remuneration or failure to pay holiday
remuneration will constitute an offence under the Act.[1] A wages
council may authorise remuneration to be paid at less than the
statutory minimum rate to persons who, as a result of infirmity or
incapacity, cannot earn such rates.[2]

The remuneration laid down by an order represents the amount
to be received in cash by the worker excepting only that deductions
may lawfully be made for income tax, unemployment or health
insurance or under other legislation requiring or authorising deductions to be made, as for example under the National Insurance
or the National Insurance (Industrial Injuries) Acts 1965. Similarly,
deductions permitted by the Truck Acts or as the result of the written
request of the worker for the purposes of superannuation, thrift or
similar schemes may be made.[3] If the worker is employed only
partly on work subject to statutory minimum remuneration he is
entitled to that proportion of the minimum wages as the time spent
on such work bears to the employment.[4]

It is clear that any agreement whereby a worker who is an
apprentice or learner protected by a wages regulation order undertook to pay his master a premium might well evade the entire
purpose of the order. It is therefore unlawful for an employer to
receive, directly or indirectly, from the apprentice or learner or his
agent any payment by way of premium. This prohibition, however,
does not apply to a payment duly made under the terms of an
instrument of apprenticeship executed not later than four weeks
after the commencement of the apprenticeship or to any payment
made at any time by an instrument of apprenticeship approved by
a wages council.[5]

Where the immediate employer of any worker is himself in the
employment of some other person the two employers are, as respects
wages regulation orders, deemed to be joint employers.

---

[1] Wages Councils Act, 1959, s. 12.
[2] *Ibid.*, s. 13.
[3] *Ibid.*, s. 14.
[4] *Ibid.*, s. 15.
[5] Wages Councils Act, 1959, s. 16. For the duties of keeping records and
posting notices see *ibid.*, s. 17.

The application of the rates set out in the orders of wages councils is checked by a wages inspectorate set up and controlled by the Secretary of State for Employment. An annual report of inspections is made to each wages council. This is a system which employers appreciate since it prevents them from suffering unfair competition. This point is in addition to the protection given to the underpaid worker. The machinery of the Terms and Conditions of Employment Act, 1959[1] has been extended to cover claims in respect of wages and conditions fixed by a wages regulation order.[2] Previously conditions governed by a wages order had been excluded.

(2) Holidays With Pay.—Another piece of legislation which is of a more general application is that embodied in the Holidays with Pay Act, 1938, the substantial provisions of which are also to be found in the Wages Councils Act, 1959.[3] Under the terms of the former Act any wage regulating authority may direct that workers for whom a statutory remuneration or minimum rate of wages is being, or has been, fixed shall be allowed such holidays as may be directed. A direction will provide for the duration of any holiday which the employer is required to allow but the duration of the holiday must be related to the duration of the period of the worker's employment or engagement by the employer. The direction may make provision as to the times at which or the periods within which, and the circumstances in which, any such holiday shall be allowed, but the holidays allowed will, unless the direction otherwise provides, be in addition to any holidays or half holidays to which the worker may be entitled under any other enactment.[4]

If an authority directs that holidays are to be allowed, it must make provision for securing that the workers shall receive pay in respect of the holiday period. Such holiday remuneration will accrue and become payable at such times and subject to such conditions as may be directed and any holiday remuneration which shall have accrued to a worker will become payable to him on his ceasing to be employed before he becomes entitled to a holiday.[5]

(3) Wages in the Mining Industry.—If a mine worker's wages depend on the amount of mineral obtained he must be paid on the actual amount of mineral he gets and the mineral must be weighed as near to the pit mouth as is practicable. The employer may, nevertheless, agree with the employees that deductions may be made for substances other than that which the worker is employed to mine, or for baskets or tubs which are improperly filled.[6] The

---

[1] See *supra*, p. 139.
[2] Industrial Relations Act, 1971, s. 152 (2).
[3] *Passim. Ibid.*, s. 15.
[4] Wages Councils Act, 1959, s. 1.
[5] Holidays with Pay Act, 1938, s. 2.
[6] Coal Mines Regulation Act, 1887, s. 12 (1) as amended. Mines and Quarries Act, 1954, Sched. 5. The Secretary of State may, on the joint representation of owners and workmen, approve other methods of payment in mines which employ fewer than thirty people underground.

contract with a coal miner is a contract to procure coal and he will be paid for the coal he mines[1] but not for incidental minerals or other substances.   For the coal he extracts he is entitled to be paid and each tub of minerals he produces must be weighed in gross and the weight of the foreign substances deducted from that weight so as to arrive at a true estimation of his wages.

In *Kearney* v. *Whitehaven Colliery Co.*[2] Kearney was employed to get coal and his wages were to be based on the weight of coal produced.   The agreement provided that deductions should be made for any dirt which he sent to the surface with the coal.   The employers and their workpeople had agreed that approximately one tub in twenty, to be selected at random, should be weighed, the coal separated from other substances and if the amount of the dirt did not exceed twenty-five pounds no deduction should be made. If that amount were exceeded but the dirt did not exceed thirty-five pounds in weight, one half of the weight of the tub was to be forfeited and if the dirt was in excess of thirty-five pounds then the whole tub was to be forfeited.   The court held that this procedure was irregular and that the provision in the Coal Mines Regulation Act, 1887 which permitted deductions for substances other than that which the miner was employed to get could not be construed as permitting an agreement to waive the right to payment on any particular tub.

Workmen employed in mines and paid according to the weight of mineral they get, may, at their own cost, appoint a check-weigher and a deputy check-weigher to be stationed at the place where minerals are to be weighed and deductions are to be determined.[3] The persons entitled to appoint and from whom the check-weigher or his deputy will be entitled to recover his wages and expenses will include not only the persons in charge of the working places but holers, fillers, trimmers and others who are paid according to the weight of the mineral they produce and where a contractor who is paid according to the weight of mineral produced employs others who are in charge of working places or are holers, fillers, trimmers or brushers, they will be entitled to assist in the appointment of a check-weigher despite the fact that they are paid by the contractor and not paid by the weight of mineral they mine.   But the contractor alone will be responsible for the due proportion of the wage of the check-weigher which will be recoverable by the latter only from the contractor.[4]

---

[1] *Brace* v. *Abercarn Colliery Co.*, [1891] 2 Q.B. 699;   *Netherseal Colliery Co.* v. *Bourne* (1889), 14 App. Cas. 228.

[2] [1893] 1 Q.B. 700; *cf. Coltness Iron Co.* v. *Dobbie*, [1920] A.C. 916.

[3] Coal Mines Regulation Act, 1887, s. 13 (1); Coal Mines (Weighing of Minerals) Act, 1905, s. 1 (1); Mines and Quarries Act, 1954, Sched. 5 and s. 187.

[4] Coal Mines (Weighing of Minerals) Act, 1905, s. 2 (1), (2); Mines and Quarries Act, 1954, Sched. 5 and s. 187.

A statutory declaration made by the person who presided at the meeting for the purpose of appointing the check-weigher or his deputy, to the effect that he presided at that meeting and that the person named was duly appointed must be delivered to the mine owner or his agent and will be *prima facie* evidence of the appointment.[1] The declaration must state whether the person appointed was chosen by a majority of those entitled to appoint and if he was not appointed by a majority must state the names by and on whose behalf he was appointed. Where the check-weigher is appointed by a majority he will be deemed to be appointed by all the persons in the mine who are entitled to appoint him, and he cannot be removed by the persons employed except by a majority ascertained by ballot.[2] Notice of the intention to appoint must be given by a notice posted at the pit head or otherwise specifying the time and place of the meeting and facilities given to enable all those entitled to do so to record their vote.[3] Employers must give the check-weigher every facility to enable him to fulfil his duties and a failure to do this will constitute an offence.[4] He must be provided with a shelter from the weather containing sufficient cubic feet for two persons, a desk or table at which he may write and a sufficient number of weights to test the weighing machine.[5]

The check-weigher may examine and test the weighing machine and check the tareing of tubs and tramways. He may not, however, impede or interrupt the working of the mine or interfere with the weighing. The absence from the place at which he is stationed is not a reason for interrupting or delaying the weighing unless the check-weigher had reasonable grounds for supposing that such operations would not be continued in his absence. If the owner or manager of a mine desires the removal of a check-weigher on the ground of his unauthorised activities he may complain to a court of summary jurisdiction and the court may, after hearing both sides, make a summary order for the removal of the check-weigher. The order does not, of course, in any way prejudice the appointment of another check-weigher in the place of the one removed.[6]

Where a check-weigher has been appointed by the majority, ascertained by ballot, of the persons paid according to the amount of mineral produced and has acted as such, he may recover from each of such persons his proportion of the check-weigher's wages even though any of the persons have left the mine and others have entered it. It is proper for the owner or manager of the mine,

---

[1] Coal Mines (Weighing of Minerals) Act, 1905, s. 1 (2).
[2] *Ibid.*, s. 1 (3), (5).   [3] *Ibid.*, s. 4.
[4] Coal Mines Regulation Act, 1887, s. 13 (2); Mines and Quarries Act, 1954, Sched. 5 and s. 187.
[5] Coal Mines (Weighing of Minerals) Act, 1905, s. 1 (4); Mines and Quarries Act, 1954, Sched. 5.
[6] Coal Mines Regulation Act, 1887, s. 13 (3); Mines and Quarries Act, 1954, Sched. 5.

notwithstanding the Truck Acts, to agree with the majority of the persons affected to deduct from their wages the agreed contribution towards the wage of the check-weigher and to pay the amounts so deducted to him.[1]

These general provisions as to check-weighing were extended to various industrial processes cognate to mining by the Check-weighing in Various Industries Act, 1919. The Act applies to such industries as the production or manufacture of iron and steel, the loading or unloading of goods (whether as cargo or stores) into and from any vessels, the getting of chalk or limestone from quarries, the manufacture of cement or lime and any other industry to which the provisions of the Act may be, by regulations, extended.[2] The workmen engaged in any of these industries, may, if they are paid according to the weight of material produced, handled or gotten by them, have a right to check the weighing.[3] The First Schedule to the Act lays down the manner in which the workmen may exercise their powers to check the weight or test the estimated weight.[4] Men engaged in the production of iron and steel may appoint a check-weigher if the iron or steel is weighed on the employer's premises, as they may if the weight is calculated by reference to the weight of materials used or if it is calculated according to the capacity of the moulds. If it is impossible to use any of these devices to weigh the minerals, disputes as to weight may be submitted to arbitration.[5]

(4) Road Haulage Wages.—The wages of those employed in the road haulage industry were originally regulated by a Central Wages Board and by certain Area Wages Boards.[6] It was, however, provided under the terms of the wages councils Act, 1948 that the Central Wages Board should become a wages council established under the Wages Councils Act, 1945, with a jurisdiction over the wages of the descriptions of workers whose wages were covered by orders made under the Road Haulage Wages Act, 1938.[7] Thus the Road Haulage industry was brought, for the purpose of wage regulation, within the general field of the law as to wages councils.

The legislation concerning workers employed on vehicles has had to be recast in relation to scope which until the Transport Act, 1968, was based on the type of licence.[8] The previous scope has been retained by including all privately-owned road haulage undertakings undertaking any work for hire or removal. There was a slight

---

[1] Coal Mines Regulation Act, 1887, s. 13; Mines and Quarries Act, 1954, Sched. 5.
[2] *Ibid.*, s. 1 (2).   [3] *Ibid.*, s. 1 (1).
[4] Checkweighing in Various Industries Act, 1919, s. 2.
[5] *Ibid.*, Sched. 1 (1).
[6] See Road Haulage Wages Act, 1938, and the Trade Boards and Road Haulage Wages (Emergency Provisions) Act, 1940.
[7] *Supra.* For the transitional provisions see Sched. 2, Wages Councils Act, 1948.
[8] Road and Rail Traffic Act, 1933, s. 2 (4): 'A', 'B', 'C' licences.

extension covering those with " C " licences under the old system who chose to do some work for hire or removal. The second part of the Road Haulage Wages Act, 1938 applies to road haulage in connection with the mechanical transport of goods under such licences. The provisions of the second part of the Act do not apply to work for which a minimum rate of wages has been fixed by any other enactment, but where this is not the case, a road haulage worker or his trade union or a trade union representing a substantial number of workers employed in road haulage work may make an application to the Minister stating that the remuneration paid in respect of his work is unfair and requesting that the matter be referred for settlement. Remuneration will not be deemed unfair if it is equivalent to that payable under a wages order made under the provisions already discussed, or if it is in accordance with an agreement made between the employer and a trade union, or if it is equivalent to the remuneration paid for similar work to similar workers by other employers in the district agreed upon by employers and a trade union or if it is equivalent to remuneration paid for similar workers as a result of a decision of a joint industrial council or similar body, or if it is equivalent to that paid in accordance with the decision of an industrial court given upon a reference to that court under the Road Haulage Wages Act.

The Secretary of State, on application being made to him, will, provided he is satisfied that it is neither frivolous nor vexatious, and provided also that it is not withdrawn after representations made to the employer, refer the matter either to an industrial court or to any machinery for the settlement of disputes which exists in the trade or industry in which the employer is engaged. The Secretary of State must refer the matter for settlement within one month unless special circumstances make postponement desirable.[1]

If the court finds that the remuneration paid was unfair it will fix the remuneration to be paid which will then become the statutory remuneration. The power of the court will cover the right to fix holiday remuneration. In determining whether any remuneration is unfair the court may compare the rate paid to the claimant and that paid as the result of agreements between employers and trade unions engaged in similar work. The court will not only specify the remuneration to be paid but also the time for which the worker must be employed in order to become eligible for the daily or weekly rate and also the number of hours of employment after which overtime payment is to be made. The statutory remuneration fixed by the court will remain in force for three years from the beginning of the week following the date on which the statutory remuneration was fixed and will apply not only to the worker who first sought the intervention of the Secretary of State but to all workers employed by the employer concerned on that work. As between the employer

---

[1] Road Haulage Wages Act, 1938, s. 4.

and the worker who initiated the proceedings, the statutory remuneration will be deemed to have been in force for such earlier period not exceeding six months as the court may direct. It is open, however, to either party any time after the expiration of three months from the date the remuneration was fixed to ask for a review of the statutory remuneration when the Secretary of State will again refer the matter to an industrial court.[1]

It is an offence under the Act to fail to pay the statutory remuneration or to pay less than that remuneration.[2]

(5) Wages in Agriculture.—The Agricultural Wages Act, 1948, provides for agricultural workers a system of wage regulation similar in outline to that provided by wages councils. This Act is a consolidation of earlier legislation.[3] The keystone of the system is now the Agricultural Wages Board. This body was originally set up under the 1924 Act but the power to fix minimum wage rates was vested in the Agricultural Wages Committees. The Act of 1940 gave the Wages Board power to fix a national minimum wage which must be observed by the Committees and two years later, by statutory instrument,[4] the powers of the Committees of fixing minimum wage rates and using power under the Holidays with Pay Act, 1938, to allow holiday remuneration up to seven days was transferred " for the period of the war emergency " to the Board. After the war, the 1947 Act made this transfer permanent.

The Wages Board is now regulated by s. 1 of the Agricultural Wages Act, 1948. Its composition is eight representatives of both employers and workers and up to five independent members appointed by the Minister[5] from whom the Chairman is to be drawn.[6] The Board has power to fix minimum rates of wages for workers employed in agriculture and to direct a period of holiday entitlement. The power to fix wages includes the power to fix time rates and to fix rates of pay in respect of holidays. The Board has also power to cancel or vary a minimum rate that has been fixed or a direction as to holidays. As far as is possible the Board must secure a weekly half holiday for the workers.[7] These powers are exercised by means of Orders made under the Act. These are not statutory instruments but are published in the London Gazette. The procedure for making such orders is laid down and provides for public notice of proposals to make an order, allowing at least fourteen days for objections to be lodged. The appropriate agricultural

---

[1] Road Haulage Wages Act, 1938, s. 5.   [2] *Ibid.*, s. 6.
[3] Agricultural Wages (Regulation) Act, 1924; Agricultural Wages (Regulation) Amendment Act, 1940; Agricultural (Miscellaneous Provisions) Act, 1944 and Agricultural Wages (Regulation) Act, 1947.
[4] S. R. & O. 1942, No. 2404.
[5] The Minister of Agriculture and Fisheries.
[6] Agricultural Wages Act, 1948, s. 1 and Sched. I.
[7] *Ibid.*, s. 3.

wages committees must also be informed. There are provisions for dispensing with this procedure where the proposal is of limited application.[1]

The Agricultural Wages Committees used to exercise the power of fixing wages for their localities. These committees are set up in each county of England and Wales except where there is provision for an amalgamation of counties for this purpose.[2] The Committees now carry out their functions as directed by the Wages Board.[3] These functions include granting and revoking permits for incapacitated persons, under which workers with mental or physical deficiencies or infirmity due to age or other cause may be paid wages less than the minimum;[4] granting and revoking certificates approving terms of employment of persons undergoing instruction;[5] approving apprenticeship agreements which require payment of a premium;[6] and revaluing houses the occupation of which is included in the payment of the minimum wage.[7] The Wages Board has statutory power to make an order defining the benefits or advantages which may be reckoned as payment of wages in lieu of cash, determining the value at which such benefits must be reckoned and limiting the amount of such advantages or benefits.[8] A Wages Committee can then hear individual claims for revaluation of houses. A Wages Committee is to consist of equal representatives of employers and workmen plus two independent members appointed by the Minister. The Chairman is appointed by the Committee itself, or in default, by the Minister.[9]

Enforcement of minimum wage rates, holiday periods and rates of pay is available to the worker as a civil action and the employer who has failed to observe the terms of the Order is also liable to a fine.[10] The Act applies to agricultural workers only. This includes boys, girls and women as well as men. The definition of agriculture has been the subject of some case law. By statute it includes dairy farming, the production of any consumable produce which is grown for sale or for consumption or other use for the purpose of a trade or business or of any other undertaking, whether carried on for profit or not, and the use of land as grazing, meadow, or pasture land or orchard or osier land or woodland or for market gardens or nursery grounds.[11] It has been held to include a private garden used as a market garden[12] and also poultry farming.[13]

---

[1] Agricultural Wages Act, 1948, s. 2 and Sched. 4.
[2] *Ibid.*, s. 3 and Sched. 2.
[3] *Ibid.*, s. 2(4).
[4] *Ibid.*, s. 5.
[5] *Ibid.*, s. 6(1).
[6] *Ibid.*, s. 6(5).
[7] *Ibid.*, s. 7(3).
[8] *Ibid.*, s. 7(1).
[9] *Ibid.*, s. 2 and Sched. 3.   [10] *Ibid.*, s. 4.
[11] Agricultural Wages Act, 1948, s. 17.
[12] *Roberts* v. *Wynn*, [1950] W.N. 300.
[13] *Walters* v. *Wright*, [1938] 4 All E.R. 116.

The principal distinctive feature of the payment of agricultural wages is not the separate system of minimum wage regulation but the greater scope for the payment of minimum wages partly in kind. The Truck Acts do not apply[1] but the fixing of value by the Wages Board serves as a safeguard against misuse of this power. An attempt to avoid this valuation by paying full cash entitlement and then accepting a greater sum than the advantage given has been held to be illegal.[2]

3. PROTECTION OF WAGES

(1) **The Truck Acts.**[3]—Legislation designed to protect the worker in the free enjoyment of his earnings represents one of the earliest manifestations of what we should now regard as industrial law. Originally, payment for services rendered was, almost invariably, in kind, and long after the payment of money wages became a characteristic element in the contract of service the consideration for services rendered often took the form of a money payment together with the supply of goods and services by the master to the workmen. It was not, as is too frequently assumed, a wholly vicious system, but it was capable of great abuse. By placing a fictitious value upon the services rendered or the goods supplied an unscrupulous employer had a ready means of reducing his labour costs. Moreover the practice was often resorted to, of paying wages, not in coin of the realm but in vouchers exchangeable at a shop of which the employer was the owner or in which he had an interest. It was against these practices that the Truck Acts were aimed and the Truck Act, 1831, is the first of the statutes on which the modern law is based. The Act makes it an offence for an employer to contract that wages payable to his servant shall be paid otherwise than in current coin of the realm and if he does purport so to contract the contract is illegal and void.[4] The recent Payment of Wages Act, 1960 has introduced certain important exceptions to meet modern conditions.[5] Nor must a contract of service contain any provision, direct or indirect, concerning the place where, or the manner in which, or the person or persons with whom, the whole or any part of the wages shall be laid out or expended.[6] The entire amount of the wages must be actually paid to the worker in current coin and not otherwise.[7]

---

[1] Truck Amendment Act, 1887, s. 4.

[2] *Williams* v. *Smith*, [1934] 2 K.B. 158.

[3] For a summary of the legislation, see Report of the Committee on the Truck Acts, 1961—a Ministry of Labour Departmental Committee under the chairmanship of D. Karmel, Q.C.

[4] Truck Act, 1831, s. 1. With the consent of the workman wages may be paid in bankers notes or drafts (*ibid.*, s. 8). This is a remote contingency at the present time, for Treasury notes are legal tender.

[5] See p. 159, *infra.*

[6] Truck Act, 1831, s. 2.

[7] *Ibid.*, s. 3.

The Act applies to any "workman", and the term workman was defined by the Employers and Workmen Act, 1875. It excludes a domestic or menial servant but means "any person who, being a labourer, servant in husbandry, journeyman, artificer, handicraftsman, miner, or otherwise engaged in manual labour has entered into or works under a contract with an employer whether it be a contract of service or a contract personally to execute any work or labour."[1] Thus a draper's packer[2] and a potter's printer engaged to do work with assistants whom he engaged is within the Act[3] as also is a motor omnibus driver who must do any repairs which may be necessary when he is with the vehicle.[4] But an omnibus conductor is not a person engaged in manual labour for "his real and substantial business is to invite persons to enter the omnibus and to take, and keep for his employers, the money paid by the passengers."[5] Such a one does not fall within the scope of the Truck Acts, nor does a grocer's assistant[6] nor a potman, though both may do certain manual work.[7] Similarly, a person employed to assist a firm as a mechanic in developing ideas which the firm wishes to perfect is not a workman nor is a man employed to do work of an engineering nature in a hospital. Such work is concerned with the maintenance of the hospital and has a character which is chiefly domestic.[8]

It is an offence under section three of the Act of 1831 for a brickmaker who also owns a public house to allow men credit for drink supplied and subsequently to deduct the amount from their wages[9]; or for a master to supply goods from his shop and to deduct the cost from the workman's wages.[10] It is equally, and perhaps more obviously, an offence for a master to give a note on a shop in payment of wages, particularly where it is his intention at the time that the wages should be paid in goods and not money.[11] It was, however, held that it was not a contravention of the Act to pay a sum less than the list wages to a weaver who wove badly and negligently, for the deduction was held to be a mode of ascertaining the true wages.[12] The same circumstances were considered and the same ruling given in *Sagar* v. *H. Ridehalgh & Son, Ltd.*[13] on the ground

---

[1] Employers and Workmen Act, 1875, s. 1.
[2] *Pratt* v. *Cook, Son & Co. (St. Paul's), Ltd.*, [1940] A.C. 437; [1940] 1 All E.R. 410.
[3] *Grainger* v. *Aynsley, Bromley* v. *Tams* (1880), 6 Q.B.D. 182.
[4] *Smith* v. *Associated Omnibus Co.*, [1907] 1 K.B. 916.
[5] *Morgan* v. *London General Omnibus Co.* (1884), 13 Q.B.D. 832.
[6] *Bound* v. *Lawrence*, [1892] 1 Q.B. 226.
[7] *Pearce* v. *Lansdowne* (1893), 62 L.J. Q.B. 441.
[8] *Cameron* v. *Royal London Ophthalmic Hospital*, [1941] 1 K.B. 350; [1940] 4 All E.R. 439.
[9] *Gould* v. *Haynes* (1889), 59 L.J. (M.C.) 9.
[10] *Wilson* v. *Cookson* (1863), 13 C.B. N.S. 496.
[11] *Athersmith* v. *Drury* (1858), 1 E. & E. 46.
[12] *Hart* v. *Riversdale Mill Co.*, [1928] 1 K.B. 176.
[13] [1931] 1 Ch. 310.

I.L.—8*

that the custom of making such deductions incorporated into the contract of employment a term which permitted the deduction.

The Truck Acts apply also where articles are made by a person at his own home or elsewhere, provided the person in question employs no one other than himself and members of his own family. Such a person will be accounted a workman and the shopkeeper, dealer or trader who buys the articles in the way of trade will be accounted, for the purposes of the Act, an employer. There must, consequently, be no deductions from the price of the articles made, for the price paid will be deemed to be wages earned. The provision applies only to articles under the value of five pounds of a kind enumerated in the Truck Amendment Act, 1887.[1]

Where, in defiance of the Act, wages have not been paid in current coin of the realm the workman is entitled to recover the whole or such part of the wages as have not been so paid.[2] In *Pratt* v. *Cook, Son & Co. (St. Paul's), Ltd.*, the plaintiff was employed for many years as a draper's packer at a wage of fifty-three shillings a week. The employer supplied dinner and tea which it was agreed were worth a further ten shillings a week. The plaintiff claimed that these meals represented a deduction from his wages which the defendants were not entitled to make. The House of Lords held that the plaintiff's view was correct and that he was entitled to recover.[3] The employer's deductions for meals would have been legal had they been supported by a contract,[4] and under the Truck Act, 1940 employers are protected in respect of transactions occurring before July 10th, 1940, involving deductions from wages for matters specified in section 23 though the transaction was not made according to the form required by that section. Apart from this, if the workman brings proceedings against his employer for such recovery the employer may not set off against the workman's claim the cost of any goods received by the workman on account of his wages, or the cost of any goods supplied to the workman at any shop or warehouse in the profits of which the employer has an interest.[5] An employer cannot maintain a suit or action against his workman for goods which he supplies to the latter as a reward for his labour or for goods supplied at a shop or warehouse kept by or belonging to the employer or in the profits of which the employer has a share or interest.[6] An employer who, directly or indirectly, enters into a contract or makes payments declared illegal by the Act is liable to a penalty, and where the offence for which the employer is liable has in fact been committed by an agent of the employer or some other

---

[1] S. 10.

[2] Truck Act, 1831, s. 4.

[3] [1940] A.C. 437; [1940] 1 All E.R. 410.

[4] See the Truck Act, 1831, s. 23.

[5] *Ibid.*, s. 5.

[6] *Ibid.*, s. 6. In certain cases where the workman or his family are in receipt of public assistance, the local authority may recover wages paid to the workman otherwise than in cash (*ibid.*, s. 7).

person that agent or person will be liable as if he were the employer.[1] The employer will not be exempt from the penalty even though he was unaware of the offence unless he lays an information against the actual offender.[2]   But the activities which were struck at by the Act of 1831, though capable of the greatest abuse, were not wholly disadvantageous to the workman.   It might be iniquitous that an employer could compel his men to make purchases the value of which was deducted from wages but there were circumstances in which an employer could render services to a workman and in which he could pass on to the workman the value of his being able to buy in gross at beneficial rates.

Consequently, despite the general provisions against the payment of the whole or any part of the workman's wages otherwise than in cash, the Act permits deductions in certain cases.   Thus an employer may contract to supply or supply to his workman (a) medicine or medical attendance; (b) fuel; (c) materials, tools or implements to be used by workmen employed in mines; (d) hay, corn or provender to be consumed by a beast of burden; or (e) he may let to his workmen the whole or any part of a tenement; or (f) he may supply to his workmen food prepared and consumed on the employer's premises. Where the employer renders any of these services he may recoup himself by deductions from the employee's wages, but the deductions must not exceed the true value of the goods supplied or the services rendered and in every case there must be a written agreement signed by the workman evidencing his consent to the deduction.[3] The written agreement need not be elaborate or specific in its particulars provided the workman's consent to the deductions is clear.   "It is sufficient if there be a contract in writing which states in general terms that the charges for the things mentioned may be deducted from the wages and the amount of these deductions may be shown by parol evidence . . . ."[4]   Where, however, the contract is for goods supplied or to be supplied, it must be a contract of sale and not of hire.[5]

No deductions other than those permitted by the Act may be made and though a master may, by agreement, deduct from his employee's wages sums owing by the worker to a third party he may not deduct from his employee's wages sums which the employee owes to himself.   In *Hewlett* v. *Allen*[6] the plaintiff was employed by the defendant on terms which required that he became a member of a club

---

[1] Truck Act, 1831, s. 9, see also the Truck Amendment Act, 1887, s. 12.
[2] *Ward* v. *W. H. Smith & Son*, [1913] 3 K.B. 154.   As to the liabilities of partners, see Truck Act, 1831, s. 13.
[3] Truck Act, 1831, s. 23.
[4] *Cutts* v. *Ward* (1867), L.R. 2 Q.B. 357, *per* BLACKBURN, J., at p. 363.
[5] *Ibid*.   An employer may not make a deduction from wages for sharpening or repairing tools except by an agreement which does not form part of the condition of hiring, Truck Amendment Act, 1887, s. 9.
[6] [1894] A.C. 383.

from which benefits might be drawn if a member had an accident or was ill.   The employer paid the plaintiff the net amount of wages after deducting the contributions to the fund and paid the contribution to the treasurer of the fund.   It was held that there was no offence under the Act.   But when employers deducted from the men's wages moneys which magistrates had held the men liable to pay under the Employers and Workmen Act, 1875, it was held that the deduction was not one which the Act sanctioned[1] and where employers made deductions from wages for medical services and normally handed the sums to the doctors but filed a liquidation petition, whilst a balance due to the doctors remained in their books, it was held that the workmen were entitled to that balance.[2]

It is not an offence for an employer to advance to his employee money which the latter contributes to a friendly society or bank or for his relief in sickness or for the education of his children.   Where the employer does so he may deduct the advances made from subsequent earnings.[3]

The Hosiery Manufacture (Wages) Act, 1874 was designed to strike at certain abuses in the hosiery trade.   Wages are to be paid in current coin of the realm without deduction except for bad and disputed workmanship.[4]   Contracts to stop wages and for frame rents and charges between employer and workman are illegal and void.[5]

An employer who deducts or bargains to deduct from the wages of his workmen frame rent or other charges or pays any part of the wages other than in current coin of the realm is liable to a penalty to be recovered by the workman or other person suing.[6]   Where the master entrusts a frame or other machine to a worker for the purpose of manufacturing hosiery for the employer, the workman must not, without the written consent of the master, use the machine to manufacture goods for any person other than the employer.[7] The Act is not designed to prevent an employer from recovering by the ordinary processes of the law a debt due to him by his employee, but no action, suit, or set-off between employer and workman will be allowed for any deduction or stoppage of wages, nor for any contract declared by the Act to be illegal.[8]

---

[1] *Williams* v. *North's Navigation Collieries (1889), Ltd.*, [1906] A.C. 136. *Cf. Penman* v. *Fife Coal Co., Ltd.*, [1936] A.C. 45.

[2] *Re Morris, Ex parte Cooper* (1884), 26 Ch.D. 693.

[3] Truck Act, 1831, s. 24. A workman against whom deductions are made for the education of his child who sends the child to a State-inspected school may have the school fees of the child deducted at the same rate and to the same extent as the other workmen from whose wages a like deduction is made: Truck Amendment Act, 1887, s. 7.

[4] Hosiery Manufacture (Wages) Act, 1874, s. 1.

[5] *Ibid.*, s. 2.

[6] *Ibid.*, s. 3.

[7] *Ibid.*, s. 4

[8] *Ibid.*, ss. 5, 6.

The abuses of the system of Truck which had led to the Act of 1831 had caused the legislature to frame that Act in terms which experience had shown to be too restrictive. At the same time new developments had occurred which required further legislation. The Acts of 1887[1] and 1896[2] were efforts to deal with the new situation.

Where by agreement, custom or otherwise a workman is entitled to receive in anticipation of the regular period of the payment of his wages an advance on account thereof it is not lawful for the employer to withhold the advance or to make a deduction on account of poundage, discount, interest or any similar charge.[3] Nor do the Truck Acts prevent a contract with a servant in husbandry by which the latter receives food, drink (not being intoxicating), a cottage, or other privileges in addition to his money wages but as a remuneration for his services.[4]

Should a workman bring an action against his employer for the recovery of wages, the employer is not entitled to any set-off or counter-claim in respect of goods supplied to the workman under an order or direction of the employer, nor is the employer or his agent entitled to sue the workman in respect of goods so supplied excepting, of course, where the goods supplied are those which are permitted by the Truck Acts.[5]

If deductions are made from wages for medicine, medical attendance, tools or for the education of children the employer must prepare accounts and submit them to the audit of two auditors appointed by the workmen.[6]

The Truck Act, 1896[7] is chiefly concerned with deductions made in respect of fines and for damaged goods. Fines are usually of a disciplinary character whilst in many industries it is usual for the employer to recompense himself for damage to materials by deductions from wages. Transactions of these kinds were not within the scope of the Truck Acts for the courts regarded them as means of ascertaining the workman's true wages. The 1896 Act defines closely the conditions under which fines and deductions might be made. The permissibility of the practice of imposing fines on workmen or shop assistants depends upon the making of a contract between the employer and employee. The terms of the contract must either be written and signed by the workman or contained in a notice which must be kept in a place where it may be seen, read and copied by any person whom it affects. It must specify the acts or omissions for which the fine may be imposed and the amount

---

[1] Truck Amendment Act, 1887.   [2] Truck Act, 1896.
[3] Truck Amendment Act, 1887, s. 3. The practice of "subbing," as it is called, is still widely practised in certain occupations. notably among bargees and certain unskilled workers.
[4] *Ibid.*, s. 4.   [5] *Ibid.*, s. 5.   [6] *Ibid.*, s. 9.
[7] *Supra.* The Secretary of State has power to exempt from the provisions of the Act, s. 9.

of the fine or particulars from which the amount may be ascertained. The fine imposed by the contract must arise out of an act or omission which causes or is likely to cause loss to the employer or interruption or hindrance to his business, and its amount must be fair and reasonable having regard to all the circumstances of the case.

An arrangement by which an employer reserves the right to suspend a workman from his employment where the latter has been guilty of misconduct and thus suffers a loss of wages is not within the Truck Acts. For in such an agreement there is no deduction from the wages; the employer, in fact, never contracted to pay wages during the period of suspension.[1]

An employer may not make any deductions or receive payment on account of a fine unless it is in accordance with the contract and unless the workman is supplied with particulars which show the acts or omissions for which the fine is imposed and the amount of the fine. These particulars must be made available to the workman on each occasion when a fine is levied.[2] The most usual offence for which a fine is levied is for lateness in arriving at the workshop or factory, but other acts of indiscipline may be included and the contract displayed to or made with the worker may be in general terms. A notice which informed workers that they were liable to a fine if they did not observe good order and decorum in the factory was held to be sufficiently explicit.[3]

Deductions or payments for bad or negligent work or injury to materials or other property belonging to the employer may not be made unless (a) the terms on which such deductions are to be made are contained in a notice displayed at places open to the workmen in such a position that it may easily be seen, read and copied or the contract is in writing signed by the workman; (b) the deduction or payment does not exceed the actual or estimated damage or loss occasioned by the workman or by some person over whom the workman has control, or for whom the workman has, by the contract, agreed to be responsible and (c) the amount of the deduction or payment is fair and reasonable having regard to all the circumstances of the case.[4] All deductions or payments must be made in pursuance of the contract and the workman must be supplied with particulars in writing on each occasion when a deduction or payment is made showing the acts or omission of which the employer complains and the amount to be deducted or paid.[5]

Deductions or payments to be made by a workman to an employer for the use or supply of materials, tools or machines, standing room, light, heat or for any other thing which the employer does or provides are legal only if made in pursuance of a contract and written

[1] *Bird* v. *British Celanese, Ltd.*, [1945] K.B. 336; [1945] 1 All E.R. 488
[2] Truck Act, 1896, s. 1.
[3] *Squire* v. *Bayer & Co.*, [1901] 2 K.B. 299
[4] Truck Act, 1896, s. 2 (1).
[5] *Ibid.*, s. 2 (2).

particulars are given to the workman showing the things for which the deduction or payment is made, and the amount of the deduction or payment. The terms of the contract must be displayed where the workmen may easily read and copy them, or the contract must be in writing signed by the workman. The sum to be paid or deducted must not exceed the actual or estimated cost to the employer or must be a fair and reasonable rent or charge.[1]

In an effort to enlist the support of the employees in the enforcement of the Act it is provided that a workman or shop assistant may recover sums deducted or paid contrary to the Act provided he begins proceedings within six months from the date of the deduction. Where however the workman has acquiesced in or consented to the deduction he has no right to recover the whole sum but only to recover the excess which has been deducted over that amount which the court finds to be fair and reasonable.[2]

On the written demand of an Inspector of Factories or Mines an employer must produce any contract, or a true copy thereof, which purports or intends to operate under the Act and the Inspector may take a copy. A workman or shop assistant who is a party to any such contract must be given by the employer at the time of the making of the contract a copy of the contract or of the notice containing its terms. The workman or shop assistant is entitled, on request, to obtain a free copy, presumably at any time subsequent to the making of the contract. The employer must keep a register of deductions or payments made in which must be specified the amount and the act or omission for which the fine was imposed. The register must be open at all times for inspection by the Inspector of Factories or of Mines.[3]

(2) Payment of Wages Act, 1960.—The advantages of paying wages by cheque or by similar documentary form are such that the government was persuaded to introduce legislation to modify the Truck Acts and to provide for payment in this way. Payment may now be made direct into a bank account standing in the name of an employee, or in his name jointly with someone else, or by postal or money order or by cheque, where the employer receives a written request from the employee that his wages should be paid in one of the ways specified.[4] It is specifically provided that such payment shall not then offend the Truck Act, 1831, the Hosiery Manufacture (Wages) Act, 1874 or the Stannaries Act, 1887, all of which, as we have seen, require that workers to whom they apply should receive their wages in coin of the realm.[4] The Act provides certain safeguards for the employee. Wages, if to be paid into a specified account must be paid into that account and no other, a cheque must name the employee as payee and there must be no deduction from

---

[1] Truck Act, 1896, s. 3.   [2] *Ibid.*, s. 5.
[3] *Ibid.*, s. 6.
[4] Payment of Wages Act, 1960, s. 1.

the gross amount of wages due arising from the method of payment.[1] At, or before, the time of payment the employee must be given a statement in writing setting out the gross amount of his wages, clear of all deductions; the amount of each deduction and the matter in respect of which it is made; and the net amount payable.[1] Where the statutory method of payment only applies to part of the wages the net amount payable otherwise must also be shown.[2] Such a statement will not be invalid where there is an error or omission which is a clerical mistake or was otherwise made accidentally and in good faith.[3] Either side has a right to cancel the arrangement by giving notice which takes effect at the end of four weeks.[4]

A further important provision deals with the payment of wages where the employee is absent either through duties which require him to be, or through illness or personal injury. In these circumstances payment may be made, even though no agreement by the employee under the earlier provisions of the Act exists, by postal or money order.[5] A statement of particulars as outlined in s. 2 must be given. Although the employee's consent is not required he may, by giving written notice to his employer, exclude the operation of this section in his case and prevent the employer from paying in this way.[6]

(3) **The Shop Clubs Act, 1902.**—An Act closely allied to the Truck Acts in that its contravention might, in certain circumstances, involve illegal deductions from wages is the Shop Clubs Act, 1902. The Act makes it an offence, punishable by a fine, for an employer to make it a condition of employment (a) that any workman shall discontinue his membership of any friendly society or (b) that any workman shall not become a member of any friendly society other than the shop club or thrift fund.[7] A friendly society is a society registered under the Friendly Societies Act, 1896. A "shop club" or "thrift fund" is any club or society for providing benefits to workmen in connection with a workshop, factory, dock or warehouse.[8] It is also an offence, under penalty of a fine for an employer to make it a condition of employment that any workman shall join a shop club or thrift fund unless the club or fund is registered under and subject to the Friendly Societies Act and is certified by the Registrar of Friendly Societies.

A certificate will not be given by the registrar unless he is satisfied that the club or fund affords to the workman substantial benefits in the form of contributions or benefits, at the cost of the employer in addition to those provided by the workman, that the club or fund is of a permanent character which does not, annually or periodically, divide its funds and that no member shall, except in accordance with

---

[1] Payment of Wages Act, 1960, s. 2.
[2] *Ibid.*, s. 2(5)(*d*).
[3] *Ibid.*, 2(6).
[4] *Ibid.*, s. 3.
[5] *Ibid.*, s. 4.
[6] *Ibid.*, s. 4(2).
[7] Shop Clubs Act, 1902, s. 1.
[8] *Ibid.*, s. 2.

section six of the Act, be required to cease his membership of the club or fund upon leaving the firm with which the club or fund is connected. Before he certifies a club or fund the registrar is required to take steps to ascertain the views of the workmen. He must be satisfied that at least seventy-five per cent of the workmen desire the establishment of the club or fund and must consider any objections to certification which the workmen may make.[1]

The Act exempts railways from its scope and its terms do not apply to compulsory membership of any superannuation fund, insurance or other society already existing for the benefit of the persons employed by any railway company to the funds of which such company contributes.[2]

Where a workman, by the conditions of his employment, is a member of a shop club he shall on leaving his employment or on dismissal therefrom, unless the rules of the club are to the contrary, have the option of remaining a member or of having returned to him the amount of his share of the funds of the club. But a member who elects to remain a member of the club will not be entitled to take any part in the management of the club or to exercise a vote in respect thereof whilst he is out of the employment of the undertaking with which the club is associated.[3]

(4) Payment of Wages in Public Houses.—Another Act which has some affinity with the objects of the Truck Acts is the Payment of Wages in Public Houses Prohibition Act, 1883. Under the terms of this Act no wages shall be paid to any workman at or within a public house, beer shop or similar place or in any office, garden or place belonging thereto, except where the wages are paid by the resident owner or occupier to a workman employed by him. And if, contrary to the provisions of the Act, wages are paid for or on behalf of an employer (*e.g.* by a cashier or foreman) the employer will himself be guilty of an offence unless he can prove that he had taken all reasonable means in his power to prevent the contravention.[4]

The Act applies to "workmen," a term which includes any person who is a labourer, servant in husbandry, journeyman, artificer, handicraftsman or is otherwise engaged in manual labour, and whether he is under or above the age of twenty-one years. The Act does not apply to domestic or menial persons. Hitherto the Act did not apply to persons engaged in or about a mine and the Mines Act, 1911, s. 96, provided for miners. Now, however, the Mines and Quarries Act, 1954,[5] removes the limiting words and mines are brought within the terms of the Act.

---

[1] Shop Clubs Act, 1902, s. 6.
[2] *Ibid.*, s. 5.
[3] *Ibid.*, s. 2.
[4] Payment of Wages in Public Houses Prohibition Act, 1883, s. 3.
[5] Sched. 5.

4. UNEMPLOYMENT INSURANCE

Compulsory insurance against ill health and unemployment became law in this country for the first time in 1911 as a result of the National Insurance Act of that year. That Act, limited in its operation to certain specified industries,[1] has been constantly amended and its scope enlarged. The law was consolidated in the Unemployment Insurance Act, 1935, which, in its turn, has been subjected to modification by later Acts. These Acts were in large part repealed and replaced by the National Insurance Act, 1946,[2] and this, and subsequent amendments, has been replaced by the National Insurance Act, 1965. This legislation is the foundation of the law of insurance against sickness, unemployment and certain other hazards. The main 1965 Act has been amended in 1966 and 1969 by further National Insurance Acts. The 1966 Act is especially important in that it introduced an earnings related supplement.[3] It is not proposed, therefore, to give, in this book, anything more than a summary of existing provisions relating to unemployment benefit together with an outline of the relevant provisions in the National Insurance Act. Until the present time there was no question that the topic of unemployment insurance was properly to be discussed in works dealing with industrial law. Now, however, unemployment insurance is merely one part of a co-ordinated system of national insurance covering many, indeed most, of the hazards of life from birth (in the guise of maternity benefits) to death (in the form of death benefits). Moreover, the scope of the system of national insurance is so comprehensive, the classes of people entitled to benefit so extended, that its incidence is no longer " industrial " in any accepted meaning of that word, but " social " in the broadest possible sense.

Thus, on the matter of insurance against unemployment, the law is that provided by the National Insurance Act, 1965, as amended. And though, in this book, we are principally concerned with employment insurance only, and though the Act covers insurance against many other eventualities it is necessary to know something of the general scope of the Act.

(1) Entitlement.—Subject to the provisions of the Act, every person who, on or after July 5th, 1948, is over the school leaving age[4] and under pensionable age (in the case of men, sixty-five, and of women, sixty years),[5] is in Great Britain and fulfils the prescribed conditions as to residence, must become and continue to be insured.[6]

The requirement that a person should be " in Great Britain " must

---

[1] National Insurance Act, 1911, Sched. VI.

[2] 9 & 10 Geo. 6, c. 67.

[3] The detailed rules are to be found in the National Insurance (Unemployment and Sickness Benefit) Regulations, 1967, S.I. 1967, No. 330.

[4] Education Act, 1944, s. 35. At present 15, but will rise to 16 this year.

[5] National Insurance Act, 1965, s. 114 (1).

[6] *Ibid.*, s. 1 (1).

be considered in relation to the provision which enables the appropriate Minister[1] by regulation, to treat as employed contributor's employment, employment outside Great Britain,[2] and must be considered also in relation to the fact that the Minister is empowered to make regulations modifying the provisions of the Act in relation to persons who are or have been outside Great Britain whilst insured under the Act.[3] Thus neither service nor residence outside Great Britain, temporarily, at least, is a complete disqualification from the benefits of the Act.

Insured persons are divided into three classes. Firstly, those who are gainfully occupied in Great Britain under a contract of service, secondly self-employed persons, *i.e.* those who are gainfully occupied in Great Britain not being employed persons, and thirdly those who are not employed. The first two classes are referred to respectively as employed persons and self-employed persons whilst the third class is referred to as non-employed persons, and into this third class are swept all insured persons who are neither employed nor self-employed.[4]

The classes of "employed" and "self-employed" persons raise, of course the familiar question whether a man is or is not a servant; whether or not he works under a contract of service or a contract of services. It was perhaps to be expected that the determination of the limits of these two categories would lead to some litigation. At first this was not so, but changes in employment patterns, the growth of various forms of self-employment for example, have led to several cases. An early example is *Gould* v. *Minister of National Insurance*[5] wherein it was held that a musical artiste employed under a form of contract in general use was a "self-employed" and not an "employed" person. The Judge was of the opinion that the authority of cases and particularly cases based upon other statutes was not of great help, but that, nevertheless a common principle might be extracted from the authorities namely "that the real question is one of the degree of control exercised . . . and this . . . means not only the amount of control, but the nature of that control and the direction in which it is exercised."[6] The control test has now been accepted as only one test, although a major one.[7]

Apparently the words "gainfully occupied" do not mean what they say and that occupation without gain may, in certain circumstances, bring one within the scope of the Acts. Thus, a victim of poliomyelitis on the advice of his doctor found a post with a salary

---

[1] Insurance is now one of the functions of the Department of Health and Social Security.
[2] National Insurance Act, 1965, s. 1(3) (a) (ii).
[3] National Insurance Act, 1965, s. 103 (2).
[4] National Insurance Act, 1965, s. 1 (2).
[5] [1951] 1 K.B. 731; [1951] 1 All E.R. 368.
[6] *Ibid.*, at pp. 734 and 371 respectively.
[7] For a discussion of these cases, see Ch. 1, *supra*, p. 5.

of £300 a year with an additional travelling allowance of £75. To do his work he required a car and someone to drive it, the total cost of which amounted to £11 a week. He was held to be gainfully occupied and employed under a contract of service within the National Insurance Acts.[1]

The Act applies to employees of the Crown in like manner as if the employer were a private person with such modifications as may be made by Order in Council.[2] Members of the forces, over school-leaving and under pensionable age, will be deemed to be insured and employed persons.[3] Regulations may modify the provisions of the Act in their application to persons who are or have been employed on board any ship, vessel or aircraft,[4] or in the new industry of exploration and exploitation of undersea resources,[5] and the participation of married women in the scheme is similarly to be regulated.

It seems likely that married women will form the largest class of what were known, in the older legislation, as "excepted persons." Unless special provisions were applied married women would rank as non-employed since they are not gainfully employed under a contract of service nor gainfully self-employed. Such an interpretation would lay upon married women the obligation to make weekly contributions under the Act. However, such an interpretation is defeated by the Act itself which, after giving the Minister power to make regulations, provides that such regulations must contain powers to except a woman if she so elects or does not elect otherwise, from insurance in any period during which she is married and a non-employed person and from liability to pay contributions as an insured person for any period during which she is married and not excepted from insurance.[6] Persons under sixteen years of age on the appointed day will not be liable to pay contributions as non-employed persons for any period before they reach that age and there are to be special provisions to deal with contributions in the year in which such persons reach the age of sixteen years.[7] The decision as to classification is one for the Department of Health and Social Security, the Government department responsible for social insurance. There is a right of appeal, but only on a matter of law.[8]

(2) Contributions.—The fund required to meet benefits payable is made up of contributions from insured persons, employers and

---

[1] *Vandyk* v. *Minister of Pensions and National Insurance*, [1955] 1 Q.B. 29; [1954] 2 All E.R. 723

[2] National Insurance Act, 1965, s. 98.

[3] *Ibid.*, s. 99.   [4] *Ibid.*, s. 100.

[5] S. 101. The explorations and exploitations under the North Sea are regulated by the Continental Shelf Act, 1964.

[6] National Insurance Act, 1965, s. 102.

[7] *Ibid.*, 1965, s. 9.

[8] *Department of Health and Social Security* v. *Walker Dean Walker, Ltd.*, [1970] 2 Q.B. 74.

moneys provided by Parliament.[1] The original rates of contribution have, of course, been varied and are now to be found in Schedule
1.[2] The Act also provides for the collection of graduation sums
dependent upon the level of earnings for those employees who are
participating in the scheme for higher retirement pensions.[3] The old
rule which makes an employer liable, in the first instance, to pay his
own and his employees' contribution subject to his right to recover
the employees' contribution by deduction from wages, is continued.[4]

(3) **Benefits.**—Benefits now fall into two categories: a flat rate
benefit under the 1965 scheme and an earnings-related benefit under
the 1966 Act.

1965 Act—Flat rate.—Benefits receivable are to be found in
Schedules 3 and 4 to the National Insurance Act, 1965 as amended
in 1969.

The 1966 Act.—The formula for arriving at earnings-related benefit
is one-third of the normal weekly earnings between £9 and £30.
Thus a worker earning £21 a week would be entitled to one-third
×£12 (21–£9). There is a device called wage stop.[5] If the benefit
arrived at by adding both sources together exceeds 85 per cent of
normal weekly earnings, the sum is reduced to that 85 per cent.
This rule, however, only applies to the earnings-related addition.
It cannot be used to cut the flat rate. The formula for normal
weekly earnings is to take one-fiftieth of total earnings for the previous tax year.[6] It follows that taxed income is not counted unless
the tax is deducted by the employer under the P.A.Y.E. scheme.
This can produce difficult results in unusual cases.[7]

Eligibility.—Eligibility for unemployment benefit arises in respect
of any day of unemployment which forms part of a period of interruption of employment provided that at the date of the claim
the applicant is under pensionable age and has satisfied the relevant
contribution conditions. The relevant contribution conditions for
unemployment benefit are (*a*) that not less than twenty-six contributions shall have been paid between his entry to the scheme
and the days for which benefit is claimed and (*b*) not less than
fifty contributions have been paid or credited in respect of the last
contribution year before the beginning of the benefit year which includes the day for which benefit is claimed.[8] The terms "benefit

---

[1] *Ibid.*, s. 2.

[2] The Treasury is given power to vary the flat rate of contribution with a
view to maintaining a stable level of employment. *Ibid.*, s. 6. There is a new
Schedule 1 in the 1969 Act.

[3] *Ibid.*, ss. 4, 5.

[4] *Ibid.*, s. 11.

[5] S. 2.

[6] Set out on income tax form P. 60.

[7] *Baker* v. *Minister of Social Security*, [1969] 2 All E. R. 836 ; [1969] 1 W.L.R.
644.

[8] National Insurance Act, 1965, Sched. 2; but see s. 45 for the power to
make regulations entitling a person to benefits at lower rates where the contribution conditions have only been partially satisfied.

year" and "contribution year" have the same meaning, that is, any such period of fifty-two or fifty-three weeks as may be prescribed.[1] But a person is not entitled to benefit for the first three days of his unemployment unless within the period of thirteen weeks beginning with the first of those days he has a further nine days of unemployment forming part of the same period of interruption of employment.[2]   No day will be treated as a day of unemployment unless the applicant is, on that day, capable of and available for employment.[3]   It must also be a day upon which he is expected to work. The period during which a person will be entitled to unemployment benefit at the flat rate will normally expire at the end of three hundred and twelve days.   Thereafter he must requalify for benefit, though regulations may increase the period during which the unemployment benefit is receivable.   To requalify for benefit the applicant must pay thirteen more contributions.[4] The earnings-related benefit is of much shorter duration.   It lasts for only six months and periods are aggregated if the gap between them is thirteen weeks or less.   The benefit does not start for thirteen days.

Disqualification.—A person who has lost his employment as the result of a trade dispute at his place of employment will not be eligible for benefit during the continuance of the stoppage of work arising from the dispute except where he shows (a) that he has become *bona fide* employed elsewhere in his usual occupation or has become regularly employed in another occupation or (b) that he is not participating in, financing or directly interested in the dispute and (c) that he does not belong to a trade or class of worker of which, immediately before the stoppage, there were members employed at his place of employment any of whom are participating in, financing or directly interested in the dispute.[5]   Disqualification for a period not exceeding six weeks will arise where a person (a) has lost his employment through his misconduct or has voluntarily left such employment without just cause; (b) has, after notification of suitable employment refused or failed to apply for the employment or refused to accept it when it has been offered to him; (c) has neglected to avail himself of a reasonable opportunity of suitable employment; (d) has, without good cause refused or failed to carry out any written recommendations given to him by an officer of a labour employment exchange with a view to assisting him to find suitable employment; or (e) has without good cause refused or failed to avail himself of a reasonable opportunity of receiving training approved by the Secretary of State for Employment for the purpose of becoming

---

[1] *Ibid.*, s. 114(1).
[2] *Ibid.*, s. 19(6).
[3] *Ibid.*, s. 20 (1).
[4] *Ibid.*, s. 21.
[5] *Ibid.*, s. 22 (1).

or keeping fit for entry into or return to regular employment.[1] In addition, regulations may provide for imposing, in the case of any class of persons, additional conditions with respect to the receipt of unemployment benefit and restrictions on the rate and duration thereof where such action appears necessary to prevent inequalities or injustice to employed or self-employed persons.[2] Employment will not be deemed suitable employment if it is either (a) in a situation vacant in consequence of a trade dispute; or (b) if it is employment in his usual occupation in the district where the person was last employed at a lower rate of remuneration or on conditions less favourable than those he would have obtained had he continued to be employed, or might reasonably have expected to obtain; or (c) employment in his usual occupation in any other district at lower rates of remuneration or on less favourable conditions than those generally observed in that district by agreement between employers and employed or, where there is no such agreement, than those generally recognised in that district by good employers. After the lapse of a reasonable period of unemployment, however, employment will not be deemed unsuitable merely because it is employment of a kind other than that in which the unemployed person is usually engaged, provided that neither rates of remuneration nor conditions are less favourable than those generally observed by agreement between employers and employed or, where there is no such agreement, than those generally recognised by good employers.[3]

The reader will recognise in these disqualifications from benefits survivals from the older law, but it is desirable to look at them now in some detail. In the past, under the Unemployment Insurance Acts, they have provided the basis of many decisions given by the umpire.[4] In the first place, an applicant is not entitled to benefit if his unemployment arises from a trade dispute in which he is actively participating, financially or otherwise.[5] A trade dispute in this connection is defined by the Act as any dispute between employers and employees, or between employees, connected with the employment or non-employment or the terms or conditions of employment of any persons whether employees of the employer with whom the dispute arises or not.[6] It should be noted therefore that where the unemployment arises from a dispute between two or more employers, the applicant is not disqualified. On the other hand, it is clear that disputes between workers in different unions or between unionists and non-unionists,[7] sympathetic strikes and the like, are trade disputes within the Act. He is not disqualified if he belongs

---

[1] National Insurance Act, 1965, s. 22 (2).
[2] *Ibid.*, s. 22 (4).
[3] *Ibid.*, s. 22 (5).
[4] Now the Commissioner.
[5] He has to be directly interested: *Punton* v. *Ministry of Pensions and National Insurance* (No. 2), [1964] 1 All E.R. 448.
[6] National Insurance Act, 1965, s. 22(6) (a).
[7] Umpire's Decisions, 1705/1911 ; 214/1926.

to a grade or class of worker not participating.[1]   The disqualification
it will be remembered, is defeated where, in good faith, the worker
takes up other work in the same occupation or becomes regularly
employed in some other occupation.   The essence of this provision
is that the new employment must be genuine.[2]   Employment taken
up merely in an attempt to defeat the disqualification will not, in
fact, do so.[3]   Whether a person is participating in or financing a
dispute is a question of fact.   Cases have shown that mere pro-
fessions of sympathy are not enough, but no doubt arises where a
man ceases to work in answer to the call of the union of which he is a
member.   All members of a union which is financing a trade dispute
are within the disqualification if they become unemployed in consequence of the dispute.

The disqualification which arises where work is lost through misconduct or where the applicant has voluntarily left his employment
should also be noted.   The types of misconduct involved have, in
large measure, been discussed in the section of this book devoted to
the duties of a servant.[4]   A man who is in breach of the duty faithfully to serve his master, who fails to render due and truthful
accounts, who is insubordinate, who is an habitually bad timekeeper
or is negligent, will obviously not be entitled to unemployment
insurance if he loses his work for any of these reasons.   Where
a man voluntarily leaves his employment experience suggests that
he does so by reason of some real or imaginary grievance against his
employer.   A reasonable grievance will no doubt afford a defence
against disqualification.   But to leave work is, in its way, a not less
drastic action than summary dismissal on the part of the master,
and ought not to be resorted to until other means have been tried
and failed.   Unreasonable action, however, on the part of the
master will provide a just cause for a servant's voluntarily leaving
the employment and enable the worker to receive unemployment
benefit.

Finally, some comment is necessary on the disqualification which
arises from failure to apply for a vacant situation or the refusal,
without good cause, to accept any suitable employment offered.
The Act itself lays down conditions which prevent insured and
unemployed workmen from being used to break a strike or to depress
the rates of remuneration or the conditions of labour of employed
persons.   What is "suitable" employment in any given case is a
question of fact but the employment clearly must be in the United
Kingdom[5] and the onus of proving suitability is on the Government
officer concerned.[6]

The administrative machinery of the older Acts is, in large

---

[1] R(u) 32/53; R(u) 22/55.
[2] R(u) 39/56.
[3] Umpire's Decisions, No. 8642.
[4] See Chapter III.
[5] Umpire's Decisions, 1195/1927.
[6] *Ibid.*, 10352/1930.

measure, reproduced in the new. The Secretary of State is responsible for the control and management of a National Insurance Fund made up of the contributions of employers, insured persons and monies provided by Parliament,[1] and there is also a National Insurance (Reserve) Fund to which were carried all the assets collected as the result of legislation prior to 1946, and to which fund the Secretary of State may pay assets from the National Insurance Fund, which assets will be maintained as a reserve.[2] The administrative bodies are firstly, a National Insurance Advisory Committee with the same functions of advice and assistance as had the earlier Unemployment Insurance Statutory Committee.[3] The constitution of the committee provides for a chairman and not less than four nor more than eight other members, one at least of whom shall be a woman, appointed by the Secretary of State. The duration of office as a member of this committee will normally be five years and no member of the committee will be capable of being elected to or of sitting in the House of Commons. Of the members of the committee, other than the chairman, one will be appointed after consultation with employers' organisations, one after consultation with workers' organisations, one after consultation with friendly societies and one, if and when reciprocal arrangements with the appropriate Northern Irish authority are in force, after consultation with that authority.[4] The advisory committee not only has the function of giving advice and assistance generally, but draft regulations which the Secretary of State proposes to make must be submitted to the committee except those which relate to reciprocal arrangements and Northern Ireland, to transitional provisions, to the transfer of assets and liabilities, to compensation for displaced employees, to consequential amendments and savings, to the power to make further consequential and transitional provisions and to consequential provisions and savings for Northern Ireland. Regulations on these matters will not be submitted to the advisory committee.[5] Where a preliminary draft is submitted the committee will publish it together with a statement of the time, not less than fourteen nor more than twenty-eight days, within which written objections may be made. The committee will consider the draft regulations and any objections made and will report to the Secretary of State who, after consideration, may make regulations or in the case of certain regulations, lay the draft before Parliament.[6] The orders and regulations which must be laid before Parliament are those concerned with the power to vary contribution rates,[7] those

---

[1] National Insurance Act, 1965, s. 83.
[2] *Ibid.*, s. 84.
[3] *Ibid.*, s. 88.
[4] *Ibid.*, Sched. 8.
[5] *Ibid.*, s. 108.
[6] *Ibid.*, s. 108 (4).
[7] *Ibid.*, s. 6.

concerned with supplementary schemes, those concerned with modifying the provisions of the Act in relation to mariners and airmen and married women, those relating to temporary provisions as to unemployment benefit and those relating to compensation for displaced employees. In each of these cases the orders and regulations must be approved by resolution of each House of Parliament.[1]

In the case of regulations which do not require to be laid before Parliament, the Secretary of State may, in cases of urgency or for any other special reason, promulgate the regulations as provisional regulations, before receiving or considering the report of the advisory committee. But provisional regulations may not remain in force for longer than three months after the Secretary of State has received the report. Wherever regulations, other than provisional regulations, are laid before Parliament there must also be laid therewith the report of the committee and a statement showing the amendments, if any, which have been made since the report of the committee and the effect given to any recommendation of the committee; and where a recommendation of the committee has not been accepted, the reasons for its non-adoption.[2]

To the National Advisory Committee will be added local committees representing employers, insured persons or both, to which questions bearing upon the administration of the Act will be submitted for consideration and advice.[3] Provision is made in the Act for reciprocal arrangements with Northern Ireland, the Dominions, Colonies and foreign countries. If legislation is passed for the co-ordination of the Northern Irish system of insurance with our own a joint authority will be set up which will have power to make any necessary financial adjustments and to discharge such other co-ordinative functions as may be provided for.[4]

Rights to benefit will be determined in the first instance by an officer of the Department of Health and Social Security who will himself determine the existence of a claim or submit the question to a local tribunal, the counterpart of the older court of referees. The local tribunal may also, as provided by regulation, hear appeals from the decisions of the insurance officers. Regulations may also provide for enabling appeals to be brought from the tribunal to a National Insurance Commissioner or deputy commissioner or to a tribunal to be presided over by one or other of these officials.[5] The Act provides for the appointment, in addition to insurance officers, of inspectors having powers of a kind with which the reader is already familiar and who will be concerned, as in the past, with investigations as to the employment or unemployment, and similar matters, of claimants for benefit.

---

[1] National Insurance Act, 1965, s. 107.
[2] *Ibid.*, s. 108 (5).
[3] *Ibid.*, s. 89.
[4] *Ibid.*, s. 104.
[5] *Ibid.*, s. 70.

CHAPTER V

RELATIONS OF MASTER AND SERVANT WITH THIRD PARTIES

The law imposes on a master liabilities towards injured persons in certain cases where the injury arises out of the tort, the contract, or the crime of his servant. Similarly the servant may, by virtue of his service, incur liabilities to persons other than the master where, but for the service, no liability would arise. Conversely, the parties to the contract of service may become possessed of rights enforceable against third parties, arising out of or by virtue of the contract of service.

1. THE MASTER'S LIABILITIES

(1) In Tort

Vicarious liability. A tort is a wrong committed by one person against another which does not arise out of contract or breach of trust and for which the appropriate remedy is a civil action for damages. Every man is responsible for his own tort whether he be a master or a servant, but the law also holds a master to be liable for such torts as his servant commits in the scope of his employment. The basis of the rule has been variously described. In *Swainson* v. *North Eastern Ry. Co.* it was said that the master was "liable for an injury done to a stranger by his servant acting within the scope of the latter's authority because the stranger has had no hand in the choice of the servant."[1] The point has been elaborated:

> "Upon the principle *qui facit per alium facit per se* the master is responsible for the acts of his servant and that person is undoubtedly liable, who stood in the relation of master to the wrongdoer—he who had selected him as his servant, from the knowledge of a belief in his skill and care, and who could remove him for misconduct, and whose orders he was bound to receive and obey . . ."[2]

But whatever be the theoretical basis of the rule, its practical convenience lies in the fact that the servant will frequently be a man of straw and the master a man of relative substance. Damages awarded against a servant might well be meaningless; against a master there is a greater probability that they will be paid.

When the master authorises the servant's act, either in prospect or retrospect, no difficulty arises. In any such case the normal

---

1 (1878), 3 Ex. D. 341, *per* BRAMWELL, L.J., at p. 348.
2 *Quarman* v. *Burnett* (1840), 6 M. & W. 499, *per* PARKE, B., at p. 509.

principles of the law of agency would fasten liability upon the master. Similarly, where the master instructs his servant to perform an act but imposes restrictions of a character with which the servant finds it difficult to comply so that the servant offends the restriction, the master will still be presumed to have authorised the act. This was the situation in *Gregory* v. *Piper*.[1] The servant was ordered to lay rubbish near to, but not touching, another's wall. In fact, the rubbish touched the wall and the master was liable to its owner in trespass. As to authorisation in retrospect, it has been held that a master who ratifies a purchase made by his servant, will be liable for conversion if the object purchased is one which the seller had no right to sell. And, apparently, it does not matter that the master, when he ratified, was unaware that the transaction constituted a tort.[2]

Scope of Employment.—The rule of vicarious liability, however, is much wider in scope than the performance of acts which are actually or by necessary implication, authorised by the master. The rule covers every such act of the servant as, doing harm to a third party, falls within the scope of the servant's employment. Litigation arising out of the rule has been extensive. The student will be concerned not with the poverty but with the multiplicity of instances, and in attempting to determine a master's liability in any given set of circumstances it is the distinctions of fact rather than the questions of law which are likely to constitute the difficulty. Decisions turn largely upon their individual facts and it has been said that there is no one test which is conclusive or exhaustive or exclusive.[3]

It has sometimes been suggested that an act which is *ultra vires* the master cannot make the master liable. The plaintiff in *Poulton* v. *London and South Western Ry. Co.*[4] was entitled, according to the defendant company's advertised regulations, to take his horse on the return journey without payment of fare provided he produced a certain certificate. At the end of the journey the company's servant demanded the fare, and on the plaintiff's refusal to pay, apprehended and detained him. Clearly in such circumstances the company had no right of arrest and

> " having no power themselves, they cannot give the station-master any power to do the act . . . the wrongful imprisonment is an act for which the plaintiff, if he has a remedy at all, has it against the station-master personally, but not against the railway company."[5]

The result was similar where a passenger holding a first-class season ticket was accused by a porter, who took him by the arm, of having

---

[1] (1829), 9 B. & C. 591.
[2] *Hilbery* v. *Hatton* (1864), 2 H. & C. 822.
[3] *Per* FINNEMORE, J., in *Staton* v. *National Coal Board*, [1957] 2 All E.R 667; [1957] 1 W.L.R. 893.
[4] (1867), L.R. 2 Q.B. 534.
[5] *Ibid.*, *per* BLACKBURN, J., at p. 540.

travelled first-class with a third-class railway ticket. The passenger brought an action against the railway company for assault and false imprisonment, but the company was held not to be liable, for it had no power of arrest itself and could not impliedly authorise the porter to make an arrest.[1] It is doubtful, however, whether the view that the master cannot be liable for the act of a servant which is *ultra vires* the master is a correct view of the law and *Poulton's* case is perhaps best regarded only as authority for the statement that a station-master who arrests a passenger for refusing to pay freight, is acting beyond his *implied* authority. He is thus acting outside the scope of his employment and cannot bind his master.

Compare these cases, however, with *Goff* v. *Great Northern Ry. Co.*[2] Goff, having travelled on the company's line tendered, by mistake, the return half of a ticket which had expired though he had the correct ticket in his pocket. He was taken to the ticket office and he there explained his mistake. He was nevertheless taken to the office of the superintendent of the line and ultimately before a magistrate. The magistrate dismissed the complaint and the company was held liable for those acts of its servants as had amounted to false imprisonment—for the company had power to apprehend in such circumstances. In *Goff's* case, the servant's act amounted to an error of judgment in the performance of his duty, for which the master must accept liability. The same approach can be seen in *Seymour* v. *Greenwood*[3] and *Bayley* v. *Manchester, Sheffield and Lincolnshire Ry. Co.*[4] In *Seymour's* case the guard of an omnibus ejected a drunken passenger who was thrown on to the ground and injured. In *Bayley's* case, a porter believing the plaintiff to be in the wrong train, ejected him so zealously as to injure him. The master was liable in both cases and in the latter, the legal grounds of liability in such circumstances were carefully considered.

> "A person who puts another in his place to do a class of acts in his absence, necessarily leaves him to determine, according to the circumstances, when an act of that class is to be done; and consequently he is held answerable for the wrong of the person so intrusted either in the manner of doing such an act, or in doing such an act under circumstances in which it ought not to have been done, provided that what was done was done, not from any caprice of the servant, but in the course of the employment."[5]

In short, if the master gives the servant a discretion he must accept the consequences of its being used inadvisedly.

An act, of course, may be so personal to the workman that it is outside the scope of his employment. Where a servant, who had

---

[1] *Ormiston* v. *Great Western Ry. Co.*, [1917] 1 K.B. 598.

[2] (1861), 3 E. & E. 672.

[3] (1861), 7 H. & N. 355.

[4] (1872), L.R. 7 C.P. 415.

[5] *Ibid., per* WILLES, J., at p. 420.

erroneously imagined that the plaintiff was trying to drive away from his employer's garage without paying for purchases supplied, was threatened that he would be reported, tempers were frayed and despite the presence of a policeman, the servant assaulted the plaintiff. It was held that this action was one of personal vengeance and so was unrelated to what the servant was employed to do.[1] Rather more surprisingly, the act of a lorry driver who crossed the road, a dual carriageway, to a transport café and, partly through his own negligence, caused an accident, was also held to be outside his employment even though he was driving his lorry on his master's business and had permission to stop for breakfast.[2] The judgment of PILCHER, J. is interesting in that he indicates various circumstances where the driver might possibly have been acting within the scope of his employment in crossing the road. He might well be within the scope of his employment if he were crossing for a tin of petrol, for example.[3]

In *Harvey* v. *R. G. O'Dell Ltd.*[4] workmen out on an all day job were regarded as within the scope of their employment when going for a meal. The point, however, is *obiter* because McNAIR, J., held that the journey to a neighbouring town for a meal also involved, as primary aim, the collection of tools. In contrast, in *Hilton* v. *Thomas Burton (Rhodes), Ltd.*[5] workmen on their way from a café some miles from their work were held to be not in the scope of their employment. DIPLOCK, J. took the view that the men were merely filling in time before the official end to their working day and so held that they were on a frolic of their own outside the scope of their employment. The law has also been firm in excluding travelling from and to work. This point has featured in many cases under the National Insurance (Industrial Injuries) Act and the rule is well established.[6] It has been illustrated in *Vandyke* v. *Fender*[7], where an employer provided a car and petrol so that two of his workers could travel 30 miles to work, and bring other workmen with them. There was an accident. Vandyke was injured, and it was held that he was not in the course of his employment as he was not obliged by his employer to travel in that way.

An act, however will be in the scope of a servant's employment when the servant does what he is employed to do though he does it in a wrongful manner. A servant who lights a cigarette whilst pouring petrol from a drum to a tin[8] or from a tank to a vehicle[9] so that the

---

[1] *Warren* v. *Henley's, Ltd.*, [1948] 2 All E.R. 935.
[2] *Crook* v. *Derbyshire Stone, Ltd.*, [1956] 2 All E.R. 447; [1956] 1 W.L.R. 432.
[3] *Ibid.*, at pp. 450, 436 respectively.
[4] [1958] 1 All E.R. 657.
[5] [1961] 1 All E.R. 74; [1961] 1 W.L.R. 705.
[6] See *infra*, p. 401.
[7] [1970] 2 Q.B. 292; [1970] 2 All E.R. 335, and see a similar case, *Nottingham* v. *Aldridge*, [1971] 2 Q.B. 739; [1971] 2 All E.R. 751.
[8] *Jefferson* v. *Derbyshire Farmers, Ltd.*, [1921] 2 K.B. 281.
[9] *Century Insurance Co., Ltd.* v. *Northern Ireland Road Transport Board*, [1942] A.C. 509; [1942] 1 All E.R. 491.

petrol ignites will render his employer liable to all those who are injured. In the earlier case of *Williams* v. *Jones*[1] the defendant was held not to be liable for the destruction by fire of a shed. He had been allowed use of the shed by the plaintiff in order that his servant might make a signboard. The defendant's servant, as a consequence of his carpentry, littered the floor of the shed with shavings which became ignited as a result of the negligent lighting of his pipe; the shed was destroyed but the master was held not to be liable. The case has been distinguished from *Jefferson* v. *Derbyshire Farmers, Ltd.* on the ground that lighting a cigarette whilst pouring petrol was a negligent way of performing an act which had intrinsically certain elements of danger, whilst lighting a pipe was not necessarily negligent in relation to the making of a signboard.

> " It was in the scope of his (the servant's) employment to fill the tin with motor spirit from the drum. That work required special precautions . . . the (servant) was doing the work of his employers in an improper way and without taking reasonable precautions. . . . *Williams* v. *Jones* is distinguishable because the making of a signboard is not in itself a dangerous operation. The act of the carpenter in lighting his pipe has no connection with the work he was engaged to perform. That act was no breach of any duty to exercise due care and caution . . . because the work on which he was engaged was not dangerous."[2]

It is, however, significant of the judicial tendency towards increasing the liability of the master in these cases that doubts have recently been expressed as to the validity of that distinction whilst the opinion has been expressed in the House of Lords that the dissenting judgment in favour of the liability of the master in *Williams* v. *Jones* was the better statement of the law.[3] The widening interpretation is perhaps illustrated by *Kay* v. *I.T.W., Ltd.*[4] where a forklift truck driver found his way blocked by a customer's lorry parked on his employer's premises. In attempting to move it he injured a fellow servant. He was held to be acting in the scope of his employment.

Provided that the act is within the scope of the employment, the master will be liable though he has expressly forbidden the servant to do it. Thus a workman who, contrary to his master's instructions, leaves his horse unattended[5] or who drives so as to harry the vehicles of a rival firm[6] or allows another to drive the

---

[1] (1865), 3 H. & C. 256; on appeal 3 H. & C. 602.
[2] *Jefferson* v. *Derbyshire Farmers, Ltd.*, [1921] 2 K.B. 281, *per* WARRINGTON, L.J., at p. 288.
[3] *Century Insurance Co., Ltd.* v. *Northern Ireland Road Transport Board*, [1942] A.C. 509; [1942] 1 All E.R. 491, *per* Viscount SIMON, L.C., at pp. 515, 495 respectively.
[4] [1968] 1 Q.B. 140; [1967] 3 All E.R. 22.
[5] *Whatman* v. *Pearson* (1868), L.R.3 C.P. 422; *Engelhart* v. *Farrant & Co.*, [1897] 1 Q.B. 240.
[6] *Limpus* v. *London General Omnibus Co.* (1862), 1 H. & C. 526; *London County Council* v. *Cattermoles (Garages), Ltd.*, [1953] 2 All E.R. 582.

master's vehicle[1] will make his master liable if others are injured.
Express prohibitions have been considered in cases concerning lifts
given to third parties.   In *Twine* v. *Bean's Express Ltd.*[2] a driver
employed by the defendants, contrary to instructions which were
displayed in the van, gave a lift to a third person who was killed
because of the driver's negligence.   It was held that the employers
were not liable for

> " it was outside the scope of the driver's employment for him to
> bring within the class of persons to whom a duty to take care was
> owed by the employer, a man to whom, contrary to his instructions,
> he gave a lift in a commercial van."[3]

The same line of argument was followed in *Conway* v. *Geo. Wimpey
& Co., Ltd.*[4] where the facts were much the same except that despite
the clear instructions to the contrary, prohibited persons were
frequently carried.   There was, however, no evidence of knowledge
on the part of the defendants of this and so they were not liable.
This would seem to suggest that liability would attach to a licensee
but not to a trespasser.

In both *Twine's* case and *Conway's* case the injured person had
been deemed to be a trespasser. DENNING, L.J., however, in *Young* v.
Edward Box & Co., Ltd.[5] doubted whether this was in any way
conclusive.   Young was a workman employed by Box & Co., Ltd.,
and by the terms of his contract he was himself responsible for
getting to and from the site of his work.   On Sunday evenings,
however, because of the pressure on the public transport service,
a practice had grown up of giving the plaintiff and his fellow workmen lifts on the defendant's vehicles.   In this practice, the plaintiff's
foreman and the driver concurred.   The employer was held to be
liable, two judges holding that the right to sanction a ride on the
lorry was within the ostensible authority of the foreman and that in
relying on that authority the plaintiff became a licensee.

> " The liability of the owner does not depend on whether the
> passenger was a trespasser or not; it depends on whether the driver
> was acting within the scope of his employment."[6]

Though, of course, there are significant distinctions of fact in the
Conway case and in the *Young* case, it cannot be said that they add
much by way of clarification to a confused state of the law.   Indeed,
perhaps their most significant contribution is to demonstrate, once
again, the accidents of litigation in England.   For the cases were
heard almost contemporaneously by different divisions of the Court
of Appeal.   It would have been valuable to have had the first case

---

[1] *Ilkiw* v. *Samuels*, [1962] 2 All E.R. 879; [1963] 1 W.L.R. 991.
[2] [1946] 1 All E.R. 202.
[3] *Ibid.*, p. 204.
[4] [1951] 2 K.B. 266; [1951] 1 All E.R. 363.
[5] [1951] 1 T.L.R. 789.
[6] *Per* DENNING, L.J., [1951] 1 T.L.R. 789 at p. 794.

in point of time discussed in the later case. It would seem, however, that any development of the law by way of discussions on the status of the injured party (*i.e.*, whether he was a licensee or trespasser) is not likely to be fruitful and thus the test of scope of the employment must still prevail.

The master, however, will have a defence where he can show that he not only forbade the act but that the act was for the exclusive convenience of the servant. In *Rand* v. *Craig*[1] carters employed by the respondents took rubbish to a piece of land which belonged to the appellants and was close at hand and tipped it there instead of on the dump provided by their employers, which was further off. They did this so that they could carry more loads in the day and earn more money. Their employers were held not to be liable. The court considered the same problem in a rather more original form in *Performing Right Society Ltd.* v. *Mitchell and Booker (Palais de Danse), Ltd.*[2] The plaintiffs accused the defendant company of infringing copyrights by permitting the performance of, or performing, certain dance music in their dance hall. The band, which the judge described as a "migratory thing," had a clause in its contract with the defendants in which it undertook not to infringe copyright. The defendants had posted in their hall a statement that no music must be played excepting such as was free of licence. It was held that the band was acting within the scope of its employment and the plea that it was acting for its own exclusive convenience failed.

> "I cannot doubt that in the present case the band were acting in the course of their employment and for the defendants' benefit, for they were engaged for the very purpose of playing dance music at the defendants' hall. I am satisfied moreover that they did not infringe copyright knowingly or wilfully. . . . This is not a case of wilful misconduct by the band for their own purposes, and it seems clear therefore that the case of *Rand* v. *Craig* . . . has no application here."[3]

The scope of a servant's employment is not narrowly construed, and, where the interests and property of the master are in danger, unusual acts may be considered as falling within the scope of the servant's employment. A railway inspector who gave a passenger into custody on the latter's refusal to pay excess fare involved his employers in liability when the charge was dismissed and the passenger brought an action for trespass and false imprisonment.[4] In *Poland* v. *John Parr and Sons*[5] one of the defendant's carters, having finished his work, was walking home behind a lorry which

---

[1] [1919] 1 Ch. 1.
[2] [1924] 1 K.B. 762.
[3] *Performing Right Society, Ltd.* v. *Mitchell and Booker (Palais de Danse) Ltd.*, [1924] 1 K.B. 762, *per* McCardie, J. at p. 772.
[4] *Moore* v. *Metropolitan Ry. Co.* (1872), L.R. 8 Q.B. 36.
[5] [1927] 1 K.B. 236.

was being driven by one of his employers.   Thinking that a youth
was stealing sugar from the lorry he struck the boy, who fell and
was injured.   The employer was held liable, though had the carter's
act been so excessive as to take it out of the class of authorised acts,
he would not have been so.[1]

In such cases it is the emergency which justifies the servant's act,
and the scope of his employment will contract as the emergency
passes.   In one case[2] the plaintiff tendered a German gold coin in
mistake for half a sovereign and asked the barman for change.
The barman, before he gave the change, called the plaintiff's attention to the coin and was given a half-sovereign.   Despite this, when
the plaintiff left the public house he was followed by the manager
and given into custody on a charge of attempting to pass false
money.   The defendant was held not to be liable for his manager's
act.   Any implied power to arrest ceased when the employer's
property was no longer in danger.   A railway clerk may bind his
master by ordering the arrest of one who robs the till, during the
act of robbery.   He cannot do so after the robbery is over for his
master's property is no longer in jeopardy.[3]   It follows that a
porter, though he be temporarily in charge of a station, has no
authority to give persons in charge on the mere suspicion that they
have stolen his employers' property.[4]

Whether an emergency exists is a question of fact.   The point
was considered with some care in *Gwilliam* v. *Twist*.[5]   A policeman,
believing the defendants' servant to be drunk, ordered him to cease
driving the defendants' omnibus.   The driver and the conductor
then permitted a bystander to drive, and as a consequence, the
plaintiff was injured.   It was held that a servant could not delegate
the performance of his duty to another except in cases of emergency,
and emergency could not arise in this connection if the servant had
an opportunity to consult his employer, as he had here.

Whether, given a state of emergency, the servant's act is justified
thereby, is also a question of fact.   The defendant in *Houghton* v.
Pilkington[6] employed a man and a boy to deliver milk.   The boy
was hurt, and the plaintiff offered to assist in taking the boy back.
For this purpose she got into the milk float.   Whilst she was doing
so the man carelessly started the horse and the plaintiff, too, was
injured.   The court admitted the emergency but denied that it gave

---

[1] *Ibid., per* SCRUTTON, L. J. at p. 242.
[2] *Abrahams* v. *Deakin*, [1891] 1 Q.B. 516, and see *Hanson* v. *Waller*, [1901]
1 K.B. 390.
[3] *Allen* v. *London and South Western Ry. Co.* (1870), L.R. 6 Q.B.65.
[4] *Edwards* v. *London and North Western Ry. Co.* (1870), L.R.5 C.P. 445.
[5] [1895] 2 Q.B. 84.   *Cf. Ricketts* v. *Thos. Tilling Ltd.*, [1915] 1 K.B. 644;
Ilkiw v. *Samuels*, [1963] 1 W.L.R. 991.   The *Beard* v. *London General
Omnibus Co.*, [1900] 2 Q.B. 530, was discussed in *Kay* v. *I.T.W., Ltd.*, [1968]
1 Q.B. 140; [1967] 3 All E.R. 22.
[6] [1912] 3 K.B. 308.

the servant authority to invite the plaintiff into the float. The latter, therefore, had no right of action against the defendant. The assessment of the situation has to depend upon modern social conditions and earlier cases are not always a good guide.

The fact that the servant's act is fraudulent or criminal will not necessarily absolve the master from liability. Two cases will illustrate the legal position arising from fraud (though, of course, the criminal element is present in both). In the first[1] a solicitor's managing clerk advised a widow, in order to improve her income, to sell certain cottages and call in certain mortgage moneys. For that purpose the widow handed the deeds to him and signed certain documents he had prepared. The documents conveyed the property and transferred the mortgage to the clerk. The client did not know this. She believed that her signature was necessary to enable the properties to be sold. The clerk then absconded with the proceeds. The employers were held liable. It was of no moment that the act was not in the masters' interest. As was said in *Barwick* v. *English Joint Stock Bank*—

" He (the master) has put the agent in his place to do that particular class of acts and he must be answerable for the manner in which the agent has conducted himself."[2]

In the second case, *Uxbridge Permanent Benefit Building Society* v. *Pickard*,[3] a solicitor employed one, Conway, to manage his branch office. Conway, by producing forged (and fictitious) title deeds, induced the plaintiffs to advance a sum of £500. Conway's employer was held to be liable though the person defrauded was not (as in *Lloyd* v. *Grace, Smith and Co.*) his client. In both cases the servant's act was one in which his authority was not, in fact, limited. There was no limitation of the servant's ostensible authority to carry through such a piece of business on behalf of his employer.[4] It may be otherwise where the employer is a limited company whose powers (and consequently those of its servants) are limited by the documents of its incorporation.[5] For a limited company has been held not to be liable on share certificates fraudulently issued by its secretary.[6]

In *Dyer* v. *Munday*[7] an employer was held liable for a criminal assault committed by his servant. The master and servant relationship was held not to have been severed, though such a possibility was foreseen; " I do not say," said Lord ESHER, M.R.,

---

[1] *Lloyd* v. *Grace, Smith & Co.*, [1912] A.C. 716; see also *United Africa Co., Ltd.* v. *Saka Owade*, [1955] A.C. 130.
[2] (1867), L.R. 2 Exch. 259 *per* WILLES, J., at p. 266.
[3] [1939] 2 K.B. 248; [1939] 2 All E.R. 344, C.A.
[4] *Ibid.*, *per* MACKINNON, L. J., at pp. 258, 351 respectively.
[5] *Ruben* v. *Great Fingall Consolidated*, [1906] A.C. 439, doubting *Shaw* v. *Port Philip Colonial Gold Mining Co. Ltd.* (1884), 13 Q.B.D. 103.
[6] *Ruben* v. *Great Fingall Consolidated, supra.*
[7] [1895] 1 Q.B. 742.

"that the criminal act may not be of such a character as to induce
the jury to say that it could not have been done in furtherance of
the master's business, or at all in the interests of the master. It
may well be that the question whether an offence is a criminal one
may be a material fact for the jury to consider from that point of
view but the mere fact that it is a criminal offence is not sufficient
to take the case out of the general rule."[1]

In an important recent case, *Morris* v. *C. W. Martin & Sons, Ltd.*,[2]
the Court of Appeal reconsidered the position of the fraudulent
servant. The case is notable for an attempt by Lord DENNING to
put the rules into order by reference to the duty of the master towards the goods or property of the plaintiff. Thus he discusses the
cases under headings such as gratuitous bailment, bailment for
reward, occupier's liability and so on. This new approach does
little to clarify the rules of vicarious liability which are themselves
adequate to deal with the question. The facts of the case were
basically that a servant of the defendants stole furs which had been
sent for cleaning. The master was held to be responsible for the
theft by the servant and an earlier authority which had caused the
County Court judge to decide otherwise was overruled.[3] The old
idea that the servant's crime must have been done for the master's
benefit or with his knowledge is now firmly rejected.[4]

In every case, however, in which the master is liable, the act out of
which his liability arises is actually or ostensibly within the scope
of the servant's employment. Consequently, cases where the
servant uses his master's time or property for purposes alien to the
employment are sharply to be distinguished. In such cases the
master will not be liable, though the decisions show niceties perplex-
ing to the student. The defendant in *Storey* v. *Ashton*[5] sent his clerk
and carman with a cart to deliver wine. This they did and, in
addition, collected certain empty bottles. Their duty was then to
return to the defendant's office, hand over the bottles, and drive
the horse to the stable. Instead (since it was after business hours),
the carman was persuaded by the clerk to drive to the clerk's house
and execute a certain commission for the clerk. Whilst doing this,
the accident occurred and the plaintiff was injured. The master
was not liable, and the same result was reached where a servant,
having taken out his master's dray for his own purposes, executed
those purposes and then, before the accident happened, collected
certain empty casks. He was employed to deliver and collect such
casks, and it was after he had collected the casks that the plaintiff
was injured. The argument that though he had set out on his own
purposes he had, by his act of collecting the casks, re-entered within

---

[1] *Supra, per* Lord ESHER, M.R., at p. 746.
[2] [1965] 2 All E.R. 725; [1965] 3 W.L.R. 276.
[3] *Cheshire* v. *Bailey*, [1905] 1 K.B. 237.
[4] For a fuller discussion, see the case note of J. A. Jolowicz, [1965] C.L.J. 200.
[5] (1869), L.R. 4 Q.B. 476; see also *Mitchell* v. *Crassweller* (1853), 13 C.B. 237.

the scope of his employment, was rejected.[1] It is submitted that when a servant uses the master's property for purposes of his own unconnected with the employment, the master will not be liable, though the master has given his consent to the use of the property.

Occasionally, the courts have been faced with situations in which the servant has injured another as a result of using his own property, whilst pursuing his master's business. In such cases the master will be liable. A servant who took out his own uninsured car on the firm's business, though three of the firm's vehicles were available and despite the publication of notices prohibiting the practice unless the vehicle was insured, made his master liable.[2]

A careful study of the cases we have just discussed will show that though they present much variety they are capable of classification, and, indeed, have been so classified by the Judicial Committee of the Privy Council. That Committee has placed them under three headings to which we would add a fourth :—

(i) Where the servant acts in the strictest conformity with the instructions of the master, or his master ratifies his acts.

(ii) Where the servant does work he is employed to do in a manner which the master has not authorised or would not have authorised had he known of it.

(iii) Where the servant, employed to do one thing, does another and thus acts outside the scope of his employment.

(iv) Where the servant uses his master's time or property for his own purposes.[3]

Acts which fit into the first and second categories will make the master liable. Those which fit into the third and fourth will not affect him. Together they comprehend, it is submitted, all those variations of fact with which the courts are likely to be faced in giving effect to the principle of the master's liability for the tortious acts of his servant committed against third persons.

The employer may be liable for his servant's tort even in those cases in which the servant himself would not be liable. A man and his wife were jointly employed and the husband negligently injured his wife, whilst acting within the scope of his employment. Now, according to the general principles of the law of tort at the time the capacity of one spouse to sue the other was strictly limited and no right of action arose as between the parties in the case of one spouse injured by the negligence of the other. The question before the court in the present case was whether the employer might be sued.

---

[1] *Rayner* v. *Mitchell* (1877), 2 C.P.D. 357; see also *Sanderson* v. *Collins.* [1904] 1 K.B. 628 and *Aitchison* v. *Page Motors Ltd.*, [1935] All E.R. Rep. 594,
[2] *Canadian Pacific Ry. Co.* v. *Lockhart,* [1942] A.C. 591; [1942] 2 All E.R. 464; see also *McKean* v. *Raynor Bros., Ltd. (Nottingham),* [1942] 2 All E.R. 650.
[3] Categories (ii), (iii) and (iv) are suggested by Lord PHILLIMORE delivering the recommendation of the J.C.P.C. in *Goh Choon Seng* v. *Lee Kim Soo,* [1925] A.C. 550 at p. 554. An express prohibition will not affect liability under category (ii).

The Court of Appeal decided that the employer was liable.[1] The case is not without its difficulties in logic, for if as between the spouses themselves there is no tort, on what points can the employer be made liable? SINGLETON, L.J., believed that as between husband and wife the difficulty lay not in the existence of a tortious act, for he accepted that there could be duties between husband and wife breach of which would be tortious, but in whether the spouses could sue thereon.   This also was the view of the other judges, though DENNING, L.J., put the position in broader, but more debatable terms:—

> "The master's liability for the negligence of his servant is not a vicarious liability but a liability of the master himself owing to his failure to see that his work is carefully and properly done . . . But even if the master's liability is a vicarious liability the husband's immunity is a mere rule of procedure . . . it is an immunity from suit and not an immunity from duty or liability, and so on that view of the law also, the master would be liable for the negligence of the servant."[2]

Where the tort is committed within a contractual relationship, for example negligence to a passenger, it is possible for the master to contract out of liability.   If he wishes to protect his servants also he must do so expressly and as their agent, otherwise the injured person retains an action against the servant.[3]

Independent Contractors.—The general rule that a master is liable only for the torts of his own servants and not for those of the servants of his independent contractors is subject to certain exceptions.[4] Wherever statute lays a duty upon an employer to perform certain work, he cannot escape liability to third parties by employing independent contractors, nor where the work itself is unlawful, or unduly hazardous, nor where he interferes in the direction of the work.   These exceptions to the general rule must be discussed with some care.

Firstly, wherever a person is under a statutory duty to perform a certain task or to perform the task in a certain way he remains responsible in the law of tort whether he does the work with the aid of his servants or employs an independent contractor.[5]   It follows that if the servant of an independent contractor injures a third person whilst pursuing the principal's statutory duty the principal will be liable.   So, where a local authority had contracted that certain sanitary duties laid upon it by Act of Parliament should be

---

[1] *Broom* v. *Morgan*, [1953] 1 Q.B. 597; [1953] 1 All E.R. 849, C.A.   The position as between husband and wife has been altered by the Law Reform (Husband and Wife) Act, 1962, and the limitations have been removed.

[2] *Ibid.*, at pp. 609 and 854 respectively.

[3] *Adler* v. *Dickson*, [1954] 1 W.L.R. 1482.   But see now Carriage of Goods by Sea Act, 1971.

[4] *Rapson* v. *Cubitt* (1842), 9 M. & W. 710.

[5] For a recent example concerning the duty of a carrier by sea to ensure the seaworthiness of his ship see *Riverstone Meat Co. Pty., Ltd.* v. *Lancashire Shipping Co., Ltd.*, [1961] A.C. 807; [1961] 1 All E.R. 495.

performed by another, the authority was responsible for the acts of that other's servants.[1] In *Hole* v. *Sittingbourne and Sheerness Ry. Co.*[2] the defendant company had, under its statute, power to construct a bridge subject to certain conditions protective of navigation on the river. They employed contractors to build the bridge according to the terms of the statute, but, before completion and because of a defect, the bridge could not be opened. As a consequence navigation was severely restricted. The defendant company was held to be liable in damages on the ground that it could not avoid its statutory responsibilities by contracting that another should observe them. Of course, the statute itself may provide that the general rule shall prevail and thus exempt the employer from liability for the torts of the contractor and the latter's servants.[3]

Secondly, wherever an employer engages a contractor to perform work, which turns out to be unlawful, he will be responsible for the acts of the contractor and the contractor's servants. The defendant company in *Ellis* v. *Sheffield Gas Consumers Co.*[4] employed contractors to open up trenches in a certain street and, when gas pipes had been laid, to fill in the trenches and make up the surface. Whilst the work was in progress the contractor's servants left a heap of rubble in the street. The plaintiff fell over this and suffered injury. It transpired that the act of opening up the street amounted to a public nuisance, since the defendants had no legal authority to do this. They were held to be liable in damages. They could not plead that the act was that of an independent contractor, for they had commissioned him to do something which was unlawful and their personal responsibility remained.

Thirdly, the employer remains liable where the work is of such a character as to be dangerous unless adequate precautions are taken. The rule has been stated in these terms—

> "A man who orders a work to be executed, from which, in the natural course of things, injurious consequences to his neighbour must be expected to arise, unless means are adopted by which such consequences may be prevented, is bound to see to the doing of that which is necessary to prevent the mischief. and cannot relieve himself of the responsibility by employing someone else."[5]

A defendant, who owned a house adjoining that of the plaintiff, owed the latter a right of support. He employed a contractor to pull down his house, excavate the foundations and build a new house. There was a clause in the contract with the contractor that the latter should give such support to the plaintiff's house as might prove necessary; should make any damage good, and should satisfy any claims which might arise. Yet the defendant was liable

---

[1] *Robinson* v. *Beaconsfield Rural Council*, [1911] 2 Ch. 188.
[2] (1861), 6 H. & N. 488.
[3] *Howitt* v. *Nottingham Tramways Co.* (1883), 12 Q.B.D. 16.
[4] (1853), 2 E. & B. 767. *Cf. Overton* v. *Freeman* (1852). 11 C.B. 867.
[5] *Bower* v. *Peate* (1876), 1 Q.B.D. 321 *per* COCKBURN, C.J., at p. 326.

on the contractor's failure to do these things.[1] In *Holliday* v.
National Telephone Co.[2] the court faced a similar problem. The
defendants were laying telephone wires along a street. They engaged a plumber to solder the wires. The plumber worked under
the general charge of the defendants' foreman and one of the
defendants' servants assisted him.   A lamp which he used for
the purposes of his work exploded because of a defect of which
the plumber ought to have been aware.   The plaintiff, who was
passing along the road, was burned, and he was held to be
entitled to recover from the defendant company, even though the
plumber was an independent contractor, for the defendant was
"under an obligation to the public to take care that persons passing
along the highway were not injured by the negligent performance
of the work."[3]

Occasionally, the courts have summarised this particular principle
by saying that if the danger arises from a casual act of negligence
on the part of the contractor, then the employer is not liable, for the
casual, or the collateral act, cannot be foreseen and guarded against
and to make the employer responsible for this would be unjust.[4]
Where, however, the act is one which the contractor was employed
to do the employer will be liable.   In *Pickard* v. *Smith*[5] the defendant occupied a refreshment room and cellar on a station platform.
A railway passenger walking along the platform fell down the
opening of the shute leading to the cellar.   The cover had been
taken from the shute by a coal merchant whose servants had
temporarily left the shute unguarded.   The defendant was liable
for the plaintiff's injuries and the ground of his liability was stated
with admirable clearness :—

> "The act of opening it (the coal shute) was the act of the em-
> ployer, though done through the agency of the coal merchant; and
> the defendant having thereby caused danger was bound to take
> reasonable means to prevent mischief . . . this duty he omitted; and
> the fact of his having intrusted it to a person who also neglected it,
> furnishes no excuse either in good sense or in law."[6]

Fourthly, and finally, an employer will remain liable for the acts
of his contractor where he personally interferes with the work.
So where A employed B to make a drain, and B's servants negligently
left a heap of gravel on a highway, A was held liable when C was
injured by driving into it, for the possible danger had been pointed
out to A, who had promised to remove the heap.[7]   The court found
that the promise of A to remove the gravel amounted to an act of
interference and an admission that he was exercising a *dominium*.

---

[1] *Ibid.*   [2] [1899] 2 Q.B. 392.
[3] *Ibid., per* HALSBURY, L.C. at p. 399.
[4] See ROMER, L.J., in *Penny* v. *Wimbledon Urban Council*, [1899] 2 Q.B. 72
at p. 78.
[5] (1861), 10 C.B. N.S. 470.
[6] *Pickard* v. *Smith* (1861), 10 C.B. N.S. 470, *per* WILLIAMS, J., at p. 480.
[7] *Burgess* v. *Gray* (1845), 1 C.B. 578.

Apart from these four exceptions, the employer is not responsible for the torts of the contractor or the latter's servants, and an injured person must look to the contractor for his damages.

(2) In Contract.—A master's liability on contracts entered into by his servant acting as his agent is, properly speaking, a branch of the law of agency. The student who wishes comprehensively to study the topic is referred to the standard books on agency, for we can do little more in this book than indicate the general principles.

The basis of the master's liability in contract, as in tort, is the maxim *qui facit per alium facit per se*. If a man charges another expressly or impliedly to act on his behalf, he must be responsible for that other's acts and if, as a consequence, third parties are injured, the master (or as the law of agency would say, the principal) must be liable. It follows that the principle of *ultra vires* applies in the law of contract. A principal may delegate to his agent all those contractual powers which he himself possesses, and the agent may assert them on his behalf.[1] But he cannot, by employing an agent of full capacity, hope to cure his own contractual disabilities. Consequently, an adult may employ an infant as an agent, and the infant, contracting on his principal's behalf, will bind his principal to the full extent of his principal's capacity. An adult principal, therefore, cannot plead his agent's infancy. Conversely an infant may employ an adult agent, but the agent will not be able to bind his principal to contracts which are void against or voidable by an infant.

The relation of master and servant does not, of itself, endow a servant with power to act as his master's agent. So where brandy was ordered by the defendant's butler in the defendant's name and consumed by the defendant's servants, the defendant was held not liable.

> "If the defendant had been in the habit of paying for goods ordered by his butler, he would be bound, but we must give up housekeeping if such evidence as this were to bind a master."[2]

The master will be liable only where it can be shown that there exists, between him and his servant, a contract of agency. That contract may arise if the master expressly authorises his servant to act in certain ways. The authority may be given in anticipation of the servant's act or after the acts have been performed, by means of ratification and adoption. Or the contract may arise impliedly from the master's dealing in such a way in relation to the servant that he is estopped from denying the servant's authority to act on his behalf. Finally, the relationship of principal and agent may arise (for it is difficult to speak of such circumstances in terms of contract) out of a necessity of which the master will be unaware.

---

[1] *Bevan* v. *Webb*, [1901] 2 Ch. 59, *per* STIRLING, L.J., at p. 77.
[2] *Maunder* v. *Conyers* (1817), 2 Stark. 281.

I.L.—9*

The form of the contract of agency is not material. Just as in the case of other contracts it may be formed by words spoken or written, though where the master wishes the servant to bind him by deed the servant's authority must be by deed.

The formation of the contract of agency where the authorisation is express and in anticipation of the servant's acts, need not detain us, but something ought to be said of agency by ratification. Such agency is of great antiquity. It was well established by the time of Henry IV[1], whilst its substance has been stated with great clearness by TINDAL, C.J., in *Wilson v. Tumman (Tummon)*[2] :—

> "That an act done, for another, by a person not assuming to act for himself, though without any precedent authority whatever, becomes the act of the principal if subsequently ratified by him is the known and well established rule of law. In that case the principal is bound by the act, whether it be tor his detriment or his advantage or whether it be founded on a tort or on a contract to the same extent as by, and with all the consequences which follow from, the same act done by his previous authority."

The ratification of a contract is ineffective unless the principal has full knowledge.[3] Here, a distinction is to be drawn between the ratification of a contractual act where the fullest knowledge is material, and the ratification of an act which turns out to be tortious in character. For, in the latter case, the master is bound by his ratification even though he was unaware, at the time, that the act was tortious.[4] A coachman who purported to pledge his master's credit for forage did not make the master liable even though the master used the goods, for he was unaware that his credit had been pledged.[5] Moreover, the agent must, at the time of entering into the contract, do so as an agent for the person who subsequently adopts the act.[6] The principal must ratify the whole contract, accepting its burdens as well as its benefits. In *Bristow v. Whitmore*, the master of a ship entered into an agreement to carry troops on behalf of the government. To fit the ship for this purpose he advanced money out of pocket as well as drawing bills on the owner. The owner adopted the transaction but contested the right of the ship's master to reimburse himself for the payments he had made out of the freights earned. The court found for the ship's master, on the ground that, if the latter had acted without authority, his employer might repudiate the contract. He could not take the benefits without performing the duties.[7]

---

[1] Year Book 7. Henry IV, fo. 35. 1.

[2] (1843), 6 Man. & G. 236 at p. 242; see also *Foster v. Bates* (1843), 12 M. & W. 226 especially *per* PARKE, B., at p. 233.

[3] *Banque Jacques-Cartier v. Banque d'Epargne de Montreal* (1887), 13 App. Cas. 111.

[4] *Hilbery v. Hatton* (1864), 2 H. & C. 822.

[5] *Wright v. Glyn*, [1902] 1 K.B. 745.

[6] *Phillips v. Eyre* (1870), L.R. 6 Q.B. 1, *per* WILLES, J., at p. 23.

[7] (1861), 9 H. L. Cas. 391.

Agency by estoppel or, as it is sometimes called, by "holding-out" arises wherever one person so acts as to lead another to believe that a third person is his agent. And wherever this results in that other contracting with the third person he will have a right of action against the principal. The question is, of course, entirely one of fact. In *Wright* v. *Glyn*[1] the master was, as we have seen, not liable on his servant's contract for the purchase of forage on credit. There was no express authority for the servant to pledge his master's credit, and though the master used the goods, the seller could not plead agency by ratification, for the master was unaware of the credit basis of the transaction. The case can be usefully contrasted with *Rimell* v. *Sampayo*,[2] where a coachman, dressed in his master's livery, hired horses which the master used. Despite the fact that the servant had agreed that he should provide the horses in consideration of the master's paying him an increased wage, the master was held to be liable when the servant did not, in fact, pay for the hire. There was no question of ratification because there was prior agreement the terms of which, it is true, had not been observed. But the man was in his master's livery, and the master was estopped from denying liability unless he could show that the lender of the horses had knowledge that the servant acted on his own behalf. In *Stubbing* v. *Heintz*[3] an employer was not liable where a servant, given money to buy goods, bought them on credit and appropriated the money, but where goods were delivered to a servant on credit and the master later paid for them, the master was held to be liable on subsequent transactions of a like character.[4]

The cases dealing with estoppel are often difficult to distinguish, and, as is so frequently the case where fact rather than law is in issue, the explanation will often be found in the weight which the court or the jury has attached to the evidence of the parties. In *Spooner* v. *Browning*[5] the defendants' clerk was paid a commission on business which was accepted on his introduction. He had no authority to accept orders on his employers' behalf. It was not usual for the defendants to give a formal notice of acceptance, and on three occasions orders given by the plaintiffs to the clerk were executed by the defendants. On each occasion payment was made by a cheque handed to the clerk; on the first two occasions made payable to the defendants, on the third to the clerk. The defendants credited the plaintiffs' account with the cheques and made no objection. Further orders were given to the clerk which the clerk did not execute, but by means of forgeries he induced the plaintiffs to pay to him cheques which he misappropriated. Despite

---

[1] *Supra.*
[2] (1824), 1 C. & P. 254.
[3] (1791), Peake, 66.
[4] *Hazard* v. *Treadwell* (1722), 1 Stra. 506.
[5] [1898] 1 Q.B. 528; see also *Farquharson Bros. & Co.* v. *King & Co.*, [1902] A.C. 325.

their previous conduct the defendants were held *not* liable, for the court found no evidence of holding out on their part.

Agency of necessity may arise where a servant is faced with an emergency in which he must act so as to preserve the interests of his employers and where he cannot communicate with his employer so as to secure the latter's authorisation. The law will not readily imply agency of necessity but if, for example, a servant held perishable goods on behalf of his master and the goods began to deteriorate, any sale made by the servant would doubtless be binding on the master. Wherever it is possible, in the emergency, for the servant to communicate with the master and he fails to do so, the master will not be bound. The resident agent of a mining company has been held not to possess the power to raise money on his employers' credit even though the alternative was the execution of warrants of distress upon the property of the mine.

> " There is no rule of law that an agent may, in a case of emergency, raise money and pledge the credit of his principal, for its repayment; and even if it were so, in this instance there was ample time and opportunity for him to have applied to his principals."[1]

It will be remembered that in *Gwilliam* v. *Twist*[2] a policeman forbade an omnibus driver, whom he believed to be drunk, to drive the vehicle. The conductor then asked a bystander to drive the bus to its destination. The bystander drove negligently so as to injure the plaintiff, but the owner of the vehicle was held not to be liable. The conductor was not an agent of necessity with power to make his master liable.

The law as to the formation of the contract of agency has been summarised, in a manner which cannot be improved on, by the learned author of Chitty on Contract[3]

> " . . . the most usual mode of employment is by an unwritten request, or by implication from the recognition of the principal or from his acquiescence in the acts of his agents,"

and he goes on to say,

> " And when the original relation of agency is once proved, an authority to do things within the scope of the agency is implied, and the question merely is, what is the scope of the agency?"[4]

That question we must now consider.

Agents are either special or general. A special agent is one who is appointed for a special or particular task.[5] A general agent is one to whom the principal delegates power to engage on his behalf in a series of transactions fitting into some general class or having

---

[1] *Hawtayne* v. *Bourne* (1841), 7 M. & W. 595, *per* ALDERSON, B., at p. 600.
[2] [1895] 2 Q.B. 84.
[3] 23rd Ed., Vol. II, p. 16.
[4] *Ibid.*; see also *Collen* v. *Gardner* (1856), 21 Beav. 540, *per* ROMILLY, M.R., at p. 543.
[5] *Acey* v. *Fernie* (1840), 7 M. & W. 151 at pp. 155–6.

some general object. Every agent, whether he be special or general, has the right to do all subordinate acts incidental to and necessary for the execution of his authority. So it has been held that the foreman of a saw mill may contract to supply timber to third parties so as to bind his master,[1] and the general manager of a railway company has a power to bind his employers to pay for surgical attendances given at his request to a fellow servant injured on the railway.[2] But neither a guard nor a superintendent has any such power.[3] Again, where money was tendered to a solicitor's clerk who refused it, saying that he had no instructions, this was held to be good tender against his master. For a solicitor's clerk is a general agent for the purposes of such transactions and nothing short of an express limitation of his authority by his master will save the latter from liability.[4]

Moreover, where the servant is employed as an agent of a kind which involves a particular authority, the master will be bound by acts arising out of that authority and it will be no defence that he has given the servant instructions not to act in that particular manner.[5] So where Jones employed Bushell to manage a business under the name of Bushell and the negotiation of bills of exchange was an incident of businesses of that type, Jones was held liable on Bushell's acceptance of a bill though he had expressly forbidden Bushell to accept or draw. In *Watteau* v. *Fenwick*[6] the defendant employed a manager in a beerhouse. The defendant was to supply all goods except bottled beers and the manager was forbidden to purchase these elsewhere. Despite this, the manager bought certain goods on credit, and the suppliers, finding that the defendant was the actual owner of the public house, sued him for the value of the goods supplied. He was held to be liable. It is, of course, otherwise if the principal has limited his agent's authority and brought that limitation to the notice of the plaintiff. But the notice of such limitation must be sufficient. In one case, importers employed a traveller to sell their goods, and when he had done so, to supply them with a sale sheet. Using this sheet the importers drew up an invoice which they followed with a monthly statement. On the statement was a notice to the effect that cheques must be crossed, made payable to the company and that receipts were not valid unless on the printed form. The traveller persuaded purchasers to pay by cash or by cheque payable to him. These payments he misappropriated. The court held that the payments were good

---

[1] *Richardson* v. *Cartwright* (1844), 1 Car. & Kir. 328.
[2] *Walker* v. *Great Western Ry. Co.* (1867), L.R. 2 Exch. 228.
[3] *Cox* v. *Midland Counties Ry. Co.* (1849), 3 Exch. 268. The surgeon would not go unpaid. He would have a right of action against the injured person who might be entitled to compensation.
[4] *Finch* v. *Boning* (1879), 4 C.P.D. 143.
[5] *Edmunds (Edmonds)* v. *Bushell and Jones* (1865), L.R. 1 Q.B. 97, *per* COCKBURN, C.J., at p. 99.
[6] [1893] 1 Q.B. 346.

against the importers, for the notices were held not to be a sufficient indication that the traveller was not authorised to receive cash or cheques drawn in his own favour.[1]

Provided that the act of the agent is within his authority, the court will not enquire into the motive which prompted him. The master will be bound though the act be in the servant's interest. So one who underwrote policies in his own, rather than in his principals' interests, nevertheless made those principals liable. [2] But an act which is outside the authority of a general agent and which is in the agent's interest will not bind the principal.[3]

The power of the agent to bind the principal terminates in many ways. Firstly, the principal may revoke his authority—but unless and until he gives notice of the fact, he will be liable on subsequent contracts entered into by his agent with those people with whom the agent contracted during the subsistence of the relationship. So a master was held liable for fodder ordered by one who had formerly been his coachman. The coachman had continued to wear his master's livery and the master had not given notice to the plaintiff that the employment had ended.[4]   Similarly, the agent may renounce the contract. The death,[5] mental disability or bankruptcy of the master and the dissolution of a company or partnership terminates the agency, whilst the death or mental disability of the agent has the same effect. Whether the agent's bankruptcy ends the contract depends, in the absence of an express term, on whether it unfits him to perform his duties as an agent. The jury will determine, in the event of litigation, whether he is so unfit.[6]   Though the principal's insanity will revoke the contract of agency, he may remain liable on his agent's contracts made after the insanity until the plaintiff is aware of his disability.[7] Where the principal dies it is, apparently, otherwise.[8]

Finally, a special agency will terminate on the completion of the special task; an agency for a fixed period, by the mere effluxion of time.

(3) In Crime.—Criminal responsibility, according to the common law, arises in consequence of two facts. There must, in the first place, be conduct which the law prohibits, and that conduct must, in the second place, be accompanied by a guilty mind. *Actus non facit reum nisi mens sit rea* is the cardinal principle of the common law, and the mere fact that a man has done an illegal thing will

---

[1] *International Sponge Importers, Ltd.* v. *Andrew Watt & Sons*, [1911] A.C. 279.

[2] *Hambro* v. *Burnand*, [1904] 2 K.B. 10.

[3] *Reckitt* v. *Barnett, Pembroke and Slater, Ltd.*, [1929] A.C. 176.

[4] *Aste* v. *Montague* (1858), 1 F. & F. 264; *Stavely* v. *Uzielli* (1860), 2 F & F. 30.

[5] *Campanari (Campanasi) v. Woodburn* (1854), 15 C.B. 400.

[6] *McCall* v. *Australian Meat Co., Ltd.* (1870), 19 W.R. 188.

[7] *Drew* v. *Nunn* (1879), 4 Q.B.D. 661.

[8] *Blades* v. *Free* (1829), 9 B. & C. 167.

not render him liable to penalty unless his mind is also guilty. If there is conduct which offends the law the criminal liability of master and servant will usually turn on their state of mind. It follows that a master (and the term will include a corporation[1]) will not generally be liable for his servant's crimes.[2] The doctrine of vicarious liability, where act and intention of the servant can be imputed to the master, does not arise except in limited instances. The master will be liable, however, under the normal rules of criminal responsibility where his servant, following orders, commits a crime, or where he knows his servant is committing a crime in the course of his employment and he fails to restrain him.[3] Whether the servant is also criminally responsible will depend upon whether he knew, or ought reasonably to have known, the criminal nature of the act. If he did not, he will be an innocent agent upon whom no penalty can fall.[4] If he knew of the criminal nature of the act and had the necessary guilty intent then his position of servant is irrelevant and he will be jointly responsible with his master.[5]

The common law liability of the master, however, extends beyond these limits in public nuisance and criminal libel.

Wherever a master employs a servant in an enterprise which is later proved to constitute a public nuisance, the master will be liable to indictment. So if he causes his servants unlawfully to erect telegraph poles[6] or a street tramway, an indictment will lie against him. It will be no defence that he obtained permission if the authority which gave permission had, in fact, no power to do so.[7] Moreover, if the servant's act amounts to a nuisance, criminal liability will accrue to the master though the act be contrary to his orders and without his knowledge[8] or represents a departure by the servant from the agreed method of working.[9] Where the nuisance is contrary to statute the question of the master's liability will depend on the terms of the statute. A master has been held liable, under the terms of a Public Health Act, for the negligence of his servant in permitting the emission of black smoke from a chimney.[10] The same facts in a charge under the earlier Smoke Nuisance Acts provoked a decision that the master was not liable for the negligent act of his servant.[11]

---

[1] *R. v. Birmingham & Gloucester Ry. Co.* (1842), 3 Q.B. 223; see *R. v. Great North of England Ry. Co.* (1846), 9 Q.B. 315 at p. 326 and *R. v. I.C.R. Haulage Ltd.*, [1944] K.B. 551 for a discussion of the limitations of a corporation's criminal responsibility.

[2] *R. v. Bennett* (1858), Bell C.C.1.; *R. v. Holbrook* (1878), 4 Q.B.D. 42.

[3] *R. v. Dixon* (1814), 3 M. & S. 11.

[4] *R. v. Manley* (1844), 1 Cox C.C. 104, *per* WIGHTMAN, J., at p. 104.

[5] *R. v. Bull and Schmidt* (1845), 1 Cox C.C. 281, *per* ALDERSON, B., at p. 282.

[6] *R. v. United Kingdom Electric Telegraph Co., Ltd.* (1862), 2 B. & S. 647, n.

[7] *R. v. Train* (1862), 2 B. & S. 640.

[8] *R. v. Stephens* (1866), L.R. 1 Q.B. 702; *Barnes v. Akroyd* (1872), L.R. 7 Q.B. 474.

[9] *R. v. Medley* (1834), 6 C. & P. 292.

[10] *Niven v. Greaves*, (1890), 54 J.P. 548.

[11] *Chisholm v. Doulton* (1889), 22 Q.B.D. 736.

A master is also responsible where his servant publishes a criminal libel. The newspaper proprietor was criminally liable at common law even though he had no guilty knowledge[1] but this harsh doctrine was modified by the Libel Act, 1843,[2] where proof that the publication was made without the master's "authority, consent or knowledge " and without " want of due care or caution on his part " was made a defence.

In statutory offences each statute has to be construed separately.[3] For an important decision on the Trade Description Act, 1968 see *Tesco Supermarkets, Ltd.* v. *Nattrass.*[4]

The position has been summarised with all his consummate ability and cogency by the late Lord ATKIN, in *Mousell Bros.* v. *London and North Western Ry.*[5]

> ". . . While *prima facie* a principal is not to be made criminally
> responsible for the acts of his servants, yet the legislature may
> prohibit an act or enforce a duty in such words as to make the
> prohibition or the duty absolute; in which case the principal is
> liable if the act is in fact done by his servants.   To ascertain
> whether a particular Act of Parliament has that effect or not regard
> must be had to the object of the statute, the words used, the nature
> of the duty laid down, the person upon whom it is imposed, the
> person by whom it would in ordinary circumstances be performed,
> and the person upon whom the penalty is imposed."

Whether the act of the servant brings possible liability to the master, leaving aside for the moment the question of guilty mind, follows in statutory offences basically the same rules as at common law.   The clearest case of liability is where a master orders the servant to act contrary to the law.   So where a mine owner orders his servants to make up an airway in contravention of statute he is criminally liable for their acts.[6]   A servant may, of course, do something forbidden by statute and purport to do it as an incident of his service.   The problem is then to determine whether such acts are attributable to the master as the basis of criminal liability.   The courts have adopted either of two tests to resolve the problem.   In some cases, the court asked whether the act was within the scope of employment,[7] in others, whether the act was authorised.[8]   The former test is clearly wider than the latter: it includes unauthorised, or even expressly forbidden acts, which fall within the employment.

---

[1] *R.* v. *Walter* (1799), 3 Esp. 21; *R.* v. *Dodd* (1724), Sess. Cas. K.B. 135.

[2] Lord Campbell's Act, s.7.

[3] For a full discussion see *Criminal Law, The General Part*, by Glanville Williams, 2nd Ed. (1961), Chapter 7, and *"Mens Rea in Statutory Offences,"* by J. Ll. J. Edwards, Chapter 10.

[4] [1972] A.C. 153.

[5] [1917] 2 K.B. 836 at p. 845

[6] *R.* v. *James* (1837), 8 C. & P. 131.

[7] *Commissioner of Police* v. *Cartman*, [1896] 1 Q.B. 655;   *Boyle* v. *Smith*, [1906] 1 K.B. 432.

[8] *Somerset* v. *Hart* (1884), 12 Q.B.D. 360; *Bond* v. *Evans* (1888), 21 Q.B.D. 249.

The effect of an unauthorised act was considered in *Barker.* v *Levinson*.[1] The latter was manager of a block of flats and authorised his servants to lease a flat if he was satisfied that the applicant would make a good tenant. The servant, contrary to statute, demanded a premium of £100 from the tenant as a condition of the grant of a lease. The court held that Levinson was not guilty, and Lord GODDARD, C.J., put the principle in these words:

" if a master chooses to delegate the conduct of his business to a servant who does an act in the course of conducting the business which is absolutely prohibited, the master is liable."[2]

Levinson had not authorised his servant to negotiate terms and so he was not responsible for the act in question.

It is necessary next to direct attention to the problem whether the offence is absolute, that is to say criminal without proof of a guilty mind. This problem is well illustrated by *James & Son Ltd.* v. *Smee*.[3] The offence in question was a breach of the Motor Vehicles (Construction and Use) Regulations, 1951, which provide that a trailer drawn behind a lorry must have an efficient braking system.[4] The regulations make any person using, causing or permitting a breach liable to penalty. The appellant company had sent out, in the charge of servants, a lorry and trailer with a braking system connected by a cable. A delivery had been made, the trailer had been disconnected and one of the servants had omitted to reconnect the brake cable, thus putting the lorry and trailer in breach of the regulations. The summons against the company alleged that they permitted the use in breach of the regulations. On appeal against the conviction the divisional court made a distinction between using and permitting. The company, which sent the servants out in charge of the vehicle, were using the vehicle and if it became in breach of the regulations they were guilty. It was held, however, SLADE, J. dissenting, that to permit involves knowledge and as the employers clearly did not know of the breach they were not guilty of permitting. Similar reasoning has been applied to aiding and abetting[5] and attempting[6] where a guilty mind is an ingredient in the offence and must be proved in the master to make him liable.

There are occasions, fortunately rare, in crimes requiring act and guilty knowledge where the guilty knowledge of the servant will be attributed to the master, thus importing criminal liability for an act of which he was not aware. This has arisen in several types of licensee cases.[7] Under the Licensing Act, 1953,[8] it is an offence to permit gaming on licensed premises. The defendant licensee in

---

[1] [1951] 1 K.B. 342; [1950] 2 All E.R. 825.
[2] At pp. 345, 827 respectively.
[3] [1955] 1 Q.B. 78; [1954] 3 All E.R. 273.
[4] Regulations 75 and 101.
[5] *Ferguson* v. *Weaving*, [1951] 1 K.B. 814; [1951] 1 All E.R. 412.
[6] *Gardner* v. *Akeroyd*, [1952] 2 Q.B. 743; [1952] 2 All E.R. 306.
[7] Publicans, slaughterers, goods vehicles.
[8] S.141.

Somerset v. *Hart*[1] was held not guilty for the act of his servant in permitting the gaming, the evidence being that the master neither knew nor ought to have known of the gaming, yet in *Bond* v. *Evans*,[2] on almost the same facts, the master was held liable. The cases were distinguished on the ground that in *Somerset* v. *Hart* the servant was not in charge of the premises, the landlord being present, whilst in *Bond* v. *Evans* he was in charge and the landlord was absent. These rules bring liability where there is sub-delegation.[3] Knowledge in anyone other than the servant to whom charge is delegated or sub-delegated will not, however, suffice.[4] It follows that where the landlord has entrusted control to the servant he must be assumed to have the same knowledge as the servant. This will not apply, however, where the landlord is present and in control: his lack of knowledge will not be altered by a servant's knowledge. This area of the law has been reviewed by the House of Lords in *Vane* v. *Yiannopoullos*.[5] The emphasis was upon the need for actual knowledge where the statutory provision required knowledge, but it was accepted that the situation of delegation by the licensee of premises to a servant was an exception in that knowledge of that servant brought liability to the licensee even though he had no actual knowledge. It was accepted as an anomaly which is too well established in case law to be altered.[6]

It must be emphasised that these examples must serve to illustrate, for they cannot define, the position of the master in respect of his servant's criminal breach of statutes.

The harshness of the doctrine of vicarious liability in criminal law is occasionally lessened by the statute providing that where a master is charged he can bring before the court the actual perpetrator, and if the master can show that he was not aware of the offence and that he used due care he will be exempt from penalty. This type of provision appears in many statutes with which this book is particularly concerned.[7] A frequent example of this procedure is to be encountered in the magistrates' courts where a servant delivers under-weight bags of coal. Under section 27(1) of the Weights and Measures Act, 1963 a master who is charged may give notice that he can show that the commission of the offence was due to the act or default of a third person. If that third person is under his control, he has to show that he used due diligence to avoid commission of the offence. If he succeeds, the servant is convicted, the employer acquitted.

---

[1] (1884), 12 Q.B.D. 360.
[2] (1888), 21 Q.B.D. 249.   See also *Bosley* v. *Davies* (1875), 1 Q.B.D. 84; *Redgate* v. *Haynes* (1876), 1 Q.B.D. 89.
[3] *Crabtree* v. *Hole* (1878), 43 J.P. 799.
[4] *Allchorn* v. *Hopkins* (1905), 69 J.P. 355.
[5] [1965] A.C. 486; [1964] 2 All E.R. 820.
[6] See *R.* v. *Winson*, [1969] 1 Q.B. 371.
[7] Truck Amendment Act, 1887, s. 12(2); Factories and Workshops Act, 1901, s. 141(1); Wage Councils Act, 1945, s. 16; Agricultural Wages Act, 1948, s. 10.

The test of control is here based on the scope of authority delegated and responsibility ends where the agent acts beyond his authority.[1]

A master or mistress who is legally liable to provide food, clothing or lodging for an apprentice or servant and who wilfully and without lawful excuse neglects this duty, or who does or causes to be done any bodily harm to him so that the life or health of the servant or apprentice is endangered, commits an offence.[2]

It is an offence at common law for one who is under the duty of caring for a person of tender years to withhold necessaries so that injury is done to the health of such person.[3]   This duty may include provision for servants.

2. THE SERVANT'S LIABILITIES

(1) In Tort.—Since every tortfeasor is liable for his torts, a servant will not be able to plead a contract of service in his own defence and his liability will remain unaffected by the fact that in certain cases, as we know, his master will be liable also.

The fact that the injured third party has successfully sued the master and obtained compensation for the servant's tort will not necessarily end the matter as far as the servant is concerned.   The tort of the servant may well be a breach of his contract of service and so the damages awarded to the third party against the master become the quantum of the loss occasioned by the breach of contract and so can be recovered by the master from the servant.[4]   The claim of the master may, however, be based on his rights in tort: that is to say he may claim contribution from his servant, either at common law or under the Law Reform (Married Women and Tortfeasors) Act, 1935.[5]   The position at common law is that under a well-established exception to the rule in *Merryweather* v. *Nixan*[6] an innocent joint tortfeasor, that is one who is unaware of the tortious nature of the act and is only a tortfeasor by implication, can recover from the actual tortfeasor.[7]   This covers the case of a master who is only a tortfeasor in respect of his servant's act as a result of the operation of the doctrine of vicarious liability.   The Act allows contribution from a joint tortfeasor and is illustrated by *Ryan* v. *Fildes*[8] where a schoolteacher used excessive corporal punishment on a child. The education authority claimed a contribution and the argument

---

[1] *Brentnall & Cleland, Ltd.* v. *London C.C.*, [1945] 1 K.B. 115; [1944] 2 All E.R. 552.

[2] Offences Against the Person Act, 1861, s. 26.

[3] *R.* v. *Friend* (1802), Russ. & Ry. 20.

[4] *Lister* v. *Romford Ice & Cold Storage Co., Ltd.*, [1957] A.C. 555; [1957] 1 All E.R. 125; and see p. 98, *supra*.

[5] 25 & 26 Geo. 5, c. 30.

[6] (1799), 8 Term Rep. 186.

[7] *Pearson* v. *Skelton* (1836), 1 M. & W. 504.

[8] [1938] 3 All E.R. 517, which case was expressly approved by Viscount SIMONDS in *Lister* v. *Romford Ice & Cold Storage Co., Ltd.*, at pp. 580, 135 respectively.

that the Act did not envisage an indemnity, and so was not applicable where the contribution was 100 per cent, was rejected.

The concurrence of these two heads of action, both in contract and in tort, has been the subject of much judicial discussion. The opinion has been growing that there is really no room for the tortious remedy of contribution since the master is protected to the full extent by his remedy in contract. This was strongly expressed by HODSON, L.J. in a dissenting judgment in *Jones* v. *Manchester Corporation*[1] and FINNEMORE, J. in *Semtex* v. *Gladstone*[2] was attracted by this argument but was bound by the majority decision. The judgments of the House of Lords in *Lister* v. *Romford Ice and Cold Storage Co. Ltd.* indicate that the contractual remedy is to be preferred.

Harvey v. *R. G. O'Dell Ltd.*[3] has removed any confusion that the judgment of Viscount SIMONDS in *Lister* v. *Romford Ice and Cold Storage Co. Ltd.* may have caused. This judgment indicates that if, in the circumstances, the contractual claim had failed the tortious remedy could not have been successful either. The failure of the contractual remedy may have been on two heads: that the servant's contractual duty of care had not been established or that a further duty to indemnify had been held to lie on the master. In *Harvey* v. *O'Dell* the first type of situation arose. As the tortfeasor was not employed to drive he could not be sued for breach of a contractual duty to drive carefully. The employer was still, however, held by McNAIR, J. to be able to recover contribution under the Law Reform (Married Women and Tortfeasors) Act, 1935. It would seem to follow that the *obiter dicta* of Viscount SIMONDS must be restricted to those cases where the master has, for some reason, a duty to indemnify the servant. In such cases the express wording of s. 6(1)(c)[4] of the Act does not defeat the effect of this indemnity and the rule in *Merryweather* v. *Nixan*[5] prevents a claim at common law.

A servant who infringes another's copyright is liable though he is acting under orders,[6] but he may, in such circumstances, have a right of indemnity from his master.[7] The ignorance of the servant and the fact that the act is solely for the benefit of the master, will not afford a defence,[8] nor will the fact that he is, by statute, bound to obey his master's orders. A striking example of this proposition occurred in *Mill* v. *Hawker*.[9] In that case a surveyor employed by a Highway Board removed, on written orders from

---

[1] [1952] 2 Q.B. p. 852 at p. 876; [1952] 2 All E.R. 125 at p. 133.
[2] [1954] 2 All E.R. 206 at 208.
[3] [1958] 1 All E.R. 657.
[4] Law Reform (Married Women & Tortfeasors) Act, 1935. The Law Reports have s. 6 (1) (b) in error; see [1957] 1 All E.R. 125 at p. 135.
[5] (1799), 8 Term Rep. 186.
[6] *Baschet* v. *London Illustrated Standard Co.*, [1900] 1 Ch. 73.
[7] *Ibid.; Dixon* v. *Fawcus* (1861), 3 E. & E. 537.
[8] *Stephens* v. *Elwall* (1815), 4 M. & S. 259.
[9] (1874), L.R. 9 Exch. 309; affirmed on appeal (1875), L.R. 10 Exch. 92.

the Board, an obstruction placed across a path in the plaintiff's field. There was no evidence that the path was a highway. He was held to be liable though statute provided that he should obey the orders of the Board. But, apparently, a servant will not be liable to third parties for his mere neglect of the duty he owes to his employer. The plaintiff in *Young* v. *Davis*[1] was injured owing to the defendant's failure to keep roads in good repair, which, as a surveyor, he was employed to do. The act was a mere omission on which the plaintiff could not sue. In such cases there are no duties but those which arise under the contract, and strangers to the contract cannot sue.[2]

A servant may be able to escape liability by showing that the master has subsequently accepted or ratified his act and, that, as a result, the act has lost its tortious character. Examples in the law of master and servant are not easy to find, but the working of the principle was clearly shown in *Hull* v. *Pickersgill*.[3] The house of a bankrupt was wrongly entered and certain of his goods seized by persons who had become creditors after the bankruptcy. These creditors were unaware of the identity of the bankrupt's assignees, but they later discovered this and secured a surrender of the assignee's interests in the seized goods. The position was not without its element of piquancy, for when the bankrupt sued the creditors in trespass he was faced with the situation that since the goods, in fact, belonged to his assignees and those assignees had parted with their interests to the creditors, the latter could not be successfully sued for trespass to their own goods.

Where the tort of defamation is in question, a servant who merely repeats a libel or slander will be liable in damages to the injured party just as will any other person. But an essential element in the tort of defamation is the fact that it has been published and the defendant may always show that he has taken no actual part in the publication. So a porter employed merely to deliver parcels which, unknown to him, contained defamatory matter was held not to be liable.[4] The question of publication was discussed in *Emmens* v. *Pottle*,[5] and it was held that there is no publication of a libel where those who disseminate it are innocent of its character, are not bound to know that character, and where their innocence does not arise from negligence.

(2) In Contract.—A servant who enters into a contract as agent for his master is not liable to be sued on the contract[6] for

---

[1] (1862), 7 H. & N. 760.
[2] See *Kelly* v. *Metropolitan Ry. Co.* (1895), 1 Q.B. 944 *per* A. L. SMITH, L.J., at p. 947.
[3] (1819), 1 Brod. and Bing. 282
[4] *Day* v. *Bream* (1837), 2 Mood. & R. 54.
[5] (1885), 16 Q.B.D. 354. This defence has been held not to apply in cases of contempt of court, *R.* v. *Griffiths*, [1957] 2 Q.B. 192; [1957] 2 All E.R. 379.
[6] *Owen* v. *Gooch* (1797), 2 Esp. 567; *Wilson* v. *Lord Bury* (1880), 5 Q.B.D. 518.

he is a mere channel and the other party must look to the master for performance.   Even where the servant induces the third person to enter into the contract by a fraudulent representation that he possesses an authority which he does not, in fact, possess, the servant is not liable on the contract.[1]   The fact that the agent declared himself unequivocally to be an agent, even though untruthfully, is conclusive, and prevents his being a party to the contract.   And in such circumstances it is not material that he fails to disclose the name of the master.   Provided his character of agent be known to the other contracting party, no liability on the contract will accrue to him.

If the servant so acts as to make himself a party, he will be responsible for the performance of the obligation or for damages in the event of its breach, and if he contracts personally along with his principal, both will be liable.[2]   Where the servant makes himself a party to a deed he will also be liable, and it will, in this case, be no defence that he described himself as acting "on behalf of another."[3]

If the question of the personal liability of an agent arises on a written contract, the question will be a matter of construction of law to be determined by the judge.[4]   Proof of a verbal contract is a question of fact for the jury.[5]

A servant who, by words or conduct, induces a third party to enter into a contract, by stating or implying that he is acting on behalf of another when this is not so, cannot, as we have seen, be sued on the contract.   The appropriate action, if the servant has acted in good faith and honestly believes he possesses an authority which he does not possess,[6] is an action against him for breach of warranty of authority; and if the purported agent's action amounts to fraud the injured person may elect whether to sue in tort for deceit or for breach of warranty.[7]   Of course a party to a contract with one who calls himself an agent may not allege a want of authority in the agent of which that party is aware when he enters into the contract.[8]

To support the action for breach of warranty of authority the words or conduct of the purported agent must amount to a misrepresentation of fact.   If the misrepresentation is made about a matter of law, no action will lie.[9]

---

[1] *Lewis* v. *Nicholson* (1852), 18 Q.B. 503.
[2] *Williamson* v. *Barton* (1862), 7 H. & N. 899.
[3] *Appleton* v. *Binks* (1804), 5 East, 148.
[4] *Bowes* v. *Shand* (1877), 2 App. Cas. 455, *per* CAIRNS, L.C., at p. 462.
[5] *Seaber* v. *Hawkes* (1831), 5 Moo. & P. 549.
[6] *Starkey* v. *Bank of England*, [1903] A.C. 114.
[7] *Lewis* v. *Nicholson* (1852), 18 Q.B 503, *per* Lord CAMPBELL, C.J., at p. 511.
[8] *Halbot* v. *Lens*, [1901] 1 Ch. 344.
[9] *Saffron Walden Second Benefit Building Society* v. *Rayner* (1880), 14 Ch.D. 406.

(3) In Crime.—The general principles of criminal liability which govern the liability of the master, apply with like force where the crime of the servant is in question. If a servant commits a crime, knowing it to be such, it will be no defence that he acted under the orders of his master, though if the servant be but an innocent agent he will not be liable;[1] unless his liability arises under a statute which is absolute in its terms, when lack of *mens rea* is no defence to criminal liability. Otherwise the mere existence of a contract of service is not material and a servant who, in failing to perform his duty, committed a crime, has been convicted of manslaughter.[2] In *Wilson* v. *Stewart* a servant who, in the absence of his master but carrying out his master's orders, harboured prostitutes was held guilty of aiding and abetting the offence of suffering prostitutes to meet together contrary to statute.[3]

Where, as in the above case, the servant's offence contravenes statute, the only guide is the statute itself, and the conditions of liability which it lays down. A drayman who, against the orders of his employers, sold and delivered beer to people who had not previously ordered it from the employer's brewery, was held guilty of selling beer without a licence and his employers were convicted of aiding and abetting in that they received payment for the beer so sold.[4] The servant of a dairy company has been convicted of selling milk containing added water though the evidence suggested it was adulterated when he received it,[5] whilst the unlicensed shop assistant of a duly registered pharmaceutical chemist has been indicted for selling poisons without a licence. The licence possessed by his master afforded no defence.[6]

A servant charged with assault may plead in his defence that the act was necessary for the protection of the life or property of his master against the complainant.[7]

A servant, like any other person, is liable if he steals either from his master or from a third person. The Theft Act, 1968 has removed the difficulties previously encountered in respect of servants under the old law of larceny. No special provision is, or needs to be, made for the position of a servant.

It is an offence for any person employed by a municipal authority or by any company or contractor who has the duty of supplying

---

[1] *R.* v. *Bleasdale* (1848), 2 Car. & Kir. 765; *R.* v. *Valler, Eurico and Harrison* (1844), 4 L.T.O.S. 35.
[2] *R.* v. *Hughes* (1857), Dears. & B. 248. A banksman failed to place a stage over a pitshaft, as he was employed to do, with the consequence that a truck of bricks fell into the shaft and a workman was killed.
[3] (1863), 3 B. & S. 913. See Metropolitan Police Act, 1839, s. 44.
[4] *Stansfeld & Co., Ltd.* v. *Andrews* (1909), 100 L.T. 529.
[5] *Hotchin* v. *Hindmarsh*, [1891] 2 Q.B. 181; see also *Melias, Ltd.* v. *Preston*, [1957] 2 Q.B. 380; [1957] 2 All E.R. 449.
[6] *Pharmaceutical Society* v. *Nash*, [1911] 1 K.B. 520.
[7] *Leewerd* v. *Basilee* (1695), 1 Salk. 407.

any place with gas, water[1] or electricity,[2] wilfully and maliciously to break a contract of service knowing or having reasonable cause to believe that the probable consequence of his so doing, either alone or in combination with others, will be to deprive the inhabitants of the place wholly or to a great extent of their supply of gas, water or electricity.   The authorities, companies or contractors must, under penalty, post up a copy of the section concerned in a conspicuous place.

It is, similarly, an offence for any person wilfully and maliciously to break a contract of service knowing or having reasonable cause to believe that the probable consequence of his so doing, either alone or in combination with others, will be to endanger human life or to cause serious bodily harm or to expose valuable property to destruction or serious injury.[3]

A master, as we know, is under no duty to supply his servant with a testimonial.[4]   It is, moreover, an offence for any person to personate a master or the executor, administrator, wife, relation, housekeeper, steward, agent or servant of such master and personally or in writing to give a false or forged or counterfeited testimonial; or for any person to assert that a servant has been hired or retained for any period or in any capacity other than that in which the servant was in fact hired; or to assert that the servant was discharged or left the service or had not been hired, contrary to the truth.[5]

A person who offers himself as a servant commits an offence if he falsely pretends that he has served in a service in which he has not actually served or if he adds, alters, effaces or erases anything contained in or referred to in a certificate given to him by a former master or mistress; or who falsely asserts that he has not been hired or retained in any previous service.[6]

It is an offence under the Merchant Shipping Act, 1894[7] to forge or fraudulently to alter or to assist in the forging or fraudulent alteration of a certificate of competency or an official copy of such certificate; or to make or assist in making a false representation for the purpose of procuring for himself or another a certificate of competency, or fraudulently to use such certificate or copy, or one to which he is not entitled or fraudulently to lend a certificate to which he is entitled or allow it to be used by third persons.   Similarly, it is an offence to forge the certificate of service or discharge of a seaman or soldier, or to obtain or seek to obtain employment

---

[1] Conspiracy and Protection of Property Act, 1875, s. 4.
[2] Electricity (Supply) Act, 1919, s. 31.
[3] Conspiracy and Protection of Property Act, 1875, s. 5.
[4] See Chapter III, page 85.
[5] Servants' Characters Act, 1792, ss. 1, 2 and 3.
[6] *Ibid.*, ss. 4 and 5.
[7] S. 104.

or other advantage by means of a forged certificate, or to personate the holder of such certificate.[1]

3. MASTER'S RIGHTS AGAINST THIRD PARTIES

(1) **Loss of Service due to Personal Injury.**—Wherever a master loses, temporarily or permanently, the services of his servant because of a tortious act of a third party, actionable by the servant, the master may recover damages from the tortfeasor. This action " appears to be a survival from the time when service was a status "[2] and has recently been the subject of considerable criticism and must now be regarded as confined to the narrow limits within which it has previously been allowed.[3] Its abolition has been recommended by a recent report of the Law Reform Committee. The actions in respect of enticement, seduction and harbouring of a spouse or child have been abolished.[4]

There must be a relationship of service and that service, it would seem, must be of a menial nature, that is to say rendered within the domestic sphere.[5] There are cases in which damages have been awarded where this last requirement was not fulfilled, for the servants were servicemen,[6] a policeman[7] and an actor,[8] but the actions turned on the damages to be awarded and the point in question was never raised. It was clearly established by the Judicial Committee of the Privy Council[9] that a public servant, in that case again a policeman, was not within the scope of this action. The same reasoning has now been applied within the strict field of English law with regard to policemen and a tax official.[10] An attempt was made to circumvent this decision in respect of policemen by taking action in the field of contract. In two cases[11] the basic facts

---

[1] Seamen's and Soldiers' False Characters Act, 1906, s. 1.

[2] *Admiralty Commissioners* v. *S.S. Amerika*, [1917] A.C. 38, *per* Lord SUMNER at p. 60.

[3] For a full discussion of the history of this action, see the judgment of DENNING, L.J., *Inland Revenue Commissioners* v. *Hambrook*, [1956] 2 Q.B. 641. See also Law Commission Working Paper No. 19.

[4] 1963, Cmnd. 2017; Law Reform (Miscellaneous Provisions) Act, 1970, s.5.

[5] *Taylor* v. *Neri* (1795), 1 Esp. 386; *I.R.C.* v. *Hambrook, supra. Cf. dictum* of DENNING, L.J., in *Lee* v. *Sheard*, [1956] 1 Q.B. 192; [1955] 3 All E.R. 777.

[6] *Admiralty Commissioners* v. *S.S. Amerika, supra*; *A.G.* v· *Valle-Jones*, [1935] 2 K.B. 209; [1935] All E.R. Rep. 175.

[7] *Bradford Corporation* v. *Webster*, [1920] 2 K.B. 135.

[8] *Mankin* v. *Scala Theadrome Co., Ltd.*, [1947] K.B. 257; [1946] 2 All E.R. 614.

[9] *A.-G. for New South Wales* v. *Perpetual Trustee Co.*, [1955] A.C. 457; [1955] 1 All E.R. 846.

[10] *I.R.C.* v. *Hambrook*, [1956] 2 Q.B. 641; [1956] 3 All E.R. 338.

[11] *Metropolitan Police District Receiver* v. *Croydon Corporation, Monmouthshire County Council* v. *Smith*, [1957] 2 Q.B. 154; [1957] 1 All E.R. 78: the appeals were consolidated and both considered at this reference. At first instance the decisions of SLADE, J., [1956] 2 All E.R. 785 and LYNSKEY, J., [1956] 2 All E.R. 800, which had been reached almost contemporaneously, had shown differing results. The decision of LYNSKEY, J., was affirmed.

were similar. A policeman had been injured whilst on duty. Whilst the policeman was away from work injured, by statute he was entitled to his full pay. This pay clearly represented a loss to the police authority caused by the defendant's negligence in each case. It was recognised that since *Inland Revenue Commissioners* v. *Hambrook*[1] no action lay under the action *per quod servitium amisit*, but an attempt was made to claim in quasi contract. This claim was rejected for the true loss was not of the pay, which had to be given to the policeman whether he was on duty or not, but of the services of the policeman, for which no action, as we have seen, lies.

The action itself, then, lies only where there is loss of service. So a father whose infant son was injured could not maintain an action where he could show no loss of the boy's services.[2] It is of no moment that the tort causing the injury amounts to an offence for which the defendant ought to be prosecuted, for the master will not have been the victim of the offence and the duty to prosecute will not lie upon him.[3]

Where the injury arises from the breach of a contractual duty the master will not be able to recover, for in actions founded on contract no stranger to the consideration can sue. If, however, the action is founded upon a tort, the master will have a claim. So in *Alton* v. *Midland Ry. Co.* a servant was injured whilst travelling on the defendant company's railway and in consequence there was a loss of service by the master. The action was based upon a breach of the contractual duty to carry safely and the master, not being a party, could not recover.[4] In *Berringer* v. *Great Eastern Ry. Co.* the plaintiff's son and servant took a railway ticket for a journey with a railway company to whom the defendant company supplied locomotives, drivers and firemen. As a result of the negligence of a driver a collision occurred, the plaintiff's son was injured and loss accrued to his father. It was held that the latter might recover, for the action arose out of a pure tort; and that it was against a company which was not a party to the contract of carriage was immaterial.[5] The position is not without its difficulties, and it has been emphasised that *Alton's* case does *not* decide

" that an action brought for personal injury against a company by a passenger who has taken a ticket is necessarily an action founded upon contract and not on tort."[6]

Thus the question is somewhat open and it may be that in appropriate circumstances the master may have a right of action despite the ruling in *Alton* v. *Midland Ry. Co.*,[7] the authority of which has greatly diminished.

---

[1] [1956] 2 Q.B. 641; [1956] 3 All E.R. 338.
[2] *Hall* v. *Hollander* (1825), 4 B. & C. 660.
[3] *Appleby* v. *Franklin* (1885), 17 Q.B.D. 93.
[4] (1865), 19 C.B. N.S. 213.   [5] (1879), 4 C.P.D. 163.
[6] *Taylor* v. *Manchester, Sheffield and Lincolnshire Ry. Co.*, [1895] 1 Q.B. 134, *per* A. L. SMITH, L.J., at p. 141.
[7] (1865), 19 C.B.N.S. 213.

The action will lie where the injury arises from an act of omission, for example the failure to keep in repair the boards of a stage whereby an actor is injured.[1]

The damages recoverable will include not merely those incurred between the occurrence of the injury and the time of judgment. If the loss of service continues they may be prospective and may take into account those likely to accrue between the date of the judgment and the time when it is anticipated that the effects of the injury will cease.[2] The damages will cover the extra costs to which the master may have been put in addition to any payment he may make to the injured servant. If he is bound to continue to pay the injured servant, he may recover such payments as damages. If he ceases to pay the servant and engages a substitute, he may recover the costs he thereby incurs.[3]

Where the injuries result in the immediate death of the servant the master cannot recover.[4]

(2) Seduction.—It is a wrong actionable at the suit of the master to seduce a servant whereby she becomes incapable of performing her contract of service, provided the master has in no way connived at the seduction.

The action for seduction, though brought in the great majority of cases by a parent in respect of a daughter, is available to any master who suffers loss by the seduction of his servant. It is not based upon blood relationship[5] nor even on the relationship of parent and child.[6] The claim is for damages arising from loss of service and wherever such loss can be shown as arising from the interruption of the relationship of master and servant, a right of action will accrue to the master.[7] So much is this so that the seduced woman will not herself have an action for seduction;[8] her remedy, if any, which she exercises in fact on behalf of her child, will lie in affiliation proceedings. It follows that if the seduced woman is not in the plaintiff's service, the aid of the courts cannot be invoked. A servant may have concurrent contracts of service with two masters, but where a daughter, who was in domestic service

---

[1] *Mankin* v. *Scala Theadrome Co., Ltd.,* [1947] K.B. 257; [1946] 2 All E.R. 614.

[2] *Hodsoll* v. *Stallebrass* (1840), 11 Ad. & El. 301.

[3] *A.-G.* v. *Valle-Jones,* [1935] 2 K.B. 209, *per* MacKinnon, J., pp. 216–7; see also *Receiver of Metropolitan District Police* v. *Tatum,* [1948] 2 K.B. 68; [1948] 1 All E.R. 612; *Post Office* v. *Official Solicitor,* [1951] 1 All E.R. 522.

[4] *Clark* v. *London General Omnibus Co., Ltd.,* [1906] 2 K.B. 648.

[5] *Fores* v. *Wilson* (1791), Peake 77.

[6] *Peters* v. *Jones,* [1914] 2 K.B. 781.

[7] *Eager* v. *Grimwood* (1847), 1 Exch. 61. See Pollock, C. B., at p. 63; *Grinnell* v. *Wells* (1844), 7 Man. & G. 1033.

[8] *Wellock* v. *Constantine* (1863), 2 H. & C. 146; see *Brownlee* v. *MacMillan,* [1940] A.C. 802; [1940] 3 All E.R. 384, for a case on appeal from an Alberta court where statute gave the injured woman the right to sue.

and lived in her master's house, was seduced it was held that her father could not recover though she assisted him in her leisure time. She was not, within the meaning of the law, his servant.[1]   In *Rist* v. *Faux*, on the other hand, the plaintiff's daughter was seduced and the evidence showed that though she did considerable work in his house attending to his wife who suffered from ill health, she was also employed as a servant in husbandry at the rate of five shillings a week during the recognised hours of labour.   The court found evidence of such service as would entitle the plaintiff to recover.[2]

In the case of a person standing *in loco parentis* to the seduced woman, the loss of service required to support the action may be very slight.   Indeed, the service frequently falls little short of the fictitious and the trend of the courts seems to be approaching a stage where, given proof of such relationship, a presumption of service may arise.[3]   Thus there seems no doubt that a wealthy father could sue in respect of the seduction of his daughter.[4]

The person standing *in loco parentis* will usually be the father, but an action of this character has been held to lie at the suit of one who has adopted the girl,[5] at the suit of an uncle in respect of his niece,[6] and at the suit of a putative father.[7]

The relationship of master and servant must exist at the time of the seduction, but nice questions have arisen, not only as to what constitutes service, but also as to what acts are sufficient to disrupt the relationship and what acts are sufficient to institute its revival. It is clear that a fraud practised on the woman will not effectively take her out of the service of her father.   Where a defendant with intent to seduce the plaintiff's daughter caused her to enter into service with him and then seduced her, it was held that the plaintiff might recover.[8]   Where the woman is seduced whilst living at home there will usually be sufficient evidence of the relationship of master and servant whether she be married or single,[9] and a permitted temporary absence from home will not necessarily destroy the relationship so as to debar the father from recovering.[10]   But residence at home is not necessary, and in *Mann* v. *Barrett* it was

---

[1] *Thompson* v. *Ross* (1859), 5 H. & N. 16; *Whitbourne* v. *Williams*, [1901] 2 K.B. 722.

[2] (1863), 4 B. & S. 409.   *Ogden* v. *Lancashire* (1866), 15 W.R. 158.

[3] See the case of *Maunder* v. *Venn* (1829), Mood. & M. 323 but note that service was, in fact, proved.

[4] *Fores* v. *Wilson* (1791), Peake 77, *per* Lord KENYON at p. 77.

[5] *Irwin* v. *Dearman* (1809), 11 East, 23.

[6] *Manvell* v. *Thomson* (1826), 2 C. & P. 303.

[7] *Beetham* v. *James*, [1937] 1 K.B. 527; [1937] 1 All E.R. 580.

[8] *Speight* v. *Oliviera* (1819), 2 Stark. 493.

[9] *Harper* v. *Luffkin* (1827), 7 B. & C. 387.

[10] *Griffiths* v. *Teetgen* (1854), 15 C.B. 344; *cf. Hedges* v. *Tagg* (1872), L.R. 7 Exch. 283.

held that a father could claim in respect of the seduction of a daughter who assisted him, though she did not live at home.[1]

Terry v. *Hutchinson*[2] is instructive as to the resumption of the relationship of master and servant between the person standing *in loco parentis* and the seduced woman. The plaintiff's daughter, who was employed in domestic service, was dismissed, and whilst returning home was seduced. It was held that the father's right to her services revived on the completion of her former service and that there was sufficient evidence of service to the father to enable him to maintain the action. It should be noticed that the plaintiff's daughter in this case was not seduced whilst in the service of another; the relationship of master and servant between her father and herself which had been disrupted when she left home and entered into a new contract of service was revived at the instant the new contract was terminated, so that technically she was in the employment of her father at the time in question. Nothing less than this would serve to re-establish the relationship. Thus, a father was held to have no claim where a daughter was seduced whilst in service, though it was the intention of both that she should return to her home if her service ended, and she did not take up any new service immediately;[3] and the mere fact that as a consequence of her pregnancy the daughter returns home and has to be supported by her father will not give him a claim.[4]

Three further points should be noted. Firstly, the action will, in all probability, lie if the servant is raped. The point cannot be said to have been authoritatively determined. The Judicial Committee of the Privy Council in *Mattouk* v. *Massad* laid down that :

> " the fact is that, in the case of rape the master would have precisely the same action basing it on the wrong done to his servant, as in the case of any other tort to the servant by which the master was deprived of her service."[5]

Great respect would be paid to that decision, but "judgments " of the Judicial Committee are not binding on the other courts. Secondly, the right of action is personal to the master and will remain with him and not pass to his assignees on his bankruptcy.[6] Thirdly, no master who has in any way connived at the seduction can recover, so that where a father had permitted a man whom he knew to be married to visit his daughter as a suitor, it was held no action would lie on her subsequent seduction.[7]

---

1 (1806), 6 Esp. 32.
2 (1868), L.R. 3 Q.B. 599.
3 *Blaymire* v. *Haley* (1840), 6 M. & W. 55.
4 *Dean* v. *Peel* (1804), 5 East 45; *Davies* v. *Williams* (1847), 10 Q.B. 725.
5 [1943] A.C. 588 *per curiam* at p. 592; [1943] 2 All E.R. 517, at p. 518.
6 *Howard* v. *Crowther* (1841), 8 M. & W. 601.
7 *Reddie* v. *Scoolt* (1794), Peake, 316.

Where the plaintiff does not stand *in loco parentis* to the injured woman his damages will be limited to the out-of-pocket expenses which arise from the loss of service.[1]   He may recover no more than his actual pecuniary loss.   In other cases it has been held that the jury must consider the injury "as done to the natural guardian, and all that can be referred to that relation. . . ."[2]   They are not restricted to the actual pecuniary loss,[3] but the plaintiff may recover for such things as his distress and anxiety of mind,[4] his injured feelings and loss of comfort,[5] any alteration in social position arising from the wrong,[6] and the cost, if any, of the maintenance of the infant.[7]

(3) Inducing a Breach of Contract; Receiving and Harbouring Another's Servant.

—A person who unjustifiably induces a servant to break his subsisting contract of service or who, with knowledge, receives and harbours another's servant, will be liable in damages to the master.[8]

However, if the breach is induced in contemplation or furtherance of an industrial dispute, the action of the inducer is protected from liability by the Industrial Relations Act, 1971, s. 132.   This section seems to replace the protection formerly given by the Trades Disputes Act, 1906 in s. 3.   Indeed it is difficult now to imagine very many cases in which action of this type is taken without it being in consequence of an industrial dispute situation.   If this is so consideration of the rules laid down anew in the Industrial Relations Act is essential.   The action, although it might be protected in tort under s. 132, could well be an unfair industrial practice under that Act, for example s. 96.   This topic has been dealt with in Chapter XI.

We have already considered the situation which arises when a master loses the services of his female servant owing to her seduction, but a master has a similar right to compensation against one who, without justification, induces his servant to depart from the obligations laid down in the contract of service.   At one time it was thought that, provided some evidence of service existed, there was no onus upon the master to prove a binding contract of service.[10]   This is probably too general a statement.   In actions of this character the only person to challenge the validity of the contract would be the defendant, and he is probably precluded from doing so on the ground

---

[1] *McKenzie* v. *Hardinge* (1906), 23 T.L.R. 15.
[2] *Terry* v. *Hutchinson* (1868), L.R. 3 Q.B. 599, *per* BLACKBURN, J., at p. 603.
[3] *Elliott* v. *Nicklin* (1818), 5 Price, 641.   [4]*Andrews* v. *Askey* (1837), 8 C. & P. 7.
[5] *Bedford* v. *McKowl* (1800), 3 Esp. 119.
[6] *Berry* v. *Da Costa* (1866), L.R. 1 C.P. 331.
[7] *Terry* v. *Hutchinson,* (1868), L.R. 3 Q.B. 599.
[8] *Lumley* v. *Gye* (1853), 2 E. & B. 216, *per* CROMPTON, J. at p. 224.   But see now the changes made by Law Reform (Miscellaneous Provisions) Act, 1970 in respect of spouses and children, s. 5.
[9] Especially pp. 486 *et seq.*
[10] See statement of BOVILL, C.J., in *Evans* v. *Walton* (1867), L.R. 2 C.P. 615.

that the tortfeasor may not take advantage of defects in the contract between the plaintiff and his servant. Such a proposition would seem to arise from the decision in *Evans* v. *Walton*.[1] The plaintiff's daughter lived at home and assisted him in the conduct of his business. As a result of a bogus letter of invitation, dictated by the defendant, the girl secured her mother's consent to a temporary absence from home, during which she cohabited with the defendant. After a short time she returned home. Her father was held to be entitled to damages. So also where a recruitment officer induced a young negro to leave his master's service it was held that the master might successfully maintain an action though the contract contained servile incidents which would doubtless have enabled the negro to avoid the contract.[2]

A master may sue and make liable in damages any person who induces his servant to disclose confidential information. In *Bents Brewery Co., Ltd.* v. *Hogan*[3] a trades union official invited certain employees to disclose particulars of the total amount of the sales made and the wages paid at the branches of the company in which they were employed. It was held that if any servant gave that information he would commit a breach of contract, and the defendant would be liable for inducing such breach. The injured employer may also obtain an injunction against a rival who is employing his workmen in their spare time and so gaining advantage of their exclusive skill.[4]

Such unjustifiable encouragements to break contracts must be distinguished from cases where a person is induced to cease working, but in such a manner that there is no breach of contract and no use of means which are unlawful,[5] and from cases in which the defendants neither knew nor ought to have known of the wrong being done. In *British Industrial Plastics, Ltd.* v. *Ferguson*[6] the plaintiff's servant after many years' service entered into a leaving agreement with them. He promised that he would not, before March 31st, 1934, interest himself in the manufacture or sale of certain chemicals used in the plaintiff's secret processes. In June, 1934, the servant went to the defendants and offered them a process for which their patent agent made application for a patent. The plaintiffs then began an action against the former servant for breach of contract and against the defendant company for inducing such breach. It was held, however, that there was no ground of action against the company which had no knowledge, either actual or constructive, that the process belonged to the plaintiffs.

---

[1] (1867), L.R. 2 C.P. 615.
[2] *Keane* v. *Boycott* (1795), 2 Hy. Bl. 511.
[3] [1945] 2 All E.R. 570.
[4] *Hivac, Ltd.* v. *Park Royal Scientific Instruments, Ltd.*, [1946] 1 Ch. 169; [1946] 1 All E.R. 350 and see p. 90, *supra*, for a discussion of this case.
[5] *Allen* v. *Flood*, [1898] A.C.1.
[6] [1940] 1 All E.R. 479.

An action will lie for receiving or continuing to employ the servant of another, after notice that he is that other's servant though the defendant has not, in fact, enticed the servant. A master who takes another's servant into his employment commits no fault whilst he remains unaware of the obligation to the first employer. But from the moment he knows of the continuing contract of service he should discharge the servant or he will be liable in damages.[1] Damage must be proved however and if the servant had no intention of returning to his first employer there is no damage and an action will fail.[2]   There can be no harbouring of another's servant if no valid contract of service exists.   The plaintiff in *Forbes* v. *Cochrane*[3] owned plantations from which certain of his slaves escaped to the defendant's ships.   The plaintiff was permitted to see the men but he failed to persuade them to return.   An action for harbouring the men failed.   Since there was no contract recognised by our law there could be no action for inducing its breach.

Where an action for inducing a breach of contract or receiving another's servant lies, the plaintiff may waive his rights in tort and sue on an implied contract for the servant's services.[4]

As to damages, the master must show loss arising from the breach but his damages are not restricted to compensation for the period during which the servants ought to have served or during which they were harboured.   In *Gunter* v. *Astor* a master whose servants were induced to leave him at a critical period received a sum equal to two years' profits.[5]   The general principle that damages are compensatory nonetheless obtains and if the master collects penalties payable on the loss of his servant he cannot recover damages also.[6]

These older cases and approaches will undoubtedly give way to the new provisions of the Industrial Relations Act except for the rare situations where the tort is not part of the fabric of industrial relations but is based on a more personal situation.

4. Servant's Rights against Third Parties

(1) Inducing the Master to Break the Contract of Service.
It is becoming increasingly difficult to envisage a situation in which action taken against a servant, by way of pressure upon his employer, is not the result of an industrial relations situation.   The new framework of law laid down in the Industrial Relations Act is

---

[1] *Blake* v. *Lanyon* (1795), 6 Term Rep. 221 *per curiam* at p. 222.
[2] *Jones Brothers (Hunstanton), Ltd.* v. *Stevens*, [1955] 1 Q.B. 275; [1954] 3 All E.R. 677.
[3] (1824), 2 B. & C. 448.
[4] *Foster* v. *Stewart* (1814), 3 M. & S. 191.
[5] (1819), 4 Moore, C.P. 12.
[6] *Bird* v. *Randall* (1762), 3 Burr. 1345.

such that the servant is protected in two ways. Both fall to be dealt with fully elsewhere in this book. Both have the point in common that they combine to give the servant protection in his employment. This protection falls short of compulsory re-instatement. There is considerable criticism of the Industrial Relations Act in that it only gives the industrial tribunal power to recommend re-engagement. There is now power to enforce it.[1]

The first area of concern is where pressure is put upon the master to dismiss the servant on the grounds of that person's personal position—his membership or non-membership of a trade union. This was the background to the leading case of *Rookes* v. *Barnard*.[2]

The plaintiff, who was employed at London Airport as a draughtsman, resigned from his Union, the Association of Engineering and Shipbuilding Draughtsmen. The Union had an understanding with British Overseas Airways Corporation, the plaintiff's employers, that certain sections should be staffed only with Union members. As the plaintiff worked in such a section the Union took steps to get him to rejoin and, failing this, finally told his employers that if he was not removed from his present office the Union would strike. In consequence of this the plaintiff was dismissed in accordance with the breach clause in his contract of employment. He sued officials of the Union for damages for wrongfully inducing the employers to terminate his employment.

He succeeded but the case led to considerable criticism. The position was changed by the Trade Disputes Act, 1965. This in turn has been repealed by the Industrial Relations Act.

The employment which is threatened by the third party's pressure is protected by Part II of the Industrial Relations Act, which gives the worker the right to take action against his employer for the unfair industrial practice of unfair dismissal.[3] In cases not involving trade union membership or non-membership the protection is delayed by a qualification period of three years.[4] In the vast majority of likely cases the root of the problem is likely to be, as in *Rookes* v. *Barnard*, trade union membership or non-membership. The action against unfair dismissal lies primarily against the employer. Where, however, that dismissal is induced by another's pressure two points arise. The employer is not permitted to rely on this pressure as a defence. He might well feel that he had to chose between dismissing the complainant or having his whole enterprise stopped by a strike. Section 33 of the Industrial Relations Act specifically provides that in determining whether the dismissal was fair or not no account has to be taken of pressure put upon the employer. This issue is to be determined as if no such pressure existed.[5]

---

[1] Industrial Relations Act, 1971, s. 116.
[2] [1964] A.C. 1129; [1964] 1 All E.R. 367.
[3] See *supra*, 105.
[4] Industrial Relations Act, 1971, ss. 28, 29.
[5] Section 33(1).

Of greater importance is the provision in the same section[1] that the putting on of pressure so as to attempt to induce an employer to commit any of the protective unfair dismissal practices under s. 5 (2)[2] or s. 22[3] should itself be an unfair industrial practice. This means that the third party becomes jointly responsible for the injury done to the workman. It gives the worker a right both against his employer and against the third party putting on the pressure.

The pressure is defined in industrial relations terms and is limited to the trade union type of action. It covers calling, organising, procuring or financing a strike or threatening to do so and organising, procuring or financing any irregular industrial action,[4] short of a strike or threatening to do so. These provisions will cover satisfactorily the position that arises where a trade union puts on pressure to dismiss, say, a non-union worker. It does not, however, appear to cover indirect pressure which is sometimes used. It is not unusual for trade union members to insist that their employer does not allow non-union labour to work in his factory and on his site. This embargo is applied to the employees of firms with whom the employer contracts who have to come on to the premises or work alongside the employer's own men. Examples occur covering the work force of a contractor, or the drivers of a transport firm. The result of non-union labour being used is sometimes industrial strife which the employer seeks to avoid. He can do this best by anticipation. That is to say he can make it a term in the contract he makes with the contractor that workers without the appropriate union membership will not be employed on the work under the contract. Although the worker in question who suffers as a result of this pressure is protected in that if he is dismissed he has an action for unfair dismissal against his own employer, it would appear that the pressure that led to this is not caught by the Industrial Relations Act. It would be expected that it would fall under s. 33 but as we have seen this section, although it applies to any person, is drawn in terms which mean that it applies to trade union type industrial pressure but not to either employer type industrial pressure, the lock-out, nor to commercial pressure. The reality of the situation is that it will be usual to use commercial pressure and to withhold the contract unless the appropriate promise is made.

The discussion so far has been confined to the worker's rights against those who put pressure against him or his employer so that he is dismissed. The acts which are actually used to achieve this will also be both potentially tortious and also unfair industrial practices under the Industrial Relations Act, 1971. The position

---

[1] Section 33(3).

[2] Preventing or detering a worker from exercising his s. 5 rights or dismissing, penalising or discriminating against him.

[3] Unfair dismissal.

[4] Section 33(2). The definition of irregular industrial action is to be found in this section, s. 33(4).

in tort is affected by s. 132 of that Act which establishes the protections which apply where the actions taken are in contemplation or furtherance of an industrial dispute.   This section replaces in a different form the protections previously to be found in the now repealed provisions of the Trade Disputes Act, 1906.   It is appropriate that situations to which s. 132 is likely to apply should be discussed along with the new provisions of the Industrial Relations Act which create unfair industrial practices which are relevant where pressure is put upon a master to break his employee's contract of service.   These matters are dealt with in Chapter XI.[1]

(2) **Injuries to the Servant.**—A servant injured by the act of a third party will normally have a right of action quite independent of his contract of service.   The action will lie wherever the wrongdoer owes the servant a duty but, generally speaking, a servant will not be able to found an action upon the negligent performance of the third party's contract with the master.   In *Earl* v. *Lubbock* the defendant failed in his contractual duty to maintain a firm's vans in good order.   The plaintiff was employed by the firm and was injured by a wheel coming off.   It was held that the plaintiff could not set up as a ground of action, negligence under a contract to which his master was a party and he was not.   The defendant owed no duty to the plaintiff.[2]   It must be added that since *M'Alister* (*or Donoghue*) v. *Stevenson*[3] the concept of duty of care in tort has been considerably widened.   The principle remains but its application has been greatly narrowed by the great development of the ambit of the tort of negligence.

Where the courts can construe the defendant's duty as embracing both the master and the servant the latter will have his remedy.   A gas fitter who negligently connected a pipe in the master's house has been held liable in damages to a servant,[4] and a coal merchant who consigned coal in a defective truck was compelled to pay damages to the servant of the buyer for it was said that the defendant must have known that the party with whom he contracted would not unload the truck himself.[5]

(3) **Rights arising in the Law of Contract.**—A servant who has entered into a contract expressly as the agent of his master cannot sue in his own name[6] but it is, of course, otherwise if he contracts personally, though he has disclosed his agency.   And where he has joined with his master in a contract he may still sue though the master has renounced the contract.[7]

---

[1] *Infra*, p. 486.
[2] [1905] 1 K.B. 253; *Winterbottom* v. *Wright* (1842), 10 M. & W. 109.
[3] [1932] A.C. 562.
[4] *Parry* v. *Smith* (1879), 4 C.P.D. 325.
[5] *Elliott* v. *Hall* (1885), 15 Q.B.D. 315.
[6] *Evans* v. *Hooper* (1875), 1 Q.B.D. 45.
[7] *Short* v. *Spackman* (1831), 2 B. & Ad. 962.

A servant who, as an agent, has a right to sue, will lose that right where his master intervenes.   Thus the captain of a ship entered into a charterparty under which the charterer agreed to pay freight generally though the captain gave him notice to pay it to no one but himself.   It was held that when the owner of the vessel demanded, and was paid the freight, the captain lost his right to sue.[1]   A servant who, acting under a mistake of fact, pays money on behalf of his principal, has the right to sue in his own name.   So a servant who was authorised by his master to pay only in satisfaction of certain acceptances, paid, owing to the misrepresentation of the defendant, against a non-existent acceptance.   It was held that either the master or the servant might recover.[2]

---

[1] *Atkinson* v. *Cotesworth* (1825), 3 B. & C. 647.
[2] *Holt* v. *Ely* (1853), 1 E. & B. 795; *Colonial Bank* v. *Exchange Bank of Yarmouth, Nova Scotia* (1885), 11 App. Cas. 84.

CHAPTER VI

THE MASTER'S LIABILITY FOR INJURY
TO HIS SERVANT

An employer of labour is responsible at law for his acts of personal negligence whether they be directed towards his servants or towards third parties. In addition, consequent upon his status, the law has, from the earliest times, laid upon him particular duties, the breach of which, should injury result to the employee, give the latter certain legal rights. To these common law duties have been added, during the last century, many duties imposed by statute. In this chapter we shall discuss the duty of the master to his servant in respect of the latter's injuries at common law, the remedies available under the Fatal Accidents Act, 1846,[1] and similar enactments.

The defence of common employment, long available to an employer where one of his servants was injured by a fellow servant upon whose care the injured man relied in the ordinary course of the employment, was abolished by the Law Reform (Personal Injuries) Act, 1948,[2] in respect of causes of action accruing on or after July 5th, 1948. This Act also repealed the Employers' Liability Act, 1880,[3] which had been passed to limit the operation of the defence of common employment.

i. At Common Law

(1) **The Master's Duties.**—The duties laid upon an employer at common law can be conveniently summarised. A master must use reasonable care in the choice of servants, must secure and maintain plant and appliances proper to the work in which they are to be used, and must, finally, combine personnel, plant and equipment in a safe system of working. Recently the Courts have tended to reject over-fragmentation and emphasis has been laid upon there being in essence one duty.[4] It is still, of course, convenient to deal with the duty under the various separate headings, at the same time bearing in mind the essential unity of the duty.

Staff

As to the master's duty to provide a competent staff, it is well established that this is a primary duty and his failure to discharge

---

1 (As amended).
2 11 & 12 Geo. 6, c. 41.
3 43 & 44 Vict. c. 42.
4 See, for example, *Wilson* v. *Tyneside Window Cleaning Co.*, [1958] 2 Q.B. 110; [1958] 2 All E.R. 265: particularly PARKER, L.J., at pp. 124 and 272 respectively.

such of his servants as provide clear evidence of their incapacity will amount to actionable negligence in the event of others being injured.

> " The master is not and cannot be liable to his servant unless there be negligence . . . in that in which he . . . has contracted with his servant to do.   What the master is . . . bound to his servant to do, in the event of his not personally superintending and directing the work, is to select proper and competent persons to do so. . . ."[1]

So there is a duty on mine owners to appoint and maintain competent persons to deal with dangers in the mine and if the owners do so they will be under no personal liability to a servant injured by the negligence of the persons properly chosen and retained.[2]

The master must, having acted reasonably in the choice of the servant, give such instruction as may be necessary in the circumstances to offset a servant's youth or inexperience or to check dangerous misbehaviour.[3]   He must, for example, instruct and warn his inexperienced workmen as to any dangers but he may delegate this duty to other servants.[4]

Plant and Tools

Having chosen a competent staff, the master must supply them with proper plant and appliances.   As far as the safety of the premises is concerned, the employer's duty is not merely that of any person in occupation of premises to a person coming upon those premises and having an interest in so doing.   He must not only use such care as the circumstances demand to prevent their injury from abnormal dangers of which he is, or ought to be aware; he must also take steps to minimise any such dangers.

> " In the case of premises that contain an element of danger a duty arises as soon as there is a probability that people will go upon them—but it is a duty only towards such people as actually do go. . . . The only obligation . . . is to take such precautions as are reasonable in each instance to prevent mischief."[5]

But if in fact the premises are not safe it will be no defence for the master to say that he appointed a competent delegate to see that they were safe.   In *Paine* v. *Colne Valley Electricity Supply Co., Ltd., and British Insulated Cables, Ltd.*[6] a workman employed by the electricity company was killed owing to the defective screening of a kiosk containing transformers which had been built for them by the Cable Company.   The first defendants were liable for breach of a

---

[1] *Wilson* v. *Merry* (1868), L.R.1 Sc. & Div. 326, *per* CAIRNS, L.C., at p. 352
[2] *Butler (or Black)* v. *Fife Coal Co., Ltd.*, [1912] A.C. 149.
[3] *Hudson* v. *Ridge Manufacturing Co., Ltd.*, [1957] 2 Q.B. 348; [1957] 2 All E.R. 229.
[4] *Cribb* v. *Kynoch, Ltd.*, [1907] 2 K.B. 548 ; *Young* v. *Hoffman Manufacturing Co., Ltd.*, [1907] 2 K.B. 646.
[5] *Thomas* v. *Quartermaine* (1887), 18 Q.B.D. 685.
[6] [1938] 4 All E.R. 803; see also *Lovell* v. *Blundells & Crompton & Co. (T.A.)*, [1944] K.B. 502; [1944] 2 All E.R. 53.

statutory duty arising from Schedule 6, paragraph 20, Factory and Workshop Act, 1901, but they were also liable at common law for their failure to provide a safe place of working—a failure which was not excused by the employment of competent contractors.

In the recent case of *Sumner* v. *William Henderson and Sons, Ltd.*,[1] there was an interesting attempt to restrict this rule to those aspects of the employer's business in which he had a special skill. Thus it was urged it did not apply where the employer delegated a job, again it was electric wiring, which he could not, as a shopkeeper, be expected to do himself. This argument was rejected and the rule re-emphasised that where an employer delegates a personal and inalienable duty to an independent contractor he remains liable for the contractor's negligence.

What, however, is the position where the unsafe premises are in the occupation, not of the employer but of a third person? It has been suggested that, in these circumstances, the employer was under no duty to the workman in respect of such premises for he could not be expected to be liable for premises over which he could not exercise control.[2] Such a view must now be qualified. The matter was considered by both the Court of Appeal and the House of Lords in *Christmas* v. *General Cleaning Contractors, and Caledonian Club Trust, Ltd.*[3] A window-cleaning company had been engaged to clean the windows of certain premises. Their workman stepped out on the sill holding the window frame whilst doing so. One of the sashes of the window, which moved at the least touch, fell on the workman's fingers causing him to lose balance, fall and be injured. There was evidence that loose sashes were not uncommon and that a safety belt which had been provided by the employers could not be used because there were no hooks affixed to the structure to which it could be attached. It was held that the occupiers were not liable.

"The window cleaner had no right to expect the windows to be in perfect condition. Windows which are often quite serviceable for ordinary purposes, may yet have some minor defect . . . making them quite unsuitable for window cleaners to put their trust in. Such defects are, for window cleaners, common recognizable dangers of everyday experience and cannot be classed as unusual. They are, therefore, dangers against which window cleaners must provide their own safeguards . . . In my opinion, therefore, the judge was wrong in finding the club liable, and their appeal should be allowed."[4]

---

[1] [1964] 1 Q.B. 450; [1963] 1 All E.R. 408 and on appeal, [1963] 2 All E.R. 712.

[2] See *Taylor* v. *Sims and Sims*, [1942] 2 All E.R. 375. *Hodgson* v. *British Arc Welding Co., Ltd., and B. & N. Green and Silley Weir, Ltd.*, [1946] K.B. 302; [1946] 1 All E.R. 95.

[3] [1952] 1 K.B. 141; [1952] 1 All E.R. 39, C.A., affirmed *sub nom. Genera Cleaning Contractors, Ltd.* v. *Christmas*, [1953] A.C. 180; [1952] 2 All E.R. 1110, H.L.

[4] [1952] 1 K.B. 141, at p. 148; [1952] 1 All E.R. 39, at p. 41.

In these words DENNING, L.J., dismissed the occupiers of the premises from the action so that they did not appear as parties to the appeal in the House of Lords. In so founding the law his Lordship relied upon *London Graving Dock Co., Ltd.* v. *Horton*,[1] wherein an experienced workman employed by sub-contractors sustained injuries whilst working on a ship because of inadequate staging. As an experienced man he knew of and recognised the risk though it was admittedly " unusual " to the work in hand.

The result was that in the appeal before the House of Lords, the window-cleaning firm alone were the appellants and this, to some extent moved the ground of contention from the duty to provide safe premises to the duty to lay out the work in such a way as to provide for the employees' safety. "The employers," said DENNING, L.J., in words which were approved by Earl JOWITT,

> "should have laid out the work more carefully. One way would have been to do the cleaning from a ladder instead of from a sill. Another way would have been to ask the householder to allow the firm to insert hooks into the brickwork so as to attach a safety belt. It is said by these employers that these suggestions are not practicable, and that it is the usual thing for men to clean windows by standing on the sill. That answer does not satisfy me. If employers employ men on this dangerous work for their own profit, they must take proper steps to protect them, even if they are expensive. If they cannot afford to provide adequate safeguards, they should not ask them to do the work at all."[2]

In *Wilson* v. *Tyneside Cleaning Co.*,[3] upon very similar facts, the workman's claim failed. He knew of the danger; he was an experienced workman, and the Court of Appeal held that on the facts of the case the employers could not be said to have failed to take reasonable care. The House of Lords decided otherwise on this point in *Smith* v. *Austin Lifts Ltd.*,[4] but only upon the particular facts of the case. The emphasis upon the responsibility of experienced workmen was approved and applied but the employers had been repeatedly told of the danger and so could not escape liability.

An employer must, further, take reasonable care to provide proper appliances and to maintain them in a proper condition.[5] This does not mean that an employer may not ask his workmen to handle implements to which some element of danger attaches. It means that where he does so the law places upon him the further duty to take whatever steps are reasonable to ensure that the danger should

---

[1] [1951] A.C. 737; [1951] 2 All E.R. 1.   The liability of occupiers to visitors to the premises is now subject to the Occupiers' Liability Act, 1957, but the employer's duty remains unaltered by this Act.
[2] [1952] 1 K.B. 141 at p. 149; [1953] A.C. 180 at p. 187.   And see *Drummond* v. *British Building Cleaners, Ltd.*, [1954] 3 All E.R. 507.
[3] [1958] 2 Q.B. 110; [1958] 2 All E.R. 265.
[4] [1959] 1 All E.R. 81; [1959] 1 W.L.R. 100; and see *Mace* v. *R. & H. Green and Silley Weir, Ltd.*, [1959] 2Q.B. 14; [1959] 1 All E.R. 655.
[5] *Smith* v. *Baker & Sons*, [1891] A.C. 325.

be reduced as much as possible.[1] Consequently where an actress
was compelled to wear, for the purposes of the film in which she was
appearing, certain highly inflammable material which ignited and
severely burned her, it was held that the employer would be liable
unless he could show that he had done everything that the exercise
of reasonable skill and care suggested to make the plant and material
safe.[2] Moreover, the duty relating to plant and appliances is a continuing duty.   In *Monaghan* v. *W. H. Rhodes & Son*[3] the plaintiff
was a dock labourer employed by the defendant stevedores.   Whilst
a vessel was being loaded, fellow servants blocked the permanent iron
ladders so that they could not be used and resort was had to a rope
ladder which did not reach the bottom of the hold.   The consequence was, that when the plaintiff used it, the ladder began to
swing and he fell and was gravely hurt.   The plaintiff, apparently,
felt that the rope ladder was unsafe and had informed his foreman
of this.   It was held that the defendants were liable for they were
aware that the original and safe ladder had gone, and knew that the
rope ladder was a dangerous substitute, yet had done nothing.
They had, that is to say, failed in their common law duty to maintain adequate appliances.

The courts had to answer the question whether the master could
discharge his duty if he obtained, in appropriate circumstances,
tools from a reputable supplier, and subsequently a latent defect in
the tool caused injury.   There was judicial disagreement as to
whether the duty was a delegation of a statutory duty, in which case
the lack of reasonable care by the independent contractor would be
no defence, or was a duty to take reasonable care, in which case buy-
ing from a reputable supplier would suffice.   The latter view was
adopted by the majority in the Court of Appeal in *Davie* v. *New
Merton Board Mills, Ltd.*,[4] where a fitter was injured because metal
flew from a drift when it was struck with a hammer.   The drift had
been obtained from a reputable supplier but was of excessive hard-
ness, a fact which could not be discovered by the employers' system
of inspection.   It followed from this decision that the employee must
sue the negligent supplier in tort and he will recover under the rules
in *M'Alister (or Donoghue)* v. *Stevenson.*[5]

This was an inconvenient decision, often putting the employee in
difficulty.   The supplier might, for example, be a foreign manufacturer.   So the decision in *Davie's* case has been reversed by

---

[1] *Naismith* v. *London Film Productions, Ltd.*, [1939] 1 All E.R. 794.
[2] *Ibid.*
[3] [1920] 1 K.B. 487.
[4] [1958] 1 Q.B. 210; [1958] 1 All E.R. 67; PARKER, PEARCE, L.JJ., JENKINS,
L.J., dissenting.   Reversing the judgment of ASHWORTH, J., [1957] 2 Q.B.
368; [1957] 2 All E.R. 38.   Followed recently in *Sumner* v. *William Henderson
and Sons, Ltd.*, [1964] 1 Q.B. 450; [1963] 1 All E.R. 408.   See " A Master's
Liability for Defective Tools," by A. L. Goodhart (1958), 74 *L.Q.R.* 397.
[5] [1932] A.C. 562.

legislation. By the Employers' Liability (Defective Equipment) Act, 1969, an employee can sue his employer who provides defective equipment which causes personal injury. The Act provides that where an employee suffers injury in the course of his employment, as a result of a defect in equipment provided by his employer for the purposes of the employer's business, then if the defect is attributable wholly or in part to the fault of a third person, who need not be identifiable, then the injury is deemed to be caused by the negligence of the employer. This provision does not affect the application of the rules of contributory negligence.[1] It is not possible to contract out of this liability,[2] which applies to the Crown.[3] Equipment for the purposes of the Act is defined as any plant, machinery, vehicle, aircraft and clothing.[4]

A defect is not latent if the employer could have discovered it by reasonable inspection and maintenance. The significance of this point has been lost as a result of the statutory liability for latent defects, but as a safety point it emphasises the need for proper inspection and maintenance.[5] The duty to provide safe appliances is not restricted to those operations which relate, in the strict sense, to the industrial processes carried on in the factory, but covers " all such acts as are normally and reasonably incidental to the work." A worker who slipped on a duck board due to the greasy condition of the floor whilst going up to a tap for the purpose of washing a tea cup for her own use, was held entitled to recover damages.[6] And where appliances are provided they must be properly contrived and erected for there is a common law duty to use reasonable care and skill in such matters.[7]

The dynamic nature of the employer's liability is well illustrated by *Stokes* v. *Guest, Keen and Nettlefold (Bolts and Nuts), Ltd.*[8] A worker had died as a result of cancer of the scrotum and his widow was suing his employers. There was medical evidence that if a person has at least five years' regular exposure to certain types of oil this condition could develop. Although that danger was known since 1941, and although the employers had a medical officer, the checks and warnings made were not very well organised or effective. It was held that the employers had failed in their duty to keep abreast with expanding knowledge and experience.

System

It is clearly not enough merely to engage competent workmen and adequate plant and machinery. The law, as we have said,

---

[1] S. 1(1).   The Act came into force on October 25th, 1969.
[2] S. 1(2).
[3] S. 1(4).
[4] S. 1(3).
[5] *Pearce* v. *Round Oak Steel Works, Ltd.*, [1969] 3 All E.R. 680; [1969] 1 W.L.R. 595.
[6] *Davidson* v. *Handley Page, Ltd.*, [1945] 1 All E.R. 235.
[7] *Pratt* v. *Richards*, [1951] 2 K.B. 208; [1951] 1 All E.R. 90, n.
[8] [1968] 1 W.L.R. 1776.

insists that they be co-ordinated in a safe system of working. Where the system is unsafe the master will be liable to an injured workman, but where a safe system is rendered defective through the incompetence of a servant engaged to control that system the master will, generally, not be liable. The rule is easy to lay down but difficult to apply and though the law on the topic has received the attention of the House of Lords—in the luminous judgments in *Wilsons and Clyde Coal Co., Ltd.* v. *English*[1]—it is to be feared that it will remain a fruitful source of litigation. None the less, as a result of *Wilsons'* case[2] and certain earlier decisions it is now possible to state the law in a series of propositions. This, indeed, has been done in the following way by MacKinnon, L.J.:

> "(i) It is the duty of an employer towards his servants to provide a safe system of working in the operation the servants are to carry out. (ii) The employer may, and in many cases must, delegate the provision of such a system to an agent, but in such a case the employer is responsible for any failure of such agent to provide such system. (iii) If the injury to a workman is caused by the failure of the employer either personally or vicariously to provide such a system of working the employer is liable to pay damages to the workman for such injury."[3]

Wilsons' case did much to define these postulates. The action was brought by a workman in respect of personal injuries. At the trial it had been found, as a fact, that there was no reasonably safe system of working; that the company's agent was aware of this, but that the directors were not. It had been found, also, that the provision of the system of working was part of the technical management of the mine, in which, the owners were, by the terms of the Coal Mines Act, 1911,[4] precluded from interfering unless they were qualified to be mine managers. The defendant company consequently pleaded that it could not be held responsible for the ill doing of that which it was not, by law, permitted to do. The master, it was urged, having delegated the duty of providing a reasonably safe system of working to a competent agent, had fulfilled his obligation. It is, indeed, difficult to imagine a more favourable case being put forward on the employer's behalf. The court had no difficulty in rejecting it. The duty as to a safe system was the master's duty which he could not, in any legal sense, delegate to another. True, he must get someone with special knowledge to advise him, but for the acts of that one he remains liable. So far as this is concerned the position is the same whether he acts *per se* or *per alios*.

What will constitute a safe system can be determined only in

---

[1] [1938] A.C. 57 ; [1937] 3 All E.R. 628.
[2] *Ibid.*
[3] *Speed* v. *Swift (Thomas) & Co., Ltd.*, [1943] K.B. 557, *per* MacKinnon, L.J., at p. 564; [1943] 1 All E.R. 539, at p. 542.
[4] S. 2 (4).

reference to particular circumstances.¹ It will vary according to the type of work performed. It may even vary in the same work at different times, but Lord GREENE, M.R. has suggested that such things as the physical lay-out of the job, the sequence in which the work is to be carried out, the provision of warnings, notices and special instructions may all be relevant.² It may apply to the long term layout of the work or to a procedure adopted for a short time to complete one job.³ The quality of the system of working, whether it be reasonably good or not, is a question of fact but there is no rule of law that suggests that an employer must adopt the latest improvements and appliances.⁴ The general practice in the particular industry will, however, be relevant. A passage from the judgment of Lord NORMAND in *Paris* v. *Stepney Borough Council* dealing with the liability of the employer for faults of omission makes this point plain:

> " that fault should be one of two kinds, either to show that the thing which he did not do was a thing which was commonly done by other persons in like circumstances, or to show that it was a thing which was obviously wanted and that it would be folly in anyone to neglect to provide it."⁵

It was emphasised in *Cavanagh* v. *Ulster Weaving Co., Ltd.*⁶ that evidence of a general practice was not conclusive, although of course it gave rise to a strong presumption.

Nice questions are bound to arise as to the difference between a bad system and the defective working of a good system. For the law only asks for the setting up of a *reasonably* safe system. It does not impose on the employer a duty to see that no one makes an error. If he supplies the material of a safe system and a servant substitutes an inferior material the master will *not* be liable.⁷

Under the rules of remoteness, neither will the employer be responsible for injuries resulting from circumstances which he could not reasonably have foreseen. This is well illustrated by the facts of *Doughty* v. *Turner Manufacturing Co. Ltd.*,⁸ where an asbestos cover fell into a cauldron of molten metal. A moment or two later there

---

¹ *Watt* v. *Hertfordshire County Council*, [1954] 2 All E.R. 368; [1954] 1 W.L.R. 835, where the duty of fire authorities was considered.
² *Speed* v. *Thomas Swift & Co., Ltd.*, [1943] K.B. 557; [1943] 1 All E.R. 539.
³ *Winter* v. *Cardiff R.D.C.*, [1950] 1 All E.R. 819.
⁴ *Toronto Power Co., Ltd.* v. *Paskwan*, [1915] A.C. 734.
⁵ [1951] A.C. 367, at p. 382; [1951] 1 All E.R. 42, at p. 49, (he is citing the judgment of Lord DUNEDIN in *Morton* v. *Wm. Dixon, Ltd.* (1909), S.C. 807, 809). Applied in *Morris* v. *West Hartlepool Steam Navigation Co., Ltd.*, [1956] A.C. 552; [1956] 1 All E.R. 385.   Approved in *Cavanagh* v. *Ulster Weaving Co. Ltd.*, [1960] A.C. 145; [1959] 2 All E.R. 745.
⁶ [1960] A.C. 145.
⁷ *O'Melia* v. *Freight Conveyors, Ltd. and Rederiaktiebolaget Svenska Lloyd,* [1940] 4 All E.R. 516.
⁸ [1964] 2 W.L.R. 240.

was an explosion and the plaintiff, who was an employee standing by, was injured by molten metal. STABLE, J. applied the rules of remoteness laid down in the leading *Wagon Mound* case[1] and held that the explosion and hence the injuries were not reasonably foreseeable and so the employer was not liable.

The question whether a given system is reasonably safe has frequently been before the courts and it is established that the object of the safety of the system is to secure the personal safety of the employees; it is not directed towards the safety of their property. It follows, therefore, that an employee could not allege that an unsafe system of working was the cause of the theft of his clothing.[2] And even where his personal safety is concerned, the workman must not ask the impossible. Where the floors of a factory were flooded by an unusually heavy rainstorm and an oily substance usually contained in a channel on the floor, rose and mixed with the rain water and the employers spread sawdust on the floors but some areas were left untreated because of an inadequate supply, it was held that it would be unreasonable to expect that the factory should be closed until absolutely safe conditions prevailed.[3]

Causation

So, also, the workman, although he is entitled to expect the work to be laid out in a manner so as to make it reasonably safe for him,[4] cannot expect to be constantly reminded to take safety precautions which are available and which his experience should tell him are essential. In *Qualcast (Wolverhampton), Ltd.* v. *Haynes*[5] the House of Lords held that the employers were not responsible in negligence to an experienced workman who was splashed on the foot with molten metal whilst not wearing protective spats. The employers had provided spats which could be had for the asking but had not ordered or advised the wearing of them. It is clear that the workman had decided not to take advantage of the protection offered. In an earlier case, *Woods* v. *Durable Suites, Ltd.*,[6] it was similarly held that employers were under no duty to provide supervision to ensure that precautions, clearly explained in notices, were taken. Two further points arise in the *Qualcast* case. The duty will vary with the experience of the workman and decisions of fact

---

[1] *Overseas Tankship (U.K.), Ltd.* v. *Morts Dock and Engineering Co., Ltd.* (The Wagon Mound), [1961] A.C. 388; [1961] 1 All E.R. 404.

[2] *Deyong* v. *Shenburn*, [1946] K.B. 227; [1946] 1 All E.R. 226; *Edwards* v. *West Herts Group Hospital Management Committee*, [1957] 1 All E.R. 541; [1957] 1 W.L.R. 415.

[3] *Latimer* v. *A.E.C., Ltd.*, [1952] 2 Q.B. 701; [1952] 1 All E.R. 1302, C.A.

[4] *Whitby* v. *Burt, Boulton & Hayward, Ltd.*, [1947] K.B. 918; [1947] 2 All E.R. 324. See also *Grant* v. *Sun Shipping Co., Ltd.*, [1948] A.C. 549; [1948] 2 All E.R. 238, H.L.

[5] [1959] A.C. 743; [1959] 2 All E.R. 38.

[6] [1953] 2 All E.R. 391, C.A. See also *Brown* v. *Rolls Royce, Ltd.*, [1960] 1 All E.R. 577; [1960] 1 W.L.R. 210.

in earlier cases are not to be taken as binding precedents. The matter is one of asking whether reasonable precautions were taken in all the circumstances of each particular case.

The refusal of the workman to adopt safety precautions raised the further problem of causation. As there was no negligence found against the employers this point did not fall to be discussed by the House of Lords. It had arisen in the Court of Appeal[1] where the county court judge's assessment that the employers' default contributed twenty five per cent towards the damages was accepted. Dicta in the House of Lords indicated that they may well have found the workman's intention not to use the precautions a complete bar, as the employers could not be said to have caused the accident.[2]

The individuality of each case is constantly being emphasised in the courts. Whilst doing this in *Machray* v. *Stewart and Lloyds, Ltd.*,[3] McNAIR, J. used as the basic test this interesting formulation by Lord REID

> . . . fault is not necessarily equivalent in this context to blameworthiness. The question really is whose conduct caused the accident, because it is now well established that a breach of statutory duty does not give rise to civil liability unless there is a proved causal connection between the breach and the plaintiff's injury.[4]

This formulation was made with breaches of statutory duty in mind but it would appear useful when the question before the court involves a consideration of an employer's failure to take certain steps on the one hand and the experience of the injured plaintiff on the other. Thus it has been held that an experienced workman may be left a discretion to select his own tools.[5]

Where work is being conducted which involves principals and contractors the question of which party is liable is sometimes raised. A crane driver was lent by his master, together with the crane he operated, to a firm of stevedores for the purpose of unloading goods into a warehouse. The crane was operated electrically from a plug placed twelve feet high in a pillar around which the stevedores had piled cargo. The crane driver was then asked to move the crane, to do which it was necessary that he should climb the cargo to disconnect the plug. Whilst doing so he fell and was injured. The question arose whether his employers or the stevedores had control of the operation which caused the injury, for if it were the latter a

---

[1] [1958] 1 W.L.R. 225.   This decision, involving the idea that supervision should have been provided, was followed shortly afterwards in *Nolan* v. *Dental Manufacturing Co., Ltd.*, [1958] 2 All E.R. 449; [1958] 1 W.L.R. 936.

[2] E.g. Lord DENNING at pp. 762 and 46 respectively.   The same problem arises in actions arising from breach of statutory duty: see *Imperial Chemical Industries, Ltd.* v. *Shatwell*, [1965] A.C. 656; [1964] 2 All E.R. 999.

[3] [1964] 3 All E.R. 716; [1965] 1 W.L.R. 602.

[4] In *Ross.* v. *Associated Portland Cement Manufacturers, Ltd.*, [1964] 2 All E.R. 452 at p. 455; [1964] 1 W.L.R. 768 at p. 777.

[5] *Richardson* v. *Stephenson Clarke, Ltd.*, [1969] 3 All E.R. 705; [1969] 1 W.L.R. 1695.

relationship *pro hac vice* of master and servant would arise and, for the operation in question, the duty to provide a safe system of working would fall upon the stevedores.[1]

The duty to provide a safe system of working may involve the preferential treatment of all workmen who have physical defects likely to render the consequences of an accident more serious than they would otherwise be. Such was the situation in *Paris* v. *Stepney Borough Council*[2] where a workman was, to the knowledge of his employers, blinded in one eye as a consequence of enemy action. Whilst working on the under part of an omnibus he struck a piece of metal from a nut which blinded him in the other eye. In the Court of Appeal it had been held that the employers were not liable and ASQUITH, L.J., in a judgment of considerable force had maintained that where there was not an increased *risk* of injury it was inequitable to impose upon employers the increased consequences of injury. Such was not the view of the House of Lords though there were dissenting judges. The majority however held that in order to render a system of working safe to the appellant he should have been provided with goggles. But it is not essential to transfer workers to other work or to dismiss them from employment because the work creates a risk. Provided the employer takes reasonable care the decision whether to accept the risk lies with the worker.[3]

Such defects may not be obvious to the employer and he will not be negligent unless he has ignored indications that should have told him. This rule is illustrated by *James* v. *Hepworth and Grandage* where the employers were not aware that a man was illiterate. This meant that notices to use safety equipment were ineffective as far as he was concerned. It was held that they had had no reason to suspect the illiteracy and so were not negligent in failing to make special provisions.[4]

A case which brings together many of the aspects of the employer's duty to his workman is *Barcock* v. *Brighton Corporation*.[5] Barcock was employed by the defendants at an electrical sub-station which was a factory to which certain special regulations made under the authority of the Factories Act, 1937, applied. These regulations covered, amongst other things, the procedure to be adopted for making the switchboard dead whenever it was necessary to work upon it. For some time the plaintiff worked with one whose duty it was to make tests and who ignored the safety regulations by removing a screen which was required to separate those parts of the equipment which remained "alive" when the rest was "dead." There was evidence that Barcock was, at first, concerned about this,

---

[1] *Holt* v. *W. H. Rhodes & Son, Ltd.*, [1949] 1 All E.R. 478, C.A.
[2] [1951] A.C. 367; [1951] 1 All E.R. 42.
[3] *Withers* v. *Perry Chain Co., Ltd.*, [1961] 3 All E.R. 676; [1961] 1 W.L.R. 1314.
[4] [1968] 1 Q.B. 94; [1967] 2 All E.R. 829.
[5] [1949] 1 K.B. 339; [1949] 1 All E.R. 251.

but, on enquiry, had been told that if no risks were taken nothing would be done. Barcock was later appointed to undertake work requiring knowledge and experience in the avoidance of danger and was informed that he must familiarise himself with the regulations, a copy of which he was given. Whilst making a test according to the usual—but illegal—practice, an explosion occurred and he was injured. He claimed damages on the grounds that his employers were in breach of their statutory duties towards him, and that they were liable at common law on their failure to provide a safe system of working. Against him his employers contended that he, not they, had removed the screen and was in breach of the statutory duty to comply with the electricity regulations and that the damage at common law arose from Barcock's contributory negligence. The case is, in many ways a strong one, particularly on the question of the workman's responsibility. HILBERY, J., held that the workman could not allege a breach of statutory duty on the part of the employers when he was himself the active cause of that breach, but that on the question of the safe system of working he must find for the plaintiff. Employers do not provide a safe system of working by telling their workmen to read the appropriate legislation and conform thereto; and even supposing that they had originally provided such a system they had clearly, and for a long period, allowed it to be disregarded. On the question of the workman's contributory negligence the judge was of opinion that Barcock's removal of the safety device gave him much to answer. But it was necessary to remember that there was no safe system of working; that the plaintiff had received no instructions and that, indeed, all that he had done was to follow the example set by his superiors. He was not, held the court, contributorily negligent. The result was that Barcock recovered damages, not under statute but at common law.

Rylands v. Fletcher

The rule in *Rylands* v. *Fletcher* will not apply to dangers arising from industrial processes where the danger is limited to the land of the defendant.[1] The rule lays down that a person

> "who for his own purposes brings on his land and collects and keeps there anything likely to do mischief if it escapes must keep it at his peril, and is *prima facie* answerable for all the damage which is the natural consequence of its escape."[2]

The facts were that the owners of land had employed contractors to construct a reservoir. Whilst doing so the contractors had discovered certain disused shafts which communicated with mines on neighbouring land, though no one was aware of this, for they were, or seemed to be, filled with earth. When the reservoir was complete the weight

---

[1] *Read* v. *J. Lyons & Co., Ltd.*, [1945] K.B. 216 ; [1945] 1 All E.R. 106; affirmed, [1947] A.C. 156; [1946] 2 All E.R. 471.
[2] *Fletcher* v. *Rylands* (1866), L.R. 1 Exch. 265 at p. 279; affirmed *sub nom. Rylands* v. *Fletcher* (1868), L.R. 3 H.L. 330.

of water burst these shafts and flooded the mines, the owner of which was held entitled to recover.

In *Read's* case[1] the respondent was working in a factory engaged in the manufacture of high explosives. An explosion occurred, the cause of which was not explained. The respondent was injured, though no negligence was alleged against the appellants. It was argued, on her behalf, that the rule in *Rylands* v. *Fletcher* gave her a remedy at common law, but the court rejected this. It was recognised that the case raised questions of a quite fundamental character and that were the proposition conceded that the employers were liable, without proof of negligence, for the consequences arising from activities which were dangerous in themselves, the mass of safety legislation to be found in industrial statutes would be of a purely declaratory character. The rule in *Rylands* v. *Fletcher* would not apply in *Read's* case because in the latter case a factor vital to the judgment in the former case was absent.

> "The vital feature in *Rylands* v. *Fletcher*, was the defendant's interference with the plaintiff's right to enjoy his land without interference by the defendant."[1]

There can be no doubt that the decision is a correct one, for any other decision would mean that employers were the insurers of their workpeople wherever hazardous industrial operations took place, and a vast amount of legislation on which Parliament has devoted much time and attention would, in fact, have been almost unnecessary. To concede the plaintiff's right said SCOTT, L.J.,

> "would be beyond the power of judges; it is a matter for Parliament if it is thought desirable."[2]

The use of the land must be extraordinary or "non natural." This requirement has been held not to be fulfilled by water pipe installations[3] and wiring to supply electric light.[4] It does, however, apply to bulk storage of water, gas or electricity.[5]

It must be emphasised that all the duties laid upon employers which we have discussed are only particular applications of the general duty laid by the law on every citizen so to conduct himself that he does not, by his negligence, injure another to whom, in the circumstances, he owes a duty of care. It follows that the employer may avail himself of any defences relevant to an action for negligence. He may reply to a common law claim for injury to his servant that the risk was incidental to the servant's employment and that the servant had accepted it as such. He may urge

---

[1] *Read* v. *J. Lyons & Co., Ltd.*, [1945] K.B. 216; [1945] 1 All E.R. 106, at pp. 238, 115 respectively, *per* SCOTT, L.J.
[2] *Ibid.*
[3] *Rickards* v. *Lothian*, [1913] A.C. 263; *Tilley* v. *Stevenson*, [1939] 4 All E.R. 207.
[4] *Collingwood* v. *Home and Colonial Stores, Ltd.*, [1936] 3 All E.R. 200.
[5] *Northwestern Utilities* v. *London Guarantee and Accident Co., Ltd.*, [1936] A.C. 108; [1935] All E.R. Rep. 196.

that the servant was himself contributorily negligent. Should he successfully prove any one of these defences he will not be liable. What then is the precise character of each of these defences?

(2) Volenti Non Fit Injuria.—A master will be able to avoid his common law liability for accident to his servant wherever he can show that the accident arose out of a risk necessarily incidental to the employment, of which risk the servant was aware and which he voluntarily accepted as part of his employment.   This defence—*volenti non fit injuria* as it is called—is based on the notion that legal injury cannot arise from a risk voluntarily incurred.

Whether a servant undertook any particular risk is a matter of fact and not of law and the onus of proving that he did so will lie on the master.[1] Nineteenth century cases such as *Thomas* v. *Quartermaine*[2] illustrate this point but the presumptions reached would not be made to-day.   Thus in that case a workman habitually working in a narrow passage by a boiling vat was said to have known and agreed to encounter the risk of falling in.   But merely to show that the servant had a knowledge of the risk is insufficient. The maxim " is not *scienti non fit injuria* but ' *volenti.*' "[3] Were mere knowledge to afford the defendant a defence then no one ought to recover for injuries received by being run over since everyone is aware of the risks incidental to crossing the road.[4]   To prevent the servant recovering from the master mere knowledge is not conclusive, the latter must show not only that the servant was aware of the nature and extent of the risk but that he willingly accepted it.   In *Smith* v. *Baker & Sons*[5] the plaintiff had worked for some time in a quarry in which it was the practice to swing large blocks of stone over the heads of the workmen.   He suffered injury and sought to make his employer liable and was met with the defence of *volenti*.   The court however rejected the defence. The plaintiff was aware of the risk but there was no evidence to show that he had accepted it.   Indeed, it was clear that whenever possible he moved away from the stone which was being swung overhead.   Knowledge may, of course, be such that it leaves no inference open except that which suggests that the risk has been voluntarily encountered.[6]   In such circumstances the defence is complete[7] as it will be wherever, two courses being open to the person subsequently injured, he elects to take the course involving most risk.   This refinement of the rule operated where a shunter who normally worked with boys chose to work without

---

[1] *Williams* v. *Birmingham Battery and Metal Co.*, [1899] 2 Q.B. 338.

[2] (1887), 18 Q.B.D. 685.

[3] *Ibid., per* BOWEN, L.J., at p. 696.

[4] *Smith* v. *Baker & Sons*, [1891] A.C. 325.

[5] *Ibid.*

[6] However, a juvenile workman may be too young to appreciate the nature of the risk.   See *Olsen* v. *Corry and Gravesend Aviation, Ltd.*, [1936] 3 All E.R. 241.

[7] *Thomas* v. *Quartermaine*, (1887), 18 Q.B.D. 685, *per* BOWEN, L.J., at p. 697.

one and was injured, though there was no negligence on his part. The injured person was doubtless unwilling to work without assistance, but though this was so, he preferred doing it to leaving it undone and in that sense he was willing to do it. In *Haynes* v. *Harwood*[1] a police constable was on duty in a busy street and was injured in an attempt to stop a runaway horse. It was held that the constable had not voluntarily accepted the risk, as he acted in pursuance of a public duty against which the defence was of no avail. Where, however, a private individual, at the request of a driver whose horse had bolted and been recaptured, attempted to quiet the horse and was injured, the defence was effective. The cause of the accident was the plaintiff's own act which was completely voluntary.[2]

Once it is shown that a worker has not accepted a risk on first taking up employment, nothing but the clearest indication that he had re-entered the employment on terms of the acceptance of the risk will enable the employer to avail himself of the defence of *volenti non fit injuria*. In *Read* v. *J. Lyons & Co., Ltd.*,[3] a worker, directed under an Essential Work Order to work in a factory, was injured by an explosion. The argument put forward was that the rule in *Fletcher* v. *Rylands*[4] gave the workman a remedy at common law. Supposing that this argument were to be accepted the court would then have to consider whether the defence of *volenti non fit injuria* would be available. It should be noted that the court rejected the view that the worker had a remedy at common law. In consequence the question of *volenti* did not arise, and what the judgments said on the matter was only obiter. None the less, MACKINNON, L.J., had little doubt that a worker who was compelled by the Ministry of Labour to take up employment under conditions in which there was no real freedom of choice, could not be *volens* within the maxim *volenti non fit injuria*.[5] Whether this is an accurate and final statement of the law is a matter of doubt. Its effect, in any future war, would be to restrict within the narrowest limits the operation of the defence of *volenti*. What is important, and what, it is submitted, is an accurate statement of principle, is that supposing any element of compulsion to have been attached to the conditions of service in the first place, a trivial incident or opportunity to change the employment will not enable the employer to avail himself of the defence. In *Read's* case[6] the appellants had argued that though the worker might not have been *volens* when

---

[1] [1934] 2 K.B. 240: [1934] All E.R. Rep. 103.
[2] *Cutler* v. *United Dairies (London), Ltd.*, [1933] 2 K.B. 297; [1933] All E.R. Rep. 594.
[3] [1945] K.B. 216; [1945] 1 All E.R. 106.
[4] (1866), L.R. 1 Exch. 265; affirmed *sub nom. Rylands* v. *Fletcher* (1868), L.R. 3 H.L. 330.
[5] *Read* v. *J. Lyons & Co., Ltd.*, *supra*, at pp. 241, 116 respectively.
[6] [1945] K.B. 216; [1945] 1 All E.R. 106.

she took up the employment, she had become so when, having been offered another kind of employment in a different part of the factory, she had refused the offer and preferred to remain as she was.

> "The plaintiff became a worker in the factory under compulsion. When she had acquired that status I do not think a subsequent incident could rid her of it unless it was clear that the compulsion was entirely withdrawn and she re-entered employment . . . purely as a volunteer."[1]

The courts have been concerned from time to time, with the defence of *volenti* as applied to an injury accruing to A's servant B when B is properly engaged on C's property, a situation which frequently arises in modern industry. This, indeed, was the central situation which exercised the House of Lords in *London Graving Dock Co., Ltd.* v. *Horton.*[2] A highly experienced workman had, for some months been working on a ship, on which his employers, a firm of sub-contractors, were working for the defendants who were re-conditioning the vessel. Because of the inadequacy of certain staging he fell and was injured. Of the danger he was fully informed and he and certain of his fellow workmen had complained. Now, though he was the servant of the sub-contractors he was merely the invitee of the defendant firm of ship repairers and their duty was limited to that of informing him of any unusual dangers. But of the danger in question he was well aware for he had protested against it and thus it was held that he could not recover from the defendants. "I accept the contention," said Lord PORTER,

> "that an invitor's duty to an invitee is to provide reasonably safe premises or else show that the invitee accepted the risk with full knowledge of the danger involved. If the parties were master and servant it may well be that one should go further and say that a full appreciation of the risk is not enough, the servant must not be put in a position in which he is obliged either to obey orders or run the risk of dismissal. But to my mind the position is different where the injured person is not a servant but an invitee. Admittedly the duty of a master to his servant is higher than that of an invitor to an invitee; the invitor, as I see it, is not concerned with the position of an invitee *vis-à-vis* his own ultroneous master: so far as he is concerned the invitee is an invitee and nothing more."[3]

But though there was no doubt that the injured workman was *sciens*, was he *volens* ? Lord PORTER felt that in the present case the question did not arise :

> "The difference between *sciens* and *volens* has by now been firmly established, but where the exact line is to be drawn is a matter of more difficulty. The accurate demarcation, however, in my opinion, need not be laid down in the present case, since it is enough to

---

[1] [1945] K.B. 216; [1945] 1 All E.R. 106, at p. 241 and p. 116 respectively. *per* MacKinnon, J.

[2] [1951] A.C. 737; [1951] 2 All E.R. 1.

[3] [1951] A.C. 737; [1951] 2 All E.R. 1 at pp. 746–7 and 5 respectively.

protect the invitor from liability if he proves that the invitee knew
and fully appreciated the risk. The further step, that he must be
shown not to have been under a feeling of constraint, or, to put it
otherwise, must have been *volens* is not an essential to the defence.
Whether the learned judge meant to find that the respondent was
volens I am not sure, nor am I sure that if he had meant to do so he
had evidence which entitled him to reach that conclusion. But, as
I have said, my view is that the question does not arise."[1]

Where, however, the workman cannot exercise free choice the
position may be different. The plaintiff in *Merrington* v. *Iron-
bridge Metal Works, Ltd.*[2] was a fireman called to a fire at a factory
which was engaged in the process of extracting the aluminium
from aluminium foil. The process created a fine dust containing
aluminium and carbon particles which lay in thick deposits over
various parts of the factory. During the fire the plaintiff was injured
by an explosion caused by the dust and against his claim for damages
it was contended that he attended the fire voluntarily and with
knowledge that risk would be incurred. It was held that there
was a duty on the defendants not to have their factory in a dangerous
condition, for this created a dangerous and unusual situation. Nor
could the defence of *volenti non fit injuria* be successfully pleaded.
In the circumstances it must be shown that the man was both *sciens*
—and *volens*. For the liability of a fireman called to the premises,
sometimes by people other than the occupiers, does not wholly
depend on the fact of his being an invitee. Referring to the defence
of *volenti*, HALLETT, J., said that he was

"satisfied that the doctrine can have no application unless the
plaintiff is at least *sciens*, that is to say, he fully appreciates the
dangerous character of the physical condition which has been
brought about by the negligence of the defendant."[3]

Accordingly the plea broke down at the outset. But knowledge was
not sufficient.

" The plaintiff must also be *volens*, that is to say a real consent to
the assumption of the risk without compensation must be shown
by the circumstances."[4]

It is a question of fact in each case and not of law. If, however, a
man acts under the compulsion of a duty, such a consent should
rarely if ever be inferred, because a man cannot be said to be willing,
unless he is in a position to choose freely.[5] Thus the defendants
were liable.

The defence is limited by the employer's duty to provide a reasonably safe system of working and any change from the normal system
which increases the risk will place a greater onus on the employer in

---

[1] [1951] A.C. 737; [1951] 2 All E.R. 1, at pp. 748 and 6 respectively.
[2] [1952] 2 All E.R. 1101.
[3] *Ibid.*, at p. 1103.
[4] *Ibid.*
[5] *Ibid.*

proving the servant's acceptance of the risk.   In other words, it is easier to prove acceptance when a servant comes to the risk than when an additional risk is added to his present employment.   So where a horseman who had been employed for twelve years to work with horses was, despite his protests, given one which was known to be restive, it was held that the defence would not apply since there was no acceptance of the risk.[1]   Nor may the defence be used to evade liability arising by reason of the breach of a duty imposed by statute.   So, even though it is shown that a servant accepted the risk of working an unfenced machine which was required by law to be fenced, the master will yet be liable.[2]

(3) **Contributory Negligence.**—It may so happen that where a servant is injured during his employment both he and his master are at fault.   The master's fault may consist in a breach of any of the standards of care we have tried to define in this chapter, or it may consist in some duty laid upon him by statute.   If in such circumstances the workman sues his master he may be met by the defence of contributory negligence, when he will find in the courts a power to apportion damages between them according to the measure of their fault.   This position represents a novel change in the law dependent upon the Law Reform (Contributory Negligence) Act, 1945.[3]

Hitherto, the position at common law had been that the courts had to ascertain whose negligence or breach of duty had been the "proximate" or "direct" cause of the accident.   If it were that of the worker he could recover nothing despite any otherwise tortious act on the part of the employer.   If the employer's breach were the substantial cause of the accident he would be liable despite any negligence on the part of the worker.

It is now provided that where a person suffers damage, partly as the result of his own fault and partly as the result of the fault of another, a claim in respect of that damage will not be defeated by reason of the fault of the person suffering that damage, but the damages recoverable will be reduced to such extent as the court thinks just and equitable having regard to the claimant's share in the responsibility for the damage.[4]   The court in awarding damages under this provision must find and record the total damages which would have been awarded had the claimant not been at fault.[5]   The damages recoverable under the Act cover those for loss of life and personal injury, but it is submitted that the Act does not here alter the existing law and if this is so, damages in respect of loss of property

---

[1] *Bowater* v. *Rowley Regis Corporation*, [1944] K.B. 476; [1944] 1 All E.R. 465.
[2] *Wheeler* v. *New Merton Board Mills, Ltd.*, [1933] 2 K.B. 669: [1933] All E.R. Rep. 28.
[3] 8 & 9 Geo 6, c. 28.
[4] *Ibid.*, s. 1 (1), but see *Mullard* v. *Ben Line Steamers*, [1971] 2 All E.R. 424, where damages were not reduced.
[5] *Ibid.*, s. 1 (2).

must also be covered though they are not referred to. "Fault" is defined as meaning any negligence, breach of statutory duty or other act or omission which gives rise to a liability in tort or would, apart from the Act give rise to the defence of contributory negligence.[1]

The Act applies a principle which had long been accepted law in relation to collisions at sea and the practices of the Admiralty Division in the assessment of damages have influenced the courts in applying the Act.[2] And the general principles of the law relating to contributory negligence evolved before the passing of the Act are still important for the courts must still determine whether one or both of the parties are negligent and if so, to what degree.

The basis of the rule, was defined by Lord ELLENBOROUGH, C.J. in *Butterfield* v. *Forrester* in these terms:

> "One person's being in fault will not dispense with another's using ordinary care for himself."[3]

So, if a master commits a breach of his duty towards the servant and the servant might, by ordinary care, have avoided the consequence of that breach his right to recover may be affected. In *Gibby* v. *East Grinstead Gas and Water Co.*[4] a workman had to move along an unfenced and unlighted gantry. A lamp was provided but the workmen were not compelled to use it and some of them preferred to use torches of their own. On the night in question a workman had brought his own bicycle lamp but used neither that nor the hurricane lamp. He died, but there was no evidence to show how exactly he met his death. It was held that his failure to use a lamp was such "contributory" negligence as would offset any claim whether at common law or under the Factories Act.

> "In going along this gantry at night without any light to guide him as he was walking back along it to the retort house, the deceased was disregarding his own safety and therefore was negligent. The only other point in the case . . . seems to me to be whether or not there was a sufficient train of causation between that negligence and the accident. . . . In my opinion, there clearly was. If you find that a person has been walking along a path on a dark night when there is no moon, and the only thing known about him afterwards is that he has fallen off the track, whether it is over a cliff side or down into a yard below a gantry, I think most people would say : 'Well, it is what comes of going along a place like this without a light.'"[5]

Gibby's case, of course, was heard before the Law Reform (Contributory Negligence) Act came into effect but its authority on the subject of the workman's negligence is not questioned. But in

---

[1] Law Reform (Contributory Negligence) Act, 1945, s. 4.
[2] See *William A. Jay & Sons* v. *J. S. Veevers, Ltd.*, [1946] 1 All E.R. 646.
[3] (1809), 11 East, 60, at p. 61.   [4] [1944] 1 All E.R. 358.
[5] *Gibby* v. *East Grinstead Gas and Water Co., supra, per* GODDARD, L.J., at p. 362.

Cakebread v. *Hopping Bros. (Whetstone), Ltd.*[1] a new point was raised before the court. The plaintiff was a woodworker of considerable skill and experience who lost part of one of his fingers whilst operating a circular saw. The saw was, by Regulation, required to be guarded with a guard so adjusted that the work might be carried on without unnecessary risk. The workman had objected to the guard being placed as low as possible, on the ground that he could not see what he was doing. The court were agreed that the employers had not carried out their statutory duty in respect of the adjustment of the guard, but they in turn maintained that had the guard been adjusted by the workman as low as possible the accident would not have occurred; that this was a wrong on the part of the workman who had aided and abetted his employers in their breach of duty and was thus defeated by the operation of the maxim *ex turpi causa non oritur actio*. OAKSEY, L.J., however said that since their foreman knew of the faulty adjustment, the employers were in continuing breach of their statutory duty, but the workman had also failed to observe the care which a prudent person would have taken for his own safety and that this constituted "fault" within the meaning of the Act. On the question of the operation of the maxim *ex turpi causa* COHEN, L.J., insisted that as the maxim was based on public policy and as on the facts of the present case, public policy did not require that the action should be dismissed, but that it should be entertained and decided on its merits, the maxim was not available to defeat the plaintiffs. Thus the damages were apportioned equally between the parties. Where, however, the breach of duty is a technical breach by the employer arising as a result of delegation of a duty to a servant, in a case where such delegation is usual or reasonable, and from the failure of that servant to act with due care, then the court will not apportion but will apply the commonsense notion that the fault is all that of the servant who is debarred from any recovery.[2] It must be emphasised that this reasoning will only apply to an action by the servant on whom the delegated duty was placed.

The workman's duty to observe the care of a prudent man was discussed and affirmed in *Davies* v. *Swan Motor Co. (Swansea), Ltd. (Swansea Corporation and James, Third Parties).*[3] The plaintiff's husband had ridden on the steps of a lorry contrary to instructions when an omnibus belonging to the defendants collided with the lorry and killed him. It was held that the driver of the omnibus was guilty of negligence but that the dead man was guilty of contributory negligence, for though by riding on the steps he was in breach of a duty which he owed to the driver of the omnibus, not to make

---

[1] [1947] K.B. 641; [1947] 1 All E.R. 389.
[2] *Johnson* v. *Croggon & Co., Ltd.,* [1954] 1 All E.R. 121.   Had contribution been appropriate the plaintiff's damages would have been reduced by 99 per cent.
[3] [1949] 2 K.B. 291; [1949] 1 All E.R. 620.

more difficult the passing of the lorry by the omnibus, it was not necessary to prove any such breach of duty to found contributory negligence. It was sufficient to show a lack of reasonable care on the part of the deceased for his own safety. The damages awarded were reduced by one-fifth on account of the deceased's culpability and the remaining damages were to be borne by the omnibus company and the driver of the lorry in the proportions of two to one. Discussing the legal effect of the Act, DENNING, L.J., said,

> "If the plaintiff's negligence was one of the causes of his damage he is no longer defeated altogether. He gets reduced damages. The practical effect of the Act is, however, wider than its legal effect. Previously, to mitigate the harshness of the doctrine of contributory negligence, the courts, in practice sought to select, from a number of competing causes which was *the* cause—the effective or predominant cause — of the damage and to reject the rest. Now the courts have regard to all the causes and apportion the damages accordingly. This is not a change in the law as to what constitutes contributory negligence—the search, in theory, was always for all the causes—but it is a change in the practical application of it."[1]

(4) Duty to Insure.—It has always been the practice of the prudent employer to cover his so-called " employer's liability " with insurance under such a policy as will include both his vicarious liability (and we have seen that most cases involve the insurance company using the employer's name in the action), and his liability to his own employees. But not all employers were prudent, and the result of a failure to insure might prejudice the ability of the injured employee to recover from a bankrupt employer.

Statutory provision has now been made for an employer to have to insure against his liability for personal injury to his employees. This is the Employers' Liability (Compulsory Insurance) Act, 1969.[2] The Act states that every employer must insure: excepted are local authorities,[3] statutory corporations and nationalised industries, and there is power to add to this list by regulations.[4] The duty is to maintain an approved policy with authorised insurers covering bodily injury or disease of an employee arising out of and in the course of employment[5] in Great Britain. The details defining such concepts as approved policy and authorised insurers, are provided by regulation.[6] For example, they prohibit certain conditions of exemption of the insurers from liability. Those to be covered by such insurance are defined in the Act as individuals working under a contract of service or apprenticeship.[7] Close relatives are ex-

---

[1] [1949] 2 K.B. 291; [1949] 1 All E.R. 620, at pp. 322, 630 respectively.
[2] Operative from January 1972.
[3] S. 3(2).
[4] S. 3(1).
[5] For a discussion of this phrase, see pp. 172 and 399.
[6] Employers' Liability (Compulsory Insurance) General Regulations, 1971, S.I. 1971, No. 1117.
[7] S. 2(1).

cluded, as are those not ordinarily resident in Great Britain, although regulations make exceptions to the latter category.[1]   The Act provides that certificates of insurance must be issued.   Again the details are to be found in the regulations.[2]   Such certificates have to be produced to an inspector, and failure to do so is a summary offence.[3]   Failure to insure, itself, is also, of course, backed by the criminal sanction of a summary offence.[4]   Any officer or servant of the employer who is a corporation, who has had a part in the failure to insure, is liable, as well as the corporation itself.

2. Fatal Accidents Acts

From the foregoing sections it is clear that, even at common law, the principles of an employer's liability for accidents to his workmen, had been worked out with some particularity.   But the system had two major defects.   In the first place, if the accident resulted in death, the death would prevent a cause of action arising.   In the second place, the defence of common employment might prevent an injured workman from making his master liable.   In both cases the common law principles were so firmly entrenched that it was hopeless to expect relief except by statute.   Such relief, however, arrived and the Fatal Accidents Acts, 1846 to 1908, were aimed at the first defect,[5] whilst the Employers' Liability Act, 1880, limited the right of the employer to avail himself of the defence of common employment in certain special cases.   The latter Act, as has been pointed out, has now been repealed consequent upon the abolition by Parliament of the doctrine of common employment.[6]

(1) Liability for Death at Common Law.—The common law gave no remedy for a civil act which resulted in the death of a human being.   Death, when it ensued, wiped out any possible tortious character in the act, for the rule at common law was that a personal action died with the person in whom the right of action rested.   This doctrine is often referred to as the rule in *Baker* v. *Bolton*[7] in which case the plaintiff sued in respect of injuries resulting in the death of his wife.   Had the wife recovered she would, of course, have been able herself to maintain an action.   Indeed the husband might maintain an action for the loss of her society to the date of her death, but for nothing further.[8]   In another case in which it was held that a master could not succeed in an action for damages for injuries which caused the immediate death of his servant it was said:

---

[1] S. 2(2) and S.I. 1971, No. 1117.
[2] S. 4 and S.I. 1971, No. 1117.
[3] S. 4(3).
[4] S. 5.
[5] The 1908 Act has been repealed by the recent Fatal Accidents Act, 1959.
[6] Law Reform (Personal Injuries) Act, 1948.
[7] (1808), 1 Camp. 493.
[8] *Baker* v. *Bolton* (1808), 1 Camp. 493.

"It may seem a shadowy distinction to hold that when the service is simply interrupted by accident resulting from negligence, the master may recover damages, while in the case of its being determined altogether by the servant's death from the same cause no action can be sustained. Still I am of opinion that the law has been so understood up to the present time."[1]

However, by the Law Reform (Miscellaneous Provisions) Act, 1934,[2] death no longer terminates the action in tort except for torts of a highly personal nature.[3] The personal representatives may take action on behalf of the deceased's estate and the sum awarded where the tort involved death will include damages for loss of expectation of life.[4]

Where the death of the servant arises from a breach of contract to which the master is a party the position at common law is different and damages may be recovered.[5]

(2) When the Action Lies.— A master might be liable at common law where, owing to accident, his servant was maimed, but could escape liability where the servant was killed. This anomaly led to the passing of the Fatal Accidents Act. Section 1 of the principal Act[6] lays down that wherever the death of a person[7] is caused by such wrongful act, neglect or default[8] as would, if death had not ensued, have entitled the injured party to recover damages, then the person responsible for the death will be liable for damages. This will be so though the death is caused in circumstances which amount to an offence.

As might be expected, the requirement that no action will lie under the terms of the Act unless the deceased himself would, but for his death, have had a right of action has led to some litigation. The test to be applied is that of the legal position of the deceased at the moment of death

"with the idea fictionally that death has not taken place. At that moment, however, the test is absolute. If, therefore, the deceased could not, had he survived at that moment, successfully have maintained his action, then the action under the Act does not arise."[9]

---

[1] *Osborn* v. *Gillett* (1873), L.R. 8 Exch. 88, *per* Pigott, B. at pp. 91-2.
[2] 24 & 25 Geo. 5, c. 41.
[3] Defamation.
[4] *Rose* v. *Ford,* [1937] A.C. 826; [1937] 3 All E.R. 359.
[5] *Jackson* v. *Watson & Sons,* [1909] 2 K.B. 193.
[6] Fatal Accidents Act, 1846.
[7] The representatives of an alien may recover under the Act where the wrongdoer is an Englishman; *Davidsson* v. *Hill,* [1901] 2 K.B. 606.
[8] These words will cover a negligent breach of contract; *Grein* v. *Imperial Airways, Ltd.,* [1937] 1 K.B. 50; [1936] 2 All E.R. 1258.
[9] *British Columbia Electric Ry. Co.* v. *Gentile,* [1914] A.C. 1034 *per* Lord Dunedin at p. 1041.

Thus if the master would have had a satisfactory defence against the deceased he can urge it in actions founded on the Act. An action, consequently, will fail where the deceased, before death, had accepted a sum of money in satisfaction of all claims.[1] The same result will ensue where the deceased had covenanted not to claim in respect of injuries,[2] and where a workman travelled on a railway with a free pass which relieved the company of all liability, an action could not be successfully maintained.[3] But supposing that an action lies, an agreement as to limitation of liability to which the deceased was a party will not bind claimants under the Fatal Accidents Acts,[4] for the Act says nothing about the quantum of damages which the deceased must have been entitled to recover.

Where the act constituting the tort is also an offence the general rule is that no action may be brought on the tort whilst the offence remains unprosecuted. To this rule there are several exceptions, and the section under discussion provides that the remedy under the Fatal Accidents Acts may be pursued though the prosecution of the felony is not undertaken.

(3) **Benefit of the Action.**—The action lies for the benefit of the following relatives of the deceased: grandparents, father, mother, uncle, aunt, wife, husband, brother, sister, children, grandchildren.[5] Relationship may be traced through step-relatives: an adopted child is to be treated as the child of his adopted parents, an illegitimate child as the child of his mother and reputed father. The relatives of the deceased's spouse have the same rights as the deceased's relatives.[6] The remedy is given to these persons as individuals and not as a class. Consequently where the deceased was of independent means, and the sources of his income were not changed by death, it was held that an action would lie if, as a result of his death, the mode of distribution of his property was changed.[7] The action should be brought in the name of the executor or administrator of the deceased.[8] Where there is no executor or administrator or where there is such and he refuses or neglects to bring an action within six calendar months of the death of the deceased, the action may be brought in the name or names of the persons for whose benefit the executor might have brought action.[9]

The jury will give such damages as are proportionate to the injury caused by the death and, after deducting costs not recoverable from

---

[1] *Read* v. *Great Eastern Ry. Co.* (1868), L.R. 3 Q.B. 555.
[2] *Griffiths* v. *Earl of Dudley* (1882), 9 Q.B.D. 357.
[3] *The Stella*, [1900] P. 161.
[4] *Nunan* v. *Southern Ry. Co.*, [1924] 1 K.B. 223.
[5] Fatal Accidents Act, 1846, s. 2 and Fatal Accidents Act, 1959, s. 1 (1).
[6] Fatal Accidents Act, 1959, s. 1 (2). See (1960) 22 *M.L.R.* 60 for notes by J. Unger and O. Kahn-Freund.
[7] *Pym* v. *Great Northern Ry. Co.* (1862), 2 B. & S. 759.
[8] Fatal Accidents Act, 1846, s. 2.
[9] Fatal Accidents Act, 1864, s. 1.

the defendant, will divide the damages into shares for the persons indicated.[1] If the defendant pays money into court it is sufficient that he pays it in one sum without specifying the shares into which it is to be divided. If the said sum is not accepted and issue is taken as to its sufficiency and the jury thinks the sum to be sufficient the defendant will be entitled to the verdict on that issue.[2] Where a dispute is settled, without an action being brought, by the payment of a lump sum of money, the court will, if asked to make a declaration, apportion the damages amongst beneficiaries just as would a jury.[3] In assessing damages under the Acts, any benefit accruing to a dependant, as a result of the death must be taken into account. This will include property devolving from the deceased's estate.[4] Similarly any pension receivable by a beneficiary from the Crown in respect of the death, even though it is dependent on the Crown's bounty.[5] However, sums payable on the death of the deceased in respect of insurance are not to be taken into account,[6] nor are any pensions, gratuities or benefits including benefits receivable under the National Insurance Acts.[7] Damages may be awarded in respect of funeral expenses if such have been incurred by the parties for whose benefit the actions are brought.[8]

These provisions have been considered by the courts in many recent cases. The basic principle was set out by Lord WRIGHT in the following terms :

> "It is a hard matter of pounds shillings and pence, subject to the element of reasonable future probabilities. The starting point is the amount of wages which the deceased was earning, the ascertainment of which to some extent may depend on the regularity of his employment. Then there is an estimate of how much was required or expended for his own personal and living expenses. The balance will give a datum or basic figure which will generally be turned into a lump sum by taking a certain number of years purchase. That sum has, however, to be taxed down, by having due regard to uncertainties, for instance that the widow might have again married and thus cease to be dependent and other like matters of speculation and doubt."[9]

But once the basic sum has been ascertained and the deductions made the amount must not be increased because of a lowered value

---

[1] Fatal Accidents Act, 1846, s. 2.
[2] Fatal Accidents Act, 1864, s. 2; *Bishop* v. *Cunard White Star Co., Ltd.,* [1950] P. 240; [1950] 2 All E.R. 22.
[3] *Bulmer* v. *Bulmer* (1883), 25 Ch.D. 409.
[4] E.g. damages awarded under the Law Reform (Miscellaneous Provisions) Act, 1934; see *supra*, p. 235; *Davies* v. *Powell Duffryn Associated Collieries, Ltd.,* [1942] A.C. 601; [1942] 1 All E.R. 657.
[5] *Baker* v. *Dalgleish SS. Co., Ltd.,* [1922] 1 K.B. 361; *Johnson* v. *Hill,* [1945] 2 All E.R. 272.
[6] Fatal Accidents Act, 1959, s. 2.
[7] *Ibid.,* s. 2 (2).
[8] Law Reform (Miscellaneous Provisions) Act, 1934, s. 2
[9] *Davies* v. *Powell Duffryn Associated Collieries, Ltd.,* [1942] A.C. 601 at p. 617; [1942] 1 All E.R. 657 at p. 665.

of the pound since the date of the accident[1] and where, for example, the widow has died between the date of the death of the husband and the judgment in the Fatal Accidents action, damages would be limited in respect of the period during which she had lived and not based on her expectation of life at his death.[2] Similarly it is proper in assessing the damages to take into account the possibility of a man being killed in war as a member of the services.[3] And where an estimate of the man's earnings has been made, a sum may be deducted covering the cost of his living expenses.[4]

There has been extensive case law on the question of what sums, accruing upon death, need not be taken into account. The formula of the 1908 Act, " any sum paid or payable on the death of the deceased under any contract of assurance "[5] had given rise to considerable difficulty and it has, in the 1959 Act, been replaced by " any insurance money, benefit, pension or gratuity which has been or will or may be paid as a result of the death."[6] Earlier decisions that pensions payable under Royal Warrant,[7] or under contributory pension schemes,[8] are to be taken into account, are no longer good law. The difficulty of including, as not to be taken into account, moneys received from a group pension scheme in which the deceased was not a party to the contract of insurance has been removed.[9] Finally, the inclusion in the new formula of the words " gratuities " and " or may be paid " has ended the doubt where the money paid was a voluntary payment rather than a legal obligation.[10]

To sustain the action the plaintiff must show a reasonable probability of pecuniary loss by the death of the deceased. A mere speculative possibility of loss is not sufficient.[11] Nor is the basis of the damage the loss of a legal right, for the damages are distributed only amongst defined persons, and others outside these, though their

---

[1] *Ibid.*

[2] *Williamson* v. *John I. Thornycroft & Co., Ltd.,* [1940] 2 K.B. 658; [1940] 4 All E.R. 61.

[3] *Hall* v. *Wilson,* [1939] 4 All E.R. 85.

[4] *Heatley* v. *Steel Co. of Wales, Ltd.,* [1953] 1 All E.R. 489, C.A.

[5] Fatal Accidents (Damages) Act, 1908 and Law Reform (Personal Injuries) Act, 1948, s. 2 (5).

[6] Fatal Accidents Act, 1959, s. 2.

[7] *Johnson* v. *Hill,* [1945] 2 All E.R. 272.

[8] *Lory* v. *Great Western Railway,* [1942] 1 All E.R. 230; *Smith* v. *British European Airways Corporation,* [1951] 2 K.B. 893; [1951] 2 All E.R. 737; *O'Neill* v. *S. J. Smith & Co. (Bideford), Ltd.,* [1957] 3 All E.R. 255; [1957] 1 W.L.R. 1204.

[9] *Bowskill* v. *Dawson (No. 2),* [1955] 1 Q.B. 13; [1954] 2 All E.R. 649; *Green* v. *Russell,* [1959] 1 Q.B. 28; [1958] All E.R. 44; affirmed, [1959] 2 Q.B. 226; (1959) 2 All E.R. 525. For a discussion of the complexities of this point see J. Unger, (1959) *M.L.R.* 96, 519.

[10] *Baker* v. *Dalgleish Steam Shipping Co.,* [1922] 1 K.B. 361 which had been distinguished in *Peacock* v. *Amusement Equipment Co., Ltd.,* [1954] 2 Q.B. 347; [1954] 2 All E.R. 689, is no longer good law.

[11] *Barnett* v. *Cohen,* [1921] 2 K.B. 461.

legal rights may have suffered, cannot claim.[1] By the same reasoning, damages may not be given under the Acts for mental suffering or the loss of the companionship of the deceased. If mental anguish were to provide the test then certain people would be deprived of damages though they were named in the Act, for example

> " not only the child without filial piety but a lunatic child and a child of very tender years, and a posthumous child on the death of the father."[2]

The onus of proof on a plaintiff that he must show a reasonable probability of pecuniary loss by death resolves all such difficulties. Whether such probability existed and if so, to what extent, are matters of fact for the jury.[3] The father of a boy of four was held not to be entitled to recover when his son was killed by the negligence of the defendants. The possibility that the father might benefit in the future was held to be merely speculative and not within the bounds of probability.[4] Yet the old and infirm father of a son was entitled to damages in respect of work which the father did, assisted by the son.[5] The jury may properly take prospective loss into account provided the loss is reasonably probable. The father of a boy aged fourteen who had earned the sum of four shillings a week was awarded damages though the boy, when he was killed, was unemployed.[6] Similarly, damages were recovered in respect of the death of a girl of sixteen years of age who was still, at the time of death, serving her apprenticeship as a dressmaker.[7]

Though based upon the probability of pecuniary loss, damages are limited neither by the value of money lost, nor the money value of things lost. They will include the monetary loss incurred by replacing services rendered gratuitously by a relative, so that a husband may claim in respect of the services of his deceased wife where he is compelled to employ and pay a housekeeper in her stead.[8]

(4) Limitation of Action.—Section 3 of the Act[9] provides that one action only shall lie for and in respect of the subject matter of complaint and the Law Reform (Limitation of Actions, &c.) Act, 1954,[10] provides that every such action shall be commenced within three years after death. In the earlier Act the period of limitation

---

[1] *Franklin* v. *South Eastern Ry. Co.* (1858), 3 H. & N. 211.
[2] *Blake* v. *Midland Ry. Co.* (1852), 18 Q.B. 93 *per* COLERIDGE J., at p. 110.
[3] *Franklin* v. *South Eastern Ry. Co.* (1858), 3 H. & N. 211 *per* POLLOCK, C.B., at p. 214.
[4] *Barnett* v. *Cohen*, [1921] 2 K.B. 461.
[5] *Franklin* v. *South Eastern Ry. Co.* (1858), 3 H. & N. 211; *Hetherington* v. *North Eastern Ry. Co.* (1882), 9 Q.B.D. 160.
[6] *Duckworth* v. *Johnson* (1859), 4 H. & N. 653.
[7] *Taff Vale Ry. Co.* v. *Jenkins*, [1913] A.C. 1.
[8] *Berry* v. *Humm & Co.*, [1915] 1 K.B. 627.
[9] Fatal Accidents Act, 1846.
[10] 2 & 3 Eliz. 2, c. 36.

had been twelve months but the Act has been generously construed and it is not unlikely that such generosity will persist. So where a shorter period was required by another Act the provision as to twelve months was held to apply and where the other Act gave a longer period this longer period was adopted as the period of limitation. Thus in *Venn* v. *Tedesco*[1] the defendants were under the general protection of the now repealed Public Authorities Protection Act, 1893,[2] which required that actions against them should be instituted within six months. It was held, nonetheless, that the period of limitation of action was that prescribed by the Fatal Accidents Act. Yet where, under section 8 of the Maritime Conventions Act, 1911, the action might be brought within two years from the date when the loss was caused, the court held that this period would apply rather than the then prevailing twelve calendar months of the Fatal Accidents Act.[3]

The same generosity of interpretation is to be found in *Lubovsky* v. *Snelling*.[4] A claim under the Fatal Accidents Act in which liability was admitted led to an action for the apportionment of damages. An action was begun before the plaintiff had taken out letters of administration and was discontinued on the error being discovered. Another writ, after the grant had been obtained, was taken out more than twelve months after the date of death and the defendant argued that this second action was barred. But the court held that after admitting liability the defendants could not set up a limitation under section 3.

> "... both of them were thereafter precluded from putting forward any defence whatever which would imperil their liability. It was just as much a contract not to plead section 3 of the Act as if that undertaking had been put in words."[5]

3. The Action for Breach of Statutory Duty

It is remarkable that though the last century saw an increasing burden of legislative duties thrust upon the employer for the benefit of his workman's welfare and safety, the legislators, until the passing of the first of the Workmen's Compensation Acts in 1897[6] did little for the injured workman himself. A few scattered provisions throughout the Acts, one or two Acts designed to limit, *e.g.*, a defence otherwise open to the employer[7] or to outwit some harsh or inconvenient rule of the common law[8] represented, so it seemed, the maximum Parlia-

---

[1] [1926] 2 K.B. 227.
[2] Repealed by the Law Reform (Limitation of Actions, &c.) Act, 1954, s.1.
[3] *The Caliph*, [1912] P. 213.
[4] [1944] K.B. 44; *sub nom. Cohen* v. *Snelling, Lubovsky* v. *Snelling*, [1943] 2 All E.R. 577.
[5] *Lubovsky* v. *Snelling*, [1944] K.B. 44, *per* Scott, L.J., at p. 46.
[6] See *infra*.
[7] *E.g.*, the Employers' Liability Act, 1880, in relation to the defence of common employment.
[8] *E.g.*, the Fatal Accidents Acts, see *supra*, p. 234.

mentary interest in the injured individual. It was otherwise with the courts. They made two significant contributions to the injured workman's code of rights. They built up the triple duty on the part of the employer in respect of the competence of his staff, the safety of the plant and the method of working, for breach of which they held the employer liable to the injured workman. And they developed the action for breach of statutory duty to which certain references have, inevitably, been made throughout this book.

Wherever a statute imposes a duty and provides for a penalty there will always be an action in the criminal courts for the breach, but this offers no consolation to the injured workman. The question is thus raised whether the criminal action is the only action available and if not, in what circumstances an action for breach of the statutory duty may be maintained by the workman or his defendants. The only sure guide is the statute itself. Thus

> ". . . The only rule which in all circumstances is valid is that the answer must depend on a consideration of the whole Act and the circumstances including the pre-existing law in which it was enacted. But that there are indications which point with more or less force to the one answer or the other . . . For instance if a statutory duty is prescribed, but no remedy by way of penalty or otherwise for its breach is imposed, it can be assumed that a right of civil action accrues . . .' '[1]

It has frequently been suggested that if the Act is of general public character then a civil remedy will not be presumed and nothing but an express provision will make such remedy available,[2] but some caution is needed, and an Act which appears to have a general public character may in fact be passed for the benefit of a limited class of persons.[3] And when the legislation is aimed at benefiting such a limited class the presumption is that a civil remedy is not excluded.

In the sphere of master and servant the increasing tendency of the courts has been to construe Acts concerned with the welfare of the worker as giving that worker a civil remedy even though the only reference is to a fine for breach. Thus actions for breach of duties imposed in the Factories and Mines and Quarries Acts have been frequent, as have actions on regulations made under those Acts. But where a Minister has power to make regulations and does not do so an action will not lie. Lord WRIGHT, discussing this matter in *Nicholls* v. *F. Austin (Leyton) Ltd.*, said,

> ". . . No regulations have been made under this clause, which is left in the air. It might indeed have been made use of to prevent the small slivers thrown off by the back of the saw being at large within

---

[1] *Cutler* v. *Wandsworth Stadium, Ltd.*, [1949] A.C. 398 at p. 407; [1949] I All E.R. 544 at p. 548.
[2] *Atkinson* v. *Newcastle Waterworks* (1877), 2 Ex. D. 441.
[3] *Read* v. *Croydon Corporation*, [1938] 4 All E.R. 631.

the metal case . . . and coming out and striking the operator . . .
the fact remains that no regulations have been made. . . . This I
think is fatal to her (the plaintiff's) claim."[1]

Where regulations modify or vary the Act which authorises their
promulgation the regulations may extend or diminish the obligations imposed by the Act.[2]   The regulations may be taken as being
incompletely exhaustive and so a situation in which the employer
has not been in breach of a particular regulation may still be
actionable as being in breach of the general duty in the Act itself.
So where regulations dealt with the fencing of a specific part of a
machine and were otherwise silent, failure to fence other parts was
held to be an actionable breach of the general duty in the Act.[3]   The
more usual result, however, is that compliance with the regulation
will be regarded as a defence, for that specific duty under the regulation is substituted for the more general duty in the Act.[4]

Liability in the action for breach of statutory duty falls upon the
person made liable by the particular statute or regulation concerned.
So, under the Factories Act normally the occupier will be liable and
the onus, in general, of displacing his liability is heavy though,
indeed, the occupier may have a right of indemnity from the party
actually causing the damage.[5]

The plaintiff in an action for breach of statutory duty must prove
that his injuries arose from a danger against which the statute intended that he should be protected and that there has been a breach
of the duty which was intended to guard against that danger.[6]   That
possible difficulties may arise from the onus of proving causation
being placed upon the plaintiff workman is illustrated by *Nolan* v.

---

[1] [1946] A.C. 493 at p. 503; [1946] 2 All E.R. 92 at p. 97

[2] See *Franklin* v. *Gramophone Co., Ltd.*, [1948] 1 K.B. 542; [1948] 1 All E.R.
353; *Miller* v. *Boothman (Wm.) & Sons, Ltd.*, [1944] K.B. 337; [1944] 1 All
E.R. 333; *Chipchase* v. *British Titan Products Co., Ltd.*, [1956] 1 Q.B. 545;
[1956] 1 All E.R. 613.

[3] *Benn* v. *Kamm & Co., Ltd.*, [1952] 2 Q.B. 127; [1952] 1 All E.R. 833;
Dickson v. *Flack*, [1953] 2 Q.B. 464; [1953] 2 All E.R. 840.   And for regula-
tions with proviso retaining the general duty see *Quinn* v. *Horsfall & Bickham,
Ltd.*, [1956] 2 All E.R. 467; [1956] 1 W.L.R. 652.

[4] *Automatic Wood Turning Co., Ltd.* v. *Stringer*, [1957] A.C. 544; [1957] 1 All
E.R. 90; *John Summers & Sons, Ltd.* v. *Frost*, [1955] A.C. 740: [1955] 1 All
E.R. 870; *Miller* v. *William Boothman & Sons, Ltd.*, [1944] K.B. 337; [1944]
1 All E.R. 333.

[5] *Whitby* v. *Burt, Boulton & Hayward, Ltd.*, [1947] K.B. 918; [1947] 2 All
E.R. 324; but see *Dorman, Long & Co., Ltd.* v. *Hillier*, [1951] 1 All E.R. 357;
and *Hopwood* v. *Rolls Royce, Ltd.* (1947), 176 L.T. 514, C.A.

[6] *Bonnington Castings, Ltd.* v. *Wardlow*, [1956] A.C. 613; [1956] 1 All E.R.
615.   The earlier case was considered here and the suggestion that the onus
of proving that the breach did not cause the injury lies in the defendant employer which is to be found in such cases as *Vyner* v. *Waldenberg Brothers, Ltd.*,
[1946] K.B. 50; [1945] 2 All E.R. 547; *Lee* v. *Nursery Furnishings, Ltd.*, [1945]
1 All E.R. 387 and *Hughes* v. *McGoff and Vickers, Ltd.*, [1955] 2 All E.R.
291; [1955] 1 W.L.R. 416 was rejected.   The plaintiff workman must prove
that the breach of duty caused or materially contributed to his injury.

Dental Manufacturing Co. Ltd.,[1] which case also provided an interesting contrast between the application of breach of statutory duty and common law negligence.

A moment's thought will show that in modern industry the employer cannot himself comply with all the duties laid upon him by statute. In the very nature of the case he must work by delegation and once this is recognised the question is immediately raised : how far, in an action for breach of statutory duty may an employer plead that he has delegated the duties to a servant and that, given the circumstances the delegation was reasonable? In *Harrison* v. *National Coal Board*[2] the plaintiff was injured as the consequence of the failure of a shot firer to give due warning as required by the Coal Mines Order, 1934. According to the evidence the Coal Board had not been aware of the breach, had done all that was reasonable to enforce discipline and compliance with the regulations in the mines and it was held that they were not liable. It would seem, therefore, that reasonable delegation to a proper official (and in the case of mines such delegation may be imposed by statute) will afford a defence except where the statute unequivocably excludes this and makes the employer liable.

But any such delegation must be clear and unambiguous. In *Manwaring* v. *Billington*[3] the plaintiff workman had been instructed not to mount ladders without putting sacking at the base so as to prevent slipping and to tie sacking also at the top. The plaintiff failed to do so and, when injured, brought action against his employers. The breach of duty was admitted but it was pleaded that the employer had delegated the duty to the workmen. The court maintained that mere instruction about the carrying out of duties does not constitute such delegation of a statutory duty as will give the employer a defence. If it is sought to delegate a statutory duty it must be made quite explicit that it is the *duty* which is being delegated. However, since in the present case it was the plaintiff who caused the accident, his employer was not liable.

On the other hand it will be remembered that the defence *volenti non fit injuria* is not available to an employer sued for breach of statutory duty.[4] The defence is based on the notion that a workman voluntarily accepts risks incidental to the work but it is obvious that in general the parties cannot by agreement stipulate that statutes shall not bind them. But a workman may be contributorily negligent for a breach of statutory duty and where he is so the general principles of such negligence will apply.

[1] [1958] 1 W.L.R. 936; [1958] 2 All E.R. 449.
[2] [1951] A.C. 639; [1951] 1 All E.R. 1102.
[3] [1952] 2 All E.R. 747; for the opposite result see *Jenner* v. *Allen West & Co., Ltd.*, [1959] 2 All E.R. 115.
[4] The leading case is *Imperial Chemical Industries, Ltd.* v. *Shatwell*, [1965] A.C. 656.

4. THE WORKMEN'S COMPENSATION ACTS[1]

The Workmen's Compensation Acts, the first of which was introduced in 1897,[2] were for half a century the chief statutory remedy
for a workman who sustained personal injury arising out of and in
the course of the employment. They introduced, at a critical period
in the development of the relations between master and servant, an
entirely new principle; namely that in respect of certain workmen
and in relation to certain risks the master became an insurer of their
safety. Hitherto his liability had been based upon negligence, but
with the constantly increasing complexity of modern industry and
with the growth of larger economic units the personal remedy against
the employer became more difficult to enforce. The Workmen's
Compensation Acts were designed, in part to meet this situation.
Originally covering only a small number of the workmen of the
country, they had been increasingly extended. The Acts gave a
remedy which existed for the benefit of the workman, or, if death
resulted, for the benefit of his dependants.[3] In this latter eventuality
compensation took the form of a lump sum, which could not, however, exceed £700.[4] Compensation payable on partial or total incapacity was a weekly payment, expressed in terms of the workmen's
average earnings during the twelve months previous to the injury
or of such lesser period during which he had been in the service of
the same employer. The workman might also agree to compromise
his claim, if it were disputed, for a lump sum payment.[5]

The system had been subject to considerable criticism and was
studied amongst other things, during the last war, originally by an
Interdepartmental Committee of civil servants of which Sir William
Beveridge was chairman and later by Sir William himself who ultimately produced a report upon which subsequent Ministerial policy
was, in some measure, founded. The criticism urged against workmen's compensation was far reaching and, from the comparative
point of view, suggested that in this field Britain compared ill with
other countries, and this though there was much in the system to
commend it. The virtues, amply recorded in the Beveridge Report,
were that in a substantial number of cases the workman received his
compensation with little delay, the employer and his employee remained connected throughout and it was usual for the injured
employee to return to the service of his original employer; the
employer was free to make what arrangements he chose as to insurance—though only in the case of mining was such insurance compulsory—and the cost of insurance to cover the liability to pay com-

---

[1] Some of the material in this section is based upon a paper prepared for the
fourth International Congress of Comparative Law. Paris 1954.

[2] 60 and 61 Vict., c. 37.

[3] The Workmen's Compensation Act, 1925, s. 2.

[4] *Ibid.*, s. 8 (1) and Workmen's Compensation (Temporary Increases) Act,
1943.

[5] Workmen's Compensation Act, 1925, ss. 2 (1), 9 (1), 21 (1) and 24.

pensation varied, of course, with the risk of accident. This was said to encourage accident prevention.

But perhaps the most fundamental criticism levelled at the sytems was that, in the ultimate, the threat or actuality of litigation was the sanction upon which the scheme depended. The hope that disputes would be settled by a friendly, informal arbitration had never been realised and the mass of litigation which resulted did much to clarify the law but little to improve relations between employer and employed. Indeed, the system of insuring against the employer's liability tended to increase litigation, for no matter how well disposed the employer might be to his workmen the word of the insurance company frequently prevailed and action was brought. Indeed the fact that the undisclosed principals were, as often as not, an insurance company and a trade union, not infrequently forced parties to fight who would have been glad to come to terms. Such considerations were decisive in keeping the post-1947 system of industrial accident insurance, in the main, outside the courts.

It was said also, that the inclusion of industrial diseases within the system of workmen's compensation merely meant that employers were sometimes ready, on early symptoms showing themselves, to dismiss unfortunate workmen.

Two other criticisms were made. It was said that a system which paid a man only a stated proportion of his salary when the need was greatest stood condemned; and though the payment of a lump sum was subject to considerable scrutiny, it was often inadequate and still more often was expended unwisely, giving rise to subsequent need on the part of the workman and his dependants.

How these criticisms were met by the national insurance system will be explained in the next chapter, but certain general observations may be made here. It was decided, as will be seen, to reserve industrial injuries for special treatment in the new system though Sir William Beveridge had said that were it not for the past there would have been much to be said for the introduction of a genuinely comprehensive system of insurance. On this issue it is submitted that when the decision to terminate the system of workmen's compensation was made, a great opportunity was missed. If the purpose of a national system of insurance is to protect against need and to compensate for pain and suffering, any distinction between industrial and non-industrial accidents and diseases would seem to be logically untenable. It would perhaps have been over-optimistic to expect that employers and employed should agree about a desirable alternative to workmen's compensation. But that neither side reached agreement within itself was bound to have unfortunate consequences. A middle course between these divergent interests became inevitable and to a consideration of the industrial injury insurance we must now turn. For though the system of workmen's compensation is not dead it has been in the greater part repealed and operates now only in respect of those injuries which accrued before July 5th, 1948.

Turning from these wider considerations it should be noted that in the matter of the risks insured against in the two schemes there is little movement to be observed. The original Workmen's Compensation Act protected the worker from personal injury arising out of and in the course of the employment; the National Insurance (Industrial Injuries) Act does the same. The phrase has been productive of a torrent of litigation, but Parliament has evolved no better definition.[1] The Act of 1906 extended the insurance to certain enumerated diseases and although the number of diseases traceable to occupational causes has increased it has not yet been found possible to attempt any comprehensive definition and it may be that no such definition will ever be achieved. For certain terms are terms of art, to be given such meaning as legislators may desire. But an industrial disease is a scientific fact and the growth of scientific knowledge will doubtless relate an increasing number of diseases to industrial contacts and environments. Indeed, it is significant that though the National Insurance (Industrial Injuries) Act gives the Minister a general power to prescribe certain diseases as being industrial in origin, it contains special provisions concerning certain respiratory diseases—a tribute to the insistence with which medical science has emphasised its view that industrially, at any rate, this is an age of dust and fume.

Finally, it is submitted that the case law to which the system of workmen's compensation gave rise may remain of some significance and will be discussed in Chapter IX

---

[1] It is true that the National Insurance (Industrial Injuries) Act, 1965, s. 6 (3), provides that an accident arising in the course of an insured person's employment will be deemed, in the absence of evidence to the contrary, also to have arisen out of that employment. But it is submitted that this does not extend the definition of an accident. At the most, it removes the burden of proof from the plaintiff.

CHAPTER VII

INDUSTRIAL LEGISLATION (1)

1. SAFETY, HEALTH AND WELFARE

(1) **Introduction.**—Legislation securing standards of safety, health and welfare for workmen at their place of work, and regulating the hours worked, is today's monument to the nineteenth-century reformers who fought so hard for progress. The history of this movement is a study in itself.[1] Unfortunately, it has left a tangle of legislation and regulation which must be outlined in the ensuing pages. The present position is the one so often found in the pattern of English law. There are great statutory peaks: the Factories Act, 1961; the Offices, Shops and Railway Premises Act, 1963; and the Mines and Quarries Act, 1954.[2] Agriculture is covered by the Agriculture (Safety, Health and Welfare Provisions) Act, 1956, and by the Agriculture (Poisonous Substances) Act, 1952. The Shops Act, 1950, a code which long pre-dated the Offices, Shops and Railway Premises Act, has provisions for hours of work. The safe working of railways, in the interests both of the travelling public and workers, is secured in several statutes, notably the Regulation of Railways Act, 1871, and the Railway Employment (Prevention of Accidents) Act, 1900. Merchant Shipping also has its own code laid down in the Merchant Shipping Act, 1970. Several specialized hazards are dealt with in statutes such as the Boiler Explosions Acts, 1882 and 1890; the Alkali Works Regulation Act, 1906; and the Radioactive Substances Act, 1960.

There are several important signs of reform of this mass of legislation. Two areas have been the subject of Bills in Parliament. In 1970 a Bill, which was lost because of the dissolution, tackled two areas together. It proposed to abolish the appointed factory doctor, as provided for in the Factories Act, 1961, and to institute in his place a more widely conceived employment medical service. This proposal has reappeared in a Bill laid before Parliament by the new Government. It will become law as this book is published and its provisions can be noted at the appropriate place.[3] The other proposal was more radical, although it had precedents in the field of mining.[4] This was for the appointment by recognized trade unions,

---

[1] There was a brief resumé in previous editions of this book, *e.g.* 5th Ed., Ch. VIII, pp. 220–229.

[2] The regulations made under these Acts have a bulk and, in some senses, an importance outweighing the Acts themselves.

[3] See *infra*, p. 264, Employment Medical Advisory Service Act, 1972.

[4] See *infra*, p. 349.

in factories of a certain size, of safety representatives and also for the establishment of joint safety committees. It met with a fair measure of opposition, but these proposals have also re-appeared, this time in a private Member's Bill. The matter has been shelved at least for the time being.

A departmental committee of the Department of Employment was set up in June, 1970, under the chairmanship of Lord Robens. Its terms of reference include the duty to review the provisions made for the safety and health of persons in the course of their employment and to consider whether any changes are needed in the scope or nature of the major relevant enactments or the nature and extent of voluntary action concerned with these matters. The committee will report in mid-1972, and it could well be that major reform will be set in train.

2. The Factories Act, 1961

(1) The Scope of the Act—*Definition of Factory*

The Factories Act, 1937, consolidated and amended the legislation of the last half century, and abolished the distinction between the textile and the non-textile factory and within the general term " factory " as defined by the Act the older categories of factories, workshops, men's workshops, women's workshops and domestic factories are all comprehended. Now, for the purposes of the 1961 Act the expression " factory " means any premises in which, or within the close or curtilage or precincts of which, persons are employed in manual labour in any process for or incidental to (a) the making of any article or of any part of any article; or (b) the altering, repairing, ornamenting, finishing, cleaning or washing, or the breaking up or demolition of any article, or the adapting for sale of any article; or (c) the slaughtering of animals[1] or (d) the confinement of such animals while awaiting slaughter at other premises,[2] being premises in which, or within the close, curtilage or precincts of which, the work is carried on by way of trade or for purposes of gain and to or over which the employer of the persons employed therein has the right of access or control.[3] The definition is an extension of definitions in use for some time so that cases which have been decided under older enactments are of value in the interpretation of this.

---

[1] Cattle, sheep, swine, goats, horses, asses or mules.

[2] Not being premises maintained primarily for agricultural purposes or premises used for holding a market. The heads (c) and (d) were added to the 1937 Act by the Slaughterhouse Act, 1958.

[3] Factories Act, 1961, s. 175(1).

Manual Labour

A place cannot be a factory unless it is one in which manual labour is performed. The courts have expressed their sense of difficulty in determining what constitutes manual labour. "It is, I think, clear," said Lord ALVERSTONE, C.J., in *Hoare* v. *Robert Green, Ltd.*,[1]

> "that there must be some limit placed on the scope of these words, and I think that the question as to the limit is best answered by saying that if the substantial purpose for which the place is used, is the employment of persons in manual labour then the Act applies. On the other hand if the place is only incidentally used for the purpose of manual labour—if, for example, the place is a shop and the manual labour is merely incidental to the general business of the shop—then different considerations apply."

The question before the court was whether the making of wreaths, crosses, bouquets and the like in a room behind the shop in which they were sold was manual labour of such a character as to make the place a workshop. The court held that this was so and it seems clear that the test is not one of the quantum of physical energy required, for it has been held that the packing of sweets into the boxes in which they were sold retail is also manual labour.[2]

In *Joyce* v. *Boots Cash Chemists (Southern), Ltd.*,[3] SLADE, J. applied the test laid down in *Hoare* v. *Green (Robert) Ltd.* and said that though a porter working in a shop was engaged in manual labour such labour was only incidental to the shop which was not therefore a factory. The back room at a grocer's shop where a bacon slicing machine was used was, however, held to be a factory.[4] The test laid down in *Hoare* v. *Green (Robert), Ltd.* has recently been doubted in a dictum of the Divisional Court decision in *Paul Popper, Ltd.* v. *Grimsey*[5] for it was thought to give rise to practical difficulties of application but in *Haygarth* v. *J. F. Stone, Lighting and Radio, Ltd.*,[6] it was accepted by Lord PARKER, C.J., as an appropriate test for the room at the rear of a shop. This situation is different from one where the work done in the back of the premises is a major service. In the room in question an engineer was employed to diagnose and repair faulty radio and television sets, the shop being one which sold or hired such sets. The room was held to be a factory. In the House of Lords it was pointed out that the definition is not limited to *unskilled* labour.[7]

---

[1] [1907] 2 K.B. 315 at p. 320.
[2] *Fullers, Ltd.* v. *Squire*, [1901] 2 K.B. 209.
[3] [1950] 2 All E.R. 719 *affd.* [1951] 1 All E.R. 682 n.
[4] *McLeavy* v. *Liptons, Ltd.* (1959), 109 L. Jo. 667.
[5] [1962] 1 All E.R. 864; [1962] 2 W.L.R. 886.
[6] [1965] 2 All E.R. 662; [1965] 3 W.L.R. 316.
[7] *Ibid.*, affirmed *sub nom. J. and F. Stone, Lighting and Radio, Ltd.* v. *Haygarth*, [1968] A.C. 157; [1966] 3 All E.R. 539.

Processes

The various processes which the statutory definition includes as proper to the character of a factory raise, with one exception, no problems. The making, altering, repairing, finishing, cleaning and washing of articles, or the breaking up or demolition of articles are all processes readily recognisable and, consequently, not likely to lead to litigation.[1] But it is otherwise where the "adapting for sale of any article" is concerned, and here the courts have had many problems to solve. Adapting for sale means, so it has been said, that something should be

" done to the article in question which, in some way makes it, in itself, a little different from what it was before."[2]

Consequently the testing and certifying of cables and anchors is not an adapting for sale, and the premises in which such testing takes place is not, by virtue of this fact alone, a factory.[3] Similarly a pumping station, where water is merely put under pressure, is not a factory although it was accepted that a filtration plant would be.[4] On the other hand the composing, printing and publishing of a newspaper is an adapting for sale,[5] as is the sorting and matching of wool,[6] the separation of the saleable from the unsaleable parts of a city's refuse,[7] and the aeration and bottling of beer,[8] but not the cleaning and bottling of milk for nothing is there done to turn an unfinished into a finished article or analogous thereto.[9] The possible fineness of the distinction is always apparent as in the case of a slaughter-house where mere killing is not adapting for sale but division into the various usable parts is.[10]

---

[1] But the mincing of meat by an electrical machine in the kitchen of a municipal hospital does not amount to the breaking up or demolition of any article: *Wood* v. *London County Council*, [1941] 2 K.B. 232; [1941] 2 All E.R. 230.

[2] *Grove (Dudley Revenue Officer)* v. *Lloyd's British Testing Co., Ltd.*, [1931] A.C. 450, *per* Viscount DUNEDIN, at p. 467. [3] *Ibid.*

[4] *Longhurst* v. *Guildford, Goldalming and District Water Board*, [1961] 3 All E.R. 545; [1961] 3 W.L.R. 915. Where a pump house is part of a works which is clearly a factory it will not be excluded under s. 175(6) on the grounds that it is used for some purpose other than that of the factory, merely on the strength of this decision. If the purpose of the pumping is incidental to the work of the factory the pump house will be part of the factory. *Newton* v. *John Stanning & Son, Ltd.*, [1962] 1 All E.R. 78; [1962] 1 W.L.R. 30.

[5] *Cardiff Revenue Officer* v. *Cardiff Assessment Committee and Western Mail, Ltd.*, [1931] 1 K.B. 47.

[6] *Weatherhead (Bradford Revenue Officer)* v. *Bradford Assessment Committee and Laycock, Son & Co., Ltd.*, [1931] 1 K.B. 386.

[7] *Henderson* v. *Glasgow Corporation* (1900), 2 F. (Ct. of Sess.) 1127.

[8] *Hoare* v. *Truman, Hanbury, Buxton & Co.* (1902), 71 L. J.K.B. 380; but *cf.* reservations of ALVERSTONE, L.C.J., in *Law* v. *Graham* [1901] 2 K.B. 327.

[9] *Wiltshire County Valuation Committee* v. *London Co-operative Society, Ltd.*, [1950] 1 All E.R. 937. This case, in so far as it relates to the cleaning of milk, is hard to reconcile with the dictum in *Longhurst's case* (see note 4, *supra*) that filtration of water is adapting for sale. Nor the opening of cases of foods and their identification and arrangement: see *Davis Cohen & Sons, Ltd.* v. *Hall*, [1952] 1 All E.R. 157.

[10] *Fatstock Marketing Corporation, Ltd.* v. *Morgan (Valuation Officer)*, [1958] 1 All E.R. 646; [1958] 1 W.L.R. 357.

Trade or Gain

To satisfy the statutory definition of a "factory" the manual labour must operate in the processes described "by way of trade or for the purpose of gain." But no distinction is to be drawn between direct and indirect gain and earlier cases must, to the extent that they rest on any such proposition be considered as over-ruled.[1] So *Nash* v. *Hollinshead*,[2] where it was held that a workman employed by a farmer to tend a movable steam engine which worked a mill to grind food for the farm stock did not work in a factory, is to be explained not because any gain was indirect, but because farm workers were not within the contemplation of the Factories Acts.[3] In *Stanger's* case it was held that a consulting engineer who, on premises in a residential area, conducted tests in the mixing of concrete, had converted those premises into a factory.[4] The barge yard of a lighterage company has been held to be worked for the purposes of gain[5] and it has been held that premises on which tramway tickets were printed[6] and those on which coffee was ground for sale in shops,[7] were factories. Finally, trade is not limited to the sale of goods, but extends also to the supplying of services for reward and will cover such activities by a transport company as a centre for the repair of vehicles.[8]

The words requiring that the work carried on be "by way of trade or for the purposes of gain" clearly impose a significant limitation in modern times when so much industrial activity is carried on in premises of which the state or a local authority is the occupier. It is, therefore, provided that premises in the occupation of the Crown or of any municipal or other public authority shall be deemed to be a factory, and building operations and works of engineering construction undertaken by or on behalf of the Crown or any such authority shall be brought within the operation of the Act though the work carried on is not carried on by way of trade or for purposes of gain.[9] Of this provision it has been said that its object is

> "to cover the numerous operations of the Crown and public authorities . . . which would fall within the general definition were

---

[1] *Stanger* v. *Hendon Borough Council*, [1948] 1 K.B. 571; [1948] 1 All E.R. 377.
[2] [1901] 1 K.B. 700.
[3] *Stanger* v. *Hendon Borough Council*, *supra*, *per* SOMERVELL, L.J., at p. 578.
[4] *Supra*.
[5] *Barton (Poplar Revenue Officer)* v. *Union Lighterage Co., Ltd.*, [1931] 1 K.B. 385, at p. 499.
[6] *Moon (Lambeth Revenue Officer)* v. *London County Council*, [1931] 1 K.B. 385, at p. 500.
[7] *Barton (Stepney Revenue Officer)* v. *R. Twining & Co., Ltd.*, [1931] 1 K.B. 385, at p. 500.
[8] *Bailey (Stoke-on-Trent Revenue Officer)* v. *Potteries Electric Traction Co., Ltd.*, [1931] 1 K.B. 385, *per* SCRUTTON, L.J., at p. 498; see also *Potteries Electric Traction Co., Ltd.* v. *Bailey (Stoke-on-Trent Revenue Officer)*, [1931] A.C. 151.
[9] Factories Act, 1961, s. 175 (9).

it not for the fact that they cannot properly be said to be carried on by way of trade or for the purposes of gain."[1]

Apart from bringing such operations within the scope of the Act, the section does not extend the definition of a factory. Thus, a technical institution conducted by a local authority is not a factory,[2] nor is the kitchen of a municipal hospital,[3] and there is no statutory duty to fence dangerous machines in such a place.

The workrooms of a prison are not within the scope of the Acts. No one with experience of the law is easily shocked by the enterprise of litigants. Nevertheless, *Pullen* v. *Prison Commissioners*[4] does represent something of a record. The plaintiff had been sentenced to a term of imprisonment during which he had worked on the making of coir mats. Dust was certainly given off as a result of the process, but an exhaust appliance was used. Some time after release from gaol Pullen was found to be suffering from tuberculosis and he brought an action for breach of statutory duty alleging that he had not been protected from dust and fumes as required by section 47 of the 1937 Act. The court had no difficulty in ruling that a prison workshop was not a factory.

> " If the definition of a factory is to apply there must exist (except in certain express cases, for instance apprentices, for there is a sub-section which deals with apprentices) the relationship of master and servant and employment for wages. There is no employment for wages in the case of prisoners."[5]

Special Instances

But the definition section of the Factories Act proceeds from the general to the particular and emphasises that certain premises, whether or not they are factories according to the foregoing definition, are to be accounted such for the purposes of the Act. So that yards and dry docks in which ships are constructed, repaired, finished or broken up, or premises in which articles are sorted incidentally to the purposes of a factory, or in which bottles or containers or packing articles are washed or filled, or in which yarn or cloth is hooked, plaited, lapped, made up or packed, are all within the scope of the Act. A laundry carried on as ancillary to another business or incidentally to the purposes of a public institution is a factory, as also are premises in which locomotives, vehicles and the like are constructed, reconstructed or repaired as ancillary to a transport undertaking.

Premises used for the purpose of housing locomotives or vehicles where only cleaning, washing, running repairs or minor adjustments

---

[1] *Weston* v. *London County Council*, [1941] 1 K.B. 608, *per* WROTTESLEY, J., at pp. 612, 3; [1941] 1 All E.R. 555.

[2] *Weston* v. *London County Council*, *supra*.

[3] *Wood* v. *London County Council*, [1941] 2 K.B. 232; [1941] 2 All E.R. 230.

[4] [1957] 3 All E.R. 470; [1957] 1 W.L.R. 1186.

[5] *Ibid.*, *per* Lord GODDARD, C.J., at pp. 471, 1190 respectively.

are carried out are not within the scope of the Act unless they are premises used for purposes of a railway undertaking where running repairs to locomotives are carried out and this is so notwithstanding the words

" any premises in which . . . persons are employed in any process for or incidental to any of the following purposes namely . . . the repairing . . . cleaning or washing of any article."[1]

Premises in which printing or bookbinding is carried on constitute a factory if the work is carried on for the purposes of gain or incidentally to any other business so carried on. The premises in which the dresses, scenery or properties incidental to the production or presentation by way of trade or for the purposes of gain of cinematograph films or theatrical performances are made, adapted or repaired, are factories, but if such operations take place on the stage or in the dressing-room of a theatre in which only occasional adaptations or repairs are made they do not make the stage or dressing-room a factory.[2]

The case of *Curtis* v. *Shinner*[3] had ruled that a chamber used by a fisherman for the repair of his nets was not a factory, but the Act now expressly brings such a room within its scope and a place in which mechanical power is used in connection with the making or repair of articles of metal or wood incidentally to a business carried on by way of trade or for purposes of gain must also be conducted according to the terms of the Act.[4] Moreover the decision in *Curtis* v. *Shinner*, in so far as it rested upon the basis that the repairing of the nets was not by way of trade and for purposes of gain, must now be considered as overruled.[5] Nevertheless

" one must always go back to the words ' work is carried on by way of trade or for the purposes of gain ' and although the explanation formerly accepted, that it must be directly for the purposes of gain, is now rejected . . . I think that . . . it may be that there has been by statutory authority, reversion to some extent to what I may describe as the older view."[6]

Premises in which cinematograph films are commercially produced are factory premises, but persons employed in them who are theatrical performers within the meaning of the Theatrical Employers Registration Act, 1925, are not deemed to be employed in a factory. Thus the Factories Act will not cover actors, singers, dancers, acrobats or performers of any kind. Finally, the term factory will include premises in which articles are made or prepared incidentally to the

---

[1] *Jones* v. *Crosville Motor Services Ltd.*, [1956] 3 All E.R. 417; Factories Act, 1961, s. 175(10).
[2] Factories Act, 1961, s. 175 (2)(*h*).
[3] (1906), 95 L.T. 31.
[4] Factories Act, 1961, s. 175 (2)(*k*).
[5] *Per* SOMERVELL, L.J., *Stanger* v. *Hendon Borough Council*, [1948] 1 K.B. 571, at p. 578; [1948] 1 All E.R. 377 at p. 379.
[6] *Jones* v. *Crosville Motor Services Ltd.*, [1956] 3 All E.R. 417 at p. 420.

carrying on of building operations or works of engineering construction and premises used for the storage of gas in a gas-holder having a storage capacity of not less than 5,000 cubic feet.[1]

Lines or sidings, used for the purposes of a factory, which are not part of a railway or tramway are deemed to be part of the factory and if they are used in connection with more than one factory belonging to different occupiers the line or siding will be considered to be a separate factory.[2]   A place in which, with the permission of the owner or occupier, two or more persons carry on work which would constitute the workplace a factory if the persons who work therein were in the employment of the owner or occupier, will also be deemed to be a factory and if such a workplace is not a tenement factory or part of a tenement factory the Act will apply as if the owner or occupier were the occupier of the factory and the persons working therein were employed in the factory.[3]

Premises may be a factory though they are in the open air; and where, within the close or curtilage of a factory, a place is used solely for some purpose other than the processes carried on in the factory, that place shall not be deemed to form part of the factory for the purposes of the Act but, if otherwise it would be a factory, it shall be deemed to be a separate factory.[4]

The last provision was considered in *Thurogood* v. *Van den Berghs and Jurgens, Ltd.*[5] where the defendants occupied a separate building within the curtilage of their factory which they used for maintenance work on plant and equipment used in the factory. The plaintiff was injured whilst testing in this maintenance shop an electrical fan brought from the factory for the purpose.   It was argued that the maintenance shop was a separate factory and that the fan was consequently a piece of equipment brought in for repairs and was not a piece of machinery requiring to be fenced.   It was held that even assuming that the maintenance shop was a "place" within the curtilage of the factory, it could only be deemed not to be part of the factory itself by showing that it was used for purposes other than processes carried on in the factory and this the defendants had failed to do.   But, in *Street* v. *British Electricity Authority*[6] a workman was employed by the second defendants to install boilers in a power station owned by the first defendants.   He worked on the second floor which was divided into bays in some of which boilers had been installed and were generating electricity

---

[1] Factories Act, 1961, s. 175 (2)(*n*).
[2] *Ibid.*, s. 175 (3).
[3] *Ibid.*, s. 175 (5).
[4] *Ibid.*, s. 175 (6), (7).
[5] [1951] 2 K.B. 537; [1951] 1 All E.R. 682.   Followed, in the case of an administrative block, where designing, drawing and technical development took place—*Powley* v. *Bristol Siddeley Engines, Ltd.*, [1965] 3 All E.R. 612; [1966] 1 W.L.R. 729.
[6] [1952] 2 Q.B. 399; [1952] 1 All E.R. 679.

whilst there were others into which boilers were to be put. In one
of these latter was an open space through which the plaintiff fell.
It was held that the place concerned was not a factory, though
those bays in which electricity was being generated might well be.
The other bays constituted a place within a factory and were
indeed, part of the factory building, but at the time they were used
for purposes other than those carried on in the factory.

These decisions followed the careful consideration given to the
section in question by the Court of Appeal in *Cox* v. *Cutler & Sons,
Ltd. and Hampton Court Gas Co.*[1] The case arose as an appeal
against both defendants for injuries suffered by the plaintiff when,
as Cutler's servant he had been injured while engaged on the repair
of a gas holder owned by the second defendants. The holder had
suffered damage from enemy action, was separated from the gas
works by a public road and was connected only by pipes which had
been sealed off when the holder was damaged. Any liability attaching to the gas company could only arise out of their infringement of
duties under the Factories Act. The Court of Appeal held that
these duties did not touch them in respect of the holder, firstly,
because they were no longer occupiers within the meaning of the
Act, secondly because even supposing that they were, a gas holder
in that condition could not store gas within the meaning of section
151 (1) (xiii) of the 1937 Act, and thirdly, because of the words under
discussion, namely that a place used for some purpose other than
the processes carried on in the factory should not be deemed to form
part of the factory. A recent clear example of the operation of these
words is to be found in *Walsh* v. *Allweather Mechanical Grouting
Co., Ltd.*,[2] where the injured workman was relaying the concrete apron
adjoining a hangar on an airfield. Although the apron was held to
be part of the factory, relaying of concrete was a purpose other
than the processes of assembling and testing aeroplanes carried on
in the factory and the Factories Act did not, therefore, apply.

Another aspect of the use of a place within a factory solely for
purposes other than the processes of the factory was considered in
Thomas v. *British Thomson-Houston Co., Ltd.*[3] Within the curtilage
of a factory was a restaurant consisting of certain dining rooms and
store rooms and a room for the use of the manageress of the restaurant as an office, a games room and a flat which was occupied by
a caretaker. Workpeople were not permitted to use the restaurant,
for a canteen was provided for them elsewhere in the factory. One
of the factory employees was injured whilst cleaning one of the
windows of the restaurant and he alleged that there was a breach of
the duty to provide a safe means of access to and a safe place at

---

[1] [1948] 2 All E.R. 665.
[2] [1959] 2 Q.B. 300.
[3] [1953] 1 All E.R. 29; but see also *Luttman* v. *Imperial Chemical Industries,
Ltd.*, [1955] 3 All E.R. 481.

which to work under the terms of section 26 of the 1937 Act. HAVERS, J., held that, as the restaurant was within the curtilage of the factory, it was thus *prima facie* within the definition of a factory within the Act. The real problem was to decide whether it was solely used for, or incidental to the purposes of the factory. He thought not, for he could not find " that it was essential for the welfare of the industrial workers." Thus he ruled that the place was not a factory. It is in accordance with these rules that office buildings in a factory are excluded from the operation of the Factories Acts. Individual offices, particularly those on the shop floor, may of course be part of the factory: it is a question of applying the tests to the individual circumstances.

Part VII of the Act contains provisions for certain special applications and extensions of the scope of the Act. Thus, specified provisions of the Act will apply to tenement factories with the significant alteration that the owner of such factory, whether or not he is one of the occupiers, shall be responsible for any contraventions of those provisions.[1] The expression "tenement factory" means any premises where mechanical power from any prime mover within the close or curtilage of the premises is distributed for use in manufacturing processes to different parts of the same premises occupied by different persons, in such manner that those parts constitute, in law, separate factories.[2] The Act details those of its provisions which apply to such factories,[3] and for the purpose of such provisions the whole of a tenement factory or, as the case may be, the whole of such factory except rooms occupied by not more than one tenant shall be deemed to be one factory. The owner may escape liability where he shows that any contravention of the Act arises from the use of any fencing appliances, machinery or plant if the use thereof is outside his control. In such a case the occupier will be liable.[4] Moreover where a part of a building which is not a tenement factory is let off as a separate factory, the occupier of that part of the building must comply in all respects with the Act. But it is clear that, in such a case, the provisions as to health and safety might be rendered completely valueless if the other parts of the building, just because they were not technically a factory, were exempt from all legal obligation. The Act, therefore, lays down that the provisions relating to cleanliness and lighting; to prime movers, transmission machinery, hoists and lifts, steam boilers, the construction and maintenance of floors, passages and stairs; to lifting machines and lifting tackles, steam receivers and steam containers and the provisions relating to the power of courts of summary jurisdiction to make Orders in cases of danger or of unsatisfactory

---

[1] Factories Act, 1961, s. 121 (1).
[2] *Ibid.*, s. 176 (1).
[3] *Ibid.*, s. 121 (1).
[4] *Ibid.*, s. 121 (2).

premises shall apply to any part of the building used for the purpose of the factory though not comprised therein. Moreover, for the purpose of these provisions, lifting machines attached to the outside of the building, and chains, ropes and lifting tackle used in connection therewith, are to be treated as though they were in the building; but a lifting machine not used for the purpose of the factory, and any tackle used for that machine shall be disregarded, so as not to fall within the provisions of the Act.

It is obvious that where part of a building which is not a tenement factory is used as a separate factory problems of liability arise. To meet these, the owner and not the occupier is held to be liable for any contravention of the relevant provisions and for any contravention of the provisions relating to sanitary conveniences, but only where they are used in common by several tenants. The owner is also liable for contravention of the law concerning hoists and lifts, means of escape in case of fire in so far as the provisions relate to matters within his control. So far as the provisions governing the use of lifting machines and tackle, steam receivers, steam containers and air receivers are concerned, the occupier will be liable where the contravention arises in respect of machinery or plant belonging to or supplied by him; in other cases liability will fasten upon the owner provided the contravention does not arise in relation to matters outside his control.[1]

The Act also applies to premises in which persons are regularly employed in or in connection with electrical stations, and in the case of premises of a like character large enough to admit the entrance of a person after the machinery or plant is in position certain detailed provisions of the Act will apply.[2]

In the case of premises attached to an institution (whether of a charitable or reformatory character) the Act will apply wherever manual labour is exercised in or incidental to the making, altering, repairing, ornamenting, finishing, washing, cleaning or adapting for sale of articles not intended for the use of the institution. If it can be shown that the persons engaged in such processes are inmates of and supported by the institution or persons engaged in the supervision of the work or the management of machinery and that such work is carried on in good faith for the support, training, or reformation of the persons engaged in it, the Secretary of State may direct that the Act shall apply as modified.[3]

Docks, wharves, quays (including warehouses belonging to owners of such docks, wharves and quays, and lines or sidings used in connection therewith and not forming part of a railway or tramway) and every warehouse (not forming part of a factory) are also within

---

[1] Factories Act, 1961, s. 122.
[2] *Ibid.*, s. 123; *Paine* v. *Colne Valley Electricity Supply Co., Ltd. and British Insulated Cables, Ltd.*, [1938] 4 All E.R. 803.
[3] Factories Act, 1961, s. 124.

the scope of the Act, provided mechanical power is used.[1] The processes of loading, unloading or coaling a ship in a dock, harbour, or canal are similarly covered and the machinery used must satisfy a large part of the provisions of the Act unless it is on board the ship and is the property of the ship owner.[2] In *Kenny* v. *Harrison*[3] an accident occurred on a piece of land separated by a space of about forty yards from the water side of a quay and in the ambit of certain docks.   At the time in question timber was stored on it, but it was possible to use it as a wharf, and it was held to be such.   The case is to be distinguished from *Haddock* v. *Humphrey*,[4] where a place one hundred and fifty yards from the water's edge and separated from the quay was held not to be a dock, wharf or quay. A floating contrivance containing cranes and grabs moored in midstream and not connected with the river banks, and used for unloading coal from ships into barges was held, in *Ellis* v. *Cory & Son, Ltd.*, to be a wharf.[5]   The process of loading or unloading a ship is not complete until the hatching is secured.[6]

Work carried out in a harbour or wet dock in constructing or reconstructing, repairing, refitting, painting, finishing, or breaking up a ship, or in scaling, scurfing, or cleaning boilers, combustion chambers and smoke boxes in a ship or in cleaning oil-fuel tanks including tanks last used for oil carried as part of the cargo, and tanks or holds last used for any substance so carried and specified in regulations as being of a dangerous or offensive nature, or to the cleaning of bilges in a ship, will be covered by the Act subject to certain indicated limitations[7] but the Act will not apply to any work of this character performed by the master or crew of the vessel or done on board a ship during a trial run.

Building Operations

Building operations and works of engineering construction are subject to the limited applications of the Act where they are undertaken by way of trade or for business or for the purpose of any industrial or commercial undertaking.   Any line or siding in connection with any such building operations or works of engineering construction is also within the Act, provided it is not part of a railway or tramway.   The requirements of the Act as to registers and the posting of notices will be complied with in the case of those engaged in building operations if the general register is kept at an office and the notices and regulations are kept posted up in a position where they can easily be read, at each office, yard, or shop at which persons employed on the operations attend.

---

[1] For a consideration of " warehouse " see *Fisher* v. *Port of London Authority*, [1962] 1 All E.R. 458; [1962] 1 W.L.R. 234.

[2] Factories Act, 1961, s. 125.   [3] [1902] 2 K.B. 168.

[4] [1900] 1 Q.B. 609.   [5] [1902] 1 K.B. 38.

[6] *Stuart* v. *Nixon and Bruce*, [1901] A.C. 79; *Manchester Ship Canal Co.* v. *Director of Public Prosecutions*, [1930] 1 K.B. 547.

[7] Factories Act, 1961, s. 126.

A person undertaking building operations and works of engineering construction to which the Act applies must inform the inspector, in writing, of the place and nature of the operations, whether mechanical power is to be used and, if so, its nature, together with such other particulars as may be prescribed. But the provision as to notices does not apply where the person undertaking the building operations has reasonable grounds for believing that they will be completed within six weeks, nor where the building operations are undertaken in a place on which similar operations in respect of which notice has been given are already in progress.[1]

Building operations more often than not take place outside a factory. The statute is regulating a dangerous operation. It is obvious that in such circumstances the duties have to be differently laid. Thus section 127(4) provides that the provisions of the Act, in their application to building operations, have effect as if the place where they are carried on were a factory and as if the person undertaking the operations were the occupier. It follows that in the often complicated relationships between various trades engaged in a building operation, it is the person responsible for the actual section of the operation who is under the statutory duty.[2]

Engineering construction is defined as construction, structural alteration or repair (including re-pointing and repainting) or the demolition of any dock, harbour, inland navigation, tunnel, bridge, viaduct, waterworks, reservoir, pipeline, aqueduct, sewer, sewage works, or gas holder except where carried on upon a railway or tramway.[3] This statutory definition was extended by the Engineering Construction (Extension of Definition) Regulations, 1960.[4]

These provisions have given rise to an interesting problem— namely the precise obligations attached to building operations as defined by section 176 of the Act when those operations are conducted in a building which is itself a factory, within the meaning of the Act. In *Whitby* v. *Burt, Boulton and Hayward, Ltd.*,[5] sub-contractors were at work on building operations in a factory. The plaintiff was employed by these sub-contractors to work in an attic the base of which was comprised of iron sheeting nailed to wooden supports; which sheeting the plaintiff was to remove. When he had almost completely done so, the wooden supports, which were clearly inadequate to support the weight of one man, collapsed so that the plaintiff fell and was injured. It was held that his employers, the sub-contractors, were liable at Common Law, because they had failed to lay out the work with due care, and that the occupiers of the factory were liable in that, under section 26 of the 1937 Act (now s.

---

[1] Factories Act, 1961, s. 127.
[2] *Fisher* v. *C.H.T., Ltd.*, (*No. 2*), [1966] 2 Q.B. 475; [1966] 1 All E.R. 88.
[3] *Ibid.*, s. 176.
[4] Applied *British Transport Docks Board* v. *Williams*, [1970] 1 All E.R. 1135; [1970] 1 W.L.R. 659.
[5] [1947] K.B. 918; [1947] 2 All E.R. 324. As to the duty under what is now s. 29 of the 1961 Act, see later.

29), they were under a duty to maintain a safe means of access to where the plaintiff had to work, namely to the place where he actually had to withdraw the nails.   Though the decision was academic in the sense that it was held that the occupiers were entitled to a contribution from the sub-contractors amounting to a complete indemnity.   DENNING, J.'s view was that section 107 of the 1937 Act (now s. 127) dealt only with building operations not conducted in a factory and as a matter of construction held that where building operations were conducted in a factory the whole of the obligations of the 1937 Act would apply.[1]

In *Lavender* v. *Diamints, Ltd.*[2] the Court of Appeal discussed much the same position. A window cleaner, who was under contract to clean the windows of a factory, was moving along a roof made of asbestos sheeting which was the only way to get to his place of work, when he slipped and fell, and suffered injuries.   He claimed under section 26 of the 1937 Act (now s. 29) that the owners of the factory were liable on their failure to provide a safe means of access.   It was held that under this section the plaintiff might recover, but TUCKER, L. J., was of the opinion that window cleaning did not fall within the definition of a building operation, though he specifically reserved the point whether or not section 26 applied to building operations carried on within a factory.

This then was the situation until the coming into operation of the Factories Act, 1948.   By section 2 of that Act, section 107 of the 1937 Act was to include references to sections 99, 126 and 127 of the Act, and section 14(4) of the 1948 Act specifically provided that the application of the 1937 Act to any building operation was not to be excluded by reason of the fact that it was undertaken on premises which were, apart from such works, a factory.

The combined effect of the two Acts was considered in *Whincup* v. *Joseph Woodhead & Sons (Engineers), Ltd. and Another.*[3] The plaintiff was employed by the first defendants to repair glass in the roof of a factory occupied by the second defendants. He fell through the roof and was injured. The judgement confirmed that section 107 applied only to building operations conducted outside a factory and did not relieve an occupier from duties imposed by the Act as a whole, and that this position was not altered by section 14(4) of the Act of 1948, which was a declaration of the law laid down by DENNING, J., in *Whitby's* case.[4]   The 1961 Act has merely combined these provisions in s. 127.

The provisions relating to the employment of women and young persons in certain processes connected with lead manufacture and the use of lead compounds, the provisions requiring notification of

---

[1] *Ibid.*, at pp. 928 and 325 respectively.
[2] [1949] 1 K.B. 585; [1949] 1 All E.R. 532.
[3] [1951] 1 All E.R. 387.
[4] [1947] K.B. 918; [1947] 2 All E.R. 324.

lead poisoning and the provisions relating to the powers and duties of inspectors, and to offences, penalties and legal proceedings apply to employment in any such processes whether in a factory or in a place other than a factory and apply as if the references to young persons included references to all persons who had not attained the age of eighteen.[1]

Throughout the Act there are provisions which further extend its scope, notably, for example, to workpeople who work on material supplied by manufacturers to be worked upon at home.   Such out-workers are dealt with in Part Eight of the Act and the additional duties which are laid upon their employers are evidence of the legislature's concern that the more unscrupulous type of employer should not, by the device of employing outworkers, injure employers to whom the provisions of the Act apply.[2]

Finally the Act applies to factories owned by or in the occupation of the Crown and to building operations and works of engineering construction undertaken by the Crown.   But the Secretary of State is given power by Order, in emergencies, to exempt to the extent and during the period named in the Order, any factory belonging to the Crown or building operations or works of engineering construction undertaken by or on behalf of the Crown.   Where works of this character are concerned the powers which the Act confers on a district council or other local authority are exercisable by an inspector and notices requiring to be served will be served on the inspector and not on the local authority.[3]

(2) The Administration and Enforcement of the Act.—The duty of administering the Act falls chiefly on four authorities.   The ultimate authority, as always, is the Government, but the actual administration of the Act is the responsibility of the Secretary of State for Employment, referred to throughout the Acts as the Secretary of State, the factory inspectors, the appointed factory doctors and the local authorities.   The overall responsibility of the Secretary of State was underlined by the 1959 Act which provided that the Secretary of State should promote health, safety and welfare in factories by collecting and disseminating information and by investigation of problems, for which purposes he may provide and maintain laboratories and other services.[4]   The chief duties of compliance with the terms of the Act lie upon the occupier of the factory, but one strikingly novel and important qualification is introduced.   For it is enacted that employed persons shall not interfere with or misuse things provided for their health and safety, and that where a means or appliance for securing health or safety is provided for the use of any such person he shall use that means

---

[1] Factories Act, 1961, s. 128.
[2] *Ibid.*, ss. 133-134.
[3] Factories Act, 1961, s. 173.
[4] S. 26, now Factories Act, 1961, s. 177.

or appliance.[1] The provision is not a strong one; it is difficult
to see how it could be satisfactorily enforced, particularly if the use of
a safety appliance in any way reduced a man's production and influenced his earning power.   Nonetheless, the refusal to use a safety
appliance now constitutes an offence for which the workman is liable
to be punished.   In addition a general duty is laid on every employed
person to refrain from doing anything wilfully and without reasonable
cause which is likely to endanger himself or others.   The courts considered these questions in *Wraith* v. *Flexile Metal Co., Ltd.*[2] A girl
employee, in an effort to recover a tube, crept under a drying oven
and, as a result, was injured.   There were the clearest instructions
that employees were not to go under the machinery but were to use
a broom to retrieve fallen articles.   In answer to the claim of the girl
for compensation the employers pleaded that the girl herself was in
breach of the statutory duty not wilfully to do anything likely to
endanger herself.   She had failed, the employers urged, to use the
appliances provided; and this failure and not the absence of fencing,
was the cause of the accident.   With this the court did not agree.
It was found that the accident arose from the failure securely to
fence the machinery.

> ". . . it is plain beyond argument that the employee suffered the
> bodily injury which she did in consequence of that failure. It is
> impossible to guarantee that workers will not be both foolish and
> reckless and the object of the Factories Act, 1937, is to protect them
> against their own folly and carelessness."[3]

Thus the precise scope of the employee's obligation under the Factories Act still awaits interpretation by the courts but it is already
clear that an employer who is himself in breach of the statute may
not excuse himself by pleading the employee's breach unless that
breach is so fundamental as to be the sole cause;[4] certainly not
where the employer's breach is the substantial cause of the accident.
Clearly the employer may not excuse the absence of a superior safety
device by proving that he has provided a device which is of a merely
auxiliary character.

The employee's duty regarding the use of safety devices was
considered by the Court of Appeal in *Norris* v. *Syndic Manufacturing
Co., Ltd.*[5] Norris was a tool setter employed by the defendants who,
whilst making adjustments removed from a power press the guard
which had been fitted by the defendants, and failed to replace it
whilst testing the press in motion. It has been suggested that an
order by the defendants to use a safety device was a condition

---

[1] Factories Act, 1961, s. 143 (1).
[2] [1943] K.B. 24; [1942] 2 All E R. 549.
[3] [1943] K.B. 24, *per* Viscount CALDECOTE, C.J., at p. 27.
[4] *Nolan* v. *Dental Manufacturing Co. Ltd.*, [1958] 2 All E.R. 449; [1958] 1
W.L.R. 936.
[5] [1952] 2 Q.B. 135;[1952] 1 All E.R. 935. For the position at common law,
see the discussion of *Haynes* v. *Qualcast (Wolverhampton) Ltd.* [1958] 1 All E.R.
441; [1958] 1 W.L.R. 225, *supra* at p. 221.

precedent to liability, but the argument was rejected and it was held that section 119 of the 1937 Act imposed an absolute duty on the workman once the device was available.[1] Again it was said that:

"the true interpretation of the second part of section 119 is . . . this: The occupier must provide the means or appliance required by the Act. Once he has provided a proper means or appliance in good condition and ready to hand in a proper place, then the workman comes under a duty to use it. This duty on the workman is imposed by the Act not by the employer. The important thing is the intention of the Act, not the intention of the employer. If the Act intends the man to use it, then use it he must, no matter what the employer thinks about it, nor even what he says or does, so long as he does not actually forbid the man to use it. Acquiescence by an employer may mitigate the man's offence, but cannot absolve him of his duty."[2]

It is probable that the courts will take the view that a safety device has not been "provided for the use of any person" within the meaning of the statute, unless it is available where it is needed. The mere fact, for example, that an appliance is available in a storeroom to which the workman has access, may or may not, in itself, absolve the occupier from liability. It is largely a question of common sense to be applied to the particular facts of the case.[3] For example, in *Ginty* v. *Belmont Building Supplies, Ltd.*,[4] equipment to be used when workmen went on roofs was kept in a store yard a few feet away from the place of work. The workmen knew the equipment was there and the court held that it had been provided because it was nearby and available for use.

Inspectorate

The Secretary of State has power, with the approval of the Treasury as to numbers and salaries, to appoint such inspectors, clerks and servants as he deems necessary for the execution of the Act.[5] Notice of appointment must be published in the London Gazette and, once appointed, an inspector is invested with considerable powers. He has a right of entry to a factory at any reasonable time, day or night, whenever he has reasonable cause to believe that any person is employed therein. He may, similarly, enter, by day, any place which he has reasonable cause to believe to be a factory, and any part of any building of which a factory forms a part and in which he has reasonable cause to believe that explosive or highly inflammable materials are stored or used. Where he reasonably apprehends

---

[1] *Ibid.*, *per* SOMERVELL, L.J., at pp. 140 and 938 respectively.
[2] *Ibid.*, *per* DENNING, L.J., at pp. 142-3 and 939 respectively.
[3] *Clifford* v. *Charles H. Challen & Son, Ltd.*, [1951] 1 K.B. 495; [1951] 1 All E.R. 72.
[4] [1959] 1 All E.R. 414.
[5] Factories Act, 1961, s. 145. S.R. & O. 1946, No. 376 transfers the functions of the Secretary of State under various Acts (including the Factories Act, 1937 and any other Act which is to be construed therewith) to the Minister of Labour and National Service, now the Secretary of State for Employment.

serious obstruction he may take with him a constable.[1]   He may also, in appropriate circumstances, take with him into the factory a medical officer of health, sanitary inspector or other officer of the district council.[2]   He may require the production of the registers and all similar documents kept in pursuance of the Act and may inspect, examine and copy them.   He may require any person whom he finds in a factory to give such information as it is in that person's power to give as to who is the occupier, and to examine either alone or in the presence of any other person, anyone whom he not only finds in a factory but whom he has reasonable cause to believe to be or to have been employed within a factory within the preceding two months.   He may require persons so examined to sign a declaration of the truth of the matters as to which they have been examined. But, of course, no person may be required to give an answer or evidence tending to criminate himself.   Wilfully to delay an inspector in the exercise of his powers, failure to comply with an inspector's requisition, failure to produce documents, wilfully to withhold information as to who is the occupier of a factory, or wilfully to conceal or prevent persons from appearing before or being examined by an inspector is an offence under the Act.[3]   An inspector may, if authorised in writing by the Secretary of State, prosecute, conduct or defend causes arising under the Act, although he is not of counsel or a solicitor.[4]   An occupier or manager of a factory may require an inspector to produce his certificate of employment.[5]

In 1948, the power of an Inspector of Factories was considerably increased, in that he was authorised to enter, inspect and examine at all reasonable times by day or night any warehouse or part thereof where or in connection wherewith he reasonably believes young persons are employed, and by day only when he has reasonable cause to believe that any young person has within the preceding two months been, but is not so employed at the time of entry.[6]

The Employment Medical Advisory Service Act, 1972 has replaced the old appointed factory doctor system.[7]   Instead the Secretary of State is given power to establish a medical advisory service.[8]   This will be based upon the existing medical inspectorate.   It will be staffed by fully registered medical practitioners.   The advisers will have the powers of a factory inspector.   Such powers, such as the right of entry, are given in Schedule 1 of the Act which also lists the places and processes that are deemed to be factories under the 1961 Act.   A close link is established with the School Health Service which has a duty to send information to the advisory service so that they have a complete medical history of school leavers.   Routine medical examinations are abolished.   The occupier must give notice

---

[1] Factories Act, 1961, s. 146 (1) (b).
[2] *Ibid.*, s. 9 (2).
[3] Factories Act, 1961, s. 146.
[4] *Ibid.*, s. 149.
[5] *Ibid.*, s. 150.
[6] Now, Factories Act, 1961, s. 147.
[7] *Ibid.*, s. 2.
[8] *Ibid.*, s. 1.

that he is employing a young person to the Youth Employment Service.[1]

The new medical advisers take over the duties of the appointed factory doctor. For example, the notification of industrial diseases under s. 82 (3) is now to the medical adviser. The medical adviser has power under s. 119 to require cesser of the employment of a young person. A medical adviser has power to serve a notice upon an occupier requiring permission to carry out a medical examination of any of his employees.[2]

The medical officer of health for every district council must, in his annual report to the council, report specifically on the administration of, and furnish the prescribed particulars with respect to matters in the Act administered by the district council[3] and must send a copy of the report or such parts of it as deal with these matters to the Secretary of State.[4] He shares the duty, as does any other officer of a district council who is concerned with the inspection of factories, of informing the inspector for the district of any factory in which an abstract of the Act is not affixed. The officers of a county council or district council have all the powers that an inspector has of entry, inspection, and taking legal proceedings, but any such officer must exercise his powers only on the written authority of the council, which authority an occupier or manager may demand to see. Any person exercising powers of inspection under the Act must exercise them in good faith, and it is an offence, punishable by fine or imprisonment, for an inspector or other officer to disclose information as to manufacturing processes or trade secrets, where the disclosure is not made in the performance of his duty.[5]

Ministerial Regulation

Throughout the Act, as we shall see, a power is given to the Secretary of State to make regulations and orders. These regulations form a substantial part of the corpus of industrial legislation and by them the general provisions of the Act are given a specialised application to various industries. The first step of every student of industrial law engaged in industry, after studying the Act, is to study those regulations, if any, which have reference to the particular industry in which he is concerned. A detailed discussion of such orders and regulations is outside the scope of this book. What must be noted are the conditions under which the Secretary of State may make regulations under the Factories Act. The regulations are made by statutory instruments which have the force of law from the date which they themselves define, but they may be annulled by a resolution of either House of Parliament[6] within forty days. But anything done between the date of the promulgation of the order and

---

[1] Factories Act, 1961, s. 5.　　　　　　[2] *Ibid.*, s. 3.
[3] See *ibid.*, particularly ss. 1 to 8, and ss. 133 and 134.　　[4] *Ibid.*, s. 153.
[5] Factories Act, 1961, s. 154.　　　　[6] *Ibid.*, s. 180.

the resolution of annulment is not made invalid by that resolution and the power of the Secretary of State to make new regulations is not, in any way, affected.

Where the Secretary of State is empowered by the Act to make special regulations he must comply with certain additional requirements set out in the Second Schedule of the Act.   In such cases he must publish notice of his proposal to make regulations, give particulars of the place where copies of the draft regulations may be obtained and of the time (which must not be less than twenty-one days) during which the objections of the persons affected may be sent to the Secretary of State.[1]   The objections must be written and must state not only the specific grounds of objection but also the omissions, additions or modifications asked for.[2]   These objections the Secretary of State must consider and, if he thinks fit, he will amend the draft regulations after which, unless an enquiry has been held, he must deal with the amended regulations in the same manner as the original draft.[3]

The procedure is varied where a general objection is made against draft regulations.   A general objection is one made by or on behalf of the majority of the occupiers of the factories affected by the regulations or employing a majority of the persons employed in those factories or by any person who satisfies the Secretary of State that he or an association on behalf of which he acts represents a majority of the persons employed in those factories.   Similarly, an objection is regarded as general where it is made by or on behalf of the majority of the occupiers of any class or description of factories affected respecting which it appears that any of the requirements of the draft regulations may be unnecessary or inappropriate in the case of that class or description, or by or on behalf of the occupier or occupiers employing a majority of the persons employed or by any person who satisfies the Secretary of State that he or an association on behalf of which he acts represents a majority of the persons employed in any such class or description of factories.[4]

Where any such general objection is made within the required time and is not withdrawn, an enquiry must be held; as it may be where the Secretary of State thinks fit though no general objection is lodged.   There is, of course, no obligation to direct that an enquiry shall be held where the Secretary of State withdraws the draft regulations or where a previous enquiry under the Fourth Schedule has been held respecting the draft or some previous draft of the regulations.[5]   The enquiry must be held in public and the Secretary of State must appoint a competent person or persons to conduct it.

---

[1] *Ibid.*, s. 180 (10) and Sched. 4, para. 1.
[2] *Ibid.*, para. 2.
[3] *Ibid.*, para. 3.
[4] Factories Act, 1961, Sched. 4, para. 6.
[5] *Ibid.*, para. 4.

The chief inspector, any objector and any other person who proves to the satisfaction of the tribunal that he is affected may appear at the enquiry, either in person or by representation. Witnesses may be examined on oath,[1] but subject to these principles the enquiry must be conducted in accordance with rules made by the Secretary of State.[2]

Assuming, however, that no general objection is made to an order and that the requisite forty days have elapsed after the order has been laid before Parliament and no resolution of annulment has been passed the order will have the effect of a statute from the date it is made or on such later date as the order itself provides. Thereafter its legal validity may be contested only on two grounds. For it may still be proved to the satisfaction of the court that the order is *ultra vires*, that is to say, completely beyond the power bestowed by Parliament on the Secretary of State or that the order is in conflict with the statute. Parliamentary authority remains supreme and power delegated to the Secretary of State must be used in strict accordance with the terms of the delegation.[3]

Although in theory the use of regulations should be a speedy, flexible way of keeping the law up to date, the practical results do not bear this out. An extreme example of delay is shown by the Abrasive Wheels Regulations. The leading case of *John Summers and Sons, Ltd.* v. *Frost*[4] indicated that the duty laid down by the fencing sections of the Factories Act was absolute and, as applied to abrasive wheels, meant that they could only be fenced to fulfil the duty if made unusable. Proposals for regulations were published promptly in 1956. These met with strong trade union opposition and a fresh set of proposals was published in 1963. Further opposition was encountered and fresh proposals were issued in 1967. An inquiry was instituted in 1968 and the report published in 1970.

Offences and Penalties

A contravention of the Act or of any regulation or order made under its provisions constitutes an offence for which the occupier or the owner (where he is responsible under the Act) is liable.[5] Apparently the occupier of a factory under the Act is not necessarily the same person as the occupier of the same factory according to a regulation made under the Act. In *Rippon* v. *Port of London Authority*

---

[1] *Ibid.*, Sched. 4, para. 5. This procedure may also be used for enquiries into the hours of labour of young persons (see s. 87) and into the overtime employment of women and young persons (see s. 89). See S.R. & O. 1938 No. 585.

[2] The Factories Act (Conduct of Enquiries) Rules, 1938 (S.R. & O. 1938 No. 586).

[3] *Patent Agents Institute* v. *Lockwood*, [1894] A.C. 347. *Mackey* v. *James Henry Monks (Preston), Ltd.*, [1918] A.C. 59. *Minister of Health* v. *R., Ex parte Yaffe*, [1931] A.C. 494.

[4] [1955] A.C. 740; [1955] 1 All E.R. 870.

[5] Factories Act, 1961, s. 155.

and Russell & Co.[1] the Authority owned a public dry-dock in which a firm of ship repairers (Russell & Co.) were repairing a vessel.   An employee of the latter firm was injured whilst walking down certain steps in the dock due to the failure to provide a safe means of access. This amounted, so it was held, to a breach of sections 25 (1) and 26 (1) of the 1937 Act (now s. 28 (1) and s. 29), and of the Shipbuilding Regulations, 1931.[2]   The point at issue was whether the Port Authority or Russell & Co. were liable as occupiers of the dock.   The court found that the Port Authority had remained the occupiers throughout and were liable under the Act.   Such a finding, the court held, was not inconsistent with a notional occupation for a limited purpose and, under the Shipbuilding Regulations, Russell & Co. must be deemed to be in occupation to the extent that, if a safe means of access were not already provided it would be their duty to provide one.   It thus only remained for the court to fix the basis of contribution as between the two defendants.

The guilt of an occupier or owner in respect of the provisions of the Act does not necessarily exhaust the liability for the offence, and where the act or default for which they are liable is in fact the act or default of some other person, that other person will be guilty and liable to the same fine as if he were the owner or the occupier.[3] This liability may be additional to the liability of the occupier or owner or may be in substitution for that liability.   For where the occupier or owner is charged under the Act he will be entitled, on giving not less than three days' written notice of his intention to the prosecution, to have any other person whom he charges as the actual offender brought before the court, and if, after the commission of the offence has been proved, the occupier or owner proves that he has used due diligence to enforce the Act and that the other person had committed the offence without his consent, connivance or wilful default, then that other person shall be liable and the occupier or owner shall not; moreover proceedings may be instituted against the actual offender without action being taken against the occupier or owner where the inspector is satisfied that the latter has used due diligence and the offence has been committed without his consent, connivance or wilful default.[4]

The Act also deals with the situation where, in a factory, the owner or hirer of a machine or implement moved by mechanical power is some person other than the occupier of the factory.   In such circumstances the owner or hirer shall be deemed to be the occupier of the factory in respect of any offence under the Act committed in relation to a person who is employed in or about or in connection

---

[1] [1940] 1 K.B. 858; [1940] 1 All E.R. 637; the Receiver and Manager for a Debenture holder may be an "occupier" within the meaning of the Act: *Meigh* v. *Wickenden*, [1942] 2 K.B. 160; [1942] 2 All E.R. 68.

[2] Reg. 1.

[3] Factories Act, 1961, s. 160 (1).

[4] Factories Act, 1961, s. 161.

with that machine or implement and is in the employment or pay of the owner or hirer.[1]

These provisions were discussed in *Whalley* v. *Briggs Motor Bodies, Ltd.*[2] The plaintiff was employed by a firm of contractors in a factory and whilst breaking up old concrete with a pneumatic pick, injured his eyes. Goggles had not been provided either by his employer, or the occupiers of the factory who were being sued. It was held, as a fact, that his employers were the hirers or the owners of the pick for the purposes of any action arising from its use. Thus section 139 of the 1937 Act (now s. 163) was fatal to his claim for it provided, in these circumstances, that the employer should be deemed to be the occupier of the factory, not the defendants.

When an employed person has duties under the Act he, and not the occupier, will be liable for infringements, except where the occupier has failed to take all reasonable steps to prevent the offence. An occupier who avails himself of any special exception allowed by the Act must comply with all the conditions attached thereto or he will commit an offence and an employer who employs persons otherwise than in accordance with the terms of the Act will be deemed to commit a separate offence in respect of every person so employed. An interesting and novel provision is that which stipulates that where an offence under the Act is proved to have been committed with the consent or connivance of or to have been facilitated by any neglect on the part of a director, manager, secretary or other officer of the company, he, as well as the company, shall be deemed to be guilty of the offence. This provision is sound in principle but its efficacy is open to doubt, for presumably it would be open to an occupier to indemnify any such officer against a fine imposed for an offence in contravention of the Act.[3] It is also difficult to apply in practice. *Wright* v. *Ford Motor Co., Ltd.*[4] illustrates this well. One of the defendant's workmen had been injured because he had entered an enclosure when power had not been cut off from the machine inside. The structure was such that the gate could only be opened by the key when the power had been cut off. Unknown to the injured workman the gate had been forced, presumably by a fellow employee. The defendants were not of course aware of this and it was held that they had taken all reasonable steps to prevent the lock being forced. The defence was based first on the point that an employee had clearly contravened a duty under the Act in forcing the gate.[5] Under s. 155 it follows that the occupier is not guilty of breach provided that he has not failed to take all reasonable steps to prevent the contravention. But it was argued:

---

[1] *Ibid.*, s. 163.
[2] [1954] 2 All E.R. 193.
[3] Factories Act, 1961. s. 155.
[4] [1967] 1 Q.B. 230; [1966] 2 All E.R. 518.
[5] Factories Act, 1961, s. 143.

". . . that the offence referred to of which the employer is not guilty
is, to take this case, not the offence for which he was prosecuted, a
breach of s. 14, but it is said, an offence which he, apart from
these words, commits whenever a servant of his wilfully interferes
with an appliance, contrary to section 143."

This argument assumes a vicarious responsibility on the part of the
occupier for the employee's breach of duty, which is itself criminal.
It was rejected by the Divisional Court. But in an interesting
passage in his judgment Lord PARKER, C. J., indicated that
Parliament may indeed have had the intention to legislate for such
vicarious responsibility.[1] If this is so, they failed to achieve it.
Equally interesting, and perhaps more effective, is the provision as to
the enforcement of fines in respect of the employment of young persons. If a young person is employed in any factory in contravention
of the Act, the parent of the young person is guilty of an offence
unless it appears to the court that the contravention occurred without
the consent, connivance or wilful default of the parent.[2]

The power of the court to deal with contraventions of the Act is
not limited to the imposition of a fine. It may, either in addition
to or instead of inflicting a fine, order that such steps shall be taken,
within a specified time, as shall remedy the matters in respect of
which the contravention occurred. During the time specified the
occupier or owner will not be liable for the continued contravention
of the Act, but if, after the expiration of the time, the order is not
complied with a fine not exceeding five pounds for each day on which
the non-compliance continues may be imposed.[3]

Proceedings under the Act are to be taken, in the first place, in a
court of summary jurisdiction with appeal to a Crown Court.[4]
Where an occupier is prevented by the terms of any agreement
with the owner from carrying out structural or other alterations
necessary to enable him to comply with the Act he may apply
to the county court, which court has power, under the Act, to make
an order setting aside or modifying the terms of the agreement as the
court considers just or equitable.[5] Where alterations are required in
order to comply with the Act and the owner or occupier alleges that
the whole or part of the expenses of the alterations ought to be borne
by the occupier or owner, the owner or occupier may apply to the
court which may make such order concerning the expenses or their
apportionment as may be just and equitable. The court must have
regard to the terms of any contract between the parties, or it may,
in the alternative, at the request of the owner or occupier, determine
the lease.[6]

---

[1] Thus attempting to overrule *Carr* v. *The Decca Gramophone Co., Ltd.*,
1947] K.B. 728; [1947] 2 All E.R. 20.
[2] *Ibid.*, s. 158.
[3] Factories Act, 1961, s. 157.
[4] *Ibid.*, ss. 164, 165.
[5] *Ibid.*, s. 169.
[6] *Ibid.*, s. 170.

(3) General Provisions as to Health.—The first part of the 1961 Act is concerned with general provisions affecting the health of the factory worker. The normal tenor of factory legislation during the nineteenth century was from the general to the particular. The 1937 Act attempted, not always with conspicuous success, to secure both. The provisions are reproduced in the 1961 Act and the particular rules for securing cleanliness are set out without prejudice to the overriding rule that every factory shall be kept in a clean state and free from effluvia arising from any drain, sanitary convenience or nuisance. Accumulations of dirt and refuse are to be removed daily from floors and benches of workrooms, staircases and passages. The floors of workrooms are to be cleaned at least once a week by washing or other effective means. Inside walls, partitions and ceilings of rooms, passages and staircases which have a smooth, impervious surface must be washed or cleaned by some other method approved by the district inspector once in every fourteen months. If they are kept painted with oil paint or varnish they must not only be washed as above but must be repainted or rewashed at least once in every period of seven years. In other cases they must be whitewashed or colourwashed at least once in every fourteen months. The obligation to wash, paint or whitewash will not apply, unless the inspector otherwise requires, in factories where mechanical power is not used and less than ten persons are employed.[1]

Carroll v. *North British Locomotive Co.*[2] laid down that damages are recoverable for breach of the duty to keep the floor clean, where the breach causes illness.

A factory must not, whilst work is being carried on, be so overcrowded as to cause risk of injury to the health of people employed. Without prejudice to this general duty, a factory will be deemed to be overcrowded if the amount of cubic space is less than four hundred cubic feet for every person employed.[3] The Secretary of State may, by regulation, increase the amount of cubic space to be provided.[4] In calculating the cubic space, no space above fourteen feet from the floor is to be taken into account and where a room contains a gallery the gallery is to be treated as though it were partitioned off from the remainder of the room and formed a separate room. Unless the inspector otherwise allows, there must be posted in the workroom a notice specifying the number of persons who, having regard to the above provisions, may be employed in that room.[5]

---

[1] Factories Act, 1961, s. 1. The Secretary of State may direct that these provisions shall not apply or shall apply as varied by himself to factories in which there is evidence that they are inappropriate. This " dispensing " power of the Secretary of State is repeated throughout the Act. And see S.I. 1958, No. 752.

[2] [1957] S.L.T. (Sh. Ct.) 2.

[3] Factories Act, 1961, s. 2. The Secretary of State may, by certificate, exempt a workroom from this provision (s. 2 (2)).

[4] *Ibid.*, s. 2 (4).

[5] *Ibid.*, s. 2 (5), (6).

A reasonable temperature must be provided and employers must make provision for this by methods which do not involve the injection into the air of injurious or offensive fumes. After the first hour the temperature should not be less than sixty degrees in rooms where much of the work is done sitting and does not involve serious physical effort. At least one thermometer must be placed in a suitable position in each workroom.[1] In the ironing rooms and wash-houses of laundries effective steps must be taken to regulate the temperature by fan or otherwise, and carry away the steam. Stoves for heating irons must be so separated from the ironing room or table as to protect the workers from the heat thereof and no gas iron which emits a noxious fume may be used.[2]

Workrooms must be adequately ventilated by securing the circulation of fresh air and steps must be taken to render harmless injurious fumes and dusts generated in consequence of the work carried on.[3] The obligation to ventilate was considered by the House of Lords in *Nicholson and Others* v. *Atlas Steel Foundry and Engineering Co. Ltd.*[4] Nicholson worked in a factory wherein there was much dust containing siliceous particles and where there were two machines with exhaust equipment. It proved not to be necessary to determine, for the purposes of the action, whether these machines gave off siliceous dust, for the only ventilation in the place was provided by the doors. There was no roof ventilation. A breach of section 4 was, to that extent, admitted. Nicholson contracted pneumoconiosis from which he died. The respondents denied that there was any connection between their breach of duty and the workman's death. This the Court rejected. The failure to ventilate had increased the hazards to which the workmen were exposed and, pneumoconiosis being a progressive disease, the dust had, in Nicholson's case, materially contributed to his death. Their Lordships were much influenced by *Bonnington Castings Ltd.* v. *Wardlaw*,[5] in which case the respondent had been subjected to dust in much the same circumstances as had Nicholson, and the respondents, as in the earlier case, had admitted a breach of the Grinding of Metals Regulations but had denied any causality between the breach and the injury. After commenting on the defective condition of the dust extractors, Lord TUCKER went on to say:

"... it follows that the quantity of silica dust discharged into the atmosphere from this source cannot be disregarded as negligible on the 'de minimis' principle. In my opinion ... the silica

---

[1] *Ibid.*, s. 3. The Secretary of State is empowered to make regulations fixing special standards: s. 3 (3).

[2] *Ibid.*, s. 71.

[3] Factories Act, 1961, s. 4. The Secretary of State again has the power to fix special standards: s. 4 (2).

[4] [1957] 1 All E. R. 776; [1957] 1 W.L.R. 613.

[5] [1956] A.C. 613; [1956] 1 All E.R. 615.

dust . . . contributed to the harmful condition of the atmosphere
. . . and was, therefore a contributory cause of the disease."[1]

and Lord REID emphasised the obligation of proof:

> " The fact that Parliament imposes a duty for the protection of em-
> ployees has been held to entitle an employee to sue if he is injured as
> a result of a breach of that duty, but it would be going a great deal
> further to hold that it can be inferred from the enactment of a duty
> that Parliament intended that any employee suffering injury can
> sue his employer merely because there is a breach of duty and it is
> shown to be possible that his injury may have been caused by it.
> In my judgment, the employee must, in all cases, prove his case by
> the ordinary standard of proof in civil actions; he must make it ap-
> pear at least that, on a balance of probabilities, the breach of
> duty caused, or materially contributed to, his injury."[2]

In these cases, it will be noticed, a breach of duty was admitted; it
was the question of causality which was in issue.   It was otherwise
in *Ebbs* v. *James Whitson & Co., Ltd.*[3]   The defendants employed
the plaintiff on work which involved the scraping and sand-papering
of monsonia wood and, because of the dust thus created, the plaintiff
contracted dermatitis.   The employers were not aware of any
special danger arising from the wood and they consequently took no
precautions.   The plaintiff alleged that they were in breach of
sections 4 and 47 of the Factories Act of 1937.[4]   It was held that
there was no liability under either section and that section 4 was
limited in its application to defects of ventilation and, there being
no such defects in the present case, liability did not arise.

It should be noticed that the injurious dusts and fumes must be
generated by the work carried on.   Consequently an employee who
had gone into a boiler room into which it was no part of his duty to
go and had closed the door of the room and opened that of the
furnace for warmth and had died from carbon monoxide poisoning,
was held not to be protected by the section.[5]

Sufficient and suitable lighting, whether natural or artificial, must
be provided in every part of the factory in which persons work or
pass.   Glazed windows and skylights used for lighting purposes must
be kept clean on both inner and outer surfaces and free from
obstruction, though such windows may be whitewashed or shaded
where the purpose is to mitigate heat or glare.[6]

---

[1] *Ibid.,* at pp. 623 and 620 respectively.
[2] *Ibid.,* at pp. 620 and 618 respectively. On that point of proof of causation
see also *Nolan* v. *Dental Manufacturing Co., Ltd.,* [1958] 2 All E.R. 449; [1958]
1 W.L.R. 936; *Cummings (or McWilliams)* v. *Sir William Arrol & Co., Ltd.,*
[1962] 1 All E.R. 623; [1962] 1 W.L.R. 295.
[3] [1952] 2 Q.B. 877; [1952] 2 All E.R. 192; see also *Graham* v. *Co-operative
Wholesale Society, Ltd.,* [1957] 1 All E.R. 654.
[4] S. 47 of the 1937 Act is now s. 63 of the 1961 Act.
[5] *Brophy* v. *J. C. Bradfield & Co., Ltd.,* [1955] 3 All E.R. 286.
[6] Factories Act, 1961, s. 5.   The Secretary of State is empowered to make
regulations fixing special standards; s. 5(2).

Where floors are wet to such an extent that drainage can provide a remedy, such drainage must be provided.[1]

Sanitary conveniences both sufficient and suitable must be provided, maintained, and kept clean, with separate accommodation for persons of each sex.[2]

Part I of the Act ends by giving the Secretary of State power to require medical supervision of persons employed in any factory or class or description of factory in which cases of illness have occurred which he believes to be due to the nature of the work carried on, or in which, by reason of any change in the processes or substances used in the processes, or by the introduction of new processes or new substances, there may be risk of injury to the health of persons employed or in which young persons are or are about to be employed in work which may cause risk of injury to their health. And where it appears that there may be risk of injury to the health of employed persons, either from any substance or material brought to the factory to be handled or used therein or from any change in the conditions of work or other conditions in the factory the Secretary of State also has a power to make regulations or orders as to medical supervision.[3]

(4) General Provisions as to Safety.—In many ways the second part of the Act is the most important, for in it a large number of sections are directed towards dealing with the problem of industrial accidents arising from mechanical and other causes in a more comprehensive and detailed way than had been attempted before 1937.

Fencing

Every flywheel directly connected to any prime mover[4] and every moving part of a prime mover must be securely fenced, whether it is situated in an engine house or not.   The head and tail races of water wheels and water turbines must be securely fenced.   Every part of electrical generators, motors and rotary converters, and every flywheel directly connected thereto,[5] every part of the transmission machinery,[6] every dangerous part of machinery other than prime movers and transmission machinery[7] and every part of a stock bar which projects beyond the head stock of a lathe, shall be securely fenced unless it is in such a position or of such a construction as to

---

[1] *Ibid.*, s. 6.

[2] *Ibid.*, s. 7.   Again the Secretary of State has power to set standards by regulation; s. 7 (2).

[3] Factories Act, 1961, s. 11.

[4] *I.e.*, an appliance which provides mechanical energy derived from **fuel, steam, water** or other source (Factories Act, 1937, s. 152).

[5] Factories Act, 1961, s. 12 (1), (2) and (3).

[6] *Ibid.*, s. 13 (1).   An electrically driven lift set in motion by a rope loop may amount to "transmission" machinery; *Deane* v. *Edwards & Co., Ltd.*, [1941] 2 All E.R. 274.

[7] Factories Act, 1961, s. 14 (1), (2).

be as safe to every person employed or working on the premises as it would be if securely fenced.[1] Provided that in so far as the safety of a dangerous part of any machinery cannot, by reason of the nature of the operation, be secured by means of a fixed guard, the law will be complied with if an automatic device is provided which prevents the operator from coming into contact with that part.[2]

In determining whether any part of a machine is safe by position or construction, account is not to be taken of any person making an examination, lubrication or adjustment which must be done whilst the machinery is in motion. In the case of processes, specified by the Secretary of State in regulations, which are of a continuous nature, so that the stopping of the dangerous part would seriously interfere with the whole process, no account shall be taken of any person carrying out, in conformity with the regulations, any lubrication or mounting of belts. But the examination, lubrication or adjustment must be carried out only by male persons over the age of eighteen years.[3]

The fencing and other safeguards provided by the employer in conformity with the Act must be of substantial construction and maintained in position whilst the parts are in motion, except whilst they are necessarily exposed for examination, lubrication or adjustment.[4]

The forerunners of these provisions in earlier Acts have led to considerable litigation, from which certain very clear principles have evolved. In the first place, the purpose of the legislation is "to provide absolute safety as far as fencing can provide it."[5] The words are "securely fenced." They are not to be interpreted as though they read "a little securely fenced" or "reasonably" or "moderately" securely fenced, and an employer will not be able to defend himself by showing that it was impossible, for commercial or mechanical reasons, to fence the machine or part. The respondent in *John Summers & Sons Ltd., v. Frost*[6] was grinding a piece of metal when his thumb came into contact with the wheel and was injured. The upper part of the machine was guarded and at the base there was an adaptable foot rest but part of the stone was un-

---

[1] *Ibid.*, s. 14 (5), (6).
[2] *Ibid.*, s. 14 (2).
[3] *Ibid.*, s. 15.
[4] Factories Act, 1961, s. 16. This section does not apply to machinery when not in motion; *Nash* v. *High Duty Alloys, Ltd.*, [1947] K.B. 377; [1947] 1 All E.R. 363, or whilst it is being turned over by hand or by mechanical power specially adapted to turn the machine over intermittently: *Knight* v. *Leamington Spa Courier, Ltd.*, [1961] 2 Q.B. 253; [1961] 2 All E.R. 666. See also for "not in motion," *Kelly* v. *John Dale, Ltd.*, [1965] 1 Q.B. 185; [1964] 2 All E.R. 497.
[5] *Findlay* v. *Newman, Hender & Co., Ltd.*, [1937] 4 All E.R. 58, *per* HEWART. L.C.J., at p. 60.
[6] [1955] A.C. 740; [1955] 1 All E.R. 870. See also *Pugh* v. *Manchester Dry Docks Co., Ltd.*, [1954] 1 All E.R. 600; [1954] 1 W.L.R. 389. Grinding wheels are now covered by the Abrasive Wheels Regulations (1970).

guarded.   The Court applied the principle that if the result of a machine being securely fenced was that it would not remain commercially practicable or mechanically possible this provided no defence to compliance with section 14 which imposed an absolute duty.

Thus, so far as these sections of the Act are concerned, the obligation to make the specified machinery safe would seem to be absolute.   But these sections do not, apparently, stand alone. They are to be read in conjunction with section 76 which gives the Secretary of State power to make regulations which may, *inter alia*, modify or extend any provisions of Parts I, II and IV of the Act. The effect of this was considered in *Miller* v. *William Boothman and Sons, Ltd.*[1]   A joiner had been injured whilst working at a circular saw.   The saw complied with the Woodworking Machinery Regulations, but the plaintiff contended that this was immaterial, since the obligation laid down by the Factories Act was absolute.   The court held, however, that this was only so where the Secretary of State had not, by regulation, modified the liability.   In the Woodworking Regulations he had done so, and, as a consequence, the plaintiff could not recover.

To whom do the regulations made under section 76 apply?   At one period and as a result of *Hartley* v. *Mayoh & Co. and Another*[2] it had seemed that an extremely restrictive view of the law was to be taken.   It had been held that a fireman called to a fire who was electrocuted because of the unlawful transposition of certain switches did not fall within the regulations.   He was not one of the persons employed for whose benefit the section conferred the power to make regulations and there was therefore no liability for breach of statutory duty. Later another series of cases came before the courts   and   a   wider   view   prevailed.   *Massey-Harris-Ferguson (Manufacturing), Ltd.* v. *Piper*[3] considered circumstances in which a painter, employed by contractors who were painting a factory, was held to be covered by regulations and affirmed the view that whilst *Hartley* v. *Mayoh & Co.* might be correct when applied to a fireman who was always liable to be called to special dangers and face special emergencies, it was not to be interpreted as meaning that only employees of the occupier of a factory could claim the benefit of the regulations.   A like decision was reached in *Bryers* v. *Canadian Pacific Steamship Co., Ltd.*[4]   The defendant's ship was in dry dock in the hands of general repairers.   The plaintiff, an able seaman employed by the shipowners, had been ordered by them to do certain work during which he fell into an unprotected well.   He complained that his employers were in breach of regulations and

---

[1] [1944] K.B. 337; [1944] 1 All E.R. 333; *Quinn* v. *Horsfall & Bickham*, [1956] 2 All E.R. 467. The provision was then s. 60 of the 1937 Act.
[2] [1954] 1 Q.B. 383; [1954] 1 All E.R. 375.
[3] [1956] 2 Q.B. 396; [1956] 2 All E.R. 722.
[4] [1957] 1 Q.B. 134; [1956] 3 All E.R. 560, affirming the decision of DIPLOCK, J., in *Bryers* v. *Canadian Pacific Steamship Co., Ltd.*, [1956] 3 All E.R. 242.

that he was protected by these.   It was held that he might recover,
and JENKINS, L.J., dealt with the question of the scope of the
regulations in these terms:

> " The question whether a given person . . . can recover damages
> from the person guilty of the breach, is a question which depends
> on the construction of the particular regulation relied on and on the
> facts of the particular case.   It would be idle to attempt to lay
> down any general rule . . . in a number of sets of regulations . . .
> the expression ' person employed ' was defined so as to mean a
> person employed in the particular process or manufacture. . . .
> Then, in contrast to that, . . . occurs the phrase ' any person
> employed in the works ' . . . in the present instance . . . the relevant
> enabling section . . . enabled protective regulations to be made in
> the widest possible terms."[1]

It has been recently emphasised that there is nothing in the section
to justify a restriction of protection to the time when an employee is
acting within the scope of his employment.[2]   Obviously there comes
a situation when the employee is no longer acting as an employee
but as a volunteer as where he operates a machine for his own purpose in his own time.[3]

Machinery must be made safe, but the obligation to fence is subject
to certain limitations, one of which is that once a secure fence has
been provided and maintained,

> "it does not cease to be secure because by some act of perverted
> and deliberate ingenuity the guard can be forced or circumvented
> and the safeguard provided thereby rendered nugatory."[4]

And the duty to fence securely will be complied with when the
machinery is fenced in such a way as to guard against all such
dangers as might be reasonably foreseen.   This has been held to
cover a situation where there was an appreciable, though not serious
risk.[5]   A divergence of judicial view grew up around this point,
but in the case of *Close* v. *Steel Company of Wales, Ltd.*[6] the House
of Lords has had an opportunity of reviewing these earlier cases
and laying down fresh principles.   The appellant in this case
was injured in the eye when the bit of a portable electric drill which
he was using shattered.   It was not an uncommon occurrence for
bits to break.   The workman's claim against his employers for

---

[1] [1956] 3 All E.R. 560 at pp. 573-4.

[2] *Uddin* v. *Associated Portland Cement Manufacturers, Ltd.,* [1965] 2 Q.B.
15; [1965] 1 All E.R. 347.

[3] *Napieralski* v. *Curtis (Contractors), Ltd.,* [1959] 2 All E.R. 426; [1959] 1
W.L.R. 835.

[4] *Carr* v. *Mercantile Produce Co., Ltd.,* [1949] 2 K.B. 601, *per* STABLE, J., at
p. 608; [1949] 2 All E.R. 531 at p. 537; *Woodley* v. *Meason Freer & Co., Ltd.,*
[1963] 3 All E.R. 636; [1963] 1 W.L.R. 1409.

[5] *Dunn* v. *Birds Eye Foods, Ltd.,* [1959] 2 Q.B. 265; [1959] 2 All E.R. 403.
A Divisional Court decision arising out of a prosecution under s. 133 of the
Factories Act, 1937.

[6] [1961] 2 All E.R. 953; [1961] 3 W.L.R. 319.   Distinguished on the facts in
Millard v. *Serck Tubes, Ltd.,* [1969] 1 All E.R. 598; [1969] 1 W.L.R. 211.

failure to comply with the duty to fence failed.   The first ground, on which all the judges concurred, was that the risk of grave injury was not reasonably foreseeable.   The Court applied the principle enunciated in *Hindle* v. *Birtwistle*[1] that " machinery or parts of machinery is and are dangerous if in the ordinary course of human affairs danger may be reasonably anticipated from the use of them without protection."[2]   Although bits commonly broke they were not usually ejected far and so the danger was held to be one that could not reasonably have been anticipated, and the part was not therefore dangerous.

The House of Lords also considered the proposition, adopted by them in previous cases,[3] that the duty to provide fencing was confined to the prevention of a workman coming into contact with moving parts of the machine and did not include the duty to protect a workman from injury caused by ejected or flying pieces of the machine itself or of the material on which the machine was working. This proposition was reaffirmed although, it should be noted, with reluctance[4] and with two strong dissenting judgments on this point.[5]   It follows that those cases which had indicated that the proposition could be modified to some extent can no longer be relied upon for this.[6]   This is plainly a matter for future amendment by legislation although it is important to note, as Lord GODDARD was at pains to point out in his judgment, that where there is a known tendency to ejection of machine or material, failure to guard against injury to workmen may well afford a cause of action at common law.

This decision has already been considered in later cases.   In *Eaves* v. *Morris Motors Ltd.*[7] the workman injured his finger in a milling machine when the block performed an " uncovenanted stroke."   The workman saw the stroke in time but in hastily withdrawing his hand he grazed his finger on an irregularity in the bolt which was being milled in the machine.   The Court of Appeal held, reversing the decision of WINN, J., that the bolt was not part of the machine and so could not be covered by the duty to fence.[8]   It was emphasised that the duty to fence was in respect of the normal operation of a machine and did not cover a situation where the machine went wrong or operated as it was not designed to do.

Although this decision is clear upon the point that the duty to

---

[1] [1897] 1 Q.B. 192.   The decision in this case cannot now be supported as good law.   See the next paragraph.

[2] [1897] 1 Q.B. 192, at p. 195, *per* WILLS, J.

[3] *Nicholls* v. *F. Austin (Leyton), Ltd.*, [1946] A.C. 493; [1946] 2 All E.R. 92. *Carroll* v. *Andrew Barclay & Sons, Ltd.*, [1948] A.C. 477; [1948] 2 All E.R. 386.

[4] See Lord GODDARD, [1961] 3 W.L.R. 319 at p. 330.

[5] Lord DENNING and Lord MORRIS.

[6] *Dickson* v. *Flack*, [1953] 2 Q.B. 464; [1953] 2 All E.R. 840; *Rutherford* v. *R. E. Glanville & Sons (Bovey Tracey), Ltd.*, [1958] 1 All E.R. 532; [1958] 1 W.L.R. 415.

[7] [1961] 2 Q.B. 385; [1961] 3 All E.R. 233.

[8] Applying *Bullock* v. *G. John Power (Agencies), Ltd.*, [1956] 1 All E.R. 498; [1956] 1 W.L.R. 171.

fence does not apply to materials in the machine it was accepted that
the insertion of materials might make the machine itself dangerous,
in which event there would be a duty to fence.   HOLROYD PEARCE,
L.J., put it like this:

> " Although *Bullock* v. *G. John Power (Agencies), Ltd.*, does not
> allow us to equate dangers from the nature of the material (namely,
> the sharp edge of the bolts) to dangers from the machinery, it does
> not compel us when deciding whether machinery is dangerous to
> disregard the nature of the machine when it is doing its normal
> appointed task, or from holding it to be dangerous if that task
> clearly involves danger from its juxtaposition with its normal
> materials."[1]

This point has now been firmly established by the House of Lords
in *Midland and Low Moor Iron and Steel Co., Ltd.* v. *Cross*[2] where it
was held that the duty to fence was not discharged in circumstances
in which the machine, though safe whilst stationary, was dangerous
whilst operating in the normal way.

Some of the problems posed in this area have been considered
afresh in *Johnson* v. *F. E. Callow (Engineers), Ltd.*[3]   The workman's
hand was injured whilst he was using a centre lathe.   The exact
cause of the accident was not clear but it appears likely that it
arose because he was using a squeezy bottle to squirt coolant rather
than the automatic system.   The trial judge could not satisfactorily
determine the cause of the accident and so he held that the accident
was clearly not foreseeable and so there was no liability for breach
of statutory duty.   The Court of Appeal rejected this approach.   It
was held that knowledge of the use of squeezy bottles which might
lead to injury was enough to found liability and it was no answer
to say that the want of a clear explanation of the cause of the accident established lack of foreseeability.   This point has been similarly
decided in two recent cases.[4]   *Johnson's* case raised, however, a
further point.   It was the article being turned which moved and
thus made the otherwise stationary machine dangerous.   This type
of situation had led to the judicial divergence of opinion which
seems so normal in this area of law.[5]   The Court of Appeal came down
clearly in favour of liability attaching to such a situation.   It was
considered wrong to view the stationary boring bar in isolation.
When seen in close proximity to the revolving material it became
a dangerous part of the machine, covered by the duty to fence.

---

[1] Cited in [1961] 3 W.L.R. at p. 663.
[2] [1965] A.C. 357; [1965] 3 All E.R. 752.
[3] [1970] 2 Q.B. 1; [1970] 1 All E.R. 129; affirmed *sub nom. F. E. Callow
(Engineers), Ltd.* v. *Johnson*, [1971] A.C. 335; [1970] 3 All E.R. 639.
[4] *Allen* v. *Aeroplane and Motor Aluminium Castings, Ltd.*, [1965] 3 All E.R.
377; [1965] 1 W.L.R. 1244; *Millard* v. *Serck Tubes, Ltd.*, [1969] 1 All E.R.
598; [1969] 1 W.L.R. 211.
[5] For liability—*Hoare* v. *M. & W. Grazebrook Ltd.*, [1957] 1 All E.R. 470;
[1957] 1 W.L.R. 638 and *Victor Lenthall* v. *Gimson & Co. (Leicester), Ltd.*,
(1956), unreported.   Against, and so not followed—*Lewis* v. *High Duty
Alloys, Ltd.*, [1957] 1 All E.R. 740; [1957] 1 W.L.R. 632.

A divergence of judicial view has also grown up around the related point of the relevance of the tool or material which the workman is presenting to the machine.   The problem is whether this is to be regarded as material in the machine or an extension of the man who has to be fenced out.   Two recent cases illustrate the difficulty.   In *Sparrow* v. *Fairey Aviation Co., Ltd.*,[1] STREATFEILD, J. took a narrow view.   In that case the plaintiff workman was cleaning the edge of a hole in the material being processed in a lathe with a small tool. The tool caught against the lathe, flinging the workman's hand on to the lathe and causing him injury.   It was held that the duty to fence a machine would protect the operator from contact but did not extend to the operator and his tool viewed as a unit.   In *Johnson* v. *J. Stone & Co. (Charlton) Ltd.*,[2] HINCHCLIFFE, J., took a divergent view.   There a casting, whilst being presented to a saw, came into contact with an unfenced pulley which dropped and injured the workman.   The judge took the view that the fence should have been adequate to keep out the workman and the material.   The House of Lords in *Sparrow's* case reaffirmed the view that the statute only required the operator to be fenced out and this term was not to include his tools although it was accepted that it must include his clothing. There is an interesting dissenting judgment by Lord MacDERMOTT and the general indication in the majority judgment is that the law is not regarded as satisfactory.

This section of the law cannot be viewed with pleasure for on each of these points there is a plain divergence between a strict interpretation of the words of the Act and the desire to make the provisions effective over a wider field.   It must be accepted that these provisions cannot be considered adequate and the only true remedy is by amendment of the Act to cover the wider field of risk. HOLROYD PEARCE, L.J., put this succinctly, saying:

> " There is no protection under section 14 against a class of obvious perils caused by dangerous machinery, namely perils which arise from a dangerous machine ejecting at the worker pieces of the material or even pieces of the machine itself.   Thus, there is now left a gap which neither logic nor common sense appears to justify."[3]

The same sentiments can be applied to the position of an injury caused through a tool or piece of material being processed coming into contact with a moving part.

A further problem arises where the machine complies with regulations as to fencing made by the Secretary of State.   Can breach of section 14 still be established?   This was considered by the House of

---

[1] [1961] 1 All E.R. 216; [1961] 1 W.L.R. 844.   An earlier case to support this decision is *Lewis* v. *High Duty Alloys, Ltd.*, [1957] 1 All E.R. 740; [1957] 1 W.L.R. 632.

[2] [1961] 1 All E.R. 869; [1961] 1 W.L.R. 849.   An earlier case to support this view is *Hoare* v. *M. W. Grazebrook, Ltd.*, [1957] 1 All E.R. 470; [1957] 1 W.L.R. 638.

[3] *Eaves* v. *Morris Motors, Ltd.*, [1961] 2 Q.B. 385; [1961] 3 All E.R. 233.

Lords in *Automatic Woodturning Co., Ltd.* v. *Stringer.*[1] The plaintiff
was injured when her hand came into contact with a saw whilst using
a push stick given to enable her to push away " off-cuts " of wood.
Originally she had brought action at both common law and under
statute.   Under the latter she alleged infringement of regulations.
The claim under the regulations was abandoned for it was subsequently admitted that the machine did not offend the regulations
and leave was given to proceed under section 14 of the 1937 Act.
Reviewing the cases Viscount SIMMONDS said[2]:

> " It was held in *Miller* v. *William Boothman & Sons, Ltd.,*[3] which
> was recently approved by this House in *John Summers & Sons, Ltd.*
> v. *Frost*[4] that the obligation of a special regulation such as regula-
> tion 10(c) if it had been duly complied with, is to be regarded as
> substituted for the more general obligation as to fencing contained
> in section 14. . . .   It was contended by the appellants and held
> by the Court of Appeal that the present case was governed by
> authority.   It had been, however, held by OLIVER, J. that he was
> enabled by two cases, *Benn* v. *Kamm & Co., Ltd.*[5] . . . and *Dickson* v.
> *Flack*[6] to distinguish the earlier case of *Miller* v. *William Boothman*
> and hold that the general obligation of section 14 of the Act had
> not, in regard to the operation on which the respondent was
> engaged, been superseded, by the specific obligation in regulation
> 10(c).   He said:
>
>> ' I find no difficulty in saying that a saw may be correctly
>> fenced for the purposes of operation as a saw, but not correctly
>> fenced for some other purpose.'
>
> . . . I agree with the unanimous opinion of the Court of Appeal that
> *Benn* v. *Kamm & Co., Ltd.,* and *Dickson* v. *Flack* decide no more
> than that compliance with a special regulation in regard to the
> fencing of some specific dangerous part of a machine does not
> absolve the employer from taking proper steps under section 14 of
> the Act to fence some other part of the machine for which no
> provision is made in the special regulation.   This is, I think, made
> particularly clear in the judgment of my noble and learned friend,
> Lord SOMERVELL of HARROW, in *Benn* v. *Kamm & Co. Ltd.*   It is a
> different thing altogether to say in regard to a single dangerous part
> of a machine which, as a whole, admittedly complies with the
> relevant regulation, that it does not comply with it for the purpose
> of what is called an ancillary activity.   The evidence left me in no
> doubt that an essential part of the industrial operation of sawing
> was the sweeping of off-cuts from the table of the saw.   It is
> impossible that that should not have been foreseen when regulation
> 10(c) was made . . . and this admission, from which we cannot in
> this case depart, that the regulation was complied with, precludes us
> from holding that, in regard to this activity, there was any room
> for the operation of section 14."

---

[1] [1957] A.C. 544; [1957] 1 All E.R. 90 at pp. 551 and 94 respectively.
[2] [1957] 3 All E.R. 470; [1957] 1 W.L.R. 1186.
[3] [1944] K.B. 337; [1944] 1 All E.R. 333.
[4] [1955] A.C. 740; [1955] 1 All E.R. 870.
[5] [1952] 2 Q.B. 127; [1952] 1 All E.R. 833.
[6] [1953] 2 Q.B. 464; [1953] 2 All E.R. 840.

The test of " foreseeability " to which reference has already been made was also applied in *Smith* v. *Chesterfield and District Co-operative Society, Ltd.*[1] when the plaintiff worked on a machine, the rollers of which were protected by a guard which came down to within three inches of the bed of the machine.   She placed her hand under the guard, despite instructions to the contrary, and was injured.   The judge who had tried the first hearing held that as the plaintiff had voluntarily put her hand within the guard she could not recover.   The Court of Appeal felt otherwise.   The conduct of the plaintiff, though deliberate, was foreseeable, and the machine was not securely fenced within the provisions of the Act.   So also in *Burns* v. *Joseph Terry & Sons, Ltd.*[2] there was a machine, guarded by a rail about four feet above ground level, and above this was a pulley wheel shaft and pinion.   These latter were guarded, but from approach by the front only, by a wire mesh.   Above the top of the pulley wheel was a shelf.   The plaintiff, a youth of seventeen, put a ladder against a shaft and climbed up to collect objects on the shelf. The ladder slipped and in searching for some support he put his hand between the wheel and the pinion.   It was held that the employers were not liable for the machine was fenced against such dangers as might be foreseen.   It is clear, however, that the fencing need not be such as to protect a man determined to come into contact with danger.   Then the failure of the normally adequate fence to prevent injury will not be accepted as the cause of the damage.[3]

It was formerly assumed that if machinery or gearing was out of normal reach it was safe by position and there was no obligation to fence.   Such an assumption cannot now be sustained.   In *Findlay* v. *Newman, Hender & Co., Ltd.*,[4] the court considered the claim of a workman injured in replacing a belt on a revolving countershaft twelve and a half feet from the ground.   The employers were held to be liable.

The words "every dangerous part of any machinery" have also received considerable judicial attention.

> "It seems to me, that machinery or parts of machinery is and are dangerous if, in the ordinary course of human affairs, danger may be reasonably anticipated from the use of them without protection."[5]

Again,

> "in considering whether machinery is dangerous, the contingency of carelessness on the part of the workman in charge of it, and the

---

[1] [1953] 1 All E.R. 447.

[2] [1951] 1 K.B. 454; [1950] 2 All E.R. 987.

[3] *Rushton* v. *Turner Brothers Asbestos Co., Ltd.*, [1959] 3 All E.R. 517; [1960] 1 W.L.R. 96.

[4] [1937] 4 All E.R. 58; see also *Hodkinson* v. *Hy Wallwork & Co., Ltd.*, [1955] 3 All E.R. 236; *Williams* v. *Sykes and Harrison, Ltd.*, [1955] 3 All E.R. 225.

[5] *Hindle* v. *Birtwistle*, [1897] 1 Q.B. 192, at p. 195 *per* WILLS, J.   This test was accepted by the House of Lords in *Close* v. *Steel Company of Wales, Ltd.*, [1961] 2 All E.R. 953; [1961] 3 W.L.R. 319, see *supra*, p. 277.

frequency with which that contingency is likely to arise are matters that must be taken into consideration."[1]

If the machine is dangerous, the obligation is to fence, and substitutes for fencing will not enable the employer to evade his liability. A workman was injured when greasing pinion wheels which were in motion. A clearly displayed notice said :

" Do not put your hands in the machinery while it is in motion. Persons disregard this notice at their own risk."

The employers were held to have committed an offence.[2]

Finally, it is not sufficient to provide a guard. The machinery must be actually guarded and where an employer ordered a workman not to use a guard the court held that the position was the same as if no guard had been provided.[3]

To what machines do the provisions as to fencing and safety apply? They do not, apparently, apply to machinery made in the factory for the purposes of sale, so that where a youth was injured whilst cleaning an unfenced but dangerous part of a machine manufactured in the factory, it was held that he could not recover for breach of statutory duty.[4] *Irwin* v. *White Tomkins and Courage, Ltd.*,[5] illustrates an intermediate situation. New machinery was being installed. A sack hoist which had been completely installed was being run, probably for testing. It was held that the Act applied even though the machine had not been taken into use for normal operation. But an overhead travelling cableway, on which materials were carried in buckets, is not machinery within the meaning of the Act.[6] This last case seems to turn merely on the question of scale: a small machine carrying things in a similar way might well have been held to be within the Act as a conveyor belt plainly is.

The law has been slow to deal effectively with mobile machinery. Now an authoritative House of Lords decision has settled the matter. In *British Railways Board* v. *Liptrot*,[7] the machinery in question was a crane mounted on a chassis with four rubber-tyred wheels. This crane was able to move from place to place under its own power, and was used in an open scrap yard for collecting and sorting metal. The general approach to the problem is important. It was first held that even though cranes and lifting machinery are specifically

---

[1] *Hindle* v. *Birtwistle, supra*; cited with approval by Du Parcq, J., in *Walker* v. *Bletchley Flettons, Ltd.*, [1937] 1 All E.R. 170, at p. 175. And see *Pearce* v. *Stanley-Bridges, Ltd.*, [1965] 2 All E.R. 594, [1965] 1 W.L.R. 931.

[2] *Chasteney* v. *Michael Nairn & Co., Ltd.*, [1937] 1 All E.R. 376; see also *Sutherland* v. *James Mills, Ltd., Executors*, [1938] 1 All E.R. 283.

[3] *Murray* v. *Schwachman, Ltd.*, [1938] 1 K.B. 130; [1937] 2 All E.R. 68; *cf.* now Factories Act, 1937, s. 16.

[4] *Parvin* v. *Morton Machine Co., Ltd.*, [1952] A.C. 515; [1952] 1 All E.R. 670, H.L.

[5] [1964] 1 All E.R. 545; [1964] 1 W.L.R. 387.

[6] *Quintas* v. *National Smelting Co., Ltd.*, [1961] 1 All E.R. 630; [1961] 1 W.L.R. 401, reversing Devlin, J.

[7] [1969] 1 A.C. 136; [1967] 2 All E.R. 1072.

dealt with under section 27 of the Act, it is possible for a crane to be subject to section 14.   To be so subject it has to be part of the equipment of the factory.   Thus a distinction is to be made between mobile transport visiting the factory and that which is part of the equipment of a particular factory.   Once the crane is accepted as part of the equipment, the question is then not whether it was machinery to which the Act applies but whether it contained machinery.   If it does, then section 14(1) is applied to that machinery. The earlier case[1] which had laid down as the crucial test whether the object in question was an independent vehicle or truck was overruled.   The point was put quite simply by Viscount DILHORNE:

> " While it would not be right to describe a vehicle as machinery, it may contain machinery; and if the vehicle forms part of the equipment of the factory, then, in my opinion, section 14 imposes an absolute obligation, subject to the proviso in that section, to fence securely every dangerous part of the machinery it contains."

The situation which arises where the workman himself provides the motive power was considered at length in *Richard Thomas and Baldwins, Ltd.* v. *Cummings.*[2]   The respondent had been ordered to adjust the position of a part of a machine which was driven, in the ordinary way, by belts passing over pulleys.   As the machine was under repair, power had been cut off, but the cover which ordinarily guarded the belts and pulleys had also been removed and it was not contested that, in the ordinary way, these must be fenced.   So as to do the work put upon him, the respondent pulled a belt by hand and whilst doing this injured himself.   Could it be said that this was transmission machinery in motion?   The Court of Appeal had thought so but the House of Lords took a different view.

> " In my opinion the appeal must succeed.   Whether or not this machinery was transmission machinery when unconnected with a prime mover, it was clearly a dangerous part of the machinery within section 14, and therefore must be fenced.   But the question, in my view, depends on the true construction of section 16, and on that I am of opinion that the belt and pulley in question were not in motion or in use at the time of this accident, within the meaning of section 16.   They were not in motion or in use for the purposes for which they were intended, but for repair and in my opinion section 16 does not prohibit the removal of fencing when such removal is necessary for repair. . . . The words ' in motion or in use ' in section 16 do not, in my opinion, refer to such movement of machinery by hand as took place in the present case, and section 16 does not deal in any way with such movement."[3]

---

[1] *Cherry* v. *International Alloys,* [1961] 1 Q.B. 136; [1960] 3 All E.R. 264.

[2] [1955] A.C. 321; [1955] 1 All E.R. 285.   And see *Knight* v. *Leamington Spa Courier, Ltd.,* [1961] 2 Q.B. 253; [1961] 2 All E.R. 666; *Kelly* v. *John Dale, Ltd.,* [1965] 1 Q.B. 185; [1964] 2 All E.R. 497.

[3] *Per* Lord OAKSEY [1955] A.C. 321 at p. 329; [1955] 1 All E.R. 285 at pp. 287-8; in consequence *Charles* v. *S. Smith & Sons Ltd.,* [1954] 1 All E.R. 499 is now of doubtful validity.

An interesting distinction was made in *Stanbrook* v. *Waterlow &
Sons, Ltd.*,[1] between being moved slowly and in motion at a fast
pace.   A printing machine was being prepared for printing and the
method used involved its revolving quickly.   It was held because
of this to be in motion under s. 16.   The test which is gaining acceptance is the character of the movement rather than its purpose.[2]

The Factories Act recognises, by implication, that however comprehensive are the requirements to secure safety, some degree of accident is inevitable.   Thus, there must be provided and maintained in
every room where work is carried on by means of mechanical power
devices which enable that power promptly to be cut off from the
transmission machinery.   Driving belts, when not in use, must not
be allowed to rest or ride on a revolving shaft forming part of the
transmission machinery and efficient mechanical devices must be
provided and used to move driving belts to and from fast and loose
pulleys and be so constructed as to prevent the driving belt from
creeping back to the fast pulley.[3]

When the Secretary of State is satisfied that there are satisfactory
safety devices which either prevent the exposure of a dangerous part
of machinery whilst still in motion or which stop a machine in case
of danger, he may make regulations to secure their use, though, if
action is brought against an employer charging him with contravention of this subsection, it will be a good defence that he used another
but equally effective device.[4]

In the case of machines intended to be driven by mechanical
power, every set screw, bolt or key on any revolving shaft, spindle,
wheel or pinion must be so sunk, cased or guarded as to prevent
danger, and all spurs and other toothed or friction gearing which
does not require frequent adjustment whilst in motion must either
be safe by position or completely encased.   Failure to comply with
this is an offence not only on the part of the employer, but also on
the part of the person who sells the machine or lets it on hire or, as
agent of the seller or hirer, causes it to be sold or let on hire for use in
a factory in the United Kingdom.   Thus, the seller or hirer will be
liable where he is in the jurisdiction or, in the case of machinery of
foreign origin, an agent who is within the jurisdiction will be liable
where the principal cannot be prosecuted.[5]

In *Biddle* v. *Truvox Engineering Co., Ltd.*[6] the court considered
a novel point arising out of these provisions, namely, whether the
seller or hirer of a machine which did not conform with the requirements of the section might, in addition to being fined, be made
liable in a civil action at the instance of an injured person. It was
held that this was not so and that the legislature had not intended

[1] [1964] I W.L.R. 825.
[2] *Mitchell* v. *W. S. Westin, Ltd.*, [1965] I All E.R. 657; [1965] I W.L.R. 297.
[3] Factories Act, 1961, s. 13 (2), (3), (4).   The Secretary of State has power to
order that these provisions shall not apply (s. 13 (5)).
[4] *Ibid.*, s. 14 (2).
[5] Factories Act, 1961, s. 17.   [6] [1952] I K.B. 101; [1951] 2 All E.R. 835.

to create between the seller and the servant of the purchaser, the duty which existed between the purchaser and his servant. In *Biddle's* case the buyer who had been made defendant by an injured servant, joined as third parties the manufacturers of the machine, the relevant part of which was alleged to consist of "toothed or friction gearing" not completely encased. FINNEMORE, J., held that the part in question was within section 17 of the 1937 Act, and that section had not been complied with, but also, for the reasons given above the sellers were not liable in damages.

It is submitted with respect, that the decision is a wrong one and that since the purpose of the Act was to protect workmen, there seems no reason in logic or in law, why the manufacturers should not be made liable to contribute to the damages.

Dangerous Substances

Vessels containing dangerous liquids have been a frequent source of industrial accidents and they are dealt with by provisions which require that every fixed vessel, structure, sump or pit which contains scalding, corrosive or poisonous liquid and of which the edge is less than three feet above the adjoining ground or platform must be securely covered or fenced to at least that height or (where neither covering nor fencing is possible) all practical steps must be taken to prevent persons falling in.[1]   In particular any ladder, stair or gangway placed above, across, or inside must be at least eighteen inches wide and must be securely fenced to a height of three feet on both sides.[2] Secure fencing means sheet fencing or an upper and lower rail and toe boards.[3]   Where two such vessels, structures, sumps or pits adjoin and the space between is less the eighteen inches in width or is not securely fenced to three feet in height, that is to say does not fulfill the safety standard for gangways, the passage must be closed by barriers.[4]

Self-acting Machines

In any factory erected after 1895, in any factory reconstructed after the passing of the Factories Act, 1937, and in any extension of or addition to a factory made after such passing of the Act, no traversing part of any self-acting machine, and no material carried thereon shall, if the space over which it runs is a space over which any person is liable to pass, be allowed to run within a distance of eighteen inches from any fixed structure not being part of the machine, except that the traversing carriage of a self-acting spinning mule may run to a point twelve inches distant from any part of the head stock of another such machine.[5]

---

[1] Factories Act, 1961, s. 18(1).   The Secretary of State has an exempting power.
[2] *Ibid.*, s. 18(2).
[3] *Ibid.*, s. 18(4).
[4] Factories Act, 1961, s. 18(3).
[5] *Ibid*, s. 19.

Machines and Women and Young Persons

No part of a prime mover or of transmission machinery shall be cleaned whilst in motion nor shall any part of any machine be cleaned by a woman or young person,[1] if they would thereby be exposed to danger from any moving part of the machine being cleaned or of any adjacent machinery.[2] This requirement represents a welcome strengthening of the law, for under the Factory and Workshop Act, 1878,[3] the prohibition had concerned children only and had been restricted to the cleaning of "any part of the machinery in a factory while the same is in motion. . . ." In *Pearson* v. *Belgian Mills Co.*[4] this had been interpreted as meaning that a child might not clean a fixed and motionless part of a machine which was in motion. The wording of the new section puts the matter beyond doubt, and the cleaning of any part of any machine is prohibited in the interests of women and young persons if they are thereby exposed to risk. The court in *Taylor* v. *Dawson (Mark)* & *Son, Ltd.*,[5] discussed a problem of some interest, namely, what amounts to cleaning a machine? Certain spinning machinery tended to become choked by fluff, which had, consequently, to be removed. When reclaimed, the fluff had a marketable value and was sold. The argument that a child, injured whilst taking the fluff from the machine, was not cleaning the machine but was engaged in a manufacturing process, was rejected.

The Secretary of State may prescribe certain machines as being of such a dangerous character that young persons ought not to work at them unless they have been instructed as to the dangers arising and the precautions to be observed and, in addition, have either had sufficient training in work at the machine or are under the adequate supervision of someone who has a thorough knowledge and experience of the machine.[6]

Hoists, Cranes and Lifting Tackle

The Act contains elaborate and detailed regulations as to hoists, lifts, cranes, lifting machines and lifting tackle, and the reader is referred to the Act for their details. Hoists must be of good construction and properly maintained; they must be thoroughly reported upon by a competent person every six months; the hoistway must be protected by a substantial enclosure fitted with gates, having some device to secure that the gate cannot be opened except when the cage is at the landing, and the cage cannot be moved therefrom until the gate is closed. This provision as to the mechanical locking of gates when the cage is away from the landing is subject

---

[1] *I.e.*, one who has reached the age of 14 and has not reached that of 18 (*ibid.*, s. 176).

[2] *Ibid.*, s. 20.

[3] 41 and 42 Vict., c. 16, s. 9 ; see also Factory and Workshop Act, 1901, s. 13.

[4] [1896] 1 Q.B. 244.

[5] [1911] 1 K.B. 145.

[6] Factories Act, 1961, s. 21.

to the exception that where, in the case of hoists built or reconstructed before the passing of the Act, it is not practicable to fit such devices, it will be sufficient if steps are taken to prevent persons falling down the hoistway, but in the case of lifts and hoists not connected with mechanical power such a device is not necessary though the gate must be closed and fastened except when the cage or platform is at rest at the landing. The hoist and its enclosure must be built so as to prevent the persons or goods carried from being trapped between the hoist and any fixed structure or between the counterbalancing weight and any other moving part of the hoist. The maximum working load must be clearly marked and the Act provides additional requirements where the hoist is to be used for carrying persons whether together with goods or otherwise.[1]

The court in *Whitehead* v. *James Stott & Co.*[2] considered the operation of the Act's requirements relating to hoists. The plaintiff was travelling in the defendants' hoist when the cage fell and the winding gear fell on him and injured him. In proceedings against the defendants he alleged them to be in breach of their statutory duty in failing to see that the hoist was of good mechanical construction, of sound material and properly maintained. It was found that there was a latent defect in the winding gear which had probably been there when it was installed many years before. The Court of Appeal held that despite this, the defendants were in breach, for the duty was absolute, and a few days later, considering the same section in *Galashiels Gas Co., Ltd.* v. *O'Donnell (or Millar)*[3] the House of Lords held that the obligation was both absolute and continuing—a point on which the earlier case had not spoken.

Chains, ropes and lifting tackle must be of good construction and free from patent defect. When they are kept in a store, a table of the safe working load of every kind of chain, rope or lifting tackle must be posted in a prominent position and the material must be used in accordance with the table. They must be examined at least once in every period of six months by a competent person, and must not be used for the first time without being examined, tested and the safe working load certified by a competent person.[4]

All parts, whether fixed or movable and including the anchoring and fixing appliances of every lifting machine,[5] must be of good construction and properly maintained. They must be examined by a competent person at least once in every period of fourteen months. The rails and track on which a travelling crane or the carriage of a transporter moves must be of the proper size and strength, be properly laid or suspended and have even running surfaces. Safe working loads must be plainly indicated and the machine must not

---

[1] *Ibid.*, ss. 22–25.
[2] [1949] 1 K.B. 358; [1949] 1 All E.R. 245.
[3] [1949] A.C. 275; [1949] 1 All E.R. 319.
[4] Factories Act, 1961, s. 26.
[5] *I.e.*, crane, crab, winch, transporter or runway, etc.

be loaded beyond its strength.   The machines must be examined before they are taken into use in any factory and their safe working load certified by a competent person.[1]   Something of the interaction of these provisions is to be seen in the case of *Gledhill* v. *Liverpool Abattoir Utility Co., Ltd. and Another.*[2]   The plaintiff was employed by the first defendants in a slaughterhouse owned and controlled by Liverpool Corporation who were the second defendants.   The slaughterhouse was a factory which had been reported as unsatis-factory in use.   The defect related to certain chains which were not defective in themselves but were of too robust a construction to permit of the tying of a satisfactory slip round an animal that was to be hoisted.   One such animal slipped through the chain and, in its fall, injured the plaintiff who brought action against his em-ployers for failure to provide a safe system of working.   His employers denied liability and contended that the Corporation was the responsible party, under both sections 23 and 24 of the 1937 Act, now ss. 26 and 27 of the 1961 Act.   The trial judge had held that both the first and the second defendants were liable and assessed the damages equally between the two.   The Court of Appeal reversed the decision insofar as the Corporation was concerned.   That body was held not to be liable for there had been no failure to provide chains " of good construction " and " adequate strength."   The words " good construction " were not to be taken as denoting suita-bility for a particular purpose—and since the evidence was that the chains were of a strength greater than required, they could hardly be said not to be of adequate strength.

The plaintiff, in an effort to bring his case within section 24, argued that the chains constituted an elevator or runway.   The court refused to determine this point but proceeded on the assumption that the chains were comprehended within the wording of the section.   It followed that they must be of good construction and properly maintained.   But even " on this approach " the court found for the Corporation, for

> " if the chains were of good construction and adequate strength, then there is no evidence at all which in any way suggests that the chains did not at all times continue to be of good construction and of adequate strength."[3]

If any person is employed or working on or near the wheel track of an overhead travelling crane in any place where he would be liable to be struck by the crane, effective measures shall be taken by warning the driver of the crane or otherwise to ensure that the crane does not approach within twenty feet of that place.[4]   In *Holmes* v. *Hadfields, Ltd.,*[5] the plaintiff worked on a platform sixteen

[1] Factories Act, 1961, s. 27.
[2] [1957] 3 All E.R. 117; [1957] 1 W.L.R. 1028.
[3] *Ibid.,* at pp. 122, 1035 respectively *per* MORRIS, L. J.
[4] Factories Act, 1961, s. 27.
[5] [1944] K.B. 275; [1944] 1 All E.R. 235.

feet above the floor and within less than twenty feet from an overhead crane which was liable to strike anyone working on the platform.   The plaintiff knew of the approach of the crane and moved
from the platform to a girder between the platform and the floor.
His signal to the crane driver was misunderstood and the crane
knocked a drill, with which the plaintiff had been working, off the
platform and injured him.   The employers contended that there
was no breach of the duty laid upon them by section 24 of the 1937
Act, now s. 27 of the 1961 Act, since when the plaintiff was injured
he was not working in a place where he would be liable to be struck
by the crane.   The court found that there was a breach of the duty
and the plaintiff could recover.

> " If a man's place of employment is partly within the twenty feet
> and partly outside the twenty feet, he may be at any given moment
> at one part or the other.   The object of the subsection is to lay
> down an absolute rule of safety and not make the obligation of the
> employer dependent upon the precise point where the workman
> may be at any given moment."[1]

Moreover the duty to warn is the duty of the occupier of the factory
and he cannot escape liability by seeking to place it upon the workman.   So where, in a factory, a large notice instructed cranemen
not to approach within twenty feet of men at work and instructed
men working in the area of the crane to inform the cranemen, and a
man was injured through another's failure to warn the crane driver
in time, it was held that the employer was liable.[2]

At the risk of stressing the obvious it should be emphasised that
an overhead travelling crane is a crane which travels overhead.
The point was of substance in the case of *Carrington* v. *John Summers
& Sons, Ltd.*,[3] in which case the plaintiff was injured when, slipping
on a piece of metal, his foot was caught in a gap between a crane and
the ground.   The crane travelled on wheels on the ground but the
crab of the crane travelled on a transverse girder supported by legs.
To such a crane the obligations concerning overhead travelling
cranes do not apply.

It will be noticed that the statutory obligation covers " All
parts . . . of lifting machines."   It is not always easy to decide what
are the parts of the machine.   In *Gatehouse* v. *John Summers &
Sons, Ltd.*,[4] an electrical cable carried current to a crane in order
to electrify its magnet.   The cable jammed and an electrician,
pulling it to make it free, caused the cable to break at a defective
joint.   He fell and was killed.   It was held that the cable did not

---

[1] [1944] K.B. 275; [1944] 1 All E.R. 235 *per* Lord GREENE, M.R., at pp. 278,
279 and p. 236 respectively.
[2] *Lotinga* v. *North Eastern Marine Engineering Co.* (*1938*), *Ltd.*, [1941] 2 K.B.
399; [1941] 3 All E.R. 1.
[3] [1957] 1 All E.R. 457; [1957] 1 W.L.R. 504.
[4] [1953] 2 All E.R. 117.

constitute one of the parts of a lifting machine and thus the defendants were not in breach of a duty imposed by that section.[1]

Floors, Stairs and Passages

Section 28 deals with floors, steps, stairs, passages and gangways and requires that such shall be of sound construction and properly maintained and that they shall be kept free from any obstruction, and from any substance likely to cause persons to slip, so far as is reasonably practicable. Every staircase whether in a building or affording a means of exit from a building must have a substantial handrail. If the staircase has an open side the handrail must be on that side; if both sides are open or if the staircase is one which owing to the nature of its construction or the condition of its surface is specially liable to cause accidents two handrails must be provided. Any open side of a staircase must be guarded by the provision and maintanance of a lower rail or other effective means. Wherever possible all openings in floors should be securely fenced and all ladders soundly constructed and properly maintained.[2] In the provisions as to floors it should be noticed that there is no reference to safety. Nevertheless the purpose of the legislation is clear. The floors are to be properly maintained and maintenance relates, in this connection, to the floors being kept in an efficient state and in good repair. A floor is in an efficient state when it is safe for people passing across or working on it and though the word "safe" is absent from the section it is to be read as though this were the end to be achieved.[3]

What are special circumstances liable to cause accident was considered in *Harris* v. *Rugby Portland Cement Co., Ltd.*[4] A factory staircase had a handrail on the open but not on the wall side. At the edge of the floor at the top of the stairs was a three-inch strip of metal which had become shiny through use. A foot or two away was a hatchway out of which tins of grease were issued from time to time. Harris slipped on some grease and was injured. No complaints had been made and Harris himself had constantly used the staircase in a four-year period of employment. The court held that the metal strip was not such a condition of the stairs as rendered them specially liable to accident, nor did the presence of the grease hatchway nor the grease on the stairs amount to the special circumstances that the section visualised.

As to what constitutes an opening in a floor it has been held that

---

[1] They were, however, in breach of one of the electrical regulations requiring joints to be of good construction.

[2] See *Rippon* v. *Port of London Authority and Russell & Co.* [1940] 1 K.B. 858; [1940] 1 All E.R. 637.

[3] *Payne* v. *Weldless Steel Tube Co., Ltd.*, [1956] 1 Q.B. 196; [1955] 3 All E.R. 612.

[4] [1955] 2 All E.R. 500.

castings dug out of deep sand spread over a foundry floor do represent such openings[1] but a dry dock does not.[2]

As might be expected, a provision having reference to the sound construction and proper maintenance of floors, steps, stairs and passages has not been easy to interpret. *Latimer* v. *A.E.C., Ltd.*[3] laid down that the duty imposed was an absolute duty, but that the defendants were not in breach of the duty imposed when one of their workmen slipped on a patch of oil and water. The decision rested on a distinction between the floor itself and substances on the floor. The 1959 Act[4] removed the effects of this case by adding the duty to keep the floor free from obstructions or substances likely to cause a person to slip. There has followed a spate of litigation on what factually constitutes an obstruction.[5]

Safe Access and Work Place

The next section provides that means of access to every place at which any person has at any time to work must be as safe as reasonably practicable and every such place of work must be similarly made and kept as safe as is reasonably practicable.[6] The last part of the section dealing with the place of work was added by the 1959 Act.[7] This does not refer merely to structural and permanent features. The plaintiff in *Callaghan* v. *Kidd* (*Fred*) & *Son* (*Engineers*), *Ltd.*,[8] tripped over certain iron bars left lying on the floor and was injured by a revolving grindstone. It was the duty of certain employees to carry iron bars to the grindstone and to proceed at once with the grinding. On the occasion in question an employee had left the bars on the floor and the plaintiff, intent on his work, did not see them. It was held that the employers were liable to the plaintiff.

The reasoning of *Callaghan's* case was applied in *Hosking* v. *De Havilland Aircraft Co., Ltd.*[9] Contractors were employed by the occupiers to conduct certain building operations on land attached to their factory. The contractors built a trench across which they laid a plank to be used by their own workmen and those of the occupier; one of the latter crossed the plank which broke, causing him to fall into the trench and injuring him. It was held that the plank was

---

[1] *Harrison* v. *Metropolitan-Vickers Electrical Co., Ltd.*, [1954] 1 All E.R. 404.

[2] *Bath* v. *British Transport Commission*, [1954] 2 All E.R. 542.

[3] [1952] 2 Q.B. 701; [1952] 1 All E.R. 1302.

[4] S. 4.

[5] *Drummond* v. *Harland Engineering Co., Ltd.*, [1963] S.L.T. 115; *Dorman Long* (*Steel*), *Ltd.* v. *Bell*, [1964] 1 All E.R. 617; [1964] 1 W.L.R. 333; *Pengelley* v. *Bell Push Co., Ltd.*, [1964] 1 All E.R. 613; [1964] 1 W.L.R. 433; *Churchill* v. *Louis Marx* (1964), 108 Sol. Jo. 334 and *Marshall* v. *Ericsson Telephones, Ltd.*, [1964] 3 All E.R. 609; [1964] 1 W.L.R. 1367.

[6] Factories Act, 1961, s. 29 (1); see *Rippon* v. *Port of London Authority and Russell & Co.*, *supra*; and also *Thomas* v. *Bristol Aeroplane Co., Ltd.*, [1954] 2 All E.R. 1

[7] S. 5.

[8] [1944] K.B. 560; [1944] 1 All E.R. 525; but where the obstruction is temporary and unusual, see *Levesley* v. *Thos. Firth and John Brown, Ltd.*, [1953] 2 All E.R. 866.

[9] [1949] 1 All E.R. 540

a " gangway " within the meaning of section 25 (1) of the 1937 Act, (now s. 28 (1)), and that the occupiers, since they were carrying on work in the vicinity and the plank had been put there for the benefit of their workmen as well as those of the contractors, were under a duty to see that it was of sound construction and properly maintained. They were also held to be in breach of their duty under section 26 of the 1937 Act, (now s. 29), in that they had not, so far as was reasonably practicable, maintained a safe means of access.[1]

It should be noticed that the duty to provide a safe means of access is qualified by the phrases "to every place at which any person has at any time to work" and "as far as is reasonably practicable." So that where an employee was walking along a passage to a canteen and slipped on a greasy substance, it was held that section 26 of the 1937 Act (now s. 29) was not applicable, for this was not a means of access to a place of work; nor was section 25 of the 1937 Act (now s. 28) applicable, for the presence of grease upon a floor did not constitute a defect in the floor itself.[2] This last point would be decided differently since the amendment of s. 25 by the 1959 Act that we have just considered.

The onus of proof is important. It has been held that the injured workman claiming breach of section 29 has not got the duty to show that it was reasonably practicable to avoid that danger. The defendant can establish that he has gone as far as is reasonably practicable, but the opposite point need not be established by the plaintiff.[3]

The words "as far as is reasonably practicable" raise more difficulty and the determination of their precise importance has not always been helped by the decisions of the courts. It will be recalled that in *Whitby* v. *Burt, Boulton and Hayward, Ltd.*[4] a workman stripping asbestos sheets from a roof was successful in sustaining an action for breach of the statutory duty imposed by section 26 of the 1937 Act, (now s. 29) when the wooden roof supports collapsed, causing a fall and injury. It was held that the occupiers were liable under section 26 (1) even though the building operations on the roof were being conducted by independent contractors. The decision raises difficulties and it may be asked whether it is reasonably practicable for the occupiers to provide a safe means of access for men who were working under the control of others and who were, so to speak, themselves engaged in removing the means of access involved. The decision was subjected to some criticism[5] because of

---

[1] It was further held that the occupiers were entitled to be indemnified by the contractors to the extent of damages awarded to the plaintiff.

[2] *Davies* v. *De Havilland Aircraft Co., Ltd.*, [1951] 1 K.B. 50; [1950] 2 All E.R. 582.

[3] *Nimmo* v. *Alexander Cowan & Sons*, [1968] A.C. 107, [1967] 3 All E. R. 187.

[4] [1947] K.B. 918; [1947] 2 All E.R. 324.

[5] See *Dorman, Long & Co., Ltd.* v. *Hillier*, [1951] 1 All E.R. 357.

the difficulty in saying that the place where the fall occurred was access as opposed to place of work. This distinction need no longer be drawn for the 1959 Act put place of work on the same footing as means of access.

It will have been noted that this section refers to " person " and is wide enough to include those who are not employed in the factory as servants of the occupier. Thus in *Whitby's* case DENNING, J., held that servants of an independent contractor, or the independent contractor himself, could sue the occupier under this section.[1]

Where work is at a place from which the worker is liable to fall a distance of more than six feet, six inches, then, unless there is a secure foothold and where necessary, secure hand-hold, all reasonably practicable means by fencing or otherwise must be taken to ensure his safety.[2]

Dangerous Fumes

Where work has to be done inside any chamber, tank, vat, pit, pipe, flue or similar confined space, in which dangerous fumes are likely to be present, a manhole must be provided unless there is other adequate means of egress. The manhole must be not less than eighteen inches long and sixteen inches wide or, if circular in shape, not less than eighteen inches in diameter. In the case of mobile plant (for example, tank wagons) the exit provided must be not less than sixteen inches long and fourteen inches wide or if circular in shape not less than sixteen inches in diameter. In addition, no person shall enter any such confined space unless he is wearing a suitable breathing apparatus and has been authorised to enter by a responsible person, and, where practicable, is wearing a belt with a rope securely attached of which the free end is held by a person outside capable of pulling him out.[3] Breathing apparatus, reviving apparatus and belts must be kept readily accessible and a sufficient number of persons employed must be trained in the use of such apparatus.[4] The breathing, reviving and rescuing apparatus must be thoroughly examined by a competent person at least once a month or at such other intervals as may be prescribed and a report of such examination signed by the person concerned shall be kept available for inspection. Moreover, without prejudice to the above requirements, no person may enter or remain in any chamber, tank, vat, etc., unless he is ensured of a supply of air adequate for respiration and the

---

[1] See also *Lavender* v. *Diamints, Ltd.*, [1949] 1 K.B. 585; [1949] 1 All E.R. 532.

[2] Factories Act, 1961, s. 29(2); *Wigley* v. *British Vinegars Ltd.*, [1964] A.C. 307; [1962] 3 All E.R. 161: And see *Ginty* v. *Belmont Building Supplies Ltd.*, [1959] 1 All E.R. 414 for a discussion of what steps constitute " providing " means for ensuring safety. Leaving provision to an employee without enough skill or experience will not avoid liability: *Ross* v. *Associated Portland Cement Manufacturers, Ltd.*, [1964] 2 All E.R. 452; [1964] 1 W.L.R. 768.

[3] Factories Act, 1961, s. 30 (1)–(3); the chief inspector may, by certificate, grant exemption from compliance with these requirements: s. 30 (8).

[4] Factories Act, 1961, s. 30 (6).

rendering harmless of fumes or he is wearing a suitable breathing apparatus.[1] No work may be permitted in any boiler furnace or flue until it has been made sufficiently safe by ventilation or otherwise.[2]

Explosive or Inflammable Gas

Where, as the result of any grinding, sieving, or other process dust is liable to escape and to explode on ignition steps must be taken to prevent the explosion, by the enclosure of the plant, by the removal or prevention of accumulations of dust and by the exclusion or effective enclosure of possible sources of ignition. If the plant is not constructed so as to withstand the pressure of any such explosion steps must be taken to restrict the spread and effects of the explosion by effective appliances. Where any part of a plant contains explosive or inflammable gas or vapour under pressure greater than atmospheric pressure the Act provides special provisions for the opening of that part of the plant as it does also when any welding, brazing, soldering or cutting operation is contemplated.[3]

Steam Boilers and Receivers

Steam boilers must be provided with suitable safety valves fixed directly to, or as close as possible to the boiler and so adjusted as to prevent the boiler working at a pressure greater than the maximum permissible working pressure; with a suitable stop valve connecting the boiler to the steam pipe; a correct steam pressure gauge indicating the pressure of steam in the boiler with the maximum permissible working pressure marked in a distinctive colour; at least one water gauge of transparent material; means for attaching a test pressure gauge; and, unless externally fixed, a suitable fusible plug or an efficient low water alarm device.[4] Elaborate provisions govern the conditions under which persons are allowed to enter a steam boiler, which is one of a range of two or more, the construction of such boilers, their periodic examination, and the use of second-hand boilers.[5] Steam receivers and containers and air containers are subject to analogous provisions.[6]

Gasholders

Gasholders must be of sound construction, properly maintained and examined externally by a competent person at least once in every period of two years and a record of the examination kept. In the case of any gasholder of which any lift has been in use more than twenty years, the internal sheeting must be examined at least once in every ten years by a competent person by cutting samples from the crown and sides of the holder or by other sufficient means. The

---

[1] *Ibid.*, s. 30 (9).
[2] *Ibid.*, s. 30 (10).
[3] *Ibid.*, s. 31.
[4] *Ibid.*, s. 32 (1), (2).
[5] Factories Act, 1961, s. 34
[6] *Ibid.*, ss. 35-37.

person making the examination must provide a report which must
be kept available for inspection. Where a factory contains more
than one gasholder, every gasholder must be marked with a distinguishing number or letters. The repair or demolition of gasholders
must be carried out under the supervision of persons of experience.[1]
The occupier of the factory or a responsible official authorised to do
so must sign a record showing the date of the construction (as
nearly as it can be ascertained) of the oldest lift of every gasholder in
the factory; the record must be kept available for inspection.

Occupier

Although the interpretation section of the Act[2] is very full it does
not define the term "occupier." For any such definition we must
turn to the cases. The "occupier" is the person who runs the
business, and this is in every case a question of fact. In *Fitton* v.
Wood[3] the defendant owned a brickyard which he leased to another.
This other gave his exclusive services to brick-making, managed
the yard and engaged his own workpeople. Wood was held not to
have contravened the Workshops Regulation Act, 1867, when the
lessee employed a child contrary to that Act. The respondents in
Turner v. *Courtaulds, Ltd.*,[4] were also charged with breach of factory
regulations relating to an electrical switchboard. Work on the
switchboard was being carried out by another company and the
switchboard, though on their premises, had not been handed over
in working order to the respondents. They were held none the less
to be its occupiers and, consequently, to be liable for the breach of
regulations. In another case the defendants owned a shipbuilding
yard in which was a vessel they were building but had not completed. They built a staging to be used by another company; the
staging was defective and the plaintiff was injured. It was held
that the respondents and not the other company were in occupation
of the staging.[5]

Fire Precautions

The provisions requiring precautions to be taken to prevent fire
and to ensure maximum safety if a fire occurs are perhaps as detailed
as any in the Act. One of the chief purposes of the 1959 Act was to
strengthen the provisions on this topic. The provisions as to means
of escape in case of fire apply (i) to every factory in which more than
twenty people are employed; (ii) to every factory completed before
the passing of the 1937 Act in which more than ten people are employed in the same building above the first floor or more than twenty
feet above the ground level; (iii) to every factory in or under which

---

[1] *Ibid.*, s. 39.
[2] *Ibid.*, s. 176.
[3] (1875), 32 L.T. 554.
[4] [1937] 1 All E.R. 467.
[5] *Smith* v. *Cammell Laird & Co., Ltd.*, [1940] A.C. 242; [1939] 4 All E.R. 381.

explosive or highly inflammable materials are stored for use and (iv) to every factory which is constructed or converted to factory purposes after the passing of the 1937 Act in which more than ten persons are employed in the same building on any floor above the ground floor.[1] Every such factory must be certified by the fire authority[2] as having such means of escape in case of fire as may reasonably be required. The fire authority may refuse the grant of a certificate unless certain alterations are carried out. A time limit is specified for these alterations and the refusal is deemed to arise at the end of that period if the alterations have not been carried out. If any premises are used as a factory in respect of which no certificate is issued, the Act provides appropriate penalties. The certificate must give in detail the means of escape provided and the maximum number of persons employed or proposed to be employed.[3] The specified means of escape must be properly maintained and kept free from obstruction.[4] The fire authority may examine the factory to see whether changed conditions have made the existing means of escape insufficient. If, after a certificate has been granted, it is proposed to make any material extension or structural alteration or materially to increase the number of persons employed, or to begin to store inflammable or explosive materials, or materially to increase such storage the occupier must give written notice to the fire authority. The fire authority must then determine whether the existing means of escape are adequate and if not, may, by written notice, require the occupier to make such alterations, within such period, as shall be specified. Where an inspector is of opinion that dangerous conditions in respect of escape from fire exist in any factory he may give written notice to the fire authority which must arrange for the examination of the factory and by written notice require the occupier to make any specified alterations. When the alterations have been carried out the fire authority must amend the certificate or issue a new one, and if the alterations are not carried out the fire authority may, without prejudice to any other proceedings which might be taken, cancel the certificate. If a fire authority does not, within one month, act upon the representations made to it by an inspector, the inspector himself may do all the things which the fire authority might have done and recover as a civil debt from the fire authority such expenses as he incurs and are not recovered from any other person provided that they are not incurred in connection with unsuccessful legal proceedings.[5] Where the inspector believes that the fire-escape conditions are so dangerous that the factory ought not to be used, he may, instead of serving notice on the fire authority, apply to a court of summary jurisdiction which

---

[1] Factories Act, 1961, s. 45.
[2] This will be determined under the Fire Services Act, 1947; see Factories Act, 1961, s. 47.
[3] Factories Act, 1961, s. 40.
[4] *Ibid.*, s. 41 (1).
[5] Factories Act, 1961, s. 42 (6).

court may prohibit the use of the factory until adequate steps have been taken to remedy the danger.[1]

An occupier who is aggrieved by the fire authority's or the inspector's use of the power given by sections 40 and 41 has a right of appeal to a court of summary jurisdiction.[2] The Secretary of State may make regulations governing means of escape in case of fire and the duty of seeing that these are complied with rests on the fire authority. The fire authorities have power to make bye-laws as to means of escape in case of fire, but such bye-laws are void in so far as they contain provisions inconsistent with regulations made by the Secretary of State.[3]

All doors in the factory must, whilst any person is in the factory either for employment or meals, be unlocked and be capable, easily and immediately, of being opened from the inside. Doors opening on to a staircase or corridor from any room in which more than ten persons are employed, and in the case of factories constructed or converted after the coming into effect of the 1937 Act all doors of exit from the factory, shall, except where they are sliding doors, be constructed to open outwards. In factories constructed or converted for use as such before the coming into operation of the 1937 Act in which more than ten persons are employed in the same building above the ground floor, any door which is not kept continuously open at the foot of a staircase affording a means of exit from the building, shall, except in the case of sliding doors, be constructed to open outwards. Hoistways in buildings constructed after the coming into operation of the 1937 Act must be completely enclosed in fire-resisting materials and means of access to the hoist must be fitted with fire-resisting doors. Windows, doors and other exits which afford means of escape or which give access to such means of escape other than means of exit in ordinary use must be marked with a notice in red letters. A warning clearly audible throughout the building must be installed in every factory where more than twenty persons are employed in the same building or in which explosive or highly inflammable materials are stored or used. The contents of rooms in which persons are employed must be arranged so that there is free passage way to a means of escape in case of fire.[4]

Where a factory has more than twenty persons employed above the first floor or more than twenty feet above ground level or has explosive or highly inflammable materials stored in it where persons are employed, effective steps must be taken to ensure that all persons employed are familiar with the means of escape, their use and the routine to be followed in case of fire.[5] The Secretary of State has power under this section to make regulations setting out the

---

[1] *Ibid.*, s. 41 (7).
[2] *Ibid.*, s. 43.
[3] *Ibid.*, s. 46.
[4] Factories Act, 1961, s. 48.
[5] *Ibid.*, s. 49.

steps to be taken. He may similarly make regulations as to measures to be taken to reduce the risk of fire breaking out or spreading, which measures may include prescribing requirements as to internal construction and the materials used in internal construction.[1]

In every factory there must be appropriate means for fighting fire, placed readily available for use and properly maintained.[2] Again the Secretary of State has wide power to specify procedures by regulation. For example regulations may be made specifying the means to be provided for notifying the fire brigade of an outbreak of fire.[3] All means of giving warning of fire are to be tested or examined at least once every three months and whenever an Inspector requires.[4] The Secretary of State has power to make special regulations requiring special provisions in factories or classes of factories where the number or nature of accidents occurring indicates the need.[5]

Finally, if on the complaint of the inspector, a court of summary jurisdiction is satisfied that any part of the ways, works, machinery or plant in a factory is in a condition or is so constructed that its use involves risk of bodily injury or that a process or work is carried on so as to cause such risk the court may prohibit its use either absolutely or until it is repaired or altered or may require the occupier to take such steps as may be specified for removing the danger.[6] And similarly the court may, on being satisfied that any factory or part of a factory is in such condition or is so constructed or placed that any process or work carried out or intended to be carried out cannot be so with due regard to the safety, health, and welfare of persons employed, by order prohibit the use thereof for the purpose of that process or work. This power is exercisable also in relation to new factory premises where they are intended to be used as a factory and any order made by the court may contain an indefinite prohibition or operate until such steps are taken as will eliminate the elements of danger.[7]

(5) General Provisions as to Welfare.—The third part of the Act is concerned with general welfare provisions. An adequate supply of drinking water, either from public mains or from some other source approved in writing by the district council, must be maintained at suitable points conveniently accessible to all persons. Where the water supply is not laid on it must be contained in suitable vessels and renewed daily and, whether the supply is laid on or not, it must, where the inspector so directs, be clearly marked

---

[1] *Ibid.*, s. 50.
[2] *Ibid.*, s. 51.
[3] *Ibid.*, s. 51 (3).
[4] *Ibid.*, s. 52.
[5] *Ibid.*, s. 53.
[6] *Ibid.*, ss. 54, 55.
[7] Factories Act, 1961, s. 55.

"Drinking Water." Unless the water is supplied from an upward jet from which the employees can conveniently drink, suitable cups and facilities for rinsing them must be provided.[1] Suitable washing facilities must be provided including clean running hot and cold or warm water, soap and clean towels or other suitable means of cleaning and drying. The facilities provided must be conveniently accessible and kept in a clean and orderly condition. The Secretary of State may prescribe a standard of adequate and suitable washing facilities; he also has a power to exempt from compliance with the provisions in those cases where their application would be unreasonable.[2] Adequate and suitable accommodation for clothing not worn during working hours must be provided and reasonable arrangements made for drying such clothing.[3]

Where employees have reasonable opportunities for sitting, not detrimental to their work, suitable facilities for sitting must be provided and maintained; and where a substantial part of any work can be done sitting a seat must be provided and maintained for the employed person of a design and construction suitable for him and the work, with a footrest where necessary. The seat must be adequately and properly supported whilst in use for the purpose for which it is provided.[4]

A first-aid box or cupboard must be provided and maintained in an accessible place and where more than one hundred and fifty persons are employed an additional box or cupboard for every one hundred and fifty persons. The box or cupboard must contain nothing but first-aid appliances or requisites and must be in the charge of a responsible person who must, if more than fifty persons are employed, be trained in first-aid treatment. The person in charge must be readily available during working hours. A notice must be affixed in every workroom stating the name of the person in charge of the first-aid box or cupboard provided in respect of that room. If an ambulance room is provided at the factory and such arrangements are made as to ensure the immediate treatment there of all injuries occurring in the factory, the inspector may exempt the factory from the requirements of this section.[5]

The Secretary of State has power to make special regulations requiring reasonable steps to be taken to secure the welfare of workers either in addition to or substitution or variation of any of the welfare provisions in this section of the Act. Such regulations,

---

[1] *Ibid.*, s. 57.

[2] *Ibid.*, s. 58 and see also s. 180.

[3] *Ibid.*, s. 59. The Secretary of State has power to prescribe standards and exempt from compliance. See also s. 180.

[4] *Ibid.*, s. 60.

[5] Factories Act, 1961, s. 61. The standard required of the responsible person who is trained in first aid is laid down by the Secretary of State.

however, will not apply to factories in which the only persons employed are members of the same family dwelling there.[1]

(6) Health, Safety and Welfare.—The first three Parts of the Act are concerned with the general provisions regarding health, safety and welfare; Part IV of the Act is concerned with special provisions and regulations covering them.

Dust

In every factory in which any injurious or offensive dust, fume or other impurity is given off or in which there is created any substantial quantity of dust of any kind, all practicable measures must be taken to protect the persons employed against inhalation of the impurities. In particular, wherever it is practicable, exhaust appliances must be provided and maintained, as near as possible to the point of origin of the impurity so as to prevent it entering the air of any workroom. Stationary internal combustion engines must not be used unless provision is made to conduct the exhaust gases into the open air, and the engine (except when it is being tested) must be so partitioned off from any room in which people are employed (other than those attending to the engine) as to prevent the fumes from entering the room.[2]

The operation of the duty to remove dusts and fumes was discussed in *Franklin* v. *Gramophone Co., Ltd.*[3] and the court had to consider three questions. The first was whether the regulations as to the grinding of metals made under the Factory and Workshop Act, 1901, and confirmed by the 1937 Act were capable of superseding the statutory requirements—for it was found as a fact that though the deceased workman had died as the result of inhaling dust from abrasive wheels—he was outside the ambit of the regulations. So far as the regulations were concerned, the occupier had fully complied with them. The second question was whether the occupier, being free from fault under the Grinding of Metals Regulations was under the duty of conforming with the obligations of the Act itself so far as the removal of dusts was concerned. This in turn raised the question whether the power to make regulations was a power to modify or even exclude the operative section of the Act. The court answered this question in the affirmative and construed the regulations as saying to the occupier of any factory where relevant processes were conducted:

> " Carry these regulations out honestly and carefully and you will have complied with all the statutory requirements incumbent on you and your factory."[4]

---

[1] *Ibid.*, s. 62.

[2] *Ibid.*, s. 63.

[3] [1948] 1 K.B. 542; [1948] 1 All E.R. 353.

[4] [1948] 1 K.B. 542; [1948] 1 All E.R. 353, *per* SCOTT, L.J., at pp. 551 and 356 respectively.

The third question discussed by the court was whether the decision that no liability arose under the statute precluded the plaintiff from recovering at common law: Could an occupier fulfil all his statutory obligations and yet be guilty of negligence at common law?   The answer of the court was that he could.   Indeed, SOMERVELL, L.J., said that

> "it is the regulation itself coupled with the evidence which, I find, establishes negligence. The regulation by saying that the appliances must be there if one or more people are employed mainly in or incidental to the process, is an indication that injury is to be apprehended by continuous proximity to an abrasive grinder. Although neither the deceased nor anyone in the shops was wholly or mainly employed at this grinder, there was, as I have said, a lathe within four or five feet of it at which the deceased . . . was continuously at work except when using the grinder . . . [and] I think in leaving this grinder as it was with someone working in close proximity, the defendants fell short of the standard of care in this matter which the law imposes."[1]

It should be noted that since *Franklin's* case the regulations have been amended with the purpose, *inter alia*, of providing that, except where they speak specifically to the contrary, the requirements of the regulations shall be in addition to and not in derogation of the Act.

In *Mist* v. *Toleman & Sons*[2] a workman employed on processes which gave off dust and in which exhaust appliances did not conform with the Act, was found to be suffering from tuberculosis. There was evidence of infection before entering the defendants' employment, but it was agreed that exertion might have made the inactive tubercle active, and though dust itself would not do this, coughing produced by dust might. It was held that the object of section 47 of the 1937 Act (now section 63), was to prevent every injurious effect of dust and not merely tuberculosis and that the plaintiff had not discharged the onus of showing that he suffered from an injury by reason of the failure of his employers to conform with section 47.

The section requires that "all practical measures" shall be taken to protect persons employed and the meaning of these words was discussed by the Court of Appeal in *Adsett* v. *K. & L. Steelfounders and Engineers, Ltd.*[3] It was

> "argued by the plaintiff that it was practicable for the defendant to install the new extractor plant because they ought to have thought of it earlier.[4] I do not think that that is the right test. In deciding whether all practicable measures were taken one must have regard to the state of knowledge at the material time, and, particularly, to the knowledge of scientific experts."[5]

---

[1] *Ibid.*, at pp. 558-9 and 360 respectively.
[2] [1946] 1 All E.R. 139; see also *Ebbs* v. *James Whitson & Co., Ltd.*, [1952] 2 Q.B. 877; [1952] 2 All E.R. 192.
[3] [1953] 2 All E.R. 320.
[4] They had in fact installed a plant of a kind embodying new ideas.
[5] [1953] 2 All E.R. 320 *per* SINGLETON, L.J., at p. 322.

Graham v. *Co-operative Wholesale Society, Ltd.*,[1] gave section 47 of the 1937 Act, (now s. 63), an extremely narrow, possibly too narrow an interpretation. The decision that dust, from a wood not known to be dangerous, which settled on the plaintiff, causing him skin trouble, did not give rise to a cause of action, was doubtless correct. But the suggestion that the obligation in section 47 was to take all reasonable measures to prevent accumulation of dust, yet not to prevent that dust settling on the plaintiff, has little to commend it. A surer basis for the decision lies in the lack of knowledge of the injurious effects of the dust. This reasoning was adopted in the case of *Crookall* v. *Vickers Armstrong Ltd.*[2] People were employed in a foundry in which quantities of siliceous sand were used though the dangers arising from the use of the sand were not known until 1942. Immediately the defendants were aware of the danger they kept in store a sufficient number of masks for use by workmen. Despite the efforts of the manager from time to time to persuade the men to use masks few did so. The plaintiff, when found to be suffering from silicosis, brought action for breach of section 47. It was held that he was entitled to succeed. Once the defendants were aware of the danger, they were under the duty to take all reasonable steps to diminish the risk. This, on the facts, they had failed to do; moreover the duty to take all practical measures included the provision of masks and the effort to induce men to use them. " There was a failure," said GLYN-JONES, J.[3]

> " to press on the men's representatives with earnestness and ardour, the need for these masks, so as to try at least to secure their strong help in persuading them to wear them."

Richards v. *Highway Ironfounders (West Bromwich), Ltd.*[4] shows clearly the dual character of the obligation as to dusts, fumes and impurities:

> " The first thing to notice about the sub-section is the dichotomy, which the learned judge observed, between cases of the emission ' of dust or fume . . . of such a character . . . as to be likely to be injurious ' on the one hand, and ' substantial quantity of dust of any kind ' on the other hand. Having regard to the state of knowledge, (until about 1950 the employers were unaware of the dangers arising) it may be taken that the dust with which we are here concerned was not, at any material date, dust within the first branch of the sub-section, since it could not fairly be regarded then as likely to cause silicosis. On the other hand there is no doubt that the dust was emitted in substantial quantities so that it fell within the second branch of the sub-section. From that it follows that, since the dust was in substantial quantities, there arose an

---

[1] [1957] 1 All E.R. 654; [1957] 1 W.L.R. 511.
[2] [1955] 2 All E.R. 12; [1955] 1 W.L.R. 659.
[3] *Ibid.*, at pp. 17, 666 respectively.
[4] [1955] 3 All E.R. 205.

obligation . . . to take ' all practical measures . . . to protect the persons employed against inhalation of the dust.' "[1]

The question whether, in the case under discussion, the defendants had committed a breach of their statutory duty by their failure to provide masks was sent back for retrial. As a result it was held that masks were not a practical measure, since at the relevant time there was no knowledge of the harmful effects of the invisible sand particles.[2]

Poisonous Substances

Where, in any room lead, arsenic or other poisonous substance is so used as to give rise to any dust or fume, a person shall not be permitted to take food or drink in the room or be allowed to remain in the room during meal or rest intervals other than rest intervals allowed in the course of a spell of continuous employment. The Secretary of State may, by regulation, prescribe certain processes as giving rise to siliceous or asbestos dust and where he does so no person may be permitted to remain in the room in which the process is carried on for meal or rest intervals. Suitable provision must be made to enable the employees to take meals elsewhere in the factory.[3]

Protection of Eyes

Where the Secretary of State specifies a process as one involving special risk of injury to the eyes suitable goggles or screens must be provided.[4] Goggles are not provided within the meaning of these requirements, where, after hanging for some time on a machine for the use of the operative, they are removed to the foreman's office to prevent abusive handling of them.[5] The process relating to which effective goggles or screens must be provided must, apparently, be a process of the occupiers of the factory, which covers only persons employed by the occupiers. Where, therefore, a workman employed by contractors was engaged in breaking up concrete with a pneumatic drill in a factory and injured his eye, goggles not being provided, it was held that he could not succeed in an action for breach of statutory duty. The process in which he was engaged was not that of the occupier of the factory, nor was he their servant.[6] The duty is to provide " suitable " goggles and " suitable " does not mean perfect. It is a defect of most goggles that, because of the heat of the face, they tend to become misty. An employee to whom this happened and who, without taking them off, pulled them sufficiently away from the eyes to wipe away the mist and was

---

[1] *Per* Sir RAYMOND EVERSHED, M.R., at p. 209.
[2] [1957] 2 All E.R. 162.
[3] Factories Act, 1961, s. 64.
[4] *Ibid.*, s. 65.
[5] *Finch* v. *Telegraph Construction and Maintenance Co., Ltd.,* [1949] 1 All E.R. 452; see also *Williams* v. *Falkirk Iron Co., Ltd.,* [1951] 1 All E.R. 294, n.
[6] *Whalley* v. *Briggs Motor Bodies, Ltd.,* [1954] 2 All E.R. 193.

injured by a fragment of metal whilst doing so, was held to be unable to recover.

"... while the obligation to provide suitable goggles is quite clearly an absolute obligation, there is no absolute obligation that the goggles so provided shall ensure protection."[1]

The Minister may also make regulations extending the provision and use in weaving factories of shuttles which are not capable of being threaded by mouth suction.[2]

The use of white phosphorus in the manufacture of matches is prohibited.[3] Matches made with white phosphorus may not be imported into the United Kingdom.[4]

Humidity

The Act then attempts to deal with the special problems arising from the maintenance by artificial means, of humidity in factories. Before or on the first occasion that artificial humidity is introduced into a factory the occupier must give written notice to the inspector. Unless special regulations apply there must be provided and maintained in every humid room two hygrometers of which one shall be fixed at the centre and one at the side or in such place as may be directed or sanctioned by the inspector so as to be plainly visible to the persons employed.[5] Near to each hygrometer the current table of humidity must be hung.[6] The hygrometers must be read twice daily, between ten and eleven o'clock in the morning and between three and four o'clock in the afternoon.[7] The readings must be noted on a record which must also be hung near the hygrometer and when filled up must be filed for reference. There must be no artificial humidification at any time when the wet bulb thermometer exceeds $72\frac{1}{2}°$ or 80°F. in the case of a room in which the spinning of cotton or in which the spinning of merino or cashmere by the French or dry process or the spinning or combing of wool by that process is carried on. Nor shall there be any humidification at any time when the difference between the readings of the dry and wet bulb thermometer is less than that indicated in the table of humidity. Water which is liable to cause injury to health or to yield effluvia must not be used for humidification.[8]

Work must not be carried on in any underground room certified by the inspector as unsuitable. An underground room is one of which one half or more than one half the whole height, measured

---

[1] *Daniels* v. *Ford Motor Co., Ltd.*, [1955] 1 All E.R. 218 at p. 221. See also *Rees* v. *Bernard Hastie & Co., Ltd.*, [1953] 1 Q.B. 328; [1953] 1 All E.R. 375.

[2] Factories Act, 1961, s. 66.

[3] *Ibid.*, s. 67.   [4] *Ibid.*, s. 77 (1).

[5] *Ibid.*, s. 68. The inspector may direct that one hygrometer is sufficient: s. 52 (3).

[6] See Schedule I of the Act.

[7] Where persons are employed before 6 a.m. or after 8 p.m., at such times other than those stated above as may be directed by the inspector.

[8] Factories Act, 1961, s. 68.

from floor to ceiling is below the surface of the ground adjoining or adjacent to the room.[1]   Without prejudice to the rule as to underground workrooms a basement bakehouse[2] must not be used as such unless it was so used at the passing of the Act and a certificate of suitability had been issued by the district council.   A basement bakehouse not used as such for a period exceeding twelve months must not be used as such again.   The district council must, in every fifth year, examine every basement bakehouse having a certificate of suitability.   If satisfied, they will give written notice sanctioning the continued use of the premises.   If the council is not satisfied written notice of the expiration of the certificate of suitability must be given and the place must not thereafter be used as a bakehouse. There is a right of appeal to a court of summary jurisdiction which may invalidate the notice of the council and direct that the certificate of suitability shall continue to operate.[3]   Apparently the court may do this though the bakehouse was unsuitable at the time of the council's notice, if, before the court hearing, the defects have been remedied.[4]

Heavy Loads

No person must be employed to carry or lift loads so heavy as to be likely to cause him injury,[5] and female young persons must not be employed in any part of a factory where glass (other than lamp-blown glass) is blown or melted or is annealed or where brine is evaporated in open pans or salt is stored[6].   Women and young persons shall not be employed in processes involving the reduction or treatment, by furnace, of zinc or lead ores, nor in the manipulation, reduction or treatment of ashes containing lead, the desilverising of lead, the manufacture of solder or alloys containing more than ten per cent. of lead, nor in the manufacture of any oxide, carbonate, sulphate, chromate, acetate, nitrate or silicate of lead, nor in mixing or pasting in connection with the manufacture or repair of electrical accumulators nor shall they be employed in the cleaning of workrooms in which any of these processes is carried on.[7]   They must not be exposed to the danger of lead dusts, fumes or splashes unless detailed safety precautions, including the use of protective clothing and periodical medical inspection, are provided.[8]

The Secretary of State is given power to make special regulations on being satisfied that any manufacture, machinery, plant, equip-

---

[1] *Ibid.*, s. 69.

[2] *I.e.*, a bakehouse any bakery room of which is more than three feet below the surface of the footway of the adjoining street (Factories Act, 1961, s. 70 (4)).

[3] Factories Act, 1961, s. 70.

[4] *Fulham Borough Council* v. *A.B. Hemmings, Ltd.*, [1940] 2 K.B. 669; [1940] 3 All E.R. 625.

[5] Factories Act, 1961, s. 72.   The Secretary of State has power to prescribe maximum weights.

[6] *Ibid.*, s. 73.

[7] Factories Act, 1961, s. 74.

[8] *Ibid.*, s. 75.

ment, appliance or process or description of manual labour causes risk of bodily injury. Such special regulations may prohibit, modify or limit hours of employment or prohibit, limit or control the use of materials.[1] If the Secretary of State uses this power to prohibit the use of any material its importation into the country may be prohibited by Order in Council and it would thereupon become an offence to sell or offer the same for sale. An inspector may take for analysis samples of materials when he suspects a contravention of regulations and which he thinks might be likely to cause bodily injury to employed persons. The occupier or his agent may require the sample to be divided into three parts : one for himself, one for future comparison and one for the analyist. The analysis made by the government chemist must not be disclosed except so far as is necessary for the purposes of a prosecution. A certificate of a government chemist is available as evidence but either party may require the maker of the certificate to be called to testify.[2] The certificate will not, of course, be conclusive evidence if the defendant gives evidence on his own behalf,[3] but it is otherwise if it is not contradicted.[4]

Plans relating to cotton cloth factories must not be approved by a local authority unless they are certified by the inspector as not contravening the regulations made under the Factory and Workshop (Cotton Cloth Factories) Act, 1929.[5]

(7) Notification of Accidents and Industrial Diseases.— Part V of the Act is concerned with industrial accidents and diseases. In considering the law relating to industrial injuries we shall discuss the legal notion of an accident as required by the National Insurance (Industrial Injuries) Act, 1946.[6] It does not follow that the word accident will be interpreted identically when it appears in different statutes, but it is extremely unlikely that the definitions of accident as evolved at the cost of much litigation would be lightly set aside. The ensuing uncertainty would be calamitous. Thus we can take it that for the purposes of the Factories Act, 1961, an accident will be " any unintended and unexpected occurrence which produces hurt or loss."[7] It will include pneumonia following upon abnormal exposure to the ventilating draught of a colliery;[8] or the nervous shock to one servant at the sight of another's injuries.[9] But to constitute an accident there must be some event or occurrence which

---

[1] *Ibid.,* s. 76.
[2] *Ibid.,* s. 78.
[3] *Hewitt* v. *Taylor.* [1896] 1 Q.B. 287.
[4] *Robinson* v. *Newman* (1917), 86 L. J. K.B. 814.
[5] Factories Act, 1961, s. 79.
[6] See *infra,* Ch. IX.
[7] *Fenton* v. *Thorley & Co., Ltd.,* [1903] A.C. 443, *per* LINDLEY, L.J., at p. 453.
[8] *Coyle (or Brown)* v. *John Watson, Ltd.,* [1915] A.C.1.
[9] *Yates* v. *South Kirkby, etc. Collieries, Ltd.,* [1910] 2 K.B 538.

can be referred to a specific time and place.[1]   The dividing line between the various sets of circumstances may be difficult to draw but a disease which is the result of malignant industrial conditions of long standing cannot, unless it is so prescribed by regulations, legally be the result of an accident.   Thus the Factories Act makes provision for industrial diseases as distinct from industrial accidents and by so doing attempts to cope with these two great hazards of industry.

Where an accident occurs in a factory, to a person employed in the factory, which causes loss of life or disablement for more than three days from earning full wages at his usual work, written notice must be sent to the inspector forthwith.   Where disablement is later followed by death the occupier of the factory must inform the inspector as soon as the death comes to his knowledge.[2]   A medical practitioner who attends a patient whom he believes to be suffering from lead, phosphorous, arsenical or mercurial poisoning, anthrax, manganese poisoning, compressed air illness or toxic anæmia, contracted in a factory, must immediately inform the chief inspector of factories, whilst the occupier of the factory in which the disease is contracted must inform the district inspector and the employment medical adviser.[3]

The task following that report will be to investigate and report upon cases of death or injury caused by exposure to fumes or other noxious substances or due to other special causes as well as those deaths and injuries as to which he receives special notice from the inspector or receives notice as arising from a disease notifiable under the Act.   Special precautions are taken in the case of inquests on persons whose death may have arisen as the result of accident or disease of which notice must be given.   The coroner must adjourn the inquest until the inspector or some other representative of the Secretary of State is present to watch the proceedings.[4]

The Secretary of State is given power to direct that a formal investigation be made into the causes and circumstances of any accident occurring, or case of disease contracted or suspected to have been contracted, in a factory.   The investigation will be in open court and the person or persons appointed to constitute the court will have all the powers of a court of summary jurisdiction when acting as a court to hear informations under the Act and, in addition, certain powers detailed by the Act.[5]

---

[1] *Eke* v. *Hart-Dyke*, [1910] 2 K.B. 677.

[2] Factories Act, 1961, s. 80.   The Secretary of State has power, by regulation, to require notice to be given of any special class of explosion, accident, collapse of buildings, etc. (*ibid.*, s. 81).

[3] *Ibid.*, s. 82.

[4] *Ibid.*, s. 83.

[5] Factories Act, 1961, s. 84.

(8) Employment of Women and Young Persons.—Subject to certain exceptions no woman or young person shall be permitted to work for more than nine hours a day or forty-eight hours a week exclusive of meal and rest intervals,[1] whilst in the case of workers under the age of sixteen the maximum period is forty-four hours.[2] The period of employment must not exceed eleven hours a day. In the case of persons under the age of sixteen the employment must not begin earlier than seven o'clock in the morning nor end later than six o'clock in the evening and in the case of others eight o'clock in the evening or one o'clock in the afternoon on Saturday.[3] There shall be no continuous work period of more than four and a half hours without an interval of at least half an hour for a meal or rest, though the spell may be increased to five hours if an interval of not less than ten minutes is allowed during the spell.[4] Male young persons over the age of sixteen who are employed with men and upon whose continuous employment the men rely to be able to carry on their work, may be employed, as respects any spell of work beginning in the morning, for a spell of five hours.[5] The period of employment fixed for the factory by the occupier must be specified in a notice displayed in the factory together with particulars of the meal and rest intervals. Once they have been fixed, such periods must not be changed without notice to the factory inspector and to the employees by means of a notice displayed in the factory. In any case if it is proposed to change the periods more frequently than once in three months special cause must be shown, and allowed in writing by the inspector. Where the inspector, in writing, names a public clock the periods of employment and the permitted intervals for meals and rest must be regulated by that clock.[6]

Despite the provisions relating to the hours of labour laid down, it is permissible to increase them, in the case of women and young persons over the age of sixteen, by means of overtime working[7] where the pressure of work in the factory demands it. But in no case must the overtime exceed one hundred hours in any calendar year or six hours in any week nor shall it take place in the factory in more than twenty-five weeks in any calendar year. Moreover the calculation of the overtime worked is to take place according to a basis generous to the worker; for every fraction of an hour less than half an hour will count as half an hour and every fraction of an hour more than half an hour will be treated as an hour. Even so,

---

[1] *Ibid.*, s. 86 (*a*).

[2] *Ibid.*, s. 81 (1). The Secretary of State may, after enquiry, sanction working periods in particular industries of up to 48 hours a week (s. 87 (2)).

[3] *Ibid.*, s. 86 (*b*). But the Secretary of State has power to sanction exceptions (ss. 101 and 102).

[4] *Ibid.*, s. 86 (*c*).

[5] *Ibid.*, s. 105.

[6] *Ibid.*, s. 88.

[7] Overtime working means any period during which a woman or young person is at work outside the period of employment fixed by notice as required by the Act.

the total hours, including overtime, to be worked by the woman or young person, exclusive of meal and rest intervals, must not exceed ten a day, nor the period of employment exceed twelve hours nor be extended outside the hours permitted by the Act,[1] except that in the case of women it may extend to nine o'clock in the evening on week-days other than Saturday.[2] If the occupier of a factory allows to any women or young persons who are to be employed overtime, on any day, a rest or meal interval in addition to any interval fixed for the day by a notice required under the Act, he may employ during that interval women or young persons who are not to be employed overtime on that day. In all other circumstances the law relating to continuous employment and intervals for meals or rest must apply to overtime employment just as it applies to other employment.

The Secretary of State may make regulations prohibiting or restricting the otherwise permitted overtime employment of young persons where he is satisfied that such employment is prejudicial to their health,[3] and where he receives representations that overtime employment may be reduced without serious detriment to an industry concerned he may direct an enquiry to be held. In reaching this decision he will consult such associations of employers or employees, such industrial councils, wages councils or similar bodies as would seem to be affected. If, as a result of the enquiry, he is satisfied, he may, by regulations, make such modification of the provisions as to overtime working in their application to the industry concerned as will secure the reduction of the amount of overtime worked by women and young persons.

Where any class or description of factory is subject to seasonal or other pressure the hours of work and period of employment allowed in a day may be increased but the increase shall only take place in such number of weeks, not exceeding eight in any year, as shall be specified by regulation, and in the same circumstances the hours of overtime employment in a calendar year may be increased to one hundred and fifty hours, except in the case of young persons who must not be employed during more than one hundred of the hours of overtime allowed for the factory.[4]

On the other hand where the Secretary of State is satisfied that the exigencies of trade or pressure of work due to some unforeseen emergency demand the measure he may, by regulation or order, increase the aggregate number of hours of overtime allowed for a factory or the number of weeks in any calendar year in which overtime employment can take place.[5] Where the nature of the work

---

[1] *I.e.*, 7 a.m. and 6 p.m. in the case of workers under sixteen years and between 7 a.m. and 8 p.m. in other cases.

[2] Factories Act, 1961, s. 89 (2) (*b*).

[3] *Ibid.*, s. 89 (4).

[4] Factories Act, 1961, s. 89 (6) (*a*) and (*b*).

[5] *Ibid.*, s. 89 (7) (*a*) and (*b*).

carried on in a factory involves the overtime employment of different persons on different occasions to such an extent as to make it unreasonable or inappropriate to limit overtime by reference to the factory as a whole, the Secretary of State may by regulations provide that a factory may, in lieu of complying with the regulations limiting overtime by reference to the factory, comply with such provisions limiting overtime employment by reference to the individual as may be specified in the regulations. Such regulations must secure that no woman shall work overtime for more than seventy-five hours and no young person for more than fifty hours in any calendar year and that no woman or young person shall, except as otherwise provided by regulations, be employed overtime in the factory for more than six hours in any week or more than twenty-five weeks in any calendar year.[1]

Before employing any woman or young person in overtime on any day the occupier of the factory must send such particulars as may be prescribed, in writing, to the inspector and must enter the particulars in the prescribed register. A notice containing the prescribed particulars must be kept posted in the factory during such time as may be prescribed.[2]

Women and young persons may not be employed outside the factory, in the business of the factory or in any other business carried on by the occupier during any interval allowed for a meal or rest, or any time not included in the period of employment fixed by a notice under the Act, on any day during which they are employed in the factory, excepting that a woman or young person who has reached the age of sixteen may be so employed in a shop outside the period of employment but any such employment shall be treated as employment in the factory. Women or young persons to whom work is given out or who take out any work to be done outside the factory will be deemed to be employed outside the factory on the day on which the work is so given or taken out.[3] Women or young persons must not remain in rooms in which a process is being carried on during rest or meal intervals so that if it is not intended that women and young persons should leave the workroom during such periods all work must cease.[4] Male young persons employed in the manufacture of wrought iron, steel or tinplate, or in the manufacture of paper or glass are, however, exempted from the benefit of this provision,[5] which does not, in any case, apply to persons employed in work of a continuous nature or where different sets of persons have different intervals for meals or rest or an interval allowed in a spell of continuous employment.[6]

---

[1] *Ibid.,* s. 89 (9) (*a*) and (*b*).
[2] *Ibid.,* s. 90 (1) and (2).   [3] *Ibid.,* s. 91 (1), (2) and (3).
[4] Factories Act, 1961, s. 92.
[5] *Ibid.,* s. 103.
[6] *Ibid.,* s. 104 (1). By s. 104 (2) the Secretary of State has a power to make further exceptions.

Women and young persons must not be employed on Sundays in a factory nor must such persons employed in any factory on any other day of the week be employed on Sunday about the business of the factory or in any other business carried on by the occupier.[1] But where the occupier of a factory is of the Jewish faith or is a member of a religious body observing the Jewish sabbath, a woman or young person of the Jewish religion or who is a member of such a religious body may be employed on Sunday provided that the factory is closed on Saturday and is not open for business on Sunday. A partnership or company will be deemed to be Jewish within the meaning of the Act if a majority of the partners or of the directors are members either of the Jewish religion or of a religious body observing the Jewish Sabbath.[2] The Act further provides that women and young persons are to have Christmas Day, Good Friday and every bank holiday as whole holidays unless the occupier of the factory in which they are employed posts a notice three weeks before any of these days intimating that he intends to substitute some other week day.[3] Moreover, persons entitled to these holidays must not be employed in a factory on a whole holiday nor must they be employed about the business of the factory or about any other business carried on by the occupier.[4] But these provisions do not apply to women engaged in responsible positions of management who are not ordinarily engaged in manual work.[5]

The Secretary of State may, by order, suspend the provisions as to the hours and holidays of women and young persons to avoid serious inconvenience with the ordinary working of the factory where this is endangered by accident, breakdown or other unforeseen emergency.[6]

To these provisions as to the employment of women and young persons the Act makes certain special exceptions. Thus male young persons who have reached the age of sixteen years, and are employed in certain industries and processes may be employed on a shift system outside the hours specified for the employment of young persons.[7] The industries and processes in which such a system may be worked are those concerned with the smelting of iron ore, the manufacture of wrought iron, steel, tinplate, paper and glass; the galvanising of sheet metal or wire[8]; and processes in which reverberatory or regenerative furnaces, kept in operation day and night, are used in connection with the smelting of ores, metal rolling, forges, or the manufacture of metal tubes or rods or in connection

---

[1] *Ibid.*, s. 93; but see also s. 112 (1).
[2] *Ibid.*, s. 109.
[3] *Ibid.*, s. 94 (1)–(4).
[4] *Ibid.*, s. 94 (6).
[5] *Ibid.*, s. 95.
[6] *Ibid.*, s. 96.
[7] Factories Act, 1961, s. 91 (1), (2).
[8] Except the pickling process.

with such other classes of work as the Secretary of State may by regulation specify.[1] All these processes within which the shift system may be applied to young males are those which demand continuous labour by day or night. The shift system which is permitted by the Act is subject to the most stringent limitations. The period of employment may end on Sunday morning not later than six o'clock or begin on Sunday evening not earlier than ten o'clock and where the young persons are employed on a system of four shifts with turns of not more than eight hours for each shift the male young persons may be employed in such shifts between six o'clock in the morning and ten o'clock in the evening on Sundays and on week days.[2] But no young male worker may work more than six turns in any week; a minimum period of fourteen hours must separate each successive turn of employment and there shall be no employment of any such young person in two consecutive weeks, between twelve midnight and six o'clock in the morning.[3] The total hours worked under these provisions may exceed forty-eight but they must not exceed fifty-six in any week or one hundred and forty-four in any continuous period of three weeks.[4] Provision is made for the examination of young persons employed on the shift system by the appointed factory doctor and for subsequent re-examination at intervals not exceeding six months. The employment of such a young person may not continue unless the doctor has certified him to be fit for such employment.

The rules as to the employment of women and young persons are subject to another exception in the case of factories which operate the five-day week, where the total hours worked each day may extend to ten and the period of employment extend to twelve hours. Women and young persons over the age of sixteen are permitted under these circumstances to work ten and a half hours a day including overtime.[5] An occupier of a factory who avails himself of this section may employ women and young persons who have attained the age of sixteen years on a sixth day in any week provided that such person is not employed overtime on any other day in that week, that the hours worked on the sixth day do not exceed four and a half and provided that the hours so worked are deemed to be overtime.[6]

A further exception to the provisions of the sixth part of the Act relating to the hours of employment of women and young persons, to notices fixing the hours of employment, overtime employment,

---

[1] Factories Act, 1961, s. 99 (8).
[2] *Ibid.*, s. 99 (1), (2), (5) and (6).
[3] *Ibid.*, s. 99 (3). For young persons employed in a system of four shifts and in the manufacture of glass the Secretary of State has power to modify these provisions.
[4] *Ibid.*, s. 99 (6).
[5] Factories Act, 1961, s. 100 (1).
[6] *Ibid.*, s. 100 (2).

prohibition of the use of rooms during intervals, prohibition of Sunday employment and annual holidays is to be found in the withdrawal from the benefits of such legislation of such male young persons as are employed as part of the regular maintenance staff of a factory or by a contractor in repairing any part of the factory or any machinery or plant therein.[1]

Where the exigencies of a trade so require, the Secretary of State may by regulation substitute some other day for Saturday as the short working day,[2] and he has a similar power in relation to factories where by custom or exigency it is deemed necessary to allow all or any of the annual whole holidays to be taken on days other than those stipulated in section 94.[3]

It has always proved difficult to bring certain industries within the scope of any comprehensive piece of legislation and in the more stubborn cases the Factory Act has met the problem not so much by solving it as by conditionally exempting them from the general requirements of the Act. Thus women employed in laundries and in the manufacture of bread or flour confectionery or sausages, may on two days other than Saturday (in the case of laundries they must be week days) in any week, work a period not exceeding ten hours and on those days the period of employment may extend to twelve hours and may begin at any time not earlier than six o'clock in the morning and end at any time not later than nine o'clock in the evening. But the total hours of work permitted by the Act must not be exceeded.[4] The general provisions of the Act as to the employment of women and young persons do not apply to the employment of women and young persons who have attained the age of sixteen in processes connected with the preserving, canning or curing of fish or the preparing of fish for sale; or the preserving or canning of fruit or vegetables during the months of June, July, August and September where it is urgent that the work should be carried on so as to prevent the goods from being spoiled.[5] So too the Secretary of State is given the power by regulations to vary the provisions of the Act in the case of factories where cream, butter, cheese, milk powder, condensed milk or any other milk product is made, or fresh milk or cream is sterilised or otherwise treated before being sold as such.[6]

The permitted exceptions to the provisions relating to women and young persons have been much criticised as providing loopholes through which employers may escape some of the burdens of the Act. It should therefore be remembered that these exceptions are themselves severely controlled and that the Act confers upon the

---

[1] *Ibid.*, s. 106.
[2] *Ibid.*, s. 107.
[3] *Ibid.*, s. 108.
[4] *Ibid.*, ss. 110 (1), 111 (1).
[5] Factories Act, 1961, s. 112, but see s. 112 (1).
[6] *Ibid.*, s. 113.

Secretary of State the power, by regulation, to require the adoption of any special provision which he believes to be necessary for the protection of the health or welfare of women or young persons employed overtime or in pursuance of the special exceptions under Part VI of the Act. Moreover an occupier of a factory must, not less than seven days before he avails himself of any such exception, serve notice on the inspector and post in his factory notice of his intention. Until such notice is served on the inspector the special exception shall not apply to the factory. The notice posted in the factory and served on the inspector must specify the period of employment, the intervals to be allowed for meals and rest, and the annual holidays where any of these differ from the ordinary hours, intervals or holidays. And, subject to the law as to overtime, no person employed under the special exceptions may be employed otherwise than in accordance with the notice. Any proposed departure from the terms of employment as set out in the notice cannot be effective until details are served on the inspector and posted in the factory and must, in any case, not be made more frequently than once in three months except for special cause allowed in writing by the inspector.[1]

In considering the Act so far it will have been noticed that, for the purposes already discussed, women and young persons are treated together. But the Act recognises that, apart from these general provisions, certain special safeguards of the health and safety of young persons are required. The sections[2] which are concerned with these safeguards either introduce principles new to the history of industrial legislation or substantially extend principles already in existence. Young persons can be employed in certain duties only under special conditions. The young persons specifically enumerated are those engaged in collecting, carrying or delivering goods or who carry messages or run errands wholly or mainly outside the factory or who are employed in connection with any business carried on at a dock, wharf or quay to which the Act applies, or at any warehouse not forming part of a factory and not covered by the Shops Act, 1950[3] or employed by a person having the use or occupation of the dock, wharf, quay or warehouse or of premises within it or forming part of it; or young persons employed in or in connection with any process[4] carried on at any such dock, wharf, quay or warehouse and by a person having such use or occupation as aforesaid, or in connection with the processes of loading, unloading or coaling any ship in any dock, harbour or canal.[5] Young persons engaged in these various ways[6] must not, apart from certain per-

---

[1] *Ibid.*, s. 115.

[2] *I.e.*, *ibid.*, ss. 116–119.

[3] 14 Geo. 6, c. 28.

[4] Not being a process covered by Factories Act, 1937, s. 106 (now s. 126 of the 1961 Act).

[5] Factories Act, 1961, s. 116 (1).

[6] Whether in receipt of wages or not—*ibid*, s. 116 (5).

mitted overtime, work more than forty-eight hours a week exclusive
of intervals for meals and rest, nor be employed in continuous spells
of more than five hours without a break of at least half an hour for
a meal or rest.　If the hours of employment cover the hours between
half-past eleven in the morning and half-past two in the afternoon
an interval of not less than three quarters of an hour must be
allowed, during those hours, for dinner.　And on one day in each
week work must cease not later than one o'clock in the afternoon.
Where the young person has attained the age of sixteen he may, in
cases of seasonal pressure, or emergency, work overtime for not
more than six hours in any week nor more than fifty hours in any
calendar year.　Where an employer has employed overtime any
young persons entitled to the benefit of these provisions in twelve
weeks (whether consecutive or not) in any calendar year neither he
nor any person succeeding to his business shall employ young persons
to whom the section applies overtime during the remainder of that
year.　In every period of twenty-four hours between mid-day of
one day and mid-day of the next the young persons must be allowed
an interval of at least eleven consecutive hours including the hours
from ten o'clock in the evening until six o'clock in the morning.　The
employer must keep proper records of the hours worked by the
young persons, of their intervals for meals and rest and of their
overtime.[1]

Where the Secretary of State is satisfied that it is desirable in the
public interest, for the purpose of maintaining or increasing the
efficiency of industry or transport, he may exempt the employment
of persons of or over the age of sixteen from these provisions of
s. 116 and from certain other legislation.[2]　Exemptions may extend
to persons generally or to classes of particular persons; the former are
termed general exemption regulations and must only be made on the
application of a joint industrial council, conciliation board or similar
body, or of a wages council or of organisations jointly representing
the employers and workers concerned or of one of these, the other
side being consulted; the latter are termed special exemption regulations, which must not extend for more than a year, although they
may be renewed.[3]

The principal change made by the Employment Medical Advisory
Service Act, 1972, in so far as it applies to regulation is the different
approach adopted in respect of the employment of young persons.
Routine medical examinations give way to a system aimed at
securing a steady flow of information and also giving the medical
adviser power to examine where he thinks fit.　It is appreciated by
the Act that the employment medical advisory is but one link in the

---

[1] *Ibid.*, s. 116 (2).

[2] *Ibid.*, s. 117. The other provisions are Employment of Women, Young
Persons, and Children Act, 1920, s. 1 (3), (see *infra*, p. 332) and Hours of
Employment (Conventions) Act, 1936 (see *infra*, p. 333).

[3] Factories Act, 1961, s. 117 (2)-(7).

chain of school medical officers and care under the National Health scheme.

Section 119 of the Factories Act, 1961, is amended so that the occupier of a factory who employs a young person in his factory, either directly or by way of transfer, must send within seven days a notice to the local careers office.[1]

The power to examine is achieved by amending section 10 of the Factories Act, 1961. Wherever the employment medical adviser feels that anyone being employed in a factory is suffering in health or has been or is likely to be injured, then he can make an examination. He is given powers to enforce this.[2] This provision applies to all age groups but it will plainly be of importance in respect of young workers.

Finally, the provisions of section 75 of the Factories Act, 1965, are amended. This section prohibited employment of women or young persons in processes involving the use of lead compounds after suspension on the medical grounds that further work would involve a special danger to health. This is continued but the responsibility falls on the employment medical adviser.[3] In fact, monitoring lead levels is one of the routine functions of the medical inspectorate.

(9) Home Work.—In the case of persons employed in such classes of work as may be specified by regulations, the occupier of every factory and any contractor employed by him in the business of the factory shall keep, in the prescribed form, lists showing the names and addresses of outworkers directly employed by him, either as workmen or as contractors in the business of the factory, outside the factory and particulars of the places where they are employed. They must also send to the inspector such copies or extracts from the lists as may be required and must send to the district council during the months of February and August in each year copies of those lists, showing outworkers employed during the preceding six months. The district council must examine such lists and must furnish the name and place of employment of every outworker included in any such list whose place of employment is outside the district of the council, to the council in whose district his place of employment is situated.[4]

In these provisions the legislature attempts to deal with a problem of considerable, though diminishing, dimensions. In 1864 the fustian cutting industry had been regulated and since fustian cutting was an industry largely conducted in the worker's home the Act represented an early attempt to grapple with the problem

---

[1] Employment Medical Services Act, 1972, s. 5.
[2] s. 3.
[3] s. 4.
[4] Factories Act, 1961, s. 133.

of outworkers. It has proved impossible to impose on such workers the standards of the Factories Acts and the most that can be done is to secure inspection by the district council. This of itself would not have proved adequate had not the growth of the factory system reduced the importance of outworking. The original protests of the factory occupiers that they could not hope to meet the rising cost incurred by conformity with the Factories Acts whilst employers who employed outworkers only were free from such obligations, are rarely heard today. The classes of work to which the obligation to keep lists of outworkers applies are still numerous—but the economic and legal importance of such classes is constantly declining.

The mere power, on the part of the district council, to inspect premises which outworkers use is valueless. The Act therefore provides that where work is carried on in connection with a factory in a place which, in the opinion of the council, is injurious or dangerous to the health of the persons employed therein, the council may give written notice to the occupier of the factory or any contractor employed by him. The notice must set out the causes of complaint and if the person to whom it is addressed gives out work after the expiration of ten days to be done in that place he will be guilty of an offence unless he can prove that the place was not injurious or dangerous. And for the purpose of these provisions any place from which work is given out shall be deemed to be a factory.[1]

(10) Particulars of Piece Work and Wages.—A long-standing source of industrial unrest is the question of piece rates and the determination of wages by methods of computation often not understood by the worker. Few provisions of industrial legislation have been more popular than those requiring an employer to give a worker the necessary particulars from which he can check the correctness or otherwise of his wages. Testimony was almost unanimous in the earlier days of industrial legislation that the workman's right to seek such particulars from his employer was not sufficient. Indeed the first "particulars" clause is to be found in the Arbitration Act of 1824 but its usefulness was limited just because it was voluntary.[2] The last century saw extensions of the device to various industries so that by the time of the Factories Act the requirements of the particulars clauses were accepted as normal in industry. In textile factories particulars of the rates of wages applicable to the work to be done must be published so as to enable the worker to compute the wages due to him. The method of publication varies. In the case of weavers in the worsted and woollen (other than hosiery) trades the rates of wages must be given to the worker in writing when the work is given out to him and must also be exhibited on a placard, whilst the same method applies to weavers in the cotton trade except that, in addition, the worker must be

---

[1] Factories Act, 1961, s. 134.
[2] 5 Geo. 4, c. 96, ss. 18, 19.

furnished with particulars of the conditions by which the prices are regulated. In the case of other workers the particulars of the rates of wages must be furnished, in writing, when the work is given out, but if the rate applies to the work to be done by each of the persons in one room it will be sufficient to exhibit the particulars on a placard. The placard must not contain any other matter and must be posted where it is easily legible. Moreover such particulars of the work to be done as affect the amount of wages payable to him must also be furnished to the worker when the work is given out except so far as these are ascertainable by an automatic indicator. If an automatic indicator is used and a placard containing particulars of the rates of wages is exhibited in each room by the mutual agreement of employers and employed, this will be sufficient compliance with the requirements set out above. The particulars either of rates of wages or of work must not be expressed by means of symbols. An automatic indicator must have marked on its case such particulars as will enable its accuracy to be checked. The fraudulent use of a false indicator or the fraudulent alteration of such, is an offence, as is the disclosure by a person employed of particulars furnished either directly to him or to a fellow workman for the purpose of divulging a trade secret. It is also an offence to solicit or procure a person employed in a factory to disclose such particulars or, with that object in view, to pay or reward such a person for disclosing such particulars. The Secretary of State has power to apply the provisions as to particulars of work and wages to non-textile factories.[1]

Every enactment for the time being in force relating to weights and measures and to weighing or measuring instruments shall apply in a factory for the purpose of checking or ascertaining wages, in like manner as if they were used for trade. Inspectors of weights and measures shall have the same powers and duties for the purpose of inspecting instruments used to ascertain or check wages as he has with respect to weights, measures and instruments used for trade.

(11) Miscellaneous Requirements.—The Act ends with a series of provisions miscellaneous in character, some of which are novel and many of which are extremely interesting.[2] Every person must, not less than one month before he begins to occupy or use premises as a factory serve a written notice on the inspector for the district, stating amongst other things, the nature of his work, whether mechanical power is to be used and if so its nature; and not less than one month before the date upon which mechanical power is first used in any factory the occupier must serve written notice on the inspector indicating the nature of the power to be used. The period of one month may be reduced with the written permission of the inspector and a person may begin to occupy a factory less than

---

[1] Factories Act, 1961, s. 135.
[2] Those dealt with here are contained in Part X. Parts XI to XIV have been dealt with earlier.

one month after notice if he takes over from another person without changing the nature of the work and the notice is served as soon as practicable and in any case within one month of his taking over.[1] An abstract of the Act must be posted at the principal entrances of the factory at which employed persons enter together with the addresses of the district inspector, the superintending inspector for the division and the appointed factory doctor. A notice must be similarly posted which specifies the clock, if any, by which the hours of labour and rest are regulated. All notices and documents which are required by the Act to be posted must be printed in such characters and hung in such places as permits them to be read conveniently. The pulling down, injuring or defacing of a notice constitutes an offence under the Act.[2] Where, under powers conferred by the Act, special regulations are issued, a copy, or the prescribed abstract, must be posted as indicated above and if any person affected by the notices so requires, the occupier must supply a copy of such regulations.[3]

Every factory must maintain a general register in the prescribed form in which must be entered the required particulars as to young persons employed, as to the washing, whitewashing, colour-washing, painting or varnishing of the factory; as to particulars of accidents and industrial diseases of which notice must be given to the inspector; as to special exemptions of which the occupier avails himself, and as to such other matters and reports as may be prescribed. The occupier must send to the inspector such extracts from the general register as the inspector may require,[4] and the register itself and any other record or register kept in pursuance of the Act must be kept available for inspection by any inspector or by the appointed doctor for at least two years after the date of the last entry, or such time as may be required.[5] At intervals of not less than one year the occupier must file with the chief inspector a record of the number of persons employed together with such other particulars as the Secretary of State may direct.[6]

---

[1] Factories Act, 1961, s. 137.
[2] *Ibid.*, s. 138.
[3] *Ibid.*, s. 139.
[4] Factories Act, 1961, s. 140.
[5] *Ibid.*, s. 141.
[6] *Ibid.*, s. 142.

CHAPTER VIII

INDUSTRIAL LEGISLATION (2)

1. LEGISLATION RELATING TO SHOPS

(1) Introduction.—The first Act regulating employment in shops was not passed until the year 1886. The smallness of the economic unit involved, the persistence of the family type of undertaking, the reluctance of the assistants to organise and combine in support of their interests all contributed to the delay in putting legislation on to the Statute Book. It is true that, thirteen years earlier, in 1873, a bill had been considered in the House of Commons, but no progress had been made. The Shop Hours Regulation Act, 1886,[1] consequently represents the first effort at reform. It provided that young persons were not to be employed for more than seventy-four hours a week including meal times, and no young person was to be employed in any shop who had previously been employed on the same day in any factory or workshop for the number of hours permitted by the Factory and Workshop Act, 1878,[2] or for a longer period than would complete such number of hours. The Act was a temporary measure but was made permanent by the Shop Hours Act, 1892,[3] which also laid the duty of administering the Act on the local authorities. An Act passed in 1893[4] merely remedied a defect in the earlier Act by giving the local authorities power to levy a rate to meet expenses incurred in the administration of the Acts. That there was, as yet, no attempt to provide more than the merely *ad hoc* solution is shown by the Seats for Shop Assistants Act, 1899,[5] which provided that in rooms where goods were actually retailed to the public and where female assistants were employed, seats were to be provided behind the counter or in other suitable positions in the proportion of not less than one seat to every three female assistants. The Shop Hours Act, 1904,[6] empowered the local authorities by Order, to fix the hours at which shops were to be closed for the serving of customers. The Act of 1911[7] represented a considerable step forward. Provision was made concerning hours of employment, and meal intervals, for a weekly half holiday[8] and for the setting up of local enquiries "to promote and facilitate the early closing of shops."

---

[1] 49 & 50 Vict., c.55.   [2] 41 & 42 Vict., c.16.   [3] 55 & 56 Vict., c.62.
[4] Shop Hours Act, 1893; 56 & 57 Vict., c.67.
[5] 62 & 63 Vict., c.21.
[6] 4 Edw. 7, c.31.   [7] Shops Act, 1911; 1 & 2 Geo.5, c.54.
[8] The Shops (Early Closing Days) Act, 1965, has substituted the term "early closing day" for "weekly half-holiday."

The Act of 1912 was a consolidating measure and proved to be the starting point of the more modern development of the law. Other Acts were passed and in 1950 the Shops Act, 1950, consolidated the Shops Acts, 1912-1928. A minor amending Act was passed in 1965: the Shops (Early Closing Days) Act.

These Acts dealt principally with employment in shops and regulated times of opening. There were similar provisions dealing with health and comfort. These have been replaced by the comprehensive provisions of the Offices, Shops & Railway Premises Act, 1963. The question of the regulation of hours is one of some political controversy. A bill was introduced into Parliament by the government in 1956 but was subsequently dropped. A White Paper has recently been published setting out further proposals.[1]

(2) Definition of Shop.—A shop includes any premises where any retail trade or business is carried on.[2] The expression " retail trade or business " includes the business of a barber or hairdresser, the sale of refreshments or intoxicating liquors, the business of lending books or periodicals when carried on for purposes of gain, and retail sales by auction, but does not include the sale of programmes and catalogues and other similar sales at theatres and places of amusement.[3]

A fair, bazaar or sale of work held for charitable or other purposes from which no private profit is derived and libraries at which the business of lending books or periodicals is not carried on for purposes of gain other than of making profits for some philanthropic or charitable object (including any religious or educational object) or for any club or institution are, in general, exempted from the operation of the Act as also are libraries registered under the Provident Societies Acts, 1893-1928.[4]

The definition, though simple when compared with that of a factory in the Factories Act, has yet given rise to much litigation. In *Fine Fare, Ltd.* v. *Brighton County Borough Council*[5] the Divisional Court considered a mixed shop. This type of shop, once found only in the largest towns, is becoming very common and the decision that it was to be regarded as one shop and not as a number of shops is important. It has been held that both a wooden booth containing games of chance in which prizes were awarded to successful players and a blacksmith's shop are not shops,[6] whilst the dining room of a residential hotel in which non-residents were served with

---

[1] Retail Trading Hours, Home Office, 1965.
[2] Shops Act, 1950, s. 74(1).
[3] *Ibid.*
[4] *Ibid*, s. 46.
[5] [1959] 1 All E.R. 476; [1959] 1 W.L.R. 223. And see *Fine Fare, Ltd.* v. *Aberdare U.D.C.*, [1965] 2 Q.B. 39; [1965] 1 All E.R., 679; *Redbridge London Borough Council* v. *Wests*, (*Ilford*), [1968] 1 Q.B. 789; [1968] 1 All E.R. 277.
[6] *Dennis* v. *Hutchinson*, [1922] 1 K.B. 693; *R.* v. *Chapman and Alderman* (1843), 7 J.P. 132.

meals fell within the definition.[1]   A stall used twice a week and consisting of a board on trestles in a market place, at which the proprietor sells medicines, is not a shop,[2] nor is a similar temporary structure on a railway station for the sale of periodicals.[3]

In *Turpin* v. *Middlesborough Assessment Committee and Bailey* the[4] appellant occupied a garage at which he sold petrol and motor accessories and did certain repairs. This was held to be a shop.

(3) **Employment in Shops.**—A shop assistant is any person wholly or mainly employed in a shop in connection with the serving of customers or the receipt of orders or the despatch of goods.[5] So, a kitchenmaid whose duties are restricted to the preparation of meals for the customers of a restaurant is, none the less, a shop assistant,[6] as is a potman who puts up and takes down the tables on which customers eat food, who cleans the cutlery and glasses and is generally responsible for the cleanliness of the premises.[7]

On at least one day in each week a shop assistant shall not be employed about the business of a shop after half past one o'clock in the afternoon.[8]   The business of the shop is not restricted to work performed within the precincts of the shop and an employer who employs his shop assistants on work other than that on which they are normally engaged may contravene the statute.   So, a shop-keeper who employed his assistants to distribute bills on the early closing day is liable under the Act though the bills did not refer to the shop at which the assistants were employed and though additional remuneration was earned.[9]   So also is the occupier of two shops who, on the weekly early closing day, employs the assistants at the first shop about the business of the second shop.[10]   Moreover, an occupier may be liable where his servant employs himself

---

[1] *George Hotel (Colchester), Ltd.* v. *Ball*, [1938] 3 All E.R. 790.

[2] *Summers* v. *Roberts*, [1944] 1 K.B. 106; [1943] 2 All E.R. 757.

[3] *W. H. Smith & Son* v. *Kyle*, [1902] 1 K.B. 286.   This case alleged failure to display a certain notice which was, in fact, displayed at a neighbouring shop owned by the appellants.   Such a trestle stall might, consequently, be a shop for certain of the provisions of the Act and if a person were employed at a temporary stall in defiance of the prescribed conditions of employment it is submitted that a breach of the Act would occur.

[4] [1931] A.C. 451; see also *M. & F. Frawley, Ltd.* v. *Ve-Ri-Best Mfg. Co., Ltd.*, [1953] 1 Q.B. 318; [1953] 1 All E.R. 50.

[5] Shops Act, 1950, s.74 (1).

[6] *Melluish* v. *London County Council*, [1914] 3 K.B. 325.

[7] *Prance* v. *London County Council*, [1915] 1 K.B. 688.   *Cf. Gordon Hotels, Ltd.* v. *London County Council*, [1916] 2 K.B. 27.

[8] Shops Act, 1950, s.17.   Special arrangements are in force concerning the week preceding a Bank Holiday. The term "Shop Assistant" will include young persons employed mainly or wholly about the business of a shop but does not apply to persons employed in residential hotels (see Shops Act, 1950, s.18). The provision as to weekly half holidays does not apply to any young person unless he is employed about the business of the shop for more than twenty-five hours a week, nor to young people employed in a theatre whose duties do not begin before mid-day (*ibid.*).

[9] *George* v. *James*, [1914] 1 K.B. 278.

[10] *London County Council* v. *Wettman*, [1922] 1 K.B. 153.

about the business of the shop in disobedience of orders though in such cases the employer may lay an information and bring the servant before the court.[1]

The occupier of a shop must fix a notice in the shop specifying the day of the week on which his assistants are not to be employed after half past one o'clock. He may fix different days for different assistants.[2] He must arrange intervals for meals so that no person shall be employed for more than six hours without an interval of at least twenty minutes during the course thereof,[3] whilst young persons[4] must not be employed for more than five hours without interval except that on the day on which employment is not to extend beyond half past one o'clock, five and a half hours may be worked without interruption.[5] This latter provision applies to any young person employed wholly or mainly about the business of a shop, (who is to be deemed a " shop assistant ") and to young persons employed in retail trade or business at a place which is not a shop but does not apply to persons employed in residential hotels who are not shop assistants, nor to those engaged in the business of selling intoxicating liquors or refreshments for consumption on the premises.[6]

The Act makes special provision for half-day holidays and meal times for those shop assistants who are themselves engaged in the sale of refreshments, whether the premises on which they work are licensed for the sale of intoxicating liquors or not.

The occupier of a shop mainly or wholly engaged in the supply of refreshments or intoxicating liquors for consumption on the premises may elect whether he will satisfy the provisions of sections 17, 18 and 19 of the Shops Act, 1950 or those of section 21 of the Act. In the latter case he must secure that no assistant is employed for more than sixty-five hours in any week exclusive of meal times, and in addition must provide every year thirty-two whole holidays on a week day of which two at least shall be given within the currency of each month and which shall comprise a holiday on full pay of not less than six consecutive days and twenty-six whole holidays on Sunday in every year so distributed that at least one out of every three consecutive Sundays shall be a whole holiday.[7]

Every assistant must be allowed intervals for meals amounting to not less than three quarters of an hour on half holidays and on

---

[1] *Ward* v. *W. H. Smith & Son*, [1913] 3 K.B. 154.

[2] Shops Act, 1950, s. 17(2).

[3] *Ibid.*, s. 19(1) and Sched. 3, Part I. This provision does not apply where the only shop assistants are members of the family of the occupier, maintained by him and dwelling in his house (*ibid.*, s. 19(1)).

[4] *I.e.* those who have not yet reached the age of 18 years. The term "young person" as used in the Act, however, does not include a child whose employment is regulated by s. 18 of the Children and Young Persons Act, 1933, or the Children and Young Persons (Scotland) Act, 1937, see Shops Act, 1950, s. 74(1).

[5] Shops Act, 1950, s. 20 and Sched. 3, Part II.

[6] *Ibid.*, s. 20.

[7] *Ibid.*, s. 21(3). Two half holidays on a week day shall be deemed equivalent to one whole holiday on a week day.

other days to not less than two hours. No assistant may be employed for more than six hours without being allowed an interval of at least half an hour. The occupier must maintain in a conspicuous place on the premises a notice in the prescribed form referring to the provisions of the section and stating the steps taken with a view to compliance therewith.[1]

(4) **Employment of Young Persons.**—Young persons (that is, persons between the ages of sixteen and of eighteen years) may not be employed about the business of a shop for more than forty-eight working hours in any week, but in periods of seasonal or exceptional pressure, persons between the ages of sixteen and eighteen may be employed overtime. Where they are so employed in any year for six weeks, whether consecutive or not, no young person shall be so employed during the remainder of the year and no young person may be employed overtime after he has been employed overtime for fifty working hours in that year, or in any week after he has been employed overtime for twelve working hours in that week.[2] A person who has not attained the age of sixteen years may not be employed about the business of a shop for more than fifty-four working hours in any week but where due notice has been posted, such persons may, for a fortnight over the Christmas period, be employed for forty-eight hours in either week provided that not more than eighty-eight hours are worked throughout the period.[3] A young person who has, in the knowledge of the occupier of a shop, been previously employed on any day in a factory, shall not be employed on that day about the business of the shop for a longer period than will, together with the time during which he has been previously employed on that day in the factory, complete the number of hours permitted by the Factories Acts, 1937 and 1948.[4]

The Secretary of State has power to prevent the hours of employment of young persons from being divided into spells so as to deprive them of reasonable opportunities of instruction and recreation.[5] Young persons employed in shops must, in every period of twenty-four hours between midday on one day and midday on the next, be allowed an interval of at least eleven consecutive hours, including the hours from ten o'clock in the evening until six o'clock in the morning, but the interval of eleven hours need not include the hour between five and six o'clock in the morning in the case of males between sixteen and eighteen years of age who are employed during that hour in the collection or delivery of milk, bread, or newspapers.[6]

The occupier of a shop engaged in the business of serving meals, intoxicating liquors or refreshments to customers for consumption on the premises may, by affixing a notice in the shop, elect to be

---

1 Shops Act, 1950, s. 21(3). The provision as to meal intervals does not apply to such assistants as are members of the family of the occupier, maintained by him and dwelling in his house.
2 Shops Act, 1950, s. 24.
3 *Ibid.*, s. 27.   4 *Ibid.*, s. 28.   5 *Ibid.*, s. 30.   6 *Ibid.*, s. 31(1), (2) and (3).

bound by alternative conditions for two consecutive weeks specified in the notice. Where he does so a young person between the ages of sixteen and eighteen wholly or mainly employed in such business will be deemed not to be employed about the business of the shop in excess of the normal maximum working hours in either week of the period specified if he is employed neither for more than sixty working hours in either week nor for more than ninety-six hours throughout the period, but the provisions of section 1, permitting overtime, shall not apply to the young persons employed.[1]

In determining the working hours for which a young person has been employed about the business of a shop he shall be deemed also to have been employed about the business thereof during any time during which he was employed about the business of any other shop, factory or workshop. An employer may, however, defend himself from a charge of contravening these provisions where he can show that he did not know and could not by reasonable diligence have ascertained that a young person was employed by another employer.[2]

The relevant provisions of the Shops Act, 1950, do not apply to the employment of persons in or about a theatre, except in relation to young persons employed wholly or mainly in connection with any retail trade or business carried on in the theatre and the provisions are so modified that, in the case of a person between the ages of sixteen and eighteen years of age employed in a theatre where a performance is taking place which begins before and ends after ten o'clock in the evening, the interval of at least eleven hours need not include any time between ten o'clock in the evening and the time at which the performance ends.[3]

(5) Hours of opening.—Subject to certain exceptions every shop must be closed for the serving of customers not later than one o'clock in the afternoon of one week day in every week. The Shops (Early Closing Days) Act, 1965, has made the occupier of the shop responsible for fixing the early closing day, a power formerly vested in the local authority.[4] Each occupier must keep a notice of the early closing day conspicuously displayed in his shop so as to be visible to customers outside the shop.[5] The occupier can change the day if he wishes but the existing day must have been effective for three months, although during the first month of a new day he can revert to the old one.[6] These provisions do not apply to shops engaged in the sale of victuals, stores or other articles necessary to a ship on her arrival or immediately before her departure from a port, nor do they apply to shops selling intoxicating liquors, refreshments, meat, fish, milk, cream and many similar articles.[7]

---

[1] Shops Act, 1950, s. 25: see s. 26 for special provisions as to the sale of accessories for aircraft, motor vehicles and cycles.

[2] *Ibid.*, s. 29(1).

[3] *Ibid.*, ss. 31(3) and 33. Theatre will include cinemas and music halls (s. 74(1)).

[4] S. 1(1).   [5] *Ibid.*, s. 1(2).   [6] *Ibid.*, s. 1(3).

[7] Shops Act, 1950, s. 1 and Sched. I.

Under the provisions of the Shops Act a grocer has been held liable when, on the weekly half holiday, he .closed his shop but sold provisions from his home.[1] The section aims at preventing the personal carrying on of the business so that a dairyman who fixes to the door of his shop a machine from which milk, stored inside the shop, may be purchased, does not commit an offence when the machine is used during the prohibited hours.[2] Interestingly, in more modern idiom, neither does the occupier of a coin operated launderette. This is certainly a shop but it is not an offence under these provisions to have it open on a Sunday, even with a cleaning woman present, for no personal service is rendered to customers.[3] In *Lucas* v. *Reubens* an auctioneer sold jewellery by auction at a time fixed by order of the local authority as a period during which jeweller's shops must be closed. It was held that he had not committed any offence.[4] An offence is not committed where a person being in the shop before one o'clock is served after that hour, even though the process of serving him is likely to take several hours.[5]

The local authority may make an Order, subject to confirmation by the Secretary of State, fixing the hours on the several days of the week at which all shops or shops of any specified class are to be closed for the serving of customers, but such order will not apply to any shops engaged in the trades or businesses mentioned in the Second Schedule to the Shops Act, 1950, for example, post offices, the sale of intoxicating liquors, of newspapers, medicines and refreshments. The hour fixed by the Order must not be earlier than seven o'clock.[6]

It is not lawful to carry on, in any place not being a shop, a retail trade or business of any class at a time when it would be unlawful in that locality to keep a shop open for the purposes of retail trade or business of that class. "Place" here indicates a position of permanence and not any spot where casual sales are made.[7] But this provision does not apply to the sale of newspapers or to a barber or hairdresser who attends a customer at the customer's home or to the auction of private effects in a private dwelling house.[8]

Where several trades or businesses are carried on in the same shop and any of the activities is such that if it were the only one the shop would be exempt from being closed, the exemption applies only so far as the carrying on of that trade or business is concerned

---

[1] *Cowden* v. *McEvoy*, [1914] 3 K.B. 108.

[2] *Willesden Urban District Council* v. *Morgan*, [1915] 1 K.B. 349

[3] *Ilford Corporation* v. *Betterclean (Seven Kings)*, [1965] 1 All E.R. 900; [1965] 2 W.L.R. 727.

[4] [1921] 2 K.B. 482; see also *Schuck* v. *Banks*, [1914] 2 K.B. 491.

[5] *Moore* v. *Tweedale*, [1935] 2 K.B. 163; [1935] All E.R. Rep. 292.

[6] Shops Act, 1950, s.8 and Sched. 2.

[7] *Eldorado Ice Cream Co., Ltd.* v. *Keating*, [1938] 1 K.B. 715; [1938] 1 All E.R. 330; *Stone* v. *Boreham*, [1959] 1 Q.B. 1; [1958] 2 All E.R. 715; *Kahn* v. *Newberry*, [1959] 2 Q.B. 1; [1959] 2 All E.R. 202.

[8] Shops Act, 1950, s. 12.

and if, in a mixed shop, an activity is exempt from a closing order, the order must be complied with in respect of all other activities. The Act recognises that peculiar difficulties may arise in the case of shops situated in holiday resorts, and in such areas the local authority may suspend, for periods not exceeding, in the aggregate, four months in any year, the obligation to close shops on the weekly early closing day.   Where the occupier of a shop in a place in which suspension is in force satisfies the local authority that it is his practice to allow all his shop assistants a holiday of not less than two weeks in every year on full pay and keeps a notice to that effect affixed in his shop, the requirement that on one day in each week a shop assistant shall not be employed after half past one o'clock shall not apply to the shop during the periods specified in the Order.[1]   The Shops (Airports) Act, 1962, gave relief from the restrictions on hours of opening to shops at designated airports.

Every shop must be closed for the serving of customers not later than nine o'clock in the evening of one day in the week (known as "the late day") and not later than eight o'clock in the evening of any other day.   The late day will be Saturday unless the local authority fixes some other day.[2]   It is, however, not an offence to serve a customer who is proved to have been in the shop before the closing hour or where the article supplied after the closing hour was required in a case of illness.   So that where, in a hairdresser's shop, two customers were in the shop before one o'clock on the half closing day, there was no offence, though the process of serving them would take several hours.[3]

But if potential customers are invited to enter a shop, to remain after the closing hour, and after that hour are invited to make purchases, an offence is committed[4] for

> "there is a wide difference between keeping a shop open after the closing hour for the purpose of inviting persons to become customers after that hour and . . . continuing in a shop which has been closed at the closing hour to serve a customer who became a customer before that hour."[5]

Special provisions refer to the selling of newspapers and periodicals.[6]   In the trade or business of selling table waters, sweets, chocolates, sugar confectionery or ice-cream, the general closing hour is ten o'clock on the late day and half past nine on every other day,

---

1 Shops Act, 1950, s. 40.
2 *Ibid.*, ss. 2 (1) (b) and 3. Section 7 provided that the general closing hours applicable to the winter months should be temporary and should expire on Dec. 10, 1950. They were extended on two occasions and were finally abolished by the Shops (Revocation of Winter Closing Provisions) Order, 1952, No. 1862.
3 *Moore* v. *Tweedale*, [1935] 2 K.B. 163; [1935] All E.R. Rep. 292.
4 *Salford Cattle Market Salerooms, Ltd.* v. *Osborne* (1923), 92 L.J. K.B. 1018.
5 *Moore* v. *Tweedale, supra, per* HEWART, L.C.J., at p. 171.
6 Shops Act, 1950, s. 5.

but the local authority may, if a majority of the occupiers of the shops affected so desire it, substitute for either of the general closing hours an earlier hour not being earlier than eight o'clock in the evening[1]; and in the case of the sale of tobacco and smoker's requisites, hours not later than ten o'clock on the late day and nine o'clock on other days may be substituted.[2]

(6) Sunday opening.—It is unlawful to carry on the business of a retail trader in butcher's meat on Sunday and where such a business is carried on in a shop, the shop must be closed for the serving of customers on Sunday.[3] A person of the Jewish faith may, however, carry on the business of a retail dealer in kosher meat and keep open a shop for the serving of customers on Sunday provided (*a*) that he is licensed by the local board of Shechita (or by a committee appointed, in the absence of such a board, by the local Jewish congregation); (*b*) that he does not carry on the business of a retail dealer in kosher meat or of a retail dealer in butcher's meat on Saturday, and if he carries on the business in a shop, closes the shop for the purpose of business on Saturday; (*c*) he has previously given notice to the local authority of his intention to carry on the business of a retail dealer in kosher meat on Sunday, and (*d*) if he carries on the business in a shop, he causes to be conspicuously posted in the shop a notice stating that it is open on Sundays for the purposes of retail dealing in kosher meat but is not open on Saturday.[4]

It is also unlawful to despatch any butcher's meat from a shop or to deliver meat so despatched at a time when the shop may not be open for the serving of customers, but this will not apply on any Sunday which is also Christmas Day or on any Sunday when the succeeding Monday is Christmas Day.[5] These provisions are not designed to prevent the sale, despatch or delivery of butcher's meat required by any person for a ship or aircraft on her arrival at, or immediately before the departure from, a port or aerodrome.[6]

In general every shop must be closed for the serving of customers on Sunday. To this rule the Fifth Schedule of the Shops Act, 1950, provides many exceptions covering such activities as the conduct of the business of a post office and a funeral undertaker and the sale of intoxicating liquors, meals and refreshments, newly cooked provisions, newspapers, guide-books and the like.[7] Moreover, a local authority may grant partial exemption orders in favour of shops

---

[1] Shops Act, 1950, s. 6.

[2] *Ibid.*, s. 4. There is a power to exempt exhibitions and holiday resorts from the hours of closing (ss. 41, 42). A similar power exists in relation to Christmas and " special " occasions, s. 43; s. 44 deals with the position of post office business.

[3] *Ibid.*, ss. 60 and 61.

[4] *Ibid.*, s. 62.

[5] *Ibid.*, s. 63.

[6] *Ibid.*, s. 65.

[7] *Ibid.*, s. 47 and Sched. 5; and see *Waterman* v. *Wallasey Corporation*, [1954] 2 All E.R. 187; *Monaco Garage* v. *Watford Borough Council*, [1967] 2 All E.R. 1291; [1967] 1 W.L.R. 1069.

selling bread and flour confectionery, fish, groceries and other provisions commonly sold in grocers' shops. A partial exemption order
will not authorise a shop to be open for the serving of customers
after ten o'clock on Sunday mornings except that the order may
authorise the serving of customers after ten o'clock in cases of
emergency and in such other cases as may be specified in the Order.[1]
The local authority may, upon terms, exempt shops open for
the serving to customers of meals or refreshments for consumption
elsewhere than at the shop at which they are sold.[2]   There is a
similar exempting power, subject to certain conditions, as to shops
in holiday resorts,[3] whilst the position of persons observing the
Jewish sabbath and of the city and county of London is specially
safeguarded.[4]   Goods sold retail may not be delivered or despatched
for delivery from a shop at any time when under the provisions of
the Act a customer could not be served with those goods in that
shop.[5]   Again, however, the restriction on Sunday trading does
not apply to the sale, despatch, or delivery of goods required for
ships or aircraft, nor to goods sold, despatched or delivered to a club
for the purpose of the club.   The Act does not prevent the cooking
on Sunday, before half past one o'clock in the afternoon, at any
shop, of any goods brought to that shop by a customer and required
by him for consumption on that date, or the despatch and delivery
before that hour of any food so cooked.   It will be a good defence
to a charge of keeping a shop open or of selling or despatching goods
in contravention of the Act, to prove that reasonable grounds
existed for believing that the goods were required in the case of
illness.[6]

No person may be employed on Sunday about the business of a
shop which is open for the serving of customers (a) unless, in the
case of a person so employed for more than four hours on any
Sunday, he receives a whole holiday on a day other than his statutory
half holiday, if any, on a week day of the week beginning with that
Sunday unless he has, in the previous week, received a whole holiday
in respect of the following Sunday employment and is not employed
about the business of a shop more than two other Sundays in the
same month, and (b) in the case of a person not so employed for more
than four hours on a Sunday in any month, that person shall receive
in respect of his employment on any Sunday in the month a half

---

[1] Shops Act, 1950, s. 48 and Sched. 6.
[2] *Ibid.*, s. 49: see s. 50 for the position of shops where several trades or businesses are carried on.   S. 50 does not itself make breach an offence, and charges
should be laid under s. 47; *Tonkin* v. *Raven*, [1959] 1 Q.B. 177; [1958] 3 All
E.R. 374.
[3] *Ibid.*, s. 51.
[4] *Ibid.*, ss. 53 and 54; and see *Miller's Cash Stores, Ltd.* v. *West Ham Corporation*, [1955] 3 All E.R. 282.
[5] *Ibid.*, s. 55.   There are exceptions when Sunday is also Christmas Day, or
when the day following is Christmas Day.
[6] *Ibid.*, 1950, s. 56.

holiday in addition to his statutory half holiday, if any, and that additional half holiday must be on a week day of the week beginning with that Sunday unless he has, in respect of his employment on that Sunday, already received such a half holiday on a week day of the previous week. These provisions do not apply to persons wholly or mainly employed in the sale of intoxicating liquor, to milk roundsmen, employees in a post office or to registered pharmacists and the like.[1]

The provisions relating to Sunday trading extend to any place where any retail trade or business is carried on as if that place were a shop and as if in relation to any such place the person by whom the retail trade or business is carried on were the occupier of a shop.[2] In *Eldorado Ice Cream Co., Ltd.* v. *Clark*[3] the court had to decide whether a warehouse from which tricycles used for the sale of ice cream were loaded was a place within the Act and whether the tricycles were "places" within the Act. In both cases the court answered in the negative. For the warehouse was not used as a place of retail trade or business and no customers were served within it and the word "place" must be construed as meaning a shop or something like a shop and the tricycles were not such. It is now clear that "place" refers to something fixed and does not include a place where a casual sale is made. So where a motor van equipped as a shop stopped to make a sale[4] or where a costermonger stopped his barrow and made sales[5] neither was selling in a "place".

(7) Health, Safety and Welfare in Shops.—Prior to 1963 the provisions for ensuring health, safety and welfare in shops were scanty. There were virtually only three sections in the 1950 Act which dealt with aspects other than hours of work.[6] This lack has been remedied by the comprehensive Offices, Shops and Railway Premises Act, 1963.

Shop premises, for the purposes of this Act, are defined in wider terms than under the 1950 Act so as to include, for example, wholesalers' premises.[7] The definition includes shops, buildings, and parts of buildings where the principal use is carrying on a retail trade or business.[8] This last phrase is specifically said to cover the sale of food and drink, sales by auction and book or periodical lending for gain.[9] It also includes a wholesalers' building where goods are kept for sale wholesale and a building to which members of the public are invited to go to deliver goods for repair or treatment or to themselves repair or treat the goods.[10] Warehouses connected with the running

---

[1] Shops Act, 1950, s. 22. [2] *Ibid.*, s. 58.
[3] [1938] 1 K.B. 715; [1938] 1 All E.R. 330.
[4] *Stone* v. *Boreham*, [1959] 1 Q.B. 1; [1958] 2 All E.R. 715.
[5] *Kahn* v. *Newberry*, [1959] 2 Q.B. 1; [1959] 2 All E.R. 202.
[6] Sections 37–39.
[7] Offices, Shops and Railway Premises Act, 1963, s. 1(3).
[8] *Ibid.*, s. 1(3)(*a*)(ii).   [9] *Ibid.*, s. 1(3)(*b*).
[10] *Ibid.*, s. 1(3)(*a*)(iii) and (iv).

of a dock, wharf or quay are exempted.   Finally included are fuel storage premises being premises where solid fuel is stored which is intended to be sold in the course of trade or business.   This does not include storage places at a dock or colliery.[1]

Buildings occupied together with those falling under this definition are to be treated as forming part of the shop.[2]   Similarly premises which are maintained for the purpose of the sale or supply for immediate consumption of food or drink wholly or mainly to persons employed to work in the premises are included even if they do not fall within the foregoing heads of definition.[3]

The Act lays down common duties applying to all the types of premises it covers.   Its detailed provisions will be covered by the section dealing with offices and reference should be made to this section for the position relating to shops.[4]

2. SPECIAL LEGISLATION RELATING TO THE EMPLOYMENT OF WOMEN, CHILDREN AND YOUNG PERSONS

(1) The Employment of Women, Young Persons and Children Act, 1920.—The 1920 Act was passed in pursuance of a Convention adopted by a general conference of the International Labour Organisation in 1920.   It lays down that no person who is not over the compulsory school age may be employed in any industrial undertaking nor in any vessel, ship or boat except upon those in which only members of the same family are employed or on school or training ships approved and supervised by public authority.[5]

No young person may be employed at night, that is during a period of at least eleven consecutive hours, including the interval between ten o'clock in the evening and five o'clock in the morning, in any industrial undertaking.[6]   The term industrial undertaking specifically includes mines, quarries, industries in which articles are manufactured, altered, cleaned, adapted for sale or demolished or broken up, shipbuilding or the generation, transformation or transmission of electricity or other kinds of motive power.   It will include undertakings for the construction, repair or demolition of railways, harbours, tramways, docks and the like, and undertakings involved in the transport of goods by road or rail.[7]   In coal and lignite mines work may be carried on in the interval between ten o'clock in the evening and five o'clock in the morning if an interval of ordinarily fifteen hours, and in no case of less than thirteen hours, separates the two periods of work.[8]

---

[1] *Ibid.*, s. 1(3)(a)(v).   Solid fuel is defined as coal, coke or solid fuel derived from them.
[2] *Ibid.*, s. 1(3).   [3] *Ibid.*, s. 1(5).   [4] *Supra*, pp. 314 *et seq.*
[5] Employment of Women, Young Persons and Children Act, 1920, s. 1 (1), (2), Schedule, Part IV; and see Education Act, 1944.
[6] Employment of Women, Young Persons and Children Act, 1920, s. 1 (3).
[7] *Ibid.*, Schedule, Part II, article 1.   [8] *Ibid.*, article 3.

Young persons under the age of eighteen years may not be employed during the night in any public or private industrial undertaking excepting in an undertaking in which only members of the same family are employed.   Young persons over the age of sixteen years may be employed in certain undertakings on work which by reason of the process must be carried on continuously by day and night.   Such undertakings will include, amongst others, those engaged in the manufacture of iron and steel, glass works, the manufacture of paper and of raw sugar and in gold mining reduction work.   Moreover, young persons between the ages of sixteen and eighteen years may be employed in what would otherwise be a contravention of these provisions as to night labour where there arises an emergency which could not have been controlled or foreseen and which has interfered with the normal working of the industrial undertaking.[1]

(2) Hours of Employment (Conventions) Act, 1936.—The Hours of Employment (Conventions) Act, 1936, was also enacted in fulfilment of a Convention adopted by the International Labour Organisation.   Women, without distinction of age, may not be employed during the night in any industrial undertaking other than one in which only members of the same family are employed, excepting where there occurs an interruption of work which it was impossible to foresee and which is not of a recurring character or where the work is concerned with materials which are subject to rapid deterioration, when the night work is necessary to preserve the materials from certain loss.   In industrial undertakings which are seasonal in character and in all cases where exceptional circumstances demand it, the night period may be reduced to ten hours on sixty days of the year.   These provisions as to the employment of women during the period of the night do not apply to women holding responsible positions of management who are not ordinarily engaged in manual work.[2]

(3) The Young Persons (Employment) Acts, 1938 and 1964.— The Young Persons (Employment) Act, 1938, deals with certain types of employment not covered by the Factories Act, 1937, nor by the Shops Acts.[3]   Part 1 of the Act applies to young persons employed in any of the following employments where the employment is wholly or mainly in that employment or in two or more of the employments taken together.   The employments detailed are those of (*a*) the collection or delivery of goods or the carrying, loading or unloading of goods incidental to their collection or delivery; (*b*) employment in connection with a business carried on at any

---

[1] Employment of Women, Young Persons and Children Act, 1920, Schedule, Part II, articles 2, 3 & 4.
[2] Hours of Employment (Conventions) Act, 1936, s. 1, Schedule, Part I.
[3] But see the Shops Act, 1950, s. 68.

premises in carrying messages or running errands, being employment
wholly or mainly outside the premises; (c) employment at a residential hotel or club in carrying messages or running errands or in
connection with the reception of guests or members in the hotel or
club; (d) employment in connection with the business carried on at
any premises where a newspaper is published in carrying messages or
running errands; (e) employment at a place of public entertainment
or amusement, or at a public swimming bath, bathing place or
turkish bath, in carrying messages or running errands or in the
reception of or attendance upon persons resorting thereto; (f) employment elsewhere than in a private dwelling house in the operation
of a hoist or lift connected with mechanical power; (g) employment
in, or in connection with the operation of cinematograph apparatus;
(h) employment at any premises occupied for the purposes of the
business of a laundry, dyeing or cleaning works or other factory in
receiving or despatching goods and, added by the 1964 Act, (i)
certain licensed premises.   But Part 1 of the Act does not apply to
the employment of a young person whose hours of employment are
regulated by the Factories Act, 1961, the Mines and Quarries Act,
1954, nor, generally to young persons whose hours of employment
are covered by the Shops Acts or who are employed in connection
with agriculture or in a ship.[1]

The total number of hours to be worked by a young person
engaged in the occupations just enumerated, exclusive of intervals
allowed for meals and rest, shall not exceed forty-four in any week
in the case of a person who has not attained the age of sixteen years,
nor forty-eight hours in the case of a young person who has attained
the age of sixteen years.   Overtime is permitted in the case of persons who have reached the age of sixteen years on occasions of emergency or seasonal or special pressure. The overtime worked must not
exceed six hours in any week nor fifty in any year and where, in any
year, a young person has engaged in overtime employment in twelve
weeks (whether consecutive or not) no further overtime employment
of such persons may be permitted during the remainder of that
year.[2]   Young persons protected by the Act may not be employed
continuously for more than five hours without an interval of at
least half an hour for a meal or rest, and where the hours of employment include the hours from half past eleven in the morning to half
past two in the afternoon, an interval of not less than three quarters
of an hour shall be allowed between those hours for dinner.   On at
least one day in each week young persons may not be employed
after one o'clock in the afternoon.   In every period of twenty-four
hours, between midday on one day and midday on the next, young
persons must be allowed an interval of at least eleven consecutive
hours which must include the hours from ten o'clock in the evening

---

[1] Young Persons (Employment) Act, 1938, s. 7.
[2] *Ibid.*, s. 1.   The Secretary of State may by regulation increase the number
of hours of overtime which may be worked. *Ibid.*, s. 1 (7).

until six o'clock in the morning. There must be no Sunday employment of a young person unless he receives, in respect of such employment, a whole holiday on a week day either in the week beginning with that Sunday or in the previous week, being a week day other than that on which he is not to be employed after one o'clock in the afternoon.[1]

An employer who employs young persons at, or in connection with the business carried on at, a residential hotel, a place of public entertainment or amusement, or a public swimming bath, bathing place or turkish bath, being a young person to whom, apart from section 68 of the Shops Act, 1950,[2] the provisions of that Act or the provisions of Part 1 of the Young Persons (Employment) Act, 1938, would apply, may elect by which of the two Acts he shall be bound in respect of such persons.[3]

3. LEGISLATION CONCERNING OFFICES

The imposition by statute of a minimum standard of welfare, safety and health has never been confined to industry in its narrow sense. In agriculture the Threshing Machines Act, 1878, provided for the sufficient and secure fencing of the drum and feeding mouth of threshing machines and the Chaff-Cutting Machines (Accidents) Act, 1897, provided for the fencing of the mouth or box, the fly-wheel and knives of chaff-cutting machines. Both these statutes laid down these duties subject to the qualification " as far as is reasonably practicable and consistent with the due and efficient working of the machine," thus laying down a standard less than that now required under the Factories Acts.

A committee under the Chairmanship of Sir Ernest Gowers reported in March 1949, and one of its terms of reference was to consider " the statutory provisions relating to health, welfare and safety of employed persons at places of employment other than those regulated under the Factories or Mines and Quarries Acts."[4] This report was a focal point in the campaign to get regulation of this type for offices.[5] Although the Government expressed support for the recommendations concerning offices nothing was done until 1959 when a private member introduced an Offices Bill. This, having received a second reading in the face of Government opposition, was given Government support and passed as the Offices Act, 1960, which came into force at the beginning of 1962.[6] This Act was repealed and replaced by the Offices, Shops and Railway

---

[1] *Ibid.*, s. 1.
[2] *Ibid.*, s. 8.
[3] Shops Act, 1950, s. 68; see also Sched. 8.
[4] Cmnd. 7664.
[5] There is a considerable history of efforts to achieve this. Between 1923 and 1936 eleven private members' bills were introduced into the House of Commons.
[6] Offices Act, 1960, s. 15.

Premises Act, 1963, before it became operative.   The new statute
has gone a considerable way to putting the regulation of offices on
the same footing as factories and the basic structure of the Act
follows the pattern of the Factories Act.

(1) Definition of Office.—The Act defines in particular detail
offices, shops and railway premises, the principal types of workplaces
to which it applies.   Office premises are a building or part of a
building the sole or principal use of which is as an office or for office
purposes.[1]   Office purposes are not exhaustively defined but are said
to include administration, clerical work, handling of money and
telephone or telegraph operating.[2]   Clerical work is further defined
as including writing, book-keeping, sorting papers, filing, typing,
duplicating, machine calculating, drawing and the editorial preparation of matter for publication.[3]

Any premises which are occupied together with office premises
for the purpose of activities carried on in the office form part of the
premises governed by this statute.[4]   In particular premises maintained in conjunction with the office premises for the sale or supply
for consumption of food or drink wholly or mainly to persons employed in the offices will be covered by the Act.[5]

Premises in which the only workers are near relatives of the employer are not included, nor is a dwelling house in which a person
living there does work he is employed to do.[6]   If the sum total of
work done by those employed on premises does not normally exceed
twenty-one hours a week, the premises in question are also excluded.[7]

To ensure proper integration it is provided that the Act shall not
apply to any premises which form part of a factory and are therefore
governed by the Factories Acts, 1961, nor to premises which are
below ground and constitute a mine under the Mines and Quarries
Act, 1954.[8]

(2) Health and Welfare.—The scheme of the Act is that general
provisions are set out in the various sections and, where appropriate,
power is also vested in the Secretary of State for Employment to
make regulations amplifying what is laid down.

The health provisions cover similar topics to those dealt with in
the Factories Act but the detail of the requirements differ.   Thus
the first provision is that all premises, furniture, furnishing and
fittings must be kept clean.[9]   No dirt or refuse must be allowed to

---

[1] Offices, Shops and Railway Premises Act, 1963, s. 1(2).

[2] *Ibid.*, s. 1(2)(*b*).

[3] *Ibid.*, s. 1(2)(*c*).

[4] *Ibid.*, s. 1(2).

[5] *Ibid.*, s. 1(5).

[6] *Ibid.*, s. 2.   The list of relatives is husband, wife, parent, grandparent, son,
daughter, grandchild, brother or sister.

[7] *Ibid.*, s. 3.   The Secretary of State has power to reduce the figure of twenty-
one by regulation.

[8] *Ibid.*, s. 85(3).

[9] *Ibid.*, s. 4.

accumulate and floors and steps must be cleaned at least weekly by sweeping or washing. The Secretary of State is further empowered to make regulations applying to premises generally or any particular class of premises to ensure that a proper standard of cleanliness is achieved. The provisions of the Act are in places quite complicated and the next section dealing with overcrowding is an example of this.[1] It says, generally, that no room in premises covered by the Act must be so overcrowded as to constitute a risk to the health of persons working there. In determining whether or not there is overcrowding attention must be paid not only to the number of persons employed in the room but also to the furniture, fittings, machinery and so on in the room. The section goes on to lay down a fairly complicated formula the effect of which is to ensure that each person employed in the room has at least 40 square feet of floor space and 400 cubic feet of breathing space.[2] These specialised formulae do not apply to rooms to which members of the public have access, but the general rule will apply.[3]

The temperature of rooms in which persons work for other than short periods must be maintained at a reasonable level.[4] This must not be achieved by any method which contaminates the air with injurious or offensive fumes. If the work done in the room is not substantially of a kind requiring severe manual effort the temperature after the first hour of work must not fall below the reasonable standard of 16 degrees Centigrade.[5] These rules do not apply to a room to which the public come in which maintenance of such a temperature is not reasonably practicable. Nor do they apply to rooms where if followed there would result a deterioration of goods.[6] Enforcement of the rules is assisted by the provision that a thermometer must be kept on any floor of premises on which there is a room governed by these rules. The thermometer must be kept in a prominent place, available to test the temperature in the rooms in question.[7] The Secretary of State is empowered to provide varying temperatures for premises generally or for different classes of premises. He can also forbid methods of maintaining temperatures which are likely to be injurious to workers and he can order special provision of additional thermometers.[8]

Every room in which persons are employed must be adequately ventilated and supplied with fresh or artificially purified air.[9] A similarly general provision covers lighting which must be sufficient

---

[1] Offices, Shops and Railway Premises Act, 1963, s. 5.
[2] *Ibid.*, s. 5(2). This subsection does not have effect for three years after the general rule comes into force.
[3] *Ibid.*, s. 5(2)(*b*).
[4] *Ibid.*, s. 6.
[5] *Ibid.*, s. 6(2)—the equivalent is 60·8 degrees Fahrenheit.
[6] *Ibid.*, s. 6(3).
[7] *Ibid.*, s. 6(4).
[8] *Ibid.*, s. 6(5).
[9] *Ibid.*, s. 7.

and suitable, whether natural or artificial.[1]   It is also provided in this section that windows and skylights which are used for lighting must be kept clean on both inner and outer surfaces as far as is reasonably practicable.   This is not to affect the practice of white-washing or shading windows to minimise heat or glare.[2]

Suitable and sufficient sanitary conveniences must be provided and the Secretary of State can, by regulation, provide that there must be separate provision for each sex.[3]   The foregoing sections correspond to those in Part I of the Factories Act—entitled Health (General Provisions) and reference should be made to the case law which has been decided on these sections for there can be no doubt that it will be a useful guide to some problems of interpretation.[4] The sections which follow correspond to those in the Factories Act, Part III—entitled Welfare (General Provisions).[5]

Washing facilities must be provided which are suitable and suffi-cient.   They are to include a supply of running hot and cold or warm water, soap, clean towels or other suitable means of cleaning or drying.[6]   The wash place must be effectively lit and kept clean and in an orderly condition and all apparatus must be properly maintained.[7]   Again in this section the Secretary of State is empowered to provide by regulation that separate facilities should be available for each of the sexes.[8]   It is not necessary in this, or the following section, that the facilities should be for the exclusive use of the workers employed in the premises concerned and the sec-tions will be satisfied if they have the use of facilities provided for others as long as all the other requirements of the sections have been fulfilled.[9]

The next section requires the provision of a supply of wholesome drinking water.   This must be piped, or, if supplied in vessels, renewed daily.[10]   Discardable drinking vessels must be supplied or washable vessels and clean water in which to rinse them.[11]

There must be provision so that persons employed on premises to which the Act applies can hang up or otherwise accommodate clothing which they do not wear during working hours.   As far as is reasonably practicable arrangements must also be made for drying this clothing.[12]   If special clothes have to be worn during work similar facilities must be provided for these clothes if they are not taken home by the worker.[13]

---

[1] Offices, Shops and Railway Premises Act, 1963, s. 8.
[2] *Ibid.*, s. 8(3).   [3] *Ibid.*, s. 9.
[4] Factories Act, 1961, ss. 1–7.   See *supra*, pp. 271 *et seq.*
[5] *Ibid.*, ss. 57–60.   See *supra*, pp. 301 *et seq.*
[6] Offices, Shops and Railway Premises Act, 1963, s. 10.
[7] *Ibid.*, s. 10(2).
[8] *Ibid.*, s. 10(4).
[9] *Ibid.*, s. 10(5) and s. 11(4).
[10] *Ibid.*, s. 11.
[11] *Ibid.*, s. 11(3).
[12] *Ibid.*, s. 12(1).
[13] *Ibid.*, s. 12(2).

Where a person's work provides opportunities for sitting without detriment to the work then facilities must be provided to enable them to sit. In a shop provision will not be reasonable unless at least one seat is provided for every three assistants. It is an offence for the employer if he fails to permit workers to use facilities provided under this section whenever use does not interfere with work.[1] Where the work is sedentary work as to the whole or a substantial part of it then a suitable seat must be provided along with a foot rest if one is necessary to support the feet.[2]

If employed persons eat in shop premises suitable and sufficient facilities must be provided.[3]

(3) Safety.—The first of the sections dealing with safety is almost identical in terms to that in the Factories Act dealing with floors, passages and stairs.[4] Briefly, these must be kept free from obstruction or slippery substances and must be soundly constructed and properly maintained. Staircases must have a hand rail or hand hold which must be on the open side if there is one, or on both sides if it has two. The open sides must also be guarded so that a person cannot slip between the hand hold or rail and the steps. All openings in floors must be securely fenced except where the nature of the work renders this impracticable.[5] These rules do not apply to fuel storage premises in the open for which there are special provisions of a more appropriate kind. The surface of the ground is to be kept in good repair, steps and platforms are to be soundly constructed and properly maintained and openings in platforms are to be securely fenced as far as is practicable.[6]

The Factories Act division of machinery into three categories— prime movers, transmission machinery and other machinery—is not reproduced in this Act.[7] The fencing section applies to every dangerous part of any machinery used as equipment in the premises.[8] These must be securely fenced unless by virtue of construction or position they are safe to every person working in the premises as if securely fenced. If the nature of the machine prevents the fixing of a fixed guard the duty will be discharged by means of an automatic guard which prevents the operator of the machine from coming into contact with it.[9] There is special provision for examining, lubricating or adjusting machinery where this can only be done whilst it is in motion. The fencing requirement does not apply where this is

---

[1] Offices, Shops and Railway Premises Act, 1963, s. 13.
[2] *Ibid.*, s. 13.
[3] *Ibid.*, s. 14.
[4] *Ibid.*, s. 16. The equivalent section in the Factories Act, 1961, is s. 28. See *supra*, p. 291.
[5] Offices, Shops and Railway Premises Act, 1963, s. 16(4).
[6] *Ibid.*, s. 16(5).
[7] For a full discussion of the fencing sections under the Factories Act, 1961, see *supra*, pp. 274. *et seq.*
[8] Offices, Shops and Railway Premises Act, 1963, s. 17.
[9] *Ibid.*, s. 17(2).

being done.[1] These operations apart, the fences, which must be of substantial construction and properly maintained, must be kept in proper position whilst the parts to be guarded against are in motion or use.[2]   No person under the age of eighteen may carry out the permitted operations with an unfenced machine nor may a young person similarly clean a machine where this exposes him to risk of injury.[3]   Persons using machinery which the Secretary of State may by regulation specify as being of a dangerous character must be sufficiently trained or adequately supervised by a knowledgeable and experienced person.[4]   For an instance of application and a discussion of the phrase " all due diligence ", see *J. H. Dewhurst, Ltd.* v. *Coventry Corporation.*[5]

The Secretary of State is empowered to make regulations protecting workers against risks to themselves or to their health arising from noise or vibration.[6]   There is also a rule that no person must be required in the course of his work to lift, carry or move a load which is so heavy as to be likely to injure him.[7]

There is an extensive section securing proper first aid provisions.[8] All premises covered by the Act must have a first aid box or cupboard and additional boxes or cupboards where the number of workers exceeds 150 so that there is one for each unit of 150 workers and one for any fraction remaining.   The contents of the box or cupboard are a matter for regulation by the Secretary of State but the container in question must only be used for first aid equipment.[9] Each box or cupboard must be in the charge of a responsible person who must have responsibility only for that one box.   At least one of the persons in charge of the boxes must have had training in first aid treatment and he must be always available during working hours.[10] A notice must be posted in a prominent position setting out the first aid provisions that have been made under the requirements of the Act.[11]   Where an employer maintains a first aid room offering immediate treatment to workers requiring it in particular premises, those premises may be excused from the requirements of this section since they clearly supersede them in provision.[12]

(4) **Fire.**—As with the Factories Act there is a long series of provisions laying down rules relating to fire precautions.   These require the provision of reasonable means of escape in case of fire, having regard to the number of persons expected to be on the premises, taking

---

[1] Offices, Shops and Railway Premises Act, 1963, s. 17(3).
[2] *Ibid.*, s. 17(4).
[3] *Ibid.*, s. 17(5).
[4] *Ibid.*, s. 18.   Young person means under eighteen.
[5] [1970] 1 Q.B. 20; [1969] 3 All E.R. 1225.
[6] *Ibid.*, 1963, s. 21.
[7] *Ibid.*, s. 23.
[8] *Ibid.*, s. 24.
[9] *Ibid.*, s. 24(2).
[10] *Ibid.*, s. 24(4).
[11] *Ibid.*, s. 24(5).
[12] *Ibid.*, s. 24(7).

account of both those working there and those likely to be there otherwise than as workers.[1]   Where premises are to be used so that at any one time more than twenty persons are employed to work there or more than ten persons are to work on other than a ground floor or where underneath any work premises explosive or highly inflammable materials are stored the premises cannot be used unless a fire certificate has been issued.   The rule applies to buildings as a whole and this means that workers in differing employment in the same premises must be aggregated when determining whether a fire certificate is required.   The fire certificate will be issued only where the fire authority is satisfied as to the provision of means of escape.[2] The certificate, when issued, must be kept on the premises, and failure on the part of the occupier of premises to obtain such a certificate where appropriate is punishable by a fine.[3]   Means of escape which are provided must be properly maintained and kept free from obstruction.[4]   A continuance of satisfactory fire pre-cautions is sought by the provision that the fire authority may in-spect the premises at any time.   It is also necessary, while a fire certificate is in force with respect to any premises, to notify an intention to make material extensions or structural alterations or to increase the number of persons employed in the premises at any one time or to store inflammable materials.   Alterations may then be required.   Failure to comply is again made an offence and on con-viction the fire authority must revoke the fire certificate, and the authority has further power to cancel a fire certificate without pro-ceedings if there has been contravention.[4]

The Act provides a right of appeal against the refusal of a fire certificate or of the amendment of a certificate or of a cancellation and also against the fire authority's requirement that alterations be made and that a fire certificate be suspended until such alterations are satisfactorily completed.   The appeal must be made within twenty-one days of the actions complained of to the magistrates in the area of the premises.[5]   Where premises under the Act are felt to be dangerous application may be made to the magistrates for an order that no one be employed in the premises or part of them, or that no one be employed on particular processes or to do some par-ticular work until appropriate steps have been taken to remove the danger.[6]   Doors through which workers may have to pass in case of

---

[1] Offices, Shops and Railway Premises Act, 1963, s. 28.

[2] *Ibid.*, s. 29(1), (8) and (9).   " Fire authority " usually means the appropri-ate body under the Fire Service Act, 1947, but some of the duties are laid elsewhere—the efficiency of alarms is the responsibility of the inspectorate, i.e. of shops, offices, factories, mines and quarries, as appropriate.   S. 39 deals with the detailed allocation of function.

[3] *Ibid.*, s. 29(6).

[4] *Ibid.*, s. 30.

[5] *Ibid.*, s. 31.   There is the usual suspension of the effect of the action pend-ing the determination of the appeal, s. 31(2).   *R.* v. *Recorder of Oxford Ex. parte Brasenose College,* [1970] 1 Q.B. 109; [1969] 3 All E.R. 428.

[6] Offices, Shops and Railway Premises Act, 1963, s. 32.

fire must not be locked or fastened so that they cannot be immediately opened whilst workers are on the premises either at work or eating a meal. The contents of rooms in the premises must be so arranged as to afford free passageway to a means of escape in case of fire. Where a fire certificate is in force all exits giving access to means of escape which are not in ordinary use must be distinctively and conspicuously marked by notices printed in letters of adequate size.[1] Effective fire alarms must be provided in premises to which a fire certificate applies and these alarms must be examined at least once every three months and whenever the fire authority requires.[2] Effective steps must be taken to ensure that all persons employed on premises to which a fire certificate applies are familiar with the means of escape, their use, and the routine to be followed in case of fire.[3]

The Secretary of State is given very wide power to make regulations. He may do so with respect to means of escape to strengthen in general or particular cases the statutory provisions,[4] he may also make regulations to reduce the risk of the outbreak of fire by prescribing requirements as to internal construction of premises and the materials to be used.[5]

All premises must be provided with appropriate fire fighting equipment, which must be placed readily available for use. Again the Secretary of State is empowered to make special regulations stengthening this general requirement.[6]

(5) Special provisions.—One of the problems which is more applicable to the types of premises governed by this Act as opposed to those coming under the Factories Act is that of buildings which are in multiple occupation by different employers. This is tackled by two lengthy sections, ss. 42 and 43. The principle used is to put the onus for compliance with appropriate provisions on the owner of the premises, rather than on the occupiers. The shift of duty applies, for example, to cleanliness, lighting and safety of common parts, washing facilities and fire precautions. Fuel storage premises in single ownership are treated in the same way.[7]

There is finally a section of the Act making provision for particular deviation from the general application of the Act. Both the Secretary of State[8] and enforcing authorities[9] are given power to allow exemptions. The Secretary of State, for instance, may by order exempt premises from any or all of the obligations about overcrowding or temperature set out in ss. 5(2) and 6. Enforcing authorities have similar powers of exemption in these instances.

---

[1] Offices, Shops and Railway Premises Act, 1963, s. 33.
[2] *Ibid.*, s. 34. Here the authority is the appropriate inspectorate.
[3] *Ibid.*, s. 35.
[4] *Ibid.*, s. 37(1).
[5] *Ibid.*, s. 37(2).
[6] *Ibid.*, s. 38.
[7] *Ibid.*, s. 44.
[8] *Ibid.*, s. 45.
[9] *Ibid.*, s. 46.

(6) Enforcement.—Any attempt by those upon whom new duties have been placed to avoid the burden is defeated by making it an offence for the owner or occupier of premises to levy employees in respect of any expense incurred.[1] The ground work for enforcement is provided by the establishment of the duty to notify accidents occurring in premises covered by the Act which cause the death of a person employed there or disablement from doing his usual work for more than three days.[2] In the same way before a person first begins to employ persons to work in premises covered by the Act he must give notice in prescribed form.[3] Notice under these sections has to be given to the " appropriate authority ". The appropriate authority is basically the local authority who must appoint an inspectorate to discharge this function.[4] Certain areas of the Act, however, are enforced by other authorities. Fire precuations[5] are the responsibility of the fire authority. The relationship between this statute and the Factories Act is achieved by making the factory inspectorate responsible for certain premises, for example those coming under this Act but which would form part of a factory but for the exclusion in s. 175(6) of the Factories Act, 1961, of premises used solely for some purposes other than the processes carried on in the factory, for office premises erected for building operations, for railway premises and for offices of railway undertakings in the vicinity of a railway and for fuel storage premises of a railway.[6] Similarly office and shop premises which form part of a mine or quarry are to be supervised by the mines and quarries inspectors.[7]

The newly created inspectorate is provided with powers similar to those of existing inspectorates. These cover entry of premises at any reasonable time, necessary examinations or inquiries, accompaniment of a constable if serious obstruction is feared, questioning of persons found on the premises, or believed to have worked on them within the previous two months, and production of a fire certificate where appropriate.[8]

There is an interesting provision aimed at securing uniformity by the local authorities' inspectors. The Secretary of State is given two specific powers to help in this. He can make regulations as to the manner of discharge of the duties of the inspectors and the exercise of their powers and he can also appoint officers charged with the task of informing the Secretary of State how the duties are being discharged—an inspectorate of the inspectors.[9]

The Act finally provides for the appropriate penalties for contravention of its provisions or of regulations made under the Act.

---

[1] Offices, Shops and Railway Premises Act, 1963, s. 47.
[2] *Ibid.*, s. 48(1).
[3] *Ibid.*, s. 49(1). For the form see S.I. 1964 No. 533.
[4] *Ibid.*, s. 52(1).
[5] *Ibid.*, ss. 28 to 38.
[6] *Ibid.*, s. 52(4).
[7] *Ibid.*, s. 52(6).
[8] *Ibid.*, s. 53.
[9] *Ibid.*, s. 63.

The basic penalty is a fine of a maximum of £60 with a daily penalty of a maximum of £15 for each day the contravention continues. Where the contravention is such that death or serious injury was likely the maximum fine is increased to £300.[1]

4. Legislation concerning Mines and Quarries

Until the year 1942, the general responsibility for the welfare of workers engaged in mines and quarries lay with the Board of Trade in which there was a Mines Department having a Parliamentary Secretary. This department exercised, on behalf of the Board, the powers of the Board relating to the Mining Industry. In 1942 a Minister of Fuel and Power was appointed and to the new Minister were transferred all the functions of the Board of Trade relating to coal, minerals, mines and the mining industry, quarries and petroleum, other than the functions relating to weights and measures. The appropriate authority is now the Secretary of State for Trade and Industry.[2]

(1) Hours and Conditions of Labour in Mines and Quarries.— There is an absolute prohibition against the employment of female workers underground and, after July 1st, 1957, in relation to mines of any class, no male young person who has not attained the age of sixteen may be employed below ground except for the purpose of receiving instructions of such description as may be prescribed.[3] A woman or young person (*i.e.* one over the compulsory school age who has not reached the age of eighteen)[4] employed above ground at a mine or employed at a quarry may not work more than nine hours a day, nor more than forty-eight in any week, exclusive of intervals for meals and rest, except that in the case of young male persons over the age of sixteen when the hours worked in the day may not exceed eight unless the intervals allowed for a meal or rest between spells amount to less than one and a half hours. A woman or young person may not be employed continuously for a spell of more than four and a half hours without a meal or rest interval of at least half an hour; but where an interval of not less than ten minutes is allowed in the course of a spell, the spell may be increased to five hours.[5]

The total hours worked by a young person below ground[6] at mines other than of coal, stratified ironstone, shale or fireclay (including meal and rest intervals), the period between the time at which he must attend for the purpose of going below ground and the time at

---

[1] Offices, Shops and Railway Premises Act, 1963, s. 64.
[2] S.I. 1970, No. 1537.
[3] Mines and Quarries Act, 1954, s. 124; S.I. 1957, No. 1093.
[4] *Ibid.*, s. 182.
[5] *Ibid.*, s. 125.
[6] See s. 132(1) for the determination of hours spent below ground for the purposes of that part of the Act under discussion.

which he arrives at his working place and the period between the time at which he leaves his working place and the time at which he returns to the surface must not exceed nine a day or forty-eight a week.[1]

A woman employed at a mine or quarry may not be employed earlier than six o'clock in the morning, nor later than ten o'clock in the evening, or on Saturday, two o'clock in the afternoon.[2]

A female young person working at a mine or quarry or a male who has not reached the age of sixteen and who is employed above ground may not be employed before six in the morning nor after nine in the evening or on Saturday after two o'clock in the afternoon.[3]

A young male who has not reached the age of sixteen and who is employed below ground at a mine may not begin earlier than six in the morning nor end later than ten o'clock in the evening or, on Saturday, two o'clock in the afternoon.[4]

A woman employed at a mine or quarry and such young persons as have been mentioned in the last two paragraphs must be given intervals of not less than twelve hours between successive periods of employment, and Sunday employment in mines and quarries is forbidden for women and such young persons.[5]

Unless special exceptions provide to the contrary a male young person above the age of sixteen whether employed above or below ground at a mine or at a quarry may not be employed earlier than six o'clock in the morning nor after ten o'clock in the evening nor after two o'clock on Saturday, nor at any time on Sunday except where the work consists of surveying, measuring, repairing or maintaining, which work must be done at that time.[6]

A responsible person[7] may, where authorised (by the Secretary of State in respect of all mines or quarries or any class of such, or by an inspector in the case of a particular mine or quarry), post a notice directing that for the reference to six o'clock in the morning may be substituted such earlier time as may be specified not being earlier than five o'clock in the morning and/or post a direction substituting for the reference to ten o'clock in the evening such later time as may be specified not being later than eleven o'clock. But any such directions will be void if their combined effect extends the period of employment of the young persons employed at the mine or quarry by more than one hour.[8]

---

[1] Mines and Quarries Act, 1954, s. 125.
[2] *Ibid.*, s. 126 (1).
[3] *Ibid.*, s. 126 (2).
[4] *Ibid.*, s. 126 (3).
[5] *Ibid.*, s. 126 (4 and 5).
[6] *Ibid.*, s. 127 (1).   The China Clay and China Stone Quarries (Employment of Young Persons) Order, 1957, No. 410 provides that male employees over sixteen but under eighteen may begin work not earlier than 5 a.m.
[7] *I.e.* the manager of a mine and the owner of a quarry: *ibid.*, s. 182.
[8] *Ibid.*, s. 127.

Moreover every male young person covered by section 127 must
be given an interval of not less than twelve hours between successive
spells of employment and where such a young person is employed
at a mine or quarry after two o'clock in the afternoon on a Saturday
he may not be employed after two o'clock in the afternoon of one
of the days falling between the next following Sunday and the next
following Saturday, and where a young person is so employed on a
Sunday he shall not be employed at the mine or quarry at any time
on one of the days falling between that day and the next following
Saturday.[1]

The person responsible must fix, within the limits of the provisions
set out, the period of employment for each day of the week for the
women and young persons employed at the mine or quarry and any
intervals allowed for meals or rest and must specify in a notice these
periods and intervals.   Every woman or young person employed
must be employed in accordance with the notice.   Different periods
of employment and different intervals may be fixed for different
classes of women and young persons and for different days of the
week.   The periods or intervals fixed may not be changed until the
responsible person has given notice to the inspector for the district
and has given notice in a conspicuous place at the mine or quarry
of his intention to make the change.   A change shall not be made
oftener than once in three months unless for special cause shown and
allowed by the inspector.[2]

Special temporary exceptions relate to the employment of male
young persons in coal mines in Durham, Northumberland and
Warwick and there are also provisions designed to enable any
accident or emergency to be dealt with.[3]

In mines of coal, stratified ironstone, shale and fireclay the general
rule is that no workman may be below ground in a mine for the
purposes of his work and of going to and from his work for more than
seven hours during any consecutive twenty-four hours.[4]   Time
underground will be reckoned, in the case of workmen working in
a shift, from the time at which the last workman in the shift leaves
the surface and the first workman in the shift returns to the surface.[5]
These provisions will not be contravened where the workman
exceeds the prescribed time underground in order to render
assistance in an accident or for the purpose of meeting any danger
actual or feared or for dealing with emergencies or work uncom-
pleted through unforeseen dangers and the like.[6]   The manager

---

[1] Mines and Quarries Act, 1954, s. 127.
[2] *Ibid.*, s. 128.
[3] *Ibid.*, ss. 129, 130 and see s. 132 for the application of certain sections of
the Act to persons holding responsible positions of management, etc.
[4] Coal Mines Regulation Act, 1908, s. 1, as amended by the Coal Mines Act,
1919, s. 1.   See also Mines and Quarries Act, 1954, Sched. 5.
[5] Coal Mines Regulation Act, 1908, s. 1.
[6] *Ibid.*

must appoint an agent or agents to direct the lowering and raising of men to and from the mine and must keep a register containing particulars of the times at which men are lowered and raised. The workmen may, at their own cost, appoint a person or persons to observe the times of lowering and raising.[1] The prescribed time of seven hours for employment below ground may be extended by not more than half an hour provided that a register of such extension of times is kept.[2] There is a power to suspend the operation of the Coal Mines Regulation Act, 1908, in the event of war, emergency, or grave economic disturbance and the period of underground employment may also be extended in the case of certain employees and certain districts.[3]

(2) Safety in Mines and Quarries

Administration

The law relating to the management and control of mines and quarries underwent the severe legislative overhaul to which factory law was subjected in the Factories Act, 1937. Formerly two separate codes existed. The law dealing with employment in mines was largely, but not exclusively, to be found in the Coal Mines Act, 1911, as amended, whilst the law governing quarries was chiefly contained in the Metalliferous Mines Regulation Acts, 1872 and 1875. The Mines and Quarries Act, 1954, reduces this legislation, and much more, to the bounds of one principal statute. The Act came into force on January 1, 1957,[4] except for sections 172 and 190, which operated from the day the Act received the Royal assent, *i.e.* November 25, 1954.[5]

No single statute, however inclusive its terms, can hope to cope with the manifold exigencies of a modern industry. Resort must be had to regulations which will define and amplify powers and provide the machinery, less cumbersome than the amendment of an Act of Parliament, by which the law may be kept abreast of changing industrial processes. The Mines and Quarries Act bestows on the Secretary of State a wide power to make regulations. These regulations are either " general " or " special " in character. A " general " regulation is not applicable to a particular mine or quarry only, whilst a " special " regulation is limited to particular mines and quarries.[6] The procedure for making regulations is laid down in the second schedule to the Act.

---

[1] Coal Mines Regulation Act, 1908, s. 2 as amended by Mines and Quarries Act, 1954, Sched. 5.

[2] *Ibid.*, s. 3, as amended by the Coal Mines Act, 1931, s. 1. Sections 1 and 3 of the 1908 Act suspended as to Coal Mines to April 30th, 1958 (S.I. 1957, No. 751).

[3] Coal Mines Regulation Act, 1908, s. 4.

[4] Mines and Quarries Act, 1954 (Commencement) Order, 1956, No. 1530.

[5] Mines and Quarries Act, 1954, s. 194. For the relationship of the Act to the Factories Acts, see s. 184.

[6] *Ibid.*, ss. 141–3.

As a consequence of the amalgamation of the law in the Mines and Quarries Act there are parts of the Act which are relevant only to mines, parts which apply to quarries alone and parts which operate on both, and it is to these general parts, applying to quarries and mines alike, or with minor amendments, that we shall first turn.

A mine is defined as an excavation or system of excavations made for the purpose of, or in connection with, the getting, wholly or substantially, by means involving the employment of persons below ground, of minerals (whether in their natural state or in solution or suspension), or the products of minerals.   A quarry is an excavation or system of excavations having the same purposes being neither a mine, nor a well nor bore hole, nor a well and bore hole combined.[1]

Inspection

The Act imposes onerous duties and responsibilities on owners, managers and officials and these we shall later discuss.   The local administration and enforcement of the Act is largely in the charge of inspectors who may be appointed by the Secretary of State in such numbers as he believes necessary.   He will assign to them their duties.   The Secretary of State must assure himself before appointment that the appointee has no interest, financial or of any other kind, which is likely to conflict with his duty.[2]   The inspector, in pursuance of his duties under the Act, may at any time, day or night, enter a mine or quarry or central rescue station and inspect it in whole or part and any animals employed for its purposes.   He may make such examination as may be necessary to assure himself that the provisions of the Act and any other regulations or notices made under it are being observed; to ascertain anything relating to the safety or health of persons employed or the care and treatment of animals, and the causes and circumstances of any accident or other occurrence.   He may take with him a constable where he reasonably fears obstruction, or where he wishes to examine the care and treatment of animals he may take a duly qualified veterinary surgeon.

The inspector may require any person whom he finds at a mine, quarry or central rescue station or whom he reasonably believes to be or to have been within the preceding two months employed at such a place to answer, in the absence of persons other than a person nominated by him to be present, all proper questions.   Answers to such questions are however not admissible in evidence against him in any proceedings.   He may take samples of articles or substances found at a mine or quarry, and in the case of a mine, samples of the atmosphere.   He may take possession of any article which appears to him to have caused or to be likely to cause danger; he may have such articles dismantled or subjected to processes or tests, notwithstanding that they are thereby damaged or destroyed.

It is within the power of an inspector to demand the production

---

[1] Mines and Quarries Act, 1954, s. 180.
[2] *Ibid.*, s. 144.

of books, records, documents, and plans,[1] and to require a manager of a mine to mark on a plan the state of the workings and to require any person having responsibilities in the mine or quarry to give him all necessary facilities and assistance, and, in addition, he may exercise such other powers as may be necessary to carry the Act into effect.

It is an offence to fail to comply with a requirement imposed by an inspector, or to prevent or to attempt to prevent any other person from appearing before an inspector or from answering any questions; or without the inspector's permission, to remove from a mine or quarry or to conceal or tamper with any machinery, apparatus, or other articles of which the inspector has taken possession, or to obstruct an inspector in the exercise of his powers or duties.[2]

Where an inspector is of the opinion that a mine or quarry is likely to become dangerous, he may serve a notice stating that he is of that opinion and imposing such prohibitions, restrictions or requirements as are necessary to safeguard safety or health.[3]

It is not the State alone which has a power of inspection. So as to enable inspections to be made on behalf of workmen, a panel of persons each of whom has not less than five years' practical experience of mining or quarrying may be appointed for that mine or quarry. The appointments will be made, where there is an association or body representative of a majority of the total number of persons employed at the mine or quarry, by that association or body; and in other cases by associations or bodies which are together representative of such a majority. The owner of the mine or quarry must permit such inspections to be carried out as will enable two of the members of the panel to inspect every part of the quarry or mine and its equipment once at least in every month—and one of the two must be employed at the mine or quarry. On the occurrence of an accident any two members of the panel (one at least of whom is employed at the mine or quarry) may together inspect the place where the accident or other occurrence occurred and, so far as is necessary for the purpose of finding the cause of the accident, they may inspect any part of the mine or quarry and any machinery and equipment, and may take samples of the atmosphere and of any dust or water.

When carrying out an inspection, members of the panel have a right to inspect documents and may take with them their advisers. But they may not, on such an inspection at a mine, preclude the attendance of the owner or his nominee, the manager and his nominee and any under-manager. Similarly, at the inspection of a

---

[1] For the general duty to keep records, etc., by owners, managers, etc., see Part IX, Mines and Quarries Act, 1954, ss. 133–140.

[2] *Ibid.*, s. 145.

[3] *Ibid.*, s. 146.

quarry they may not preclude the owner and his nominee and the manager and his nominee from accompanying them.   All employed persons are under obligation to afford to members of the panel all requisite facilities and assistance, and the manager of the mine or quarry has special obligations to furnish the panel with information as to the nature and extent of the workings.   The members of the panel, when they have finished their inspections, must make, in a book provided for this purpose by the owner, a full and accurate report, one copy of which will be sent to the inspector for the district and a second of which must be posted in a conspicuous position at the mine or quarry, for a period of twenty-four hours.[1]

Notification and Investigation

The general rules as to the notification and investigation of accidents and disease apply to both mines and quarries.   Where an accident causes death or serious bodily injury to an employed person notice must be given to the inspector and to such other person as may, for the time being, be nominated.   This latter person will be nominated, where there is an association or body representative of a majority of employed persons, by that association, and in other cases jointly by the associations or bodies which are together representative of such a majority.   Where an accident which has been notified as involving serious bodily injury ultimately results in death, notice of the death shall forthwith be given to the inspector and the nominated person.   Where an accident occurs to a person employed at a mine or quarry the owner of which is not the employer of that person, the actual employer will commit an offence if he fails to report the death to the responsible person immediately.[2]

If the Secretary of State believes that a special class of occurrences at mines and quarries is of so dangerous a nature as to make it desirable that they should be made notifiable, he may, by order, require such notification whether death or serious bodily injury occurs or not.   Where proceedings are brought in consequence of a failure to give notice it will be a defence to prove lack of knowledge of the occurrences and that the defendant had taken all reasonable steps to have occurrences of the kind in question brought to his notice.[3]   The Secretary of State may also, by order, apply the provisions as to notification of accidents to such diseases as he may specify.[4]

A coroner who holds an inquest on a person whose death may have been caused by an accident at a quarry or mine must adjourn the inquest unless an inspector or some other person on behalf of the Secretary of State is present to watch the proceedings.   Where he adjourns the inquest he must give to the inspector at least four days' notice of the time and place of the adjourned hearing.   But before adjournment, the coroner may take evidence of identification and

---

[1] Mines and Quarries Act, 1954, s. 123.
[2] *Ibid.*, s. 116; see also S.I. 1957, No. 1095.
[3] *Ibid.*, s. 117.
[4] *Ibid.*, s. 118.

order burial, and if the inquest relates to the death of only one person the coroner need not adjourn the inquest if twenty-four hours' notice was given to the district inspector of the time and place of the hearing. Should evidence be given, at an inquest at which an inspector is not present, of any neglect as having caused or contributed to the accident, or of any defect which appears to require remedy, the coroner shall inform the inspector of the facts.[1]

Where there occurs an accident or occurrence of which notice must be given no person may disturb the place of occurrence and anything thereat before three clear days have expired after notification, or the place has been visited by an inspector, whichever first occurs. But anything may be done, despite these rules, to which an inspector consents, and in proceedings arising out of contravention of these requirements it is a defence to prove that the doing of the act to which exception is taken was necessary in the interests of safety.[2]

The Secretary of State may always direct the making and publication of a special report made by an inspector on an accident or other occurrences at a mine or quarry and the Secretary of State may also direct that a public enquiry be held.[3]

The conduct of any industrial undertaking involves some element of risk to the people employed. In mining and quarrying the risks are obvious and constant. An element of danger is something to which, in greater or lesser degree, the employees must get accustomed. Mining, moreover, is a highly skilled occupation and mine management demands considerable technical knowledge. In perhaps no other industry would interference by an unskilled proprietor be fraught with so much hazard.

Such considerations have led to the rule that the owner[4] of every mine and quarry must make such provision, financial and otherwise, and take such other steps as may be necessary to secure that the mine is managed and worked according to the terms of the Mines and Quarries Act, 1954, and orders and regulations made thereunder and is so planned and laid out that this purpose may readily be secured, and that all other provisions of the Act, orders made under it and regulations are, so far as applicable to any mine or quarry, duly complied with. In particular, the owner without prejudice to the general duty just defined must give to any person he appoints to carry out statutory responsibilities, written instructions defining the matters with respect to which that person is charged with securing the fulfilment of those responsibilities. A copy of such instructions must be sent to the inspector for the district, and to

---

[1] Mines and Quarries Act, 1954, s. 119.
[2] *Ibid.*, s. 120.
[3] *Ibid.*, s. 122.
[4] See *ibid.*, s. 181, for definition of the word " owner."

the manager of the mines or quarry or, where there is more than one manager, to each of them.[1]

Mines: Manager

No mine shall be worked unless there is a sole manager of the mine, who shall be an individual duly appointed with such qualifications (if any) as are required by the provisions of the Act.   The manager shall have the management and control of the mine, which he shall exercise subject to any instructions given to him by or on behalf of the owner.   The manager also has the responsibility of seeing that all others discharge the duties imposed on them by the provisions of the Act and in addition the manager has such duties relating to the appointment of persons to carry out mine inspections and to be in charge of or supervise operations at the mine, and has also such other duties as are imposed or conferred on him by the Act.

The manager is appointable by the owner who, if an individual, may appoint himself provided that, where the Act requires the manager to hold qualifications for the office, he possesses those qualifications.[2]

Where instructions affecting the performance of statutory responsibilities are given to the manager by or on behalf of the owner, they must, if not written, be confirmed in writing by the person by whom they were given forthwith on request by the manager.[3] Excepting in the case of an emergency neither the owner nor a person acting on his behalf shall give instructions to persons working at the mine and responsible to the manager except through the manager.   The manager may agree that instructions may be given direct to some other person but in these cases of emergency and the manager's consent the person who gave the instructions must, forthwith, inform the manager of the substance of the instructions, and on the manager's request confirm them in writing.[4]

The purpose of provisions such as these is obvious: it is to safeguard the position of the manager in the techniques of mine management, but the Act goes further.   In the case of an owner giving or authorising the giving of instructions to a manager required to hold qualifications or an under-manager or person appointed by the manager, the latter may, if he believes such instructions likely to prejudice the health or safety of the workers or to impede the discharge of his statutory duties, if the instructions are given to him refuse to perform them unless they are confirmed in writing as provided by the Act, and in any other case direct that they be not executed until they are so confirmed.

---

[1] Mines and Quarries Act, 1954, s. 1.   This section is not to be construed as derogating from any obligation imposed by or by virtue of any other provision of this Act upon the owner of a mine or quarry, s. 193.

[2] *Ibid.*, s. 2.   For temporary appointments see s. 7.   [3] *Ibid.*, s. 3(1).

[4] *Ibid.*, s. 3 (2) (3).   These provisions do not apply to instructions given by an under-manager or a person appointed by the manager of a mine.

These provisions do not apply where the owner of a mine is an individual or where the person giving written confirmation to a manager is himself a person qualified for appointment as manager of the mine. Where instructions given are confirmed in writing the manager is under a duty to preserve the confirmatory document (as also is the owner of the mine) for three years after the instructions cease to be operative.[1]

No person may be appointed manager of a coal, stratified iron-stone, shale or fireclay mine unless he fulfils the prescribed conditions which will include, where more than thirty persons are employed below ground, the holding of a first-class certificate of competency[2] and the attainment of an age of twenty-six years. Where the number of persons employed underground exceeds fourteen but is less than thirty, the manager must be at least twenty-three years of age and hold either a first- or second-class certificate of competency—and even in this case, if an inspector so directs, the manager must hold a first-class certificate and be aged at least twenty-six. If the number of persons employed underground does not exceed fourteen an inspector may nevertheless direct that the manager must possess a first- or second-class certificate and have reached the age of twenty-three. Regulations may direct that no person shall manage a mine other than of coal, ironstone, shale or fireclay unless he satisfies such conditions as may be prescribed.[3]

Except where an inspector so approves a person shall not manage more than one mine unless the total number of persons at all the mines of which he is manager does not exceed one thousand; and the surface entrances to all the shafts and outlets for the time being in use at all the mines lie within a circle whose radius is two miles.[4]

One or more under-managers may of course be appointed, by the owner, for any mine. A recent Act has also provided for managers' assistants who may be delegated some of the manager's powers.[5] A mine which, by virtue of the Act, requires a manager holding a first-class certificate of competency, being a mine in which the manager is also the manager of another mine, and a mine subject to direction by an inspector that, on the ground of its size, condition or system of working at least one under-manager is required, may not be worked unless there is at least one under-manager employed. The jurisdiction of an under-manager may be limited to part of the mine, but a mine which it is unlawful to work unless at least one under-manager is employed, may not be worked unless every part below ground is within the jurisdiction of the under-manager or, where

---

[1] Mines and Quarries Act, 1954, s. 3.
[2] For the law as to the granting of certificates, etc., see *ibid.*, Part XII, ss. 147–150.
[3] *Ibid.*, s. 4; but see also s. 192.
[4] *Ibid.*, s. 5, which see also for the powers of an inspector where he believes that management of more than one mine is acting to the prejudice of statutory obligations.
[5] Mines Management Act, 1971.

more than one is employed, under the jurisdiction of one of them.
The under-manager must, to the extent of his jurisdiction, supervise
all work carried on, and carry out the provisions of the Act to the
best of his ability.

A mine which requires as manager a person holding a first-class
certificate of competency may not be worked so long as a person is
employed as under-manager who does not fulfil the prescribed
conditions, namely, that he holds a first- or second-class certificate,
has attained the age of twenty-three years and satisfies such other
conditions as may be prescribed. Regulations may, in addition,
provide that mines other than those described may not be worked
unless the under-manager satisfies such conditions as may be
prescribed.[1]

A manager or, where the statute requires his employment, an
under-manager must exercise daily personal supervision. During
absence on leave, sickness or absence from causes beyond his
control, a person appointed by the owner must exercise such supervision, such person being an under-manager or one who could be
appointed as such without the working of the mine being rendered
unlawful. Any arrangement for supervision in the absence of the
manager must not persist for a period greater than seventy-two days
unless an inspector so authorises.[2]

No mine shall be worked when neither the manager, nor an under-
manager, nor their substitute is present unless the mine is in charge
of a competent person appointed by the manager and having such
qualifications as may be prescribed.[3]

In *Bassett* v. *Evans*[4] the court considered similar provisions to
those just outlined and contained in earlier legislation. Before a
temporary absence the manager appointed a duly qualified substitute and gave instructions for certain work, saying, amongst other
things, " we will pull these half rings out and then those that are in
the cement I will have burnt out."   The rings were burnt out during
the manager's absence with an oxy-acetylene burner, some ten yards
inside the entrance to the mine—though the authority of the
inspector for the use of the burner had not been secured. The
manager was charged with the offence committed in his absence.
He set up the defence provided by the earlier Act, that he had taken
all reasonable means to prevent the contravention of or non-
compliance with the Act.[5] The Court held the defence to be valid.
In appointing a duly qualified person to act in his absence the
responsibilities under the Act were assumed by the person appointed.

---

[1] Mines and Quarries Act, 1954, s. 6. See s. 7 for provisions as to temporary
appointments during vacancy in the office of manager and under-manager.
[2] *Ibid.*, s. 8.
[3] *Ibid.*, s. 9.   These provisions will not prevent the working of the mines
when no persons are employed below ground.   As to the duty to read reports,
etc., see s. 10.
[4] [1956] 2 All E.R. 899; [1956] 1 W.L.R. 925.
[5] The present Act affords a not dissimilar defence (s. 156).

No mine shall be worked unless the owner has appointed a surveyor for the mine having such qualifications as may be prescribed, provided that in the case of death, resignation or other cause the mine may be worked for a period not exceeding twenty-eight days or such longer period as an inspector may allow pending the filling of the vacancy. The main duty of the surveyor shall be the preparation of plans and other documents.[1]

The manager of the mine must ensure to the best of his ability that persons appointed by him in pursuance of the Act understand the nature and scope of their duties.[2]

The owner is under a duty to inform the inspector of the district when he appoints a manager or under-manager and certain other officers or when he appoints persons to exercise the duties attaching to such offices.[3]

The law is always concerned to minimise the circumstances in which interest and duty may conflict and an example of this is to be seen in the provision that where a mine is worked, in whole or part, by a contractor and a person is required by the Act to possess qualifications for appointment to any office in the mine, neither the contractor nor a person employed by him shall be capable of being appointed to that office notwithstanding that he possesses the necessary qualifications.[4]

Outlets

It is unlawful to employ any persons below ground in a coal, stratified ironstone, shale or fireclay mine unless there are available for affording to them alternative and ready means of ingress and egress, two shafts or outlets (though not necessarily exclusive to that particular mine), which, except when the shafts were sunk before January 1st, 1865, are at no point separated from each other by less than 45 feet or (where the sinking began before the first day of January, 1888) ten feet.

Where, as a consequence of accident or breakdown, the employment of persons in a mine would be unlawful as a consequence of a shaft or outlet having become unavailable, but the manager is of opinion that the employees will not be exposed to undue risk then, subject to satisfying certain conditions people who were underground at the time of the accident or breakdown may work on until the end of their period of work, or, until the expiration of twenty-four hours beginning with the time at which the accident or breakdown occurred where the work is necessary to secure the safety of the mine, or the welfare of animals or in rendering the shaft or outlet

---

[1] Mines and Quarries Act, 1954, s. 11. For duties as to the keeping of plans, etc., see ss. 17, 18, 19, 20. Statutory provision is also made for the appointment of various officials and technicians. See ss. 12 and 13.

[2] *Ibid.*, s. 14.

[3] *Ibid.*, s. 15.

[4] *Ibid.*, s. 16.

again available. The conditions to be complied with are the posting at the mine and in a conspicuous position of a notice specifying the accident or breakdown and stating that the manager is satisfied with the position and his reasons for being so satisfied and sending a message to the same effect by the quickest available means to the inspector of the district and to the person, if any, nominated to receive on behalf of persons employed at the mine, notification of accidents.

But no person may continue to be employed in such circumstances underground after the manager has received notice from the inspector that that person should be withdrawn.[1]

Regulations may be made with respect to a particular mine and provide that such number of persons, not exceeding thirty, may be employed below ground as shall be prescribed, being persons to whom only one shaft or outlet is available—but there are severe rules limiting the number of persons so employed.

For the purpose of these provisions a shaft or unwalkable outlet at a mine provided with apparatus for carrying persons through the shaft or outlet shall be deemed not to be available to those below ground for affording to them ingress or egress if that apparatus is not available for use by them.

None of these provisions apply to persons actually employed in a shaft or outlet or in the insets of a shaft or outlet, but there is a strict limitation on the number of persons who may be employed in such places.[2]

So long as more than one shaft or outlet is available to underground workers there must be provided and maintained between them a communication not less than five feet high and not less than four feet wide, following a reasonably short and convenient route, but there is a power to exempt from these requirements.[3]

An inspector has power to require the provision of additional ways out from the working faces of coal mines and such faces may not be worked unless the additional roads are provided according to the terms of a notice served by the inspector.[4]

Shafts and unwalkable outlets in coal, stratified ironstone, shale or fireclay mines provided to enable a means of ingress and egress to underground workers must be provided with apparatus for carrying people from the top of the shafts and the entrances to the workings. In other types of mines such shafts and outlets, where the distance between the top of the shaft and the bottom of the lowest entrance thereto exceeds one hundred and fifty feet, must be provided with similar apparatus. All such apparatus must be kept properly maintained and, when not in use, kept constantly available for use.[5]

---

[1] Mines and Quarries Act, 1954, s. 22 (1) and (2). For exemptions see s. 22 (3).

[2] *Ibid.*, ss. 22, 24, 25.

[3] *Ibid.*, s. 23.   [4] *Ibid.*, s. 27.

[5] Mines and Quarries Act, 1954, s. 28. There is a power to grant exemptions.

Mine shafts and staple-pits[1] must be made and kept secure except where the natural conditions of the strata render this unnecessary.[2] This duty applies not only to the walls but to dangers in the airspace, where there is scaffolding placed there, for example.[3] In a prosecution arising out of an alleged infringement of this provision, it is a good defence that at the time in question the insecure part of the shaft or staple-pit was not in use, or was the site of work in progress to drive or extend the shaft or staple-pit.

Entrances and Roads

The surface or other entrances to the mine shafts and staple-pits must be fitted with an enclosure or barrier and designed and built so as to prevent persons accidentally falling down the shaft or coming into contact with moving parts of the winding apparatus. Such enclosures or barriers must be properly maintained and where any part is removable or openable there is a duty to see that such parts are kept securely in position or securely closed, except in so far as the removal or opening may be necessary for the purpose of using the shaft, or working or inspecting the shaft or staple-pit. These requirements have no application to shafts, outlets or staple-pits in abandoned mines not worked for a period of twelve months but apart from this they will apply to such places when they are used, even though they are not used as shafts, outlets and staple-pits.[4] There is a power to make regulations with the object of preventing persons being injured by the accidental fall of articles down shafts and staple-pits.[5]

Entrances to parts of mines which are not maintained in a state fit for persons to work in or pass through must be provided with efficient enclosures or barriers, built so as to prevent anyone from accidentally entering that part of the mine. Again there is the duty of proper maintenance and the duty to see that removable or openable parts are kept closed or secured in position except where the manager, under-manager or person in charge of that part of the mine authorises opening or removal.[6]

Mine managers must ensure in respect of every road in a mine along which vehicles or conveyors run or which is used at the beginning or end of a shift by not less than ten persons to walk to or from their places of work (*a*) that if the road is made after January 1st, 1957, it shall be made and maintained so as to avoid sudden changes of direction, height, width and gradient except where it is unnecessary to do so or the system of working or the natural conditions of the strata make it inadvisable from the point of view of safety to do so; and (*b*) that the road be kept free from obstruction and the floor be

---

[1] This includes a winze. *Ibid.*, s. 182.
[2] *Ibid.*, s. 30.
[3] *Coll* v. *Cementation Co. and National Coal Board*, 1963 S.L.T. 105.
[4] *Ibid.*, s. 31.
[5] *Ibid.*, s. 32.
[6] *Ibid.*, s. 33.

kept in good repair and condition so that persons and animals can tread with safety and reasonable convenience.[1]   In the case of roads made before January 1st, 1957, an inspector may direct that any sudden change in height, width or gradient be eliminated.[2]

Roads used at the beginning or end of a shift by not less than ten persons to walk to or from their work and made after January 1st, 1957, must be not less than five and a half feet high, but there is a power to exempt from this provision either by regulation or by inspector's notice and in the case of roads made before January 1st, 1957, the inspector may require by notice that lengths of road be heightened to not more than five and a half feet.   When an inspector is of opinion that a length of road in a mine requires widening, irrespective of when it is made, an inspector may serve a notice requiring the widening of the road.[3]

Vehicles may not run in a road if they, or their loads or the ropes to which they are attached or the animals which draw them or the harness of such animals, rub against the roof or sides of the road or supports to such roof or sides; nor may a conveyor be operated in a road if the conveyor or its load rubs against the roof or sides of the road or anything supporting them.   It will be a defence to prosecutions for contravention of this section of the Act to show that the vehicles were being run or the conveyor operated for the purpose of carrying out repairs the object of which was to enable vehicles to run or a conveyor to work in that road without contravention of the requirement.   It will also be a defence to show that the rubbing occurred because of a sudden and unavoidable decrease in height, that there was no ground for believing that bodily injury to persons or animals would result and that there was no avoidable delay in remedying the situation.[4]

Mine managers may make what are known as " transport rules " governing the use of vehicles and conveyors in the mine, defining the conditions under which they may be used and generally to secure the safe operation of vehicles and conveyors and the avoidance of bodily injury.[5]   Regulations may require the provision, in prescribed cases, of travelling facilities so that underground workers may proceed to and from their working places with safety and without incurring excessive fatigue.[6]

In the case of lengths of road in a mine in which vehicles run otherwise than by hand or animal traction certain safety provisions must be observed.   Thus whilst vehicles are moving in that road

---

[1] A haulage rope has been held not to be an obstruction; *Cook* v. *National Coal Board*, [1961] 3 All E.R. 220; [1961] 1 W.L.R. 1192.

[2] *Ibid.*, s. 34.   Changes of gradient will be construed as including references to deviations (upwards or downwards) from the horizontal.

[3] *Ibid.*, s. 35.

[4] *Ibid.*, s. 36.

[5] *Ibid.*, s. 37.

[6] *Ibid.*, s. 38.

otherwise than by these means no unauthorised person may pass on foot along the road unless the vehicles are specially stopped for the purpose, and if the road is used at the beginning and ending of a shift by not less than ten persons the manager must fix periods within which they may use the road in safety and no vehicle may be moved during such periods. The provisions do not apply to " authorised persons." Such persons are mine officials, workers themselves engaged in the running of the vehicles, persons engaged in repairs of immediate importance and persons carrying out workmen's inspections.[1]

Vehicles may not run in lengths of road in the mine unless, at prescribed intervals, refuge holes are provided. Such refuges need not be provided within seventy-five feet of the working face served by the road, but the working face here referred to does not include a place in a road at which ripping or repair work is in progress.[2]

When vehicles are used in a mine, unless there be good reason to the contrary there must be provided, maintained and used, either in the mine or on the vehicles, or in both, such safety devices as are necessary to prevent the danger of bodily harm caused by vehicles running away, the devices being so constructed that they automatically assume the position which enables them to fulfil their purposes. There must also be taken, in respect of persons who, otherwise than as a matter of routine, work in a place through which vehicles run or are accustomed to run, such steps as are necessary to prevent them suffering bodily injury should a vehicle run away.[3]

Winding Apparatus

Mechanically or gravity operated winding apparatus provided in a mine shaft or staple-pit and mechanically or gravity operated rope haulage apparatus may not be worked when persons are carried thereon except by a competent male person who has reached the age of twenty-two years, and it is the duty of the manager to appoint such number of competent male persons as will enable the following provisions to be complied with. The manager of every mine to and from which persons gain ingress or egress by being carried through a shaft or unwalkable outlet by means of mechanically or gravity operated winding or rope haulage apparatus or in which persons gain access thereto by being carried through a staple-pit by means of similar apparatus, must make and secure the efficient carrying out of arrangements whereby a person is in attendance to operate the apparatus so long as anyone is below ground who it is intended should come out through that shaft, outlet or staple-pit. An inspector may require that, at the times he specifies, a person who is in attendance at the mine for the discharge of duties under these

---

[1] Mines and Quarries Act, 1954, s. 39. See this section also for the power of exemption and defences.

[2] *Ibid.*, s. 40.

[3] *Ibid.*, s. 41. *Jones* v. *National Coal Board*, [1965] 1 All E.R. 221; [1965] 1 W.L.R., 532.

provisions does not operate more than one set of mechanically or gravity operated winding or rope haulage apparatus. Such persons may not work for more than eight hours a day in any day on which his duties consist of or include the operation, when people are being carried, of winding apparatus.[1]

Winding apparatus not used for the carriage of persons must be operated by or under the constant supervision of a competent male person who has reached the age of twenty-one years, and no rope haulage apparatus may be used in similar circumstances except by or under the constant supervision of a competent male person who has attained the age of eighteen years.[2] Conveyors may not be operated along working faces except by or under the supervision of a male who has reached the age of eighteen years.[3] There are elaborate requirements governing the provision and maintenance of signalling systems in shafts, outlets and roads.[4]

Support

It is the duty of the manager to take, in respect of roads and working places, such steps to control the movements of strata and to support the roof and sides of the road or working place as may be necessary to keep the place secure,[5] and a manager must ensure that he possesses all the information necessary to enable him to determine what steps he must take to secure compliance with the provisions of the Act in the matter of safety.[6] The duty under s. 48 is not an absolute one "to ensure that the road or working place is secure." So where, in *Brown* v. *National Coal Board*,[7] a tub knocked down a prop in what had been a secure road until then, it was held that as immediate steps were taken to remedy the insecurity the manager had complied with the duty laid upon him. The electrician who was working to remedy the insecurity by removing a light so that a fallen girder could be replaced could not, therefore, succeed in an action brought because he was injured by a falling stone.

In coal, shale and fireclay mines there is a duty to provide systematic support for the roof and sides of every place where minerals are worked, for every roadhead, every junction of two or more lengths of road through any one of which vehicles or a conveyor run or runs and every length of road in which persons work otherwise than occasionally or for short periods. In addition an inspector may serve notice that in his opinion a length of road, not being a length mentioned in the last sentence, requires systematic support, and

---

[1] Mines and Quarries Act, 1954, s. 42.
[2] *Ibid.*, s. 43. [3] *Ibid.*, s. 44. [4] *Ibid.*, ss. 45, 46, 47.
[5] This does not apply to places to which s. 33 is applicable.
[6] Mines and Quarries Act, 1954, s. 48.
[7] [1962] A.C. 574. This case has established itself as the basic statement of the duty under s. 48; see e.g. *Tomlinson* v. *Beckermet Mining Co., Ltd.*, [1964] 3 All E.R. 1; [1964] 1 W.L.R. 1043. There is a good review of the case law in G. H. L. Fridman, Security in Mines (1969), 32 M.L.R. 174.

regulations may require or empower inspectors to require the provision and maintenance of systematic support in mines not being of coal, shale or fireclay.[1]

Although the provisions of section 49 do not apply to anywhere which is not a working place, any place to which a man may be sent to work or is expected to work, is included in the cover.[2] The duty of the mine manager only applies to dangers which should have been foreseen.[3]

Subject to regulations providing for the contrary, all support materials must be provided by the owner, who may not levy a charge upon any employee for support materials provided. The manager must secure a sufficient supply of support materials and have them readily available to every workman for use at the place where he is working. In the case of a workman not having a supply readily available for use where he is working the workman is required to withdraw to a place of safety and report to an official of the mine that he has done so; and where it appears to a person in charge of a mine that the necessary supply is not available, that person may cause the workman to withdraw to a place of safety. Once withdrawn the workman may not be permitted to return to the working place until those in authority are satisfied that the supply of support materials will be readily available.[4] Support may not be withdrawn from the roof or sides of any place without the adoption of some device or method which permits the withdrawal to be done from some place of safety.[5]

The Act has been in operation for some time now. It must be remembered that its provisions are not entirely novel, much of it is declaratory of existing law and much of it reproduces, fairly closely, provisions in earlier legislation. Thus *Wraith* v. *National Coal Board*,[6] though decided according to the terms of s. 49 of the Coal Mines Act, 1911, covers points contained in the 1954 Act and, indeed, is interesting generally as showing the impact of the law on a number of technical problems to deal with which the present Act and its predecessors were enacted. The facts themselves show something of the hazards which mining entails. The plaintiff, an employee of the defendants, was working with another miner in bringing into use a roadway which had been abandoned and allowed to fall into disrepair. This disrepair showed itself chiefly in two ways, namely by the crumpling of the steel arches which had supported the roof and sides because of pressure of earth, and by resulting falls of roof, covering or partly covering the arches and leaving an almost con-

---

[1] Mines and Quarries Act, 1954, ss. 49, 50. See the former section for the power to make regulations and also for exemptions.

[2] *Venn* v. *National Coal Board*, [1967] 2 Q.B. 557; [1967] 1 All E.R. 149.

[3] *Robson* v. *National Coal Board*, [1968] 3 All E.R. 159.

[4] Mines and Quarries Act, 1954, s. 51. For the duties of officials and technicians concerning safety and for the provisions as to "Support Rules" see ss. 52, 53, 54.

[5] *Ibid.*, s. 52.   [6] [1954] 1 All E.R. 231.

tinuous cavity in the roof.   The method of repair used was to clear
a length of the roadway by removing the debris, then the roof and
sides were made so that a new arch, girder or ring could be fitted,
above which horizontal timbers were laid.   Across these timbers
further timbers were laid so as to form a continuous strip of covering
which would protect a man working in the centre of the roadway
from any fall of the roof immediately above him and which also
projected about eighteen inches or two feet towards the next arch
to be installed.   The workmen then cleared the roadway sufficiently
to make room for the next girder which was placed some three feet
from the first.   Then the old distorted arch or arches were removed.
Whilst clearing debris before the removal of an old arch the plaintiff
was injured by the fall of a stone some six or seven feet away from
the last new arch girder.

The problems raised by the facts are many and varied.   But chief
amongst them were clearly: " when does a road cease to be a road and
when does it re-become one? " and " what is meant by ' a working
place,' where the legislative provisions as to the security of roof and
sides are concerned? "

> " I am of opinion that if a roadway in a mine has ceased to be used
> as a roadway but has been allowed to fall into disrepair because it is
> no longer needed, it ceases to be a roadway . . . and there is no duty
> on a mine owner to keep the roof and sides of a disused roadway
> secure.   So much of it as has been reconstructed, but only so much,
> became a roadway and the defendants then came under a duty to
> keep the roof and sides of that much of it secure, but the point at
> which the stone fell was beyond the point at which the recon-
> structed roadway ended."[1]

The judge then went on to consider whether the place might be a
working place within the Act:

> " If the spot where the plaintiff . . . (was) working is to be called a
> working place rather than a roadway it seems to me that the
> expression ' the roof of a working place ' cannot be limited to the
> reconstructed roof but must be construed as extending at least to
> that area of roof above and beyond the spot where the plaintiff was
> working, from which a fall might put the plaintiff in peril.   In my
> opinion, this section, however, draws a distinction between a road
> and a working place.   I do not think that a roadway becomes at
> any given point a working place merely because at that point men
> are employed to repair it . . . "[2]

Grant v. *National Coal Board*[3] involved also the consideration of
s. 49 of the 1911 Act—now substantially re-enacted in s. 48(1) of the
1954 Act.   The appellant was travelling on a man haulage bogey at
the end of his shift and was injured as a consequence of the bogey

---

[1] [1954] 1 All E.R. 231. *per* GLYN JONES, J., at p. 234.
[2] *Ibid.*, see also *Sidor* v. *National Coal Board and Associated Tunnelling Co.*,
[1956] C.L.Y. 5536.
[3] [1956] A.C. 649; [1956] 1 All E.R. 682.

being derailed because of a fall of redd or stone from the roof. His plea was that the fall of stone demonstrated that at some time the roof was not secure. The questions were whether the employer was in breach of duty to keep the roof secure and what was the purpose of the legislation. Was it generally for the safety of men at work or only to protect them from a particular danger, *i.e.* that of being injured by a fall? Viscount SIMONDS pointed out that protection from the direct consequences of a fall was no doubt the primary end of the section but a fall which prevented a workman reaching the shaft was equally to be apprehended, and once this is conceded it follows that the safety of the workman depends on roads being kept free from obstruction. Hence the plaintiff could recover damages.

As to what constitutes a haulage road see *Stoisavljevic* v. *National Coal Board.*[1] It was held that the use of a conveyor belt made the road a haulage road so that the plaintiff who was injured whilst crossing, as he alleged, a stationary intake road conveyor belt which began to move without warning could recover.

The wording of section 48 of the Act is, of course, absolute in terms as was the older legislation, but there are circumstances in which the obligation as to safety cannot prevail. Walsh[2] was engaged in ripping the roadway at the coal face. During the course of certain operations, a boulder was observed in the roof. As it would be dangerous to dislodge the boulder it was decided to prop and wedge it with timber. Later, when Walsh was making the roof and sides secure the boulder fell and injured him. He claimed that his employers had failed in their duty to make the roof and sides secure, but the court held that though these words imposed an absolute duty, the owners did not violate their duty by setting the plaintiff to make the roof and sides secure. Similarly in *Jackson* v. *National Coal Board*[3] a shot firer was killed by an explosion which was, in large measure, caused by his own failure to observe regulations designed for his own and other people's safety. The explosion resulted in props which supported the roof being dislodged and the roof collapsed and killed him. It was found that the insecurity of the roof was due to the deceased's conduct against which the defendants could not be expected to provide and his widow was not able to recover damages.

Ventilation

It is the mine manager's duty to take all necessary steps for securing ventilation (*a*) to dilute, render harmless and remove inflammable or noxious gases and (*b*) to provide air containing a sufficiency of oxygen.   This provision is of general application and without prejudice to its generality the ventilation in a part of a mine will be deemed

---

[1] [1956] C.L.Y. 5535.
[2] In *Walsh* v. *National Coal Board*, [1956] 1 Q.B. 511; [1955] 3 All E.R. 632.
[3] [1955] 1 All E.R. 145.

inadequate for the purpose of diluting carbon dioxide so as to render it harmless unless the amount thereof in the general body of the air in that part is not more than one and a quarter per cent by volume or if a smaller percentage is prescribed, that percentage; and unless the amount of oxygen in the general body of air is not less than nineteen per cent by volume it will not be deemed adequate.[1] The manager must also aim at securing (consistently with the discharge of his general duty as to ventilation) working conditions that are reasonable so far as regards the temperature, the degree of humidity and the amount of dust in the mine. The duty to ventilate does not apply in any part of a mine which is stopped-off or stowed-up, in any waste, or in such other parts of the mine as may be prescribed. Should the ventilation in any part of the mine become inadequate the manager must, until it is restored, restrict access to the affected part of the mine so as to prevent entry to any person not engaged in restoring the ventilation—or to those passing through on an emergency.[2] An inspector may serve a notice requiring that the ventilation in any part of the mine be improved.[3] Unless adequate ventilation is available by natural means there must be provided and maintained on the surface of the mine mechanically operated apparatus which can produce sufficient ventilation (apart from ventilation produced mechanically underground) to enable all underground workers at any one time in the mine to leave safely. If the apparatus is not normally used to produce ventilation, it shall be used at least once a week and must be kept constantly available for use. Unless the apparatus provided on the surface is designed to enable it both to force air into the mine and to exhaust air from the mine, then additional associated machinery must be provided for reversing the direction of flow. It is not lawful to use a fire for ventilation in a mine, or, except with the consent of an inspector, to release compressed air into a mine for the purpose of diluting or removing inflammable or noxious gases.[4]

Where, in a coal, stratified ironstone, shale or fireclay mine, of two lengths of road one is made after January 1st, 1957, then, unless there is no or no appreciable leakage of air between them, it is not lawful to use one as an intake airway and the other as a return airway, unless any necessary steps are taken to minimise the leakage of air between them. But this does not make it unlawful to use as an airway so much of any passage in a mine as lies within a distance of four hundred and fifty feet (or such other distance as an inspector may prescribe) from a working face to which air is supplied or from which air is drawn off through that airway.[5]

---

[1] Mines and Quarries Act, 1954, s. 55; which see also for the formula concerning other gases.

[2] Mines and Quarries Act, 1954, s. 55; as to avoidance of danger from gas in waste see s. 56.

[3] *Ibid.*, s. 57.

[4] *Ibid.*, s. 58, which see also for power to grant exemptions.

[5] *Ibid.*, s. 59.

Lights

At every other mine of coal and fireclay and at mines other than of coal and fireclay being either a safety lamp mine or a mine containing any waste, a barometer must be provided in a conspicuous place where it can easily be seen and read by employed persons.[1] Suitable and sufficient lighting, natural or artificial, must be provided in every part of the mine above ground in which persons walk or pass (taking into account any lamps carried by such persons), and suitable and sufficient artificial lighting must be provided below ground except where the installation of artificial lighting is inadvisable for reasons of safety or is unnecessary because of the light given by lamps normally carried. All apparatus installed at the mine for producing artificial light must be properly maintained.[2]

No lamps or lights other than permitted lights[3] may be allowed or used underground in coal mines opened after January 1st, 1957. And similarly no lamps or lights other than those permitted may be used in a mine (whether of coal or any other mineral) first opened after the same date which is either (*a*) a mine in which immediately before that date no lights might be used except locked safety lamps or some other means of lighting authorised by the then existing legislation or (*b*) a mine in which locked safety lamps were being used otherwise than by way of a purely temporary precaution.

No lamps or lights other than permitted lights may be used in mines first opened before January 1st, 1957 (not being a mine to which the above provision applies), after an underground ignition or explosion of gas naturally present in the mine; or the introduction in any part of the mine of locked safety lamps, otherwise than by way of temporary precaution; or after notice served by an inspector.[4]

It is forbidden to take below ground safety lamps not provided by the owner and the only safety lamps permitted below ground are those for the time being approved by the Secretary of State.[5] A person who damages, destroys or loses or permits to be damaged, destroyed or lost a safety lamp given out to him at a mine commits an offence, but it is a defence to show that reasonable steps were taken for the care and preservation of the lamp and that immediately after the occurrence of the damage, destruction or loss he informed a mine official. It is also an offence to tamper with a safety lamp given out at a mine.[6]

It is also an offence to take, or have in possession below ground in a safety lamp mine a cigar, cigarette, pipe or other smoking contrivance or a match or mechanical lighter. The manager of a safety

---

[1] *Ibid.*, s. 60.

[2] Mines and Quarries Act, 1954, s. 64.

[3] That is a locked safety lamp or other means of lighting authorised by regulation; s. 182.

[4] *Ibid.*, s. 62. For making of regulations, see s. 63.

[5] *Ibid.*, s. 64.

[6] *Ibid.*, s. 95.

lamp mine must make arrangements whereby all persons employed below ground are searched in an authorised manner immediately before or after they go below ground, and where such arrangements are not in operation to ensure that no person goes below ground. And the manager of a safety lamp mine, or a mine containing a safety lamp part, may cause any person who is below ground and any article he has with him to be searched in the authorised manner. If the prohibited articles are found upon any person that person commits an offence, and any article found may be seized and dealt with in such manner as the manager may direct. No person may search another person on any occasion unless he has given an opportunity to two other persons to search himself and if searched by them has not been found by them to have any prohibited article in his possession. One who refuses to allow himself or an article he has with him to be searched commits an offence and where he refuses before he goes underground shall not be allowed to go underground, or if the refusal occurs in a mine shall not be allowed to remain in that mine.[1]

Subject to certain exceptions no article which produces an unprotected flame or spark may be taken or used below ground in a safety lamp mine or in a safety lamp part of a mine.[2]

In recent years much electrical lighting and equipment has been introduced into mines and the new Act contains an extensive provision for the making of regulations governing them.[3] Similarly regulations may make provision for prohibiting or restricting the supply, storage or use at mines of blasting materials and for prohibiting and restricting the use of such materials.[4]

Fire Precautions

It is unlawful to employ more than one hundred persons below ground in a coal mine in circumstances in which, if there were a fire in any length of intake airways through which the air supply to all those persons passes, none of them would be able to withdraw from the mine without either passing through the fire or following a way to the surface through which the air might become so contaminated by the fire as to prejudice seriously their safe withdrawal. This will not apply where the length of intake airway and everything with which it is equipped are so constructed, treated, maintained and used that that length of airway is, so far as can reasonably be foreseen, free from the risk that should a fire break out it will develop so as to endanger the withdrawal of persons from the mine; nor will it apply where means are provided to ensure that if there is a fire in that length of intake airway, those persons will be able to withdraw in safety.[5]

The Secretary of State may by order prohibit the use of brattice

---

[1] Mines and Quarries Act, 1954, s. 66.
[2] *Ibid.*, s. 67. [3] *Ibid.*, s. 68. [4] *Ibid.*, s. 69.
[5] *Ibid.*, s. 70, and see this section and s. 72 generally for fire precautions.

sheeting other than that of a type which he approves and he has similar powers with regard to the use of conveyor belting.[1] Wherever there is special danger of fire or escape of steam, or of noxious gas in a dangerous concentration involving the risk of a person being trapped, steps must be taken to minimise the risk.[2]

The manager must ensure that the giving off of inflammable dust and dust of such a character and in such quantity as to be likely to be injurious to persons employed is minimised. Where in connection with any operations or process below ground in a mine or in a building on the surface of a mine inflammable dust or dust noxious in quantity is produced, then the manager must take steps as near as possible to the point of origin of the dust to minimise its entry into the air or its accumulation in any place. He must take steps to ensure that dust entering the air is trapped or dispersed and that dust not prevented from accumulating is either systematically cleared up and removed or treated in a manner approved by the Secretary of State with the object of making it harmless.[3]

The manager of a mine must put himself in possession of information about disused workings, rock or stratum containing or likely to contain water, and any material such as peat, moss, sand, gravel or silt which is likely to flow when wet. On any information of the above character coming into the possession of the owner or the manager each must inform the other forthwith, and of the steps taken and any conclusions reached as a result of taking such steps. Both owner and manager are under the duty of ascertaining the total depth of strata lying between the workings and the surface water wherever a mine is in the vicinity of the sea, a lake, a river bed, or other surface water, and all information discovered in pursuance of this duty must be exchanged between owner and manager. Steps must be taken to prevent inrushes of gas or water or material that flows, when wet, from disused workings of any kind, and additional powers are given to inspectors in this regard.[4]

Where inflammable gas is present in excessive quantity a person in charge of the mine or part of the mine affected must cause all employed persons to leave and immediately thereafter, unless he is the manager, inform his superior and other persons in charge of areas likely to be affected, and thereafter he must, as soon as is possible without undue risk, ascertain the condition of the area concerned and any measures necessary to render the area safe. Re-entry to an affected area is not permitted until it is clear that inflammable gas in dangerous quantity no longer exists and the appropriate person is satisfied that no other danger exists.[5] There

---

[1] *Ibid.*, s. 71.   [2] *Ibid.*, s. 73.
[3] Mines and Quarries Act, 1954, s. 74.   [4] *Ibid.*, ss. 75, 76, 77, 78.
[5] *Ibid.*, s. 79, which also see for the keeping of records and for technical definitions of gas in excessive quantities.

is a duty on all mine workers where a danger has arisen or is about to arise either, if such is within his normal duties, to take steps to make the mine safe or to prevent the danger arising, and if this is not part of his duties to report the matter at once to an official.[1]

Safety of Machinery

All parts and working gear, fixed or moveable, of all machinery and apparatus forming part of the equipment of a mine and all foundations of such machinery and apparatus must be of good construction, suitable material, adequate strength, free from patent defect and must be properly maintained.[2] This section has been considered in several recent cases. In *Hamilton v. National Gas Board*[3] the House of Lords held that " properly maintained " imposed an absolute duty to keep the machinery in a proper and efficient state. This duty will not be discharged by routine maintenance which allows the machine to deteriorate in condition. In *Sanderson v. National Coal Board*,[4] the Court of Appeal considered the phrase " free from patent defect " and held that this meant an observable defect. This implies the use of an objective test rather than a subjective one which the use of the word "observed" would have implied. Thus patent defects are defects which were seen or ought to have been seen. Every flywheel and every other dangerous exposed part of any machinery must be securely fenced, maintained and kept in position whilst the parts are in motion or use, except where such parts are exposed for examination or adjustment which must be undertaken whilst they are under examination or in use.[5]

If the machinery is not so fenced it will not be a defence that an injured person was acting in a wrong manner, for the legislation is designed to protect such a person as one who acts in a right manner.[6] A machine is dangerous within the provision if it is of such a character that an employer might reasonably foresee it as a potential source of injury to those in its neighbourhood.[7]

Internal combustion engines, steam boilers and locomotives may not be used below ground except in accordance with regulations made for the purpose or with the consent of the Secretary of State or an inspector.[8]

Apparatus producing air, gas, or steam at greater than atmospheric pressure must be so constructed, installed, maintained and used as to obviate risks from fire, bursting, explosion, collapse or the production

---

[1] *Ibid.*, s. 80.

[2] *Ibid.*, s. 81.

[3] [1960] A.C. 633; [1960] 1 All E.R. 76, and see *Edwards* v. *National Coal Board*, [1949] 1 K.B. 704; [1949] 1 All E.R. 743.

[4] [1961] 2 Q.B. 244; [1961] 2 All E.R. 796.

[5] Mines and Quarries Act, 1954, s. 82.

[6] *Carey* v. *Ocean Coal, Ltd.*, [1938] 1 K.B. 365; [1937] 4 All E.R. 219.

[7] *Smithwick* v. *National Coal Board*, [1950] 2 K.B. 335, C.A.

[8] Mines and Quarries Act, 1954, s. 83.

of noxious gases. The Secretary of State may at any time cause the apparatus to be examined by a person nominated by him and the manager must give all the necessary facilities. Should the examination reveal the apparatus to be inadequate or inaccurate in a material particular the cost of the examination is recoverable by the Secretary of State from the owner.[1]

Every crane, crab and swivel must be plainly marked with the safe working load, except that in the case of a jib crane in which the safe working load may be varied by raising or lowering the jib, there must be attached an automatic indication of the safe working load or a table indicating safe working loads at corresponding inclinations of the jib or corresponding radii of the load. The safe working loads must not be exceeded, except for the purposes of a test. These provisions do not apply, however, to working apparatus with which a mine shaft or staple-pit is provided nor to any rope haulage apparatus, and regulations may provide for further exemptions.[2]

Safety of Structures

All buildings and structures on the surface of a mine must be kept in safe condition, and there must be provided and maintained safe means of access to every place in or on a building or structure on the surface of a mine at which any person has at any time to work. Where a person is to work at any place from which he will be liable to fall a distance of more than ten feet, then, unless the place itself affords secure foothold and, where necessary, secure handhold, means, by fencing or otherwise, for ensuring safety must be devised.[3]

The hazards and dangers of mining are increased a hundredfold by incompetence and indiscipline amongst employees and so the Act provides that all persons employed at a mine must either have received adequate instruction in or, where necessary, training for the work they are doing and hence be competent to do it without supervision or work under the instruction and supervision of a competent person.[4] An employee commits an offence who contravenes transport or support rules, or directions given to him by or on behalf of the owner or manager being directions given or rules made for securing compliance with the Act or for securing the safety or health of employed persons. It is also an offence under the Act negligently or wilfully to do anything likely to endanger the safety of the mine or the safety or health of persons at the mine or to omit to do anything necessary for securing the safety of the mine or health of persons thereat. Offences are also committed by anyone (not being a mine-official and not having the permission of such an official) who removes, alters or tampers with anything provided at a mine for securing the safety or health of persons employed thereat.[5]

---

[1] *Ibid.*, s. 84.
[2] Mines and Quarries Act, 1954, s. 85.   [3] *Ibid.*, ss. 86, 87.
[4] *Ibid.*, s. 88.
[5] *Ibid.*, ss. 89, 90. See s. 91 concerning the provision of First Aid Equipment.

I.L.—15

Provision may be made by regulation for requiring young persons employed or seeking employment at mines to submit themselves for medical examination and for prohibiting the employment at a mine of a young person who fails, when required, to submit himself for medical examination without reasonable cause and of a young person who is unfit, by reason of physical or mental condition, for employment.[1]   A woman or young person may not be employed at a mine to lift, carry or move a load so heavy as to be likely to cause injury to that woman or young person.[2]

With legislation so detailed as that already discussed on the Statute Book it is understandable that the general welfare provisions of the Act are few in number.   Suitable and adequate sanitary conveniences, both below and above ground, must be provided affording separate accommodation for persons of each sex and these shall be kept clean, properly maintained and reasonable lighting provision made for them.

All necessary steps must be taken to keep down vermin and insects. Regulations may impose requirements concerning washing facilities, facilities for changing, storing and drying clothes, for canteens and facilities for feeding.   Supplies of drinking water must be assured.[3]

(3) Quarries.—Many of the provisions of the 1954 Act relate both to mines and quarries, but necessarily certain sections have particular reference to quarries alone and we proceed now to discuss these.[4]

No quarry may be worked unless there is a sole manager, an individual having every part of the quarry under his jurisdiction, or there are two or more managers.   In the latter case every part of the quarry must be within the jurisdiction of some one of the managers but not within the jurisdiction of any of the others, and the various jurisdictions must be defined in a written instrument executed by the owner and lodged with an inspector for the district and approved by him.   An inspector may not withhold or withdraw approval unless satisfied that his failure to do so might result in prejudice to the safety or health of employed persons.   The manager is appointed by the owner, who, if an individual, may appoint himself.   A sole manager must have the management and control of the quarry, subject to instructions given to the owner, and must see that all others discharge duties imposed on them by the Act, and any manager who is not sole manager must have the management and control of that part of the quarry over which he has jurisdiction within which he also has the duty of securing that other people discharge their obligations.[5]

---

[1] *Ibid.*, s. 92.
[2] *Ibid.*, s. 93.
[3] Mines and Quarries Act, 1954, ss. 94, 95, 96, 97.
[4] *Ibid.*, ss. 98–115.   With minor modifications ss. 73, 80–82, 84–88, 89, 90–91, 92, 93, 96, 97 apply to quarries as well as mines.
[5] *Ibid.*, ss. 98, 99.

There may be excepted from the management and control vested in the manager any matter, the responsibility for which is reserved for the time being by the owner. Such reservation must be in writing and lodged with the inspector, and the manager will not be concerned to secure compliance with the requirements of the Act in matters reserved by the owner to himself. In the interests of health and safety an inspector may direct that the instrument or a defined part shall be of no effect. Instructions given by an owner to a manager affecting the fulfilment by the manager of statutory responsibilities must either be written or confirmed in writing when the manager so requests. Excepting in emergencies, neither the owner nor anyone acting on his behalf may, except with the consent of the manager, give otherwise than through the manager any instructions to a person affecting that person's duties. And where instructions are so given the person giving them must forthwith inform the manager and, if requested, confirm them in writing.[1]

Where a manager dies, resigns or otherwise ceases to hold office the quarry may be worked for a period not exceeding seventy-two days (or such longer period as an inspector allows) until a successor is appointed if at that time there is a person appointed by the owner to exercise, in the event of the manager's ceasing to hold office, his powers and duties until a successor is appointed, being a person who has the like jurisdiction as that manager had immediately before he ceased to hold office. A person so appointed will be treated, if acting in the place of the sole manager, as if he were sole manager and, if not, as if he were manager of a quarry with jurisdiction the same as the manager in whose place he is acting.[2]

The law requires quarry managers to give close and effective supervision over all operations at the quarry. In the event of the absence of the manager the owner must appoint a person in his stead. Where a quarry has two or more managers the same principles operate with the necessary modifications as to jurisdictions—but every part of the quarry must, at all times, be under close supervision.[3] Regulations may prohibit prescribed operations unless that part of the quarry in which they are conducted is within the jurisdiction.[4] Where the Act requires the keeping of reports, records and the like, it is the duty of the manager to read these, or to ensure that they are read by a competent person who will bring to his notice relevant information.[5] Regulations may require the appointment of officials, engineers, technicians and other competent persons.[6] There are rules also as to the notification of certain appointments to the district inspector.[7]

The manager must so conduct operations in the quarry that the danger of falls is avoided and without prejudice to the generality of

---

[1] Mines and Quarries Act, 1954, ss. 100, 101.   [2] *Ibid.*, s. 102.
[3] *Ibid.*, s. 103.   [4] *Ibid.*, s. 104. There is a power to exempt.
[5] *Ibid.*, s. 105.   [6] *Ibid.*, s. 106.   [7] *Ibid.*, s. 107.

this, the work must be so conducted that there is no overhanging on the face, or sides, of the quarry or of any gallery in the quarry.[1] Safe means of access must be maintained to every working place in the quarry.[2]   After January 1st, 1959, no ropeway and no vehicle running on rails may be used at a quarry for the purpose of carrying employed persons to or from their working places, except in accordance with prescribed conditions.   So long as vehicles running on rails are in use in a quarry, there must be provided, maintained and used, either at the quarry or on the vehicles, such safety devices as are necessary to prevent the occurrence of accidents caused by vehicles running away and likely to do bodily harm to employed persons.   Such devices must be automatic in operation except where there is good reason to the contrary and except where persons are employed as a matter of routine in places in which vehicles on rails run, all necessary steps must be taken to protect persons from bodily injury by a vehicle running away.   This duty is additional to the duty to provide automatic safety devices and is aimed at the protection of the worker who does not habitually work at the place in question.[3]

Wherever natural light in the quarry is insufficient to enable safe working, and wherever workers pass at a time when such light is insufficient, there is a duty to provide suitable and sufficient artificial lighting and to secure also the proper maintenance of apparatus installed.[4]

Where injurious dust is given off the manager must take whatever steps are necessary to protect persons against the inhalation of the dust, but if the dust is given off in a building at a quarry then the manager must ensure that the entry of the dust into the air and the accumulation of it must be minimised by means of steps taken as near as possible to the point of origin of the dust; that any of the dust which enters the air is trapped or dispersed so as to make it harmless, and that any dust which does accumulate is either systematically cleared up and removed, or treated so as to make it harmless.[5]

If a person in charge of a quarry is of opinion that danger exists he must withdraw persons from the affected area, and, unless he is the manager, must immediately thereafter inform his superior and after this, as soon as it is possible to do so without undue risk, ascertain, either personally or by some competent substitute, the condition of the affected area and what measures are necessary to

---

[1] *Ibid.*, s. 108, which see also for exemptions.   See *Marshall* v. *Gotham Co., Ltd.*, [1954] A.C. 360; [1954] 1 All E.R. 937; *Brazier* v. *Skipton Rock Co., Ltd.*, [1962] 1 All E.R. 955 *Sanderson* v. *Millom Hematite Ore and Iron Co.* [1967] 3 All E.R. 1050.

[2] Mines and Quarries Act, 1954, s. 105.

[3] Mines and Quarries Act, 1954, s. 110.

[4] *Ibid.*, s. 111.

[5] *Ibid.*, s. 112.

make it safe. After withdrawal on suspected danger no person may re-enter the dangerous zone until the responsible person is satisfied that danger no longer exists, though this will not prevent entry for the purpose of saving life, ascertaining the extent of the danger and removing the danger.[1]

Provision may be made by regulation with regard to the generation and use of electricity at quarries, the supply, storage and use of blasting materials, and the provision and maintenance of equipment for the prevention of fire.[2]

Every abandoned mine and quarry must be fenced, as must places which are not abandoned but which have not been worked for a period of twelve months.[3]

(4) Penalties.—Finally the rules as to offences, penalties and legal proceedings contained in the Act are grouped together, though certain particular rules have application to mines and others to quarries. Where, in relation to a mine, the Act, or an order or regulation made under its terms, not being a provision which itself actually provides that a person shall be guilty of an offence; or where there is contravention of a direction, prohibition, restriction or requirement given or imposed by notice served by an inspector; or where there is contravention of a condition attached to an exemption, consent, approval or authority granted or given by the Secretary of State or an inspector, the owner, any person to whom written instructions have been given by the owner under the Act, the manager of the mine, any person who for the time being is treated as manager, every under-manager and any person treated as such shall be guilty of an offence.[4]

In the case of like contraventions relating to quarries the persons whom the Act makes, subject to its provisions, guilty of an offence are the quarry owner, any person to whom the owner has given written instructions as provided by the Act, every manager of the quarry and every person for the time being treated as manager. Though neither the manager of a quarry, nor a person treated as such, shall be guilty of offences taking place outside his jurisdiction and neither the manager, nor a person treated as such, shall be guilty of an offence in matters reserved by the Act to the owner.[5]

In the case of contraventions arising in relation to mines by persons not mentioned above, that person will be guilty of an offence in addition to those mentioned wherever the contravened provision expressly imposes a duty on that person or on persons of a class to which he belongs or expressly prohibits him from doing a specified act.[6]

---

[1] *Ibid.*, s. 113.   [2] *Ibid.*, s. 114.   [3] *Ibid.*, s. 151.
[4] Mines and Quarries Act, 1954, s. 152 (1).
[5] *Ibid.*, s. 152 (2); and see s. 100.
[6] *Ibid.*, s. 152 (3).

But neither a manager nor under-manager of a mine or quarry, nor a person for the time being treated as such, will be guilty of an offence where the owner of the mine or quarry contravenes the Act's provisions or an order or regulations made thereunder which expressly imposes on the owner a duty, requirement or prohibition or contravenes any prohibition, restriction or requirement served by an inspector.[1]

Where the offence consists in the employment of persons at a mine or quarry otherwise than in accordance with the terms of the Act there will be deemed to be a separate contravention in respect of every person so employed, and if a person is employed as manager in contravention of the Act, there will be deemed to be a separate offence in relation to each mine in which he acts as manager.[2]

In any proceedings under the Act in which a person is charged in respect of a contravention by some person other than himself, it will be a defence for the person charged to prove that he used all due diligence to secure compliance with the law.[3]   Similarly it is a defence in proceedings to recover damages and in any prosecution to prove that it was impracticable to avoid or prevent the contravention.[4]

Thus a manager has been held not to be liable under the older legislation for failure systematically to clear relevant parts of the mine of coal dust where he proved that it was impracticable for him to do so.[5] An under-manager of a mine whose jurisdiction is limited may avail himself of the defence that the contravention did not take place in, or in relation to the part of the mine over which he had jurisdiction and that nothing he did or omitted to do contributed to the contravention.[6]

So that there shall be no doubts as to the position the Act specifically lays down that the owner of a mine or quarry is not absolved from liability to pay damages in respect of a breach of statutory duty by a person employed by him by reason only of the fact that the provision contravened was one which expressly imposed on that person, or on persons of a class to which he belonged, a duty or a

---

[1] *Ibid.*, s. 152 (4).   See s. 153 as to accessories.
[2] *Ibid.*, s. 154.   For penalties see s. 155.
[3] Mines and Quarries Act, 1954, s. 156.
[4] *Ibid.*, s. 157.   For a discussion of the meaning of " practicable " see *Brown* v. *National Coal Board*, [1961] 1 Q.B. 303; [1960] 3 All E.R. 594; particularly the judgment of HOLROYD PEARCE, L.J., at p. 332.   This case is reported in the House of Lords, [1963] A.C. 574.   See also *Sanderson* v. *National Coal Board*, [1961] 2 Q.B. 244; [1961] 2 All E.R. 796, where it was emphasised that exercise of reasonable care did not establish that the act not done was impracticable.   The standard required is higher than in the tort of negligence.   And see *Jayne* v. *National Coal Board*, [1963] 2 All E.R. 220; *Morris* v. *National Coal Board*, [1963] 3 All E.R. 644; [1963] 1 W.L.R. 1382.
[5] *Atkinson* v. *Shaw*, [1915] 2 K.B. 768.
[6] Mines and Quarries Act, 1954, s. 158; the section also applies to one who is being treated as an under-manager with limited jurisdiction.

requirement or expressly prohibited that person from doing a specified act or as the case may be that the prohibition, restriction or
requirement was expressly imposed on that person or that that
person was appointed by someone other than the owner.[1]

Another provision of some interest as affecting legal proceedings
is that if a young person is employed at the mine or quarry in
contravention of the Act, the parents are guilty of an offence unless
it appears to the court that the parent had not consented, connived
or been guilty of wilful default in respect of the contravention.[2]

Finally, an owner or manager who institutes proceedings against
a person employed at the mine or quarry for an offence under the
Act must, within twenty-one days after the conclusion of the trial,
give written notice to the inspector of the district of the result of
the trial. And should the case go to appeal, similar formalities
must be observed.[3]

Events have led to two developments which affect safety and
therefore employment. The tragic Aberfan disaster led to the
Mines and Quarries (Tips) Act, 1969. This Act is consolidated with
Part I of the Mines and Quarries Act, 1954. The aim of the Act
is to ensure public safety.

The search for oil and natural gas in the sea bed has led to the
recent Mineral Workings (Offshore Installations) Act, 1971.

5. LOCAL EMPLOYMENT ACT, 1972

The twentieth century has seen a movement of some magnitude
of industrial enterprise away from the older established industrial
areas to new areas. This movement has reflected itself, not
unnaturally, in a movement of population, but industry has not
followed population, at least, not in a sufficient degree. In addition
there has been a marked change in the relative importance of
industry throughout the country. Many industries, including some
which had hitherto been regarded as basic industries, have declined
sharply as the result of foreign competition, scientific discovery and
other factors. The result has been the creation, throughout the
country, of areas in which unemployment, during periods of depres-
sion, has reached great proportions. To combat this there were passed
Distribution of Industry Acts in 1945 and 1950, which marked out
these areas as "development areas," to promote their continued
industrial liveliness and to secure, throughout the country as a whole,
a proper distribution of industry. These original development
areas were listed in the First Schedule to the Act, and included
areas in the north-east of England, in West Cumberland, in Scotland
and in Wales. These Acts were replaced by the Local Employ-

---

[1] *Ibid.,* s. 159.
[2] *Ibid.,* s. 160; and see s. 166.
[3] *Ibid.,* s. 165.

ment Act, 1960. This Act continued the policy of attempting to make provision for areas in England, Scotland and Wales where high and persistent unemployment exists or is likely to exist. It was further extended by the Local Employment Act, 1963.[1]

The process was continued by the Industrial Development Act, 1966. Employment was further dealt with by the Local Employment Act, 1970 whilst financial aspects of regional policy were contained in the Investment and Building Grants Act, 1971. The whole code has now been consolidated in the Local Employment Act, 1972 as far as it affects employment.[2] The basis of the policy is, as we have seen, the concept of development areas. To these the 1966 Act added the idea of 'grey' or intermediate areas. The Secretary of State for Trade and Industry is empowered to designate these development or intermediate areas.[3] The aim is to encourage the growth and proper distribution of industry. Designation of the areas can be by reference to employment exchange areas. The Act provides for the advisory committee set up in 1960 to continue.[4] Its duty is to advise the Secretary of State as to the use of his powers. The criteria to be taken into account are the relation between the expenditure involved and the employment likely to be provided, as well as the effects upon other areas.

The assistance provided includes building grants for undertakings to be carried on in the area.[5] There is also power to make loans or grants to undertakings which benefit employment in the area. Power is also granted to subscribe for or otherwise acquire shares in such undertakings.[6] The Secretary of State is given the authority to acquire land and to erect buildings in the designated areas. In this way too help can be given to undertakings in the areas.[7] In a similar way there is power given to any government department to improve what tends now to be called the infrastructure. This is called 'basic services' in the Act and these are defined to cover transport (road, rail, water or air), power, lighting, heating, water, and sewerage disposal.[8] Attention is also given to derelict land. This may be tackled for aesthetic reasons, to make the area more attractive or because it will directly aid the development of industry in the area.[9]

The 1960 Act set up, and the 1972 Act continues, the industrial estate corporations. There is one each for England, Scotland and Wales.[10] Their functions are to manage land leased to them by the

---

[1] It has also been followed by specialist Acts *e.g.* Fort William Pulp and Paper Mills Act, 1963; Shipbuilding Credit Act, 1964.
[2] The earlier Acts have only been repealed in part.
[3] Local Employment Act, 1972.
[4] S. 2(3).
[5] S. 3.
[6] S. 4.
[7] S. 5.
[8] S. 7.
[9] S. 8.
[10] S. 10.

Secretary of State or vested in them by the 1960 Act so that buildings may be erected, land developed or services provided to benefit undertakings in the designated areas.

The most direct impact on a worker is provided in s. 6.[1]   The aim is to assist the transfer of persons from employment elsewhere to employment in the designated area, whether with an existing firm or one to start operations.   Payment may in appropriate cases be made under the Employment and Training Act, 1948 towards the cost of removal and resettlement expenses of the workers and their dependents.   Payment may also cover maintenance and welfare of the workers and their dependents during the resettlement period.

The 1972 Act is purely a consolidating measure.   It was passed without debate in the Houses of Parliament and so no new policy matters arise.   These have been the subject of considerable political and economic debate from time to time.   Nevertheless, they have survived hostile criticism, and remain a useful way of tackling the problem of heavy regional unemployment which arises from seasonal trades or from the decline of heavy industry such as coal mining or shipbuilding upon which certain areas have relied heavily.

6. The Disabled Persons (Employment) Acts, 1944 and 1958

An interesting experiment in the social control of employment is contained in the Disabled Persons (Employment) Act, 1944.   The Act embodies an effort to secure employment for people whose disablement might make it difficult for them to do so, and to find employment for them suited to their degree of capacity or incapacity. The first object is achieved by compelling employers to engage a stipulated quota of disabled persons, whilst the second object is realised by a power given to the Secretary of State to designate certain types of employment as affording special opportunities for the employment of disabled persons.

A disabled person, within the terms of the Act, is one who, on account of injury, disease or congenital deformity, is substantially handicapped in obtaining or keeping employment, or in undertaking work on his own account, of a kind which, apart from that injury, disease or deformity, would be suited to his age, experience and qualifications.   The word "disease" is to be construed as including a physical or mental condition arising from the imperfect development of any organ.[2]

The Secretary of State may provide or make arrangements with other persons to provide vocational training courses for the benefit of

---

[1] Again from the 1960 Act.
[2] Disabled Persons (Employment) Act, 1944, s. 1.

disabled persons, provided they are over compulsory school age,[1] so as to fit them to undertake employment or work on their own account.   He may also provide or make arrangements for others to provide industrial rehabilitation courses for the benefit of disabled persons, so as to enable them to take up work of a kind in which they were engaged before they became disabled, or of some other kind suited to their age, experience and qualifications.[2]   The Secretary of State may defray or contribute towards the expenses of persons attending the courses.[3]

The Act requires the Secretary of State to maintain a register of disabled persons.[4]   An application for registration must be made by the disabled person or someone acting on his behalf.   To secure registration a person must satisfy the definition of a disabled person; that is to say, he must be substantially handicapped in obtaining or keeping employment, and must show that he is likely to be so for at least twelve months.[5]   A disability pensioner of the 1914–18 war will be deemed to be substantially handicapped in obtaining employment, and will be entitled to registration without further proof that his disablement is likely to continue for twelve months. His name may be registered without his making an application.[6]   An applicant for registration must be ordinarily resident in Great Britain; he must desire to obtain paid employment or to work on his own account, and must have a reasonable prospect of obtaining and keeping some form of such employment.   Men and women who served in the forces and, in the case of women, in certain associated services, are not required to satisfy the condition as to residence unless they are foreign nationals.   A foreign national who is at the time of the application in Great Britain and who, since September 1st, 1939, has served a minimum period of twelve months in the British or Allied Armed Forces or mercantile marine or in work of national importance is eligible for registration.   Other foreign nationals may qualify for registration only in exceptional cases.[7]   Persons under the school-leaving age who unreasonably refuse or fail to attend a vocational training or industrial rehabilitation course, or are of habitually bad character, are not eligible for registration.   A similar disability attaches to lunatics, the inmates of prisons and to whole-time patients in hospitals, sanatoria and the like.[8]

---

[1] At present 15: Education Act, 1944, s. 35 but to be raised to 16.

[2] Disabled Persons (Employment) Act, 1944, s. 3. Claimants for and persons in receipt of benefits under the National Insurance (Industrial Injuries) Act may be required to attend vocational and rehabilitation courses.   The age limit was changed from 16 to 15 by the 1958 Act.

[3] Disabled Persons (Employment) Act, 1944, s. 4.

[4] *Ibid.*, s. 6.

[5] Prior to 1958 the period was six months.

[6] *Ibid.*, s. 7.   His employer may make application for registration.

[7] S.R. & O., 1945, No. 940.

[8] Disabled Persons (Employment) Act, 1944, s. 7; S.R. & O., 1945, No. 938, and 1959, No. 1510.

Persons who are registered will be retained on the register for so long as the Secretary of State shall direct or, in the case of a pensioner of the 1914-1918 war, for so long as he continues to be such. Where the Secretary of State is satisfied after considering the recommendations of the district advisory committee[1] that a registered person has become disqualified from registration, his name may be removed from the register.[2]   The disabled person is entitled to have his name removed from the register on making written application to the Secretary of State for Employment.[3]

Every employer of twenty or more persons must give employment to a quota of disabled persons and where he is not doing so he must allocate vacancies for that purpose.   He must not, at any time, take or offer to take into his employment any person other than a registered person if, after offering such employment, the result would be that he was employing less than his quota.   Despite this an employer may take or offer to take into his employment any person whom he is under an obligation to employ (*a*) by virtue of any Act of Parliament, or (*b*) by virtue of an agreement to reinstate him in his employment before the date of operation of the Disabled Persons Act, and (*c*) any person for whose employment he has a permit issued by the Secretary of State under the terms of the Act.[4] An employer may make application for a permit to employ other than a disabled person even though the effect would be that he employed fewer than his quota of disabled persons.   The permit may be unconditional or subject to such conditions as the Secretary of State may direct.[5]   An employer may not, under penalty of a fine, discontinue the employment of a registered person, except for reasonable cause, if the consequence would be that he was employing less than his quota of disabled persons.   No proceedings against an employer for discharging a registered person without reasonable cause may be instituted unless the matter has been referred to a district advisory committee and the employer has been given an opportunity of making representations to the committee and the committee has reported to the Secretary of State.[6]

The quota of persons to be employed is ascertained in the following manner.   There is a standard percentage and a special percentage. The special percentage may be greater or smaller than the standard percentage and will be applied to trades, industries or occupations which in the opinion of the Secretary of State, after consultation with the interests concerned, offer employment suitable to disabled persons.   To estimate his personal quota the employer must apply the

---

[1] S.R. & O., 1945, Nos. 939 and 1471 and S.I. 1960 No. 1380.
[2] Disabled Persons (Employment) Act, 1944, s. 8.
[3] Disabled Persons (Employment) Act, 1958, s. 2 (2).
[4] Disabled Persons (Employment) Act, 1944, s. 9
[5] *Ibid.*, s. 11.
[6] *Ibid.*, s. 9.

standard percentage to the total number of his staff affected by
such percentage and the special percentage (if any) to the total
number of his staff affected thereby. If the number so ascertained
produces a fraction less than one half the fraction may be ignored,
if more than one half the quota will be the nearest higher whole
number.[1] Suppose therefore that an employer employs 894
persons, and that the standard percentage applies to 500 and the
special percentage applies to 394 of them, because they are employed
in work particularly suitable to disabled persons. Suppose, further,
that the standard percentage is two per cent. and the special
percentage is four per cent. Of the five hundred workers, ten
should be registered persons and of the 394, sixteen should be
registered persons.[2]

The Secretary of State has power to designate classes of employment as offering specially suitable opportunities for the employment
of disabled persons.   Where he does so an employer may not take or
offer to take into that class of employment a person who is not
registered as disabled or cause or permit a person in his employment
other than a registered person to take up that class of employment,[3]
unless he is under a duty to reinstate the person employed or has
secured a permit from the Secretary of State.[4]

7. Legislation as to Training and Development

**(1) The Industrial Organisation and Development Act,
1947.**—The Industrial Organisation and Development Act, 1947, is
an interesting Act, having for its purpose the strengthening of private
industry by providing methods for enabling such industries to bring
themselves up to date and to meet some of the problems which arise
as a result of inequalities of standard between different industrial
units. Some of these units are so small as to be unable to utilise,
let alone provide themselves with, existing services of research,
design, training and the like. Concerned with the relative industrial
efficiency of this country compared with others, the then President
of the Board of Trade, Sir Stafford Cripps, had set up various committees of enquiry (known as "working parties") and many of these
had referred, in their reports, to the need for some central body to
deal with such questions as would arise in the effort to make the
industry concerned an integrated team of producers instead of
isolated units of production. One of the chief factors working against
such integration is a deep-seated fear amongst many industrialists
that any suggestion of pooling of resources may carry with it the

---

[1] Disabled Persons (Employment) Act, 1944, s. 10.
[2] For provisions as to part-time workers see S.R. & O., 1945, No. 1558.
[3] Disabled Persons (Employment) Act, 1944, s. 12.
[4] *Ibid.*, ss. 9 (3), (4), 11. For regulations as to the keeping of records, see s. 14.

need to pool knowledge of trade secrets and industrial processes and the lack of compulsion in the Industrial Organisation and Development Act arises from the effort to meet this fear.[1]

The Act authorises the establishment, in any industry in which the majority of the persons engaged desire it, of a development council to which council there may be assigned any functions of a kind specified in the First Schedule to the Act. The list contained in this Schedule is an exhaustive list and is thus not to be exceeded and whilst it is too long for detailed comment, it covers such things as the promotion of research, the production and marketing of standard products, the better definition and use of trade descriptions, the training of personnel, the adoption of better and safer working conditions, promotion of the export trade and generally advising on matters relating to the industry (questions of remuneration or conditions of employment excluded).[2]

Because the responsibility for industry in this country is not the exclusive concern of one government department the power to make orders establishing development councils was given initially to the Board of Trade, the Minister of Agriculture and Fisheries, the Minister of Supply, the Minister of Food, the Minister of Works, the Admiralty, the Secretary of State, and the Minister of Power. The development council, once established, is a body corporate, with members appointed by the Board or Minister concerned, who must, however, draw his members from persons capable of representing those carrying on business in the industry, from those capable of representing employed persons in the industry, and independent members whose objectivity is sought to be assured by the requirement that they shall have no financial or industrial interest likely to affect them.

Representative members must always be in a majority on the council and the chairman, who is appointed by the Minister, must be drawn from the independent members.[3]

Under the powers given by the Act, development councils have been established in the Cotton,[4] Furniture,[5] Jewellery and Silverware,[6] and Clothing Industries.[7]

The Order establishing the council may provide for the registration of those carrying on business in the industry and for requiring such persons to furnish such returns and information as may be required to enable the council to exercise its functions, but in the latter case

---

[1] For a full discussion see Commons Debates, 1946–7, Vol. 433, p. 547
[2] Industrial Organisation and Development Act, 1947, s. 1; see *Thorneloe and Clarkson, Ltd.* v. *Board of Trade*, [1950] 2 All E.R. 245.
[3] Industrial Organisation and Development Act, 1947, s. 2.
[4] S.I. 1948, No. 629; 1951, No. 2173; 1953, No. 421; 1957, No. 508.
[5] S.I. 1948, No. 2774.
[6] S.I. 1948, No. 2801.
[7] S.I. 1949, No. 2124.

the Minister must approve the use of the power and the form in which the returns or other information will be furnished.[1]

There may also be a power to levy charges to meet the expenses of the council, and in order to do so equitably amongst the participants in the industry concerned, these may be required to produce books and documents, to keep records and to produce them for examination.[2]

These powers are, of course, vital to the work of a council, but they are the powers around which most contention has centred and about which most disquiet has been felt. It has, therefore, been provided that when a council is given power to require the production of information and the discovery of books and records or to furnish information relating to an individual business, the returns or other information must be furnished to, and any examination done by, independent members of the council or to or by officers of the council specially authorised in that behalf. The returns and the information furnished and the information obtained as a result of any examination may not, unless the person concerned consents, be disclosed (except in the form of a summary of similar information obtained from others and so framed as to prevent the identification of individual business) and even then only to independent members of the council or to officers of the council or to an officer of the Board or Minister concerned or to an officer of the Board of Trade to enable government departments more readily to obtain information for the appreciation of economic trends. And no person is to be prejudiced by a refusal to disclose what he claims to be a secret process unless the form of the requirement and the making of it in that form have been approved by the Board or Minister concerned after consideration of his claim.[3]

The development council must prepare and transmit annually to the Minister concerned, a report setting out the manner in which they have discharged their functions.[4]

In the case of industries not possessing a development council in which it appears that funds should be made available for scientific research, for the promotion of the export trade, or for the improvement of design, and there is, or is about to be created, a body capable of carrying out any of these purposes, the Minister concerned may make an order imposing on persons carrying on the industry such charges as may be specified to carry out the required activity.[5] Levies have been authorised in respect of the lace,[6] the woollen

---

[1] Industrial Organisation and Development Act, 1947, s. 3.

[2] *Ibid.*, s. 4.

[3] Industrial Organisation and Development Act, 1947, s. 5.

[4] *Ibid.*, s. 7. For power as to the amendment or termination of a development council, see s. 8.

[5] *Ibid.*, s. 9.

[6] S.I. 1951, No. 1125. This instrument, as amended, is now replaced by S.I. 1958, No. 2116.

textiles[1] and cutlery[2] industries. And a power is given to the Board of Trade with the approval of Parliament to make grants of monies to the Council of Industrial Design and to any association or body, corporate or unincorporate, the objects of which include promoting the improvement of design in any industry or activities appearing to the Board to be conducive thereto and as to which the Board is satisfied that it does not carry on its business for the purpose of making a profit.[3]

(2) The Employment and Training Act, 1948.—The Employment and Training Act, 1948,[4] has for its purpose the provision of such facilities as the Secretary of State for Employment may deem expedient to assist persons to select, make themselves fit for, obtain and retain employment suitable to their age and capacity, to assist employers to obtain suitable employees and generally to promote employment in accordance with the requirements of the community.[5] To fulfil these purposes the Secretary of State is empowered to maintain employment exchanges, to collect and furnish information and to provide registers of employments vacant and of persons seeking work. It is specifically provided that no person shall be disqualified or otherwise prejudiced in respect of facilities provided at a labour exchange because he refuses to accept employment found for him by the exchange if the ground of refusal is that there is an existing dispute which affects his trade, or that the wages offered are lower than those current in the trade in the district where the employment is found.[6]

The Secretary of State may provide training courses for persons, whether employed or not, who are above the upper limit of the compulsory school age. This is an interesting development. The provision of training courses was not, of course, a new thing but until the passing of the present Act, their purposes had been restricted to the training of unemployed or disabled persons. The new legislation had a wider purpose in that the Secretary of State would be concerned not only with the unemployed but also with the training of unskilled persons to follow trades requiring skill.[7] And where a scheme promoting greater regularity of employment in any industry is approved by the Secretary of State on the joint application of employers and workmen, he may assist in the administration of the scheme either by attaching officers of the Department of Employment to the scheme or in such other ways as he thinks fit.[8] In an effort to

---

[1] S.I. 1950, No. 1739; This instrument, as amended, is now replaced by S.I. 1957, No. 1378.

[2] S.I. 1960, No. 2384.

[3] Industrial Organisation and Development Act, 1947, s. 11.

[4] 11 & 12 Geo 6, c. 46.

[5] *Ibid.*, s. 1.

[6] Employment and Training Act, 1948, s. 2. The first Act establishing labour exchanges had been enacted in 1909.

[7] *Ibid.*, s. 3.

[8] *Ibid.*, s. 4.

produce a greater geographical mobility of labour, the Secretary of State may make provision by grant, loan or otherwise, to facilitate the removal and resettlement of persons, with or without their dependants, for the purpose of obtaining employment.[1]

The Second Part of the Act is concerned with the provision of a Youth Employment service and applies to persons under the age of eighteen years and persons over that age who are for the time being attending school. Such a service would be useless unless it were reasonably comprehensive and so the Act empowers the Secretary of State to make arrangements with the Minister of Education and the Secretary of State for the performance of any of the functions under the Act, through an executive body, to be known as the Central Youth Employment Executive. This executive will consist of such persons, being officers of the Minister, the Minister of Education or the Secretary of State as may be appointed.[2]

The Secretary of State is required to provide in such areas as he may determine for the constitution of Youth Employment Committees which shall advise him in those areas as to his functions under the Act. The Secretary of State will appoint to membership of the Committees persons who have experience and knowledge of education, employment and other conditions affecting the welfare of those to whom the second part of the Act applies, but he will not appoint a Youth Employment Committee for any area in respect of which he has approved a scheme set up as follows.[3] For the Secretary of State might authorise a local education authority to undertake in its own area, any of the functions conferred upon him in respect of the Youth Employment Service. But any such scheme had to be submitted to the Secretary of State for his approval within six months of the commencement of the Act.[4]

Without prejudice to the power to set up advisory committees the Act requires the Minister to set up a National Youth Employment Council and Advisory Committees on Youth Employment for Scotland and Wales respectively.[5] This Council will advise the Secretary of State in the performance of his duties under the Act and as to the function of local education authorities under the Act and will make such reports as the Secretary of State may require and such representations as they consider expedient, whilst the advisory committees for Scotland and Wales will advise the Council on matters relating to Scotland and Wales respectively.[6]

(3) **The Industrial Training Act, 1964.**—This short Act has laid the foundations of what will undoubtedly be far-reaching develop-

---

[1] *Ibid.*, s. 5.
[2] Employment and Training Act, 1948, **s.** 7.
[3] *Ibid.*, s 9
[4] *Ibid.*, s. 10.
[5] For the constitution see *ibid.*, Sched. I, Part II.
[6] See also Part II of Sched. I.

ments in the organised training of workers. This is to be achieved through the medium of industrial training boards. The Secretary of State for Employment is empowered to make orders establishing boards to improve training of persons over compulsory school age.[1] He must appoint a Central Training Council to advise him on the exercise of his functions under the Act.[2]

The functions of the boards are to provide or secure courses and other training facilities for persons employed in particular industries or intending to be so employed. They may approve courses provided by others. They have also a deliberative function and must consider the needs of the industry in question and make recommendations as to the nature and length of training, the persons to give and receive such training, the methods to be used and the standards to be attained. They may apply tests for ascertaining these standards and may award certificates. The scope is very wide indeed and covers almost every aspect of training from the training courses themselves to research into improvements.[3]

A board may pay maintenance and travelling expenses to students attending approved courses, make grants or loans to those providing courses and pay fees to others who provide the courses.[4]

It is envisaged that the boards may work through a system of appointed committees to whom various aspects of the functions will be delegated. Boards may find it convenient to set up joint committees.[5]

The work of the boards is to be financed by a levy on employers. This will be secured by the Secretary of State making, on the advice of the board, a levy order.[6] This procedure is backed by power vested in the Secretary of State to obtain information from employers so that the levy may be assessed and collected.[7] The Secretary of State is also given power to make grants and loans to boards to assist them with their work.[8]

Boards have been quickly established under the Act for wool, iron and steel, construction and engineering.[9] Others will soon follow and there is bound to be significant growth here.

(4) The Reinstatement in Civil Employment Act, 1944.— The Reinstatement in Civil Employment Act, 1944, was designed to secure the reinstatement in civilian employment of persons who,

---

[1] Industrial Training Act, 1964, s. 1.
[2] *Ibid.*, s. 11.
[3] Industrial Training Act, 1964, s. 2.
[4] *Ibid.*, s. 2(4).
[5] *Ibid.*, s. 3.
[6] *Ibid.*, s. 4.
[7] *Ibid.*, s. 6.
[8] *Ibid.*, s. 5.
[9] S.I.s 1964 Nos. 907, 949, 1079 and 1086 respectively. There are now 13 such Boards.

because of the war and the claims of national service, had been in the service of the Crown or in a civil defence force. Though originally in the nature of emergency legislation the Act embodied a principle which became permanent and remained so as long as conscripted national service remained an obligation of the adult citizen in this country.   It provides an example of the type of legislation which is devised to meet the problems of demobilisation and conscription.[1]

---

[1] A full treatment will be found in the 3rd Ed. pp 261–274.

CHAPTER IX

THE NATIONAL INSURANCE (INDUSTRIAL INJURIES) ACT, 1965[1]

The former system of compensation for industrial injuries and diseases was replaced by that provided by the National Insurance (Industrial Injuries) Act, 1946.[2] It was subsequently amended and the law was consolidated by the 1965 Act, which has itself been subjected to amendment and extension. The former law, which we have considered in our discussion of Workmen's Compensation and in which the main principle was that of insurance by an employer against injuries to his servant, has been superseded, in great measure, by a system of state insurance on a contributory basis. Despite the comprehensive character of the National Insurance Act, 1965, it has been noted that industrial accidents and diseases are still reserved for special treatment and that though a sickness benefit is payable under the latter Act it is, in the main, less substantial in amount than that receivable in the case of sickness arising from injuries received in the course of the claimant's employment. This two-tier system is frequently criticised and the logic (and justice) of providing more generous benefits for one group of casualties by reference to the place where their misfortunes occurred is not easy to understand.[3] In these circumstances, it is not surprising that the system has given rise to a temptation to insured persons to bring their claims, where possible, within the scope of the Industrial Injuries rather than the more general Act.

1. INSURED PERSONS AND LIABILITY FOR CONTRIBUTIONS

(1) Insured Persons.—The Act divides employments into those which are insurable and those which are excepted from insurance. All persons employed in insurable employment are to be insured, in the manner provided by the Act, against personal injury caused on or after the appointed day, by accident arising out of and in the course of the employment.[4] Insurable employments are of eight kinds. Firstly, employment under any contract of service or apprenticeship whether written or oral and whether expressed or implied. The contract of apprenticeship will present little difficulty

---

[1] 1965, c. 52.
[2] For surviving compensation in respect of pre-1948 accidents, see Industrial Injuries and Diseases (Old Cases) Act, 1967.
[3] For criticism of the arguments originally used to justify the two-tier system, see Aikin and Reid, *Employment, Welfare and Safety at Work*, Penguin, 1971, Ch. 14.
[4] National Insurance (Industrial Injuries) Act, 1965, s. 1(1).

for it represents a legal relationship not easily to be confused with any other relationship.   However, as we have already seen, the existence of a contract of service is often an issue of some difficulty, and the tests used to determine the question have reached a stage of fluidity and, consequently, great uncertainty.   Significantly, many of the cases in recent years have arisen in the context of liability to pay National Insurance contributions.[1]   The resort by the courts to criteria such as " integration " and " economic reality " has already been considered.[2]   It follows that any agent who is an independent contractor will not be within this provision,[3] nor will a partner even though he performs services which might, in other circumstances, form the basis of a contract of service.[4]   Where, however, there is a deed of assignment of partnership property, the trustee under the deed may employ a partner on such terms as to bring the latter within the scope of the Act.[5]

Secondly, insurable employment may consist of employment under a contract of service either as master or member of the crew or in any other capacity[6] on board ships (a) belonging to Her Majesty (b) whose port of registry is a port in Great Britain and (c) all other British ships of which the owner, managing owner, charterer or manager resides, or has his principal place of business in Great Britain, provided that the employment is for the purposes of the ship or her crew or of any passengers, cargoes or mails she carries and that the contract is entered into in Great Britain with a view to its performance wholly or in part while the ship is on her voyage.   This provision will apply to any prescribed ships whether British or not provided that the person by whom remuneration is paid, or in the case of employment as master or member of the crew, either that person or the vessel's owner or managing owner if there is more than one, has a place of business in Great Britain.[7]

The third category covers employment as a pilot on board any ship where the person employed holds a licence or deep sea certificate from a pilotage authority in Great Britain covering that employ-

---

[1] See, e.g., Amalgamated Engineering Union v. Minister of Pensions and National Insurance, [1963] 1 All E.R. 864; [1963] 1 W.L.R. 441; Whittaker v. Minister of Pensions and National Insurance, [1967] 1 Q.B. 156; [1966] 3 All E.R. 531; Argent v. Minister of Social Security, [1968] 3 All E.R. 208; [1968] 1 W.L.R. 1749; Ready Mixed Concrete v. Minister of Pensions and National Insurance, [1968] 2 Q.B. 497, [1968] 1 All E.R. 433; Market Investigations, Ltd. v. Minister of Social Security, [1969] 3 All E.R. 732; [1969] 2 W.L.R. 1.

[2] See Ch. 1.

[3] Vamplew v. Parkgate Iron and Steel Co., [1903] 1 K.B. 851; Ready Mixed Concrete, Ltd., v. Minister of Pensions and National Insurance, [1968] 2 Q.B. 497; [1968] 1 All E.R. 433.

[4] Ellis v. Joseph Ellis & Co., [1905] 1 K.B. 324.   Cf. the sham partnership in E. Rennison & Son v. Minister of Social Security (1970), 10 K.I.R. 65.

[5] Easdown v. Cobb, [1940] 1 All E.R. 49.

[6] The Secretary of State is empowered to make special provision by regulations for the inclusion or exclusion of persons " in any other capacity " in this context.   See National Insurance Act, 1967, s. 2(2).

[7] National Insurance (Industrial Injuries) Act, 1965, Sched. 1.

ment and in such other cases as may be prescribed. Fourthly, employment as a regular or enrolled member of the crew of any lifeboat stationed in Great Britain under the control of the Royal National Lifeboat Institution.

Fifthly, employment under a contract of service either as pilot, commander, navigator or member of the crew of any aircraft or in any other capacity[1] on board such aircraft where the employment is for the purposes of the aircraft or its crew or of any passenger, cargo or mails carried, and the contract is entered into in the United Kingdom with a view to its performance wholly or in part while the aircraft is in flight, provided that the aircraft belongs to Her Majesty or is registered in England and the owner, managing owner or hirer resides or has his principal place of business in Great Britain. The provision concerning employment in connection with an aircraft may apply to any prescribed aircraft whether registered in England or not where the person by whom the remuneration of that employment is paid, or in the case of employment as commander, navigator or member of the crew of that aircraft either that person or the owner (or if there is more than one) the managing owner has a place of business in Great Britain.[2]

Sixthly, employment in Great Britain under any public or local authority constituted in Great Britain. Seventhly, employment in Great Britain in plying for hire with any vehicle or vessel the use of which is obtained under a contract of bailment, not being a hire purchase agreement, in consideration of the payment of a fixed sum or a share in the earnings or otherwise. The final category of insurable employment covers employment in Great Britain as a member or as a person training to become a member of any such fire brigade, rescue brigade, first aid party or salvage party at a factory, mine or works as may be prescribed or of any such similar organisation as may be prescribed.[3] Membership of such organisations is frequently quite voluntarily undertaken by persons employed under contracts of service not inclusive of such activities. By this provision they are clearly brought within the terms of the Act.

Certain employments are specifically exempted from the operation of the Act. Firstly, any employment in Great Britain under a public or local authority constituted in Great Britain which is prescribed as exempt. Secondly, employment in ships and vessels not falling into the category of insurable employment. Thirdly, employment in aircraft of a character not coming within the definition, outlined above, of insurable employment. Fourthly, employ-

---

[1] Again, the Secretary of State is empowered to make special provision by regulations for the inclusion or exclusion of persons " in any other capacity ". See National Insurance Act, 1967, s. 2(2).

[2] National Insurance (Industrial Injuries) Act, 1965, s. 1, Sched. 1. The Secretary of State has power under s. 75 to modify as he thinks fit the provisions of the Act in their application to mariners and airmen.

[3] *Ibid.*, Sched. 1, Part I.

ment of a casual nature not being employment (a) for the purpose of the employers' trade or business; or (b) as a pilot on board a ship or vessel; or (c) for the purposes of any game or recreation where the persons are engaged or paid through a club; or (d) as a member of any such organisation as may be prescribed under the power given to the Minister to prescribe organisations similar to fire or rescue brigades as insurable employment.   Casual employment in this connection cannot easily be defined.   In *Hill* v. *Begg*[1] a man earned his livelihood by doing odd jobs and was employed at irregular intervals over a period of two years to clean the windows of a private house.   It was usual to summon him by post when the windows required cleaning.   Whilst cleaning the windows he met with an accident from the result of which he died.   The employment was held to be of a casual nature not entitling his dependants to compensation under the Workmen's Compensation Acts.

Fifthly, employment in the service of the husband or wife of the employed person is also excepted employment as is also employment by the father, mother, grandfather, grandmother, stepfather, stepmother, son, daughter, grandson, granddaughter, stepson, stepdaughter, brother, sister, half-brother or half-sister of the person employed, insofar as the employment is employment in a private dwelling house in which the person employed and the employer reside and is not employment for the purposes of any trade or business carried on there by the employer; and sixthly, employment which is prescribed as being in the nature of subsidiary employment only; and employment which is prescribed as being inconsiderable.[2]

The Secretary of State may also, by regulation, define classes of employment as being insurable or excepted where it appears that anomalies are resulting from the operation of the Act.[3]   Thus, provision has been made for the inclusion of office-cleaners in the class of insurable employment.[4]

The Act will apply to those persons employed by or under the Crown to whom it would apply were their employer a private person, but employment in the armed forces of the Crown and any other prescribed employment under the Crown will be excepted employments, and where the Act does apply to servants of the Crown the Act may be modified by Order in Council so that its provisions may be adapted to the case of such persons.[5]   It will also apply, subject to such modification as may be prescribed, to members of a police force.[6]   The Secretary of State has recently been given power to

---

[1] [1908] 2 K.B. 802.

[2] National Insurance (Industrial Injuries) Act, 1965, s. 1 and Sched. 1, Part II.

[3] *Ibid.*, s. 1 (2) and Sched. 1, Part III.

[4] National Insurance (Industrial Injuries) (Insurable and Excepted Employments) Amendment Regulations, 1968 (S.I. No. 1723).   See also S.I. 1970, No. 222, for special provision in respect of office staff supplied by an agency.

[5] National Insurance (Industrial Injuries) Act, 1965, ss. 74.

[6] *Ibid.*, s. 77.

make regulations for treating as insurable those working on exploration or exploitation of the Continental Shelf[1] and for modifying the application of the rules to them.[2] Where a claim for benefit is made under the Act or an application made for a declaration that an accident was an industrial accident, the Secretary of State may direct that the employment of the person concerned was an insurable employment notwithstanding that the relevant contract of service was void or the employed person not lawfully employed therein.[3] Though there is a scarcity of authority on a similar provision in the Workmen's Compensation Act, 1925[4] the purpose is clearly to protect a worker who is subjected to industrial risks under a contract which is, for some reason or other, invalid.

(2) **Contributions.**—The funds required to pay the benefits provided by the Act will be built up out of contributions from persons engaged in insurable employments, their employers and the Treasury. The latter will pay, in such manner and at such times as may be determined, the monies provided by Parliament for the purposes of the Act.[5] The Secretary of State is required to maintain a fund to be known as the " Industrial Injuries Fund " into which he will pay all monies received for the purposes of the Act and out of which he will pay claims for benefit and other authorised payments.[6] The contributions of employers and employees vary according to the sex and age of the insured person. There are four kinds of contribution, five pence being paid by men over eighteen years of age and three pence by boys under that age. Women over eighteen will contribute four pence a week and girls under that age two pence. Employers will pay six pence in respect of men over the age of eighteen years and three pence for boys under that age. They will pay five pence for women employees over the age of eighteen and three pence for girls under that age.[7] The Treasury will contribute a sum equal to one-fifth of the aggregate amount of the contributions made by employers and employed.[8]

An insured person may be exempted from the liability to pay contributions either because of the subsidiary or inconsiderable character of his employment or because the Secretary of State has exercised his power to make regulations modifying the provisions of the Act. Thus, the Secretary of State has power, by regulation, to exempt from insurance or from the payment of contributions mariners or airmen who are neither domiciled nor have a place of residence in the United Kingdom, and he has power, in the case of a mariner employed as a master or a member of the crew of a fishing

---

[1] Governed by the Continental Shelf Act, 1964.
[2] National Insurance (Industrial Injuries) Act, 1965, s. 76.
[3] *Ibid.*, s. 80.
[4] S. 3(3).
[5] National Insurance (Industrial Injuries) Act, 1965, s. 2.
[6] *Ibid.*, 1965, s. 59.
[7] National Insurance Act, 1971, s. 7 and Sched. 3.
[8] National Insurance (Industrial Injuries) Act, 1965, s. 2.

vessel who is remunerated wholly or partly by a share in the profits or gross earnings of the vessel, to remove the restriction on the right of deducting or otherwise recovering the employer's contribution in respect of him.[1]

The employer's liability is, in the first instance, to pay the contribution of himself and his employees. It is an offence for an employer or an insured person to fail to pay within the prescribed time contributions for which he is liable,[2] and it is an offence for an employer to deduct, or attempt to deduct, any part of his own contribution from the employee's remuneration.[3] The employer is entitled to recover from his employees the amount of any contributions paid or to be paid by him on their behalf, despite the Truck and similar Acts, by deductions from wages or other remuneration. Where an insured person does not receive pecuniary remuneration from the employer but receives remuneration from some other person, the employer may treat contributions, made by him on the insured person's behalf, as a civil debt to be recovered summarily provided he institutes proceedings within three months of the date on which the contribution was payable. If an insured person receives no pecuniary remuneration, either from the employer or from anybody else, the employer will be liable for the full contribution without the right to recover any part from the insured person.[4]

Contributions will not be payable either by a child or his employer when the child has not reached the upper limit of the school-leaving age and such a child will not be entitled to injury benefits except insofar as regulations may provide.[5]

The employer liable to pay the contributions will usually be the person with whom the insured person has entered into a contract of service, but the Act makes provision for cases which are not so clear. Thus, where a person is an insured person otherwise than by virtue of a contract of service, or is employed for the purpose of a game and recreation and engaged or paid through a club, the Secretary of State may, by regulation, prescribe who shall be treated as the employer. If an insured person is employed in any one contribution week by more than one person, the first person employing him, or such other person as may be prescribed, will be liable to pay the contributions. Should insured persons work under the general control and management of a person other than their immediate employer, regulations may provide that that other person shall be treated as the employer

---

[1] *Ibid.*, s. 2 and Sched. 2, Part II.

[2] *Ibid.*, s. 3(4).   The maximum punishment for this offence was raised from a fine of £10 to £50 by the Social Security Act, 1971, s. 8.

[3] *Ibid.*, s. 4.

[4] National Insurance (Industrial Injuries) Act, 1965, s. 3(7), incorporating s. 12 of the National Insurance Act, 1965.   For the arrangements as to the return of contributions paid erroneously see s. 3 (5) and Sched. 2, Part III. For payment of contributions through an Employment Exchange see National Insurance Act, 1965, s. 11(4).

[5] *Ibid.*, s. 78.

and be permitted to deduct the amount of contributions (other than the employer's contributions), he is liable to pay, from sums payable by him to the immediate employer. In such a case the immediate employer may recover from the insured persons the sums which he would have to pay if he were liable to pay contributions.[1]

Contributions may be made by means of stamps or by such alternative method as regulations may provide. Where the adoption of an alternative method of paying contributions results in greater cost than would be the case were payment made by means of stamps, a person adopting the alternative method may be required to pay such fees as would indemnify the Secretary of State against those costs.[2] If a person buys, sells, exchanges, pawns or takes into pawn an insurance card or stamp or affixes a used stamp to a card or knowingly makes a false statement or false representation or produces, furnishes, causes or knowingly allows to be produced or furnished any document or information which he knows to be false in a material particular he will commit an offence. Should the offence be committed by a body corporate and it is proved that it was committed with the consent, connivance or negligence of a director or officer thereof, that person, as well as the body corporate will be liable to be proceeded against and punished.[3] This provision, though attempting to fasten responsibility upon the actual delinquent, is open to the criticism that the Act does not make it an offence for the corporate body to indemnify a director or officer so punished.

The provisions as to offences, penalties and legal proceedings are governed by the appropriate provisions in the Insurance Act, 1965.[4] An employer convicted of the offence of failing to pay contributions will be liable to pay to the Industrial Injuries Fund a sum equal to the amount he failed to pay, as he will if he forges, or prints, a die or stamp or commits similar offences[5] or uses defaced or cancelled stamps whether they had actually been used for the purpose of payment or not. Moreover, an employer who is convicted of any of these offences may be faced with evidence that he has failed to pay other contributions in respect of the same person during the two years preceding the date of the offence and in the case of an employer convicted of failure to pay contributions, evidence may be brought in proof of a like failure to pay other contributions during those two years in respect of any other person employed by him.

---

[1] *Ibid.*, s. 79. See National Insurance (Industrial Injuries) (Insurable and Excepted Employments) Amendment Regulations, 1970 (S.I. No. 222), which makes special provision for office staff supplied through an agency.

[2] *Ibid.*, s. 67.

[3] National Insurance (Industrial Injuries) Act, 1965, s. 68, which makes the offences under the National Insurance Act, 1965, applicable here.

[4] Ss. 93, 94 and 96.

[5] National Insurance Act, 1965, s. 93 and see the Stamp Duties Management Act, 1891, s. 13.

If the offence be proved he will again be liable to pay to the Industrial Injuries Fund a sum equal to the total of all the contributions he has failed to pay. The payment to the fund will be treated as a payment in satisfaction of the unpaid contributions, but the employer will not be permitted to recover from the insured person that person's share of the contribution. A corporate body failing to pay a sum required by these provisions to be paid to the Fund may be sued for the debt jointly and severally with any directors who knew or could reasonably be expected to know of the failure to pay the contributions.[1]

All sums due to the Fund under the Act are recoverable as debts due to the Crown and without prejudice to any other remedy may be recovered summarily as a civil debt.[2] Proceedings for such recovery may be brought within three years from the time when the matter complained of arose. An inspector or other authorised officer may institute proceedings and, although not of counsel nor a solicitor, may conduct the proceedings.

Amounts due in respect of contributions payable during the twelve months before the date of a receiving order or the relevant date in winding-up will be payable in priority to other debts.

2. THE RISKS INSURED

The Act insures persons engaged in insurable employment (i) against personal injury caused by accident arising out of and in the course of their employment[3] and (ii) against any prescribed disease and any personal injury not so caused but being a disease or injury due to the nature of the employment and developed on or after the appointed day.[4]

(1) Industrial Accidents.—To enable an insured person to recover he must show that he has suffered a personal injury which has been caused by accident arising out of and in the course of his employment. There have, of course, been many hundreds of cases decided by the Commissioner since 1948, but few new principles of law have been evolved. Indeed, the law on the subject which grew up around the similar provisions in the Workmen's Compensation Acts, still influences the Commissioner and his deputies, although some recent cases have given rise to previously unconsidered problems. Borderline disputes are sometimes attributable to the imperfection of the definition of the risks insured, but such disputes can also be seen as the inevitable consequence of the " two-tier " system referred to at the beginning of this chapter.[5]

---

[1] National Insurance (Industrial Injuries) Act, 1965, s. 69(8).
[2] National Insurance Act, 1965, s. 96. See also p. 417 for other rules relating to proceedings under the Act.
[3] National Insurance (Industrial Injuries) Act, 1965, s. 5.
[4] *Ibid.*, s. 56—the appointed day is July 4th, 1948.
[5] For a recent statement of this view, see Atiyah, *Accidents, Compensation and the Law,* (Weidenfeld and Nicholson, 1970), p. 355: " The fact is that the

Personal Injury

The significance of the words " personal injury " is that mental as well as physical injuries are included. The point was considered in *Ex parte Haines*[1] where the evidence showed a member of the National Fire Service to be suffering from nervous debility as a consequence of his work in a relief fire crew during air raids. The Act which provided compensation in the relevant circumstances was the Personal Injuries (Emergency Provisions) Act, 1939 and in that Act reference was made "to any physical injury." The court found that the use of these words precluded any recovery in the case of injuries which were exclusively mental in character. The court drew a distinction between the use of the words "physical injuries" in the Personal Injuries Act and the use of the words "personal injury" in the Workmen's Compensation Act—from which Act the definition we are now discussing was borrowed.

> "I find that the legislature . . . has deliberately rejected the phrase 'personal injury' used in the Workmen's Compensation Acts . . . and has instead used the words 'physical injuries.' By so doing it has, I think purposely excluded injuries which are purely mental."[2]

In another case a miner, hearing a cry of distress, discovered an injured fellow worker whom he picked up and carried away. The man was still alive but died later. The miner, in consequence, suffered nervous shock and it was found that he was suffering from a personal injury. "In my opinion," it was said "nervous shock due to accident which causes incapacity is as much 'personal injury' by accident as a broken leg."[3]

Thus, there is no doubt that under the present Act all injuries whether physical or mental in character are included, but in addition the Act specifies that any references to loss of physical faculty shall be construed as including references to disfigurement, whether or not accompanied by any actual loss of faculty.[4] However, damage to an artificial limb is not a personal injury.[5]

Accident

The personal injury must arise out of an accident to enable an insured person to recover benefits under the Act. The word accident is to be construed "in the popular and ordinary sense of the

---

absence of any clear and sound policy reason for distinguishing between employment risks and non-employment risks makes it almost impossible to draw a satisfactory criterion for distinguishing accidental injury within the scheme from accidental injury outside the scheme in many borderline situations."

[1] [1945] K.B. 183; [1945] 1 All E.R. 349.
[2] *Ex parte Haines*, [1945] K.B. 183; [1945] 1 All E.R. 349, at pp. 187 and 351 respectively, *per* TUCKER, J.
[3] *Yates* v. *South Kirkby, etc., Collieries, Ltd.*, [1910] 2 K.B. 538, *per* FARWELL, L.J., at p. 542 ; see also *Re Drake*, [1945] 1 All E.R. 576.
[4] National Insurance (Industrial Injuries) Act, 1965, s. 5 (3).
[5] R(I) 7/56.

word as denoting an unlooked-for mishap or an untoward event which is not expected or designed."[1]   The court, when these words were spoken, was considering the case of a man who had ruptured himself by an act of over-exertion.   The wheel he was employed to turn became stuck, and in the effort to turn it he was injured.   The argument used against his claim was that there was nothing accidental in the occurrence. This view the court rejected.

> "The word accident is not a technical legal term with a clearly defined meaning.   Speaking generally, but with reference to legal liabilities, an accident means any unintended and unexpected occurrence which produces hurt or loss.   But it is often used to denote any unintended and unexpected loss or hurt apart from its cause; and if the cause is not known the loss or hurt itself would certainly be called an accident. . . .   The great majority of what are called accidents are occasioned by carelessness; but for legal purposes it is often unimportant to distinguish careless from other unintended and unexpected events."[2]

An occurrence may be accidental though its effect is to produce a disease.   The facts in *Brintons, Ltd.* v. *Turvey*[3] were that whilst a workman was sorting wool a bacillus entered his eye and resulted in anthrax from which he died.   He was held to have died from an accident.   Insisting that the word accident must be interpreted in its ordinary and popular meaning, HALSBURY, L.C., remarked that the use of language preceded scientific investigation.

> "Probably it is true to say that in the strictest sense and dealing with the region of physical nature there is no such thing as an accident.   The smallest particle of dust swept by a storm is where it is by the operation of physical causes, which if you knew beforehand you could predict with absolute certainty that it would alight where it did. . . .   It does not appear to me that by calling the consequences of an accidental injury a disease one alters the nature or the consequential results of the injury that has been inflicted."[4]

A workman who is killed by design may yet be said to have died as the result of an accident, for the meaning of that word must connote an unlooked-for or untoward event, that is to say it must have been unexpected and unlooked-for by the sufferer.   In *Trim Joint District School Board of Management* v. *Kelly*[5] a master at an industrial school was killed whilst superintending the boys in the school yard.   The killing was the result of a premeditated act by boys whom the schoolmaster had threatened to punish.   It was held that the dependent mother of the schoolmaster was entitled to recover and that a contrary decision would amount to reading into the Work-

---

[1] *Fenton* v. *Thorley & Co., Ltd.*, [1903] A.C. 443, *per* Lord MACNAGHTEN at p. 448,
[2] *Ibid., per* Lord LINDLEY, at p. 453.
[3] [1905] A.C. 230.
[4] [1905] A.C. 230, at pp. 233-4.
[5] [1914] A.C. 667.

men's Compensation Acts a proviso that an accident is not to be deemed within the Acts if it arises from the mischievous act of a person not in the service of the employer. This principle has been applied repeatedly by the Commissioner under the Industrial Injuries Acts. An insurance agent who was attacked and robbed of the premiums collected when on his way home after making the last call of the day was held to have suffered an industrial injury[1] as also was a van driver injured by a stone thrown deliberately by a small boy.[2] A workman who asked another for assistance which was refused called the other a 'lazy swine' and had certain teeth knocked out in consequence. It was held that the truculent attitude of the first workman converted the dispute into a personal quarrel and that there was, in consequence, no accident.[3] On the other hand where two workmen were conversing and one pointed a finger at the other who said, "Don't point your finger at me," struck it and broke the finger, it was held that this was an industrial accident even though the evidence suggested that the assaulting workman did not intend to harm the other's finger.[4] These cases show that injuries caused by the misconduct or skylarking of others can nevertheless be classified as "accidents". Whether or not they can be said to arise "out of and in the course of employment" is considered later.

It is, therefore, clear that where one person deliberately injures another the resulting injury may yet be an accident within the law as to industrial injuries. It is perhaps more surprising to learn that there are circumstances in which the law will regard intentional self injury, when it results in death, as entitling claimants to benefits under the Acts. However, in order to establish suicide as an industrial accident it must be shown that the suicide was causally related to the injury, that, for example, it was caused by insanity, which in turn resulted from the accident.[5] So when a man committed suicide after brooding on a doctor's decision that he must stay away from work for a further period it was held that his widow was not entitled to death benefits.[6] Conversely, where a miner, whose eye had been almost blinded and who was suffering intense pain, committed suicide by gas poisoning, death benefit was given. He had brooded over the loss of sight, but this was not, in itself, sufficient. The shock of the accident had disturbed his mind and had established a causal relationship between the original accident and the subsequent suicide.[7]

---

[1] C.S.I. 63/49, but *cf. Dunning* v. *Binding* (1932), 25 B.W.C.C. 361; (*No. 2*) (1932), 25 B.W.C.C. 655.
[2] C.I. 88/50.
[3] C.I. 5/50 but *cf.* C.I. 248/50 and R. (I) 41/53.
[4] C.I. 3/48.
[5] See *Withers* v. *London, Brighton and South Coast Railway Co., Ltd.*, [1916] 2 K.B. 772; *cf. Coulter* v. *Coltness Iron Co., Ltd.* (1938), 31 B.W.C.C. Supp. 111.
[6] C.I. 256/49.
[7] C.I. 172/50.

There is a presumption against suicide and where a man's death is unexplained, as where he dies by drowning from a vessel at sea the presumption will operate in favour of the claims of the dependants.

A condition may amount to an accident though it is the result of a continued series of happenings provided its occurrence can be related to some approximate point of time.   So a packer in a colliery who worked in a confined space and who lost the power to raise the front part of his foot upwards was deemed to have done so as the result of an accident.[1]   Thus, a single specific act to which the injury is referrable is no longer required as a condition precedent to the recovery of benefits.   A dock labourer who had left home for his work in an apparently sound condition and who, after raising his arm to move a sack, fell forward and died was held to have suffered an accident.   There was evidence that the man suffered from heart disease, though what particular form of disease was not diagnosed. Medical evidence, however, testified that it was inconceivable that the work had no effect on the disease.   It was held that the work affected him and caused his death.[2]   But though it is not necessary, in the effort to prove death by accident, to show a single untoward event, there will be no accident where it can only be proved that a man's work had contributed to a progressive deterioration of health ultimately causing incapacity or death.

The difference between an accidental occurrence and one which arises by way of "process", as it is called, is often of acute significance where diseases are in question.   No difficulty, perhaps, presents itself in the case of the workman who was an habitual victim of asthma and who left his ordinary occupation to attempt to quell a fire on his employer's property.   The fumes began an attack of asthma which made him incapable of working.   The incapacity was held to be derived from an "accident"[3].   So a trainee nurse at a day nursery who developed infantile paralysis seven days after one of the children whom she had nursed had done so was held to have suffered an industrial accident,[4] but a doctor who contracted tuberculosis as a result of a series of penetrations of the lung by bacilli at various times was not entitled to industrial injury benefit.[5]   A case which moved nearer to the dividing line between a single occurrence and a process was that in which a lorry driver had to drive with a broken window and during the course of one morning an attack of fibrositis was set up.   The evidence showed that the draught was continuous and varied in intensity, but the period was so short as to negative the notion of a process.

---

[1] *Fife Coal Co., Ltd.* v. *Young,* [1940] A.C. 479; [1940] 2 All E.R. 85; see also *Whittle* v. *Ebbw Vale Steel, Iron and Coal Co., Ltd.,* [1936] 2 All E.R. 1221.   But *cf.* R.(I) 7/66, *infra,* p. 399.
[2] *Falmouth Docks and Engineering Co., Ltd.* v. *Treloar,* [1933] A.C. 481.
[3] C.S.I. 1/48.
[4] C.I. 159/50.
[5] C.I. 83/50 but see 196/50.

"The physiological change which occurred took place in a single morning. That is . . . a sufficiently identifiable incident to be treated as an accident . . .".[1]

However, the dividing line was crossed in a case in which a man who had been employed for 18 years in the blasting department of a chemical factory (during which he had been continuously exposed to chemicals known as E.G.D.N. and N.G.) died after a weekend away from work. Although doctors were unable to establish the cause of death, experts in toxicology and industrial medicine showed that prolonged exposure to these chemicals can cause sudden death, which tends to occur after a short break in the exposure. The Commissioner held that although death was caused by employment, it was not the result of an accident.[2] Thus the distinction between " accident " and " process " is particularly important in relation to diseases which are as yet insufficiently understood to be prescribed under section 56.

Out of and in the Course of Employment

Finally, the personal injury by accident must arise out of and in the course of the insured person's employment, though when it is proved that an accident arises in the course of the employment it will be deemed, in the absence of evidence to the contrary, also to have arisen out of that employment.[3] The latter provision is of considerable importance and represents a change in the burden of proof from the position under the Workmen's Compensation Acts. Under those Acts both the requirement of showing that the accident arose "out of" the employment and "in the course of" the employment had to be met. Now, provided the insured person can show that the accident arose in the course of the employment the onus of proving that it did not arise out of that employment will fall upon the persons contesting the insured person's claim. It would seem that we are only a short step away from broadening the risks covered even further by making " out of " and " in the course of " alternatives.

In the case of *Thom (or Simpson)* v. *Sinclair*[4] a woman at work in a shed belonging to her employer was injured by the collapse of a wall owned by another. It was argued, in support of the case, that no compensation was payable, that the collapse of an adjoining wall had nothing to do with her employment but was a risk which would attach to anyone who happened to be in the vicinity. This point of view did not prevail and the accident was held to have arisen out of her employment. There was no doubt that the accident arose in

---

[1] R. (I) 31/52.
[2] R.(I) 7/66.
[3] National Insurance (Industrial Injuries) Act, 1965, s. 6; *R.* v. *National Insurance (Industrial Injuries) Commissioner, Ex parte Richardson*, [1958] 2 All E.R. 689; [1958] 1 W.L.R. 851.
[4] [1917] A.C. 127.

the course of her employment.   It was acknowledged that there are many kinds of accident which have no causal relation with the employment and cannot be said to arise out of it, but if the accident from which the man suffers would not have happened to him if his employment had not compelled him to be where he was, he will be entitled to benefit.   Thus it was found that since the fall of the wall could only happen in one place, if a person were in that place owing to the demands of his employment he must be permitted to recover.   "The question really turns," said Viscount HALDANE,

> "on the character of the causation through the employment which is required by the words 'arising out of' . . . it is to be observed that it is the employment which is pointed to as to be the distinctive cause, and not any particular kind of physical occurrence. The condition is that the employment is to give rise to the circumstance of injury by accident.   If, therefore, the statute when read as a whole excludes the necessity of looking for remoter causes . . . the question becomes a simple one."[1]

And in the same case, Lord SHAW OF DUNFERMLINE defined the expression "arising out of the employment" as applying

> "to the employment as such—to its nature, its conditions, its obligations and its incidents.   If by any of these the workman is brought within the zone of special danger and so injured or killed . . . the broad words of the statute 'arising out of the employment' apply.   If the peril which he encountered was not an added peril . . . a case for compensation under the statute appears to arise."[2]

The requirement that the accident should arise out of the employment was further considered in *Lancashire and Yorkshire Ry. Co.* v. *Highley*.[3]   A workman employed on a railway had orders to work down the line and to take a train to do so.   Arriving at a station where he had to change, he crossed the line (though there was an alternative but longer route) to reach a mess room in order to obtain breakfast.   Whilst attempting to pass under the trucks of a train which moved, he was killed.   It was held that the accident did not arise out of his employment inasmuch as the workman's own act created an added peril.   Lord SUMNER doubted, as subsequent cases have shown, correctly, whether any universal test could be found by which to determine what acts did and what did not arise out of the employment, but he suggested that one test might be :

> "Was it part of the injured man's employment to hazard, to suffer or to do that which caused his injury ? . . .   To ask if the cause of the accident was within the sphere of the employment, or was one of the ordinary risks of the employment, or reasonably incidental to the employment, or, conversely, was an added peril and outside the sphere of the employment, are all different ways of asking whether it was a part of his employment that he should have acted as he was acting, or should have been in the position in

---

[1] [1917] A.C. 135.   [2] *Ibid.*, at p. 142.   [3] [1917] A.C. 352.

which he was, whereby in the course of that employment he sustained injury."[1]

Thus, one of the chief tests is to determine whether what happened to the workman was one of the risks of his employment. If so, and injury arises, then injury benefit will be available. If, however, the injury arises from a hazard not incidental to the employment, benefit will not normally be payable. So, where a colliery worker, complaining of headache, accepted a bottle of smelling salts from a friend and the liquid splashed and injured his eye, it was held that the accident was not an industrial accident. It would doubtless have been so had the workman availed himself of the firm's first aid facilities.[2] Similarly a laundry worker who tripped over a carpet before she had " clocked-on " in the sorting room of the laundry in which she worked, to which room she had gone to deposit her personal laundry so as to avail herself of the cheap rates which were given to employees, was held not to have suffered an industrial injury. The accident did not befall her in the course of her employment and thus could not be said to have arisen out of, or in its course.[3]

However, where injury is caused during a digression which can be seen as beneficial to the employer, the accident may still be considered to have arisen out of and in the course of employment. So when an agricultural worker was injured while helping an independent contractor who was repairing his (the agricultural worker's) tractor, the Commissioner held that he was entitled to benefit. Even though he had no duties to perform at the time, his conduct was reasonable and beneficial to his employer in that, by helping, he was expediting his return to work.[4]

Under the legislation concerned with workmen's compensation, employment was generally deemed to begin when the workman reached his place of employment and to continue until he left that place. Where such place began was the subject of much litigation but the Industrial Injuries Act gives an insured person, in this connection, greater security and renders much of the earlier case law of limited significance. For an accident which occurs to an insured person, who is, with the express or implied permission of his employer, travelling as a passenger on any vehicle to or from his place of work may, in certain circumstances, be deemed an accident arising out of and in the course of the employment, notwithstanding that the worker is under no obligation to his employer to travel by that vehicle. Such an accident, however, will only entitle the injured person to benefit where it is of a kind which would be deemed to have arisen out of and in the course of the employment had the insured person been under an obligation to travel in the vehicle and it is not being operated in the ordinary course of a public trans-

---

[1] [1917] A.C., 352, at p. 372. [2] R. (I) 43/57. [3] R. (I) 45/55.
[4] R.(I) 13/68.

port service.   The reference to a vehicle will include reference also to a ship, vessel or aircraft.[1]

These provisions have been the object of considerable litigation. A railwayman who was injured on his employer's premises whilst on his way to catch a train which was reserved for railwaymen and which would have taken him to the actual place where he had to report for duty, was held not to have suffered an accident within the course of the employment, for the provisions of section 9 of the 1946 Act (now replaced by section 8 of the 1965 Act) would not operate until the train was reached.   These provisions are limited to those who are travelling as passengers[2] and a roadman who was required to equip himself with a bicycle, who sprained his foot on the pedal on his way home from work was held to be not within the Acts for he was not travelling as a passenger and " the phrase would be otiose if it included the driver of a vehicle ".[3]

An agricultural labourer who was injured whilst in a lorry provided by the Agricultural Executive Committee of the county which was taking him to the farm where he was to work, was held not entitled to injury benefit.   His employer was not in any way responsible for the travelling arrangements.[4]   Another aspect of the same question arises in the case of a workman who jumped from a bus before it had stopped.   The bus was one operated in pursuance of an agreement made with the claimant's employers and it was held he might have benefit under the Act for what he did was not so perverse as to take him outside the scope of his employment.[5]

Accidents which occur whilst a person is moving to or from his employment occasion difficulty from time to time.   Thus a seaman on shore leave ceases to be within the scope of the Acts for his employment is interrupted from the time when he leaves the ship until he returns again to what is, in a fair sense, the provided means of access to the ship[6] or as Lord SUMNER said in *Parker* v. *Ship Black Rock (Owners)*:

"until he has so nearly approached the means of access to the ship as to make it reasonable to hold that he has returned to the sphere in which his employment operates."[7]

And where a seaman whilst returning from shore leave slipped and injured himself when about to step from a jetty to a boat provided by his employers to take him back to his work, it was held that he might recover industrial injury benefit even though the quay and the jetty were open to the public.   For the boat was the means of

---

[1] National Insurance (Industrial Injuries) Act, 1965, s. 8(2).
[2] R. (I) 67/52.   [3] C.I. 33/50.
[4] C.I. 101/49.   [5] C.I. 182/49.
[6] See Lord DUNEDIN, *Davidson & Co.* v. *M'Robb or Officer*, [1918] A.C. 304, at p. 322.
[7] [1915] A.C. 725 at p. 731.   This and the immediately preceding case were cited by the Commissioner in C.I. 105/49.

access provided and he had so nearly reached it that he was virtually in his sphere of employment.[1]

This doctrine, however, must not be pushed too far, for where a workman fell on an icy footpath belonging to his employers and within a hundred yards of the building in which he was to " clock on," it was held that this was not an industrial accident for, though the path was owned by the employers and was not a public right of way, the public were permitted to use it. In consequence there was no greater risk to the workman than to the general public and he could not claim to have suffered an industrial injury.[2]

This may be contrasted with a case in which a worker was injured while cycling to work along a road owned by his employers, at a point just outside the factory gates. The road provided vehicular access to the factory, but only a pedestrian right of way to the public. There was no evidence that the public used the road. The Commissioner held that the accident had arisen out of and in the course of employment. At the place where it occurred, the worker was exposed to a risk of his employment, which was different from a risk to which the general public was exposed.[3]

Such facts may usefully be compared with those where a painter was working too far from his base to permit his employers to give him tea, so that he was permitted to go to the nearest café and was paid whilst so engaged. Whilst crossing the road to the café he was injured. It was held that this was not an industrial injury, he had succumbed to a mere risk of the street.[4]

Recently the Commissioners have had to adjudicate upon claims by persons whose employment involves visiting the homes of several other persons in the course of a day. In one case a home help employed by a local authority was injured when she fell in the road on the way to the first house at which she was to work that day. She was given instructions in advance as to what calls she was to make and she was not required to report to her employers before making her first call of the day. The Commissioner held that her injury had not arisen out of and in the course of her employment. He was not concerned whether the claimant's home was the base from which she worked, but rather with the nature of her employment and her obligations with reference to it. Thus the journey to her first call was merely preparatory to her employment.[5] This case may be contrasted with another in which a civil servant, whose duties entailed his working both in his office and in visiting persons in their homes, was injured in a street accident within his defined visiting sub-area when travelling from his home to his first visit of

---

[1] R. (I) 13/53.
[2] R. (I) 20/57.
[3] R.(I) 1/68.
[4] C.I. 282/49. See also R.(I) 39/59.
[5] R.(I) 2/67.

the day.   He had a discretion as to which of his duties he performed
on a particular day and in which order he performed them.   The
Commissioner considered that the accident had arisen out of and in
the course of the claimant's employment.   It had occurred during
his hours of employment when he was acting within the terms of his
discretion and doing what he was employed to do.[1]   The previous
case was distinguished as a case in which the claimant had to commence work at a prescribed place and time.   However, a worker
who was injured in a road accident while driving home from a
temporary place of employment 100 miles away was not within the
insured risk, even though his employer paid him a mileage allowance
and for time spent in travelling.   This was because he was not
contractually obliged to travel in his own car.[2]   It is apparent that
problems of the borderline in this area are particularly acute and
that they have not yet been resolved in a way which makes decisions
predictable.

Another possible place of injury away from the employer's
premises is an educational institute attended by a worker on a day-
release basis.   The Commissioner has taken a generous atittude
towards an apprentice who was injured while attending a day-
release class which his contract permitted but did not oblige him to
attend.   He was paid by his employer whether or not he attended
the class, but if he did not, he was expected to report to his employer
for work.   The Commissioner allowed his claim, considering attendance to be incidental to his employment, even though it was not
obligatory.[3]

An accident which happens to an insured person in or about
premises at which he is employed for the purposes of his employer's
trade or business will also be deemed an accident arising out of and
in the course of the employment if it happens whilst the insured
person is taking steps, during an actual or supposed emergency, to
rescue, aid or protect persons who are, or are thought to be, im-
perilled or to avert or minimise serious danger to property.   Consequently, an insured person who, after the hours of his employment
are over, hearing that his place of employment is on fire, goes to offer
assistance will be within the protection of the Act not only whilst
he is actually engaged in that place of employment but also, it
is submitted, whilst on premises about those in which he is
employed.[4]

An insured person who acts in contravention of regulations does
not necessarily bar himself from benefit.   An accident may still be

---

[1] R.(I) 4/70.   The Commissioner expressed no opinion on what would have
been the position if the accident had occurred outside the claimant's working
hours and outside his sub-area.
[2] R.(I) 3/71, applying the analogous common law decision in *Vandyke* v.
Fender, [1970] 2 Q.B. 292; [1970] 2 All E.R. 335.
[3] R.(I) 2/68.
[4] National Insurance (Industrial Injuries) Act, 1965, s. 9.

deemed to arise out of and in the course of the employment notwithstanding that it occurs when the injured person is acting in contravention of statutory or other regulations applicable to his employment, or of any order given by or on behalf of his employer or that he is acting without instructions from his employer. But this will not be so unless the accident would have qualified the injured person for benefits under the Act had he not been acting in contravention of the regulations or orders or without instructions, and provided that the accident arises out of something done for the purposes of, and in connection with, the employer's trade or business.[1]

Two recent cases illustrate the scope of section 7. In one, a dock labourer, employed in the loading of a ship, met with an accident while driving an electric truck to fetch two slings necessary for the loading operation. He was not authorised or permitted to drive the truck, which was owned by the port authority and not by his employers. The Commissioner held that, by reason of section 7, the accident should be deemed to have arisen out of and in the course of the claimant's employment. In fetching the slings he was acting in the course of his employment, notwithstanding that he went about it in a prohibited manner.[2] But in *R. v. D'Albuquerque, Ex parte Bresnahan*[3], the worker went beyond the reach of the section. He was a dock labourer who, without authority or permission, decided to drive an unattended fork lift truck in order to remove an obstruction. Unfortunately he drove over the side of the quay and was drowned. The Commissioner decided that the act of driving the truck had taken the claimant right outside the course of his employment and beyond the reach of what is now section 7.[4] This decision survived an application to the Divisional Court for certiorari. The distinction between these two cases is a fine one which, it is submitted, runs counter to the spirit of section 7.

The Act makes one further provision for treating an accident arising " in the course of " an insured person's employment as also arising " out of " such employment, in spite of circumstances which would otherwise give rise to a contrary conclusion. If an accident is caused by another person's misconduct, skylarking or negligence or by steps taken in consequence of any such misconduct, skylarking or negligence, then it will be treated as having arisen out of the insured person's employment, provided that he did not directly or indirectly induce or contribute to the happening of the accident by his conduct outside the employment or by any act not incidental to the employment.[5] This provision is well illustrated by a case

---

[1] *Ibid.*, s. 7. As to the position of workmen acting without instructions see R (I) 41/55.
[2] R.(I) 1/70.
[3] [1966] 1 Lloyd's Rep. 69.
[4] R.(I) 1/66.
[5] S. 10, which makes similar provision in relation to injuries caused by animals, birds, fish, insects, missiles and lightning.

decided by the Commissioner in 1967.   While a factory worker was
smoking in a corridor (with permission), he was hit by a snowball
which had been thrown by a young fellow-employee.   He went after
the youth in order to remonstrate with him, but the youth slammed
a toilet door, thus injuring the worker's hand.   The Commissioner
considered that benefit should be paid.   The worker had not taken
himself beyond the reach of section 10 either by smoking in the
corridor or by taking a few steps after the youth.   Such action did
not amount to contributory conduct.[1]

Finally, it is important to note some recent decisions concerning
injuries sustained during a " break " from work when the employee
remains on the employer's premises.   Normally, short " breaks ",
provided that they are allowed by the employer, will not interrupt
employment for the purposes of the Act.   The above illustration
concerning the man permitted to smoke in the corridor is a good
example.   But as " breaks " get longer and as the activities engaged
in during them become more various, questions of degree begin to be
determined by fine distinctions.   In one case, a fireman was injured while playing volley-ball during a recreation period.   Firemen
were expected to keep themselves physically fit and were encouraged,
but not compelled, to play volley-ball during the extensive recrea-
tional periods provided for in their daily time-table.   The injury was
considered by the Commissioner to warrant payment of benefit,
reliance being placed, as in many recent cases, on the fact that it is
not necessary for the employee to be involved in contractually
obligatory conduct at the time of the accident.[2]   On the other
hand, a laboratory technician who was injured while playing football
during his lunch hour in the grounds of the hospital where he was
employed, was refused industrial injury benefit, even though such
activity was encouraged by the hospital authorities for the hospital
football team, of which the claimant was a member.[3]   The fireman's
case was distinguished on the ground that he had been playing not
merely for his own purposes, but as part of his duty to keep fit.

Although industrial injury benefit may well be payable in respect
of an injury sustained during a permitted " break," a strict view has
been taken of the boundaries of such breaks.   In *R. v. Industrial
Injuries Commisioner, Ex parte Amalgamated Engineering Union
(No. 2)*,[4] a fitter went to some special smoking booths during a
permitted ten minute break.   When he found all the booths to be
full, he waited outside and started to roll a cigarette, at which point
he was struck and injured by a negligently driven fork lift truck.
This accident took place five minutes after the end of the ten minute
break.   The Commissioner[5] considered that by extending the break

---

[1] R.(I) 3/67.
[2] R.(I) 13/66.
[3] R.(I) 2/69.
[4] [1966] 2 Q.B. 31; [1966] 1 All E.R. 97.
[5] R.(I) 4/66.

by at least a half again of the permitted time, the employee had caused an interruption in his employment and so the claim for industrial injury benefit was disallowed. The Court of Appeal dismissed an application for certiorari.[1]

(2) Industrial Diseases.—A person insured against personal injury arising out of and in the course of his employment will also be insured against any prescribed disease and against any prescribed personal injury not so caused being an injury or disease due to the nature of his employment and developed on or after the appointed day. A disease or injury may be prescribed in relation to insured persons if the Secretary of State is satisfied that it ought to be treated as an occupational risk and not as a risk common to all persons and it is such that, in the absence of special circumstances, the attribution of particular cases to the nature of the employment can be established or presumed with reasonable certainty.[2]

Regulations may provide that a person who developed a disease or injury, on or at any time after a date specified in the regulations, being before the regulations came into force but not before the appointed day, may be treated as if the regulations had been in force when he developed the disease or injury. Where a disease is such as would entitle an insured person to benefit under these provisions and is also a disease which is a personal injury by accident within the meaning of the Act he will not be entitled to benefit in respect of the disease as being an injury arising by accident if, at the time of the accident, it is a prescribed disease by virtue of the occupation in which the insured person is engaged.[3] The benefits payable in respect of prescribed diseases and injuries and the conditions to be fulfilled for the receipt of such benefits will be the same as in the case of personal injury by accident, but regulations may make different provisions with regard to matters which may be prescribed. It is probable that such regulations will include provisions for presuming whether a prescribed disease is (unless the contrary is proved) due or not due to the nature of a person's employment, for the establishment of special medical boards and for such matters as appear to the Secretary of State to be incidental to or consequential upon such matters.

As regards certain respiratory diseases regulations may provide that where a person is suffering from pneumoconiosis[4] accompanied by tuberculosis the effects of the tuberculosis shall be treated as if

---

[1] For a criticism of this decision, see Reid, (1966) 29 *M.L.R.* 389.

[2] For examples see R.(I) 3/55; 19/55; 44/55. For an example of regulations prescribing a disease, see National Insurance (Industrial Injuries) (Prescribed Diseases) Amendment Regulations, 1966, S.I. No. 987 (diffuse mesochelioma from exposure to asbestos dust).

[3] **National Insurance (Industrial Injuries) Act, 1965**, s. 56 (5).

[4] *I.e.*, fibrosis of the lungs due to silica, asbestos or other dusts and including the condition of the lungs known as dust-reticulation.

they were effects of the pneumoconiosis.[1] Persons may be required within a prescribed period of their becoming employed in an occupation in relation to which pneumoconiosis is prescribed, to submit themselves for medical examination and to be medically examined periodically whilst they are so employed and to furnish information required for the purpose of such examinations. But the Act is not solely concerned with the payments of benefits to injured or diseased persons. It attempts, though perhaps in only a tentative way, to enter the field of preventive medicine. Thus, regulations may provide for the suspension of persons from employment in prescribed occupations where they are found to be suffering from pneumoconiosis or tuberculosis or are unsuitable for such employment. Special benefits may be awarded to such persons where they are not otherwise entitled to benefit. And benefits in respect of pneumoconiosis may be forfeited by a person who, without reasonable cause, fails to submit himself to medical examination or refuses to furnish required information or engages in employment from which he has been suspended. Employers may be required to provide facilities for medical examinations; not to employ suspended persons or those who, without reasonable cause, have refused to submit themselves for examination and to give notice to a medical board or officer of the commencement of any prescribed industry or process. An insured person suffering from byssinosis will not be entitled to injury or disablement benefit under the provisions as to industrial diseases unless he is a man totally and permanently incapacitated for work as a result of the disease.[2]

3. Benefits Receivable Under the Act.

The Act provides for three kinds of benefit, namely, industrial injury benefit, industrial disablement benefit and industrial death benefit.[3] These replace and extend the compensation payable under the Workmen's Compensation Acts but, apart from regulations made under the Act, applying to seamen, mariners and workers on the Continental Shelf, benefits will not be payable for an accident which happens outside Great Britain.[4]

(1) Industrial Injury Benefit.—Whilst an insured person is, as a result of the injury or disease, incapable of work he may, during the injury benefit period, be entitled to industrial injury benefit. Thus the test is one of incapacity and if the injury does not produce such incapacity the benefit will not be receivable. Moreover, an

---

[1] See, for example, National Insurance (Industrial Injuries) (Prescribed Diseases) Amendment Regulations, 1967, S.I. No. 1187 (emphysema or chronic bronchitis).

[2] National Insurance (Industrial Injuries) Act, 1965, s. 58 (2).

[3] *Ibid.*, s. 5(1). For the abatement of these benefits in order to prevent duplication with supplementary benefits, see the Ministry of Social Security Act, 1966, s. 16 (1) (*b*).

[4] *Ibid.*, s. 5(4). The exceptions are in ss. 75 and 76.

insured person is not entitled to injury benefit in respect of any day during the injury benefit period where that day is one of the first three days of a period of interruption of employment.[1]   In determining whether the injured person is incapable of work on the day of the accident, any part of that day before the accident happened will be ignored.[2]   The injury benefit period is a period of 156 days (disregarding Sundays) beginning with the day of the accident, or the part of that period during which disablement benefit in respect of the accident is not available.

The benefit will be at the weekly rate of £8.75 and the amount payable for any day of incapacity will be one-sixth the weekly sum. In the case of a beneficiary who is not over the age of eighteen and is not entitled to an increase of benefit in respect of a child or adult dependant, the benefit will be at the weekly rate of £5.50.[3]   Injury benefit will be increased where the insured person has a child, children[4] or adults[5] dependent on him.[6]

Regulations may be made for the purpose of treating a person as incapable of work by reason of some specific disease or bodily or mental disablement, or as incapable of work as the result of an accident or injury, when he would not be so treated apart from the regulations. Provision may also be made by regulation as to the days which are or are not to be treated as days of incapacity for benefit purposes and as to the day which, in the case of night workers and other special cases, is to be treated for the purpose of benefit as the day of the accident.[7]

Earnings-related Supplement.—Persons in receipt of industrial injury benefit also qualify for an earnings-related supplement under the National Insurance Act, 1966. This supplement was considered earlier in this book when dealing with unemployment benefit.[8]

(2) Disablement Benefit.—An insured person is entitled to disablement benefit if he suffers, in consequence of the relevant accident, a loss of physical or mental faculty which is assessed at not less than one per cent.   Indeed, for the purpose of the provisions of the Acts dealing with disablement benefit, disablement is not considered to have resulted where its assessment would not reach that figure.   Disablement benefit is not available to an insured

---

[1] *Ibid.,* s. 11.
[2] Social Security Act, 1971, s. 7(2).
[3] The present rates are set out in National Insurance Act, 1971, s. 8 and Sched. 4.
[4] National Insurance (Industrial Injuries) Act, 1965, s. 17.
[5] *Ibid.,* s. 18.
[6] For the present rates, see the National Insurance Act, 1971, Sched. 4.
[7] National Insurance (Industrial Injuries) Act, 1965, s. 5.
[8] See Ch. IV, *ante.*

person until after the third day of the period of one hundred and fifty six days (disregarding Sundays) beginning with the day of the accident, nor until after the last day of that period on which he is incapable of work. But, where the injured person makes a claim for disablement benefit before the end of the injury benefit period, and does not withdraw it before it is finally determined, any days following the claim on which he is capable of work will be disregarded.[1]

The benefit is either a lump sum not exceeding £660, when it is known as a "disablement gratuity"[2] payable in cases where the disablement is assessed at less than twenty per cent, or a pension referred to as a disablement pension where the disablement equals twenty per cent or more.[3] Where a claimant had been awarded an assessment of twenty per cent for life by a medical board, and the medical appeal tribunal reduced this to nineteen per cent for life at the claimant's request so that he would obtain a gratuity to enable him to start a business, the Commissioner held the tribunal's decision to be erroneous in law as being contrary to the scheme of the Act.[4] As with injury benefit, disablement pensions will be increased where the insured person has a child, children or adults dependent upon him.[5]

The Act contains elaborate provisions for the assessment of disablement on a percentage basis and the assessment may be provisional where circumstances do not allow of a final assessment. The disablement pension will vary from £2 per week in the case of a twenty per cent disablement in an adult person of the age of eighteen and over to £10 per week where the disablement is assessed at one hundred per cent. Should the degree of disablement be limited by reference to a definite date the pension will cease on the death of the insured person before that date. During any part of the period of disablement in which the beneficiary is under the age of eighteen years and not entitled to an increase of the pension in respect of a child or adult dependant, the rate will range from £1.20 per week for a twenty per cent disablement, to £6 per week for a one hundred per cent disablement.[6]

The rate of the disablement pension will be increased by a basic " unemployability supplement " of £6 weekly where the beneficiary is incapable of work and likely to remain so incapable, and a person may be treated as incapable of work even though he is capable of work in which the earnings do not exceed £104 in a year. If, on the qualifying date, the beneficiary is a man under the age of 60 or

---

[1] National Insurance (Industrial Injuries) Act, 1965, s. 12.

[2] *Ibid.,* s. 12 (3) and National Insurance Act, 1971, Sched. 4.

[3] National Insurance (Industrial Injuries) Act, 1965, s. 12 (5) and National Insurance Act, 1971, Sched. 4, where the present rates are set out.

[4] R.(I) 6/65.

[5] National Insurance (Industrial Injuries) Act, 1965, ss. 17 and 18. For present rates see the National Insurance Act, 1971, Sched. 4.

[6] National Insurance Act, 1971, Sched. 4.

a woman under the age of 55, the weekly rate of the unemployability supplement is increased by a further sum of up to £1.[1] The unemployability supplement will be payable for such period as may be determined but can be renewed from time to time.[2] Persons who are, on the appointed day, entitled to weekly payments under the Workmen's Compensation Act, or any similar injury pension, may be entitled to an unemployability supplement if they are incapable of work and likely to remain so.[3]

The weekly rate of the disablement pension may be increased by an amount not exceeding two pounds, fourteen shillings in cases of special hardship if for example the beneficiary (*a*) is incapable and likely to remain permanently incapable of following his regular occupation and is incapable of employment of an equivalent standard which is suitable in his case; or (*b*) is and has at all times since the end of the injury benefit period been incapable of following the said occupation or any such employment. Of course a beneficiary may not at the same time receive an increase of pension under these particular provisions and an unemployability supplement. The increased disability pension is payable for such period as may be determined at the time it is granted and is renewable from time to time. The amount of the increase is determined by reference to the beneficiary's probable standard of remuneration (account being taken of his reasonable prospects of advancement) during the period for which it is granted in the insurable employments, if any, suitable in his case and which he is likely to be capable of following as compared with that of his regular occupation.[4]

The variety of misfortunes to be found in special hardship cases is endless. Reference may be made to two recent decisions illustrating the comparisons which have to be made. In *R.* v. *Deputy Industrial Injuries Commissioner, Ex parte Humphreys*,[5] a man had always worked as a ripper at Wrexham. He received an industrial injury which prevented him from following that employment, whereupon he moved to Doncaster and took a job as a welder-burner at an equivalent wage. Later, for personal reasons, he moved back to Wrexham and applied for an extension of his industrial injuries benefit. The Court of Appeal held that the benefit should be measured by the difference between the wages of a ripper generally and a welder-burner generally, and as in Wrexham the latter's wages were lower, an allowance should be ordered. A similar point was

---

[1] National Insurance Act, 1971, s. 9 and Sched. 4. Note also that the rate of unemployability supplement will be reduced where the beneficiary's wife (with whom he is living) earns in excess of £9.50 per week: *ibid.*, s. 8(3).

[2] *Ibid.*, s. 13 and Sched. 3.

[3] *Ibid.*, s. 81(1). Persons who on the appointed day are entitled to weekly payments under the Workmen's Compensation Acts may be eligible for the extra benefit in respect of constant attendance: s. 81(2).

[4] *Ibid.*, s. 14; and note that for the first thirteen weeks after death a higher rate of pension is payable; S.I. 1957, No. 2074.

[5] [1966] 2 Q.B. 1; [1965] 3 All E.R. 885.

decided far less generously in *R.* v. *National Insurance Commissioner Ex parte Mellors.*[1]   The applicant, a chargeman ripper in the coal-mining industry sustained an injury at work as a result of which he was unable to continue working underground.   He transferred to surface work at the same mine and was paid £26 for a 65 hour week, whereas, if he had remained a chargeman ripper, he would have earned £28 for a 36 hour week.   He claimed that a comparison should be made on a " common time basis," *i.e.* by taking the same number of hours per week and making a *pro rata* deduction in the post-accident earnings.   However, the Court of Appeal refused to take account of the longer hours in the post-accident employment.

An example of the availability of the special hardship allowance can be seen in the case of a joiner who, following an industrial injury, was restricted to inside bench work.   Hitherto he had been mainly employed on outdoor work and although the same rate of pay was available to inside and outdoor workmen, those who worked outside had considerable opportunities for overtime working.   It was held that he was incapable of following his regular employment. There was no separate category of outside joinery but a joiner who could not work outside did not fulfil the ordinary requirements of employers.[2]   A workman who was in receipt of a forty per cent disablement benefit resumed his regular occupation but could not renew his voluntary membership of the works fire brigade.   In consequence he lost twenty-five shillings a week remuneration.   He was held not to be eligible for the special hardship allowance.   His work in the brigade was not part of his regular occupation.[3]

The weekly rate of the disablement pension may also be increased, in certain circumstances where the beneficiary requires constant attendance,[4] and where a person is receiving disablement benefit at an assessment of less than one hundred per cent it will be treated as being assessed at one hundred per cent for any period during which he receives approved hospital treatment, subject to an adjust-ment where a disablement gratuity is awarded.[5]

(3) Death Benefit.—Industrial death benefit will be payable if the death of the insured person results from the injury.   The benefit will be payable to the widow if at his death she was either residing with the deceased person or was receiving or entitled to receive from him periodical payments for her maintenance by any order of a court, trust or agreement which the widow has taken reasonable

---

[1] [1971] 2 Q.B. at p. 415; [1971] 1 All E.R. 740.
[2] R. (I) 39/55.   *Cf.* 6/66.
[3] R. (I) 58/54.   For other recent illustrations in Commissioner decisions, see R. (I) 11/65, 8/67, 6/68, 7/68, 7/69.   In cases of exceptionally severe dis-ablement, a further increase is possible under the National Insurance Act, 1966, s. 6.   The present rates for both these benefits are to be found in the National Insurance Act, 1971, Sched. 4.
[4] National Insurance (Industrial Injuries) Act, 1965, s. 15.
[5] *Ibid.,* s. 16.

steps to enforce. Her benefit will consist of a pension[1] payable for life or until she remarries or cohabits with a man as his wife and a gratuity payable on her remarriage of an amount equal to fifty-two times the weekly rate of the pension to which she was then entitled.[2] If the deceased person was a married woman leaving a husband permanently incapable of self-support wholly or mainly maintained by her or who would, but for the accident, have been so maintained he will be entitled to a pension for life at the rate of £6.55 a week. It will be noticed that under the terms of the Act a widower seems to be in a better position than a widow for the pension accrues to him during his life without qualification and neither his remarriage nor a return of his capacity to support himself would, apparently, terminate his right to the pension. For the requirement that he should be permanently incapable of self-support refers to his position at the date of his wife's death.[3]

Where the deceased leaves a family which included a child or children then for any period during which a person has a family which includes that child or one or more of those children, that person will be entitled, in respect of the child or the elder or eldest of the children, to an allowance at the rate of £1.85 with 95p in respect of the second qualifiying child and 85p in respect of each additional child. The legitimate son or daughter of a deceased man's wife who was not his child or a child born to him posthumously will be treated for the purpose of the death benefit as having been a child of the deceased as will an illegitimate son or daughter born of him and any woman residing with him at his death, provided that the child was a child of her family and was wholly maintained by the deceased.[4]

A parent (including a step-parent and, if the deceased was illegitimate, his mother) of the deceased will be entitled to death benefit if at the deceased's death he or she was being to a substantial extent maintained by the deceased or would, but for the accident, have been so maintained. If the parent was wholly or mainly maintained by the deceased the benefit will be a pension beginning from the date of death and payable for life or in the case of the mother until she remarries or marries. The parent who was substantially maintained will receive the death benefit in the form of a gratuity of fifty-two pounds and in the case of the parent wholly or mainly maintained the benefit will be a pension of 75p a week for any period in which the parents are living together and are both entitled to such a pension and £1 a week for any other period.[5] These provisions include parents by adoption.

---

[1] For rates of pension see National Insurance Act, 1971, Sched. 4.
[2] National Insurance (Industrial Injuries) Act, 1965, s. 19(3).
[3] National Insurance (Industrial Injuries) Act, 1965, s.20.
[4] *Ibid.*, s. 21 and National Insurance Act, 1971, Sched. 4.
[5] *Ibid.*, s. 22.

Any such relative of the deceased as may be prescribed will be entitled to death benefit if at the deceased's death the relative was being wholly or mainly maintained by the deceased, or was being to a substantial extent maintained by him and, in the case of a man, was permanently incapable of self-support or in the case of a woman was herself permanently incapable of supporting herself or was living with her husband who was so permanently incapacitated. The benefit will be a pension where the relative was wholly or mainly maintained by the deceased or, in the case of a married woman living with her husband, she or her husband was, at the date of death, permanently incapable of supporting herself. The pension will be at the rate of £1 a week, will begin at the date of death and be payable for the period determined at the time it is granted, but it may be renewed from time to time. Should the beneficiary die within the period for which the pension was granted it will cease, as it will, in the case of a woman, if she marries or re-marries. If the pension was granted to a woman on the grounds of her husband's incapacity, it will cease on the termination of their marriage, otherwise than by his death, or on their ceasing to live together and in these circumstances it will not be renewed. The benefit to a relative who was being to a substantial extent maintained by the deceased or would have been so maintained but for the accident and, in the case of a man, was permanently incapable of self-support and, in the case of a woman, was permanently incapable of self-support or was living with her husband who was so incapable, will be a gratuity of £52. If the relative was being wholly or mainly maintained by the deceased or would, but for the accident, have been so maintained the benefit will be an allowance payable for thirteen weeks at the rate of £1.80 a week.

The term "relation" will not include a husband or wife or parent who is otherwise entitled to the death benefit but will include relatives by adoption or marriage and those who would have been relatives if some person born illegitimate had been born legitimate. A relative who was a child at the date of death will not be entitled to death benefit until he ceases to be a child or unless he was at the deceased's death, and is, on ceasing to be a child, permanently incapable of self-support. In such cases the pension will begin only from the date on which he ceases to be a child. If the deceased was a man a posthumous son or daughter, legitimate or illegitimate, may be entitled to the benefit.[1]

Finally where between the date of the accident and the death the deceased had a family which included a child or children and a woman was residing with the deceased and had the care of the child or one or more of the children, the woman will be entitled to death benefit if she was wholly or mainly maintained by the deceased. It should be noticed that the deceased may have been either a man or

---

[1] National Insurance (Industrial Injuries) Act, 1965, s. 23.

woman but if he were a man his illegitimate son or daughter of whom the woman is the mother will be treated as a child of his family during any period in which the child was a member of the woman's family and was, or would have been, but for the accident, wholly or mainly maintained by the deceased. The benefit payable to this final category of beneficiaries will be an allowance of £1 a week commencing from the death and payable during the period in which the woman has the care of the child or one or more of the children unless or until she marries or remarries.[1] The Act contains provisions limiting the payment of the death benefit in cases where, for example, two or more persons satisfy the conditions for the receipt of the benefit.[2]

(4) General Provisions on Benefits.—Where a person suffers two or more successive accidents against which he is insured by the Act he will not be entitled, if he is over the age of eighteen or is for the time being entitled to an increase of benefit in respect of a child or adult dependant, to pensions exceeding an aggregate of £10. Whilst if he is not over eighteen and not entitled to the increased child or dependant benefit the maximum payment will be £6.[3]

A person will not be entitled to benefit for any period during which he is absent from Great Britain or is undergoing imprisonment or detention in legal custody.[4] A workman who went to France to stay with a relative whilst convalescing, after securing a note from his doctor recommending a change of air and after receiving an assurance from the local office of the Ministry that all would be well, was held to have disentitled himself to benefit during his absence from the country. The Commissioner, though sympathetic towards the claimant, pointed out that no discretion was bestowed by the Act on the statutory authorities and thus the disqualification could not be waived.[5] It is true that regulations provide that a person shall not be disqualified where he is temporarily absent from Great Britain for the purpose of undergoing medical treatment.[6] In the present case, however, it could not be held that the claimant was undergoing treatment which required that the beneficiary should

> "perform or subject himself to an act or series of acts recommended to him by a person professing to be skilled in healing. I do not think that a beneficiary who merely changes his residence for a period because his doctor has recommended a change of air can be said to be absent from his usual residence for the purpose of undergoing medical treatment during that period."[7]

---

[1] National Insurance (Industrial Injuries) Act, 1965, s. 24.
[2] *Ibid.*, Sched. 5. And see new Family Allowances and National Insurance Act, 1967.
[3] 1965 Act, s. 29. and National Insurance Act 1971, Sched. 4. As to overlapping benefits see 1965 Act, s. 30.
[4] 1965 Act, s. 31 (1).
[5] C.I. 275/49.
[6] S.I. 1948, No. 1372, reg. 23 (1).
[7] C.I. 275/49, *per* the Commissioner.

Behaviour in a manner likely to retard recovery may also disqualify a person from the receipt of benefits.[1]

The Secretary of State may by regulations make provision for any purpose of the Industrial Injuries Act as to the circumstances in which a marriage celebrated under a law which permits polygamy is to be treated as having the same consequences as a marriage celebrated under a law which does not.[2]

The scheme of industrial insurance created by the Act is designed to be as comprehensive as possible.   And though it is quite contrary to the policy of the Act to permit the continuance of such contracting out schemes as were possible in the case of workmen's compensation, there is no intention that the Act should be exclusive of other benefits.   Thus any body of persons claiming to represent insured persons and their employers may submit schemes for supplementing the rights bestowed by the Act.   The schemes may cover risks against which the Act protects the insured persons, as will be the case where the purpose is to provide additional payments to those made under the Act, or they may provide for benefits to be payable in circumstances not contemplated by the Act.   The Secretary of State may approve the scheme, approve it with amendments or, presumably, reject it.   Before doing so he should take such steps as are practicable to ascertain the views of workers and employers who would be affected by the scheme but who are not, in his opinion, represented by the body which submits the scheme.   No part of the funds for providing benefits under a supplementary scheme may be derived from monies provided by Parliament except in the indirect sense that the Act preserves the right of government servants and their employers to submit a supplementary scheme for consideration.   A supplementary scheme may apply in its administration any of the provisions of the Act with or without modifications, and may make provision for the constitution of such a body to administer the scheme as the Secretary of State may consider necessary.   It may provide for the participation of the Secretary of State and contain such other provisions as he deems necessary.   Any supplementary scheme approved by the Secretary of State will continue in force until it is determined according to its own provisions and the Secretary of State on representation by the body which submitted the scheme or the body charged with its administration, may vary or amend its terms.   He has power, having regard to any periodic audit and valuation and after consultation with the body which administers the scheme, to modify the rates of contribution or the rates or periods of benefit.[3]

---

[1] National Insurance (Industrial Injuries) Act, 1965, s. 31 (2).
[2] National Insurance Act, 1971, s. 12.
[3] National Insurance (Industrial Injuries) Act, 1965, s. 82.   See National Insurance (Industrial Injuries) (Colliery Workers' Supplementary Scheme) Amendment and Consolidation Order, 1970, S.I. No. 376, for the sole example of a supplementary scheme.

4. ADMINISTRATION AND THE DETERMINATION OF CLAIMS.

The Act as amended divides the power to determine questions and claims arising out of its operation between the Secretary of State for Social Services, medical boards and medical appeal tribunals, the National Insurance Commissioner, local tribunals and Insurance Officers. Since the National Insurance Act, 1966, the settlement of disputes under the Industrial Injuries Act has been largely integrated with the settlement of disputes under the Insurance Act.

(1) Secretary of State.—Whether a person is in insurable employment, liability for contributions, and the rate of contribution payable in particular cases, the grant and renewal of increased disablement pensions in respect of the need of constant attendance, the amount of such increase and the period for which it shall be payable and questions arising out of the provisions limiting the payment of death benefits contained in the Fifth Schedule to the Act, are matters reserved for the decision of the Secretary of State.[1] If a question of law is involved the question may, if he thinks fit, be referred to the High Court and there is a right of appeal to the courts by a person who is aggrieved by the decision of the Secretary of State on a question of law which is not so referred.[2]   The Secretary of State will be entitled to appear and be heard on any reference or appeal made to the court and the decision of the High Court will be final.   The general provision which provides that where there is a right of appeal to the High Court the appeal shall be heard and determined by a divisional court will not apply to appeals against the Secretary of State under the Industrial Injuries Act.   Should new facts be brought to the notice of the Secretary of State he may review any decision which he has given in exercise of the powers just enumerated, but he may not review a decision on which an appeal is pending on a question of law or before the time for bringing such an appeal has expired.[3]

The Secretary of State may review any decision given by him, also, where he is satisfied that the decision was given in ignorance of, or was based on a mistake as to some material fact in any case being considered or on the ground that new facts have emerged.[4]

The question of whether a person is or was a child or is or was under the upper limit of the compulsory school age and whether any person has or had a family including a child or children or is or was a child of some other person's family, though not the question of whether any person is to be treated for the purpose of any provision of the Industrial Injuries Acts as having a family or as being a child of some other person's family, will be determined in the same

---

[1] National Insurance (Industrial Injuries) Act, 1965, s. 35 (1) (a).
[2] This part of the administration is governed by the rules in the National Insurance Act, 1965, s. 65.
[3] National Insurance Act, 1965, s. 65.
[4] *Ibid.*, s. 66.

manner, unless modifications are prescribed, as would a corresponding question under the terms of the Family Allowances Act, 1965. The Act lays down that all such questions shall be decided by the Secretary of State with an appeal to one or more referees selected from a panel and whose decision in general will be final.[1]   This Act also provides that a person shall be treated as a child during any period in which he or she is under the upper limit of the compulsory school age and during any period before he or she attains the age of eighteen years whilst he or she is undergoing full-time instruction in a school or is an apprentice, and in the case of one who because of illness of body or of mind has not attended or has before reaching eighteen years ceased to attend school, and is not treated under any regulations made under the Act as undergoing full-time instruction in a school or full-time training during any period whilst he or she is under the age of sixteen years and is incapacitated by that illness or disability both for attendance at a school or for employment.[2]   The Act also provides that a family may consist of (a) a man and his wife living together, any child or children being issue of theirs, his or hers, and any child or children being maintained by them; (b) a man not having a wife or not living together with his wife, any child or children being issue of his and any child or children being maintained by him; and (c) a woman not having a husband or not living together with her husband, any child or children being issue of hers and any child or children being maintained by her. Issue means issue of the first generation.[3]

(2) Medical Boards and Appeal Tribunals.—A medical board or medical appeal tribunal has jurisdiction to determine what are known as disablement questions including whether an accident has resulted in a loss of faculty, whether a loss of faculty is likely to be permanent, at what degree the extent of disablement resulting from a loss of faculty is to be assessed and what period is to be taken into account by the assessment.[4]

A difficult problem which has arisen in this context is the relationship between a medical appeal tribunal and a local tribunal.[5] The problem is illustrated by *Jones* v. *Secretary of State for Social Services.*[6] The appellant lifted a heavy piece of metal during the course of his work.   He felt a pain in his back and appeared pale and ill.   He was subsequently admitted to hospital where myocardial infarction was diagnosed.   When he claimed injury benefit, his claim was at first refused by an insurance officer, but later allowed

---

[1] National Insurance Act, 1966, s. 8; the procedure is that laid down in National Insurance Act, 1965, s. 76.

[2] National Insurance (Industrial Injuries) Act, 1965, s. 86, and Family Allowances Act, 1965, s. 2.

[3] Family Allowances Act, 1965, s. 3(1).

[4] National Insurance (Industrial Injuries) Act, 1965, s. 37.

[5] As to which, see *infra*, p. 428.

[6] [1972] 1 All E.R. 145; [1972] 2 W.L.R. 210, H.L.

by a local appeal tribunal after a full investigation and the hearing of medical evidence. When, at a later date, the appellant claimed disablement benefit in respect of the accident, the medical board rejected the finding of the local appeal tribunal and considered that the appellant had suffered two separate disabilities—strained chest and myocardial infarction—and that the former was, but the latter was not, caused by the work he had been doing. This view was confirmed by the medical appeal tribunal and upheld by the National Insurance Commissioner. However, when the Act provides for the division of jurisdiction between the various authorities, it goes on to say that " any decision of a claim or question as provided by the foregoing provisions . . . shall be final."[1] The appellant argued that this prevented the medical appeal tribunal from taking a different view from the " final " decision of the local appeal tribunal on the question of causation. This argument was successful before the House of Lords and an order of certiorari was granted.[2] It would seem, therefore, that, in spite of its medical expertise, a medical appeal tribunal has no jurisdiction to re-open such questions of causation.

The medical boards will be appointed by the Secretary of State and will consist of two or more medical practitioners of whom one will be appointed to act as chairman, and it is open to the Secretary of State to arrange with any other government department that medical boards recognised by that department shall act for the purposes of the Industrial Injuries Act. Medical appeal tribunals will also be composed of medical practitioners but must consist of a chairman and two others.[3] The normal procedure will be that a claim for disablement benefit will be made to an insurance officer who will refer it to the medical board for determination of the disablement questions involved. If the board provisionally assesses the disablement, the claim must be laid before the board again not later than the end of the period taken into account in the provisional assessment. If the claimant is dissatisfied he may appeal in the prescribed manner and within the prescribed time to the medical appeal tribunal. An appeal will not lie against a provisional assessment before the expiration of two years from the date on which the case was first referred to the board, nor where the period taken into account by the assessment falls wholly within the two years. The Secretary of State may, however, within the prescribed time, notify the insurance officer that he is of opinion that a decision of a medical board ought to be considered by a medical appeal tribunal, when the officer must refer the case to the appeal tribunal which may confirm, reverse or

---

[1] National Insurance (Industrial Injuries) Act, 1965, s. 50(1). The case actually concerned the equivalent section in the 1946 Act.

[2] Following (albeit reluctantly in the case of some of their Lordships, and with two of the seven dissenting) *Minister of Social Security* v. *Amalgamated Engineering Union*, [1967] 1 A.C. 725; [1967] 1 All E.R. 210, H.L.

[3] *Ibid.*, s. 38.

vary the decision in whole or in part as it would in the case of an appeal.[1]   An appeal on points of law now lies from the medical appeal tribunal to the National Insurance Commissioner.[2]   It may be brought by the claimant, his Union or the Secretary of State, with the leave of either the tribunal or the Commissioner.

The decisions of a medical board or a medical appeal tribunal may be reviewed at any time by a medical board if satisfied by fresh evidence that the decision was given in consequence of the fraudulent or innocent non-disclosure or misrepresentation of a material fact.[3] An assessment of disablement may be reviewed by the medical board if the latter is satisfied that there has been an unforeseen aggravation of the results of the relevant injury since the making of the assessment.   But an assessment made, confirmed or varied under these provisions may not be reviewed without the leave of a medical appeal tribunal.   The medical board may deal with a case on a review in any manner in which they could deal with it on an original reference and they may, in such circumstances, make a provisional assessment, notwithstanding that the assessment they are reviewing purported to be final.[4]

Regulations provide that, where the claimant consents, disablement questions may be referred to a single medical practitioner appointed by the Secretary of State but the assessment made by the doctor, in such a case, cannot take into account a period exceeding six months.   The doctor's decision has the same effect as though it were a decision of a medical board and is similarly subject to appeal, review and reference to a medical appeal tribunal.[5]

(3) Commissioners,   Local   Tribunals   and   Insurance Officers.—Subject to the determination of the questions reserved to the Secretary of State, to the medical boards and to the medical appeal boards, any claim for benefit and questions arising in connection with a claim for or award of benefit will be determined by an insurance officer, a local National Insurance tribunal or a Commissioner.[6]   The National Insurance Act, 1966, authorises the appointment of a Chief National Insurance Commissioner and such other National Insurance Commissioners as may be necessary.[7]

---

[1] National Insurance (Industrial Injuries) Act, 1965, s. 39.

[2] *Ibid.*, s. 42, as amended by the National Insurance Act, 1966, ss. 8, 9, 13, enacting the recommendations of the Franks Report (Cmnd. 218) introduced first in 1959.

[3] For a discussion of " fresh evidence " see *R.* v. *Medical Appeal Tribunal (North Midland Region), Ex parte Hubble,* [1959] 2 Q.B. 408; [1959] 3 All E.R. 40.

[4] National Insurance (Industrial Injuries) Act, 1965, s. 40.

[5] *Ibid.*, s. 41, and S.I. 1967, No. 1571, reg. 6.

[6] *Ibid.*, s. 43, as amended by the National Insurance Act, 1966, s. 8, which assimilates most of the administrative provisions of the Insurance Act and the Industrial Injuries Act of 1965.

[7] National Insurance Act, 1966, s. 9(1).

If it appears to the Chief National Insurance Commissioner that any appeal falling to be heard by one Commissioner involves a question of law of special difficulty, he may direct that the appeal shall be dealt with not by that Commissioner alone, but by a tribunal consisting of any three Commissioners.[1]

The local tribunal is now the same body as for the purposes of the Insurance Act.[2] It will consist of one member chosen to represent employers and one chosen to represent employed persons. The Secretary of State will set up panels of persons chosen to represent these two interests, and the members of the tribunal will be selected from these panels. In addition, the tribunal will have a chairman appointed by the Secretary of State.

A claim for benefit and all questions arising will be submitted, in the first instance, to an insurance officer, who is now the same person as for the purposes of the Insurance Act.[3] He will consider the claim and decide it in favour of the claimant, decide it adversely to him or refer it to a local tribunal. Where the insurance officer has decided any claim or question adversely to the claimant, the claimant may appeal to a local tribunal.[4]

An appeal from a decision of the local tribunal will lie, at the instance of an insurance officer, at the instance of a claimant, or at the instance of an association of employed persons of which the claimant is a member and was so immediately before the question at issue arose or was a member at the time of his death. The appeal must be brought within three months of the decision appealed against.[5] Leave to appeal is not now required.[6] Where it is decided that an accident was or was not an industrial accident, the fact must be expressly declared and a claimant is entitled to have this question decided despite the fact that his claim is disallowed on other grounds. Moreover where an injured person claims that the accident occasioning the injury was an industrial accident he is entitled to have this question determined notwithstanding that no claim for benefit has been made, a provision designed to protect an insured person from the effects of an accident which, though of apparently innocuous consequences in the first place, later becomes of greater significance. The right of the insured person to have the question whether the accident was industrial or not determined is qualified

---

[1] National Insurance Act, 1966, s. 9(3).

[2] National Insurance Act, 1966, s. 8(1) (*b*); National Insurance Act, 1965, s. 77.

[3] National Insurance Act, 1966, s. 8(1) (*b*), National Insurance Act, 1965, ss. 67 and 68.

[4] National Insurance Act, 1965, s. 69, which also contains formal and temporal requirements. For the position where a " special question " is involved, see *ibid.*, s. 64, s. 69(1) and s. 71.

[5] National Insurance Act, 1965, s. 70, which also contains formal and temporal requirements. For the position where a " special question " is involved, see, *ibid.*, ss. 64 and 71.

[6] The Franks Report (Cmnd. 218) recommended this provision.

in that an insurance officer, local tribunal or the Commissioner may refuse to determine the question upon being satisfied that is unlikely that it will be necessary to determine the question for the purpose of any claim for benefit. A power of this character, vested in the officials responsible for the administration of the Act, is clearly necessary to avoid frivolous applications, but the refusal to determine the question is subject to appeal from an insurance officer to the local tribunal and from such a tribunal to the Commissioner. An industrial accident is one which arises out of and in the course of employment which is insurable and as to which benefit is not precluded because the accident happened whilst the injured person was outside Great Britain.[1]

The decision of an insurance officer, a local tribunal, or the Commissioner may be reviewed at any time by an insurance officer, or on a reference from an insurance officer, by a local tribunal on the emergence of fresh evidence, or on a relevant change of circumstances or where the decision was based on the decision of a special question and the decision of the special question has been revised.[2]

(4) Advisory Council.—The Industrial Injuries Act authorises the establishment of an Industrial Injuries Advisory Council consisting of a chairman appointed by the Secretary of State and such number of other members so appointed as he may determine including an equal number of persons appointed by him, after consultation with such organisations as he thinks fit, to represent employers and insured persons. In all cases, excepting those of great urgency, the Secretary of State will submit to this Council any proposed regulations and refer to the Council such questions relating to the Act as he thinks fit.[3] However, it has become usual for subsequent enabling Acts temporarily to dispense with the obligation to refer to the Council regulations made under those Acts.[4] The Secretary of State may promote research into the causes, incidence and methods of prevention of such accidents, injuries and diseases as fall within the scope of the Act or which it is contemplated might be prescribed for the purposes of the Act. He may himself employ such research workers or contribute to the expenses of other persons engaged in such work.[5] He may make arrangements that persons entitled to disablement benefit may take full advantage of vocational training courses, industrial rehabilitation courses and facilities in connection with employment or work under special conditions coming

---

[1] National Insurance (Industrial Injuries) Act, 1965, s. 48; see *Minister of Social Security* v. *Amalgamated Engineering Union,* [1967] 1 A.C. 725; [1967] 1 All E.R. 210, H.L.

[2] National Insurance Act, 1966, s. 72. On the point of " special questions," see *ibid.*, ss. 64 and 66.

[3] National Insurance (Industrial Injuries) Act, 1965, s. 62.

[4] See, *e.g.*, National Insurance Act, 1966, s. 14(6); National Insurance Act, 1969, s. 10(1).

[5] National Insurance (Industrial Injuries) Act, 1965, s. 71.

within the terms of the Disabled Persons (Employment) Act, 1944. The Secretary of State is authorised to secure the provision and maintenance, either free of charge or at reduced costs, of equipment and appliances for persons who have lost limbs as the result of an injury or disease in respect of which they were insured under the Act.[1]

(5) Inspectors.—Inspectors may be appointed and such inspectors will have power to enter, at all reasonable times, premises or places in which there is reasonable ground for supposing that insured persons are employed or that an injury or disease has been or may have been received or contracted and out of which a claim for benefit has arisen or may arise.[2]   But they may not enter a private dwelling house not used by or by the permission of the occupier for the purposes of a trade or business.   In addition, inspectors may make examinations and enquiries necessary for determining whether the provisions of the Act have been complied with or for investigating the circumstances in which an injury or disease, on which a claim may be made, has been received or contracted.   An inspector may examine alone, or in the presence of another, persons found in premises or places liable to inspection, or whom he has reasonable cause to believe to be or to have been an insured person or employed by the employer of an insured person.   The inspectors may also exercise such other powers as may be necessary to carry the Act into effect.

The occupier of premises liable to inspection, and a person who is employing or has employed insured persons together with their servants and agents, and any insured person, must furnish to an inspector all information, and produce such documents as the inspector may reasonably require for the purpose of ascertaining whether contributions are or have been payable or paid or whether benefit is payable to or in respect of any person.   It is an offence to obstruct or delay the inspector, to fail to answer a question or furnish a document, though, of course, no person can be compelled to answer questions or give evidence tending to incriminate him.[3]

The powers given to inspectors are extremely wide and are not unlike those conferred upon inspectors appointed under the provisions of the Factories Act, 1961.[4]   It is submitted no charge will lie against a person who refuses to answer a question not material to the enquiry upon which the inspector is engaged.   Nor will a charge lie where a person affirms that the answer to a question might expose him to any penalty or criminal charge likely to be made against him.   The person questioned must not obstruct the

---

[1] *Ibid.*, s. 72.
[2] *Ibid.*, s. 64.
[3] National Insurance (Industrial Injuries) Act, 1965, s. 64.
[4] S. 146 *et seq.*

inspector but he should be advised to be careful where he fears crimination.[1] As one judge has said,

> "I should almost prefer a man to be careful and say the answer might tend to criminate, and I should be slow to commit him to prison for not doing that which the law says he is not bound to do".[2]

Similarly no person may be compelled to produce a document which is not material to the issue in dispute or which relates solely to his own case.[3]

An inspector must carry with him his certificate of appointment and, on applying for admission to any premises for the purpose of carrying out his duties, may be required to produce the certificate.[4]

Legal proceedings for an offence under the Act may not be instituted except by or with the consent of the Secretary of State or by an inspector or other officer duly authorised. Such an inspector or officer may also prosecute or conduct the proceedings before a court of summary jurisdiction. They may be commenced at any time within a period of three months from the date on which evidence sufficient to justify the prosecution comes to the knowledge of the Secretary of State or within a period of twelve months after the commission of the offence, whichever period is the last to expire. A certificate signed by or on behalf of the Secretary of State will be conclusive evidence of the date on which evidence sufficient to justify the prosecution came to his notice. Although the general rule of evidence is that where one spouse is the defendant in criminal proceedings the prosecution cannot compel the other to give evidence, the Act provides that a husband or wife of a person charged with an offence may be called as a witness for either party whether for or against the accused but will not be compellable either to give evidence or in giving evidence to disclose communications made during marriage by the accused.[5]

In proceedings for an offence under the Act, or involving a question as to the payment of contributions or for the recovery of sums due to the Industrial Injuries Fund, the Secretary of State's decision on a question which the Act requires to be determined by him subject to appeal on a question of law to the High Court, will be conclusive except where such an appeal is pending or the time within which the appeal may be brought has not expired. If the decision of the Secretary of State has not been obtained and it is necessary for the determination of the proceedings that the question must be referred to the Secretary of State, the court must adjourn the proceedings until the Secretary of State's decision is made known.[6]

---

[1] See *Lamb* v. *Munster* (1882), 10 Q.B.D. 110. [2] *Ibid.*, at p. 111.
[3] *A.-G.* v. *Newcastle-upon-Tyne Corporation*, [1897] 2 Q.B. 384.
[4] National Insurance (Industrial Injuries) Act, 1965, s. 64(6).
[5] National Insurance (Industrial Injuries) Act, 1965, s. 68, incorporating the National Insurance Act, 1965, s. 94.
[6] National Insurance (Industrial Injuries) Act, 1965, s. 70. See *Department of Health and Social Security* v. *Walker, Dean & Walker, Ltd.*, [1970] 2 Q.B. 74; [1970] All E.R. 757.

5. ALTERNATIVE REMEDIES

Under the Workmen's Compensation Acts, the amount of compensation which might be recovered by the injured workman or his dependants was limited. Nothing in these Acts, however, affected the civil liability of the employer who, by his negligent or wilful act, had caused injury, but the workman might exercise an option to proceed under the 1925 Act or independently thereof. The employer was nevertheless, not liable to pay damages and compensation.[1] If an action were brought independently of the Act and it was held that the injury was one for which the employer was not liable in such an action, but that he would have been liable to pay Workmen's Compensation the action must be dismissed. The court in such circumstances, might, however, proceed to assess such compensation subject to its right to deduct from the compensation the whole or any part of the costs caused by the plaintiffs bringing the action instead of proceeding under the Act.[2]

It will be remembered that under the provisions of the Law Reform (Contributory Negligence) Act, 1945, where a person suffers injury partly as the result of his own fault and partly of the fault of another, a claim for damages will not be defeated by reason of the fault of the injured person but that damages recoverable may be reduced to such extent as the court thinks just and equitable.[3] The Act further provided that where, within the time limited for the taking of proceedings under the Workmen's Compensation Acts an action was brought to recover damages independently of those Acts in respect of an injury or disease giving rise to a claim under the Acts and it was determined (a) that damages were recoverable independently of the Workmen's Compensation Acts subject to a reduction on account of the injured person's contributory negligence; and (b) that the employer would have been liable to pay compensation under the Workmen's Compensation Acts, then, if the claimant consented, the court might proceed to assess and award the compensation payable under those Acts and no independent damages would be awarded.[4]

On the introduction of the system of National Insurance, the problem of alternative remedies occasioned some difficulty and gave rise to confusions which have not been resolved. In July, 1944, a Departmental Committee on Alternative Remedies was set up to consider amongst other things

"how far the recovery or proceedings for the recovery of damages or compensation in respect of personal injury should affect or be affected by, the provision made or professed to be made under

---

[1] Workmen's Compensation Act, 1925, s. 29 (1).
[2] *Ibid.*, s. 29 (2).
[3] Law Reform (Contributory Negligence) Act, 1945, s. 1 (1).
[4] Law Reform (Contributory Negligence) Act, 1945, s. 2 (1) (repealed by the National Insurance (Industrial Injuries) Act, 1946, s. 89 and Sched. 9 as from July 5th, 1948).

Workmen's Compensation Legislation or under any social insurance or other statutory schemes for affording financial or other assistance to persons incapacitated by injury or sickness or their dependants."

The report of this Committee was presented to Parliament in July 1946,[1] but unfortunately the Committee was divided in its recommendations and in consequence the problem of alternative remedies has been shelved. The effect of the Report to date has been one, quite minor, legislative provision. For the feeling amongst the representatives of workpeople has been that the National Insurance Scheme is a scheme of insurance and thus quite independent of any alternative remedies to which the injured person might have access. If, it is argued, a successful common law action can be maintained this has nothing to do with the contributory scheme of insurance from which a new and distinct body of rights and duties emerges. The representatives of employer's organisations have, not unnaturally, contested this view and have said that even if there were any truth in the contention of the workpeople, the contention could not operate in respect of the employer's contribution to the National Insurance Scheme.

And it is along this line that the inevitable compromise has been made. The Law Reform (Personal Injuries) Act, 1948, provides that in any action for damages for personal injuries (including any such action arising out of a contract) there shall, in assessing those damages be taken into account, against any loss of earnings or profits which have accrued or probably will accrue to the injured person from the injuries, one half of the value of any rights which have accrued or probably will accrue to him, therefrom, in respect of industrial injury benefit, industrial disablement benefit or sickness benefit for the five years beginning with the time when the cause of action accrued.[2] However, if an injured person fails because of ignorance to claim such benefits before they become time-barred, he will not have his common law damages reduced for failing to mitigate his loss.[3]

---

[1] Cmnd. 6860.
[2] Law Reform (Personal Injuries) Act, 1948, s. 2 (1).
[3] *Eley* v. *Bedford,* [1972] 1 Q.B. 155; [1971] 3 All E.R. 285.

CHAPTER X

INDUSTRIAL RELATIONS

Previous editions of this book have included only a short section on the traditional area where quasi-legal forms impinge upon industrial relations. There was little to say, for in 1968 it could be said that:

> " The British system of industrial relations is based on voluntary agreed rules which, as a matter of principle, are not enforced by law. This is an outstanding characteristic which distinguishes it from the systems of many comparable countries. . . . In short, it has been the traditional policy of the law as far as possible not to intervene in the system of industrial relations."[1]

The Royal Commission, under the chairmanship of Lord DONOVAN, reported in June, 1968. It proposed a continuance of the voluntary system, but with progressive reform. The report itself, and the research papers published along with it,[2] will remain an important source for the study of the place of law in industrial relations. But by the time the report was published, the pace of political interest was increasing and was moving in a different direction. Even before the publication of the Donovan report, the Conservative policy, on markedly different lines, was outlined in a policy statement, " Fair Deal at Work."[3] The Labour Government's reaction to the Donovan report was published as a White Paper.[4] The reception of the White Paper was stormy. It was followed by a Bill which left out certain controversial aspects previously proposed. The change of Government in June, 1970 meant that the Bill was lost.

Attention turned to Conservative thinking. A consultative document was published in October, 1970; a Bill the following month. After a stormy passage through Parliament, the Industrial Relations Act, 1971 became law. It came into force in stages during the following months. The new Act provides a new framework of law for industrial relations: it is this framework which must be described and considered in this chapter.

I. GENERAL PRINCIPLES

The Act, in conformity with much modern legislation, first sets out general principles. These principles are to guide all the institu-

---

[1] Royal Commission on Trade Unions and Employers' Associations, 1968, Cmnd. 3623.

[2] See especially Nos. 1, 2, 4, 6, 8.
There is a great deal of importance in the written evidence which was also published.

[3] C.P.C., April, 1968.   [4] *In Place of Strife*, Cmnd. 3888.

tions charged with functions under the Act.[1]   They are:

(a) collective bargaining freely conducted on behalf of workers and employers and with due regard to the general interests of the community;

(b) developing and maintaining orderly procedures in industry for the peaceful and expeditious settlement of disputes by negotiation, conciliation or arbitration with due regard to the general interests of the community;

(c) free association of workers in independent trade unions and of employers in employers' associations, so organised as to be representative, responsible and effective bodies for regulating relations between employers and workers.[2]

(d) the principle of freedom and security for workers, protected by adequate safeguards against unfair industrial practices, whether on the part of employers or others.

The Act itself is built around these and other basic principles.[3] Of even greater importance is the provision for a Code of Industrial Relations Practice.[4]   The Code clearly places the responsibility for the promotion of good industrial relations on management.   The detailed provisions of the Code lie outside the scope of this book, but this should not be taken to indicate that the Code is not of the greatest importance.   Its status is that failure to observe it is not itself ground for action in the tribunals or courts.   It can, however, form the subject of comment, for failure to observe it is admissible as evidence before the Industrial Court or an Industrial Tribunal.[5] These bodies have to take the provisions of the Code into account.

The Code itself covers the responsibilities of managements, trade unions, employers' associations and individual workers in securing good industrial relations.   It deals, *inter alia*, with employment policies including recruitment, training and payment systems, with shop stewards and their facilities,[6] and with communication and consultation, of greatest interest to the lawyer are the three sections dealing with disputes procedures—collective disputes arising from collective agreements, grievance procedures and disciplinary procedures. The Code does little more than lay down suggested lines these procedures should take but the flavour is very much that of the rules of natural justice familiar to the constitutional lawyer.

2. MACHINERY

(1) Courts and Tribunals.—The Act sets up and refurbishes machinery to deal with the tasks that arise.   There are several important innovations.   Chief of them is the setting up of the National Industrial Relations Court.   This is a branch of the High

---

[1] S. 1(2).   For a description of these institutions, see *infra*.   [2] S. 1(1).
[3] The eight basic principles underlying the Act were set out in the Consultative Document.   [4] S. 2.   [5] S. 4.
[6] There is a C.I.R. report on this subject—No. 17, Cmnd. 4668, May, 1971.

Court with as its President a High Court Judge (or Judge of the Court of Appeal) and in Scotland, a Judge of the Court of Session. The other members of the court are persons appointed by the Lord Chancellor and the Secretary of State who have special knowledge or experience of industrial relations.[1]   The normal court will consist of the judicial chairman and two other members.[2]   It has no set location but may sit anywhere convenient.   It will be seen that the new Industrial Court has a wide jurisdiction under the Act.   It is the principal organ to which legal matters will go where collective relationships are in issue.   Thus it receives applications concerning recognition of trades unions, or for an approved closed shop or an agency shop.   It hears complaints of unfair industrial practices. Thus wherever a trade union wishes to complain against the action of an employer, or *vice versa*, the appropriate venue will be the Industrial Court.   The court has also an appellate jurisdiction and will act as the court of appeal from the Industrial Tribunals and from decisions of the Registrar of trade unions and Employers' Associations.[3] An appeal lies from the Industrial Court to the Court of Appeal[4] in the normal way on a point of law.   The new court is to provide a forum which has both the necessary technical legal ability and the background industrial relations knowledge.   The proceedings will have a minimum of formality, for example representation may be by anyone the litigant wants.   The relationship between the new court and the old is ensured by two provisions.   Any court, which finds proceedings in tort before it which have been, or could be brought before an industrial court or Tribunal may stay the proceedings.[5] In the same way the Industrial Court is expressly said to have no jurisdiction except that given by the Industrial Relations Act. Thus it has no power to hear actions in tort nor those arising from contracts or collective agreements not specially dealt with by that Act.[6]

The powers of the Industrial Court are threefold.   It may grant an order determining the rights of the parties in relation to the action; it may award compensation;[7] it may make an order directing the respondent to refrain from specified actions.[8]   A trade union official acting within his capacity cannot be the subject of an award of compensation or a restraint order.[9]

The enforcement of these orders is to be achieved in the usual manner of the High Court.   It has the same power to order the attendance of witnesses and enforce it.   An award of costs against a

---

[1] S. 99.

[2] Schedule 3, Part II, para. 17.   One lay member is enough if the parties consent.   There may be up to four.

[3] Ss. 114, 115.

[4] In Scotland to the Court of Session.

[5] S. 131.

[6] S. 136.

[7] Subject to the limits in respect of registered trade unions set out in s. 117.

[8] S. 101.

[9] S. 101(4) only applies to registered trade unions.

party is, however, regarded as appropriate only where the court feels the proceedings were unnecessary, improper or vexatious or there was unreasonable conduct or delay.[1]

The Industrial Tribunals have already been described. They were set up in 1964 and have acquired an important jurisdiction under a long list of statutes but principally the Contracts of Employment Act, 1963 and the Redundancy Payments Act, 1965.[2] This will continue along with new and important functions under the Industrial Relations Act. Their chief new function will be the hearing of complaints of violation by way of unfair industrial practice, of the rights of the workers set out in section 5 and those of the right not to be unfairly dismissed. There is an interesting provision in the Act under which the Lord Chancellor is given power to extend the jurisdiction of the Tribunals to actions for damages for breach of contracts of employment except those concerning death or personal injury. It is not anticipated that this section will be quickly brought into force. The result would apparently give concurrent, not exclusive, jurisdiction over such actions.[3]

The old Industrial Court so-called was in effect an arbitration tribunal. It is renamed by the Act the Industrial Arbitration Board.[4] Its previous work will continue unaltered[5] but it will have certain added functions under the Industrial Relations Act, 1971, where an employer fails to bargain with a trade union or joint negotiating panel in breach of an order of the Industrial Court to recognise such body: then the Industrial Court may refer a complaint to the Industrial Arbitration Tribunal.[6] There is similar power to refer a complaint where the allegation is that the employer has failed to disclose information to a trade union as required by section 56.[7] Matters so referred then take the form of an arbitration and the award becomes a legally binding part of the appropriate conditions of service.[8]

(2) Commission on Industrial Relations.—The Commission on Industrial Relations was a body set up as a result of the recommendations of the Donovan Royal Commission. It was established in 1969 in the form of a Royal Commission. Its purpose was to consider references from the Secretary of State concerning the functioning and development of institutions and procedures for the

---

[1] Schedule 3, Part II, para. 24.
[2] Also Industrial Training Act, 1964 (their creator); Docks & Harbours Act, 1966; Selective Employment Payments Act, 1966; Equal Pay Act, 1970.
[3] S. 113.
[4] S. 124.
[5] See *infra*, pp. 446 *et seq.*
[6] S. 125.
[7] S. 126.
[8] To complete a somewhat improbable code they can then be amended by agreement between employer and employee: s. 127(3) (*b*).

conduct of industrial relations and to promote improvements in these institutions, procedures and relations. It had two years of life as a Royal Commission and published in this time some twenty-five reports.[1] The character of the work has concerned trade union recognition by employers, reform of institutions within industry and several general matters.

The Industrial Relations Act, 1971 turned the Commission into a statutory body. The Commission is to consist of between six and fifteen members. It is in effect a continuation of the Royal Commission but with another set of functions under the Act. The old procedure is continued in the Act, which provides that the Secretary of State[2] may refer to it questions on industrial relations generally or on relations in a particular industry or undertaking.[3] A detailed list of topics appropriate for reference is set out. This includes, for example, organisation of employers and workers in relation to collective bargaining procedure agreements, recognition and negotiating rights, and disclosure of information.[4] The Commission has a duty to report on matters referred to it, and such reports are, where appropriate, to be published.[5] The Commission also has a duty to present to the Secretary of State an annual report.[6]

The Commission has also several important new functions under the Act. These will appear during the course of this chapter and need only be summarised here. It will be the recipient of references from the Industrial Court. These will follow from applications to the court for recognition as bargaining agent or for the establishment of an agency shop or approved closed shop. They will also follow applications to the court to improve procedures. The Commission will have as one of its principal functions the conduct of ballots. It will also perform this function in situations where the Industrial Court provides for a strike ballot in a national emergency. A small amendment in the law also gives the Commission the duty to consider proposals to establish, vary or wind up Wages Councils.[7]

(3) Conciliation Officers.—One of the underlying principles of the Act is the stress on conciliation as a means of settling disputes and differences and of avoiding as far as possible litigation before the courts and tribunals. Provision is specifically made for the appointment of conciliation officers.[8] The function in mind in this section is the consideration of disputes arising under section 5 (trade union

---

[1] The reports are published as White Papers. The two annual reports, Cmnd. 4417 and Cmnd. 4803, give useful summaries of all other reports.

[2] Alone or jointly with another Minister.

[3] S. 121.

[4] S. 121(2).

[5] S. 122.

[6] S. 123.

[7] Schedule 3, para. 40.

[8] S. 146. This is in effect an extension of a service already provided by the Department of Employment.

membership rights) and section 22 (unfair dismissal). The Act specifically provides that communications to a conciliation officer are protected and cannot be given in evidence without consent.[1]

It is clear that the role of conciliation officers will not be confined to the matters set out in section 146. They have in the past offered their assistance in every type of dispute where this has been felt appropriate. No doubt this practice will continue.

3.   Collective Bargaining

The Act sets out in certain ways to encourage and improve collective bargaining.[2] The basic aim to encourage the recognition of trade unions for negotiating purposes is implicit in the principles. The law has never dealt with this topic, with the exception of certain provisions in nationalisation statutes.[3] It now provides a procedure by which recognition for bargaining purposes can be enforced.

The procedure is based on two concepts: the bargaining unit and the sole bargaining agent. The bargaining unit is defined as employees, or descriptions of employees of an employer or of associated employers for whom collective bargaining is or could be appropriately carried out by an organisation of workers or by a joint negotiating panel or partly by one and partly by the other.[4] Several points are noteworthy. The aim is to gather into a negotiating group those who can properly be treated, as far as normal bargaining is concerned, together. The Code of Industrial Relations Practice has a fairly substantial section devoted to the principles underlying this. It favours larger rather than smaller units and considers that factors that are to be considered include the nature of the work, its organisation, the structure of management and unions and the wishes of those concerned.[5] The drawing of boundaries of units will not always be easy and will be a matter for individual situations. A unit can stretch over associated employers. These are defined as including companies of which one controls the other, whether directly or indirectly, as well as companies jointly controlled by a third person.[6] It is not to apply to matters dealt with under wider bargaining arrangements. An example would be that a company-wide pension scheme established by bargaining at that level could be excluded from a bargaining unit established in one factory or branch of that company.

The phrase " sole bargaining agent " is slightly misleading because it must always be qualified by the addition of " or joint negotiating

---

[1] S. 146(6).

[2] It will be recalled that this constitutes the first of the general principles.

[3] They give little positive protection: *Gallagher* v. *Post Office*, [1970] 3 All E.R. 712. S. 60 ensures that the Industrial Relations Act provisions shall prevail over earlier provisions which may be narrow in scope or effect.

[4] S. 44 (*a*).

[5] Para. 78.

[6] S. 167(8).

panel ". The word " sole " refers to its *exclusive* right to bargain. This right may be granted to a trade union[1] or to a panel of unions.

It will be obvious that there is a need to identify a bargaining unit. Once this is done, an application may be made to the Industrial Court for reference to the Commission on Industrial Relations of the recognition problem.[2] Reference may be made by one or more registered trade unions, by the employer, jointly by the registered union or unions and the employer or by the Secretary of State, after he has consulted the employer and the trade unions apparently concerned.[3] The two questions to be determined are whether a specified group of employees should be recognised as a bargaining unit, either as a whole or in part, or as a number of separate units, and secondly whether an agent should be recognised and if so what trade union or joint panel should constitute that agent.[4] Although the application to the court is only available to a registered trade union, it must be noted that recognition may be given to an organisation of workers. It cannot, however, enforce it.

When the Industrial Court receives an application it must first ensure that notice has been given to the Secretary of State. This is so that before court proceedings start, the Secretary of State may attempt to achieve an appropriate voluntary agreement between the parties.[5] This is a good example of the Act's attempt to achieve settlement of problems voluntarily without recourse to the legal machinery.

The court has to be satisfied about certain points before it refers the matter to the Commission. It must be satisfied that attempts have been made to settle the matter voluntarily and have used appropriate methods of conciliation including that offered by the Secretary of State under section 45(4) (*a*). It must be satisfied that reference to the Commission is necessary to produce a satisfactory settlement and it must check that the application is not barred by these provisions under section 53(5)[6] which are meant to prevent continuous applications.[7] A similar aim is expressed in the rule that the court is not required to refer an application to the Commission if a previous reference relating to the same or substantially similar group of employees had been considered within the previous two years and the short interval did not give rise to the need for further consideration.[8]

---

[1] There is difficulty in that the Code uses the term trade union to mean both registered (trade union to the Act) and unregistered (organisation of workers to the Act) trade unions. Wherever the word trade union is used in this chapter, it will follow the practice of the Code and mean all unions. The adjective " registered " will be used to indicate special discrimination.

[2] S. 45.

[3] S. 45(2) (3).

[4] S. 45(1).

[5] S. 45(5).

[6] See *infra*, p. 436.

[7] S. 46(1).

[8] S. 46(2).

Once the matter is referred to the Commission, the emphasis again is on the search for a voluntary agreement between the parties. The Commission is empowered to apply to the court to withdraw the reference on the ground that a satisfactory and lasting settlement has been agreed. If the court is satisfied that this is so, the reference is withdrawn.[1]

The Commission is working within terms of reference presented to it by the court. But it can, if it thinks fit, send to the court proposals for extending the scope of the reference.[2] Such proposals, which will inevitably involve new parties, must be published so that persons claiming to be affected may make representations to the court.[3] The proposals must not aim at widening the scope to another employer unless he falls within the definition of associated employer.[4] The court has power to extend the scope as proposed, to a lesser extent, or not at all.

The report of the Commission has to be made in conformity with certain principles. The extent to which the different groups of employees within the scope of the reference have interests in common has to be considered, with particular regard being paid to the nature of their work and their training, experience and qualifications.[5] A trade union or joint panel recommended for recognition must be independent.[6] Such recognition must appear also to be in accordance with the general wishes of the employers within the bargaining unit and to be such as to promote a satisfactory and lasting settlement.[7] To achieve these aims, the Commission has to consider whether the body has or would have the support of a substantial proportion of the employees concerned and also whether it has sufficient resources to provide effective representation. The Commission's report may be made subject to conditions.[8] The limits of these are not specified, but are said to include the requirement that sufficient trained officials should be available for bargaining purposes, and a requirement that the recognised agent should not pursue claims for recognition in respect of another bargaining unit. The Commission may also specify matters which are to be excluded from bargaining because of the existence of more extensive bargaining arrangements.[9] The report is made to the Secretary of State, the employers concerned and the trade unions concerned, and may be published.[10]

When the report contains a recommendation for recognition, there

---

[1] S. 47(1).
[2] S. 47(2).
[3] S. 47(4).
[4] S. 47(3). Definition of associated employer is in s. 167(8).
[5] S. 48(3).
[6] For a discussion of independence, see s. 167(1) (a).
[7] S. 48 (4).
[8] S. 48(7).
[9] S. 48(8).
[10] S. 48(2).

arises a period of six months within which the employer or trade union may apply to the Industrial Court for a binding order.[1] Although the recommendation may, as we have seen, recommend recognition be granted to an unregistered trade union, only a trade union which is registered may make this type of application. Similarly a joint negotiating panel must consist solely of registered trade unions before it can apply.[2] Once the court is satisfied that any conditions have been complied with, it must ask the Commission to hold a ballot of the employees within the bargaining unit as to whether the recommendation should be made binding. The responsibility of arranging for the ballot then falls on the Commission which must allow a reasonable time for consideration to elapse before balloting.[3] The ballot requires a simple majority in favour of the recommendation for it to be made binding by the court. This order will specify the bargaining unit, the employer and the agent and will be effective two months after it is made in securing sole rights as specified. Any conditions laid down in the recommendation of the Commission will be added to the order. There is an interesting provision that the order will cease to have effect if one of the designated agents ceases to be a registered trade union.

It is apparent that this procedure has underlying it two principles. The first seeks to secure, as far as possible, agreed recognition. The second denies to the unregistered trade union use of the machinery, although the Secretary of State or employer might make application specifying an unregistered trade union as agent.

Once recognition is secured, it by no means follows that that solution will be appropriate for all time. So the Act goes on to provide for the withdrawal of recognition. There are two situations to consider: where sole bargaining rights have been given voluntarily, and where they follow an order under section 50. Any employee within the bargaining unit is entitled to apply to the Industrial Court on the grounds that the bargaining agent for his unit does not adequately represent either the employees in the whole unit or those in a particular section to which he belongs.[4] To be effective for consideration, one-fifth of the employees in the unit must have signified in writing their agreement with the application if the agency is voluntary;[5] the figure rises to two-fifths where the agency is secured by a court order. In this event too, two years must have elapsed from the date of the making of the section 50 order. This important provision is to avoid continuous turmoil. The procedure that follows is similar in nature to that of initial recognition. The question is passed by the court to the Commission, whose first task is to try and secure an agreed settlement. The

---

[1] S. 49(1).
[2] S. 49(2).
[3] S. 49(5).
[4] S. 51.
[5] S. 51(2).

court has to allow a period of time for these efforts to be made.[1]
A successful settlement has to be reported to the court. If the time
fixed elapses without settlement, the Industrial Court may decide
to test the position by way of balloting. It asks the Commission
to decide whether one ballot of the whole unit or sectional ballot
involving parts of the unit would be appropriate. This decision,
which is an important one since it could cause or prevent fragmenta-
tion of bargaining, is to be decided having regard to the nature of
work of the employees in question and their training, experience
and qualifications.[2] There follows a ballot. The question as to an
unsplit unit is the same one of whether the existing agent[3] should
continue to be recognised. To a section of the unit the question to
be asked is whether it should continue to be included within the
existing unit. The results of the ballots are reported to the court.

If the bargaining unit is balloted as a whole and the majority vote
against continuance of the agency then the court makes an order
to the employer to cease recognition and not to grant recognition
again for two years from the date the ballot was reported to the
court.[4] If a section of the unit is balloted and a majority favours
exclusion from the unit, a similar order is made in respect of that
section.[5] These orders revoke any previous section 50 orders in
so far as they are inconsistent and they too are effective two months
after being made.[6] Again the orders are followed by a two year
standstill as far as the trade unions which have lost recognition are
concerned.[7]

These procedures are protected against industrial pressure under
the Act by the creation of unfair industrial practices. These are
set out in sections 54 and 55 of the Act. It is provided that it is
an unfair industrial practice for an employer directly concerned in
dispute relating to a question in issue[8] to institute, carry on, organise,
procure or finance a lock-out or to threaten to do so.[9] Similarly
any person, and this phrase is said to include registered or unregistered trade unions or their officials, who calls, organises, procures or
finances a strike or other irregular industrial action short of a strike
or threatens so to do[10] is committing an unfair industrial practice.[11]

---

[1] S. 52(2).

[2] S. 52(5). The same criteria used in the original decision as to unit—
s. 48(3).

[3] Used to cover either a trade union or a joint negotiating panel.

[4] S. 52(1).

[5] S. 53(2).

[6] S. 53(4).

[7] S. 53(5).

[8] Question is defined in s. 54. It covers matters to be determined by the
Commission as a result of a proposal to apply to the court under s. 45.

[9] These are the employers' ways of committing the usual unfair industrial
practice.

[10] These are the trade unions' methods.

[11] S. 54(4). The content is common to most unfair practices.

A recognition order made under section 50 is similarly protected. An employer commits an unfair industrial practice if he bargains with any other than the recognised trade unions. He also commits an unfair industrial practice if he fails to take all such reasonable action to carry on collective bargaining.[1] The balancing unfair industrial practice covers any person[2] using the acts mentioned in the last paragraph knowingly to induce or try to induce the employer to do what would be an unfair industrial practice under this section by him.[3]

It is also an unfair industrial practice within the two-year period following the Commission's report to the court for any person[4] by the same means knowingly to induce or try to induce an employer to recognise as sole bargaining agent a trade union or joint negotiating panel which was not recommended for recognition even where no other body was in fact recommended for recognition, or to bargain with such a body.[5] A similar unfair industrial practice arises where an order withdrawing recognition has been made under section 53. Any person[6] who uses the specified methods to attempt to induce or to induce the employer to disregard the order commits an unfair industrial practice.[7]

Finally the right to use the procedure is protected by making it an unfair industrial practice for the employer to use his prohibited industrial actions knowingly to induce or attempt to induce any person to refrain from making application for recognition under section 47 or reconsideration under section 51.

4. THE COLLECTIVE BARGAIN

The problem of the incorporation of the collective bargain into the individual worker's contract of service has already been discussed.[8] That problem arises whether the collective agreement is legally binding or not. This question, whether a collective bargain was binding in law or not, has been the subject of some dispute amongst academic commentators.[9] The matter fell for discussion in an important case: *Ford Motor Co.* v. *Amalgamated Union of Engineering*

---

[1] S. 55(1). He may bargain with any points of a joint panel if the panel as a whole agrees: s. 55(2). The Code has an important section on that topic.
[2] Again defined to include registered and unregistered unions and their officials.
[3] S. 55(3).
[4] Again defined to include registered and unregistered unions and their officials.
[5] S. 55(6) (a), (b).
[6] See footnote 4, above.
[7] S. 55(7).
[8] *Supra*, p. 120.
[9] *E.g.* Prof. O. Kahn Freud in *The System of Industrial Relations in Great Britain*, Flanders and Clegg.

and Foundry Workers.[1]   In this case the strongly held view that collective agreements were not legally binding because the parties did not intend them to be, was followed.   Agreements between employers' associations and trade unions had always been unenforceable directly under section 4 of the Trade Union Act, 1871 which defined both bodies as trade unions and regulated agreements between them.   This approach will presumably still apply to pre-Industrial Relations Act, 1971, bargains.   They are unlikely to be held legally binding, for a subsequent piece of legislation can hardly be said to have changed their intentions.[2]

The Industrial Relations Act has clarified the position and has put the emphasis on the legally binding nature of such agreements whilst giving the parties the power to achieve the opposite effect. Every collective agreement which is in writing made after the Act comes into force[3] is conclusively presumed to be intended by the parties to be legally enforceable unless it contains a provision to the opposite effect.[4]   The provision may apply to the whole or merely to a specified part of the agreement.

A collective agreement is defined in the Act.[5]   It is said to be any agreement or arrangement made in whatever way and in whatever form[6] made by or on behalf of trade unions and employers.[7]   Such agreement must prescribe, wholly or in part, terms and conditions of employment of the workers or must relate to procedure between the parties which is defined in the section.[8]   The remarkable feature of this definition is its width.   Despite its being restricted to written agreements, the phrase made in whatever way or whatever form does mean that almost every written document evidencing bargaining could well be construed as an agreement.   There will be practical difficulties in distinguishing agreements from mutually accepted " custom and practice ".

The same presumption as to legal enforceability is also applied by the Act to the proceedings of joint negotiating bodies.[9]   Where a joint body of trade unions[10] and employers is established under a collective agreement for the purpose of regulating terms and conditions of employment or determining matters appropriate for a procedure agreement,[11] then there is a conclusive presumption that

---

[1] [1969] 2 Q.B. 303, [1969] 2 All E.R. 481.
[2] For a different view, see Selwyn, *Guide to the Industrial Relations Act 1971*, p. 83.
[3] December, 1971.
[4] S. 34(1).
[5] S. 166(1).
[6] S. 34 only applies to *written* collective agreements.
[7] All employers or trade unions represented by the agreement are parties to s. 161(4).
[8] S. 161.   Procedure agreement is defined in s. 161(5).
[9] S. 35.
[10] Both unregistered and registered.
[11] Set out in s. 166(5).

decisions on these matters which are recorded in writing and do not have a provision excluding legal enforceability will in fact be enforceable. Decision is widely defined to include any award or resolution whatever it may be called.[1]

The use of the term " conclusive presumption " prohibits the possibility of the argument being brought that legal enforceability was not indeed intended. There is strong trade union opposition to the idea of legally enforceable contracts, so the inclusion of exclusion clauses will be strongly pressed. Where the agreement is binding, the appropriate court for disputes is the Industrial Court. Internal arbitration arrangements are not affected, and will probably be provided for, but where the dispute leads to litigation it is provided that no court other than the Industrial Court should entertain a case which involves the agreement's construction or effect, or its enforcement, or for damages for breach.[2]

One of the new concepts of the Act is the protection of the legally binding collective agreement against unfair industrial practices. Any party to the agreement commits an unfair industrial practice if he breaks a legally binding agreement, or part of an agreement.[3] The parties must also attempt to exercise control over their constituent parts.[4] It is also an unfair practice for a party not to take all reasonably practicable steps to prevent persons acting or purporting to act on their behalf taking action contrary to the agreement.[5] Where such action is in fact taken, it is an unfair industrial action not to take all reasonably practical steps to end it.[6]

Special attention is given by the Act to procedure agreements. These are defined as that part of collective agreements relating to the machinery for consultation regarding the settlement of terms and conditions of employment by negotiation or arbitration, to negotiating rights, to facilities for trade union officials, to dismissal procedures, and to disciplinary procedures.[7] The Act provides for remedial action where procedure agreements are non-existent or defective. Application may be made to the Industrial Court by the Secretary of State or by an employer or by a registered trade union recognised as having negotiating rights in the unit of employment concerned and, if there is a procedure in existence, a party to the procedure agreement.[8] It may be made on the grounds that in a particular unit of employment[9] there is no procedure agreement or

---

[1] S. 35(4).
[2] S. 129.   Appeals go to the usual Court of Appeal.
[3] S. 36.
[4] Members of an employers' association or trade union.
[5] S. 36(2) (a), (b).
[6] S. 36(2) (c).
[7] S. 166(6).
[8] S. 37.
[9] Defined not too helpfully as an undertaking or part of one. The rules discussed below may also be applied to composite units, that is to say two or more associated undertakings: s. 43.

an unsuitable agreement for the prompt and fair settlement of disputes. It may also be made where a procedure agreement exists but there is recourse to industrial action—strikes, lock-outs or irregular action short of a strike contrary to the agreement.

Again the initial aim is to secure conciliation. So where the application is not made by the Secretary of State[1], the Industrial Court cannot entertain the application unless notice has been given to the Secretary of State whose duty it is to give advice and assistance and do what he feels necessary to obtain agreement including, if he thinks fit, referring the matter to the Commission on Industrial Relations. The Industrial Court, once it entertains an application, has to be satisfied that there are reasonable grounds to believe that the basic problems exist and that the result is that orderly industrial relations have been seriously impeded either as to development or maintenance, or that there have been substantial and repeated losses of working time. If it is, then the matter is referred to the Commission to investigate whether the defects do indeed exist and to recommend, if that is so appropriate, remedies.[2] The Commission, if given power, may put to the Industrial Court proposals to extend the unit of employment under consideration.[3] Such proposals have to be made public so that affected persons may make representations to the court. In formulating recommendations it is for the Commission to determine the parties concerned. These will be parties to existing procedure agreements and other employers, employers' associations, or trade unions, as appear appropriate.[4] Again the emphasis is upon the search for voluntary accord. The Commission must promote and assist discussion between the designated parties to achieve agreement upon a new provision so formulated as to be capable of being legally enforceable.[5] If such agreement is achieved, the Commission tells the Industrial Court and then the application may be withdrawn on the application of any party. If there is no withdrawal, the Commission has to make a report setting out its proposals as to new or revised provisions.[6] The report is made to the court and is given to the parties to the reference. Within the ensuing six months, any employer or registered trade union may apply to the Industrial Court to make an order defining the unit, specifying the parties upon whom the provisions set out in the report will be binding.[7] The Industrial Court must be satisfied that such an order is required to secure acceptance and observance of the recommended procedures. If it is, it makes the order and specifies a date upon which the provisions

---

[1] Who has himself a duty to consult the parties.
[2] S. 37(5).
[3] S. 38(1), (2).
[4] S. 39.
[5] S. 39(3).
[6] S. 40.
[7] S. 41.

will become effective as a legally enforceable contract between the parties.[1] There is a bar on further applications under section 37 once the Commission has reported under section 40 for two years in respect of the same or a substantially similar unit.[2] The order can be revoked or varied on a joint application by the parties.[3] If one partly alone applies, the court has power to revoke the order but only if it feels that it is no longer necessary to secure observance. The Commission may be asked to help by exercising this question and reporting to the court.[4]

It was one of the proposals of the Donovan Commission that work should be done on the improvement of procedure agreements. This process was furthered by the notification of agreements to the Department of Employment. Section 58 provides that the Secretary of State may make regulations furthering this process.[5]

Disclosure of Information.—A particular aspect of collective bargaining is the availability of information to enable the representatives of the workers to bargain effectively with their employers. Proposals were made by the Labour Government[6] and the Industrial Relations Act has two sections dealing with different aspects of this problem.

Section 57 applies to larger employers, that is to say those with more than 350 employees.[7] Employees are defined as not including part time workers employed for less than 21 hours weekly and those full time workers who have been employed for less than thirteen weeks and those ordinarily working outside Great Britain.[8] The section provides for an annual statement in writing to be issued to each employee within six months of the end of the financial year to which it related.[9] The exact content of the statement is to be determined by regulations issued by the Secretary of State, and he is empowered to include rules that the information shall cover other undertakings owned by a company and associated companies.[10] The effect of this section is to equate the employee more readily with the shareholder as far as the right to information is concerned.

Section 56 is of infinitely greater importance as far as bargaining is concerned, for the trade union will no doubt have been able to obtain much of the information under section 57 through other channels.

---

[1] S. 41(2).
[2] S. 42(1).
[3] S. 42(2).
[4] S. 42(3), (4).
[5] The Act provides for penalties for failure to apply with such regulations: s. 59.
[6] See *In Place of Strife*, para. s. 47-48.
[7] There is power on the part of the Secretary of State to alter the figure 350: s. 57(7).
[8] S. 57(9).
[9] S. 57(1), (2), (3).
[10] There is also power to exclude nominated employers of particular descriptions, s. 57(5), (6).

Section 56 concerns information required specifically for collective bargaining. An employer, and there is no requirement of size, has a duty to disclose to representatives of registered trade unions information relating to his own undertaking and to any associated undertakings. The information required to be disclosed is that without which the trade union representative would be to a material extent impeded in bargaining and that which it is in accordance with good industrial relations practice to disclose.[1] The latter head is said to be construed in accordance with the provisions of the Code of Industrial Relations Practice.[2] The Code adds a further important head, for it provides that an employer should not refuse to provide information in response to reasonable requests.

There are several rules which limit the scope of these provisions. In section 56 itself, it is provided that the section gives no right to inspect documents or demand copies. The employer may also be able to resist the collection or compilation of information if the work or cost involved is out of reasonable proportion to its value.[3] There are in these provisions several points, for example " reasonable requests " and " reasonable proportion to its value " which are very much matters of opinion and will undoubtedly give rise to heated discussion between the bargaining parties on occasion.

The question of the disclosure of information under both these sections is subject to a general immunity of certain confidential information.[4] This covers matters of national security, information covered by other statutes, information confidentially obtained by the employer, information relating to specified individuals without their consent being obtained, information obtained for the purpose of legal proceedings. Most general and therefore perhaps important is the protection of information, disclosure of which would be seriously prejudicial to the employer's interest.[5] This is a provision which is sure to lead to controversy. There is, perhaps an overstated concern on the part of an employer that the union representative may well also negotiate with his competitors.

The general question of the disclosure of information was referred to the Commission on Industrial Relations shortly after it was set up.[6]

5. SETTLEMENT OF DISPUTES[7]

There have been statutory attempts to improve and provide ways of settling industrial disputes once they have arisen. These include

---

[1] S. 56(1). There is a duty to provide the information in writing if so requested: s. 56(3).

[2] See paras. 96–98.

[3] S. 56(4).

[4] S. 158.

[5] S. 158(1) (c).

[6] By the Labour Government in 1970. The report is awaited at the time of writing. It will undoubtedly be of considerable importance.

[7] Reference should be made to the Industrial Relations Handbook, H.M.S.O. 1961.

particularly conciliation, which is the use of third party help to bring the parties together, and is sometimes called mediation, and arbitration which is the submission to a third party of a dispute for settlement. They are devices which have long been used. The advent of the Industrial Relations Act and the changes discussed in the earlier part of this chapter have not detracted from the need for these functions. They must be considered. The only important changes made by the Act are the granting of certain rights in the Secretary of State to apply to the Industrial Court for a so-called cooling off period or strike ballot.[1] These additional powers are not likely to play a frequent role in the settlement of disputes, their place is one for selective use.

(1) Conciliation.—The first modern statute bearing upon the settlement of disputes in industry is the Conciliation Act, 1896. The Act bestowed on the Board of Trade certain powers to be exercised towards the prevention and settlement of trade disputes. These powers are now exercised by the Secretary of State for Employment. Where a difference exists between employers and workmen or between different classes of workmen, the Secretary of State may (a) enquire into the circumstances of the dispute; (b) take such steps as may be expedient to bring the parties together under the presidency of a chairman mutually agreed upon or nominated by the Secretary of State or by some other person or body with a view to the amicable settlement of the dispute; (c) on the application of the interested employers or workmen and, after taking into account existing means of conciliation, appoint a conciliator or a board of conciliation; (d) on the application of both parties to the difference, appoint an arbitrator.[2]

It will be noted that the power of the Secretary of State in the matter of conciliation is wider than the powers relating to arbitration. For the power to appoint a conciliator arises at the request of either party to the dispute whilst the power to appoint an arbitrator can be exercised only on the application of both parties. The reason is clear and is of some significance to the student of industrial law. The function of the conciliator is confined to the effort to bring the parties together in the hope that a common discussion will reveal a means of settlement acceptable to both parties. The arbitrator generally fulfils a judicial role; he is concerned with law and facts and the parties, before the submission to arbitration normally agree, in advance, to accept and act upon his findings. There cannot, therefore, be arbitration unless the parties have fully agreed to such procedure. The result is that in normal circumstances the decision of an arbitrator may, by leave of the court or a Judge, be enforced in the same manner as a judgment.[3] These provisions do not, in fact,

---

[1] Industrial Relations Act, 1971, Part VIII.
[2] Conciliation Act, 1896, s. 2 (1).
[3] Arbitration Act, 1950, s. 26.

necessarily apply to submissions made under the Conciliation Act, but such submissions must either be in accordance with such of the provisions of the Arbitration Act, 1950 or such of the regulations of any conciliation board or under such other rules or regulations as may be mutually agreed upon by the parties.[1] It is clearly the policy of the Act that submission to arbitration shall not lightly be undertaken. The Act provides that a conciliator will enquire into the causes and circumstances of the difference between the parties by communication with them and will attempt a settlement, reporting his proceedings to the Secretary of State.[2] If a settlement is reached whether by arbitration or conciliation, a memorandum of the terms must be drawn up, signed by the parties and delivered to the Secretary of State.[3]

Any board, whether established before or after the passing of the Act, which is constituted for the purpose of settling disputes between employers and workmen or any association or body authorized by the written agreement of employers or workmen may apply to the Secretary of State for registration. He keeps a register of conciliation boards.[4] Where he is of opinion that in any trade or district adequate machinery for the settlement of disputes does not exist an enquiry may be set up with the employers and employed and, if so desired, with any local authority or body, as to the expediency of establishing a conciliation board.[5]

In 1919 the Industrial Courts Act was passed. The Act set up a standing Industrial Court which consists of persons appointed by the Secretary for Employment, some of whom are independent persons, some represent employers and some represent workmen. The court has been recently renamed the Industrial Arbitration Board.[6] In addition there must be one or more women. The chairman is drawn from one of the independent persons.[7] A trade dispute is defined by the Act as any dispute or difference between employers or workmen, or between workmen and workmen connected with the employment or non-employment, or the terms of employment or with the conditions of labour of any person. A workman, for the purposes of the Act, is any person who has entered into or works under a contract with an employer whether the contract be by way of manual labour, clerical work or otherwise. The contract may be expressed or implied, oral or written. It may be a contract of service or apprenticeship or a contract personally to execute any work or labour.[8]

---

[1] Conciliation Act, 1896, s. 3.
[2] *Ibid.*, s. 2 (2).
[3] *Ibid.*, 1896, s. 2. (3).
[4] *Ibid.*, s. 1.
[5] Conciliation Act, 1896, s. 4.
[6] Industrial Relations Act, 1971, s. 124.
[7] Conciliation Act, 1896, s. 1.
[8] Industrial Courts Act, 1919, s. 8.

Any trade dispute as defined by the Act, whether it exists or is apprehended, may be reported to the Secretary of State by or on behalf of the parties to the dispute. The Secretary of State will then take the matter into his consideration and, if he thinks fit, and if both parties consent, either (a) refer the matter for settlement by the Industrial Arbitration Board or (b) refer the matter to arbitration by one or more persons appointed by him; or (c) refer the matter for settlement by a Board of Arbitration. Such a board will consist of persons nominated by or on behalf of the employer with an equal number nominated by or on behalf of the workmen concerned, with an independent chairman nominated by the Secretary of State. The Secretary of State may set up panels of persons ready to act and women must be included on the panels. If machinery for conciliation or arbitration already exists the Secretary of State will not, without the consent of both parties and unless and until the existing machinery has failed to reach a settlement, refer the matter by the means provided by the Act.[1]

Any trade dispute whether it exists or is merely apprehended may, on being reported to or coming to the notice of the Secretary of State for Employment, be submitted to an enquiry into its causes and circumstances. The Secretary of State may, if he thinks fit, refer matters connected therewith to a court of enquiry which will report to the Secretary of State. Such a court of enquiry consists of a chairman and such other persons as the Secretary of State thinks fit or may consist of one person appointed by the Secretary of State. The court of enquiry may, if rules so authorise, require evidence to be given on oath. It may make interim reports and its report, together with any minority report, must be laid before the Houses of Parliament.[2]

The Industrial Relations Act has added two functions to the newly renamed Industrial Arbitration Board. Section 55 of the Act makes it an unfair industrial practice for an employer to ignore an order to recognise a trade union or joint negotiating panel[3] and to refuse to carry on collective bargaining with the recognised agent or to bargain with some body other than the specified agent. A complaint relating to such an unfair industrial practice is made to the Industrial Court,[4] when a restraint order cannot be made. Instead the court may, if it thinks it just and equitable, make an order authorising the presentation of a claim to the Industrial Arbitration Board specifying when the unfair industrial practice first occurred.[5] Such a claim to the Board is then presented under section 125 by the registered trade union, or joint negotiating panel which made the original complaint to the Industrial Court. The claim has to be in

[1] *Ibid.*, s. 2. The Arbitration Act, *supra*, does not apply to submissions to Arbitration under the Industrial Courts Act, 1919.

[2] Industrial Courts Act, 1919, ss. 4, 5.

[3] Made under s. 50: see above, p. 435.

[4] Under s. 101.

[5] S. 105(5).

writing and should set out proposed terms and conditions of employment for specified employers.

Section 56 of the Act relates to the disclosure of information.[1]
Failure to comply may be the basis of a claim to the Industrial
Court under section 102 (1) (b).   If the court finds the complaint
justified, it may make an order authorising the presentation of a
claim to the Industrial Arbitration Board.[2]   Such a claim is then
made under section 126.

In these two instances, claims are brought before the Board under
the procedure of the Act.   The Board is empowered to make an
appropriate award, either in the form of the claim made or in other
terms deemed to be more appropriate.[3]   Such award must specify
the parties to whom it applies.[4]   These terms are by statute implied
in contracts of service to which they apply from the date specified
in the award.   They will be effective until superseded or varied
by agreement or by a subsequent award by the Board.[5]

(2) Arbitration.—Mention must now be made of provision for
compulsory arbitration which lasted from 1940 until its abolition in
1958.   The abolition of compulsory arbitration was regarded with
disfavour by many trade unions, and in particular by those non-
industrial trade unions, such as National Association of Local
Government Officers, for whom such arbitration was a useful
alternative to striking, a method of action they wished to avoid.

In the early months of the war the State had not interfered with
the then existing machinery for the settlement of disputes which
was voluntary in character.   Following the fall of France and a
quickened sense of emergency, a power was given by an additional
defence regulation to the Minister of Labour and National Service
to make orders with a view to preventing interruptions of work
because of trade disputes.[6]   The power to refer trade disputes or
other matters for settlement or advice under the Industrial Courts
Act, 1919, was however specifically reserved and nothing in any
Order was to affect this.

Under this power many orders were made, the chief one being S.R.
& O. 1940, No. 1305.[7]   The machinery set up by the order worked
with some success during the war but it deprived both employers and
employees of liberties to which they were much attached.   The order

---

[1] See *supra*, p. 441.
[2] S. 102(2).
[3] S. 127.
[4] S. 127(2).
[5] S. 127(3).
[6] S.R. & O. 1940, No. 1217, reg. 58 AA.
[7] Conditions of Employment & National Arbitration Order as amended by
S.R. & O. 1941, No. 1884; 1942, Nos. 1073 and 2673; 1944, No. 1437 and S.I.
1950, No. 1309.

established what was, in effect, compulsory arbitration and prohibited strikes and lock-outs except where a dispute had been
reported to the Minister in accordance with the terms of the order,
twenty-one days had elapsed and the dispute had not, during that
time, been referred by the Minister for settlement. Thus arose the
"illegal" strike or lock-out, for to contravene the provisions of the
order constituted an offence under the Defence (General) Regulations. The system worked well during and immediately after the
war but the advent of a labour government and the readiness of the
trade union leaders to subscribe to the policies of that government
led, perhaps, inevitably to the growth of some discontent amongst
members of the unions. Unofficial strikes grew in number and
importance and at the same time the practice grew up of not prosecuting workmen infringing the order. Strikes reached dimensions
which could not be ignored and early in 1951 prosecutions were
brought following strikes in the London docks.

Order No. 1305, it was patent, could not remain on the Statute
Book unless it were enforced and the Minister of Labour certainly
did not exaggerate when he told the House of Commons that experience showed "that the enforcement of penal sanctions against persons taking part in strikes and lock-outs gives rise to extreme difficulties."[1] Prosecutions based upon it had rarely been brought and
the dockers' case showed how fortuitous the result of such prosecutions might be. Indeed, between the original hearings in the magistrates courts and the final hearing before the Lord Chief Justice,
discussions had been taking place between the government, the
trade unions and the employers. In the end the order and its
amendments were repealed and S.I. 1951, No. 1376 took its place.

The Instrument provided that where a dispute existed in a trade or
industry or section of a trade or industry or in an undertaking it
might be reported to the Minister in accordance with the order by
(*a*) an organisation of employers, on behalf of employers who were
parties to the dispute, or (*b*) by an employer who was in dispute with
his employees, or (*c*) a trade union representing workpeople who were
parties to the dispute. Then if the Minister thought that there was
machinery for the voluntary settlement of the terms and conditions
of employment and that the employers (or single employer) or trade
union habitually took part in the settlement or that there was no
such machinery but that the reporting organisation of employers or
trade union represented a substantial proportion of those in the relevant trade or industry, then, in either case the dispute might be
dealt with as provided by the Order.[2]

---

[1] Parliamentary Debates, August 2nd, 1951.
[2] S.I. 1951, No. 1376, art. 1: a trustee savings bank is an "undertaking"
within the order, see *R.* v. *Industrial Disputes Tribunal, Ex parte East Anglian
Trustee Savings Bank*, [1954] 2 All E.R. 730; [1954] 1 W.L.R. 1039.   As to
the definition of the word "section" in "section of a trade or industry," see
R. v. *Industrial Disputes Tribunal, Ex parte Courage & Co., Ltd.*, [1956] 3 All
E.R. 411; [1956] 1 W.L.R. 1062.

Again, where, within a trade or industry, conditions of employment had been settled by machinery of negotiation to which the parties were organisations of employers and trade unions representing a substantial proportion of the employers and workers engaged in that trade or industry and an issue whether an employer should observe those terms and conditions was reported to the Minister and the Minister was of opinion that the organisation of employers or trade union reporting the issue habitually took part in the settlement of terms and conditions of employment, then, also, the issue might be dealt with as provided by the Order.[1]

Any report of a dispute or issue had to be made to the Minister in writing and where the report did not contain sufficient particulars it would not be deemed to be made in accordance with the order until the Minister was satisfied that the particulars so required had been duly given.   On receiving the report the Minister might take such steps as he could to promote a settlement of that dispute or issue, except that where he was of opinion that suitable machinery of negotiation or arbitration existed and that all practical means of reaching a settlement through that machinery had not been exhausted, he must refer the dispute to that machinery for settlement.[2] And where the machinery of negotiation or arbitration had been evoked and an agreement, decision or award reached, this, for the purposes of the Order, would be treated as constituting a final settlement of the dispute.[3]

The Order also set up an Industrial Disputes Tribunal which consisted of three appointed members, one of whom was chairman, one representative of employers and the other of the workpeople, but all were appointed by the Minister from a panel of members constituted by him after consultation with the British Employers Confederation and the Trade Union Congress.   The Tribunal had to make its award without delay and, if possible, within fourteen days.[4]

Where a dispute was reported to the Minister and he had not referred it to voluntary machinery of settlement already existing, or if it had been so referred but no settlement reached, the Minister must, within fourteen days, refer it to the Tribunal for settlement, though there was a power to extend the period of fourteen days where this appeared desirable.   And if the Minister thought, that, in respect of a reported dispute, action was being taken by either of the parties designed to compel the acceptance of terms and conditions of employment which were the subject of the dispute resulting in a stoppage of work or a substantial breach of agreement, the Minister was not to refer the dispute to the Tribunal while such action continued if in his opinion it would be undesirable to do so; and where the Minis-

---

[1] S.I. 1951, No. 1376, art. 2.
[2] S.I. 1951 No. 1376, arts. 3, 4 and 5.
[3] *Ibid.*, art. 6.
[4] *Ibid.*, art. 7 and Sched. I.

ter had referred a dispute to the Tribunal and subsequently informed the Tribunal that one of the parties was taking such action, proceedings must be stayed until the Minister cancelled his notification.[1]

The Order contemplated that either "disputes" or "issues" should be referred for settlement. A dispute was defined as not including a dispute as to the employment or non-employment of any person or as to whether any person should or should not be a member of any trade union, but save as aforesaid meant any dispute between an employer and workmen in the employment of that employer, connected with the terms of the employment or with the conditions of labour of any of those workmen.[2] An issue related to whether an employer, in a district or trade in which agreed terms and conditions of employment operate, should observe such terms and conditions.[3]

Whenever an issue was reported to the Minister, the Minister, if it was not otherwise settled, had to refer it to the tribunal which might require an employer who was not observing recognised terms and conditions, or terms and conditions which were not less favourable, to observe such terms and conditions as might be defined.

When the tribunal made an award on a dispute or an issue it became an implied term of the contract between the employer and workers to whom the award applied that the terms and conditions of employment to be observed under the contract should be in accordance with the award until varied either by agreement between the parties or by a subsequent award of the tribunal.[4]

The importance of these provisions was that they restored voluntary collective bargaining and abolished any general obligation to observe recognised terms and conditions of employment. The two are, of course, related for it is known that the employers had insisted that if the right to strike was restored the obligation to observe recognised terms and conditions should be repealed. But though the general obligation disappeared the order did provide for the situation in which an individual employer failed to observe already established terms. And it should be noticed that though the order contained no provision prohibiting strikes and lock-outs the Minister retained power to refuse access to the tribunal in certain circumstances.

The courts did not succeed in drawing any clear line of demarcation between "issues" and "disputes" under the order. Thus in *R. v. Industrial Disputes Tribunal, Ex parte Technaloy, Ltd.*[5] SOMERVELL and BIRKETT, L.JJ., held that an "issue" was raised

---

[1] *Ibid.*, art. 8 and Sched. I.
[2] *Ibid.*, art. 12.
[3] *Ibid.*, art. 2.
[4] S.I. 1951 No. 1376, art. 10, but see *R. v. Industrial Disputes Tribunal, Ex parte Kigass, Ltd.*, [1953] 1 All E.R. 593; [1953] 1 W.L.R. 411.
[5] [1954] 2 Q.B. 46; [1954] 2 All E.R. 75.

when the question was whether or not an employer was bound by the recognised terms and conditions within the industry and must implement them as a whole, whereas a dispute was concerned with the implementation of one given aspect of the terms and conditions. ROMER, L.J., took a wider view. For him the term " issue " could not be confined to the question of enforcing a code in its entirety and a failure to implement some part only of the code might constitute either an issue or a dispute.

This latter view was endorsed in *R. v. Industrial Disputes Tribunal, Ex parte Portland Urban District Council.*[1] The facts were that an employee (a Mr. Carter) might be fitted into either of two trade categories, one " miscellaneous " the other " waterworks "; each class having different conditions of service. The effort to secure grading under the category " miscellaneous " being refused by the employers, the matter was referred to the Whitley Council which recommended the " miscellaneous " grading. The local authority applied the award, but for a short period. They dismissed the man, advertised for a maintenance fitter in language similar to that which they had used when advertising for a station engineer. They appointed the dismissed employee and in the new contract attempted to ensure that he was graded under the " waterworks " category. The man's union would not accept the position and reported the matter to the Minister as an " issue." The employer denied this and took objection to the jurisdiction of the Tribunal. The court, however, took the view that there was a considerable overlap in the definitions of " dispute " and " issue,"

> " Some matters may give rise to an ' issue ' only, as, for instance when all employers in a particular trade observe the recognised terms and conditions, but a trade union wishes an employer in an allied trade to observe these terms also. In such a case there is no ' dispute ' . . . because there is no dispute between an employer and the workmen in his employ: but there is clearly an ' issue.' Other matters may give rise to a ' dispute ' only, as, for instance when the workmen are dissatisfied with their pay or conditions, but there are no recognised terms or conditions with which they can be compared.
>
> Apart from those cases, there are many matters which can properly be described either as a ' dispute ' or as an ' issue.' The *Technaloy* case is, I think, a good instance. It raised an ' issue ' whether the employers should pay their men the recognised rates. That is how the Divisional Court looked at that case. It also raised a ' dispute ' between an employer and some of his workmen connected with the terms of their employment. That is how this court looked at it. So also with the present case. It could, I think, be described as a ' dispute ' because it is, as I understand it, a dispute between the local authority and some of their staff connected with the terms of employment of Mr. Carter. It can also be described as an ' issue ' because the trade union claim that

---

[1] [1955] 3 All E.R. 18; [1955] 1 W.L.R. 949.

the local authority should observe the recognised terms and conditions in regard to Mr. Carter."[1]

It had been accepted that since the end of the war, although the nature of the scheme involved compulsory arbitration, the continued existence of it depended upon the agreement of both sides of industry. It was the trade unions' dislike of the prohibition of official strike action which led to revision in 1951 and it was almost certainly the pressures of the employers which led to the final abolition of the scheme. The feeling had grown that disputes always ended in an award of some size for the workmen and it was thought that it could no longer be supported. The Government accordingly put an end to the system by a Statutory Instrument[2] that was effective from the end of February, 1959.

The end of the system was contrary to the wishes of union opinion and most particularly to the wishes of those unions which felt they could not use strike action. The Government felt, however, that they must honour the undertaking to end the system when it ceased to have the support of both sides. At the same time it was emphasised that every encouragement would be given to joint negotiating machinery set up in individual industries.

One feature of the old system remains. Under the Terms and Conditions of Employment Act, 1959 the " issues " procedure has been made permanent.[3] An " issue " is now termed a claim but the structure of the procedure is substantially retained. The Industrial Disputes Tribunal has been abolished but the Industrial Court has taken over the work of hearing claims. The procedure is that a claim is reported to the Secretary of State. It must allege that in a trade or industry terms or conditions of employment have been established, either by an award or by agreement. The parties to the award must be organisations of employers and workmen representing a substantial proportion of their side of the industry to which the award or agreement relates. Finally it must be alleged that a particular employer is not observing the terms or conditions of employment that have been established.

(5) Emergency Procedures.—Amid considerable controversy, the Industrial Relations Act has added two new procedures available for the settlement of disputes. Both presuppose an emergency situation. This is defined as a situation in which industrial action has caused or will cause an interruption in the supply of goods or the provision of services of such a nature or on such a scale that it is likely to be gravely injurious to the national economy, to imperil national security, to create a serious risk of disorder, to endanger lives of a substantial number of persons or to expose a substantial

---

[1] [1955] 3 All E.R. 18; [1955] 1 W.L.R, 949, at pp. 22, 955 respectively, *per* DENNING, L.J

[2] S. I. 1958, No. 1796.

[3] S. 8.

number to serious risk of disease or personal injury.[1]   Where he is
of the opinion that such conditions exist as a result of a strike, of
irregular industrial action short of a strike, or of a lock-out having
begun or being likely to begin and that it would be conducive to
settlement by negotiation, conciliation or arbitration if this action
were discontinued or deferred, the Secretary of State may make an
application to the Industrial Court.[2]   The application must specify
the persons apparently responsible for the action or threatened
action.   These become parties to proceedings on the application.

The Industrial Court has to satisfy itself that there is indeed an
emergency situation.[3]   It may then make an order specifying the
area of employment to which it shall apply, the parties to be bound,
the date it is to be effective and the period it is to last.   This period
cannot exceed 60 days.[4]   The terms of the order, which must only
be applied to persons deemed to have responsibility,[5] prohibit the
calling, organising, procuring or financing of a strike, or any irregular
industrial action short of a strike or threatening to do so,[6] and the
instituting, carrying on, authorising, organising or financing of a
lock-out or the threat to do so.[7]   The order may also require anyone
within a directed time, to take steps to ensure that the order is carried
out.   Thus previously issued instructions are to be withdrawn.[8]

An order originally made for less than 60 days may be extended
up to this period and an order may be extended to apply to persons
not already specified in the original order.[9]   It is not possible to
make more than one application under section 138 relating to any
one dispute, otherwise the 60-day period could be prolonged.[10]

The other procedure available in the same type of emergency
situation is a ballot.   This, by its nature, does not apply to the
lock-out situation, merely to the strike, irregular industrial action or
threat of either.[11]   The Secretary of State may apply for a ballot
when the situation is that the conditions appear to be, or likely to be,
seriously injurious to the livelihood of a substantial number of
workers employed in a particular industry.[12]   If the Industrial
Court is satisfied of the grounds for the application it must order a
ballot to be taken.   The order has to specify the area of employment concerned, the question to be asked in the ballot and the period
for holding the ballot.[13]   The order has also to enable the workers

---

[1] S. 138(2).
[2] S. 138(1).
[3] S. 139(1).
[4] S. 139(2).
[5] S. 139(3).
[6] S. 139 (4).
[7] S. 139(5).
[8] S. 139(6).
[9] S. 140.   The original order is called " the principal order ".
[10] S. 140(7).
[11] S. 141.
[12] S. 141(2).
[13] S. 142.

eligible to vote to be determined.[1]   If it thinks fit, the Government
may ask the Commission on Industrial Relations to assist in formulating the order.[2]   With the order that a ballot be taken goes a provision that until the result of the ballot is reported to the court no
trade union[3] or person specified in the order shall take strike action,[4]
and no employer shall institute a lock-out.[5]   The order may require
reasonable steps to be taken to discontinue action already taken or
to defer instructions already issued.[6]   Again, as with the cooling
off period procedure, the original order can be extended to cover
other workers.[7]   The conduct of the ballot is set out in section 144.
If all the workers concerned are members of a registered trade union
recognised by the employer and with rules approved by the Registrar[8]
then the Commission may ask the trade union to conduct the ballot
under the Commission's supervision.   The ballot is the responsibility
of the Commission and it must report the result to the Industrial
Court.[9]

One of the problems introduced by these new procedures is that
of enforcement should the orders of the Industrial Court be broken.
No special rules are laid down, the court will use the normal methods
used to enforce orders—normally appearance before the court to
show cause followed eventually by possible committal for contempt.
This would be a very unpopular step in this field of industrial
relations.

---

[1] S. 142(3).
[2] S. 142(5).
[3] Registered or unregistered.
[4] The usual actions by the workers' side are set out.
[5] S. 143(1).
[6] S. 143(2).
[7] S.143(4).
[8] Under Part IV of the Act.
[9] S. 145(4).

CHAPTER XI

THE LAW OF TRADE UNIONS[1] AND LIABILITIES IN RESPECT OF INDUSTRIAL ACTION

1. THE POSITION OF TRADE UNIONS UNTIL 1871[2]

In former times the association of workmen in defence of their interests was deemed to be contrary to public policy as was the association of employers for the maintenance of prices and similar objects. But before the beginning of the nineteenth century such associations had little in common with the modern trade union and in addition they were few in number and readily dealt with by the ordinary law of the land. It was the Industrial Revolution with its creation of an urban working class which brought about the beginnings of the movement which has resulted in modern trade unionism. The ordinary law and *ad hoc* legislation were, by the end of the eighteenth century, no longer competent to deal with the new organisations. The first legislative attempt to meet the situation was the enactment of the Combination Act of 1799,[3] the policy of which was to prevent unlawful combinations of workmen. The Act had a brief life for it was repealed by the Combination Act, 1800,[4] which made illegal and void all contracts, covenants and agreements between journeymen, manufacturers, or other persons for obtaining an advance of wages, or for an alteration in or the lessening of working hours, or for decreasing the quantity of work, or for hindering or preventing others from employing whom they wished, or for controlling or affecting in any way another's control or management of his business.[5] It was made an offence for any person to attend a meeting for the purpose of making any such contract or to summon or, by intimidation, to persuade or induce anyone to attend such a meeting.[6] Various other offences

---

[1] For the purposes of the Industrial Relations Act, 1971, " trade union " means an organisation of workers registered as a trade union under the Act and does not embrace unregistered organisations of workers (s. 61(3)). In this chapter, " trade union " is used in relation to both registered and unregistered organisations, except where the provisions of the Industrial Relations Act are being considered, in which circumstances it is used in the sense of the Act. Also, although this chapter is concerned only with organisations of workers, it should be noted that the Act makes extensive parallel provision in respect of employers' associations.

[2] See *The Legal History of Trade Unionism*, by R. Y. Hedges and Allan Winterbottom, Longmans, London, 1930, for a detailed legal history of trade unionism.

[3] 39 Geo. 3, c. 81.

[4] 39 & 40 Geo. 3, c 106.

[5] *Ibid.*, s 1.

[6] *Ibid.*, s. 4.

were created but the Act was not entirely negative. The fear of alliances between workmen or manufacturers is clear in its provisions, but it is not less clear that the legislature perceived that there were problems to be faced which a merely hostile attitude could not solve. Thus the Act set out to establish a cheap and summary mode of settling disputes between master and workmen by way of arbitration proceedings. If the arbitrators could not decide the matter within three days of the submission of the dispute, the matter in dispute was to go before justices of the peace whose decision should be final. The failure of one party to sign the submission and to appoint an arbitrator might lead to conviction and a forfeiture of ten pounds. A failure to perform the terms of an arbitral award might lead to committal to prison.[1]

The operation of the Act of 1800 was not successful either in its negative or its positive aspects. In the first years of the nineteenth century summary proceedings under the Act were surprisingly few whilst throughout, the provisions as to arbitration were but little observed. Moreover, there were changes in the political and economic opinion in the country. The Acts of 1799 and 1800 had been passed under the shadow of the French Revolution. The first reaction to that revolution in this country had been one of considerable fear, expressing itself in a desire to prevent any combination which might attempt to invade the sphere of, or coerce, the central government. This reaction was not long lived. If the first effect of the French Revolution was to induce the feeling that the working class of this country must be the object of some discipline, the second effect (and it was not long delayed) was to produce the notion that the reasonable desires of the urban workers should be met as quickly as possible. It was no longer a question of making it impossible for the urban workers of this country to emulate the French peasantry. It was a question of removing their grievances so that there would be no desire amongst them to do so. And this change of attitude in the political sphere was concomitant with a change in the sphere of economic thought. The years between 1800 and 1820 were years in which Benthamism grew as an effective influence. Both capital and labour were to be free to make their own terms and to be free, moreover, to combine, provided their freedom did not impinge upon the like freedom of others. These were the views which led, in 1824, to the passing of yet another Combination Act,[2] an Act which repealed the laws relating to combinations of workmen. It was specifically provided that combinations of workmen and others to obtain an advance, to fix the rate of wages and so on should no longer be subject to prosecution for conspiracy or any punishment whatever either under common or statute law,[3] and that combina-

---

[1] 39 & 40 Geo. 3, c. 106, s. 18.
[2] 5 Geo. 4, c. 95.
[3] *Ibid.*, s. 2.

tions of masters should enjoy a like freedom.[1] It was made an
offence for any person, by violence, threats or intimidation to force
another to depart from his work, or to spoil or destroy goods, or to
prevent others from accepting work,[2] and it was also made an offence
on the part of workmen to combine to do any of these prohibited
acts.[3] Barely a year passed before the Act was repealed. It cannot be said that the workmen used their new freedom with discretion. The Act of 1824 was followed by many strikes and some
violence and it was not many months before a demand for a new
Act was made. The result was that, barely twelve months afterwards, the Combination Act, 1825[4] repealed the Act of the previous
year and it was only by the most determined action on the part of
those who had fought for the repeal of the Combination Laws that a
compromise solution was secured. The Act of 1825 followed,
broadly, the lines of its predecessor in 1824, the most significant
changes being those which strengthened the authorities against
combinations not declared legal by the Act. The method adopted
was to define with more care the combinations which were protected
by the Act. It was still an offence for any person to compel another
to leave his work, or to return his work unfinished, or to prevent
others from hiring themselves, or to compel others to belong to clubs
or associations, or by violence, threats or intimidation to endeavour
to force another to alter the manner in which he conducted his
business. But the provision which was made in the early Act
making it an offence also to do these things in combination was not
re-enacted, perhaps because it was felt better to rely on the common
law rules relating to conspiracy.

The general effect of the Act was to permit collective bargaining
merely over matters of wages and hours but there was no statutory
means of enforcing collective agreements, for neither the right of
striking nor of locking-out was recognised by the Act. Yet such a
right, with its necessary apparatus of "picketing,"[5] came to be
judicially recognised. The interpretations of the Act of 1825 produced their own difficulties and in 1859 the Molestation of Workmen
Act[6] was passed to amend and explain the Combination Act, 1825
as interpreted by the courts. *R.* v. *Duffield*[7] had held that whilst
workmen not employed had a right, in combination, to agree that
they would not accept employment except on specified terms, they
had no right to combine to persuade others who were employed to
leave that employment. Such an agreement would amount to conspiracy. The Molestation of Workmen Act clarified and amended

---

[1] *Ibid.*, s. 3.

[2] *Ibid.*, s. 5.

[3] 5 Geo. 4, c. 95, s. 6.

[4] 6 Geo. 4, c. 129.

[5] See the judgment of BRAMWELL, B., in *R.* v. *Druitt, Lawrence and Adamson* (1867), 10 Cox, C.C. 592.

[6] 22 Vict., c. 34.

[7] (1851), 5 Cox, C.C. 404.

the legal position by providing that any person whether employed or not might enter into an agreement with others for the purposes of fixing wage rates and went on :

"no workman or any other person whether actually in employment or not shall . . . by reason merely of his endeavouring peaceably or in a reasonable manner and without threat or intimidation direct or indirect, to persuade others to cease or abstain from work in order to obtain the rate of wages or the altered hours of labour . . . be deemed or taken to be guilty of 'molestation' or 'obstruction' . . . and shall not therefore be subject or liable to any prosecution or indictment for conspiracy."[1]

The Act cleared up certain difficulties, but what was still significant was that according to statute, combinations of workmen were still only protected if their disputes turned upon the questions of wages or hours of employment. In fact, in the middle years of the century, judges used their judicial discretion to the full and were increasingly reluctant to find workmen guilty of conspiracy when they had combined in an effort to end grievances other than those relating to wages and hours. In consequence of the growth of societies established by workmen to defend their interests, the general question of the legal status of trade unions came to the fore. Such a society would be legal if it were not in restraint of trade and that fact placed an extreme restriction upon the objects which a trade union might pursue. It would be criminal if its objects went further than those permitted by the Combination Act, 1825. If it were legal it enjoyed certain statutory rights but since it could only enforce its rights by the aid of the court through its members and not as a legal entity distinct in itself, the position of the trade union was one of considerable difficulty. In dealing with the malefactions of its own members the trade union had, virtually, no legally enforceable rights at all, for a member of a union who failed to account for moneys he had received could not be convicted of embezzlement.[2] Such a member was held to be a joint owner of the property of the unions and, in consequence, could not be proceeded against. Two statutes were passed which favourably influenced the position of the union in this matter. In 1868 the Larceny and Embezzlement Act[3] laid down that should a person who was a member of a co-partnership or being one of two or more beneficial owners of property, steal or embezzle any property belonging to the co-partnership or beneficial owners he would be liable to be tried and convicted as though he were not such a member or beneficial owner.[4] The following year the Trades Unions Funds Protection Act, 1869[5] provided that an association of persons should not, by reason only that any of

---

1 22 Vict., c. 34, s. 1.
2 *R.* v. *Blackburn* (1868), 11 Cox, C.C. 157.
3 31 & 32 Vict., c. 116.
4 *Ibid.*, s.1.
5 32 & 33 Vict., c. 61.

its rules might operate in restraint of trade, be deemed for the purpose of section 24 of the Friendly Societies Act, 1855, for the punishment of frauds and impositions, to be a society established for illegal purposes or not to be a friendly society within the meaning of section 44 of the said Act.[1]   Thus a trade union, though possessed of objects in restraint of trade, might now proceed against its members for misappropriation or embezzlement of its funds.   The defect of its position being that the union could not sue in its own name but only in the names of all its members, a procedure which was clumsy in the extreme.

This, then, was the general position until the passing of the Trade Union Act, 1871.   This Act was the product of much political ferment.   In 1867 a Royal Commission had been set up under the chairmanship of Sir William Erle.   As a result the Commission produced a majority and a minority report.   It was the latter which resulted in the greatest legislative change and which had most influence on the 1871 Act.

For the hundred years between the passing of the 1871 Act and the Industrial Relations Act, 1971, trade unions were free to register or not under section 6 of the 1871 Act.   The consequences of registration were limited in importance.[2]   The law relating to membership rights and duties and to liability for instituting or participating in industrial action was for the most part the same, whether or not a particular union was registered.   The law developed in the last hundred years has been the subject-matter of the present chapter in the previous editions of this book.   Much of it remains important and is considered at appropriate places in this edition.   Broadly speaking, membership rights received increasing judicial protection and were (except in the special circumstances of political fund rules and amalgamations)[3] largely unaffected by legislation.   Liability in relation to industrial action, on the other hand, was characterised by judicial extension of common law liabilities, subsequent to which Parliament sometimes enacted immunities.[4]   With the passing of the Industrial Relations Act the common law, while being amended, has receded in importance and a new conceptual approach has come into being.   Its salient features are specially created heads of liability called unfair industrial practices, a much tighter system of administrative control and the establishing of new agencies of enforcement.   Whilst the amended common law will continue to be administered in the ordinary courts, the new concepts and institutions of the Industrial Relations Act are designed to preponderate over the common law,[5] and accordingly are given greater prominence in this chapter.

---

[1] *Ibid.*, s. 1.

[2] See Grunfeld, *Modern Trade Union Law*, p. 44 *et seq.*.

[3] As to which special provision was made in the Trade Union Act, 1913, and the Trade Union (Amalgamations, etc.) Act, 1964, respectively.

[4] Notably in the Trade Disputes Acts, 1906 and 1965.

[5] See Industrial Relations Act, 1971, s. 131.

2. REGISTRATION: MACHINERY AND LEGAL CONSEQUENCES

Under the Industrial Relations Act, only those organisations of workers which register with the new Chief Registrar of Trade Unions and Employers' Associations become " trade unions " within the meaning of the Act,[1] and, as we shall see, the Act accords vastly different treatment to the two types of organisation, registered and unregistered. Although the mere existence of an unregistered organisation is not unlawful, the scheme of the Act is to place such an organisation in such a vulnerable legal position that registration might seem, on balance, to be advantageous.

An organisation is eligible for registration as a trade union if(*a*) it is an independent organisation of workers,[2] and (*b*) it has power, without the concurrence of any parent organisation,[3] to alter its own rules and to control the application of its own property and funds.[4] The requirement of independence is a safeguard against the registration of employer-dominated organisations. Also a federation of workers' organisations is eligible to register, but only if all its constituent or affiliated organisations are themselves registered trade unions or are entered in the special register.[5] Any organisation of workers, whether formed before or after the passing of the Act, may apply for registration.[6] The manner and form of such an application may be determined by the registrar, to whom there must be sent with every application—(*a*) a copy of the rules of the organisation and a list of its officers;[7] (*b*) the names and addresses of the branches (if any) of the organisation; and (*c*) if the organisation has been in operation for more than a year before the date of the application, a statement of information along the lines of that which is required annually of all unions once registered.[8] If the registrar is satisfied that the applicant organisation is eligible for registration and that the above requirements have been complied with, he will register the organisation as a trade union and issue to it a certificate of registration.[9]

A certificate of registration as a trade union will state whether the body registered is a federation of workers' organisations or an organisation other than such a federation. It will specify the name by which the trade union is registered, provision being made for the

---

[1] Industrial Relations Act, 1971, s. 61(3).
[2] For the meaning of " workers," see s. 167(1)–(4).
[3] " Parent organisation " means an organisation of which the organisation in question is a branch or section. *Ibid.*, s. 67(3).
[4] S. 67(1).
[5] S. 67(2). The special register is considered, *infra*, p. 467.
[6] S. 68(1).
[7] " Officers " are a narrower group than " officials." See s. 167, and Sched. 4, para. 6.
[8] S. 68(3). The annual return which must be made by all trade unions once registered under the 1971 Act is dealt with by s. 88 and Sched. 5, as to which, see *infra*.
[9] S. 68(4). There is also a registration fee of, at present, £25 (s. 68(5)).

avoidance of names which are identical with, or closely resemble, the names of bodies already registered.[1]   On receipt of a certificate of registration, the organisation, if it is not already a body corporate, will become one by the name specified in the certificate.   It will have perpetual succession and a common seal.   On incorporation, all property and funds, of whatsoever nature, for the time being held by any person in trust for the organisation will vest in the organisation itself without further assurance, and any liability or obligation to which any person is for the time being subject in his capacity as a trustee for the organisation will be transferred to the organisation. Moreover any legal proceedings which are pending by or against the trustees of an organisation immediately before its incorporation may be continued by or against the organisation in its registered name.[2]   Thus the problems connected with the personality of trade unions which had registered under the 1871 Act[3] have been avoided by the extension of the corporate form to trade unions registered under the Industrial Relations Act.

(1) Examination of Rules by the Registrar.—In contrast with the 1871 Act,[4] the Industrial Relations Act gives the registrar wide powers of scrutiny and control over the rules of registered trade unions.   In the past, trade unions were free to devise their own rule books, with only a minimum of administrative control in the case of registered trade unions, and a fairly remote prospect of judicial control in a small but ill-defined area in which the courts were prepared to find particular rules void on grounds of public policy.[5]   This led to union rule books being extremely various in their quality and subject-matter, not least in important areas such as the relationship between different organs of the union, the authority of officials, admission to membership, discipline and election procedures.[6] Under the Industrial Relations Act, registered trade unions are still free to devise their own rules, but subject to their satisfying the registrar that they are consistent with two sets of criteria laid down by the Act.   Thus emphasis is placed on a stringent system of administrative control.

As soon as practicable after issuing to an organisation a certificate of registration under the Act, the registrar must examine the rules of the organisation.   If, on such examination, it appears to the registrar that the rules are defective in that they are in any way

---

[1] S. 73.
[2] S. 74.
[3] See *Bonsor* v. *Musicians' Union*, [1956] A.C. 104; [1955] 3 All E.R. 518, and Wedderburn, (1957) 20 *M.L.R.* 105.
[4] For the registration requirements of the 1871 Act, see Grunfeld, *Modern Trade Union Law*, p. 44 *et seq.*
[5] The possibility of litigation of domestic disputes in the ordinary courts has not disappeared and is considered *infra.*
[6] *Cf.* rules relating to the political activities of trade unions which have been subjected to scrutiny and control since the Trade Union Act, 1913.   See *infra*, p. 483.

inconsistent with the principles set out in section 65 or do not comply
with the requirements set out in Schedule 4, then he will serve
notice on the organisation, indicating what alterations are needed
for the purpose of remedying the defect.[1] Of the two sets of criteria,
section 65 provides a collection of " guiding principles in the conduct of every organisation of workers, other than federations of
workers' organisations." These guiding principles apply to both
registered and unregistered organisations and victims of trans-
gressions of them can claim in respect of an unfair industrial practice.[2] Accordingly, they are described in detail later when we come
to consider conduct in relation to internal affairs. For the moment,
it is sufficient to point out that they prescribe safeguards for individuals in relation to admissions, elections, disciplinary action and
procedure, termination of membership and restrictions upon resort
to legal process. In the present context, they empower the registrar
to impose a qualitative check on rules dealing with these topics.
Schedule 4, on the other hand, itemises certain matters on which
the organisation must have rules, without in itself prescribing the
qualitative content of such rules.

Under Schedule 4, the rules must specify the name of the organisation, the address of its principal office and the objects[3] for which it
was established. If the organisation has branches, the rules must
so indicate, and must also indicate the extent to which, and the
manner in which, it has power to control the activities of its branches.
Provision must be made for the election of a governing body and
for its re-election at reasonable intervals, and for the manner in
which members of the governing body can be removed from office.
Similarly, the rules must provide for the election or appointment of
officers and for the manner in which they can be removed from
office. If the organisation has officials who are not officers of the
organisation (whether they are shop stewards, workplace representatives or other officials) provision must be made for their election or
appointment and for the manner in which they can be removed
from office. The rules must specify the powers and duties of the
governing body of the organisation, of each of its officers and of
officials who are not officers of the organisation. They must provide
for the manner in which meetings for transacting any business of
the organisation are to be convened and conducted, and the manner
in which any rules of the organisation can be made, altered or
revoked. They must specify any body by which, and any official
by whom, instructions may be given to members of the organisation
on its behalf for any kind of industrial action, and the circumstances
in which any instructions may be so given.[4] On the question of

---

[1] Industrial Relations Act, 1971, s. 75(1).
[2] S. 66.
[3] Specification of objects will have the effect of delimiting the union's
capacity and will bring into play the *ultra vires* doctrine.
[4] This requirement (para. 10) will be crucial in ascertaining those who have
a defence in respect of the unfair industrial practice under s. 96. See *Infra* p. 489.

elections, provisions must be made as to the manner in which, for any purposes of the organisation, these are to be held or ballots taken, including eligibility for voting in any such election or ballot, the procedure preparatory to any such election or ballot, the procedure for counting and scrutiny of votes and ballot papers and the procedure for the declaration or notification of the result of any such election or ballot.   If the organisation is a federation of workers' organisations its rules must specify the circumstances (if any) in which the organisation has power to enter into agreements on behalf of its constituent or affiliated organisations.   Provision must also be made for the circumstances and the manner in which the organisation can be dissolved.

Schedule 4 goes on to require provision to be made in the rules for certain matters relating to members of the organisation.   Thus, they must specify the descriptions of persons who are eligible for membership and the procedure for dealing with applications for membership, including provision for appeals against decisions of the committee or other body responsible for determining such applications.   They must also specify the contributions payable in respect of membership and the procedure and penalties in case of default in payment of contributions.   On the question of discipline, there must be itemised (a) any descriptions of conduct in respect of which disciplinary action (whether by way of suspension, expulsion or otherwise) can be taken by or on behalf of the organisation against any of its members; (b) the nature of the disciplinary action which can be so taken in respect of each such description of conduct; and (c) the procedure for taking disciplinary action, including provision for appeals against decisions of the committee or other body responsible for taking it.   The rules must also specify the circumstances in which, and the procedure, other than expulsion by way of disciplinary action, by which membership of the organisation can be terminated.   Also, a procedure must be provided for inquiring into any complaint of a member of the organisation that action contrary to the rules of the organisation has been taken by the organisation or by any official of the organisation.

The final concern of Schedule 4 is that the rules contain certain provisions relating to the property and finances of the organisation. Thus, there must be defined the purposes for which, and the manner in which, any property or funds of the organisation are authorised to be applied or invested.   If any financial benefits are to be available to members of the organisation out of its property or funds, the rules must make provision as to the amounts of those benefits and the circumstances in which they are to be available to members. The rules must also provide (a) for the keeping of proper accounting records, and for the preparation and auditing of accounts, in accordance with the provisions of the Act,[1] (b) as to the rights of members

---

[1] See ss. 87 and 88 and Sched. 5.

to inspect the accounting records and the register of members; and (c) for the distribution of the property and funds of the organisation in the event of its being dissolved.

Where, by reason of special circumstances relating to a particular trade union, it appears to the registrar that a particular requirement of Schedule 4 would be inappropriate, he may waive that requirement.

It will be recalled that, if the registrar considers an organisation's rules to be inconsistent with the guiding principles of section 65, or not to comply with the requirements of Schedule 4, he will serve notice on the organisation, indicating what alterations in the rules are necessary. Such notice will specify a reasonable period for the organisation to alter its rules in accordance with the notice and to submit them as altered to the registrar for his approval.[1] If an organisation then submits its altered rules before the end of the specified period, but the registrar considers that they still do not comply with the requirements of the notice, he may, if he thinks fit, allow the organisation a further reasonable period to alter and submit its rules.[2] Only when he is satisfied that the rules comply with the statutory criteria and have been altered in the manner required by him, will the registrar approve the rules of an organisation.

The registrar may apply to the Industrial Court for an order directing the registration of a trade union to be cancelled on the grounds—(a) that the organisation has not submitted its rules to him within the period specified by him in a notice requiring alteration of the rules; or (b) that the rules submitted to him were defective and that the defect was not remedied within the period so specified.[3] If the Industrial Court finds that the grounds of the application are well-founded, the court will, at its discretion, either (a) make an order allowing a further period for alteration of the rules and submitting them as altered to the registrar; or (b) make an order directing the registrar to cancel the registration.[4] Conversely, where a trade union has submitted its rules to the registrar within the specified period, but the registrar has not approved the rules, the union itself may apply to the Industrial Court for an order (a) allowing it a further period for altering its rules and submitting them as altered to the registrar, or (b) directing the registrar to approve the rules as already submitted to him.[5]

(2) The Provisional Register.—The Act also provides for the

---

[1] S. 75(2). Where the organisation's own rules require a longer period for amendment than that specified as " reasonable " by the registrar, the organisation's own rules will be dispensed with s. 94.

[2] S. 75(3).

[3] S. 76(1). Extensions of the specified period under s. 75(3) must also have expired.

[4] S. 76(2).

[5] S. 76(3). For the role of the registrar in relation to subsequent amendments to a union's rules, see ss. 89 and 93, considered, *infra*.

institution of a provisional register to facilitate the period of transition following the coming into force of the Act, and to make it more difficult for organisations to remain outside the reach of registration. The registrar is charged with the duty of establishing this provisional register and maintaining it until all entries in it have been cancelled.[1] He is bound to enter in it every organisation which, immediately before the passing of the Industrial Relations Act, was registered as a trade union under the Trade Union Acts, 1871–1964, and any organisation which was not so registered, but which makes application to him within six months of the passing of the Industrial Relations Act to enter it on the grounds that it is a trade union within the meaning of the Trade Union Acts.[2] In the case of each organisation which is entered in the provisional register, the registrar will consider its eligibility for full registration within the meaning of section 67.[3] If, within six months of its entry in the provisional register, the registrar is satisfied as to such eligibility, he will cancel the entry, register the organisation under the Industrial Relations Act as a trade union, and issue to it a certificate of such registration.[4] If, on the other hand, the registrar is not satisfied as to such eligibility, he will serve on the organisation a notice stating that fact. He will then cancel the entry in the provisional register unless, within six months of the service of the notice, he is satisfied that the organisation would have to alter its rules in order to attain eligibility and that it is taking all necessary steps for the purpose of so altering its rules.[5] Where the registrar refrains in this way from cancelling an entry in the provisional register, he will serve on the organisation another notice, allowing it such further period as he may consider appropriate for enabling it to make the requisite alterations in its rules.[6] If by the end of this period, the organisation does not make an application for registration under section 68,[7] the registrar will cancel its entry in the provisional register. If the organisation does make an application for registration under section 68 within the notice period, and as a consequence of that application the organisation is registered as a trade union, the registrar will cancel its entry in the provisional register as soon as the organisation is so registered. But if such an application for full registration is not successful, the registrar will cancel the entry in the provisional register as soon as he has given his decision on the application and the time for appealing against that decision has expired without

---

[1] S. 78(1).
[2] S. 78(2) and (3). In either case, the registrar must cancel the registration if requested to do so by the organisation—s. 92(1) (a). See *infra*, p. 467.
[3] As to which, see *supra*, p. 459.
[4] S. 79(1).
[5] S. 79(2).
[6] S. 79(3). Again, if the organisation's own rules require a longer period for alteration than that specified by the registrar, the organisation's own rules will be dispensed with—s. 94.
[7] As to which, see *supra*, p. 459.

any such appeal having been brought or, on any such appeal, his decision has been upheld by the Industrial Court.[1]

Although entry in the provisional register does not constitute registration as a trade union under the Act, it does provide a transitional status with some of the consequences of full registration, in that provisional registration is deemed to be the equal of full registration for some purposes[2] of the Act, but not for others.[3]

(3) Administrative Provisions Relating to Registered Trade Unions.—Trade unions which are registered as such under the Industrial Relations Act become obliged to comply with certain administrative requirements designed to institutionalise accountability to the membership, the registrar and members of the public. To this end, every trade union must cause to be kept proper accounting records with respect to its transactions and its assets and liabilities and must establish and maintain a satisfactory system of control of its accounting records, its cash holdings and all its receipts and remittances. " Proper accounting records " must be such as to give a true and fair view of the state of the affairs of the trade union and to explain its transactions. There must also be kept a register of members in such form as the registrar may require.[4] Having thus ensured the keeping of proper records, the Act goes on to provide for the dissemination of certain information. Every trade union must send to the registrar an annual return relating to its affairs and must appoint an auditor or auditors to audit the accounts contained in its annual return.[5] It must also publish an annual report[6] relating to its activities either by supplying a copy free of charge to every member or by including it in a journal relating to its affairs which is available to all its members.[7] Furthermore, it is bound, at the request of any person, whether he be a member or not, to supply to him a copy of its rules either free of charge or on payment of a reasonable charge.[8] Any person may

---

[1] S. 79(4). For further provision in respect of cancellation of entry in the provisional register, see *Cancellation of Registration, infra.*

[2] In particular, ss. 5 (rights of workers), 96 and 97 (two general unfair industrial practices), 117 (limitation on awards of compensation), 153 (recovery of sums awarded in proceedings involving trade unions) and 155 (nominations by members of trade unions).

[3] The officials of such organisations do not receive the protection provided by sections 101(4) and 119(4). Nor can the organisations themselves conclude enforceable agency shop agreements or closed shop agreements eligible for approval, or apply for sole bargaining agencies.

[4] S. 87.

[5] S. 88(1) and (2).

[6] Every annual report must include, *inter alia*, a full reproduction of the last annual return sent to the registrar before the publication of the annual report—Sched. 5, para. 23(1).

[7] S. 88(3). The registrar may exempt unions with small memberships from this obligation, but, if he does so, they are under a duty to supply to each member free of charge a copy of the current annual return—s. 88(4) and (5).

[8] S. 88(6).

also apply to a trade union of which he is not a member for a copy of its latest annual report and will be entitled to receive a copy of it on payment of such sum as may be prescribed.[1]   Detailed provision is made in Schedule 5 with respect to the compilation of the annual return, the qualifications, appointment, removal and functions of auditors, the contents of the annual report, and the maintenance of members' superannuation schemes.

In addition to its annual return, a trade union must send to the registrar—(a) a copy of all changes which it makes in its rules, whether by altering or revoking existing rules or adding new rules; (b) a note of all changes in its officers; and (c) a note of any change in the address of its principal office.   Any such copy or note must be sent within one month of the change occurring and must be accompanied by the appropriate fee.[2]   On receipt of a copy of a change in a union's rules, the registrar will register the change and, as soon as practicable thereafter, examine the rules as they have effect in consequence of the change.[3]   The provisions of sections 75 and 76 (which we saw operating in the context of the examination and approval of rules by the registrar as soon as practicable after the first issue of a certificate of registration) apply also in respect of examination and approval of changes in the rules.[4]

If a trade union refuses or wilfully neglects to perform a duty imposed by sections 87 to 89 or by Schedule 5, it will be guilty of an offence, and any such offence committed by a trade union will be deemed also to have been committed by any officer of the union who is bound by its rules to perform on its behalf the duty of which the offence is a breach.[5]   However, the officer will have a defence if he can prove that he had reasonable grounds to believe, and did believe, that some other person, who was competent and reliable, was authorised to perform the duty instead of him and would perform it.[6]   The penalty for this offence is a fine not exceeding £100.[7]

It is also an offence for any person, with intent to falsify it or to enable a trade union to evade any of the statutory duties under consideration, wilfully to alter any document which is required for the purposes of any of such duties.[8]   The penalty for this more serious offence is a fine not exceeding £400.[9]

---

[1] Sched. 5, para. 24.
[2] S. 89.   The fee laid down in the Act is £10 or such other sums as may be prescribed.
[3] Ss. 89(3) and 93.
[4] Once again temporal restrictions on amendment in the union's own rules may be dispensed with—s. 94.
[5] S. 91(1) and (2).
[6] S. 91(3).
[7] S. 91(5) (a).
[8] S. 91(4).
[9] S. 91(5) (b).

If it appears to the registrar that there are reasonable grounds for believing that a trade union is insolvent, he may appoint an inspector to examine into and report on its affairs. If such a report confirms the belief that the union is insolvent, then, unless it is already in the course of being wound up, the registrar may petition for its winding-up.[1]

(4) Cancellation of Registration.—In addition to his right to seek from the Industrial Court an order under section 76 directing him to cancel the registration of an organisation,[2] the registrar may also cancel a registration in pursuance of either of two other provisions. First, the registrar may apply to the Industrial Court for an order directing a registration to be cancelled on the grounds that—(*a*) the registration was obtained by fraud or mistake; or (*b*) by reason of a change in its rules or other change of circumstances, the organisation has ceased to be eligible for registration under the Act; or (*c*) the organisation has refused or failed to comply with any requirement (other than a requirement relating to its rules) imposed on it by or under Part IV[3] of the Act, and has persisted in its default after the registrar has given it notice specifying the default and fixing a time of not less than two months for remedying the fault, and that time has expired.[4] This latter ground should become particularly important as a sanction in respect of the provisions establishing the accountability of a registered union which we considered earlier. If the Industrial Court is satisfied that the grounds of the registrar's application are well-founded, then, if the grounds are those specified in (*a*) or (*b*), above, it will order cancellation; but if the grounds are those specified in (*c*), above, it may order either an extension of the time for remedying the default or cancellation, as it considers appropriate in the circumstances.[5]

Secondly, the registrar will cancel the entry of an organisation on either the provisional register or the full register if—(*a*) he is requested by the organisation to do so,[6] or (*b*) he is satisfied that the organisation has ceased to exist. In either case, he must publicise the cancellation in the London and Edinburgh Gazettes.[7]

(5) The Special Register.—Another duty of the registrar is to institute and maintain a register to be known as "the special

---

[1] S. 90. An inspector appointed under this section may require production of books and documents of the union, examine on oath any of its officers, members or employees, and may administer such oath. The winding-up of registered unions is carried out under Part IX of the Companies Act, 1948, the union being regarded as an unregistered company—Industrial Relations Act, 1971, s. 156.

[2] As to which, see *supra*, p. 463.   [3] *I.e.* Ss. 61–95.   [4] S. 77(1).

[5] S. 77(2) and (3).

[6] The T.U.C. policy on non-registration has led to a large number of unions leaving the register. At the time of writing the position is very fluid.

[7] S. 92.

register,"[1] the aim of which is to apply some of the provisions of the Industrial Relations Act in respect of registered trade unions, to certain other bodies, notably professional associations. To be eligible for entry in the special register, an organisation must in the first place be either a company which was registered as such under the Companies Act, 1948, before the passing of the Industrial Relations Act, or an organisation not so registered, but incorporated by charter or letters patent before or after the passing of the Industrial Relations Act.[2]   An organisation which falls into one of these categories will be eligible if (*a*) it is an independent organisation consisting wholly or mainly of workers of one or more descriptions; (*b*) its activities include the regulation of relations between such workers and employers or organisations of employers;[3] and (*c*) it has power, without the concurrence of any parent organisation, to alter its own rules and to control the application of its own property and funds.[4] Alternatively, it will be eligible if it is a federation of similar bodies.[5]

Any organisation which establishes its eligibility under the above provisions may apply for entry in the special register.   Its application must be accompanied by a copy of its rules, a list of its officers and the names and addresses of its branches (if any).[6]   If the registrar is satisfied as to eligibility and compliance with these formalities, he will, on payment of the appropriate fee, enter the organisation in the special register as an organisation of workers or a federation of workers' organisations, as the case may be, and issue to it a certificate of such registration.[7]

For the most part, the provisions of the Industrial Relations Act operate in relation to an organisation entered in the special register in precisely the same way in which they operate in relation to a registered trade union.[8]   However, some provisions do not apply to organisations on the special register.[9]   Significantly the provisions as to the keeping of accounts and a register of members,[10] the annual return, audit, annual report and members' superannuation schemes,[11] and the power of the registrar to inspect and apply for a winding-up order,[12] are among those which do not apply.   The organisations in

---

[1] S. 84(1).
[2] S. 84(2).
[3] Regard is to be had to the activities actually carried on by the organisation and not to whether or not they are in accordance with the organisation's memorandum and articles of association or its charter on letters patent—s. 85(4).
[4] S. 84(3).   For the meaning of " parent organisation," see s. 84(5).
[5] S. 84(4).
[6] S. 85(2).
[7] S. 85(3) and (5).   The appropriate fee is £25 or such other amount as may be prescribed.
[8] S. 86(2).
[9] S. 86(3).
[10] S. 87.
[11] S. 88.
[12] S. 90.

question, however, will still be subjected to the provisions as to accountability comprised in the Act, charter or letters patent under which they exist.

(6) Restrictions on Registration under other Acts.—Registration as a trade union under the Industrial Relations Act is the only course of statutory registration open to an organisation of workers. Such organisations are prohibited from registering in the future as a company under the Companies Act, 1948, or under the Friendly Societies Act, 1896, or under the Industrial and Provident Societies Act, 1965.[1] Also any such registration of an organisation of workers which was effected before the commencement of the Industrial Relations Act is rendered void,[2] except that registration as a company under the Companies Act, 1948, will survive if the organisation is entered in the special register pursuant to an application made within six months of section 85 coming into force.[3]

(7) Summary of Legal Consequences of Registration and of Non-Registration.—As we have already noted, the Industrial Relations Act accords vastly different treatment to trade unions registered under its provisions, as against organisations which are not so registered. The aim is to make registration the more attractive course to follow. It is therefore convenient at this stage to summarise the main consequences of registration and non-registration or de-registration.

Registration confers upon a trade union corporate status, with the immediate legal consequences which such status implies.[4] Once registered, a union will be permitted, unlike an unregistered organisation, to enter into agency shop agreements and approved closed shop agreements;[5] to invoke the machinery for remedying non-existent or defective procedure agreements;[6] to be appointed a sole bargaining agent by order of the Industrial Court;[7] and to go to the Industrial Court to complain of certain breaches of duty on the part of employers in connection with agency shops, sole bargaining agencies and the disclosure of information for purposes of collective bargaining.[8] Furthermore, a registered trade union is incapable of committing the very general unfair industrial practice of inducing or threatening to induce a breach of contract,[9] and is given some protection in respect of industrial action in support of

---

[1] S. 157(1).
[2] S. 157(3).
[3] S. 157(2).
[4] See s. 74, *supra*, p. 460.
[5] See ss. 11–18, *supra*, pp. 58.
[6] See ss. 37–43.
[7] See s. 50, *infra*, p. 497.
[8] See ss. 101 and 102, the " enforcement sections " in respect of, *inter alia*, ss. 13, 16, 54, 55 and 56. Access to the Industrial Arbitration Board under ss. 125 and 126 is also restricted to registered unions.
[9] See s. 96, *infra*, p. 489.

another unfair industrial practice.[1]   The members of a registered
trade union benefit from the rights as against their employers, of
membership and participation in trade union activity,[2] and also from
consequential protection under the unfair dismissal provisions.[3]
Also officials of registered trade unions are less exposed to actions in
the Industrial Court than are their brethren in unregistered
organisations.[4]   Moreover, the funds of registered trade unions
receive the protection of the statutory limitation as to the quantum
of compensation which may be awarded against such unions.[5]   In
addition to these advantages of registration which arise from the
Industrial Relations Act itself, certain other enactments provide
for the preferential treatment of registered trade unions (which
now means registered under the 1971 Act).   Thus, the tax exemptions in relation to provident funds is restricted to registered unions,[6]
as is the capacity to report claims to the Secretary of State under
section 8 of the Terms and Conditions of Employment Act, 1959.[7]

The other side of the registration coin is characterised by the
requirements as to accountability to members, the registrar and
the public, along the lines which we saw earlier in this chapter.[8]
Unregistered organisations are not susceptible to any similar
requirements.

3.   CONDUCT IN RELATION TO INTERNAL AFFAIRS AND THE SETTLE-MENT OF INTERNAL DISPUTES

In common with all large organisations, trade unions, by their very
nature, generate a measure of internal conflict.   Our next concern
is to see the extent to which the law provides a basis for the resolution of such conflict. In other words, how far does membership of a
trade union give rise to legally enforceable rights and duties?   To
answer this question it is first necessary to understand the legal
nature of union membership.

Membership of all unions, registered or unregistered, is founded
on contract.   In the case of a union registered under the Industrial
Relations Act, the member is in a contractual relationship with the
union itself, which, by virtue of its incorporation, is a distinct legal
entity.   As we have already seen, the rule book upon which member-

---

[1] See s. 97, infra, p. 494.   [2] See s. 5, supra, p. 105.
[3] See ss. 22 et seq., supra, p. 105.   For a further benefit to individual
members, see s. 155 (nominations).
[4] See ss. 96, 101(4), 119(4), 139(5) and 143(6).
[5] See s. 117, infra, p. 512.
[6] Income and Corporation Taxes Act, 1970, s. 338.
[7] For further examples, see Insurance Companies Act, 1958, s. 1 and Companies Act, 1967, s. 60, concerning the provident activities of trade unions, both
of which are restricted to unions registered under the 1971 Act by amendments
to them enacted in Sched. 8 to the Industrial Relations Act.
[8] See also the extensive inquisitorial powers of the registrar under s. 83,
considered and his role in the settlement of domestic disputes in registered trade
unions under ss. 81–82 considered infra, p. 479.

ship of a registered trade union is based will, as soon after registration as is practicable, be subjected to scrutiny by the registrar to ensure that it conforms to the requirements of Schedule 4 and contains nothing inconsistent with the guiding principles set out in section 65. However, in an unregistered organisation, such is not the case. The organisation does not possess corporate personality, and therefore membership of it is based on a multilateral contract of association between all the members at any particular time. The legal problems, both substantive and procedural, which this raises are well-known, particularly those relating to the holding of property, suing and being sued and vicarious liability.[1] Also the rule book of an unregistered organisation will not have been subjected to the scrutiny and control of the registrar. Consequently, it is more likely to be silent, obscure, contradictory, unfair or otherwise defective or deficient on important points dealt with in Schedule 4 and section 65. However, regardless of what an unregistered organisation's rule book may provide, such an organisation must conform in its conduct with the guiding principles of section 65 and with its own rules to the extent that these are not inconsistent with section 65.

The picture which emerges is that members of both registered and unregistered unions have rights and duties which arise from the rules of the organisation and from section 65, but, in the case of unregistered unions, no system of administrative control exists to ensure that the rules are consistent with section 65. Members and certain other persons,[2] who are aggrieved by any internal act or omission of, or on behalf of, the organisation, will be able to seek redress on the ground that the act or omission amounts to either a breach of the organisation's rules or an unfair industrial practice under section 66 which provides that it is unfair for any organisation of workers, or any official or a person acting on behalf or such an organisation, to take or threaten to take any action against any member of the organisation or other person in contravention of the principles set out in section 65.[3]

(1) The " Guiding Principles."—The principles set out in section 65 are to be guiding principles in the conduct of every organ-

---

[1] See Grunfeld, *Modern Trade Union Law*, pp. 38–49, for a consideration of these problems, especially that of suing an unregistered union, and see Industrial Relations Act, s. 154. However, the difficulty of suing an unregistered union does not affect the right of a member to sue other members and officials whom he considers to have damaged him by acting in contravention of the union's rules. Such personal liability is not hampered by the lack of incorporation.

[2] Notably (*a*) persons who were members but whose membership has been terminated otherwise than by voluntary registration, and (*b*) rejected applicants for membership.

[3] Although breach of rules and the s. 66 unfair industrial practice will be the most common causes of action in domestic disputes, other possibilities remain, *e.g.* tortious situations such as *Huntley* v. *Thornton*, [1957] 1 All E.R. 234; [1957] 1 W.L.R. 321, and actions against the trustees of the property of an unregistered organisation.

isation of workers', other than federations of workers, organisations.[1] The first topic dealt with is that of admission. It is provided that any applicant for membership who is (a) a worker of the description or one of the descriptions of which the organisation is, in accordance with its rules, intended wholly or mainly to consist, and (b) appropriately qualified for employment as a worker of that description, shall not be excluded from membership by way of any arbitrary or unreasonable discrimination.[2] Traditionally at common law, a rejected applicant for membership was unable to complain that his application had been improperly processed or that the decision to reject him (or the rule upon which it was based) was unreasonable. As he was not a party to the rule book contract, he could not sue upon it. Nor were any other common law concepts able to assist him. This was particularly serious in closed shop situations, where the union concerned could regulate the supply of labour by its control over admissions to membership, even to the extent of excluding workers who had been trained at Government training centres.[3] Although trade unionists have been vociferous in seeking to justify this power, there were signs in recent years of the courts beginning to eschew common law notions in the search for legal protection. In *Nagle* v. *Fielden*[4] a female trainer of racehorses was refused a licence by the Jockey Club Stewards because of her sex. The Court of Appeal considered that *prima facie* it was arguable that the courts could prevent such discrimination. Lord DENNING, M. R., said:[5]

> " We live in days when many trading or professional associations operate ' closed shops '. No person can work at his trade or profession except by their permission. They can deprive him of his livelihood. When a man is wrongly rejected or ousted by one of these associations, has he no remedy? I think that he may well have, even though he can show no contract. The courts have power to grant him a declaration that his rejection and ouster was invalid and an injunction requiring the association to rectify their error. He may not be able to get damages unless he can show a contract or a tort; but he may get a declaration and injunction."

Although this statement was made in a case which did not involve a trade union in the conventional sense, it was expressed in terms which were referable to trade unions and is entirely consistent with other judgments of Lord DENNING which purport to establish wide judicial control over the rules and internal conduct of unions.[6]

---

[1] S. 65(1).
[2] S. 65(2).
[3] See Report of Royal Commission on Trade Unions and Employers' Associations, 1965–1968, Cmnd. 3623, paras. 345–348.
[4] [1966] 2 Q.B. 633; [1966] 1 All E.R. 689. These were interlocutory proceedings. The parties settled their differences before they could come to trial.
[5] [1966] 2 Q.B. at p. 646.
[6] See *Bonsor* v. *Musicians' Union*, [1954] Ch. 479, at p. 488; *Edwards* v. *Society of Graphical and Allied Trades*, [1971] Ch. at p. 365; [1970] 3 All E.R. 689.

However, the approach of Lord DENNING, based on "the right to work ", is not shared by all his fellow judges and, in particular, it is difficult to reconcile with the judgment of DIPLOCK, L. J., in *Faramus* v. *Film Artistes' Association*[1] which was subsequently supported in the House of Lords.[2] The position immediately before the Industrial Relations Act was therefore one of considerable uncertainty. The new guiding principle on admission has removed the problem of *locus standi* in that a rejected applicant now has an enforceable right not to be arbitrarily or unreasonably discriminated against at the admission stage. However, it has brought with it a new uncertainty, for it will be some time before the criteria of arbitrariness and unreasonableness are elucidated by a process of interpretation, especially since the eclipse of the closed shop as hitherto understood should reduce the seriousness of rejection.[3] Finally on the subject of admission, it will be recalled that, by virtue of Schedule 4,[4] all *registered* trade unions will have rules specifying the descriptions of persons who are eligible for membership and the procedure for dealing with applications for membership, including provision for appeals against decisions of the committee or other body responsible for determining such applications.

The second guiding principle gives to every member the right, on giving reasonable notice and complying with any reasonable conditions, to terminate his membership of the organisation at any time.[5] This provision requires no explanation. It is probable that in the past the courts would have considered any union rule which purported to deprive a member of such a right, to be void on grounds of public policy.[6]

There follows a group of guiding principles, the aim of which is to secure fairness in the conduct of union elections and meetings.[7] Previously, such matters were regulated by the union's own rules, over which it had complete freedom. A member who wished to complain about the conduct of an election would have to establish a breach of the rules (which might have been archaic, skeletal or otherwise defective) or some contravention of the general law.[8] The guiding principles seek to guarantee to individual members the right to basic democratic safeguards. Thus, no member may, by

---

[1] [1963] 2 Q.B. 527 at pp. 554–556.
[2] [1964] A.C. 925 at pp. 940, 943 and 947–948.
[3] The guiding principle applies of course regardless of whether or not there is an agency shop or approved closed shop in existence.
[4] Para. 14.
[5] S. 65(3).
[6] See Grunfeld, *Modern Trade Union Law*, pp. 35–36.
[7] For the extent to which the rules of a registered trade union must have provisions as to elections and meetings, see Sched. 4, paras. 4, 5, 6, 8 and 11, considered *supra*, p. 461.
[8] The *cause celebre* of *Byrne and Chapple* v. *Foulkes et al.* (1962), unreported concerning ballot-rigging in the Electrical Trades Union, was an action in conspiracy. For an account, see Rolph, *All Those in Favour? The E.T.U. Trial.*

way of any arbitrary or unreasonable discrimination, be excluded from—(a) being a candidate for, or holding any office in the organisation, or in a branch or section of it; (b) nominating candidates for any such office; (c) voting in any election for any such office or in any ballot of members; or (d) attending and taking part in meetings of the organisation or of any branch or section of it.[1]   The voting in any ballot of members must be kept secret;[2] and in any ballot, and in any motion, in respect of which he is entitled to vote, every member of the organisation must be given a fair and reasonable opportunity of voting without interference or constraint.[3]

The guiding principles then go on to deal with disciplinary action.[4] Members must not be subjected by or on behalf of the organisation to any unfair or unreasonable disciplinary action.[5]   Again as a general principle, this will need to be given meaning by the process of interpretation.   However, without prejudice to the generality of this principle, three grounds of disciplinary action are stated to be unreasonable: refusing or failing—(a) to take any action which would constitute an unfair industrial practice on the part of the member himself; (b) to take part in a strike which the organisation, or any other person, has called, organised, procured or financed otherwise than in contemplation or furtherance of an industrial dispute, or in such circumstances as to constitute an unfair industrial practice on the part of the organisation or of that person; and (c) to take part in any irregular industrial action short of a strike which the organisation, or any other person, has organised, procured or financed as mentioned in (b), above.[6]   Thus, disciplinary measures may not be taken against members who will not participate in industrial action which is *either* an unfair industrial practice on the part of the member, the organisation or any person instituting such action, *or* taken otherwise than in contemplation or furtherance of an industrial dispute.   The latter provision would be particularly relevant to " political " strikes.   In this way, the hold of the organisation over its members in the context of industrial action which is in any way unfair has been loosened to a considerable extent.   It should also be remembered that, in contrast to the duty to refrain from disciplining non-participants under the present provisions, an organisation may find itself obliged to take disciplinary action against members who, without authority, break legally

---

[1] Industrial Relations Act, 1971, s. 65(4).
[2] *Ibid.*, s. 65(5).
[3] *Ibid.*, s. 65(6).
[4] Reference should again be made to the extent to which the requirements of Sched. 4 (paras. 14–18) will govern the rules of registered trade unions in this area.   See p. 461 *supra*.
[5] Industrial Relations Act, 1971, s. 65 (7).
[6] For these purposes, the statutory definitions of " strike " (s. 167(1)) and " irregular industrial action short of a strike " (s. 33(4)) are amended, so as to embrace non-industrially-motivated action (s. 65(11)).   The normal definitions of these terms are considered later in this chapter.

binding, collective agreements.[1] The combination of these provisions represents an immense change in the relationship between organisation and member.

This regulation of the substance of disciplinary action is novel. The ensuing concern with procedural fairness is not and is, for the most part, reflective of the manner in which the courts were developing the law in the years leading up to the Industrial Relations Act. Dealing with disciplinary action for reasons other than non-payment of contributions, the Act provides that a member must not be subjected to disciplinary action by or on behalf of the organisation unless—(a) he has had written notice of the charges brought against him and has been given a reasonable time to prepare his defence; (b) he is afforded a full and fair hearing; (c) a written statement of the findings resulting from the hearing is given to him; and (d) where under the rules of the organisation he has a right of appeal,[2] his appeal has been heard or the time for appealing has expired without his having exercised that right.[3] Insofar as these provisions make it clear beyond all doubt that rules akin to the rules of natural justice must be observed in disciplinary procedures, they are most welcome. In the past there was considerable uncertainty as to the circumstances in which, and the basis upon which, the courts would insist upon compliance with natural justice.[4] Section 65 makes it clear that disciplinary action (except in cases of non-payment of contributions) must always be conducted in conformity with the Act's version of natural justice. However, some areas of doubt still remain. No mention is made in the Act of the right to legal representation before domestic tribunals—a question on which the common law is unclear.[5] There is no statutory insistence on compliance with natural justice in circumstances other than disciplinary proceedings, although there have been recent suggestions of the need for observance of at least some rules of procedural fairness in certain other circumstances.[6] Nor is the opportunity taken to

---

[1] Industrial Relations Act, 1971, s. 36(2).

[2] In the case of a registered trade union, the member is bound to have such a right—Sched. 4, para. 16(c).

[3] *Ibid.*, s. 65(8).

[4] Compare *Russell* v. *Duke of Norfolk*, [1948] 1 All E.R. 488, affirmed [1949] 1 All E.R. 109; *Lawlor* v. *Union of Post Office Workers*, [1965] Ch. 712; [1965] 1 All E.R. 353; *Gaiman* v. *National Association for Mental Health*, [1971] Ch. 317; [1970] 2 All E.R. 362 at p. 378; *John* v. *Rees*, [1969] 2 All E.R. 274; [1969] 2 W.L.R. 1294; *Edwards* v. *Society of Graphical and Allied Trades*, [1971] Ch. 354; [1970] 3 All E.R. 689, C.A.

[5] Compare *Pett* v. *Greyhound Racing Association, Ltd.* [1969] 1 Q.B. 125; [1968] 2 All E.R. 545; *Pett* v. *Greyhound Racing Association, (No. 2),* [1970] 1 Q.B. 46; [1969] 2 All E.R. 221; *Enderby Town Football Club, Ltd.* v. *Football Association, Ltd.,* [1971] Ch. 591; [1971] 1 All E.R. 215.

[6] See *Breen* v. *Amalgamated Engineering Union,* [1971] 2 Q.B. 175; [1971] 1 All E.R. 1148, in which the majority of the Court of Appeal held that a district committee should have observed the rules of natural justice when vetting the plaintiff member's election of a shop steward.

provide for the situations where non-compliance with the rules of natural justice (or their statutory equivalent) by an inferior decision-making body within the organisation is followed by an appeal to a superior domestic tribunal which, after full observance of the rules, reaches the same decision on the merits as did the inferior body. In *Leary* v. *National Union of Vehicle Builders*,[1] it was held that in such circumstances the deficiency of natural justice before the inferior tribunal could not be cured by a sufficiency of natural justice before the appellate tribunal. This decision will be equally applicable after the Industrial Relations Act.

The procedural requirements of Section 65 which we have just considered are not applicable to disciplinary action in respect of non-payment of contributions. However, the guiding principles go on to provide more generally that a person's membership must not be terminated unless reasonable notice of the proposal to terminate it, and the reason for it, has been given to him.[2]   This covers, *inter alia*, termination for non-payment of contributions and requires a sort of attenuated natural justice. It proscribes the practice of " automatic forfeiture " of membership for falling into serious arrears with one's contributions, but it does not go as far as the recent judicial consideration of this practice. In *Edwards* v. *Society of Graphical and Allied Trades*[3] an " automatic forfeiture " rule was found unacceptable by the Court of Appeal and compliance with natural justice was held to be a prerequisite of exclusion, even for non-payment of contributions.[4]

The final guiding principle prohibits the placing of any restriction whether by the rules of the organisation or otherwise, on any member in respect of his instituting, prosecuting or defending proceedings before any court or tribunal or giving evidence in any such proceedings.[5]   One of the consequences of this provision is that an organisation is not able, by its rules, to oblige a member to exhaust his rights of appeal within the organisation before seeking redress from the appropriate court. Thus, the doctrine of exhaustion of domestic remedies, which had already been emasculated by the courts,[6] has now been finally laid to rest, notwithstanding the fact that registered trade unions at least are under a statutory obligation to provide

---

[1] [1971] Ch. 34; [1970] 2 All E.R. 713.   See Kay, (1971) 34 *M.L.R.* 86.
[2] Industrial Relations Act, 1971, s. 65(9).
[3] [1971] Ch. 354; [1970] 3 All E.R. 689, C.A.
[4] The case was decided against the background of a closed shop.   " Automatic forfeiture " rules became common mainly as a matter of administrative convenience.   However, from 1871 until 1971, unions were unable to sue members in respect of arrears of subscription (Trade Unions Act, 1871, s. 4(2)). This is no longer so since the Industrial Relations Act.
[5] S. 65 (10).
[6] See *Annamunthodo* v. *Oilfield Workers' Union*, [1961] A.C. 945; [1961] 3 All E.R. 621, P.C.; *Lawlor* v. *Union of Post Office Workers*, [1965] Ch. 712; [1965] 1 All E.R. 353; *Leigh* v. *National Union of Railwaymen*, [1970] Ch. 326; [1969] 3 All E.R. 1249; *Leary* v. *National Union of Vehicle Builders*, [1971] Ch. 34; [1970] 2 All E.R. 713.

domestic appellate machinery.[1] Resort to such machinery is, it would seem, entirely voluntary.[2]

(2) Restraint of Trade.—From what has been said, it will be appreciated that the two main sources of legal obligation in relation to the internal affairs of unions are the unions' own rules and the guiding principles of section 65. When considering the legal enforceability of union rules, it is necessary to remind ourselves of the historical origins of such enforceability. To reach the stage where union rules were lawful, let alone legally enforceable, the unions had to fight off the common law doctrine of restraint of trade, under which they had laboured in the middle of the nineteenth century.[3] Release from the doctrine was given by the legislature in the 1871 Act,[4] one of the aims of which was to render union rules lawful, while keeping some of them unenforceable.[5] However, it was not long before the ambit of statutory unenforceability was narrowed by judicial interpretation,[6] thus rendering most union rules both lawful and legally enforceable. The Industrial Relations Act, 1971, provides release from the doctrine of restraint of trade in the same way as did the 1871 Act. The purposes of any union (whether registered or not) will not, by reason only that they are in restraint of trade, be unlawful so as—(*a*) to make any member of the organisation or body liable to criminal proceedings for conspiracy or otherwise, or (*b*) to make any agreement or trust void or voidable.[7]

Unlike the 1871 Act, the Industrial Relations Act does not go on to itemise certain rules as to which there is restriction on enforceability. However, some restriction is placed on the remedies which are available in one circumstance, for it is provided that no court shall, by granting an injunction restrain an employee from working in accordance with a lawful contract of employment, compel him to take part in a strike (whether lawful or otherwise) or in any irregular industrial action short of a strike.[8] Thus, the courts are again saved from the embarrassment of being asked to bolster union solidarity by compelling participation in industrial action, although it is hardly likely that they would ever have been asked, and, even if they had, it would have been within their discretion to decline. Apart from this provision and the paramountcy of the guiding principles of section 65, there is no statutory

---

[1] Schedule 4, para. 16(*c*).

[2] *Cf.* the duty of the registrar to defer consideration of complaints pending exhaustion—s. 82(3), as to which, see *infra*, p. 479.

[3] Culminating in *Hornby* v. *Close* (1867), L.R. 2 Q.B. 153.

[4] S. 3. Release from possible criminal consequences was provided by s. 2.

[5] *Ibid.*, s. 4.

[6] The milestones were *Wolfe* v. *Matthews* (1882), 21 Ch. D. 194; *Yorkshire Miners' Association* v. *Howden*, [1905] A.C. 256; *Russell* v. *Amalgamated Society of Carpenters and Joiners*, [1912] A.C. 421; and *Amalgamated Society of Carpenters, Cabinet Makers and Joiners* v. *Braithwaite*, [1922] 2 A.C 440.

[7] S. 135, replacing ss. 2 and 3 of the 1871 Act.

[8] S. 128(3).

restriction on the enforceability of union rules.[1]   However, since the remedies sought by aggrieved members are often discretionary, it may well be that courts and Tribunals will refuse to grant them in some circumstances.

Whilst this account of the release of unions from the doctrine of restraint of trade and the consequent rendering of union rules enforceable by the courts and Tribunals is believed to be representative of the intentions of Parliament, a recently ventilated piece of statutory interpretation would, if correct, have the effect of placing additional restrictions on the legality and enforceability of union rules.   In *Edwards* v. *Society of Graphical and Allied Trades*,[2] SACHS, L.J., rationalised his refusal to accept the " automatic forfeiture " rule by reference to the doctrine of restraint of trade.   To the point that this rule, along with all the others, was released from the consequences of the doctrine by section 3 of the 1871 Act, he replied that the release provided by that section[3] was referable only to rules giving expression to the " purposes " of the union.

> " It cannot be said that a rule that enabled such capricious and despotic action is proper to the ' purposes ' of this or indeed of any trade union.   It is thus not protected by section 3. . . . It is thus void as in restraint of trade."[4]

This argument seems to be based on reasoning which had commended itself to Lord DENNING, M.R., in his dissenting judgment in *Faramus* v. *Film Artistes' Association*,[5] but it is strange to see it re-emerge in the light of the views of the majority of the Court of Appeal[6] in that case and their subsequent approval by the House of Lords.[7]   It is submitted, therefore, that the approach of SACHS, L.J., is of dubious validity.

(3) The Processing of Complaints against Unions in respect of their Internal Affairs.—Having ascertained that all unions, whether registered or not, must act in compliance with their own rules and with the guiding principles set out in section 65 of the Industrial Relations Act, it is next necessary to consider the ways in which complaints of non-compliance may be processed.[8]   It must

---

[1] But there may be further common law restrictions as to substance because of illegability, although the extent to which the courts will interfere with union rules is, as we saw when considering admissions, *supra*, p. 472, far from clear.

[2] [1971] Ch. at p. 365; [1970] 3 All E.R. 689.

[3] And, therefore, by the Industrial Relations Act, 1971, s. 128(3), which is, to all intents and purposes, the same.

[4] [1970] 3 All E.R. at p. 700.

[5] [1963] 2 Q.B. 527 at p. 541.

[6] See especially the views of DIPLOCK, L.J., to the effect that s. 3 of the 1871 Act " does . . . give a trade union *carte blanche* to make any rule it likes, however unreasonable it may be in restraint of trade, provided that there is no other ground of illegality " (at p. 559).

[7] [1964] A.C. 925.   See especially Lord EVERSHED (at p. 942).

[8] The processing of complaints in respect of the political fund and amalgamations are dealt with under a separate heading, *infra*, p. 483.

be said that many such complaints will be disposed of without resort to outside bodies. However, our concern is with cases in which the domestic machinery of the organisation has not produced a result satisfactory to the complainant. In these circumstances, a variety of procedural possibilities is born, especially if the particular union is registered.

4. COMPLAINTS AGAINST REGISTERED TRADE UNIONS

(1) Application to the registrar to investigate.—This first possibility is akin to a conciliation stage which is available at the option of the aggrieved person. It is available to any person who (*a*) is a member; or (*b*) was a member and has ceased to be so otherwise than by voluntary resignation; or (*c*) has sought to become a member and has been refused admission or has been prevented (by action taken by or an behalf of the organisation) from obtaining admission to it.[1] Such a person may apply to the registrar on the grounds that action taken against him by or on behalf of the organisation amounted to either an unfair industrial practice under section 66 or a breach of the rules of the organisation.[2] The registrar will not proceed with the application unless he is satisfied that it was made within four weeks after whichever is the latest of the following dates—(*a*) the date, or latest date, of the action to which the application relates; (*b*) the earliest date on which that action came to the knowledge of the applicant; and (*c*) the date on which a complaint made by the applicant to the organisation, having been referred for determination in accordance with a domestic procedure, was finally determined.[3] Moreover, if the registrar considers that an adequate domestic procedure exists for determining such complaints and that there has been no utilisation of that procedure, he will defer consideration of the application. In such circumstances, he will only resume consideration of it if it is re-submitted after the complaint has been referred to the domestic procedure and a reasonable time has been allowed for it to be determined by that procedure.[4] Thus, exhaustion of adequate domestic procedures is required before resort to this conciliation machinery and, consequently, before resort to the other possibilities which are based upon it.[5] However, such exhaustion may be circumvented by a complainant who opts for one of the further possibilities discussed later.

---

[1] Industrial Relations Act, 1971, s. 81(1). Note that this procedure has no application to a federation of workers' organisations—s. 81(2) (*a*).
[2] S. 81(3) But the procedure does not apply to breaches of political fund rules or rules in respect of taking a vote on a resolution to approve an instrument of amalgamation or transfer. Such disputes are considered separately, *infra*, p. 483.
[3] S. 82(2). However, the registrar may waive this limitation period if he is satisfied that in the circumstances it was not practicable for the application to be made before the end of the four week period—*ibid*.
[4] S. 82(3).
[5] See *infra*, p. 480.

Where the registrar proceeds with an application under these provisions,[1] he will investigate the matter to which the application relates and will give notice of his conclusions to the applicant and to the organisation.[2] If he considers that the grounds of the application are well-founded, he will endeavour to promote a settlement of the matter without its becoming the subject of a complaint to an Industrial Tribunal.[3] At this stage, anything communicated to the registrar or his agent will not be admissible in evidence in any subsequent proceedings before the Industrial Court or an Industrial Tribunal, except with the consent of the person who communicated it.[4]

(2) Complaint by the registrar to the Industrial Court.— Where there has been an application to the registrar under section 81 and he considers the grounds of it to be well-founded, then he may present a complaint against the trade union to the Industrial Court if—(*a*) a settlement has not been reached within such time as the registrar considers reasonable in the circumstances, and (*b*) no complaint has been presented to an Industrial Tribunal and it appears to the registrar that the matter is of *such a serious character* that it ought to be brought before the Industrial Court.[5] Where the Industrial Court considers that the grounds of the original application were well-founded, it may, if it considers that it would be just and equitable to do so, grant to the original applicant one or more of the following remedies, viz. (*a*) an order determining the rights of the original applicant and the trade union; (*b*) an award of compensation to be paid by the trade union; or (*c*) an order directing the trade union to refrain from continuing to take the offensive action and any other action of a like nature in relation to the original applicant.[6] It will be noticed that this procedure, like the next one, may be invoked by the registrar without regard to the wishes of the original applicant.

(3) Complaint by the registrar to an Industrial Tribunal.— The distinction between this procedure and the one previously considered is that complaints may only be made to the Industrial Court in cases of " a serious character " or where a mandatory order is sought. Accordingly, the registrar may present a complaint to an Industrial Tribunal if the same conditions (other than the requirement of a " serious character ") are satisfied, the only real difference being that there is one less remedy available.[7]

---

[1] Note that he is not required to proceed with any application which he considers to be frivolous or vexatious—s. 82(4).
[2] S. 82(5).
[3] S. 82(6).
[4] S. 82(7).
[5] S. 103(1).
[6] S. 103(2) and (3).
[7] Ss. 108 and 109.

(4) Investigation initiated by the registrar.—In addition to his powers to take complaints to the Industrial Court or an Industrial Tribunal subsequent to an application having been made to him under section 81, the registrar also has power to act on his own initiative. Where he has reason to suspect *either* that there has been a serious breach, or have been persistent breaches of the rules of a trade union,[1] *or* that there has been a serious contravention or persistent contraventions of the guiding principles set out in section 65, the registrar must investigate the matter.[2] If his investigation confirms his suspicion, he will give notice of his conclusions to the trade union and endeavour to secure such action or such an undertaking on its part as, in his opinion, would be appropriate to remedy or mitigate the consequences and/or to prevent a continuance or repetition of the breaches of rules or of the action in question.[3] Where he is unable to secure such action or such an undertaking and he is satisfied that, in default of such action or such an undertaking, it would be an appropriate case for him to present a complaint to the Industrial Court under section 104,[4] he must give notice to the union to the effect that, unless the necessary action or undertaking is forthcoming within a specified period, it is his intention to present such a complaint.[5] If he then finds that the necessary action or undertaking has not been taken or given within the specified period or that such an undertaking has been given but it has not been fulfilled, the registrar may present a complaint to the Industrial Court.[6] If the court upholds the registrar's contentions, it may make an order directing the union to take such action as, in the opinion of the court, would be necessary to remedy or mitigate the consequences and/or to prevent a continuance or repetition of the breaches of the rules or of the action to which the complaint relates.[7]

In this way, the registrar is empowered to intervene to restrain irregularities about which no member feels sufficiently strongly to institute proceedings. The consequences of this provision could be profound. In addition to serious or persistent irregularities of an undeniably internal nature, it also embraces, for example, persistent breaches of rules delimiting the authority of officials to institute industrial action. As we have seen,[8] all registered trade unions must amend their rules so as to comply with, *inter alia*, the requirements of Schedule 4, paragraph 10 of which insists that the rules specify the persons or bodies authorised to give instructions for any kind of industrial action, and the circumstances in which

---

[1] Other than political fund rules and rules relating to voting on an instrument of amalgamation or transfer, as to which see *infra*, p. 483.
[2] S. 83(1).
[3] S. 83(3).
[4] As to which, see *infra*.
[5] S. 83(4).
[6] S. 104(1).
[7] S. 104 (2).
[8] *Supra*, p. 461.

such instructions may be given.   One presumes that the registrar is empowered to act under sections 83 and 104 in cases where unauthorised persons have "seriously or persistently" instituted industrial action.   Moreover, if the pre-conditions of the registrar's powers under section 83 are satisfied, then he *must* use his powers, for the provision is not couched in terms of discretion.

(5) Application by an individual to the Industrial Court.— As we saw earlier, an application to the registrar to use his powers of conciliation under section 81 is not a prerequisite to the presentation by an individual of a complaint to either the Industrial Court or an Industrial Tribunal.   Any person may present a complaint to the Industrial Court that action has been taken by the respondent which constituted an unfair industrial practice[1] and that the complainant is the person against whom the action was taken.[2]   If the court considers the grounds of the complaint to be well-founded, it may if it considers that it would be just and equitable so to do, grant one or more of the following remedies, viz. an order determining the rights of the parties, an award of compensation, or an order directing the respondent to refrain from continuing the offensive action and any other action of a like nature in relation to the complainant.[3]   However, where the respondent is an official of a registered trade union who took the offensive action within the scope of his authority, only the first of the three remedies may be awarded against him.[4]

(6) Application by an individual to an Industrial Tribunal.— Any person who is eligible to apply to the registrar under section 81 is also eligible to present a complaint against the trade union concerned to an Industrial Tribunal on the same grounds.[5]   However, the Tribunal will not entertain the complaint if it relates to a matter in respect of which an application has been made to the registrar under section 81 and the registrar has proceeded or is proceeding with it and has not yet given notice of his conclusions.[6]   That possibility apart, the determination of the complaint by the Tribunal is covered by the same provisions as where the registrar presents a complaint to the Tribunal, the important point again being the unavailability of a mandatory order as a remedy.[7]

(7) Action in the ordinary courts.—Finally, there is nothing in the Industrial Relations Act to prevent a person from pursuing an action in the ordinary courts on the basis of a breach of contract.

---

[1] This provision is general, except that the unfair practices under ss. 5 and 22 are excluded.

[2] S. 101(1).

[3] S. 101(2) and (3).

[4] S. 101(4).   But this does not affect the availability of the other two remedies in the same or other proceedings against the trade union itself—s. 101(5).

[5] S. 107.

[6] S. 107(4).

[7] See s. 109, considered *supra*, p. 480.

Indeed, with the repeal of section 4 of the 1871 Act, the jurisdiction of the ordinary courts has been considerably widened in this area.[1]

5. COMPLAINTS AGAINST UNREGISTERED ORGANISATIONS

Since the registrar may only act along the above lines in relation to *registered* trade unions, the procedural possibilities open to an aggrieved person in respect of an unregistered organisation are less various. His choice is restricted to (5), (6) and (7) of the headings considered above. Within those confines, he is in broadly the same position as he would be if he were dealing with a registered trade union.[2]

6. SPECIAL SITUATIONS: POLITICAL FUNDS AND AMALGAMATIONS

The preceding consideration of the law relating to the rules and conduct of organisations of workers, together with the processing of complaints in respect of their internal affairs, has been illustrative of the changes made by the Industrial Relations Act, 1971, in connection with the concept and consequences of registration, the role of the registrar and the system of administrative control over which he presides. In these respects, the new law is markedly different from that which it replaces. However, in two areas, the pre-1971 law contained special statutory provisions which, with minor consequential amendments, have survived the 1971 Act. The areas in question are the application of funds for political purposes, which is governed by the Trade Union Act, 1913, and the amalgamation of unions and the transfer of engagements from one union to another, which are governed by the Trade Union (Amalgamations, etc.) Act, 1964. In both cases, the special statutory provisions give the registrar powers to control the substance of rules and to determine the complaints of members in manners which were wholly exceptional at the time of their enactment.[3]

(1) The Political Fund.—After the political activities of trade unions had received a setback in the famous case of *Amalgamated Society of Railway Servants v. Osborne*,[4] the unions looked to the legislature to provide them with the means of lawfully carrying on such activities, while at the same time safeguarding the political independence of individual members. The solution was found in the Trade Union Act, 1913.

This Act provides that union funds may not be applied directly or in conjunction with any other union in furtherance of certain political objects unless those objects have been approved by a

---

[1] But the courts are still forbidden to compel a man by injunction to take part in industrial action—s. 128(3).

[2] But officials of unregistered organisations do not have the protection of s. 101(4), in Industrial Court actions. For the organisations' procedural position see s. 154.

[3] It is not possible within the compass of this book to consider these Acts in detail. Reference should be made to Citrine, *Trade Union Law*, 3rd Ed. (ed. M. A. Hickling), Chs. 6 and 7, and Grunfeld, *Modern Trade Union Law*, Chs. 13, 14, 15, 16 and 17.   [4] [1910] A.C. 87.

resolution, passed on a ballot, of a majority of the members voting. Where such a resolution applies, rules, to be approved by the registrar (whether the union is registered or not), which provide certain safeguards, must be enforced.   So, where a union, by resolution, approves the expenditure of its funds for political objects there must also be in existence rules providing (*a*) that payments in furtherance of political objects shall be paid out of a separate " political " fund and for the exemption of any member who does not wish to contribute to that fund if he gives notice, and (*b*) that a member who is exempted from making contributions to the political fund shall not be excluded from any benefits of the union or placed at a disadvantage (except in relation to the control or management of the political fund) and that contribution to the political fund of the union shall not be made a condition of admission to the union.[1]

The political objects which require express approval by a majority of the members voting are (*a*) the payment of expenses incurred by parliamentary candidates or candidates for election to any public office; (*b*) the payment of money on the holding of any meeting or the distribution of literature in support of such candidates; (*c*) the payment of money on the maintenance of any such persons; (*d*) the payment of money in connection with the registration of electors or the selection of candidates for Parliament or any public office; or (*e*) the payment of money in connection with the holding of political meetings or the distribution of political literature unless the main purpose of the meetings or the literature is the furtherance of the statutory objects of the union.[2]

A member of a union is free, at any time, to give notice that he objects to making contributions to the political fund.   This notice will be effective from the beginning of the following year unless given when he joins, when it operates immediately.   When a resolution is adopted providing for the furtherance of political objects, notice must be given to members informing them of the right of exemption.[3]

Any member who alleges that he is aggrieved by a breach of any rule made in pursuance of section 3 of the 1913 Act may complain to the registrar.   The registrar, after giving the complainant and any representative of the union an opportunity of being heard, may, if he thinks that such a breach has been committed, make such order for remedying the breach as he thinks just in the circumstances. Subject to any appeal under section 115(1) of the Industrial Relations Act, 1971,[4] any such order will be binding and conclusive on

---

[1] Trade Union Act, 1913, s. 3 (1), and see *Birch* v. *N.U.R.*, [1950] Ch. 602; [1950] 4 All E.R. 253.
[2] Trade Union Act, 1913, s. 3 (3).
[3] *Ibid.*, s. 5.
[4] Which provides for appeals to the Industrial Court.

all parties and shall not be removable into any court of law or restrainable by injunction.[1]

(2) Amalgamations and Transfers of Engagements.—It has been a frequent criticism of trade unions in this country that they have been too numerous. However, the rationalisation movement in recent years has seen a steady decline in the number of trade unions. At common law, there were difficulties in the way of mergers between unions, particularly the need to obtain the consent of every member of each of the merging organisations. For this reason, legislation has been introduced at various times in the last century so as to mitigate the difficulties while still safeguarding to a reasonable extent the interests of individual members.[2] The statute currently in force is the Trade Union (Amalgamations, etc.) Act, 1964.

Under the 1964 Act (as modified by the Industrial Relations Act),[3] two or more organisations of workers may amalgamate or merge by a transfer of engagements after a proper ballot which resulted in support for the proposed measure[4] by a simple majority of those voting.[5] This provision applies, regardless of more stringent existing requirements in the rules of an organisation. However, more stringent requirements introduced into the rules since 1964 and expressly excluding the Act, override the Act and may therefore require a special majority.[6] A ballot will only satisfy the requirements of the Act if—(a) every member is entitled to vote on the resolution; (b) every member is allowed to vote without interference or constraint and is, so far as is reasonably possible, given a fair opportunity of voting; (c) the method of voting involves the marking of a voting paper by the person voting; and (d) all reasonable steps have been taken by the union to secure that, not less than seven days before voting on the resolution begins, every member of the union is supplied with a notice in writing approved for the purpose by the registrar.[7] Any member who considers that a ballot is irregular may, within six weeks, complain to the registrar. Apart from this, and the power of the registrar, at the request of the complainant or the union, to state a case for the opinions of the Industrial Court, the validity of a resolution may not be questioned in any legal

---

[1] Trade Union Act, 1913, s. 3(2).
[2] Previous provisions are to be found in the Trade Union Amendment Act, 1876, s. 12 ; Trade Union (Amalgamation) Act, 1917 ; and the Societies (Miscellaneous Provisions) Act, 1940, which introduced the idea of transfer of engagements.
[3] See Industrial Relations Act, 1971, Sched. 8.
[4] Trade Union (Amalgamation, etc.) Act, 1964, s. 1(1).
[5] Note the provisions relating to the automatic disposal of property on an amalgamation or transfer—s. 5.
[6] *Ibid.*, s. 2.
[7] *Ibid.*, s. 1(2).

proceedings whatsoever on any ground on which a complaint could be made to the registrar.[1]

7. LIABILITIES IN RELATION TO INDUSTRIAL ACTION

We are concerned here with liabilities resulting from industrial action or the threat of industrial action, or, put another way, with the legal limitations upon such action or threats. This difficult area is complicated by the fact that, since the Industrial Relations Act, there exist two distinct sources of liability, viz. the specially-created unfair industrial practices of the 1971 Act and the common law, which has itself undergone amendment in that Act. On the question of providing for the preponderance of litigation based on the unfair industrial practices, the Act authorises the ordinary courts to stay proceedings in tort if they are satisfied that (*a*) the act complained of is one in respect of which proceedings have been brought before the Industrial Court or an Industrial Tribunal, whether those proceedings have been disposed of or not, or (*b*) the act is one in respect of which (as being an unfair industrial practice or a breach of a duty imposed by the Act), proceedings *could* be brought before the Industrial Court or an Industrial Tribunal.[2] Thus, although the unfair industrial practice may be expected to replace liability at common law, in most instances, this will depend upon the choice of forum by injured persons and, if their preference be for the common law, the readiness of the ordinary courts to exercise their discretion to stay proceedings under section 131.[3] These factors will, in turn, be influenced by the future development of both systems by the courts concerned. However, all things being equal, the natural expectation is that the new system will preponderate. For this reason it is given proportionately greater emphasis in the following pages.[4]

8. UNFAIR INDUSTRIAL PRACTICES ARISING OUT OF INDUSTRIAL ACTION OR THE THREAT THEREOF

Before considering the unfair industrial practices in detail, a distinction must be drawn between (i) those which are general in application in that they render unlawful certain methods of pressurising employers,[5] regardless of the issue at stake, and (ii) those which are more specific in that they are aimed at illegalising the use of certain forms of industrial action as means to certain specified ends.

---

[1] *Ibid.*, s. 4 and Sched. 1.

[2] S. 131(1) and (2). Similar provision is made for acts alleged to be threatened or intended—s. 131 (3).

[3] In one situation, however, the courts are bound to stay proceedings in conspiracy. See s. 132(4).

[4] Note the six-month limitation period in respect of unfair industrial practices—Sched. 3, para. 25.

[5] This chapter is not concerned with the commission of unfair industrial practices by employers.

We shall consider first the three most general unfair industrial practices,[1] but, as a preliminary question, it is necessary to examine the words " in contemplation or furtherance of an industrial dispute", for it is a pre-condition of all three that the acts or threats complained of were done or issued in such circumstances.

(1) " In Contemplation or Furtherance of an Industrial Dispute. "—This formula is of the utmost importance both as a pre-condition of liability in the present context, and, as we shall see later, as a pre-condition of immunity in respect of common law liabilities. " Industrial dispute", which replaces the previous concept of " trade dispute,"[2] is defined as a dispute between one or more employers or organisations of employers and one or more workers[3] or organisations of workers, where the dispute relates wholly or mainly to any one or more of the following—(a) terms and conditions of employment, or the physical conditions in which any workers are required to work; (b) engagement or non-engagement, or termination or suspension of employment, of one or more workers; (c) allocation of work as between workers or groups of workers; (d) a procedure agreement, or any matter to which such an agreement can relate.[4] No doubt this definition will give rise to some problems of interpretation. However, it can be said with reasonable certainty that it excludes " political " strikes[5] and disputes which are essentially between workers and workers, such as demarcation disputes, unless the employer becomes a party to, and not just a victim of, the dispute. On the other hand, recognition disputes, which caused difficulty under the 1906 Act, are included, for one of the matters to which a procedure agreement can relate is negotiating rights.[6]

In addition to the question of whether or not there is an industrial dispute, problems also arise as to whether or not particular action is taken " *in contemplation or furtherance of* " such a dispute. When considering these words in connection with the 1906 Act's " trade dispute " requirement, Lord LOREBURN, L.C., said:

> " . . . they mean that either a dispute is imminent and the act is done in expectation of and with a view to it, or that the dispute is already existing and the act is done in support of one side to it. In either case the act must be genuinely done as described, and the dispute must be a real thing imminent or existing. . . . If, however,

---

[1] Between which there may be considerable overlap.

[2] As defined in the Trade Disputes Act, 1906, s. 5 (now repealed).

[3] For the meaning of " workers," see the Industrial Relations Act, 1971, s. 167(1), (2), (3) and (4). The group is considerably wider than those of " employees " or " workmen ".

[4] Industrial Relations Act, 1971, s. 167(1). For the meaning of " procedure agreement," see s. 166(5).

[5] For the difficulty of separating the " political " and " industrial " content of some strikes, see Wedderburn, *The Worker and the Law*, 2nd Ed. (Pelican), pp. 327–329.

[6] S. 166(5) (c).

some meddler sought to use the trade dispute as a cloak beneath which to interfere with impunity in other people's work or business, a jury would be entirely justified in saying that what he did was done in contemplation or in furtherance, not of the trade dispute, but of his own designs, sectarian, political, or purely mischievous, as the case might be.   These words do, in my opinion, in some sense import motive, and in the case I have put, a quite different motive would be present."[1]

This search for the dominant motive of those responsible for industrial action has resulted in a dispute being considered outside the formula in several cases.   Thus, in *Huntley* v. *Thornton*,[2] the members of a trade union's district committee who damaged the employment prospects of the plaintiff (a fellow-member) by threats of industrial action which resulted in his dismissal and non-engagement, were considered to be beyond the scope of the formula. There was no " *trade* dispute", nor had any action been taken " in contemplation or furtherance " of one.   HARMAN, J. said:

" The defendants were not asserting a trade right, for they knew they would not procure the plaintiff's expulsion from the union.[3] The dispute, if it could be so called, had become an internecine struggle between the members of the union and no interests of ' the trade ' were involved.   It was a personal matter.

Behind these considerations lies a more fundamental point, namely, whether the committee's actions were ' in *furtherance* of a trade dispute ' . . . If, as I have held, the paramount object of the committee was to injure the plaintiff, then that was the object in furtherance of which they acted . . . they intended to injure the plaintiff in his trade by their embargo, and it was to that end their actions were directed.   They were not furthering a trade dispute, but a grudge . . ."[4]

In *Torquay Hotel Co., Ltd.* v. *Cousins*,[5] union officials went outside the formula when they organised industrial action against the plaintiff company which did not employ any of their members, but whose managing director had made public statements in support of another concern which did employ some of their members and was in dispute with the union over negotiating rights.   The Court of Appeal considered that, although there was a trade dispute concerning the negotiating rights, there was none with the plaintiff company, nor was the action " in contemplation or furtherance of " the trade dispute with the other concern.[6]   Thus, Lord DENNING, M.R., said:

---

[1] *Conway* v. *Wade*, [1909] A.C. 506, at p. 512.
[2] [1957] 1 All E.R. 234.
[3] They had, in fact, tried to expel the plaintiff, but the executive committee refused to endorse their resolution.
[4] [1957] 1 All E.R. at p. 256.
[5] [1969] 2 Ch. 106; [1969] 1 All E.R. 522.
[6] It seems to have been irrelevant that the plaintiff company was a member of the same employers' association as the other concern. *Cf.* the Industrial Relations Act, 1971, s. 98(3) (*b*).

" The only question is whether the acts done by the defendant union officials against the [plaintiff company] were done in *further-ance* of the trade dispute with [the primary concern]. I do not think they were. They were done in furtherance of the anger which they felt towards [the managing director of the plaintiff company] for having, as they said, ' intervened ' in the dispute. They were not furthering a trade dispute, but their own fury . . ."[1]

These cases were decided when the only function of the formula " in contemplation or furtherance of a trade dispute " was to delimit the immunity from common law liabilities which was given to organisers of industrial action. Now that the formula itself has been amended and its functions extended to the delimitation of liability in relation to certain unfair industrial practices, its develop-ment may take on a different appearance. However, the judicial interpretations of the 1906 Act which have survived amendment by the Industrial Relations Act, should continue to give meaning to the formula. Indeed, the search for the dominant motive has been given a new impetus by the words " wholly or mainly " in the definition of " industrial dispute".

With this in mind, we can return to our consideration of the unfair industrial practices concerned with industrial action.

(2) Section 96: Inducement and Threats to Induce.—" It is an unfair industrial practice for any person, in contemplation or furtherance of an industrial dispute, knowingly to induce or threaten to induce another person to break a contract to which that other person is a party, unless the person so inducing or threatening to induce the breach of contract—(*a*) is a trade union . . . , or (*b*) does so within the scope of his authority on behalf of a trade union . . ."[2] It is, of course, a tort to induce another to break a contract.[3] However, as we shall see, there is statutory immunity from liability for the tort in the context of the " industrial dispute " formula,[4] whereas the present unfair industrial practice is founded on the same concepts of " inducement " and the " industrial dispute " formula.

This unfair industrial practice is extremely wide in its applica-tion, extending to the inducement of all breaches of contract, not just breaches of contracts of employment. Moreover, it embraces the common law notions of both " direct " and, to some extent, " in-

---

[1] [1969] 2 Ch. at p. 136. See also RUSSELL, L.J., at p. 143, and WINN, L.J., at p. 148. Also *J.T. Stratford and Son, Ltd.* v. *Lindley*, [1965] A.C. 269; [1964] 3 All E.R. 102.
[2] Industrial Relations Act, 1971, s. 96(1). Wherever the section refers to a trade union, it refers also to an employers' association, but as our prime con-cern is with the effect of these provisions on labour, consideration from the point of view of employers' associations is omitted.
[3] *Lumley* v. *Gye* (1853), 2 E. & B. 216.
[4] S. 132(1) (*a*).

direct " inducement.[1] Thus, an unprotected[2] official who induced
his members to strike in breach of their contracts of employment
would commit this unfair industrial practice, as would one who
induced his or another employer to break a commercial contract,[3]
or, in some circumstances, one who indirectly induced the breach
of a commercial contract by his direct inducement of breaches of
employment contracts.   In this latter case, his conduct would be
actionable at the suit of the employer whose workers had broken
their contracts of employment, and, possibly, at the suit of the other
party to a commercial contract which the employer was caused to
break by the withdrawal of labour.   However, the field of potential
complainants is limited by the requirements that the breach must
be " knowingly " induced and that the complainant is "the person
against whom the action was taken."[4] Of these two requirements,
" knowingly " is, in the light of recent experience, likely to receive
a rather loose interpretation.[5] On the other hand, " the person
against whom the action was taken " should, it is submitted,
receive a strict interpretation, so that the only outside party to a
commercial contract who could claim under section 96[6] would be
one who was himself the intended object, rather than a consequential victim, of the industrial action.[7] Thus, if workers who are in
dispute with X attempt to hit at X by inducing breaches of contracts
of employment by employees of Y, X's main supplier or customer, as
a result of which a commercial contract between X and Y is broken
by Y, the inducers will be liable to X under section 96 because he is
" the person against whom " the action was taken, albeit indirectly.[8]

Having considered the nature of the section 96 unfair industrial
practice, it is necessary to have regard to the following related
matters:

(i) The meaning of " induce "

It was for a long time considered that " inducement " was a
strong word which was distinguishable from less coercive (and,
therefore, perfectly lawful) forms of communication such as " advice ".
Thus, in *D.C. Thomson & Co., Ltd.* v. *Deakin*,[9] EVERSHED, M.R.,
said:

---

[1] The common law position is considered later in this chapter.
[2] *I.e.* unprotected by reason of not being an authorised official of a registered
trade union. See *infra.*
[3] See *e.g.*, the facts of *Torquay Hotel Co., Ltd.* v. *Cousins*, [1969] 2 Ch. 106;
[1969] 1 All E.R. 522.
[4] Industrial Relations Act, 1971, s. 101(1) (*c*).
[5] See *e.g.*, Lord DENNING, M.R., in *Emerald Construction Co., Ltd.* v.
Lowthian, [1966] 1 W.L.R. 691, at p. 701 and in the *Torquay Hotel* case, *supra*,
at p. 138.   See also *J. T. Stratford and Son, Ltd.*, v. *Lindley*, [1965] A.C. 269,
[1964] 3 All E.R. 102.
[6] The possibility of claims under other heads is considered *infra.*
[7] *Cf.* the Industrial Relations Bill as first published, cl. 90(1) (*c*).
[8] A comparable factual situation existed in *Square Grip Reinforcement Co., Ltd.*
Macdonald, 1968 S.L.T. 65.
[9] [1952] Ch. 646; [1952] 2 All E.R. 361.

" I appreciate that in these matters there is a difficult question of distinguishing between what might be called persuasion and what might be called advice, meaning by the latter a mere statement of, or drawing of the attention of the party addressed to, the state of facts as they were."[1]

Indeed, one of the things which led to the defendants not being liable in that case was the absence of any " pressure, persuasion or procuration on the part of these defendants, as would in any event cause them to be liable in tort."[2]   However, in recent years the courts seem to have required far less coercive overtures as the foundation of liability for inducement. A particularly diluted (but vivid) statement was made by WINN, L.J., in the *Torquay Hotel* case:

" It was one of counsel for the defendants' main submissions that mere advice, warning or information cannot amount to tortious procurement of breach of contract. Whilst granting *arguendi causa* that a communication which went no further would, in general, not, in the absence of circumstances giving a particular significance, amount to a threat or intimidation, I am unable to understand why it may not be an inducement. In the ordinary meaning of language it would surely be said that a father who told his daughter that her fiancé had been convicted of indecent exposure, had thereby induced her, with or without justification, by truth or by slander, to break her engagement. A man who writes to his mother-in-law telling her that the central heating in his house has broken down may thereby induce her to cancel an intended visit."[3]

There is, therefore, reason to believe that the Industrial Court will inherit a readiness to characterise apparently mild communications as " inducements". Moreover, little regard seems to have been had recently to the fact that the course of action induced may often, at the option of the person induced, be carried out lawfully, rather than in breach of contract.[4]

(ii) Breach and Exemption Clauses

A point of considerable importance in relation to inducing breach of commercial contracts is that a contract against which an inducer moves may contain a clause exempting the person induced from liability to the other contracting party in the event of industrial action. In such circumstances, can the inducer be said to have induced a *breach* of contract? In the *Torquay Hotel* case, union officials who induced the plaintiffs' fuel supplier not to deliver were considered by the majority of the Court of Appeal to have induced

---

[1] [1952] Ch. at p. 686.
[2] [1952] Ch. at p. 686.
[3] [1969] 2 Ch. at p. 147.   See also *Square Grip Reinforcement Co., Ltd.* v. *Macdonald*, 1968 S.L.T. 65, at pp. 72–73 (*per* Lord MILLIGAN) ; *J.S. Stratford and Son, Ltd.* v. *Lindley*, [1965] A.C. 269 at p. 333 (*per* Lord PEARCE).
[4] *Cf.* JENKINS, L.J., in *D.C. Thomson and Co., Ltd.* v. *Deakin*, [1952] Ch. at pp. 696–697. " Induce " is not the only problematical verb in s. 96(1). "Threaten " may also prove difficult to distinguish from " warn".

a breach of contract, notwithstanding the existence in the contract of a *force majeure* clause which operated to the benefit of the supplier in the event of industrial action. RUSSELL L.J. said:

" . . . the exception clause . . . *assumes* a failure to fulfil a term of the contract—*i.e.* a breach of contract—and excludes liability— *i.e.* in damages—for that breach in stated circumstances. It is an exception from liability for non-performance rather than an exception from obligation to perform."[1]

(iii) Industrial Action and the Contract of Employment

It is now necessary to consider whether persons who induce industrial action thereby induce breaches of contract of employment on the part of the participants in that action, for if there is no breach, there can be no liability under section 96. Before the Industrial Relations Act, the common view was that a strike was probably in breach of contract,[2] unless it took the form of a lawful termination, viz. termination after proper notice.[3] However, in *Morgan* v. *Fry*,[4] Lord DENNING, M.R., took the view that a strike after proper notice (*i.e.* notice of a period not less than that necessary to terminate the contract) had the effect of *suspending* the contract.

" The truth is that neither employer nor workmen wish to take the drastic action of termination if it can be avoided. The men do not wish to leave their work for ever. The employers do not wish to scatter their labour force to the four winds. Each side is, therefore, content to accept a ' strike notice ' of proper length as lawful. It is an implication read into the contract by the modern law as to trade disputes. If a strike takes place, the contract of employment is not terminated. It is suspended during the strike: and revives again when the strike is over."[5]

However much this view may be said to have reflected the reality of the situation, it was difficult to reconcile with common law principles, which know nothing of a unilateral right of suspension.[6] If such a notion was to be imported into our law, it could only really be as a result of legislation.

Legislative reform has now become a reality in section 147 of the Industrial Relations Act, 1971, which provides that due notice[7] given by or on behalf of an employee of his intention to take part in a

---

[1] [1969] 2 Ch. at pp. 143.   See also WINN, L.J. (at p. 146 *et seq.*).
[2] See, *e.g.*, Lord DEVLIN in *Rookes* v. *Barnard*, [1964] A.C. 1129, at p. 1204; Lord DENNING, M.R., in *J.S. Stratford and Son, Ltd.* v. *Lindley*, [1965] A.C. at p. 285; WIDGERY, J., in *Morgan* v. *Fry*, [1968] 1 Q.B. 521, at p. 546.
[3] See *White* v. *Riley*, [1921] 1 Ch. 1.
[4] [1968] 2 Q.B. 710.
[5] [1968] 2 Q.B. at p. 728.
[6] For a discussion of problems inherent in adoption of the suspension approach see Report of Royal Commission on Trade Unions and Employers' Associations, 1965–1968, Cmnd. 3623, para. 943.
[7] " Due notice " means notice of a duration not less than that which the employee would be required to give in order to terminate the contract—s. 147(5).

strike[1] will not, unless it otherwise expressly provides, be construed as a notice of termination of the contract or as a repudiation (*i.e.* an *anticipatory* breach) of it.[2] As a corollary, participation in a strike after due notice will not be regarded as a breach of contract for the purposes of, *inter alia*,[3] section 96, unless the employee's action is contrary to a term of his contract of employment (including any term implied or incorporated in that contract by reference to a collective agreement) excluding or restricting his right to take part in a strike.[4] Although, in the past, such incorporation of " no strike " clauses (either in absolute form or pending exhaustion of procedure) has been thought to have been the exception rather than the rule,[5] it is submitted that in the future express incorporation is likely to become more common, not least because of section 20(2) of the Act.[6] Two other points to be noted in relation to section 147 are, firstly, that it does not derogate from an employer's right to dismiss strikers;[7] and, secondly, that since it refers only to strikes, it does not determine the question of the effect of other forms of industrial action on the contract of employment. This question will, as a rule, depend on the terms of the contract in question.[8]

(iv) Collective Agreements

Although, as we have seen, section 96 applies to, *inter alia*, the inducement of breach of contracts of employment, including terms in those contracts which are derived by a process of incorporation from collective agreements, it does not apply to the inducement of a breach of a collective agreement as such.[9]

(v) Registered Trade Unions

Registered trade unions and persons acting within the scope of their authority on behalf of such trade unions cannot commit the unfair

---

[1] As defined in s. 167(1), which definition is considered later in this chapter. It confines " strikes " to the " industrial dispute " formula.

[2] Industrial Relations Act, 1971, s. 147(1).

[3] The other purposes are (*a*) any proceedings in contract brought against the employee in respect of breach of that contract; (*b*) any proceedings in tort, whether brought against the employee or against any other person; and (*c*) s. 5 of the Conspiracy and Protection of Property Act, 1875.

[4] S. 147(3).

[5] *Cf. Rookes* v. *Barnard*, [1964] A.C. 1129; [1964] 1 All E.R. 367, where incorporation of such a clause was conceded by counsel for the defendants.

[6] Which requires the written statement of particulars given to employees pursuant to s. 4 of the Contracts of Employment Act, 1963, to include a note describing, *inter alia*, any grievance procedure applying to the employee. Although this statement is not the contract, but merely evidence of it, (*cf.* Lord Denning, M.R., in *Camden Exhibition and Display, Ltd.* v. *Lynott*, [1966] 1 Q.B. 555; [1965] 3 All E.R. 28, it is a mechanism which frequently leads to express incorporation of other documents into the contract.

[7] Industrial Relations Act, 1971, s. 147(4). *Cf.* s. 26.

[8] See, *e.g.*, *Camden Exhibition and Display, Ltd.* v. *Lynott*, [1966] 1 Q.B. 555; [1965] 3 All E.R. 28.

[9] S. 96(3).

industrial practice created by section 96.[1] Its targets are un-official action and unregistered organisations.

(3) Section 97: Industrial Action in support of an Unfair Industrial Practice.—It is an unfair industrial practice for any person, in contemplation or furtherance of an industrial dispute, to take or threaten to take certain steps if his purpose or principal purpose is to further any action which has been taken, whether by him or by any other person, and which constituted an unfair industrial practice.[2] The forbidden steps are (a) calling, organising, procuring or financing a strike, and (b) organising, procuring or financing any irregular industrial action short of a strike.[3] Mere participation in these forms of industrial action is not covered. Moreover, if a registered trade union takes any of these steps for the purpose of furthering any action which (a) has been taken by one or more of its officials or members, and (b) constituted an unfair industrial practice by virtue *only* of section 96, it does not thereby commit the unfair industrial practice under section 97.[4] Thus, if an un-authorised official of a registered trade union called a strike, thereby committing the section 96 unfair industrial practice *but no other*, and his union later adopted his act and started to finance the strike or organise other supporting action, the union would not commit the section 97 unfair industrial practice. However, if the initial action were tainted by the commission of any other unfair industrial practice, the union, in coming to its support, would commit the section 97 unfair industrial practice. Given the complexity of some of the unfair industrial practices, it may, of course, be extremely difficult for a union to assess whether or not action which it is asked to support is of such a nature as to put the union at risk under section 97.

(4) Section 98 Industrial Action against Extraneous Parties.— It is an unfair industrial practice for any person, in contemplation or furtherance of an industrial dispute, to take or threaten any of the same steps[5] if—(a) he knows or has reasonable grounds for believing that another person has entered into a contract[6] with a party to that industrial dispute; (b) his purpose or principal purpose is knowingly to induce that other person to break that contract or to prevent him from performing it;[7] and (c) that other person is an

---

[1] S. 96(1).   Registration, for this purpose, includes provisional registration—s. 96(2).   The " scope of authority " question should be read in conjunction with s. 167(9) and Sched. 4, para. 10.

[2] S. 97(1).

[3] Industrial Relations Act, 1971, s. 97(2), which also includes organisation of lockouts.   The meaning of " irregular industrial action short of a strike " is considered later in this chapter.

[4] S. 97(3).

[5] *I.e.* those mentioned in s. 97(2), *supra.*

[6] Other than a contract of employment.

[7] *Quaere:* If A persuades B lawfully to terminate his contract with C, does A prevent B from performing it?

extraneous party in relation to that industrial dispute.[1] A person will be regarded as an extraneous party to an industrial dispute if he is not a party to that dispute and has not, in contemplation or further-ance of it, taken any action in material support of a party to it.[2] The tendentious expressions " party " and " material support " are clarified to some extent by a provision that a person will not be regarded as a party or as having taken action in material support of a party by reason only that he—(*a*) is an associated employer[3] in relation to an employer who is a party to the industrial dispute; or (*b*) is a member of an organisation of employers of which a party to the industrial dispute is also a member; or (*c*) has contributed to a fund which may be available to such a party by way of relief in respect of losses incurred in consequence of the dispute, where the fund was established, and his contribution to it was paid, without specific reference to that industrial dispute; or (*d*) supplies goods to, or provides services for, a party to the industrial dispute in pursuance of a contract entered into before the industrial dispute began, or is a party to such a contract under which he is or may be required to supply goods to, or provide services for, a party to the industrial dispute.[4]

This unfair industrial practice clearly places severe limitations on the extent to which workers may seek to apply pressure against their employer by acting through a secondary employer (or his employees). It is difficult to speculate upon its ambit.   Much will depend on the development of the concept of " extraneous party."[5]

(5) Sections 96, 98 and Future Contracts.—The unfair indus-trial practices created by sections 96 and 98 are founded on the notions of inducements and threats to induce breaches of contract. In addition to their obvious application to contracts existing at the time of the inducements or threats, they can extend also, by reason of the references to " threats " and the provisions as to remedies,[6] to contracts unmade at such time.   In this, they can be seen to develop the potentialities realised in the *Torquay Hotel* case.[7]

(6) The Unfair Industrial Practices relating to Specific Types of Dispute.[8]—The unfair industrial practices of sections 96, 97 and 98 have their unlawfulness based on the means of the pressure applied, regardless of the subject-matter of a particular

---

[1] S. 98(1).   Several of the problems considered in relation to " inducement " in the context of s. 96 are also relevant here.

[2] S. 98(2).

[3] As defined in s. 167(8).

[4] S. 98(3).

[5] The crucial word is " only " in s. 98(3).

[6] See ss. 101(3) (*c*) and 105(3).

[7] [1969] 2 Ch. 106; [1969] 1 All E.R. 522.   See also *J.T. Stratford & Son, Ltd.* v. *Lindley*, [1965] A.C. 269; [1964] 3 All E.R. 102.

[8] Again, no reference is made to the possible commission of these, or similar, or other unfair industrial practices by employers.

dispute. We must now catalogue the unfair industrial practices which exist so as to render unlawful the application of certain types of pressure *for specific purposes*. Many of these are considered throughout this book at the points where the specific subject-matter is under discussion. They are all gathered together here so as to present a full account of possible liabilities incurred by workers and their unions in connection with industrial action.

It is an unfair industrial practice for any person (including any trade union, registered or unregistered) to call a strike or to organise, procure or finance a strike or any irregular industrial action short of a strike[1] or to threaten any of these things in order knowingly to induce or to attempt to induce an employer to do any of the following:

(a) not to take the requisite steps to conclude and operate an agency shop agreement when, as a result of a ballot, he has a duty so to do;[2]

(b) to enter into an agency shop agreement in respect of workers of any description after an application relating to workers of that description has been made under section 11, unless a statutorily-required ballot results in the necessary majority in favour within the meaning of section 13(1);[3]

(c) to refrain from making an application for the establishment of an agency shop under section 11(2);[4]

(d) to take any action which is or would be an unfair practice in accordance with section 5(2) (interference with the three basic workers' rights of union membership, non-membership and activity) or section 22(1) (unfair dismissal);[5]

(e) to comply with any provision in an agreement in so far as that provision is void by virtue of section 7(1) (pre-entry closed shops) or to enter into an agreement containing such a provision;[6]

(f) to comply with a provision declared to be void by an order of the Industrial Court under section 7(3) (pre-entry closed shop);[7]

(g) to join in making an application under Part I of Schedule 1 (application for approval of closed shop agreement);[8]

---

[1] The statutory meanings of " strike " and " irregular industrial action short of a strike " are considered *infra*.

[2] Industrial Relations Act, 1971, s. 13(2).

[3] S. 16(2) (a).

[4] S. 16(2) (b).

[5] Industrial Relations Act, 1971, s. 33(3) (a). This also applies to the similar inducement of a person acting on behalf of an employer.

[6] S. 33(3) (b).

[7] S. 33(3) (c).

[8] S. 33(3) (d), which also applies to the similar inducement of an employers' association.

(*h*) (where the employer is bound[1] to recognise a sole bargaining agent) to do anything which would constitute an unfair industrial practice on his part under section 55(1);[2]

(*i*) (within two years after the Industrial Court receives a C.I.R. report on the recognition of a sole bargaining agent)[3] to recognise as a sole bargaining agent for the bargaining unit to which the report related, an organisation of workers or a joint negotiating panel which was not recommended for such recognitions in the C.I.R. report;[4]

(*j*) (within the same two-year period) to carry on, with any organisation of workers or joint negotiating panel which was not so recommended, any collective bargaining in relation to employees of any description comprised in the same bargaining unit;[5]

(*k*) not to comply with an order under section 53 (withdrawal of recognition as a sole bargaining agent).[6]

It is also an unfair industrial practice for any person to call organise, procure or finance a strike, or organise, procure or finance any irregular industrial action short of a strike, whilst there is reference pending in respect of the establishment of a sole bargaining agent, and for six months after the Industrial Court receives the C.I.R. report, to the extent that such action is taken in furtherance of the same dispute.[7]

Finally, in this context, reference should also be made to the unfair industrial practices which are committed by a party to a legally enforceable collective agreement who breaks the agreement[8] (by, *inter alia*, organising industrial action in breach of procedure) or fails to take all such steps as are reasonably practicable for the purpose of preventing others (*i.e.* a union's agents, purported agents and members) from taking action contrary to an undertaking given by the party in the agreement.[9]

(7) " Strikes " and " Irregular Industrial Action Short of a Strike ".—Many of the foregoing unfair industrial practices concern the organisation, etc. of a " strike " or " any irregular industrial action short of a strike ". Both these expressions are terms of art and are defined in the Industrial Relations Act.

---

[1] By an order under s. 50.   For a general discussion see Ch. X.
[2] S. 55(3).
[3] Under s. 48.
[4] S. 55(6) (*a*).
[5] S. 55 (6) (*b*).
[6] Industrial Relations Act, 1971, s. 55(7).
[7] S. 54(4) (*b*).
[8] S. 36(1).
[9] S. 36(2).

A strike is a concerted stoppage of work by a group of workers *in contemplation or furtherance of an industrial dispute*, whether they are parties to the dispute or not, *whether (in the case of all or any of them) the stoppage is or is not in breach of their terms and conditions of employment*, and whether it is carried out during, or on the termination of their employment.[1]

Although a strike does not necessarily involve any breach of contract by the participants, " irregular industrial action short of a strike " does require at least some of the participants to commit breaches.   The statutory definition of such irregular action is any concerted course of conduct (other than a strike) which, in contemplation or furtherance of an industrial dispute, (*a*) is carried on by a group of workers with the intention of preventing, reducing or otherwise interfering with the production of goods or the provision of services, and (*b*) in the case of some or all of them, is carried on in breach of their contracts of employment or (where they are not employees)[2] in breach of their terms and conditions of service.[3] This final requirement is bound to cause difficulty in cases where contractual terms are elusive or do not lend themselves to certain interpretation.   For example, since a ban on overtime will only be irregular when it involves a breach of contract, it is necessary to ascertain whether there is an obligation to work overtime.   This may be difficult.[4]   Similarly, it is necessary to discover whether workers who " work to rule " or " go slow " have correctly interpreted the minimum obligations which their contracts impose upon them. The problem is particularly acute when one considers that it only needs some (presumably two) of the workers involved to commit breaches in order to render the action of the whole group " irregular ".

9.   COMMON LAW LIABILITIES

Before the invention of the unfair industrial practice and the establishment of the Industrial Court by the Industrial Relations Act, 1971, liability in respect of industrial action was governed by the law of crime and, to a greater extent in modern times, the law of tort.[5]   The 1971 Act has reduced the significance of the older liabilities[6] but most of them still exist and must now be considered.

(1) Criminal Liabilities.—As we have seen it was originally criminal for workmen to combine to obtain better wages or shorter working hours, to prevent any person from employing whom he

---

[1] Industrial Relations Act, 1971, s. 167(1).
[2] For the distinction between " employees " and " workers ", see s. 167 and Ch. 1, *supra*.   [3] S. 33(4).
[4] See *e.g.*, *Camden Exhibition and Display, Ltd.* v. *Lynott*, [1966] 1 Q.B. 555; [1965] 3 All E.R. 28.
[5] As we have already seen, industrial action also frequently involved breaches of contract on the part of those involved, but these were rarely litigated as such.
[6] See *supra*, p. 486.

chose or wilfully and maliciously to attempt to prevent a person from taking employment or to persuade any person to leave his employment.[1] The Trade Union Act, 1871, however, provided that the purposes of a union should not be deemed unlawful merely because they were in restraint of trade so as to render members liable to criminal prosecution for conspiracy or otherwise.[2] In the same year the Criminal Law Amendment Act was passed with the object of amending the law as to violence, threats and molestation and of dealing with the offences likely to occur during strikes and lock-outs. The use of violence to person or property, of threats or intimidation such as would justify a justice of the peace in binding over the accused person to keep the peace, of molestation or obstruction, were made offences wherever they were committed by either a master or workman in certain defined circumstances. The Act had only a short life and with its details we are not concerned. It was the object of great criticism, though in certain ways it improved the law and in particular the use of threats and intimidation were to be regarded as offences only where they were of such a character as would justify a justice of the peace in binding over the defendant.[3]

> "The statute . . . was not conceived in any weak spirit of tenderness to workmen but . . . limits intimidation . . . to such as would justify a magistrate in binding over the intimidator to keep the peace towards the person intimidated—in other words, to such intimidation as implies a threat of personal violence."

But in one important respect the criticisms levelled at the Act had some justification. It will be remembered that the Molestation of Workmen Act, 1859, s. 1 had provided that a workman should not be guilty of molestation or obstruction merely because he had endeavoured peaceably and in a reasonable manner to persuade others to cease or abstain from work. No such provision was to be found in the new Act, and it was assumed, in consequence, that all picketing was prohibited. This assumption was strengthened by the decision in *R. v. Bunn*,[5] wherein it was held that the servants of a gas company who had come out on strike as a protest against the dismissal of a fellow servant and who, in striking, had broken their contracts, were guilty of common law conspiracy. The judgment gave a most grudging interpretation to the Criminal Law Amendment Act, 1871[6] and a most liberal interpretation to the notions of molestation and obstruction. The result was a considerable public agitation

---

[1] Combination Act, 1800 (39 & 40 Geo. 3, c. 106).
[2] S. 2, now repealed but in substance re-enacted by Industrial Relations Act, 1971, s. 135.
[3] See *Legal History of Trade Unionism*, by Hedges & Winterbottom, at pp. 112–113.
[4] *Gibson* v. *Lawson*, [1891] 2 Q.B. 545, *per* Lord COLERIDGE, C. J., at p. 559.
[5] (1872), 12 Cox, C.C. 316.
[6] *Passim*.

which led to the passing of the Conspiracy and Protection of Property Act, 1875. The Act provides that an agreement or combination by two or more persons to do or to procure to be done any act in contemplation or furtherance of a trade dispute will not be indictable as a conspiracy if such an act, committed by one person would not be punishable as a crime.[1]   A crime for the purposes of this provision was defined as an offence, punishable on indictment or summary conviction and for the commission of which the offender is liable to be imprisoned either absolutely or at the discretion of the court, as an alternative to some other punishment.[2]

It was clear now that a strike, agreement or combination in furtherance of a trade dispute was legal excepting in any one of three sets of circumstances laid down by the Act.   For an agreement or combination would still be illegal if its object was the procuration or commission of an act which if done by one person would constitute a crime, as would an agreement or combination which amounted to a conspiracy for which some Act of Parliament had laid down a punishment, as would also any agreement or combination which amounted to a breach of the law relating to riot, unlawful assembly, breach of the peace, sedition, or was an offence against the State or the Sovereign.[3]

A breach of contract is usually a ground for civil proceedings but the Act provided that, in certain cases, breaches of contract could be of such a character as to be criminal.   The only one of these which survives is that it is a criminal offence wilfully and maliciously to break a contract of service or of hiring, knowing or having reasonable cause to believe that the consequence will be to endanger human life or cause serious bodily injury or to expose valuable property to destruction or serious injury.[4]

The Conspiracy and Protection of Property Act also created other offences.   It was made an offence for any person wrongfully and without legal authority, with a view to compel any other person to do or abstain from doing any act which that other person has a legal right to do or abstain from doing, (*a*) to use violence to or intimidate such other person or his wife or children or to injure his property; or (*b*) persistently to follow such other person about from place to place; or (*c*) to hide any clothes, tools or other property owned or used by such other person, or to deprive him of or hinder him in the use thereof; or (*d*) to watch or beset the house or other place where such other person resides, or works or carries on business, or happens to be or the approach to such house or place; or

---

[1] S. 3.   " Trade dispute" has now been replaced by " industrial dispute " within the meaning of the 1971 Act.

[2] *Ibid.*

[3] *Ibid.*

[4] Conspiracy and Protection of Property Act, 1875, s. 5   The " breach " provision must now be read subject to Industrial Relations Act, 1971, s. 147(2) (*c*), considered earlier in this chapter.

(e) to follow such other person with two or more other persons in a disorderly manner in or through any street or road.[1]

In 1906 the Trade Disputes Act modified the criminal law in certain respects, as in turn has the Industrial Relations Act, 1971, and in consequence it is advisable to consider these Acts together with the Conspiracy and Protection of Property Act, 1875 and to treat in some detail the specific statutory offences created. We have noted that the latter Act made it an offence to do certain things when they were done with a view to compel without legal authority some other person to do or to abstain from doing acts which that other has a legal right to do or abstain from doing. For such ends it is illegal to use violence to, or to intimidate, such other person or his wife or children, or to injure his property.[2] In the now repealed Trade Disputes and Trade Unions Act, 1927 intimidation was defined as that which caused

"in the mind of a person a reasonable apprehension of injury to him or to any member of his family . . . or of violence or damage to any person or property. . . ."[3]

Such a definition is no longer available and resort must be had to cases considered by the courts before 1927. In *Gibson* v. *Lawson*[4] the appellant and respondent were both employed as fitters in the same company. The members of the respondent's union passed a resolution not to work unless the appellant joined their union and the respondent informed the foreman of this and he and the manager told the appellant. The appellant asked the respondent to let the matter stand in abeyance until he had consulted his own union. This request was refused, whereupon the appellant refused to leave his union and join that of the respondent. To prevent a strike the appellant was discharged. The appellant agreed that no violence or threats of violence were used to him but he gave evidence that he was afraid that he would lose his work. It was held that there was no intimidation. The word "intimidate" was held to be a word of common speech which ought to receive a reasonable and sensible interpretation and, in consequence, the court refused to attempt an exhaustive definition. In *Curran* v. *Treleaven*[5] the prosecution had suggested that the secretaries of three trade unions had intimidated Mr. Treleaven by telling him that if he did not cease to employ non-union labour they would bring out of employment all members of their unions employed by him. This they did. The strikers were instructed by the union to use no violence, no immoderate language, but quietly to cease work and go home. Again, it was held that there was no intimidation. Thus, though it cannot be said that actual violence is an essential ingredient of intimidation there must

---

[1] *Ibid.*, s. 7.
[2] Conspiracy and Protection of Property Act, 1875, s. 7 (1).
[3] Trade Disputes and Trade Unions Act, 1927, s. 3 (2).
[4] [1891] 2 Q.B. 545.
[5] *Ibid.*

be a threat of such a character as to produce reasonable fear in men of normal courage.[1] It is also an offence for a person with a view to compel another to do or abstain from doing what that other has a right to do or abstain from doing, persistently to follow that other person about from place to place.[2] So in *R.* v. *Wall*[3] the offence was held to have been committed by persons who had followed an employer from his place of business to his residence with the intention that he should take back into his employment a dismissed employee. The respondent in *Smith* v. *Thomasson*,[4] whilst a picket during a strike, had silently followed for a short distance a workman who had taken the place of the strikers. A crowd had also followed and had shown some hostility. It was held, on appeal, that the respondent was rightly convicted of " persistently following." Thus the act of persistently following may be committed by one person.

It is an offence for any person with a view to compel another to do or to abstain from doing that which that other has a right to do or abstain from doing, to hide any tools, clothes, or other property owned or used by such other person or to deprive him of or hinder him in the use thereof.[5] On this offence there is a scarcity of authority. In *Fowler* v. *Kibble*[6] the defendant was a checkweigher at a mine at which the plaintiff and others were employed. They were members of different unions and certain unions had entered into an agreement with the owners of collieries that only members of the unions should be employed. To check membership, periodical inspection of union cards took place. Kibble warned one of the plaintiffs who was a member of a breakaway and not recognised union that unless he joined the union to which Kibble belonged he would not get work. Then another defendant saw the union card of another plaintiff and told him that unless he joined the union to which the defendant belonged he would not get his safety lamp to enter the pit. The lamp was withheld. Other plaintiffs to whom lamps had been given were asked by the defendant, when waiting to enter the pit, quietly and without violence, to give up their lamps. This they did. The result was that although two unions were recognised, men who did not belong to the same union as the defendants were deprived of employment. The court held that a miner's safety lamp was a "tool" within the section but that no offence had been committed because there had been no violence or threat of violence. Moreover, the acts of the defendants were not done with a view to compel the defendants to do or abstain from doing that which they were legally entitled to do or abstain from

---

[1] See *Legal History of Trade Unionism*, by Hedges and Winterbottom, p. 123.
[2] Conspiracy and Protection of Property Act, 1875, s. 7 (2).
[3] (1907), 21 Cox, C.C. 401.
[4] (1891), 16 Cox, C.C. 740.
[5] Conspiracy and Protection of Property Act, 1875, s. 7 (3).
[6] [1922]1 Ch. 140.

doing.   The defendants had acted as they had only in furtherance of
the agreement which existed between the two recognised unions
and the colliery owners.

Any person who, with a view to compel any other person to do
or abstain from doing any act which that other person has a legal
right to do or abstain from doing, watches or besets the house or
other place where such other person resides, or works, or carries on
business or happens to be or the approach to such house or place,
commits an offence under the Act.[1]   Here, of course, we are concerned with the law as to picketing and the position was modified by
a provision of the Trade Disputes Act, 1906,[2] which enacted that
it was lawful for one or more persons, acting on their own behalf or
on behalf of a trade union or of an individual employer or firm, in
contemplation or furtherance of a trade dispute, to attend at or
near a house or place where a person resides or works or carries on
business or happens to be if they so attend merely for the purpose
of peacefully obtaining or communicating information or of peacefully persuading any person to work or abstain from working.

However, this provision has been repealed by the Industrial
Relations Act, 1971, and replaced by a narrower provision, which
applies when one or more persons, in contemplation or furtherance
of an industrial dispute, attend at or near (*a*) a place where a person
works or carries on business, or (*b*) any other place where a person
happens to be, *not being a place where he resides.*   If such attendance
is merely for the purpose of peacefully obtaining information from
the person, or peacefully communicating information to him, or
peacefully persuading him to work or not to work, then it will not
of itself constitute an offence under section 7 of the 1875 Act or under
any other enactment or rule of law, nor will it of itself constitute a
tort.

Of course, if the attendance is accompanied by the commission
of *other* crimes (*e.g.* malicious damage) or torts (*e.g.* trespass), then
the person committing them is in no way protected.[3]

Finally it is an offence for a person, with a view to compel any
other person to abstain from doing or to do any act which such
other person has a legal right to do or abstain from doing, to follow
such other person with two or more other persons in a disorderly
manner in or through any street or road.[4]

It is a defence to a charge under any of the sections we have just
considered to show that the acts complained of were not done

---

[1] Conspiracy and Protection of Property Act, 1875, s. 7 (4).
[2] S. 2.
[3] For an example of pickets going beyond the scope of the statutory protection, see *Tynan* v. *Balmer,* [1967] 1 Q.B. 91; [1966] 2 All E.R. 133.   See also
the power of the police to limit pickets when there is a risk of breach of the
peace: *Piddington* v. *Bates,* [1960] 3 All E.R. 660; [1961] 1 W.L.R. 162.
[4] Conspiracy and Protection of Property Act, 1875, s. 7 (5).

"wrongfully and without legal authority." The result is that the onus on the prosecution in any of these offences is to give proof of the overt acts complained of and to prove that the acts were done with a view to compel the abstention from or commission of an act which another had the right to do. Then, if the defence cannot show justification for the overt acts, the defence will fail.[1]

(2) **Tortious Liabilities.**—The character and objects of trade unions are such that their activities constantly tend to interference with the labour and trade activities of others and in relation to these they are in danger of infringing the law of tort and the law of crime. Many of the criminal aspects of their activities were dealt with by the Trade Union Act, 1871, and the Conspiracy and Protection of Property Act, 1875.[2] The latter Act had, in certain circumstances, removed from the fear of prosecution for criminal conspiracy, persons engaged in a trade dispute; it had, however, no application to civil actions.[3] This proposition had a considerable influence on the subsequent legal history of trade unionism for if the Act protected trade unionists from criminal proceedings, it did not protect the unions from the payment of damages in respect of the tort of conspiracy. And, not unnaturally, it was to the civil remedy that aggrieved persons now turned. The decisions in such actions caused disquiet amongst trade unionists and the disquiet reached considerable proportions after the judgment of the House of Lords in the *Taff Vale* case.[4] For it was there decided that a trade union could be sued in tort and its assets taken in satisfaction of the judgment. Any other decision would have placed trade unions in a preferential position compared with that occupied by other associations; but the *Taff Vale* decision meant that all the funds of the union, including those to which the members had subscribed for the receipt of benefits, were available to injured parties as damages in appropriate circumstances. The dilemma was a real one, and a Royal Commission was set up under the chairmanship of Lord DUNEDIN. The Commission reported in 1906. The Commission did not propose that legislation should be introduced the effect of which would be to reverse the Taff Vale decision. Its proposals were more modest and in particular it was suggested that the funds of the unions should be divided into those appropriated for the payment of benefits and those not so appropriated. The benefit funds, it was suggested, should be protected from the liability of being taken in execution but not so the non-benefit funds. The Government, however, went further, and by

---

1 See *J. Lyons & Sons* v. *Wilkins*, [1899] 1 Ch. 255, *per* LINDLEY, M.R., at p. 267.
2 *Supra*, p. 458.
3 *Quinn* v. *Leathem*, [1901] A.C. 495, per Lord LINDLEY at p. 542.
4 *Taff Vale Railway Co.* v. *Amalgamated Society of Railway Servants*, [1901] A.C. 426.

the Trade Disputes Act, 1906 gave complete immunity to the unions in respect of actions in tort.[1]

The Industrial Relations Act, 1971, has now repealed the 1906 Act *in toto* and has not provided unions with any general immunity in respect of actions in tort. Trade unions are therefore now in precisely the same position as individuals in respect of tortious liability, that is to say they are answerable to the general law of tort except to the extent that the Industrial Relations Act (following but modifying the pattern of the 1906 Act) provides limited immunities in respect of certain acts done in contemplation or furtherance of an industrial dispute. It is therefore necessary to discuss the torts which are likely to be committed in the course of industrial action.[2]

Inducing Breach of Contract

It is unlawful for a person (X), who knows of a contract between the plaintiff and a third party, intentionally to induce the third party to break the contract and cause loss to the plaintiff, unless X's action can be justified. This is the tort which has developed from the case of *Lumley* v. *Gye*[3] and has now been re-created in the form of the unfair industrial practice of section 96 of the Industrial Relations Act, which we considered earlier.[4]

In its simplest form, this tort will be committed where X induces a group of workers to take industrial action in breach of their contracts of employment[5] or an employer to break a commercial contract which he has with another concern with which X's union is in dispute.[6] The defence of justification is only likely to succeed in an extreme case.

In *South Wales Miners' Federation* v. *Glamorgan Coal Co.*[7] colliers, in breach of their contracts, ceased work on the directions of the appellant federation. The object of the federation was to keep up the price of coal according to which wages were regulated. The appellants were held to be liable in damages. The fact that there

---

[1] S. 4. However, doubts remained on the question whether this provision embraced immunity from injunctions. Recently, the better view became that it did. See *Torquay Hotel Co., Ltd.* v. *Cousins*, [1969] 2 Ch. 106; [1969] 1 All E.R. 522.

[2] Only a brief discussion is possible in the space available. For a more detailed discussion of the position shortly before the 1971 Act, see A. D. Hughes, (1970) 86 *L.Q.R.* 181.

[3] (1853),), 2 E. & B. 216.

[4] Many of the problems considered earlier are equally relevant here, *e.g.* the meaning of " induce ", the effect of strikes on the contract of employment, the requirement of knowledge.

[5] *Eg. Camden Exhibition and Display Co.* v. *Lynott*, [1966] 1 Q.B. 555; [1965.] 3 All E.R. 28, where, however, the defendants were protected by s. 3 of the 1906 Act, as to which see *infra*.

[6] *E.g. Torquay Hotel Co., Ltd.* v. *Cousins*, [1969] 2 Ch. 106; [1969] 1 All E.R. 522.

[7] [1905] A.C. 239; and see *British Motor Trade Association* v. *Salvadori*, [1949] Ch. 556; [1949] 1 All E.R. 208.

was no ill will towards the employers and that the men were acting in furtherance of their own interest was held not to amount to justification. The only case in which the defence of justification has been accepted is *Brimelow* v. *Casson*[1] where, in an effort to compel a theatrical manager to pay reasonable wages, the defendants induced owners of theatres to refuse the use of their theatres to the plaintiff either by declining to enter into contracts with him or breaking contracts already in existence. The defendants were a committee representative of certain associations of actors and there was evidence that the plaintiff was paying wages so low that members of his company could not live without resorting to vice. "As has been pointed out," said RUSSELL, J.,

> "no general rule can be laid down as a general guide in such cases, but I confess that if justification does not exist here I can hardly conceive the case in which it would be present. These defendants, as it seems to me, owed a duty to their calling and to its members, and, I am tempted to add, to the public, to take all necessary peaceful steps to terminate the payment of this insufficient wage. . . ."[2]

But, as is clearly shown by the *Glamorgan Coal* case, though a duty may amount to justification, a mere self-interest cannot do so.

In cases where there is an inducement to industrial action without the commission of a breach of contract or any other unlawful act, this tort is clearly not committed. The new provisions relating to strikes after due notice[3] are of the utmost importance here.

The situations which we have considered so far are all examples of simple or " direct " inducement, in which X induces Y to break Y's contract with Z. Direct inducements of this kind are (subject to the defence of justification and the statutory immunities considered later) wrongful in themselves. It is also necessary to consider the more complicated situations of " indirect " inducement, the best example of which is where X, by directly inducing Y to break Y's contract with Z, indirectly induces Z to break a contract between himself and, say, his commercial customer. In *J.T. Stratford & Son, Ltd.* v. *Lindley*[4] the defendant union officials induced some of their members to break their contracts of employment, thus causing the members' employers to break their commercial contracts with the plaintiff company (which was associated with another company which was the real target of the defendants' actions). The House of Lords held that the plaintiffs were entitled to an injunction to restrain this indirect inducement of breach of the

---

[1] [1924] 1 Ch. 302; *Camden Nominees, Ltd.* v. *Forcey*, [1940] Ch. 352; [1940] 2 All E.R. 1. It was suggested in *British Industrial Plastics, Ltd.* v. *Ferguson* (1938), 160 L.T. 95, at p. 98 that a desire not to break the law might amount to justification. This is very doubtful.
[2] [1924] 1 Ch. 302, at p. 313.
[3] Industrial Relations Act, 1971, s. 147, as to which see consideration of the s. 96 unfair industrial practice, *supra*, p. 489.
[4] [1965] A.C. 269; [1964] 3 All E.R. 102.

commercial contracts.[1] The significant difference between direct and indirect inducement is that, whereas the former is tortious in itself, the latter is only so if it is brought about by the employment of unlawful means. In the *Stratford* case, such unlawful means were found in the direct inducement of the breaches of employment contracts.[2] This may be contrasted with the earlier case of *D. C. Thomson & Co., Ltd.* v. *Deakin*.[3] The plaintiffs made it a condition of employment that their workpeople should not join a union, though the condition was disregarded by certain employees and one such employee was discharged. His union, in his support, called out on strike those of its members who were employed by the plaintiffs and sought aid from other unions concerned with the supply of raw materials. Bowaters Sales, Ltd. supplied the plaintiffs, with papers and certain of their employees objected to loading and delivering goods of Thomson's. In these circumstances Bowaters decided not to ask their employees to effect such loading and delivering and they ceased to supply the plaintiffs, thus being in breach of their commercial contract. The plaintiffs then sought an injunction against Deakin and certain other union officials, restraining them from procuring breaches of contract between Thomson's and Bowaters. The union officials replied (*a*) that in approaching other unions they had merely asked for help and that (*b*) in so far as Bowaters' employees were concerned they had not given instructions to them not to load or deliver paper.

The Court of Appeal was quite clear that whilst an action would have lain had the defendants with knowledge of actual contracts contrived by wrongful acts a situation which made it impossible for Bowaters to perform the contract, no such action would lie if the loaders and carters acted lawfully even though a breach of contract might ensue. In the present case there was no evidence of the procurement of wrongful acts, and in these circumstances an injunction could not be given. Although, as we have seen, the courts have in recent years appeared to dilute the requirement of " knowledge " and the meaning of " induce,"[4] this case remains an outstanding illustration of the principle that for an indirect inducement to be actionable, it must have been accompanied by unlawful means. Since the defendants had not induced Bowaters' employees to break their contracts of employment, the element of unlawful means was missing.

The organisation of industrial action is, of course, particularly susceptible to the tort of inducement. Thus, since 1906, legislation has provided a limited immunity from liability. This immunity

---

[1] *Cf.* Lord PEARCE, who treated the case as one of *direct* inducement of breach of the commercial contract.

[2] The defendants were not protected by the 1906 Act because they were not acting in furtherance of a trade dispute.

[3] [1952] Ch. 646; [1952] 2 All E.R. 361.

[4] These developments were considered in the context of the s. 96 unfair industrial practice, *supra*, p. 489.

has been extended by the Industrial Relations Act, 1971, which provides that an act done by a person in contemplation or furtherance of an industrial dispute shall not be actionable in tort on the ground only that it induces another person to break a contract to which that other person is a party, or prevents another person from performing such a contract.[1] The previous protection, which was contained in section 3 of the now repealed Trade Disputes Act, 1906, was limited to the inducement of breaches of contracts *of employment.* The new provision, on the other hand, is wide enough to embrace commercial contracts. However, it remains tied to the " industrial dispute " formula, with the result that in some situations the possibility of liability survives. Since the unfair industrial practices of sections 96 and 98 can only give rise to liability within the industrial dispute formula, liability for inducement at common law is especially important when the inducement was not in contemplation or furtherance of an industrial dispute. In other words, the statutory immunity is withheld from the situations in which defendants are most vulnerable to an action at common law.

Interference with Contracts

The tort of inducing a breach of contract has been well established for over a hundred years. However, there is recent authority to the effect that it is tortious in some circumstances to interfere with the performance of a contract without causing any actual breach. This is the basis of the judgment of Lord DENNING, M.R., in *Torquay Hotel Co., Ltd.* v. *Cousins.*[2] Whereas WINN and RUSSELL, L.JJ., found the defendants liable for inducing breaches of contract (notwithstanding the presence of the *force majeure* clause in the supply contract), the Master of the Rolls preferred to innovate.

> " The time has come when the principle should be further extended to cover ' *deliberate and direct interference with the execution of a contract without that causing any breach.*' ... The principle can be subdivided into three elements: First, there must be *interference* in the execution of a contract. The interference is not confined to the procurement of a *breach* of contract. It extends to a case where a third person *prevents* or *hinders* one party from performing his contract, even though it be not a breach. Secondly, the interference must be *deliberate.* The person must know of the contract or, at any rate, turn a blind eye to it and intend to interfere with it; see *Emerald Construction Co., Ltd.* v. *Lowthian.*[3] Thirdly, the interference must be *direct.* Indirect interference will not do ... *Indirect* interference is only unlawful if unlawful means are used."[4]

---

[1] Industrial Relations Act, 1971, s. 132(1).
[2] [1969] 2 Ch. 106; [1969] 1 All E.R. 522.
[3] [1966] 1 All E.R. 1013; [1966] 1 W.L.R. 691.
[4] [1969] 2 Ch. 106 at pp. 137–138. But see now *Acrow (Automatic), Ltd.* v. *Rex Chainbelt Inc.,* [1971] 3 All E.R. 1175; [1971] 1 W.L.R. 1676, where Lord DENNING, M. R., appears to restate the principle with the difference that unlawful means are made a prerequisite to liability for both direct and indirect interference with contracts, trade or business. *Cf. Brekkes* v. *Cattell,* [1972] Ch. 105; [1971] 1 All E.R. 1031.

Whether one considers this to be an extension of the tort of inducement or the creation of a new tort, it is clearly of the utmost significance in the context of industrial action. Once again, however,
it is only likely to arise outside the scope of the " industrial dispute "
formula, since the immunity in respect of inducing breaches of
contracts applies also to the prevention of performance of contracts.[1]
Furthermore, it is provided that an act done by a person in contemplation or furtherance of an industrial dispute is not actionable in
tort on the ground only that it is an interference with the trade,
business or employment of another person, or with the right of
another person to dispose of his capital or his labour as he wills.[2]

Intimidation

The tort of intimidation is committed when the plaintiff suffers
damage as a result of action taken by X in response to an unlawful
threat made to X by the defendant. The case of *Rookes* v. *Barnard*[3]
established that this tort embraced not only threats of criminal
or tortious conduct, but also threats to break contracts. The
appellant was (lawfully) dismissed by his employer as a result of
an ultimatum in the form of a threat of industrial action emanating
from the respondents. It was conceded that the industrial action
would have involved breaches of their contracts of employment
by the participants (who included two of the three respondents). It
was held by the House of Lords that the respondents had committed
the tort of intimidation in that Rookes had suffered damage (loss
of employment) as a result of action taken by his employer (lawful
dismissal) in response to an unlawful threat made to the employer by
the respondents. This decision opened up a vast new potentiality
of liability in respect of industrial action. The 1906 Act had not
provided any immunity in relation to intimidation, which was
hardly surprising since the tort had seen no development since
1793, when it appeared to be confined to threats of physical violence.[4]
In 1965 a stop-gap immunity was introduced in the Trade Disputes
Act of that year, but the 1965 Act has now been repealed. In its
place, the Industrial Relations Act, 1971, provides that an act done
by a person in contemplation or furtherance of an industrial dispute
shall not be actionable in tort on the ground only that it consists in
his threatening that a contract (whether one to which he is a party
or not)[5] will be broken or will be prevented from being performed,

---

[1] Industrial Relations Act, 1971, s. 132(1). *Supra*, p. 508.

[2] S. 132(2). This subsection is based on limb 2 of s.3 of the Trade Disputes
Act, 1906, which appeared to have lost all significance after *Rookes* v. *Barnard*,
[1964] A.C. 1129; [1964] 1 All E.R. 367, but which may have found a rôle in the
aftermath of Lord DENNING's innovation. For the background to this
development, see Wedderburn, *The Worker and the Law*, 2nd Ed. (Pelican),
pp. 358–360 and 368.

[3] [1964] A.C. 1129; [1964] 1 All E.R. 367.

[4] *Tarleton* v. *M'Gawky* (1794), Peake 270.

[5] Thus covering both the respondents who had contracts to break in *Rookes*
and the one who had no such contract.

or that he will induce another person to break a contract to which that other person is a party or will prevent another person from performing such a contract.[1] So, once again, legislation has provided an immunity in the "industrial dispute" situation, thus leaving liability to develop only in other situations.[2]

Conspiracy

The tort of conspiracy may take either of two forms. First, it is committed when two or more persons combine so as to damage the plaintiff by the employment of means which are lawful in themselves, but with a predominant purpose other than that of advancing the legitimate interests of the combiners. Secondly, it is committed when two or more persons combine so as to damage the plaintiff by the employment of means which are unlawful in themselves, in which case the purpose of the combiners is irrelevant.

Conspiracy to injure by the employment of lawful means constituted a serious impediment to the lawfulness of industrial action after the case of *Quinn* v. *Leathem*[3] in 1901, but some of the sting was taken out of that decision by section 1 of the Trade Disputes Act, 1906. The immunity provided by that section has now been replaced by a provision in the Industrial Relations Act, 1971, to the effect that an agreement or combination by two or more persons to do or procure to be done any act in contemplation or furtherance of an industrial dispute shall not be actionable in tort, if the act in question is one which, if done without any such agreement or combination, would not be actionable in tort.[4] Moreover, in the last fifty years or so, the courts have adopted a more liberal approach to the legitimate interests which may be pursued by organised labour.[5] Consequently, conspiracy to injure by the employment of lawful means should only raise its head in the context of industrial action when the defendants act other than in contemplation or furtherance of an industrial dispute. However, once the defendants step outside that formula, they may find that they have also exceeded the pursuit of legitimate interests, even in the modern sense. Such a case is *Huntley* v. *Thornton*,[6] which we met when considering the " industrial dispute " formula.

Conspiracy to injure by *unlawful* means was not neutralised by any provision of immunity in the 1906 Act. Its scope is as wide as the

---

[1] Industrial Relations Act, 1971, s. 132(1).
[2] *Morgan* v. *Fry*, [1968] 2 Q.B. 710; [1968] 3 All E.R. 452, was an action on pre-1965 intimidation, but it failed because of the Court of Appeal's views on the legality of the strike notice. A post-Industrial Relations Act worker in the position of *Rookes* or *Morgan* finds his remedy in ss. 5, 33, 106 and 119.
[3] [1901] A.C. 495.
[4] Industrial Relations Act, 1971, s. 132(3).
[5] See, *e.g.*, *Reynolds* v. *Shipping Federation*, [1924] 1 Ch. 28; *Crofter Handwoven Harris Tweed* v. *Veitch*, [1942] A.C. 435; [1942] 1 All E.R. 142.
[6] [1957] 1 All E.R. 234; [1957] 1 W.L.R. 321.

scope of unlawful means. Thus, any conspiracy to injure by means that are criminal or tortious[1] and have not been neutralised by the provision of a statutory immunity, is actionable. Thus, the respondents in *Rookes* v. *Barnard*[2] were liable on the basis of a conspiracy to intimidate, since intimidation was not at that time the subject of a statutory immunity. However, the future development of unlawful means not covered by such an immunity is curtailed by a provision in the Industrial Relations Act. Where, in any court, proceedings in tort are brought in respect of an agreement or combination by two or more persons to do or procure to be done an act in contemplation or furtherance of an industrial dispute and the immunity in respect of conspiracy to injure by the employment of lawful means[3] does not provide a defence to the proceedings, the court *must* nevertheless stay the proceedings if the act is (*a*) the subject-matter of proceedings before the Industrial Court or an Industrial Tribunal,[4] *or* (*b*) one which could be made the subject-matter of proceedings before either of those bodies as an unfair industrial practice or other breach of duty imposed by the Act.[5] It seems, therefore, that yet again the development of a common law liability in relation to industrial action will only take place outside the " industrial dispute " formula.

10. Recovery of Sums Awarded against Unions and Limitation of Liability

Generally speaking, any judgment, order or award which is made against a registered trade union in any proceedings (*i.e.* either under the Act or otherwise) is enforceable against any property belonging to, or held in trust for, the trade union. However, where an award of compensation or damages, or for the payment of any costs or expenses, is made against a registered trade union, or its trustees *qua* trustees (but not in respect of a breach of trust), or some of its members on behalf of themselves and all the others, the Act protects certain property from enforcement. The protected property is any property (*a*) belonging to a trustee of the trade union otherwise than in his capacity as trustee; (*b*) belonging to any member otherwise than jointly or in common with the other members; (*c*) belonging to an official who is neither a member nor a trustee; or (*d*) comprised in a fund belonging to the trade union, if, under the rules of the trade union such property is precluded from being used for financing strikes or other industrial action.[6]

---

[1] In *Rookes* v. *Barnard*, Lord Devlin said that although a breach of contract was unlawful means for the purposes of intimidation, this did not necessarily mean that it was so for purposes of conspiracy: [1964] A.C. at p. 1210.
[2] [1964] A.C. 1129.
[3] *I.e.* the immunity provided by s. 132(3).
[4] Neither of which can entertain proceedings in tort—s. 136.
[5] S. 132(4).
[6] Industrial Relations Act, 1971, s. 153.

Civil proceedings by or against *unregistered* unions may be brought in the name of the organisation. Generally, any judgment, order or award made in any such proceedings against an unregistered union is enforceable, by way of execution, diligence, punishment for contempt or otherwise, against any property belonging to, or held in trust for, the organisation, to the like extent and in the like manner as if the organisation were a body corporate. However, protection is again provided for (*a*) any property comprised in a fund belonging to or held in trust for the organisation, if, under the rules of the organisation, such property is precluded from being used for financing strikes or other industrial action; and (*b*) property belonging to any member of the organisation otherwise than jointly or in common with the other members.[1]

Statutory Limits on Compensation.—*Registered* trade unions, including those on the provisional register, enjoy statutory limits on the amount of compensation which may be awarded against them in any proceedings before the Industrial Court (but not before the ordinary courts). The appropriate limit (*a*) in the case of a trade union having a membership of less than 5,000 is £5,000; (*b*) in a case of a trade union having a membership of 5,000 but less than 25,000, is £25,000; (*c*) in the case of a trade union having a membership of 25,000 but less than 100,000, is £50,000; and (*d*) in the case of a trade union having a membership of 100,000 or more, is £100,000.[2]

---

[1] S. 154.
[2] Industrial Relations Act, 1971, s. 117.

INDEX

ABSENCE FROM WORK
    contract of service, in, 74, 75, 79
ACCEPTANCE. *See* OFFER AND ACCEPTANCE.
ACCIDENTS. *See also* INDUSTRIAL INJURIES ACT, 1965.
    arising out of and in the course of the emoloyment, 244–246
    factories, in, notification of, 307–308
    fatal, limitation of time, 239–240
        master's liability for, 234, *et seq.*
    mines, in, 348, 349, 350–351
        notification of, 350–351
    offices, in, notification of, 343
ADAPTING FOR SALE
    meaning of, 250
ADVISORY COMMITTEES ON YOUTH EMPLOYMENT, 384
AGENCY
    estoppel, agency by, 187
    form of contract of, 186
    holding-out, agency by, 187
    necessity, agency of, 188
    ratification of contract of, 186
    servant's liability arising from contract of, 197–198
        rights arising from contract of, 211–212
    termination of, 190
AGENCY SHOP AGREEMENT
    categories of, 58–59
    meaning, 58
    power to enter into, 469
AGENT
    Crown servant as, 31–32
    diplomatic, capacity to enter into contract of service, 32–33
    distinguished from servant, 18–19
    general, 188–190
    infant, adult may employ as, 185
    meaning, 17
    servant's authority as, 185, *et seq.*, 197–198
    special, 188–190
AGRICULTURAL WAGES BOARD, 150–151
AGRICULTURAL WAGES COMMITTEES, 150–151
AGRICULTURE
    apprenticeship agreements, 151
    definition, 151
    holidays, 150, 151
    minimum wage rates, 150, 151
    wages in, 150–152
AIR CONTAINERS
    factories, in, 295
ALIEN
    contract of service with, 33
    enemy, disabilities, 34
    meaning, 33, 34
ALTERNATIVE REMEDIES
    legal position when plaintiff has choice of remedies, 425–426
ANALYSIS
    inspector may take samples for, 307
APPRENTICE
    capacity of, to enter into contract, 61
    consent to be bound, 61

[1]

APPRENTICE—*continued*
drunkenness of, justifying dismissal, 62
illness of, effect on contract of apprenticeship, 62
insurance of, 233
master's remedies against, 64
minimum age, 61
misconduct of, effect on contract of apprenticeship, 62–63
wages council, powers concerning, 144
APPRENTICESHIP. *See* CONTRACT OF APPRENTICESHIP.
APPROVED CLOSED SHOP AGREEMENT
application for, inducing, 496
exemption for, 57
power to enter into, 469
ARBITRATION
compulsory, 446
abolition of, 446
settlement of disputes by, 443, 446
ARMED FORCES
Equal Pay Act, 1970, application of, 123
Industrial Injuries Act, excepted employment, 390
National Insurance Acts, application of, 164
reinstatement in civil employment after service in, 386
unfair dismissal rules inapplicable to, 31, 108
ARREST
by servant, liability of master for, 172–173, 177, 178
ASSAULT
by servant, in defence of master or property of master, 199
liability of master for, 179
BAILMENT
contract of, 18, 19, 21
BAKEHOUSE
basement, not generally to be used as, 306
BALLOT
agency shop agreement, on, 59
continuance of, 60
amalgamations and transfers of engagement, 485
approved closed shop agreement, on, 58
political objects, application of funds for, 484
recognition of sole bargaining agent, 435
withdrawal, 436
strike, 443, 452–453
trade union rules, as to, 462, 474
BANKRUPTCY
of master, effect on contract of apprenticeship, 62
service, 68
servant, 68
BASEMENT
not generally to be used as a bakehouse, 306
BENEFITS
National Insurance Acts, under. *See* NATIONAL INSURANCE.
National Insurance (Industrial Injuries) Act, 1965, under, 408, *et seq.*, [415–416
BONUS
illness, effect on, 125
right to, 125
BREACH OF CONTRACT. *See also* CONTRACT OF SERVICE.
actual, 111
anticipatory, 111, 112, 493
criminal, when, 199–200, 500
damages for, 113, 114–116

[**2**]

[3]

CLOAKROOMS
mines, in, 370
offices, in, 338
CLOSED SHOP
agency shop agreement, 58–59, 469
approved closed shop agreement, 57, 469, 496
pre-entry agreement void, 56–58, 496
pre- 1971 concept, 472, 473
COAL MINE. *See* MINES.
CODE OF INDUSTRIAL RELATIONS PRACTICE
bargaining unit, 432
disclosure of information, 442
provision for, 428
scope of, 428
trade union employee–representation at workplace, 55
COLLECTIVE AGREEMENT
collective bargaining. *See* COLLECTIVE BARGAINING.
breach of, inducement of, 493
unfair industrial practice, as, 497
definition, 438
Industrial Relations Act, 1971, under, 438
joint negotiating bodies, decisions of, 438–439
establishment of, 438
legally binding, whether, 24, 437–438
procedure agreements, 439–441, 469
relation with contract of service, 24, 120–121, 437
COLLECTIVE BARGAINING
bargaining unit, definition, 432
recognition of, 433–435
withdrawal of, 435–436
collective agreement. *See* COLLECTIVE AGREEMENT.
disclosure of information, 441–442, 469
Industrial Arbitration Board, reference to, 445
Industrial Relations Act, 1971, under, 432, *et seq.*
joint negotiating panel, 432–433
recognition for purposes of, 432–435, 437
order, 435, 437
unfair industrial practice, 497
withdrawal of, 435–436
settlement of disputes, 442, *et seq.*
sole bargaining agent, 432–433, 469
recognition of, 433–435
withdrawal of, 435–436
unfair industrial practices as to, 436–437, 445, 498
wage regulating legislation to implement, 139
COLOUR WASHING
factories, in, 271
COMMISSION
advance of repayment, 125
determination of proper amount, 125
illness, effect of, 125
COMMISSION OF INQUIRY
powers, under Wages Councils Acts, 140
COMMISSION ON INDUSTRIAL RELATIONS
agency shop agreement, ballot for, 59
continuance of, 60
approved closed shop agreement, approval of, 57–58
bargaining unit, recognition of, 433–435
disclosure of information, question of, 442
establishment of, 430–431

Index

Index

DRUNKENNESS
apprentice, of, justifying dismissal, 62
effect on capacity to contract, 38–39
servant, of, justifying dismissal, 103
DRY DOCK
may be within definition of factory, 252
DURESS
service, contract of, effect on, 28
DUST, FUMES AND OTHER IMPURITIES
exhaust appliances, provision of, in factory, 272–273, 301–304
explosive, in factory, 295
suppression of, in mines, 364, 367
           quarries, 372
DUTIES
master, of, under contract of service, 82, *et seq.*
servant, of, under contract of service, 88, *et seq.*
EARLY CLOSING DAY
shops, for, 326 *et seq.*
EARNINGS-RELATED SUPPLEMENT
industrial injuries benefit, 409
unemployment benefit, 162, 165, 166
ELECTRIC GENERATORS AND MOTORS
fencing of, 274
ELECTRICAL STATIONS
Factories Act, 1961, application to, 257
ELECTRICITY
use of, in mines, 365
           quarries, 373
EMBEZZLEMENT
theft, replaced by, 6 n.   *See* THEFT.
EMPLOYED PERSON.   *See also* SERVANT.
definition, 41
employee, meaning, 108, 441
information to be given to, 441
medical supervision of, in factory, 274
obligations of, under Factories Act, 1961 . . . 261–263, 269, 270
offences, liability under Factories Act, 1961 . . . 269–270
safety appliances, must use, 261–263
EMPLOYER.   *See* MASTER; MASTER AND SERVANT.
EMPLOYMENT
common, abolition of defence of, 213, 234
industrial accident out of and in the course of, 399–407, 422
local, provision of, 375–377.   *And see* DEVELOPMENT DISTRICT.
normal working hours, under contract of service, 78–79
particulars as to terms of, 41, 42
reinstatement in civil.   *See* REINSTATEMENT IN CIVIL EMPLOYMENT.
servant acting within scope of, 172, *et seq.*
shops, in, 323–325
EMPLOYMENT AND TRAINING ACT, 1948 . . . 383–385
ENGINEERING CONSTRUCTION
definition, 259
works of, application of Factories Act, 1961, to, 254, 258–261
EQUAL PAY ACT, 1970
effect of, 122–124
job evaluation, 122
like work, meaning, 122
work rated as equivalent, 122
EQUIPMENT
defective, liability for, 217–218
master's duty to supply and maintain proper, 188, 214–218

Index

[12]

Index

Index

Index

INDUSTRIAL ACCIDENT. *See* INDUSTRIAL INJURIES ACT, 1965.
INDUSTRIAL ARBITRATION BOARD
   collective agreement, powers as to discrimination in, 123–124
      bargaining, disputes as to, 445–446
   disclosure of information, failure to comply, 446
   industrial court renamed, 123 n., 430, 444
   Industrial Relations Act, 1971, functions under, 430, 444–446
INDUSTRIAL COURT
   Industrial Arbitration Board, renamed, 123 n., 430, 444
   Industrial Relations Act, 1971, under. *See* NATIONAL INDUSTRIAL
      [RELATIONS COURT.
   redundancy fund rebate for award by, 138
   reference to, under Road Haulage Wages Act, 1938 . . . 149
INDUSTRIAL DISEASES. *See also* INDUSTRIAL INJURIES ACT, 1965.
   notification of, 307–308
INDUSTRIAL DISPUTES. *See also* IRREGULAR INDUSTRIAL ACTION;
      [LOCK-OUT; STRIKE.
   contract of service, in, 76–77, 492
   Contracts of Employment Act, 1963, effect of, 76–77
   definition, 487
   in contemplation or furtherance of, 487–489
   unfair dismissal following, 107–108, 470
      industrial practice, industrial action, extraneous parties, against,
         [494–495
         in support of, 494
         [*See also* TRADE DISPUTE.
INDUSTRIAL DISPUTES TRIBUNAL
   abolition, 451
   former function of, 448–449
INDUSTRIAL ESTATES MANAGEMENT CORPORATIONS, 377
INDUSTRIAL INJURIES ACT, 1965
   accident arising out of and in the course of the employment, 394, 399, *et seq.*
      process compared, 398–399
   accidents, successive, 415
   administration of the Act, 417, *et seq.*
   alternative remedies in relation to, 425–426
   benefits, adoptive parents, for, 413
      disqualification from, 415
      receivable under, 408, *et seq.*
      relatives eligible, 412–415
      those working on Continental Shelf, for, 408
   compensation for pre-1948 accidents, 387
   contract of service void, does not necessarily debar from benefits, 391
   contracting out prohibited, 416
   contributions, employers' liability to pay, 391–393
      exemption from liability to pay, 391–392
      offences arising from liability to pay, 393–394
      payable, 391–394
         by stamps or alternative methods, 393
   deliberate injury, 396–397
   determination of claims, procedure for, 420–422
      under, 417, *et seq.*
      questions by medical appeal tribunal, 418–420
         board, 418–420
         Secretary of State, 417–418
   disablement pension, 410, 411, 412
   earnings-related supplement, 409
   exempted employments, 389–390
   industrial accident, 394, 399, *et seq.*
      definition, 422

[17]

Index

INDUSTRIAL INJURIES ACT, 1965—*continued*
  industrial accidents, successive, 415
    death benefit, when and by whom receivable, 412–415
    disablement benefit, when receivable, 409–412
    diseases, accident producing, 396, 398
      benefits payable in respect of, 407–408
      byssinosis, 408
      generally considered, 407
      pneumoconiosis, 407–408
      respiratory diseases, 407–408
  Industrial Injuries Advisory Council, constitution and powers, 422–423
    Fund, 391, 393, 394, 424
  industrial injury benefit, 408–409
  inspectors, powers and duties, of 423–424
  insurable employments, 8, 387–391
  insurance officer, 420–422
  insured person acting in contravention of regulations, position of, 404–405
  legal proceedings under, 424
  local tribunal, constitution and powers of, 420, 421
    medical appeal tribunal, relationship between, 418–419
  medical appeal tribunal. *See* medical board, *infra*.
    board, appointment of, 419
    jurisdiction of, 418
    review of decisions of, 419–420
  National Insurance Commissioner, 420–422
  offences, 393–394
  penalties, provisions for, under, 393, 394
  personal injury, definition of, 395
  regulations, for those working on Continental Shelf, 391
    power to make, 409, 416
  research, powers of Secretary of State relating to, 422
  risks insured against, 394, *et seq.*
  special hardship allowance, 411–412
  suicide, 397
  supplementary schemes, 416
  treatment of person incapable of work, 408–409
  unemployability supplement, 410–411
INDUSTRIAL ORGANISATION AND DEVELOPMENT ACT, 1947 . . .
                             [380–383
INDUSTRIAL RELATIONS ACT, 1971
  agency shop agreement, categories of, 58–59
    meaning, 58
    power to enter into, 469
  approved closed shop agreement, application for, inducing, 496
    exemption for, 57
    power to enter into, 469
  ballot, sole bargaining agent, as to, 435, 436
    strike, 443, 452–453
  breach of contract, inducing, 209, 211, 469, 489–494, 495, 505–508
  closed shop, approved agreement, exemption for, 57
    pre-entry agreement void, 56–58, 496
  Code, 428
    bargaining unit, 432
    disclosure of information, 442
    trade union employee-representation at workplace, 55
  collective agreements, 24, 437, *et seq.*
    procedure agreements, 439–441, 469
    bargaining, 428, 432, *et seq. See also* COLLECTIVE BARGAINING.
  Commission on Industrial Relations, 430–431. *See also* COMMISSION ON
                            [INDUSTRIAL RELATIONS.

[18]

Index

INDUSTRIAL RELATIONS ACT, 1971—*continued*
complaints procedure. *See* TRADE UNIONS.
conciliation officers, 431–432
cooling off period, 443, 451–452
courts, 428–430
Crown, application to, 31, 108
dismissal, meaning, 105–106
 unfair, protection against, 102, 105–110
employee, information to be given to, 441
 meaning, 108, 441
formation of contract of service, effect on, 54–60
general principles, 427
history of, 427
industrial action, liabilities in relation to, 486
 unfair industrial practices arising out of, 486 *et seq.*
 relations and law, effect on, 3, 486
irregular industrial action. *See* IRREGULAR INDUSTRIAL ACTION.
joint negotiating bodies, agreements between, 438–439
lock-out, cooling off period, 451–452
machinery, 428, *et seq.*
National Industrial Relations Court. *See* NATIONAL INDUSTRIAL RELA-
        [TIONS COURT.
organisation of workers, meaning, 55 n.
   non-membership, right of, 55. *See also* ORGAN-
         [ISATION OF WORKERS.
particulars of employment, effect on, 42
picketing, 503
pre-entry closed shop agreement void, 56–58, 496
procedure agreements, 439–441, 469
    disputes as to, 487
provisional register, 463–465
registrar, amalgamation, ballot for, 485
  complaints, application to, 479–480, 482, 484
   by, Industrial Court, to, 480, 481
     Tribunal, to, 480
  trade unions, insolvent, 467
   rules, alterations required by, 461, 463
    examination of, 460
registration of trade unions, 459, *et seq.*, 469–470
settlement of disputes under, 443, 451–453
    internal, 478, *et seq.*
strike. *See* STRIKE.
trade union, meaning, 55, 454
  membership, right of, 54–55, 462, 470
  non-membership, right of, 55
  registered. *See* TRADE UNIONS.
  registration, 459, *et seq.*, 469–470
   former provisions, 458
  unregistered. *See* ORGANISATIONS OF WORKERS.
tribunals, 428–430. *See also* INDUSTRIAL ARBITRATION BOARD; INDUS-
         [TRIAL TRIBUNALS.
unfair dismissal, 100, 102, 105–110, 470. *See also* UNFAIR DISMISSAL.
 industrial practices, 458, 486 *et seq. See also* UNFAIR INDUSTRIAL
         [PRACTICES.
unit of employment, definition, 439
    procedure agreements, 439–441
unregistered trade unions. *See* ORGANISATION OF WORKERS.
worker, meaning, 55
INDUSTRIAL TRIBUNALS
agency shop agreement, contributions under, 59

[19]

Index

I.L.—20*   [21]

Index

OFFER AND ACCEPTANCE
  apprenticeship, contract of, in relation to, 61
  duress, effect of, on, 28
  general offer, 23
  generally considered, 22, *et seq.*
  misrepresentation, effect of, on, 27
  mistake, effect of, on, 24
  particular offer, 23
  rejection of offer, effect of, 24
  unconditional, must be, 23
  undue influence, effect of, on, 28
OFFICES
  accidents in, notification of, 343
  cleanliness of, 336–337
  cloakrooms, 338
  definition, 336
  enforcement of provisions as to, 343
  factories, in, excluded from Factories Act, 1961 . . . 256
      responsibility for, 256
  fencing of machinery, 339–340
  fire certificate, qualification for issue, 341
      right of appeal for refusal, 341
    means of escape in case of, 341–342
    precautions against, 340–342, 343
    regulations, powers to make, 342
  first-aid facilities, provision and maintenance of, 340
  floors, passages and stairs in, 339
  fuel storage, 339, 342
  health and welfare provisions, 336–339
  heavy loads in, 340
  inspectorate created, 343
  legislation concerning, 335, *et seq.*
  lighting, 337–338
  noise and vibration, provisions against, 340
  Offices, etc., Act, 1963, provisions for enforcement of, 343–344
      relationship with Factories Act, 1961 . . . 343
  overcrowding, 337
  regulations, power to make, 336, 337, 340, 342
      scope of, 340
  safety provisions, 339–340
  sanitary conveniences, 338
  seats, 339
  special provisions, powers to make, 342
  temperature, 337
  underground, 336
  ventilation, 337
  washing facilities, 338
  water supply, 338
ORGANISATION OF WORKERS
  action for breach of contract against, 483
  amalgamations and transfers of engagements, 485
  ballots, 474
  complaints, individual, by, Industrial Court, to, 483
      Tribunal, to, 483
      ordinary courts, to, 483
  disciplinary action, 462, 474–476
  elections, 461, 473–474
  federation of, registration, 459
      special, 468
  guiding principles in conduct of, 461, 463, 471, *et seq.*

[26]

[27]

[28]

Index

QUARRIES—*continued*
tips, safety of, 375
ventilation, 372
working operations, 371–372
young persons, hours of work in, 344–347
    parents, liability of, 375
RACIAL DISCRIMINATION
contract of service and, 53–54
unfair industrial practice, as, 54
RAILWAY LINE AND SIDING
may be within definition of a factory, 254
RAILWAY RUNNING SHEDS
Shop Clubs Act, 1902, inapplicable to, 161
within definition of factory, 253
RECEIVING AND HARBOURING ANOTHER'S SERVANT, 206, *et seq.*
REDUNDANCY. *See also* REDUNDANCY PAYMENTS ACT, 1965.
cessation, 127
definition, 126–128
place of work, meaning, 127
prior notice of, effect, 128
replacement, whether rebutted by, 128
unfair dismissal, statutory rules inapplicable to, 106, 107
REDUNDANCY PAYMENTS ACT, 1965. *See also* REDUNDANCY.
aims of, 126
application to contract of service, 42–43
change of employment, whether transfer effects, 77
dismissal, constructive, 128
    definition of, 128–130
    employee justified in leaving as, 129–130
dock workers, not applicable to, 133
effect on unlawful strikes, 77
    wages, 126, *et seq.*
exceptions to, 133
lay-off, provisions for, 131–132, 134, 136, 137
notice under, intention to claim, of, 131–132
    strikes during, 137
offer of new employment refused, 130–131
presumptions under, 135–136, 137
private schemes, exemption for, 136
provisions of, 126
redundancy, definition of, 126–128
Redundancy Fund, establishment of, 138, 139
    rebates, 138
    for termination payment, 138
redundancy payment, computation of, 134–136
    provisions for, 73
requisite period of employment, 132–133
relation to the Contracts of Employment Act, 1963 . . . 77, 126
short-time, provisions for, 131–132, 134, 136, 137
special provisions, 136–137
strikes during notice, 137
    where lay-off or short-time, 136
tribunal, reference to, 42–43, 137, 138, 139
REGISTERS
conciliation boards, of, 444
disabled persons, of, 378–379
employments vacant, of, 383
Factories Act, 1961, kept under, 258, 264, 320
persons seeking work, of, 383
special, Industrial Relations Act, 1971, under, 467–469

[29]

Index

SAFE SYSTEM OF WORKING
  general practice in industry relevant to, 220
  master's duty to provide, 213, 218, *et seq.*, 241
                causation, 221–224
                physical defects, workman with, 223
                refusal of workman to adopt, 221–222
SAFETY
  coal mines, in, 347, *et seq.*, 375,
  factories, in, 274, *et seq.*, 292–294, 301, *et seq.*
  introduction, 247–248
  offices, in, 339–340
  quarries, in, 347, *et seq.*, 375
  shops, in, 331–332
SAFETY DEVICES
  Factories Act, 1961, employee's duty to use, under, 261–263
                regulations for the use of, 285
  refusal to use, 221–222
  vehicles in mines, for, 359
SAFETY LAMPS. *See* MINES.
SAMPLES
  inspector may take, for analysis, 307
SANITARY CONVENIENCES
  factory, cleanliness, 271
                provision of, in, 274
  mines, in, 370
  offices, in, 338
SEAL
  gratuitous service, in, necessity for, 39
  release by deed, 118
SEAMAN
  contract of apprenticeship, 61, 62
                service with, 39–41
  forgery of certificates, 200
SEATS
  offices, in, 339
SEDUCTION
  servant, of, action for, 203, *et seq.*
  spouse or child, of, abolition of action for, 201
SERVANT. *See also* EMPLOYED PERSON.
  agent, authority as, 185, *et seq.*
                distinguished from, 18–19
  arrest by, master's liability for, 172–173, 177, 178
  assault by, when justified, 199
  bankruptcy of, effect on contract of service, 68
  breach of contract by, inducing, 206–209
  contract made by, 185, *et seq.*, 197–198
  control, right of, 7–8
                test, 5–10, 11
                rejection of, 9
  criminal act of, master's liability for, in law of tort, 178, *et seq.*
                orders no defence to, 199
                servant's liability for, 199
  death of, effect on contract of service, 67
                master may be liable for, 234, *et seq.*
  defamation by, 197
  dismissal of. *See* DISMISSAL.
  drunkenness of, justifying dismissal, 103
  duties of, under contract of service, 88, *et seq.*
  fraudulent servant, liability of master for, 179–180
  general hiring, 70

[31]

Index

Index

WASHING FACILITIES
  factory, provision of, in, 300
  mines, provision of, in, 370
  offices, provision of, in, 338
WATER SUPPLY
  factories, in, 299–300
  mines, in, 370
  offices, in, 338
WEEKS WHICH COUNT
  contract of service, in, 74–77
WELFARE
  factories, in, general provisions, 299, *et seq.*
       special regulations, 300
  introduction, 247–248
  mines, in, 370
  offices, in, 336–339
  shops, in, 331–332
WET DOCK
  factory, when within definition of, 258
WHITE PHOSPHORUS
  import of matches made with, prohibited, 305
  use forbidden in manufacture of matches, 305
WHITEWASHING
  factories in, 271
WINDING MACHINERY
  mines, in, 359–360
WOMEN
  bread and flour confectionery, employment in, 314
  cleaning of moving machinery, 287
  employment of, lead manufacture, in, 260–261, 306
       mines, in, 344–345
       prohibited in dangerous processes, 306
       on Sunday, 312, 345
  equal terms and conditions of employment for, 122–124
  heavy weights, lifting, 306, 340, 370
  hours of labour of, 309, *et seq.*
  laundries, employment in, 314
  married, national insurance, 164
  mines, employment underground in, prohibited, 344
       hours of work in, 344–345
  night work, when prohibited, 333
  overtime, 309–312, 313
  sausages, manufacture of, employment in, 314
  Sunday employment of, prohibited, 312, 345
WORK
  equal terms for like work, 122
       work rated as equivalent, 122
  master's duty to provide, 83–84
WORKER
  definition of, in Wages Council Act, 1959 . . . 143
WORKING HOURS
  holidays, effect on, under contract of service, 79
  minimum rate of payment under notice based on, 78–80
  normal working hours, 78, 135
WORKING PARTIES, 381
WORKMEN'S COMPENSATION. *See also* INDUSTRIAL INJURIES.
  criticisms of, 244–245
  generally, 244–246
WORKROOMS
  ventilation of, 272–273

[40]

Index